# THE WORLD'S GREATEST
# AIRCRAFT

# THE WORLD'S GREATEST
# AIRCRAFT

Christopher Chant &
Edited by Michael J.H. Taylor

Published in 2005 by

Regency House Publishing Ltd

24-26 Boulton Road

Stevenage

Hertfordshire

SG1 4QX

United Kingdom

ISBN 1 85361 490 4

Printed in China

# CONTENTS

# EARLY
# FIGHTERS

# Piston-Engined Fighters

Tremendous pioneering achievements in the field of aeroplane development during the first decade of the 20th century meant that it took under six years from the first flight of the Wright *Flyer* to put a military aeroplane into service with the U.S. Army, in the form of a Wright Model A in 1909. Just two years later, reconnaissance and light bombing using aeroplanes had been extensively practised within America and by others abroad, and in the same year Italy flew the world's first operational missions against Turkish forces, observing positions and dropping explosives. With land warfare conducted by vast ground armies, aeroplanes were seen as convenient 'eyes in the sky', of greater worth than tethered observation balloons but not so vital that they should be allowed to *frighten the horses*.

Meanwhile, in 1910 a rifle had been fired from a U.S. Army Curtiss biplane. Little significance was drawn from the event and no immediate thought was given to the possibility of arming aeroplanes with guns. Reconnaissance, light bombing and artillery spotting, therefore, continued to be the official roles for aeroplanes up to and beyond the outbreak of World War I. Similarly, when in Britain in 1911 Major Brooke-Popham of the Air Battalion, Royal Engineers, attempted to fix a gun to a Blériot monoplane, he was ordered to remove it in no uncertain terms. Apathy also attended experiments in America in June 1912, when the newly-invented Lewis machine-gun was fired from an Army Signal Corps Wright Model B by Captain Charles de Forest Chandler. However, the day of the fighting aeroplane was drawing close.

The British Admiralty became an early driving force for arming offensive aeroplanes, and in November 1912 contracted Vickers to design and produce an experimental fighting biplane. The Vickers EFB1 Destroyer, as it became, was put on display at the February 1913 Olympia Aero Show, featuring a rear-mounted pusher engine/propeller and a nose-mounted Vickers-Maxim machine-gun with a 60° angle of vertical/horizontal movement. Also appearing

at the Show was Claude Grahame-White's Type 6 Military Biplane, which offered a wider field of fire for its Colt gun. It was, however, the Destroyer that is best remembered, leading eventually to the development of the famed wartime FB5 Gun Bus fighter which joined British forces in France in early 1915.

Both British fighters at Olympia in 1913 featured pusher engines and propellers, allowing the nose gun in each to be fired forwards without the worry of hitting the propeller. Other countries later adopted combat aircraft of similar layout, notably the French Voisin that, in early form in October 1914, claimed the first-ever air-to-air victory by gunfire, shooting down a German two-seater.

Since 1913 several countries had produced 'scouting' aeroplanes, front-engined biplanes and monoplanes of more modern streamlined design than the pusher types, often single-seaters and intended mainly for high-speed unarmed reconnaissance but also capable of other uses including 'nuisance' raids and light bombing. Because of their front-turning propellers, fitting them with forward-firing guns had not appeared possible. But, if this could be done, a deadly new weapon would emerge, capable of catching and destroying enemy reconnaissance aircraft and even scouts before they reported back to base. The problem to be faced, however, looked daunting; how to fire a machine-gun through the arc of a turning propeller without damaging the blades and thereby destroying the aircraft.

Raymond Saulnier of the Morane-Saulnier company in France and Franz Schneider of LVG in Germany worked separately on the problem and in 1913/14 devised systems, but for various technical reasons neither was adopted. Instead, with war declared, Morane-Saulnier came up with a simple alternative and fitted deflector plates (wedges to divert striking bullets) to the propeller of a Morane-Saulnier monoplane, providing a solution of sorts without technical difficulty. Given an early machine, Frenchman Roland Garros shot down his first enemy aircraft on April 1 1915, the first-ever air victory by a fighter firing a gun through the propeller arc.

Unfortunately, he made an emergency landing behind enemy lines on the 19th, thereby passing the secret to the Germans.

Though Germany viewed the deflector system with interest, Fokker returned to the better synchronized 'interrupter' gear method of timing bullets to fire between the turning blades and quickly convinced the authorities that he had a workable system. First combat tested on a converted Fokker M5K reconnaissance monoplane with great success, it lead to the production of the world's first operational

fighter with a synchronized gun, the single-seat
Fokker E series Eindecker. Though not fast, the
small number of Eindeckers soon widened their role
from merely offering defence for German
reconnaissance two-seaters to searching the skies for
vulnerable Allied aircraft. For ten months from the
summer of 1915 Eindeckers dominated the Western
Front, a period that became known to the Allies as
the 'Fokker Scourge' due to extremely heavy losses.
The true fighter had exploded onto the scene.

*Picture: Fokker E.III, the improved and most produced version
of the famous Eindecker fighter of the First World War.*

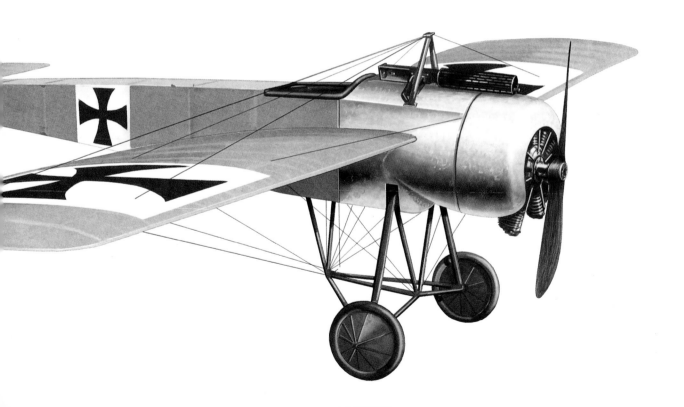

# NIEUPORT 11 BEBE and 17 (France)

*Nieuport Type 17*

The Type 11 was the fighter largely instrumental for the defeat of the 'Fokker Scourge' in 1916. Planned as a competition sesquiplane to take part in the Gordon Bennett Trophy race of 1914, the first Type 11 was designed and built in a mere four months. The outbreak of World War I led to the race's cancellation, but the Type 11 was nonetheless recognized as possessing the performance and flight characteristics to make it a useful military aircraft. Early Type 11 aircraft were powered by the 60-kW (80-hp) Le Rhône rotary engine, and were used by the French and British as scouts from 1915. The aircraft's apparent daintiness led to the nickname Bébé (Baby). The Type 11 was then turned into a fighter by the addition of a machine-gun on the upper-wing centre section to fire over the propeller's swept disc.

Many more aircraft were built under licence in Italy by Macchi with the designation Nieuport 1100. The Type 16 was a version with the 82-kW (110-hp) Le Rhône rotary for better performance. The Type 17 was a further expansion of the same design concept with a strengthened airframe but the same 82-kW (110-hp) Le Rhône. The new model retained its predecessors' excellent agility but offered superior performance, including a sparkling rate of climb. The fighter's 7.7-mm (0.303-in) Lewis gun was located on a sliding mount that allowed the pilot to pull the weapon's rear down, allowing oblique upward fire and also making for easier reloading.

The slightly later Type 17bis introduced the 97-kW (130-hp) Clerget rotary and a synchronized machine-gun on the upper fuselage. Still later models were the Type 21 with the 60-kW (80 hp), later the 82-kW (110 hp), Le Rhône and larger ailerons, and the slightly heavier Type 23 with 60- or 89-kW (120 hp) Le Rhône engines.

**NIEUPORT TYPE 11**
**Role:** Fighter
**Crew/Accommodation:** One
**Power Plant:** One 80 hp Gnome or Le Rhône 9C air-cooled rotary
**Dimensions:** Span 7.55 m (24.77 ft); length 5.8 m (19.03 ft); wing area 13 m² (140 sq ft)
**Weights:** Empty 344 kg (759 lb); MTOW 550 kg (1,213 lb)
**Performance:** Maximum speed 156 km/h (97 mph) at sea level; operational ceiling 4,600 m (15,090 ft); range 330 km (205 miles) with full bombload
**Load:** One .303 inch machine gun

*Nieuport 11.*

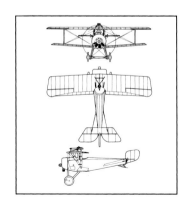

*Nieuport Type 11 Bébé*

# SPAD S.7 AND S.13 (France)

*SPAD S.13*

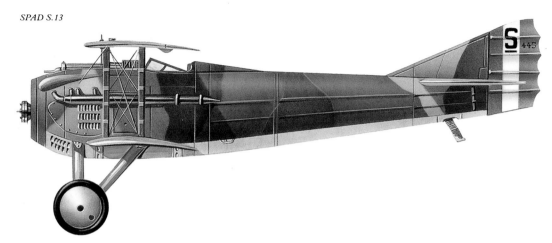

Vickers machine-gun, and was a sturdy two-bay biplane with unstaggered wings, fixed tailskid landing gear, and a wooden structure covered with fabric except over the forward fuselage, which was skinned in light alloy. Delivery of the essentially similar first production series of about 500 aircraft began in September 1916, being followed by some 6,000 examples of an improved model with the 134-kW (180-hp) HS 8Ac engine and wings of slightly increased span. In 1917 the company flew two development aircraft, and the S.12 with the 149-kW (200-hp) HS 8Bc paved the way for a production series of some 300 aircraft including some with the 164-kW (220-hp) HS 8Bec engine between the cylinder banks of which nestled a 37-mm *moteur canon*. Further development produced the S.13 that first flew in April 1917 for service from May of the same year. This has two guns rather than one, more power, slightly greater span and a number of aerodynamic refinements. Production of this superb fighter totalled 8,472 aircraft.

These two closely related aircraft were France's best fighters of World War I, combining high performance and structural strength without too great a sacrifice of agility. The result was an excellent gun platform comparable with the S.E.5a in British service. After experience with the A1 to A5 aircraft, designer Louis Béchereau turned to the conventional tractor biplane layout for the S.5 that first flew in the closing stages of 1915 and became in effect the prototype for the S.7, which was the first genuinely successful warplane developed by the Société Pour l'Avions et ses Dérives which is what the original but bankrupt Société Pour les Appareils Deperdussin became after its purchase by Louis Blériot.

The first S.7 flew early in 1916 with a 112-kW (150-hp) Hispano-Suiza 8Aa inline and a single synchronized 7.7-mm (0.303-in)

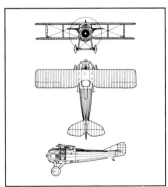

*SPAD S.7*

### SPAD S.13
**Role:** Fighter
**Crew/Accommodation:** One
**Power Plant:** One 220 hp Hispano-Suiza 8BEC water-cooled inline
**Dimensions:** Span 8 m (26.3 ft); length 6.2 m (20.33 ft); wing area 21.1 m² (227.1 sq ft)
**Weights:** Empty 565 kg (1,245 lb); MTOW 820 kg (1,807 lb)
**Performance:** Maximum speed 222 km/h (138 mph) at sea level; operational ceiling 5,400 m (17,717 ft); range 402 km (250 miles)
**Load:** Two .303 inch machine guns

*SPAD S.13*

# ALBATROS D III and D V (Germany)

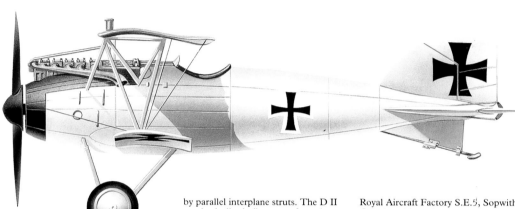

The first Albatros fighter was the excellent D I with virtually identical but staggered upper and lower wings connected toward their outboard ends

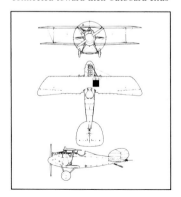

*Albatros D Va*

by parallel interplane struts. The D II was basically similar, apart from the lowering of the upper wing to provide the pilot with improved forward and upward fields of vision. In an effort to improve manoeuvrability, designer Robert Thelen then moved to the D III with a revised and unstaggered wing cellule in which an increased-span upper wing was connected to the smaller and narrower-chord lower wing by V-section interplane struts.

The D III entered service in spring 1917 and proved most successful until the Allies introduced types such as the

**ALBATROS D III**
**Role:** Fighter
**Crew/Accommodation:** One
**Power Plant:** One 175 hp Mercedes D.IIIa water-cooled inline
**Dimensions:** Span 9.05 m (29.76 ft); length 7.33 m (24 ft); wing area 20.5 m² (220.7 sq ft)
**Weights:** Empty 680 kg (1,499 lb); MTOW 886 kg (1,953 lb)
**Performance:** Maximum speed 175 km/h (109 mph) at 1,000 m (3,280 ft); operational ceiling 5,500 m (18,045 ft); endurance 2 hours
**Load:** Two 7.92 mm machine guns

Royal Aircraft Factory S.E.5, Sopwith Camel and Spad S.13 in the late summer of the same year. During the course of the fighter's production,

engine power was raised from 127- to 130-kW (170- to 175-hp) by increasing the compression ratio, and the radiator was shifted from the upper-wing centre section into the starboard upper wing so that the pilot would not be scalded if the radiator was punctured.

Albatros introduced the D V in May 1917 with features such as a still further lowered upper wing, a modified rudder, a revised aileron control system, and a larger spinner providing nose entry for a deeper elliptical rather than flat-sided plywood fuselage to reduce drag and so boost performance. Greater emphasis was then placed on this model and its D Va derivative with the upper wing and aileron control system of the D III. In fact the D V and D Va were outclassed by Allied fighters, and their lower wings were structurally deficient in the dive.

*Albatros D Va.*

# BRISTOL F.2 FIGHTER Series (United Kingdom)

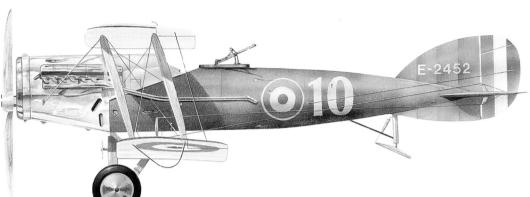

The F.2 Fighter was the best two-seat combat aircraft of World War I, even though it was designed in 1916 as a reconnaissance type. The design was an equal-span biplane of fabric-covered wooden construction, and in its original R.2A form it was planned round an 89-kW (120-hp) Beardmore engine. The availability of the 112-kW (150-hp) Hispano-Suiza engine resulted in the concept's revision as the slightly smaller R.2B sesquiplane, and further revision was then made so that the R.2B could also be fitted with the 142-kW (190-hp) Rolls-Royce Falcon engine. In August 1916, two prototypes and 50 production aircraft were ordered. Before the first prototypes flew in September 1916 the type had been reclassified as the F.2A fighter. All 50 aircraft were delivered together with the Falcon engine, and

the F.2A entered service in February 1917.

The type's combat debut was disastrous, four out of six aircraft being lost to an equal number of

Albatros D III fighters. But as soon as pilots learned to fly their F.2As as if they were single-seaters, with additional firepower provided by the gunner, the type became highly successful. The rest of the Fighter's 5,308-aircraft production run was of the F.2B variant with successively more powerful engines and modifications to improve fields of vision and combat-worthiness. Other designations were F.2C for a number of experimental re-enginings, F.2B Mk II for 435 new and reconditioned and tropicalized machines for army co-operation duties in the Middle East and India, Fighter Mk III for 80 strengthened aircraft delivered in 1926 and 1927, and Fighter Mk IV for Mk III conversions with strengthened structure and landing gear as well as a balanced rudder and automatic leading-edges slots. The RAF retired its last Fighters in 1932.

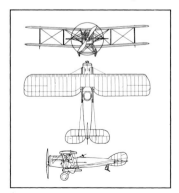

*Bristol F.2B Fighter*

**BRISTOL F.2B**
**Role:** Fighter
**Crew/Accommodation:** Two
**Power Plant:** One 275-hp Rolls-Royce Falcon III water-cooled inline
**Dimensions:** Span 11.96 m (39.25 ft); length 7.87 m (25.83 ft); wing area 37.6 m² (405 sq ft)
**Weights:** Empty 875 kg (1,930 lb); MTOW 1,270 kg (2,800 lb)
**Performance:** Maximum speed 201 km/h (125 mph) at sea level; operational ceiling 6,096 m (20,000 ft); endurance 3 hours
**Load:** Two or three .303 inch machine guns plus up to 54.4 kg (120 lb) of bombs

*Bristol Fighter Mk III.*

17

# ROYAL AIRCRAFT FACTORY S.E.5 (United Kingdom)

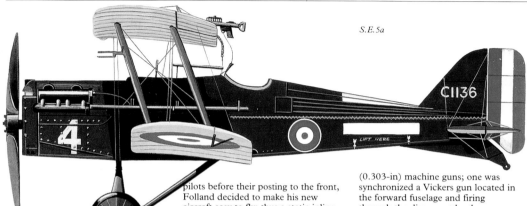

*S.E.5a*

The best aircraft to be designed by the Royal Aircraft Factory, and also the mount of several celebrated British aces of World War I, the S.E.5 was designed by H.P. Folland. Given the minimal levels of training received by pilots before their posting to the front, Folland decided to make his new aircraft easy to fly; thus a static inline engine was preferred to a rotary engine with all its torque problems, and a fair measure of inherent stability was built into the design. At the same time, Folland opted for an extremely strong airframe that was also easy to manufacture. Construction was entirely orthodox for the period, with fabric covering over a wooden primary structure. The result was a fighter that was an exceptionally good gun platform but, without sacrifice of structural strength, possessed good performance and adequate agility. The armament was an unusual variant on the standard pair of 7.7-mm (0.303-in) machine guns; one was synchronized a Vickers gun located in the forward fuselage and firing through the disc swept by the propeller, while the other was a Lewis located on a rail over the centre section and firing over the propeller. The Lewis gun could be pulled back and down along a quadrant rear extension of its rear so that the pilot could change ammunition drums. The S.E.5 was powered by a 112-kW (150-hp) Hispano-Suiza 8 inline and began to enter service in April 1917.

From the summer of the same year it was complemented and then supplanted by the S.E.5a version with a 149-kW (200-hp) engine. There were at first a number of teething problems with the engine and the Constantinesco synchronizer gear, but once these had been overcome the S.E.5a matured as a quite superlative fighter that could also double in the ground-attack role with light bombs carried under the wings. Total production was 5,205 aircraft.

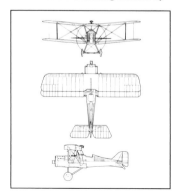

*Royal Aircraft Factory S.E.5*

**ROYAL AIRCRAFT FACTORY S.E.5a**
**Role:** Fighter
**Crew/Accommodation:** One
**Power Plant:** One 200 hp Wolseley W.4A Viper water-cooled inline
**Dimensions:** Span 8.12 m (26.63 ft); length 6.38 m (20.92 ft); wing area 22.84 m² (245.8 sq ft)
**Weights:** Empty 635 kg (1,399 lb); MTOW 880 kg (1,940 lb)
**Performance:** Maximum speed 222 km/h (138 mph) at sea level; operational ceiling 5,182 m (17,000 ft); endurance 2.5 hours
**Load:** Two .303 inch machine guns, plus up to 45 kg (100 lb) of bombs

*The Royal Aircraft Factory S.E.5a was an outstanding fighter*

# SOPWITH CAMEL (United Kingdom)

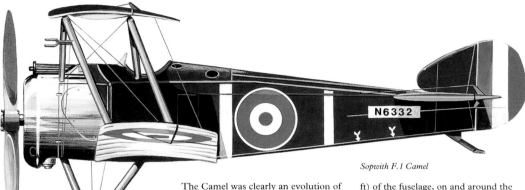

*Sopwith F.1 Camel*

The Camel was clearly an evolution of the Pup's design concept and was in fact designed to supplant this type, but had all its major masses (engine, fuel/lubricant, guns/ammunition and pilot) located in the forward 2.1 m (7 ft) of the fuselage, on and around the centre of gravity to offer the least inertial resistance to agility. The type was therefore supremely manoeuvrable; the torque of the powerful rotary meant that a three-quarter turn to the right could be achieved as swiftly as a quarter turn to the left, but this also meant that the type could easily stall and enter a tight spin if it was not flown with adequate care.

In configuration Camel was a typical single-bay braced biplane with fixed tailwheel landing gear, and was built of wood with fabric covering except over the forward fuselage, which had light alloy skinning. The type was more formally known to its naval sponsors as the Sopwith Biplane F.1, the nickname deriving from the humped fuselage over the breeches of the two synchronized 7.7-mm (0.303-in) Vickers machine guns that comprised the armament. Production of 5,490 aircraft made this the most important British fighter of late 1917 and 1918. The type was powered in its production forms by a number of Bentley, Clerget, Gnome and Le Rhône rotary engines in the power class between 75 and 112 kW (100 and 150 hp), though some experimental variants had engines of up to 134-kW (180-hp) rating. Some F.1s were operated from ships, but a specialized derivative for this role was the 2F.1 with folding wings. Other variants were the F.1/1 with tapered wing panels, and the TF.1 trench fighter (ground-attack) model with a pair of 7.7-mm Lewis guns arranged to fire obliquely downward and forward through the cockpit floor, but neither of these entered production.

## SOPWITH F.1 CAMEL

**Role:** Fighter
**Crew/Accommodation:** One
**Power Plant:** One 130 hp Clerget 9B air-cooled rotary
**Dimensions:** Span 8.53 m (28 ft); length 5.71 m (18.75 ft); wing area 21.5 m² (231 sq ft)
**Weights:** Empty 436 kg (962 lb); MTOW 672 kg (1,482 lb)
**Performance:** Maximum speed 168 km/h (104.5 mph) at 3,048 (10,000 ft); operational ceiling 5,486 m (18,000 ft); endurance 2.5 hours
**Load:** Two .303 inch machine guns

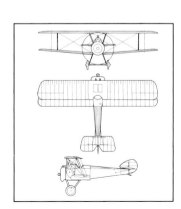

*Sopwith F.1 Camel*

*The Sopwith F.1 Camel.*

# FOKKER Dr I (Germany)

*Dr I*

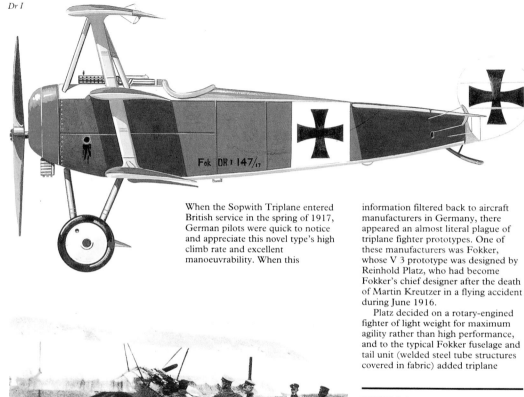

When the Sopwith Triplane entered British service in the spring of 1917, German pilots were quick to notice and appreciate this novel type's high climb rate and excellent manoeuvrability. When this information filtered back to aircraft manufacturers in Germany, there appeared an almost literal plague of triplane fighter prototypes. One of these manufacturers was Fokker, whose V 3 prototype was designed by Reinhold Platz, who had become Fokker's chief designer after the death of Martin Kreutzer in a flying accident during June 1916.

Platz decided on a rotary-engined fighter of light weight for maximum agility rather than high performance, and to the typical Fokker fuselage and tail unit (welded steel tube structures covered in fabric) added triplane wings. These were of thick section and wooden construction, with plywood covering as far aft as the spar, and were cantilever units that did not require bracing wires or interplane struts. In flight the wings vibrated, however, and Platz added plank-type interplane struts on the V 4 second prototype that also incorporated a number of aerodynamic refinements. The type was put into production during the summer of 1917 as the F I, though this designation was soon altered to Dr I. The new triplane soon built up a phenomenal reputation, though this was the result not of the type's real capabilities, which were modest in the extreme, but of the fact that it was flown by a number of aces who had the skills to exploit the Dr I's superb agility in the defensive air combat waged by Germany over the Western Front. The type was grounded late in 1917 because of structural failures in the wing cellule, but with this defect remedied, the type was swiftly restored to service. Production ended in May 1918 after the delivery of about 300 aircraft.

*Fokker Dr I*

**FOKKER Dr I**
**Role:** Fighter
**Crew/Accommodation:** One
**Power Plant:** One 110 hp Oberursel U.R. II air-cooled rotary
**Dimensions:** Span 7.17 m (23.52 ft); length 5.77 m (18.93 ft); wing area 16 m² (172.2 sq ft)
**Weights:** Empty 405 kg (893 lb); MTOW 585 kg (1,289 lb)
**Performance:** Maximum speed 185 km/h (115 mph) at sea level; operational ceiling 5,975 m (19,603 ft); range 210 km (130 miles)
**Load:** Two 7.92 mm machine guns

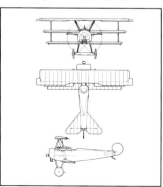

*Fokker Dr I*

# FOKKER D VII (Germany)

*Fokker D VII*

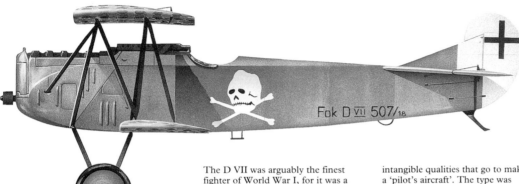

The D VII was arguably the finest fighter of World War I, for it was a package that featured great structrual strength, considerable agility, good firepower and a combination of those intangible qualities that go to making a 'pilot's aircraft'. The type was developed for Germany's first single-seat fighter competition, and the VII prototype made its initial flight just before this during January 1918. This machine had many similarities to the Dr I triplane in its fuselage, tail unit and landing gear. Reinhold Platz, designer of the D VII, intended his new fighter to offer considerably higher performance than that of the Dr I, and for this reason a more powerful inline engine, the 119-kW (160-hp) Mercedes D.III, was installed. This dictated the use of larger biplane wings. Despite the N-type interplane struts, these were cantilever units of Platz's favourite thick aerofoil section and wooden construction with plywood-covered leading edges.

As a result of its success in the competition, the type was ordered into immediate production as the D VII. Within three months, the type was in operational service, and some 700 had been delivered by the time of the Armistice. The type proved a great success in the type of defensive air fighting forced on the Germans at this stage of World War I.

It was particularly impressive in the high-altitude role as it possessed a good ceiling and also the ability to 'hang on its propeller' and fire upward at higher aircraft. Later examples were powered by the 138-kW (185-hp) BMW III inline for still better performance at altitude, and a number of experimental variants were built. Fokker returned to his native Netherlands at the end of the war, in the process smuggling back components for a number of D VIIs as a prelude to resumed construction.

*The Fokker D VII was perhaps the best fighter of World War I*

**FOKKER D VII**
**Role:** Fighter
**Crew/Accommodation:** One
**Power Plant:** One 160 hp Mercedes D.III water-cooled inline
**Dimensions:** Span 8.9 m (29.2 ft); length 6.95 m (22.8 ft); wing area 20.25 m² (218 sq ft)
**Weights:** Empty 700 kg (1,543 lb); MTOW 878 kg (1,936 lb)
**Performance:** Maximum speed 188 km/h (117 mph) at 1,000 m (3,281 ft); operational ceiling 6,100 m (20,013 ft); range 215 km (134 miles)
**Load:** Two 7.9 mm machine guns

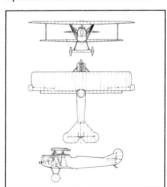

*Fokker D VII*

# ARMSTRONG WHITWORTH SISKIN (United Kingdom)

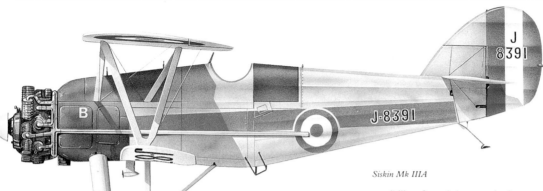

J 8391

B

J-8391

*Siskin Mk IIIA*

The Siskin was the mainstay of the Royal Air Force's fighter arm in the mid-1920s, and originated from the Siddeley Deasy S.R.2 of 1919. This was designed to use the 224-kW (300-hp) Royal Aircraft Factory 8 radial engine, a promising type whose final development was later passed to Siddeley Deasy but then put to one side so that the company could concentrate its efforts on the Puma.

The type first flew with the 239-kW (320-hp) A.B.C. Dragonfly radial and then as the Armstrong Siddeley Siskin with the definitive 242-kW (325-hp) Armstrong Siddeley Jaguar radial in 1921. The Siskin offered promising capabilities but, because the Air Ministry now demanded a primary structure of metal to avoid the

possibility of wood shortages in the event of a protracted war, had to be recast as the Siskin Mk III of 1923 with a fabric-covered structure of aluminium alloy.

The 64 examples of the Siskin Mk III began to enter service in May 1924 with the 242-kW (325-hp) Jaguar III. These were later supplemented by 348 examples of the Siskin Mk IIIA, together with the supercharged Jaguar IV and 53 examples of the Siskin Mk IIIDC dual-control trainer variant. The Siskin Mk IIIB, Mk IV and Mk V were experimental and racing machines. In October 1924, Romania placed an order for the Siskin, however unfortunately the balance of the 65-aircraft contract was cancelled after the fatal crash of one of the first seven aircraft to be delivered. In British service, the Siskin was replaced by the Bristol Bulldog from October 1932, but in Canadian service the type was not replaced by the Hawker Hurricane until as late as 1939.

**ARMSTRONG WHITWORTH SISKIN Mk IIIA**
**Role:** Fighter
**Crew/Accommodation:** One
**Power Plant:** One 400 hp Armstrong Siddeley Jaguar IVS
**Dimensions:** Span 10.11 m (33.16 ft); length 7.72 m (25.33 ft); wing area 27.22 m² (293 sq ft)
**Weights:** Empty 997 kg (2,198 lb); MTOW, 1,260 kg (2,777 lb)
**Performance:** Maximum speed 227 km/h (141 mph) at sea level; operational ceiling 6,401 m (21,600 ft); endurance 2.75 hours
**Load:** Two .303 inch machine guns

*Armstrong Whitworth Siskin Mk IIIA*

*Armstrong Whitworth Siskin is here represented by a Siskin Mk IIIAMk IIIA.*

# BOEING PW-9 and FB (U.S.A.)

*Boeing PW-9D*

by 25 PW-9As with the D-12C and duplicated flying and landing wires, 40 PW-9Cs with the D-12D and revised fittings for the flying and landing wires, and 16 PW-9Ds with a balanced rudder that was retrofitted to earlier aircraft. A total of 14 FB-1s was ordered for the U.S. Marines, this model being virtually identical to the PW-9. Only 10 were delivered as such, the last four being used for experimental purposes with different engines (the Packard 1A-1500 inline in the first three and the Wright P-1 then Pratt & Whitney Wasp radial in the last) and designations in the sequence from FB-2 to FB-6 except FB-5. This was reserved for 27 aircraft with the Packard 2A-1500 engine, revised landing gear and in addition to this increased wing stagger.

After learning the craft from the manufacture of other company's designs, most notably the Thomas-Morse MB-3A, Boeing entered the fighter market with the Model 15 that first flew in June 1923 as an unequal-span biplane with a massive 324-kW (435-hp) Curtiss D-12 inline engine. The fixed landing gear was of the through-axle type, and while the flying surfaces were of wooden construction the fuselage was of welded steel tube; most of the airframe was covered in fabric. Performance was impressive, and after the type had been evaluated by the U.S. Army as the XPW-9, two more XPW-9s were ordered.

The second of these aircraft had divided landing gear, and it was this type that was ordered into production for the U.S. Army as the PW-9 series and the U.S. Marine Corps as the FB series. The 30 PW-9s were followed

**BOEING PW-9**
**Role:** Fighter
**Crew/Accommodation:** One
**Power Plant:** One 435 hp Curtiss D-12 water-cooled inline
**Dimensions:** Span 9.75 m (32 ft); length 7.14 m (23.42 ft); wing area 24.15 m² (260 sq ft)
**Weights:** Empty 878 kg (1,936 lb); MTOW 1,415 kg (3,120 lb)
**Performance:** Maximum speed 256 km/h (159.1 mph) at sea level; operational ceiling 5,768 m (18,925 ft); range 628 km (390 miles)
**Load:** One .5 inch and one .303 inch machine guns

*Boeing PW-9D*

*Boeing PW-9D.*

# CURTISS P-1 and F6C HAWK Series (U.S.A.)

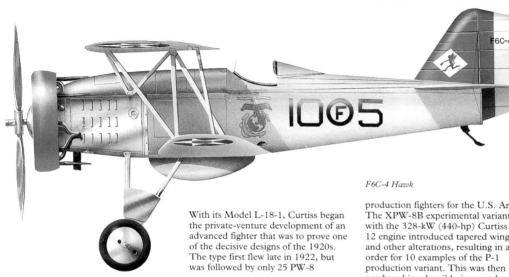

*F6C-4 Hawk*

With its Model L-18-1, Curtiss began the private-venture development of an advanced fighter that was to prove one of the decisive designs of the 1920s. The type first flew late in 1922, but was followed by only 25 PW-8

production fighters for the U.S. Army. The XPW-8B experimental variant with the 328-kW (440-hp) Curtiss D-12 engine introduced tapered wings and other alterations, resulting in an order for 10 examples of the P-1 production variant. This was then produced in a bewildering number of developed variants, of which the most significant were the 25 P-1As with detail improvements, the 25 P-1Bs with the 324-kW (435-hp) Curtiss V-1150-3 engine and larger-diameter wheels, and the 33 P-ICs with the V-1150-5 wheel brakes and provision for alternative ski landing gear. The type was also developed as the AT-4 advanced trainer. The type was based

on the P-1A but engined with the 134-kW (180-hp) Wright-Hispano E, and of the 40 aircraft ordered, 35 became P-1Ds when re-engined with the V-1150, and the other five became AT-5s with the 164-kW (220-hp) Wright Whirlwind J-5 radial; they were later converted to P-1Es with the V-1150 engine. Some 31 AT-5As with a longer fuselage were ordered, but soon became P-1F fighters with the V-1150 engine.

The army's P-1 series was also attractive to the U.S. Navy, which ordered the type with the designation F6C. The F6C-1 was intended for land-based use by the U.S. Marine Corps and was all but identical with the P-1, but only five were delivered as such, while the four others were delivered as F6C-2s with carrier landing equipment including an arrester hook. The F6C-3 was a modified F6C-2, and these 35 aircraft were followed by 31 of the F6C-4 that introduced the 313-kW (420-hp) Pratt & Whitney R-1340 Wasp radial in place of the original D-12 inline.

## CURTISS F6C-3

**Role:** Naval carrierborne fighter
**Crew/Accommodation:** One
**Power Plant:** One 400 hp Curtiss D.12 Conqueror water-cooled inline
**Dimensions:** Span 9.63 m (31.6 ft); length 6.96 m (22.83 ft); wing area 23.41 m² (252 sq ft)
**Weights:** Empty 980 kg (2,161 lb); MTOW 1,519 kg (3,349 lb)
**Performance:** Maximum speed 248 km/h (154 mph) at sea level; operational ceiling 6,187 m (20,300 ft); range 565 km (351 miles)
**Load:** Two .303 inch machine guns

*Curtiss Hawk F6C-3.*

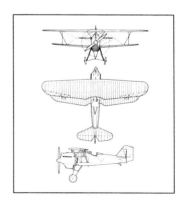

*Curtiss F6C Hawk*

# BRISTOL BULLDOG (United Kingdom)

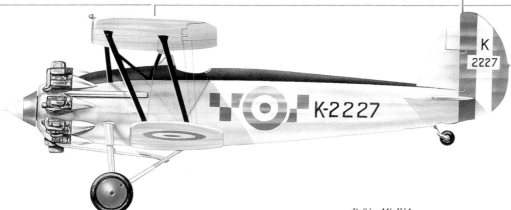

*Bulldog Mk IVA*

By the mid-1920s, the performance of light day bombers such as the Fairey Fox was outstripping the defensive capabilities of fighters such as the Armstrong Whitworth Siskin, and in an effort to provide the British fighter arm with a considerably improved fighter, the Air Ministry in 1926 issued a fairly taxing specification for a high-performance day/night fighter armed with two fixed machine guns and powered by an air-cooled radial engine. Several companies tendered designs, and the Type 105 proposal from Bristol narrowly beat the Hawfinch from Hawker. The Type 105 was a conventional biplane of its period, with a fabric-covered metal structure, unequal-span wings and fixed landing gear of the spreader-bar type. The Bulldog Mk I prototype first flew in May 1927, and was later fitted with larger wings for attempts on the world altitude and time-to-height records. A second prototype introduced the lengthened fuselage of the Bulldog Mk II production model, which was powered by the 328-kW (440-hp) Bristol Jupiter VII radial, and had a number of modern features such as an oxygen system and short-wave radio.

The Bulldog Mk II entered service in June 1929, and the Bulldog became the U.K.'s most important fighter of the late 1920s and early 1930s. Total production was 312, including 92 basic Bulldog Mk IIs, 268 Bulldog Mk IIAs of the major production type with a strengthened structure and the 365-kW (490-hp) Jupiter VIIF engine, four Bulldog MK IIIs for Denmark with the Jupiter VIFH, two interim Bulldog MK IIIAs with the 418-kW (560-hp) Bristol Mercury IVS.2, 18 Bulldog Mk IVAs for Finland with strengthened ailerons and the 477-kW (640-hp) Mercury VIS.2, and 59 Bulldog TM trainers with a second cockpit in a rear fuselage section that could be replaced by that of the standard fighters in times of crisis.

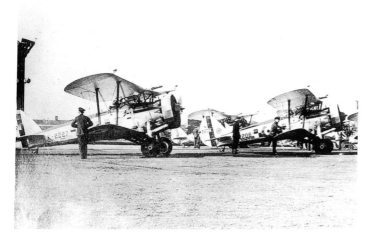

*Bristol Bulldog Mk IIA.*

**BRISTOL BULLDOG Mk IVA**
**Role:** Fighter
**Crew/Accommodation:** One
**Power Plant:** One 640 hp Bristol Mercury VIS2 air-cooled radial
**Dimensions:** Span 10.26 m (33.66 ft); length 7.72 m (25.33 ft); wing area 27.31 m² (294 sq ft)
**Weights:** Empty 1,220 kg (2,690 lb); MTOW 1,820 kg (4,010 lb)
**Performance:** Maximum speed 360 km/h (224 mph) at sea level; operational ceiling 10,180 m (33,400 ft); endurance 2.25 hours
**Load:** Two .303 inch machine guns, plus up to 36 kg (80 lb) of bombs

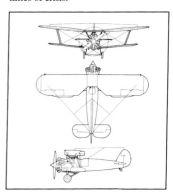

*Bristol Bulldog Mk IIA*

# BOEING F4B and P-12 (U.S.A)

6-F-4  U.S.NAVY

*F4B-4*

In an effort to produce replacements for the PW-9 and F2B/F3B series, Boeing developed its Models 83 and 89; the former had through-axle landing gear and an arrester hook, while the latter had divided main landing gear units and an attachment under the fuselage for a bomb. Both types were evaluated in 1928, and a hybrid variant with divided main units and an arrester hook was orderd for the U.S. Navy as the F4B-1 with tailskid landing gear. These 27 aircraft were followed by 46 F4B-2s with a drag-reducing cowling ring and through-axle landing gear with a

tailwheel, 21 F4B-3s with a semi-monocoque fuselage and 92 F4B-4s with a larger fin and, to be found in the last 45 aircraft, a liferaft in the pilot's headrest.

The U.S. Army ordered the type as the P-12, the first 10 aircraft being generally similar to the Model 89; later aircraft were 90 P-12Bs with revised ailerons and elevators, 95 P-12Cs similar to the F4B-2, 36 improved P-12Ds, 110 P-12Es with a semi-monocoque fuselage, and 25 P-12Fs with the Pratt & Whitney SR-1340 engine for improved altitude performance. There were also several experimental and even civil models, and also a number of export variants in a total production run of 586 aircraft. The aircraft began to enter American service in 1929, and were the mainstay of the U.S. Army's and U.S. Navy's fighter arms into the mid-1930s, and at that time they were replaced by more modern aircraft. Many aircraft were then used as trainers, mainly by the U.S. Navy, right up to the eve of the entry of the U.S.A. into World War II.

**BOEING F4B-4**
**Role:** Naval carrierborne fighter bomber
**Crew/Accommodation:** One
**Power Plant:** One 500 hp Pratt & Whitney R-1340-D Wasp air-cooled radial
**Dimensions:** Span 9.14 m (30 ft); length 7.75 m (25.42 ft); wing area 21.18 m² (228 sq ft)
**Weights:** Empty 1,049 kg (2,312 lb); MTOW 1,596 kg (3,519 lb)
**Performance:** Maximum speed 301 km/h (187 mph) at sea level; operational ceiling 8,382 m (27,500 ft); range 941 km (585 miles)
**Load:** One .5 inch and one .303 inch machine guns, plus one 227 kg (500 lb) bomb

*Boeing P-12E*

*Boeing F4B-3.*

# CURTISS P-6 HAWK and F11C Series (U.S.A.)

Curtiss P-6E Hawk.

Further development of the Model 34 (P-1 and F6C series) led to the P-6 series with the Curtiss V-1570 Conqueror engine. The development was pioneered in two P-1 conversions, namely the XP-6 with tapered wings and the XP-6A with the uptapered wings of the PW-8 and low-drag wing surfaced radiators. Both these aircraft were successful racers in 1927, and paved the way for the production series later on.

The main variants were the original P-6 of which nine were delivered with refined fuselage lines, the nine P-6As with Prestone-cooled engines, and the P-6E of which 46 were delivered in the winter of 1931-32 with the 522-kW (700-hp) V-1570C Conqueror. This was the finest of the army's Hawk fighters, and was the Curtiss Model 35.

There were many experimental variants including the radial-engined P-3 and P-21, and the turbocharged P-5 and P-23.

The type also secured comparatively large export orders under the generic designation Hawk. The Hawk I was sold to the Netherlands East Indies (eight aircraft), Cuba (three) and Japan (one), while the same basic type with a Wright Cyclone radial was sold with the name Hawk II to Bolivia (nine), Chile (four plus licensed production), China (50), Colombia (26 float-equipped aircraft), Cuba (four), Germany (two), Norway (one), Siam (12) and Turkey (19).

In addition, the U.S. Navy ordered a version of the Hawk II with the 522-kW (700-hp) Wright R-1820-78 Cyclone radial and the designations F11C-2 (28 aircraft), and with manually operated landing gear that retracted into a bulged lower fuselage, another type, the BF2C-1 (27 aircraft).

**CURTISS P-6E**
**Role:** Fighter
**Crew/Accommodation:** One
**Power Plant:** One 700 hp Curtiss V-1570C Conqueror water-cooled inline
**Dimensions:** Span 9.6 m (31.5 ft); length 6.88 m (22.58 ft); wing area 23.4 m² (252 sq ft)
**Weights:** Empty 1,231 kg (2,715 lb); MTOW 1,558 kg (3,436 lb)
**Performance:** Maximum speed 311 km/h (193 mph) at sea level; operational ceiling 7,285 m (23,900 ft); range 393 km (244 miles)
**Load:** Two .303 inch machine guns

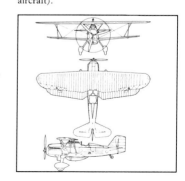

Curtiss P-6E

# HAWKER FURY I and II biplanes (U.S.A.)

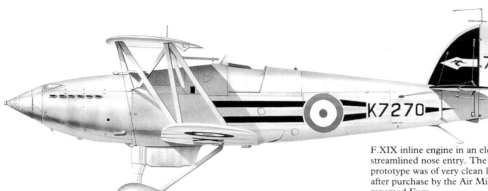

This single-seat fighter resulted from a 1927 requirement that led to the construction of prototype first flew with the 336-kW (450-hp) Bristol Jupiter radial specified by the Air Ministry. The aircraft failed to win a production contract, but its experience with this prototype stood the company in good stead. After its Hart high-speed day bomber had entered service as a pioneer of a new breed of high-performance warplanes, Hawker developed as a private venture fighter prototype. Sydney Camm decided not to follow current Air Ministry preference for radial engines, but instead opted for the Rolls-Royce F.XIX inline engine in an elegantly streamlined nose entry. The whole prototype was of very clean lines, and after purchase by the Air Ministry was renamed Fury.

Trials confirmed the type's capabilities as the first British fighter capable of exceeding 200 mph (322 km/h) in level flight, and the type was placed in production for service from May 1931. The fighter was of metal construction covered with panels of light alloy and with fabric, and the powerplant was a single 391-kW (525-hp) Rolls-Royce Kestrel IIS engine driving a large two-blade propeller. Production of the Fury (later the Fury I) for the RAF totalled 118, though another 42 were built for export with a number of other engine types. Hawker developed the basic concept further in the Intermediate Fury and High-Speed Fury prototypes that led to the definitive Fury II with the 477-kW (640-hp) Kestrel VI and spatted wheels. This entered service in 1937, and the 98 aircraft were used as interim fighters pending large-scale deliveries of the Hawker Hurricane monoplane fighter. The Fury II was exported to Yugoslavia, which took 10 aircraft. The Nimrod was a naval equivalent; 100 were produced for British and Danish service.

*Hawker Fury Mk I*

**HAWKER FURY Mk II**
**Role:** Interceptor
**Crew/Accommodation:** One
**Power Plant:** One 525 hp Rolls-Royce Kestrel IIS water-cooled inline
**Dimensions:** Span 9.15 m (30 ft); length 8.13 m (26.67 ft); wing area 23.4 m² (251.8 sq ft)
**Weights:** Empty 1,190 kg (2,623 lb); MTOW 1,583 kg (3,490 lb)
**Performance:** Maximum speed 309 km/h (192 mph) at 1,525 m (5,000 ft); operational ceiling 8,534 m (28,000 ft); range 491 km (305 miles)
**Load:** Two .303 inch machine guns

*The Fury series was always notable for the elegance of its lines.*

# BOEING P-26 'PEASHOOTER' (U.S.A.)

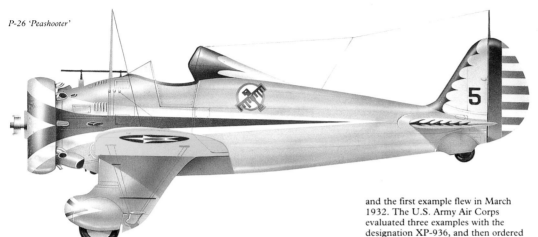

*P-26 'Peashooter'*

The Model 266 was a step, but only an interim step, towards the 'modern' monoplane fighter of all-metal construction that appeared in definitive form during the mid-1930s.

*Boeing P-26A*

The Model 266 was indeed a monoplane fighter, but the wing was not a cantilever structure and had, therefore, to be braced by flying and landing wires. This bracing was in itself an obsolescent feature, and so too were the open cockpit and fixed landing gear, though the latter's main units were well faired. Boeing began work on its Model 248 private-venture prototype during September 1931,

and the first example flew in March 1932. The U.S. Army Air Corps evaluated three examples with the designation XP-936, and then ordered 111 examples of the Model 266

production version with a revised structure, flotation equipment, and radio. The P-26As were often known as 'Peashooters', and were delivered between January 1934 and June 1934.

Later aircraft had a taller headrest for improved pilot protection in the event of a roll-over landing accident, and were produced with the trailing-edge split flaps that had been developed to reduce landing speed; in-service aircraft were retrofitted with the flaps. Other variants were two P-26Bs with the fuel-injected R-1340-33 radial, and 23 P-26Cs with modified fuel systems.

Some 11 aircraft were also exported to China, and surplus American aircraft were later delivered to Guatemala and Panama. Ex-American aircraft operated by the Philippine Air Corps saw short but disastrous service in World War II.

**BOEING P-26C**
**Role:** Fighter
**Crew/Accommodation:** One
**Power Plant:** One 600 hp Pratt & Whitney R-1340-33 Wasp air-cooled radial
**Dimensions:** Span 8.52 m (27.96 ft); length 7.24 m (23.75 ft); wing area 13.89 m² (149 sq ft)
**Weights:** Empty 1,058 kg (2,333 lb); MTOW 1,395 kg (3,075 lb)
**Performance:** Maximum speed 378 km/h (235 mph) at sea level; operational ceiling 8,230 m (27,000 ft); range 1,022 km (635 miles)
**Load:** Two .5 inch machine guns, plus 90.8 kg (200 lb) of bombs

*Boeing P-26A.*

# FIAT CR.32 and CR.42 FALCO (Italy)

*CR.32*

The CR.32 was Italy's finest fighter of the late 1930s, and marks one of the high points in biplane fighter design. The type was planned as successor to the CR.30 with smaller dimensions and reduced weight so that the type would have a comparably high level of agility but better overall performance on the same power. The prototype first flew in April 1933 with the 447-kW (600-hp) Fiat A.30 RAbis inline engine, and the successful evaluation of this machine led to production of slightly more than 1,300 aircraft in four series. These were about 350 CR.32 fighters with two 7.7-mm (0.303-in) machine guns, 283 CR.32bis close-support fighters with two 12.7-mm (0.5-in) and two 7.7-mm guns as well as provision for two 50-kg (110-lb) bombs, 150 CR.32ter fighters with two 12.7-mm (0.5-in) guns and improved equipment, and 337 CR.32quater fighters with radio and reduced weight. Another 100 or more of this last type were built in Spain as Hispano HA-132-L 'Chirri' fighters.

The Spanish Civil War led to the CR.42 Falco (Falcon) that first flew in prototype form during May 1938. This could be regarded as an aerodynamically refined version of the CR.32 with cantilever main landing gear units and more power in the form of a 626-kW (840-hp) Fiat A.74 R1C radial. More than 1,780 aircraft in five series were produced. The original CR.42 was armed with one 12.7-mm and one 7.7-mm machine guns. The CR.42AS was a close-support fighter with two 12.7-mm guns and two 10-kg (220-lb) bombs. The CR.42bis fighter was produced for Sweden with two 12.7-mm guns. The CR.42CN night fighter had two searchlights in underwing fairings. And the CR.42ter was a version of the CR.42bis with two 7.7-mm guns in underwing fairings.

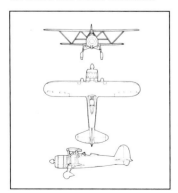

*The Fiat CR.42bis Falco*

**FIAT CR.32bis**
**Role:** Fighter
**Crew/Accommodation:** One
**Power Plant:** One 600 hp Fiat A30 RAbis water-cooled inline
**Dimensions:** Span 9.5 m (31.17 ft); length 7.47 m (24.51 ft); wing area 22.1 m² (237.9 sq ft)
**Weights:** Empty 1,455 kg (3,210 lb); MTOW 1,975 kg (4,350 lb)
**Performance:** Maximum speed 360 km/h (224 mph) at 3,000 m (9,840 ft); operational ceiling 7,700 m (25,256 ft); range 750 km (446 miles)
**Load:** Two 12.7 mm and two 7.7 mm machine guns, plus provision to carry up to 100 kg (220 lb) of bombs

*The Fiat CR.42 bis Falco.*

# POLIKARPOV I-16 (U.S.S.R.)

*I-16 Type 24*

The I-16 was the first low-wing monoplane fighter to enter full service with retractable landing gear. The aircraft had a cantilever wing of metal construction married to a monocoque fuselage of wooden construction and, in addition to the manually retracted main landing gear unit, the type had long-span split ailerons that doubled as flaps. The type first flew in 1933 as the TsKB-12 with the 358-kW (480-hp) M-22 radial. The TsKB-12bis flew two months later with an imported 529-kW (710-hp) Wright SR-1820-F3 Cyclone radial and offered better performance. The handling qualities of both variants were tricky, because the short and very portly fuselage reduced longitudinal stability to virtually nothing, but its speed and rate of climb ensured that the machine was ordered into production, initially as an evaluation batch of 10 I-16 Type 1 fighters with the M-22.

Total production was 7,005 in variants with progressively more power and armament: the I-16 Type 4 used the imported Cyclone engine, the I-16 Type 5 had the 522-kW (700-hp) M-25 licensed version of the Cyclone and improved armour protection, the I-16 Type 6 was the first major production model and had the 544-kW (730-hp) M-25A, the I-16 Type 10 had the 559-kW (750-hp) M-25V and four rather than two 7.62-mm (0.3-in) machine-guns, the I-16 Type 17 was strengthened and had 20-mm cannon in place of the two wing machine guns plus provision for six 82-mm (3.2-in) rockets carried under the wings, the I-16 Type 18 had the 686-kW (920-hp) M-62 radial and four machine guns, the I-16 Type 24 had the 746-kW (1,000-hp) M-62 or 820-kW (1,100-hp) M-63 radial, strengthened wings and four machine guns, and the I-16 Types 28 and 30 that were reinstated in production during the dismal days of 1941 and 1942 had the M-63 radial. There were also SPB dive-bomber and I-16UTI dual-control trainer variants.

**POLIKARPOV I-16 TYPE 24**
**Role:** Fighter
**Crew/Accommodation:** One
**Power Plant:** One 1,000 hp Shvetsov M-62 air-cooled radial
**Dimensions:** Span 9 m (29.53 ft); length 6.13 m (20.11 ft); wing area 14.54 m² (156.5 sq ft)
**Weights:** Empty 1,475 kg (3,313 lb); MTOW 2,050 kg (4,519 lb)
**Performance:** Maximum speed 525 km/h (326 mph) at sea level; operational ceiling 9,000 m (29,528 ft); range 700 km (435 miles)
**Load:** Two 20 mm cannon and two 7.62 mm machine guns, plus six rocket projectiles

*The I-16 was the world's first 'modern' monoplane fighter.*

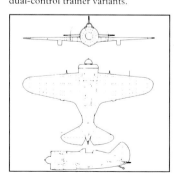

*Polikarpov I-16 Type 24*

# DEWOITINE D.500 and D.510 Series (France)

*D.510*

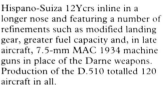

The ungainly but impressive D.500 spanned the technological gap between the fabric-covered biplanes of the 1920s and the all-metal monoplane fighters of the mid-1930s. Designed as a successor to the Nieuport 62 and 622, the D.500 was of all-metal construction with a low-set cantilever wing, but these modern features were compromised by obsolescent items such as an open cockpit and fixed tailwheel landing gear the main legs of which carried large fairings. The D.500.01 prototype first flew in June 1932 with the 492-kW (660-hp) Hispano-Suiza 12Xbrs inline engine, and the type was ordered into production. The initial D.500 was produced to the extent of 101 aircraft, later aircraft with 7.5-mm (0.295-in) Darne machine guns in place of the original 7.7-mm (0.303-in) Vickers guns. There followed 157 D.501s with the 515-kW (690-hp) Hispano-Suiza 12Xcrs engine and a hub-mounted 20-mm cannon in addition to the two machine guns.

Projected variants were the D.502 catapult-launched floatplane fighter, the D.504 parachute trials aircraft, and the D.505 to D.509 with different engines. The main variant in service at the beginning of World War II was the D.510 based on the D.501 but powered by the 641-kW (860-hp) Hispano-Suiza 12Ycrs inline in a longer nose and featuring a number of refinements such as modified landing gear, greater fuel capacity and, in late aircraft, 7.5-mm MAC 1934 machine guns in place of the Darne weapons. Production of the D.510 totalled 120 aircraft in all.

An interesting experimental derivative was the D.511 of 1934: this had a smaller wing, cantilever main landing gear units, and the HS 12Ycrs engine. The type was never flown, as it was modified as the D.503 with the HS 12Xcrs and proving inferior to the D.501 aircraft.

**DEWOITINE D.510**
**Role:** Fighter
**Crew/Accommodation:** One
**Power Plant:** One 860 hp Hispano-Suiza 12Y crs water-cooled inline
**Dimensions:** Span 12.09 m (39.67 ft); length 7.94 m (26.05 ft); wing area 16.5 m² (177.6 sq ft)
**Weights:** Empty 1,427 kg (3,145 lb); MTOW 1,915 kg (4,222 lb)
**Performance:** Maximum speed 402 km/h (250 mph) at 4,850 m (15,912 ft); operational ceiling 8,350 m (27,395 ft); range 985 km (612 miles)
**Load:** One 20 mm cannon and two 7.5 mm machine guns

*Dewoitine D.500*

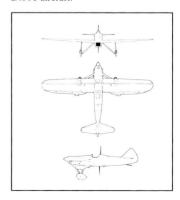

*Dewoitine*

# MESSERSCHMITT Bf 109 (Germany)

*Bf 109F-2*

The Bf 109 was Germany's most important fighter of World War II in numerical terms, and bore the brunt of the air war until supplemented by the Focke-Wulf Fw 190 from 1941. The type went through a large number of production variants, and in common with other German aircraft was developed within these basic variants into a number of subvariants with factory- or field-installed modification packages.

The Bf 109 was designed from 1934 to provide the German Air Force with its first 'modern' fighter of all-metal stressed-skin construction with a low-set cantilever wing, retractable landing gear and enclosed cockpit. The first prototype flew in May 1935 with a 518-kW (695-hp) Rolls-Royce Kestrel inline, but the second had the 455-kW (610-hp) Junkers Jumo 210A for which the aircraft had been designed. The overall production figure has not survived, but it is thought that at least 30,500 aircraft were produced, excluding foreign production. The limited-number Bf 109A, B and C variants can be regarded mostly as pre-production

and development models with differing Jumo 210s and armament fits. The Daimler-Benz DB 600A inline was introduced on the Bf 109D, paving the way for the first large-scale production variant, the Bf 109E produced in variants up to the E-9 with the 820-kW (1,100-hp) DB 601A. The Bf 109F introduced a more refined fuselage with reduced armament, and in addition was powered by the DB 601E or N in variants up to the F-6.

The most important production model was the Bf 109G with the DB 605 inline and provision for cockpit pressurization in variants up to the G-16. Later in the war there appeared comparatively small numbers of the Bf 109H high-altitude fighter with increased span in variants up to the H-1, and the Bf 109K improved version of the Bf 109G with the DB 605 inline in variants up to the K-14.

---

**MESSERSCHMITT Bf 109G-6**
**Role:** Fighter
**Crew/Accommodation:** One
**Power Plant:** One 1,475 hp Daimler-Benz DB605A water-cooled in line
**Dimensions:** Span 9.92 m (32.55 ft); length 9.02 m (29.59 ft); wing area 16.5 m² (172.75 sq ft)
**Weights:** Empty 2,700 kg (5,953 lb); MTOW 3,150 kg (6,945 lb)
**Performance:** Maximum speed 623 km/h (387 mph) at 7,000 m (22,967 ft); operational ceiling 11,750 m (38,551 ft); range 725 km (450 miles)
**Load:** One 30 mm cannon, two 20 mm cannon and two 13 mm machine guns. plus a 500 kg (1,102 lb) bomb

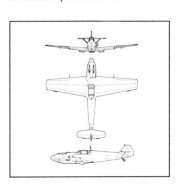

*Messerschmitt Bf 109E-3*

*Bf 109F.*

# HAWKER HURRICANE (United Kingdom)

*Hurricane Mk I*

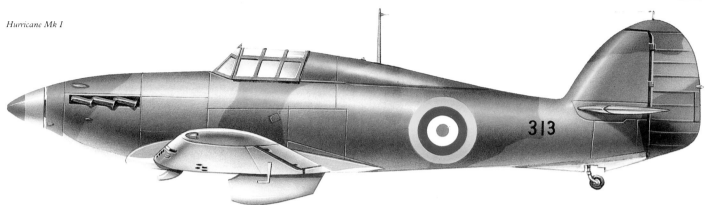

The Hurricane was the first British example of the 'modern' monoplane fighter, even though it lacked the stressed-skin construction of later machines such as the Supermarine Spitfire. The initial design was created as a private venture, and offered such advantages over current biplane fighters that a 1934 specification was written round it. The prototype first flew in November 1935 and revealed itself as a mix of advanced features (retractable landing gear, flaps and an enclosed cockpit) and an obsolescent structure of light alloy tube covered in fabric. This last did facilitate construction and repair, but limited the Hurricane's longer-term development potential despite an overall production total of 14,232 aircraft.

The Hurricane Mk I entered service in December 1937 with an armament of eight 7.7-mm (0.303-in) machine guns and the 768-kW (1,030-hp) Rolls-Royce Merlin II inline driving a two-blade propeller, and in the Battle of Britain was the RAF's most important and successful fighter with the 767-kW (1,029-hp) Merlin III driving a three-blade propeller. British production of 3,164 Mk Is was complemented by 140 Canadian-built Hurricane Mk Xs and a few Belgian- and Yugoslav-produced machines. Adoption of the 954-kW (1,280-hp) Merlin XX resulted in the Hurricane Mk II, of which 6,656 were produced in the U.K. in variants such as the Mk IIA with eight 7.7-mm machine-guns, the Mk IIB with 12 such guns and provision for underwing bombs, the Mk IIC based on the Mk IIB but with four 20-mm cannon, and the Mk IID with two 40-mm cannon in the anti-tank role; Canadian production amounted to 937 similar Hurricane Mks X, XI and XII aircraft. The final version was the Hurricane Mk IV, of which 2,575 were built with the 1208-kW (1,620-hp) Merlin 24 or 27 and a universal wing allowing the use of any of the standard armament combinations. About 825 aircraft were converted into Sea Hurricane Mks I and II.

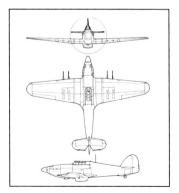

*Hawker Hurricane Mk IIB*

### HAWKER HURRICANE Mk II B
**Role:** Fighter bomber
**Crew/Accommodation:** One
**Power Plant:** One 1,280 hp Rolls-Royce Merlin XX water-cooled inline
**Dimensions:** Span 12.19 m (40 ft); length 9.75 m (32 ft); wing area 23.9 m² (257.5 sq ft)
**Weights:** Empty 2,495 kg (5,500 lb); MTOW 3,311 kg (7,300 lb)
**Performance:** Maximum speed 722 km/h (342 mph) at 6,706 m (22,000 ft); operational ceiling 10,973 m (36,000 ft); range 772.5 km (480 miles) on internal fuel only
**Load:** Twelve .303 inch machine guns, plus up to 454 kg (1,000 lb) bombload

*The Hawker Hurricane was the RAF's first 'modern' monoplane fighter.*

# NAKAJIMA Ki-27 'NATE' (Japan)

*Ki-27 'Nate'*

The Ki-27 was the Imperial Japanese Army Air Force's equivalent to the Navy's Mitsubishi A5M, and though it was an interim 'modern' fighter with

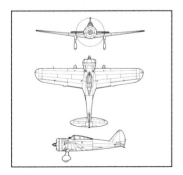

*Nakajima Ki-27b 'Nate'*

fixed landing gear (selected because of its light weight) it had more advanced features such as flaps and an enclosed cockpit. The type was evolved from the company's private-venture Type PE design, and the first of two prototypes flew in October 1936 with the 485-kW (650-hp) Nakajima Ha-1a radial. Flight trials with the prototypes confirmed the Ki-27's superiority to competing fighters, and 10 examples of the type with a modified clear-vision canopy were ordered for evaluation. These aircraft proved highly effective, and the first full-production type was ordered with the

**NALAJIMA Ki-27 'NATE'**
**Role:** Fighter
**Crew/Accommodation:** One
**Power Plant:** One 710 hp Nakajima Ha-1b air-cooled radial
**Dimensions:** Span 11.3 m (37.07 ft); length 7.53 m (24.7 ft); wing area 18.6 m² (199.7 sq ft)
**Weights:** Empty 1,110 kg (2.447 lb); MTOW 1,650 kg (3,638 lb)
**Performance:** Maximum speed 460 km/h (286 mph) at 3,500 m (11,480 ft); operational ceiling 8,600 m (28,215 ft); range 1,710 km (1,050 miles)
**Load:** Two 7.7-mm machine guns, plus up to 100 kg (220 lb) of bombs

company designation Ki-27a and the service designation Army Type 97 Fighter Model A.

The production programme lasted from 1937 to 1942 and totalled 3,384 aircraft in the original Ki-27a and modestly improved Ki-27b variants. The Ki-27a had an uprated Ha-1b (Army Type 97) engine and a metal-faired canopy, while the Ki-27b reverted to the clear-vision canopy and featured light ground-attack capability in the form of the four 25-kg (55-lb) bombs that could be

carried under the wings. A number of the fighters were converted as two-seat armed trainers, and two experimental lightweight fighters were produced with the designation Ki-27 KAI. The Ki-27 was used operationally up to 1942, when its light structure and poor armament forced its relegation to second-line duties. The type was initially known to the Allies in the China-Burma-India theatre as the 'Abdul', but 'Nate' later became the standard reporting name.

*The Nakajima Ki-27.*

# CURTISS P-36 MOHAWK and HAWK 75 (U.S.A.)

*P-36C*

In 1934 Curtiss decided on the private-venture design of a modern fighter that might interest the U.S. Army Air Corps as a successor to the Boeing P-26 and would also have considerable export attractions.

The Model 75 prototype first flew in May 1935 as a low-wing monoplane of all-metal construction with an enclosed cockpit, retractable landing gear and a 671-kW (900-hp)

Wright XR-1670-5 radial. The type was evaluated by the USAAC as the Model 75B with the 634-kW (750-hp) Wright R-1820 radial, but was initially beaten for a production order by the Seversky prototype that became the P-35.

The Curtiss machine was reworked into the Model 75E with the 783-kW (1,050-hp) Pratt & Whitney R-1830-13 derated to 708 kW (950 hp) and then re-evaluated as the Y1P-36. This was clearly a superior fighter, and in July 1937 the type was ordered into production as the P-36A with the fully rated version of the R-1830-13 driving a constant-speed propeller. Some 210

of the type were ordered, but only 31 were completed to P-36C standard with the 895-kW (1,200-hp) R-1830-17 engine and the two fuselage-mounted guns (one of 12.7-mm/0.5-in and the other of 7.62-mm/0.3-in calibre) complemented by two wing-mounted 7.62-mm guns.

The type was exported in fairly large numbers as the H75A, principally to France and the United Kingdom, but in smaller numbers to other countries. British aircraft were

named Mohawk and comprised four main variants. Some 30 repossessed Norwegian aircraft were taken in charge by the Americans with the designation P-36G. In addition to this, Curtiss developed a less advanced version as the Hawk 75, in the main similar to the pre-production Y1P-36 but with a lower-powered 652-kW (875-hp) Wright GR-1820 radial and fixed landing gear.

**CURTISS P-36C (RAF MOHAWK)**
**Role:** Fighter
**Crew/Accommodation:** One
**Power Plant:** One 1,200 hp Pratt & Whitney R-1830-17 Twin Wasp air-cooled radial
**Dimensions:** Span 11.35 m (37.33 ft); length 8.72 m (28.6 ft); wing area 21.92 m² (236 sq ft)
**Weights:** Empty 2,095 kg (4,619 lb); MTOW 2,790 kg (6,150 lb)
**Performance:** Maximum speed 501 km/h (311 mph) at 3,048 m (10,000 ft); operational ceiiing 10,272 m (33,700 ft); range 1,320 km (820 miles) at 322 km/h (200 mph) cruise
**Load:** Four .303 inch machine guns

*Curtiss P-36C*

*Curtiss P-36C.*

# SUPERMARINE SPITFIRE and SEAFIRE (United Kingdom)

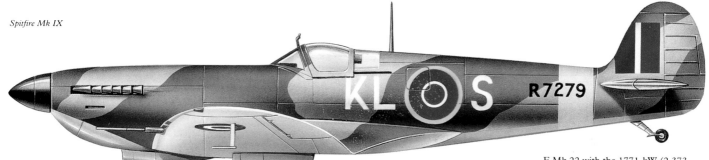

*Spitfire Mk IX*

The Spitfire was the most important British fighter of World War II and remained in production right through the conflict for a total of 20,334 aircraft bolstered by 2,556 new-build Seafire naval fighters. The prototype first flew in March 1936 with a 738-kW (900-hp) Rolls-Royce Merlin C engine, and was soon ordered into production as the Spitfire Mk I with the 768-kW (1,030-hp) Merlin II and eight 7.7-mm (0.303-in) machine guns or, in the Mk IB variant, four machine guns and two 20-mm cannon, the suffix A indicated eight 7.7-mm machine-guns, B four such machine-guns and two 20-mm cannon, C four cannon, and E two

cannon and two 12.7-mm (0.5-in) machine-guns.

Major fighter variants with the Merlin engine were the initial Mk I, the Mk II with the 876-kW (1,175-hp) Merlin XII, the Mks VA, VB and VC in F medium- and LF low-altitiude forms with the 1974-kW (1,440-hp) Merlin 45 or 1096-kW (1,470-hp) Merlin 50, the HF.Mk VI high-altitude interceptor with the 1055-kW (1,415-hp) Merlin 47 and a pressurized cockpit, the HF.Mk VII with the two-stage Merlin 61, 64 or 71, the LF, F and HF.Mk VIII with the two-stage Merlin 61, 63, 66 or 70 but an unpressurized cockpit, the LF, F and HF.Mk IX using the Mk V

airframe with the two-stage Merlin 61, 63 or 70, the LF and F.Mk XVI using the Mk IX airframe with a cutdown rear fuselage, bubble canopy and Packard-built Merlin 226.

The Spitfire was also developed in its basic fighter form with the larger and more powerful Rolls-Royce Griffon inline, and the major variants of this sequence were the LF.Mk XI with the 1294-kW (1,735-hp) Griffon II or IV, the LF and F.Mk XIV with the 1529-kW (2,050-hp) Griffon 65 or 66 and often with a bubble canopy, the F.Mk XVIII with the two-stage Griffon and a bubble canopy, the F. Mk 21 with the Griffon 61 or 64, the

F.Mk 22 with the 1771-kW (2,373-hp) Griffon 85 driving a contra-rotating propeller unit, and the improved F.Mk 24.

The Spitfire was also used as a unarmed reconnaissance type, the major Merlin-engined types being the Mks IV, X, XI and XIII, and the Griffon-engined type being the Mk XIX. The Seafire was the naval counterpart to the Spitfire, the main Merlin engined versions being the Mks IB, IIC and III, and the Griffon-engined versions being the Mks XV, XVII, 45, 46 and 47.

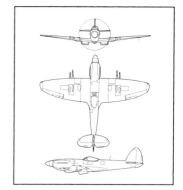

*Supermarine Spitfire F.Mk 24*

---

**SUPERMARINE SPITFIRE F.Mk XIV E**
**Role:** Fighter
**Crew/Accommodation:** One
**Power Plant:** One 2,050 hp Rolls-Royce Griffon 65 water-cooled inline
**Dimensions:** Span 11.23 m (36.83 ft); length 9.96 m (32.66 ft); wing area 22.48 m² (242 sq ft)
**Weights:** Empty 2,994 kg (6,600 lb); MTOW 3,856 kg (8,500 lb)
**Performance:** Maximum speed 721 km/h (448 mph) at 7,925 m (26,000 ft); operational ceiling 13,106 m (43,000 ft); range 740 km (460 miles) on internal fuel only
**Load:** Two 20 mm cannon and two .303 machine guns, plus up to 454 kg (1,000 lb) of bombs

*Supermarine Spitfire F.Mk XIV*

# DEWOITINE D.520 (France)

*Dewoitine D.520*

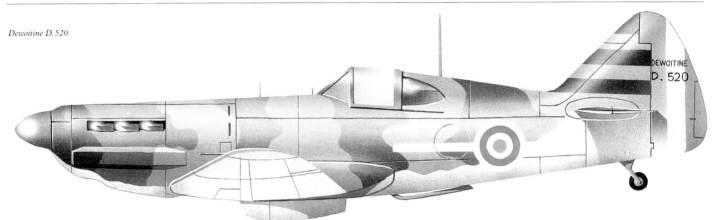

Dewoitine's first 'modern' low-wing monoplane fighter was the D.513 that first flew in January 1936 with a 641-kW (860-hp) Hispano-Suiza 12Ycrs inline. The type introduced advanced features such as an enclosed cockpit and retractable landing gear, but its low performance and severe instability problems proved very disappointing. The type was extensively revised but still had problems, so it was abandoned.

The company used the lessons learned from the D.513 fiasco in the creation of the D.520 which proved a far more satisfactory type and was ordered in substantial numbers. One of the most advanced fighters to serve with the French Air Force in the disastrous early campaign of 1940, the D.520 was a modern fighter of considerably trimmer and more pleasing lines than the D.513. It embodied an enclosed cockpit, trailing-edge flaps, retractable tailwheel landing gear and a variable-pitch propeller for the engine located in a much cleaner nose installation.

The D520.01 prototype first flew in October 1938 with the 664-kW (890-hp) Hispano-Suiza 12Y-21 inline, though the two following prototypes had wing, vertical tail and cockpit canopy modifications as well as the 746-kW (1,000-hp) HS 12Y-51 and 619-kW (830-hp) HS 12Y-31 engines respectively. Substantial orders were placed for the D.520 with the 686-kW (920-hp) HS 12Y-45 or -49, but only 403 aircraft had been delivered before the fall of France in June 1940. The in-service fighters did well in combat with German aircraft, and 478 aircraft were built for the Vichy French Air Force. Surviving aircraft remained up to the early 1950s. There were several experimental variants including the very promising D.524 with the 895-kW (1,200-hp) HS 12Y-89.

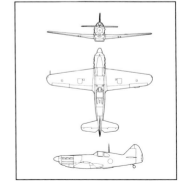

*Dewoitine D.520.*

**DEWOITINE D.520**
**Role:** Fighter
**Crew/Accommodation:** One
**Power Plant:** One 920 hp Hispano-Suiza 12Y45 water-cooled inline
**Dimensions:** Span 10.2 m (33 ft); length 8.76 m (28 ft); wing area 15.95 m² (171.7 sq ft)
**Weights:** Empty 2,092 kg (4,612 lb); MTOW 2,783 kg (6,134 lb)
**Performance:** Maximum speed 535 km/h (332 mph) at 6,000 m (19,685 ft); operational ceiling 11,000 m (36,090 ft); range 900 km (553 miles)
**Load:** One 20 mm cannon and four 7.5 mm machine guns

*Dewoitine D.520*

*Dewoitine D.520.*

# BLOCH M.B. 151 and M.B. 152 (France)

*M.B. 152 C1*

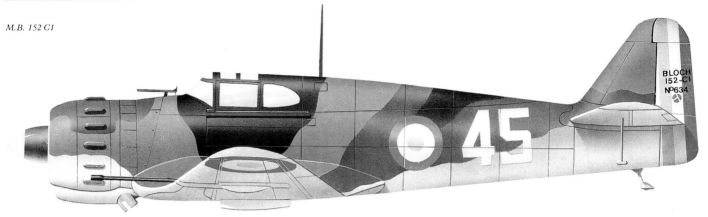

The M.B. 151 was one of France's first 'modern' monoplane fighters, and resulted from the unsuccessful M.B. 150 prototype produced to meet a 1934 requirement. The M.B.150 could not at first be persuaded to fly, but after it had been fitted with a larger wing, revised landing gear and a 701-kW (940-hp) Gnome-Rhône 14N radial, the type first flew in October 1937. In 1938 further improvement in flight performance was achieved with a slightly larger wing and the Gnome-Rhône 14N-7 engine, and a pre-production batch of 25 M.B. 151 fighters was ordered with slightly reduced wing span and the 695-kW (920-hp) Gnome-Rhône 14N-11 radial. The first of these flew in August 1938, and there followed 115 production aircraft with the identically rated Gnome-Rhône 14N-35 radial.

The type was deemed to lack the performance required of a first-line fighter, and was generally used as a fighter trainer. An improved version was developed as the M.B. 152 with the more powerful 768-kW (1,030-hp) Gnome-Rhône 14N-25 or 790-kW (1,060-hp) Gnome-Rhône 14N-49. Production was slow, and only a few M.B. 152s were combat–ready in time for the German invasion of May 1940; more than 30 aircraft had been delivered by January 1940, but most lacked the right propeller. The airworthy examples served with success during the German invasion of mid-1940, and then remained operational with the Vichy French air force. Some aircraft were used by the Luftwaffe as trainers, and 20 were passed to Romania.

*The Bloch M.B. 151.*

**BLOCH M.B. 152**
**Role:** Fighter
**Crew/Accommodation:** One
**Power Plant:** One 1,000 hp Gnome-Rhône 14N-25 air-cooled radial
**Dimensions:** Span 10.54 m (34.58 ft); length 9.1 m (29.86 ft); wing area 17.32 m² (186.4 sq ft)
**Weights:** Empty 2,158 kg (4,758 lb); MTOW 2,800 kg (6,173 lb)
**Performance:** Maximum speed 509 km/h (316 mph) at 4,500 m (14,765 ft); operational ceiling 10,000 m (32,808 ft); range 540 km (335 miles)
**Load:** Two 20 mm cannon and two 7.5 mm machine guns

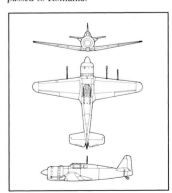

*Bloch M.B. 155*

# BOULTON PAUL DEFIANT (United Kingdom)

*Defiant Mk II*

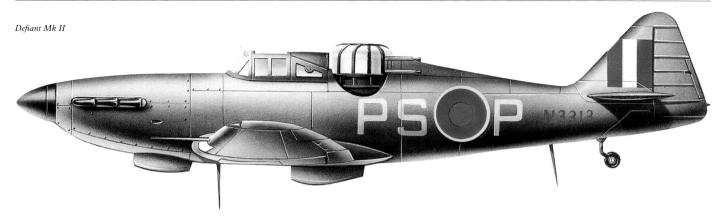

In the mid-1930s there was considerable enthusiasm among Royal Air Force planners for the two-seat fighter in which all the armament would be concentrated in a power-operated turret. Such a fighter, its protagonists claimed, would be able to penetrate into enemy bomber streams and wreak havoc. A first expression of this concept was found in the Hawker

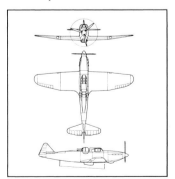

*Boulton Paul Defiant Mk I*

Demon, of which 59 were manufactured in 1934 by Boulton Paul with a Frazer-Nash turret. The company was therefore well placed to respond to a 1935 requirement for a more advanced two-seat turret fighter. The P.82 design was for a trim fighter of the 'modern' monoplane type, little larger than current single-seaters and fitted with a four-gun turret immediately aft of the cockpit. The first of two Defiant prototypes flew in

**BOULTON PAUL DEFIANT Mk II**
**Role:** Night fighter
**Crew/Accommodation:** Two
**Power Plant:** One 1,280 hp Rolls-Royce Merlin XX water-cooled inline
**Dimensions:** Span 11.99 m (39.33 ft); length 10.77 m (35.33 ft); wing area 23.23 m² (250 sq ft)
**Weights:** Empty 2,850 kg (6,282 lb); MTOW 3,773 kg (8,318 lb)
**Performance:** Maximum speed 507 km/h (315 mph) at 5,029 m (16,500 ft); operational ceiling 9,251 m (30,350 ft); range 748 km (465 miles)
**Load:** Four .303 inch machine guns in power-operated turret.
**Note:** The Defiant Mk III was retrofitted to embody AIMk4 radar.

August 1937 with a 768-kW (1,030-hp) Rolls-Royce Merlin I inline engine, and the Defiant Mk I fighter began to enter service in December 1939.

After early encounters with German warplanes, in which the Defiant scored some success because of the novelty of its layout, operations soon revealed the inadequacy of a type in which the turret's weight and drag imposed severe performance and handling limitations and also left the pilot without fixed forward-firing

armament. It was decided to convert existing fighters to Defiant NF.Mk IA night fighter standard with primative AI.Mk IV or VI radar. Mk I production totalled 723, and another 210 night fighters were built as Defiant NF.Mk IIs with the more powerful Merlin XX engine and larger vertical tail surfaces. Many were later converted to Defiant TT.Mk I target-tugs and another 140 were built as such; similarly converted Mk Is became Defiant TT.Mk IIIs. Total production was 1,075.

*Boulton Paul Defiant Mk I*

# GRUMMAN F4F WILDCAT (U.S.A.)

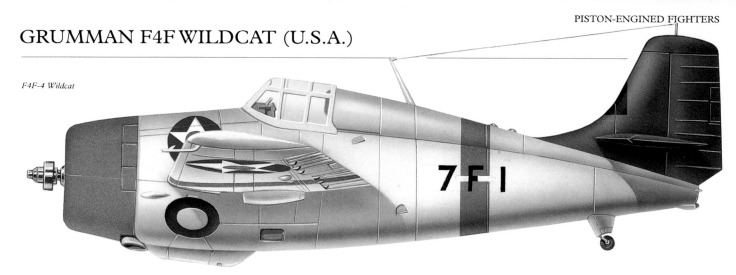

*F4F-4 Wildcat*

The F4F designation was first used for the G-16 biplane ordered as the XF4F-1 in competition to the Brewster monoplane prototype that was accepted for service as the F2A Buffalo carrierborne fighter. Grumman did not build the biplane prototype, but instead reworked the design as the G-18 monoplane. Re-evaluation of Grumman's proposal led the U.S. Navy to call for an XF4F-2 monoplane prototype, and this first flew in September 1937 with a 783-kW (1,050-hp) Pratt & Whitney R-1830-66 Twin Wasp radial. This initial model was judged slightly inferior to the Buffalo, but was revised as the G-36 with a redesigned tail, a larger wing and the XR-1830-76 engine.

This XF4F-3 first flew in March 1939, and its performance and handling were so improved that the type was ordered as the F4F-3, the British taking a similar version as the Martlet Mk I; the armament was four 12.7-mm (0.5 in) machine guns and production totalled 369 excluding 95 F4F-3As with the R-1830-90 engine. The F4F/Martlet was the first Allied carrierborne fighter able to meet land-based opponents on anything like equal terms, and proved invaluable during the early war years up to 1943 in variants such as the 1,169 examples of the F4F-4 (Martlet Mks II, III and IV) with wing folding, armour, self-sealing tanks and six rather than four machine guns, and the 21 examples of the F4F-7 unarmed long-range reconnaissance version. The Eastern Aircraft Division of General Motors built 1,060 of the FM-1 (Martlet Mk V) equivalent to the F4F-4 with the R-1830-86 engine, four wing guns, and provision for underwing stores, and 4,127 of the FM-2 (Martlet Mk V) based on Grumman's XF4F-8 prototype with the 1007-kW (1,350-hp) Wright R-1820-56 Cyclone, taller vertical tail surfaces and, on the last 826 aircraft, provision for six 127-mm (5-in) rockets under the wings.

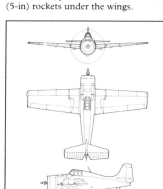

*Grumman F4F-4 Wildcat*

*Grumman F4F-4 Wildcat.*

**GRUMMAN F4F-4 WILDCAT**
**Role:** Naval carrierborne fighter
**Crew/Accommodation:** One
**Power Plant:** One 1,200 hp Pratt & Whitney R-1830-86 Twin Wasp air-cooled radial
**Dimensions:** Span 11.58 m (38 ft); length 8.76 m (28.75 ft); wing area 24.16 m² (260 sq ft)
**Weights:** Empty 2,624 kg (5,785 lb); MTOW 3,607 kg (7,952 lb)
**Performance:** Maximum speed 512 km/h (318 mph) at 5,913 m (19,400 ft); operational ceiling 10,638 m (34,900 ft); range 1,239 km (770 miles) on internal fuel only
**Load:** Six .5 inch machine guns

# BRISTOL BEAUFIGHTER (United Kingdom)

*Beaufighter Mk I*

The Beaufighter was born of the Royal Air Force's shortage of heavy fighters (especially heavily armed night fighters and long-range escort fighters) as perceived at the time of the 'Munich crisis' late in 1938. The Type 156 was planned round the wings, tail unit and landing gear of the Type 152 Beaufort torpedo bomber married to a new fuselage and two Hercules radials.

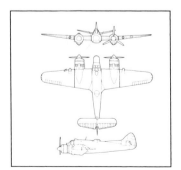

*Bristol Beaufighter TF.Mk X*

The first of four prototypes flew in July 1939, and production was authorized with 1119-kW (1,500-hp) Hercules XI engines. Development of the Beaufighter at this time divided into two role-orientated streams. First of these was the night fighter as exemplified by the 553 Beaufighter Mk IFs with Hercules XIs, nose radar and an armament of four 20-mm nose cannon and six 7.7-mm (0.303-in) wing machine-guns. This model entered service in July 1940, and

**BRISTOL BEAUFIGHTER Mk IF**
**Role:** Night fighter
**Crew/Accommodation:** Two
**Power Plant:** Two 1,400 hp Bristol Hercules XI air-cooled radials
**Dimensions:** Span 17.63 m (57.83 ft); length 12.60 m (41.33 ft); wing area 46.7 m² (503 sq ft)
**Weights:** Empty 6,382 kg (14,069 lb); MTOW 9,525 kg (21,000 lb)
**Performance:** Maximum speed 520 km/h (323 mph) at 4,572 m (15,000 ft); operational ceiling 8,839 m (29,000 ft); range 2,413 km (1,500 miles) internal fuel only
**Load:** Four 20 mm cannon and six .303 machine guns (interception guided by AI Mk IV radar)

further evolution led to the 597 Beaufighter Mk IIFs with 954-kW (1,280-hp) Rolls-Royce Merlin XX inlines, and finally the 879 Beaufighter Mk VIFs with 1245-kW (1,675-hp) Hercules VIs or XVIs and improved radar in a 'thimble' nose.

With its high performance and capacious fuselage, which made the installation of radar a comparatively simple matter, the Beaufighter night fighter provided the RAF with its first truly effective method of combating nocturnal German bombers. More significant in the longer term,

however, was the anti-ship version first developed as the 397 Beaufighter Mk ICs and then evolved via the 693 torpedo-carrying Beaufighter Mk VICs and 60 Beaufighter Mk VI (ITF)s with eight 27-kg (60-lb) rockets in place of the wing guns, to the 2,205 Beaufighter TF.Mk Xs with search radar and an armament of one torpedo plus light bombs or eight rockets. The 163 Beaufighter TF.Mk XIs were similar, while the 364 Beaufighter TF.Mk 21s were the Australian-built equivalents of the TF.Mk X.

*TF.Mk X.*

# MACCHI MC.200 to MC.205 Series (Italy)

*MC.200 Saetta*

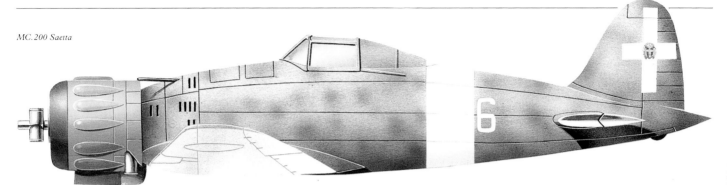

In 1936 the Italian Air Force belatedly realized that the day of the biplane fighter was effectively over, and requested the development of a 'modern' monoplane fighter with stressed-skin metal construction, a low-set cantilever monoplane wing, an enclosed cockpit and retractable landing gear. Macchi's response was the MC.200 Saetta (lightning) that first flew in December 1937 with the

649-kW (870-hp) Fiat A.74 RC 38 radial engine. The type was declared superior to its competitors during 1938 and ordered into production to a total of 1,153 aircraft in variants that 'progressed' from an enclosed to an open and eventually a semi-enclosed cockpit.

The MC.200 was a beautiful aircraft to fly, but clearly lacked the performance to deal with the higher-performance British fighters. There was no Italian inline engine that could offer the required performance, so the MC.202 Folgore (Thunderbolt) that flew in August 1940 with an enclosed

cockpit used an imported Daimler-Benz DB 601A engine. About 1,500 production aircraft followed, initially with imported engines but later with licence-built Alfa-Romeo RA.100 RC 41-I Monsone engines rated at 876-kW (1,175-hp). The MC.205V Veltro (Greyhound) was a development of the MC.202 with the 1100-kW (1,475-hp) DB 605A engine and considerably heavier armament. The

MC.205 was first flown in April 1942 but production had then to await availability of the licensed DB 605A, the RA.1050 RC 58 Tifone, so deliveries started only in mid-1943. Production amounted to 252, and most of these aircraft served with the fascist republic established in northern Italy after the effective division of Italy by the September 1943 armistice with the Allies.

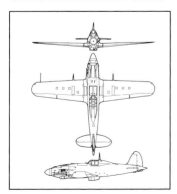

*Macchi Mc.205V Veltro*

**MACCHI MC.205V VELTRO Series II**
**Role:** Fighter
**Crew/Accommodation:** One
**Power Plant:** One 1,475 hp Fiat-built Daimler-Benz DB605A water-cooled inline
**Dimensions:** Span 10.58 m (34.71 ft): length 8.85 m (29.04 ft); wing area 16.8 m² (180.8 sq ft)
**Weights:** Empty 2,581 kg (5,690 lb): MTOW 3,224 kg (7.108 lb)
**Performance:** Maximum speed 642 km/h (399 mph) at 7,200 m (2,620 ft); operational ceiling 11,000 m (36,090 ft); range 950 km (590 miles)
**Load:** Two 200 mm cannon, plus up to 320 kg (706 lb) of bombs

*The Macchi MC.205V Veltro*

# CURTISS P-40 WARHAWK Family (U.S.A.)

*P-40 B Warhawk*

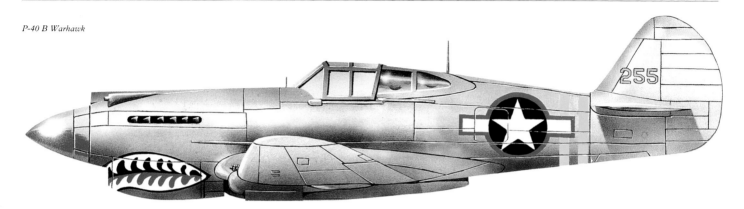

The P-40 series was in no way an exceptional warplane, but nonetheless proved itself a more than adequate fighter-bomber. It was exceeded in numbers by only two other American fighters, the Republic P-47 Thunderbolt and North American P-51 Mustang. The basis for the P-40 series was the Model 75I, a Model 75/

*Curtiss P-40E Warhawk*

XP-37A airframe modified to take the 858-kW (1,150-hp) Allison V-1710-11 inline engine. This became the first U.S. fighter to exceed 300 mph (483 km/h) in level flight, and the type was ordered by the U.S. Army Air Corps in modified form with the designation P-40 and the less powerful V-1710-33; export versions were the Hawk 81-A1 for France and Tomahawk Mk I for the UK.

Improved models were the P-40B (Tomahawk Mk IIA) with self-sealing

**CURTISS P-40F WARHAWK**
**Role:** Fighter
**Crew/Accommodation:** One
**Power Plant:** One 1,300 hp Packard-built Rolls-Royce V-1650-1 Merlin water-colled inline
**Dimensions:** Span 11.38 m (37.33 ft); length 10.16 m (33.33 ft); wing area 21.93 m² (236 sq ft)
**Weights:** Empty 2,989 kg (6,590 lb); MTOW 4,241 kg (9,350 lb)
**Performance:** Maximum speed 586 km/h (364 mph) at 6,096 m (20,000 ft); operational ceiling 10,485 m (34,400 ft); range 603 km (375 miles)
**Load:** Six .5 inch machine guns, plus up to 227 kg (500 lb) of bombs

tanks, armour and better armament, the P-40C (Tomahawk Mk IIB) with improved self-sealing tanks and two more wing guns, the P-40D (Kittyhawk Mk I) with the 858-kW (1,150-hp) V-1710-39 with better supercharging to maintain performance to a higher altitude, and the P-40E with four wing guns plus the similar Kittyhawk Mk IA with six wing guns. The P-40 series had all along been limited by the indifferent supercharging of the V-1710, and this situation was remedied in the P-40F and generally similar P-40L

(Kittyhawk Mk II) by the adoption of the 969-kW (1,300-hp) Packard V-1650-1 (licence-built Rolls-Royce Merlin). The type's forte was still the fighter-bomber role at low altitude, and further developments included the P-40K (Kittyhawk Mk III) version of the P-40E with the V-1710-33 engine, the P-40M with the V-1710-71 engine, and the definitive P-40N (Kittyhawk Mk IV) with the V-1710-81/99/115 engine and measures to reduce weight significantly as a means of improving performance.

*Curtiss P-40 Warhawk*

# FOCKE-WULF Fw 190 and Ta 152 (Germany)

*Focke-Wulf Fw 190A*

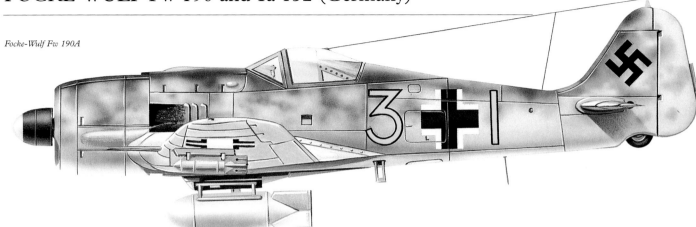

The Fw 190 was Germany's best fighter of World War II, and resulted from the belief of designer Kurt Tank that careful streamlining could produce a radial-engined fighter with performance equal to that of an inline-engined type without the extra complexity and weight of the latter's water-cooling system. The first of three prototypes flew in June 1939, and an extensive test programme was required to develop the air cooling system and evaluate short- and long-span wings, the latter's additional 1.0 m (3 ft 3.7 in) of span and greater area reducing performance but boosting both agility and climb rate. This wing was selected for the Fw 190A

production type in a programme that saw the building of about 19,500 Fw 190s. The Fw 190A was powered by the BMW 801 radial, and was developed in variants up to the Fw 190A-8 with a host of subvariants optimized for the clear- or all-weather interception, ground-attack, torpedo attack and tactical reconnaissance roles, together with an immensely diverse armament.

The Fw 190B series was used to develop high-altitude capability with longer-span wings and a pressurized cockpit, and then pioneered the 1304-kW (1,750-hp) Daimler-Benz DB 603 inline engine. The Fw 190C was another high-altitude development

model with the DB 603 engine and a turbocharger. The next operational model was the Fw 190D, which was developed in role-optimized variants between Fw 190D-9 and Fw 190D-13 with the 1324-kW (1,776-hp) Junkers Jumo 213 inline and an annular radiator in a lengthened fuselage. The Fw 190E was a proposed reconnaissance fighter, and the Fw 190F series, which preceded the Fw 190D model, was a specialized ground-attack type based

on the radial-engined Fw 190A-4. Finally in the main sequence came the FW 190G series of radial-engined fighter-bombers evolved from the Fw 190A-5. An ultra-high-altitude derivative with longer-span wings was developed as the Jumo 213-engined Ta 152, but the only operational variant was the Ta 152H.

*Focke-Wulf Fw 190*

**FOCKE-WULF Fw 190 A-8**
**Role:** Fighter
**Crew/Accommodation:** One
**Power Plant:** 1,600 hp BMW 801C-1 air-cooled radial
**Dimensions:** Span 10.5 m (34.45 ft); length 8.84 m (29 ft); wing area 18.3 m² (196.98 sq ft)
**Weights:** Empty 3,170 kg (7,000 lb); MTOW 4,900 kg (10.805 lb)
**Performance:** Maximum speed 654 km/h (408 mph) at 6,000 m (19,686 ft); operational ceiling 11,400 m (37,403 ft); range 805 km (500 miles)
**Load:** For 20 mm cannon and two 13 mm machine guns, plus up to 1,000 kg (2,205 lb) of bombs

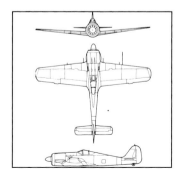

*Focke-Wulf Fw 190A*

# LOCKHEED P-38 LIGHTNING (U.S.A.)

*P-38J Lightning*

The Lightning was one was the more important fighters of World War II and, though it was not as nimble as a machine as single-engined types, found its métier in the long-range role with heavy armament and high performance. The machine resulted from a 1937 specification issued by the U.S. Army Air Corps for a high-

performance fighter providing such speed, climb rate and range that a single-engined aircraft was virtually out of the question. Having opted for the twin-engined configuration, the design team then chose an unconventional layout with a central nacelle and twin booms extending as rearward extensions of the engine nacelle to accommodate the turbochargers and support the wide-span tailplane and oval vertical surfaces.

The XP-38 prototype flew in

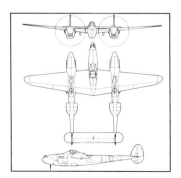

*Lockheed P-38J Lightning*

**LOCKHEED P-38L LIGHTNING**
**Role:** Long-range fighter bomber
**Crew/Accommodation:** One
**Power Plant:** Two 1,475 hp Allison V-1710-111 water-cooled inlines
**Dimensions:** Span 15.85 m (52 ft); length 11.53 m (37.83 ft); wing area 30.47 m² (327 sq ft)
**Weights:** Empty 5,806 kg (12,800 lb); MTOW 9,798 kg (21,600 lb)
**Performance:** Maximum speed 666 km/h (414 mph) at 7,620 m (25,000 ft); operational ceiling 13,410 m (44,000 ft); range 725 km (450 miles) with 1,451 kg (3,200 lb) of bombs
**Load:** One 20 mm cannon and four .5 inch machine guns, plus up to 1,451 kg (3,200 lb) of bombs

January 1939 with 716-kW (960-hp) Allison V-1710-11/15 engines driving opposite-rotating propellers. Development was protracted, and the first of 30 P-38s, with V-1710-27/29 engines, did not enter service until late 1941. Production totalled 10,037 in variants that included 36 P-36Ds with a revised tail unit and self-sealing fuel tanks, 210 P-38Es with the nose armament revised from one 37-mm cannon and four 12.7-mm (0.5-in) machine guns to one 20-mm cannon and four machine guns, 527 P-38Fs for tropical service with V-1710 49/53 engines, 1,082 F-38Gs with V-1710-

55/55 engines and provision for 907-kg (2,000-lb) of underwing stores, 601 P-38Gs with 1062-kW (1,425-hp) V-1710-89/91s and greater underwing stores load, 2,970 P-38Js with an improved engine installation and greater fuel capacity, 3,810 P-38Ls with 1193-kW (1,600-hp) V-1710-111/113s, provision for underwing rockets and, in some aircraft, a revised nose accommodating radar or a bomb-aimer for use as a bomber leader, the P-38M conversions of P-38L as two-seat night fighters, and the F-4 and F-5 conversions.

*Lockheed P-38L Lightning*

# MITSUBISHI A6M REISEN 'ZEKE' (Japan)

*A6M5 Reisen 'Zeke'*

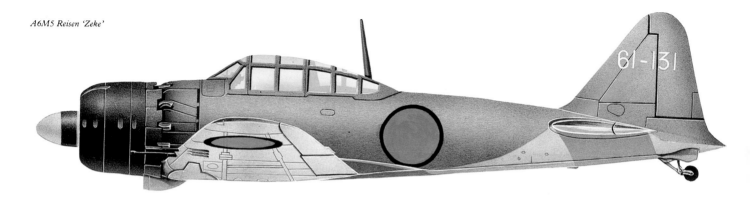

The A6M Reisen (Zero Fighter) will rightly remain Japan's best known aircraft of World War II, and was in its early days, without doubt, the finest carrierborne fighter anywhere in the world. The A6M was the first naval fighter able to deal on equal terms with the best of land-based fighters, and was notable for its heavy firepower combined with good performance, great range and considerable agility. This combination could only be achieved with a lightweight and virtually unprotected airframe. Thus from 1943 the Zero

could not be developed effectively to maintain it as a competitive fighter.

The A6M was planned to an Imperial Japanese Navy Air Force requirement for a successor to the Mitsubishi A5M, a low-wing fighter with an open cockpit and fixed landing gear. The first of two A6M1 prototypes flew in April 1939 with a 582-kW (780-hp) Mitsubishi Mk2 Zuisei radial. The new fighter was a cantilever low-wing monoplane with retractable tailwheel landing gear, an enclosed cockpit and powerful armament. Performance and agility

were generally excellent, but the type was somewhat slower than anticipated. The sole A6M2 prototype therefore introduced the 690-kW (925-hp) Nakajima NK1C Sakae radial, and this was retained for the first series-built A6M2 aircraft that entered service with the designation Navy Type 0 Carrier Fighter Model 11. Production of the series amounted to 11,283 aircraft to the end of World War II, and major variants after the A6M2 were the A6M3 with the 843-kW (1,130-hp) Sakae 21 and clipped wingtips, the A6M5 with improved

armament and armour in three subvariants, the A6M6 with the Sakae 31, and the A6M7 dive-bomber and fighter. There were also a number of experimental and development models as well as the A6M2-N floatplane fighter built by Nakajima. The principal Allied reporting name for the type was 'Zeke'.

**MITSUBISHI A6M5 'ZEKE'**
**Role:** Naval carrierborne fighter
**Crew/Accommodation:** One
**Power Plant:** One 1,130 hp Nakajima Sakae 21 air-cooled radial
**Dimensions:** Span 11 m (36.09 ft); length 9.09 m (29.82 ft); wing area 21.3 m² (229.3 sq ft)
**Weights:** Empty 1,894 kg (4,176 lb) MTOW 2,952 kg (6,508 lb)
**Performance:** Maximum speed 565 km/h (351 mph) at 6,000 m (19,685 ft); operational ceiling 11,740 m (38,517 ft); range 1,570 km (976 miles)
**Load:** Two 20 mm cannon and two 7.7 mm machine guns

*A Mitsubishi A6M5 Reisen*

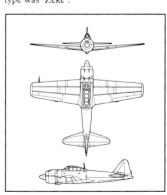

*Mitsubishi A6M3 32 Reisen*

# BELL P-39 AIRACOBRA (U.S.A.)

*P-39 Airacobra Mk I*

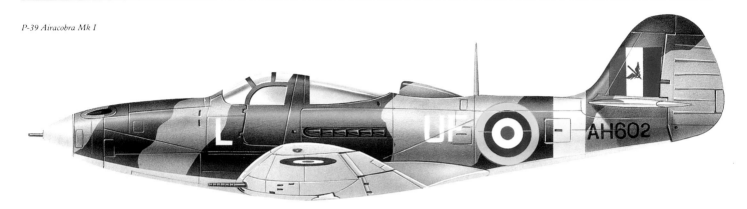

The P-39 Airacobra was an attempt to create a fighter that possessed greater manoeuvrability and more powerful nose-mounted armament than contemporary fighters. The engine was located behind the cockpit on the aircraft's centre of gravity. It drove the propeller by means of an extension shaft, and the nose volume was left free for the forward unit of the retractable tricycle landing gear and

also for heavy fixed armament including one 37-mm cannon firing through the propeller shaft. The XP-39 prototype flew in April 1938, and was followed by 13 YP-39 pre-production aircraft including one YP-39A with an unturbocharged Allison V-1710 engine. This last became the prototype for the production version, which was ordered in August 1939 as the P-45. These aircraft were in fact delivered as 20 P-39Cs and 60 P-39Ds with heavier armament and self-sealing

tanks. Large-scale production followed. Total P-39 production was 9,590, even though the Airacobra was never more than adequate as a fighter and found its real mileu in the low-level attack role.

The main models were the 229 P-39Fs modelled on the P-39D but with an Aeroproducts propeller, the 210 P-

39Ks with the V-1710-63 engine and a Curtiss propeller, 240 P-39Ms with the V-1710-83 engine and a larger propeller, 2,095 P-39Ns with the V-1710-85 engine but less fuel and armour, and 4,905 P-39Qs with two underwing gun gondolas. Large numbers were supplied to the U.S.S.R. in World War II.

### BELL P-39D AIRACOBRA
**Role:** Fighter
**Crew/Accommodation:** One
**Power Plant:** One, 1,150 hp Allison V-1710-35 water-cooled inline
**Dimensions:** Span 10.36 m (34 ft); length 9.19 m (30.16 ft); wing area 19.79 m² (213 sq ft)
**Weights:** Empty 2,478 kg (5,462 lb); MTOW 3,720 kg (8,200 lb)
**Performance:** Maximum speed 592 km/h (368 mph) at 4,206 m (13,800 ft); operational ceiling 9,784 m (32,100 ft); range 1,287 km (800 miles) with 227 kg (500 lb) of bombs
**Load:** One 37mm cannon, plus two .5 inch and four .303 inch machine guns, along with 227 kg (500 lb) of bombs

*P-39N of the Italian Air Force*

# MIKOYAN-GUREVICH MiG-1 and MiG-3 (U.S.S.R.)

*MiG-3*

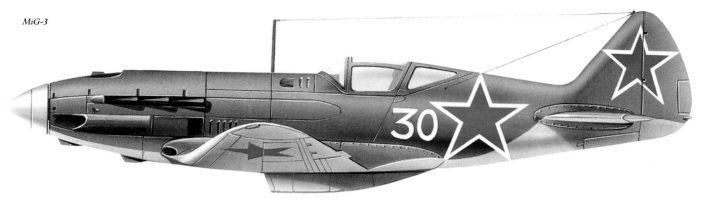

To design the new interceptor fighter requested by the Soviet Air Force in 1938, Artem Mikoyan and Mikhail Gurevich started a collaboration that led eventually to a succession of world-famous fighters. The two men's first effort was not so successful. As the starting point for the new interceptor, the MiG team produced

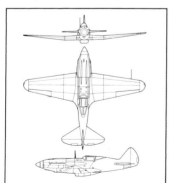

*Mikoyan-Gurevich MiG-3*

I-65 and I-61 design concepts, the latter in variants with the Mikulin AM-35A and AM-37 inlines. The I-61 was deemed superior and ordered in the form of three I-200 prototypes.

The first of these flew in April 1940, and on the power of the AM-35A the type proved to have the excellent speed of 630 km/h (391 mph), making it the world's fastest interceptor of the period. The type was ordered into production as the MiG-1 with an open cockpit or a side-hinged canopy, and an armament of one 12.7-mm (0.5-in) and two 7.62-

### MIKOYAN-GUREVICH MiG-3
**Role:** Fighter
**Crew/Accommodation:** One
**Power Plant:** One 1,350 hp Mikulin AM-35A water-cooled inline
**Dimensions:** Span 10.3 m (33.79 ft); length 8.15 m (26.74 ft); wing area 17.44 m² (187.7 sq ft)
**Weights:** Empty 2,595 kg (5,720 lb); MTOW 3,285 kg (7,242 lb)
**Performance:** Maximum speed 640 km/h (398 mph) at 7,000 m (22,965 ft); operational ceiling 12,000 m (39,370 ft) range 820 km/h (510 miles) with full warload
**Load:** Three 12.7 mm machine guns, plus up to 200 kg (441 lb) of bombs or rockets

mm (0.3-in) machine guns. But range and longitudinal stability were both minimal, and structural integrity was inadequate after battle damage had been suffered, so only 100 were delivered before the MiG-1 was superseded by the strengthened and aerodynamically refined MiG-3. This had a rearward-sliding canopy, increased dihedral on the outer wing panels, greater fuel capacity, better armour protection and provision for

weightier armament in the form of 200-kg (440-lb) of bombs or six 82-mm (3.2-in) rockets carried under the wings. Some 3,322 such aircraft were built, but these saw only limited use; the MiG-3 performed well at altitudes over 5000 m (16,405 ft), but most air combats with the generally better flown German fighters of the period took place at the low and medium altitudes below this height.

*Mikoyan-Gurevich MiG-3*

# VOUGHT F4U CORSAIR (U.S.A.)

*A-7P Corsair II*

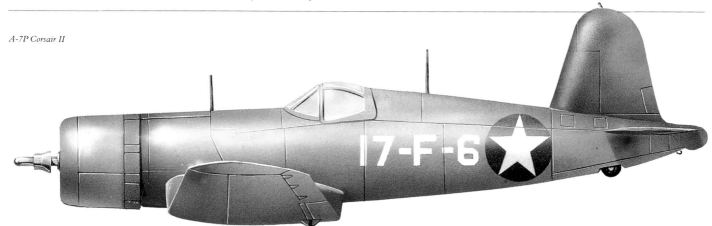

One of several fighters with a realistic claim to having been the best fighter of World War II, the Corsair was certainly the war's best fighter-bomber and a truly distinguished type in this exacting role with cannon, bombs and rockets. The type originated as the V.166A design in response to a U.S. Navy requirement of 1938 for a high-performance carrierborne fighter. The design team produced the smallest possible airframe round the most powerful engine available, the 1491-kW (2,000-hp) Pratt & Whitney XR-2800 Double Wasp radial. This engine required a large-diameter propeller, and to provide this with adequate ground clearance without recourse to stalky main landing gear legs, the design team opted for inverted gull wings that allowed short main gear legs and also helped to keep the type's height as low as possible with the wings folded.

The V.166B prototype first flew in May 1940 as the XF4U-1, and after a troubled development in which the U.S. Navy refused to allow carrierborne operations until after the British had achieved these on their smaller carriers, the type entered service as the F4U-1. Total production was 12,571 up to the early 1950s, and the main variants were the baseline F4U-1 (758 aircraft), the F4U-1A (2,066) with a frameless canopy, the F4U-1C (200) with four 20-mm cannon in place of the wing machine-guns, the F4U-1D (1,375) fighter-bomber, the F4U-1P photo-reconnaissance conversion of the F4U-1, the FG-1 built by Goodyear in three subvariants (1,704 FG-1s, 2,302 FG-1Ds and FG-1E night fighters in the FG-1 total), the F3A built by Brewster in two subvariants (735 F3A-1s and F3A-1Ds), the F4U-4 (2,351) with the 1827-kW (2,450-hp) R-2800-18W(C), a few of the F25 Goodyear version of the F4U-4, and several F4U-5, F4U-7 and AU-1 post-war models.

## VOUGHT F4U-1D CORSAIR
**Role:** Naval carrierborne fighter bomber
**Crew/Accommodation:** One
**Power Plant:** One 2,000 hp Pratt & Whitney R-2800-8 Double Wasp air-cooled radial
**Dimensions:** Span 12.50 m (41 ft); length 10.16 m (33.33 ft); wing area 29.17 m² (314 sq ft)
**Weights:** Empty 4,074 kg (8,982 lb); MTOW 6,350 kg (14,000 lb)
**Performance:** Maximum speed 578 km/h (359 mph) at sea level; operating ceiling 11,247 m (36,900 ft); range 1,633 km (1,015 miles)
**Load:** Six .5 inch machine guns plus up to 907 kg (2,000 lb) of bombs

*Vought F4U-1D Corsair*

*A Vought AU-1 Corsair with the markings of the US Marine Corps*

# NORTH AMERICAN P-51 MUSTANG (U.S.A.)

*P-51D Mustang*

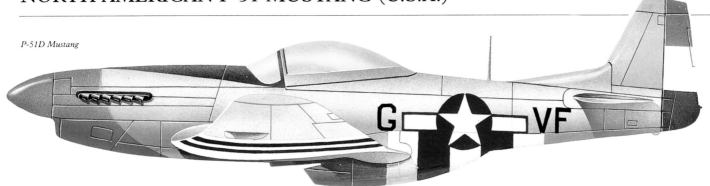

The Mustang was perhaps the greatest fighter of World War II in terms of all-round performance and capability, and resulted from a British requirement of April 1940 that stipulated a first flight within 120 days of contract signature. The NA-73X flew in October of the same year with an 820-kW (1,100-hp) Allison V-1710-F3R inline. Mustang production totalled 15,469, and the first variant was the Mustang Mk I reconnaissance fighter with an armament of four 12.7-mm (0.5-in) machine-guns; two of these 620 aircraft were evaluated by the U.S. Army Air Corps with the designation XP-51. The next variants were the 93 Mustang Mk IAs and 57 equivalent P-51s with four 20-mm cannon, and the 50 longer-range Mustang Mk IIs and 250 equivalent P-51As with more power and four machine-guns. U.S. Army offshoots were the F-6 and F-6A reconnaissance aircraft and the A-36A Apache dive-bomber and ground-attack aircraft.

Tactical capability was hampered by the V-1710 engine, so the basic airframe was revised to take the Rolls-Royce Merlin built under licence in the United States by Packard as the V-1650. Production versions were the 910 Mustang Mk IIIs with four machine-guns and the equivalent P-51B and P-51C, respectively 1,988 and 1,750 aircraft with original and bubble canopies; there were also F-6C reconnaissance aircraft. The classic and most extensively built variant was the P-51D (7l,966, of which 875 became British Mustang Mk IVs) with a cutdown rear fuselage, a bubble canopy, six machine-guns, greater power and more fuel; the F-6D was the reconnaissance version. The P-51D had the range to escort U.S. bombers on deep raids, and was the decisive fighter of the second half of World War II.

Later variants expanded on the theme of the P-51D: the 555 P-51Hs were of a lightened version, the 1,337 P-51Ks were of a similarly lightened variant with an Aeroproducts propeller, and the F-6K was the reconnaissance conversion of the P-51K. The type was also built under licence in Australia with designations running from Mustang Mk 20 to Mustang Mk 24.

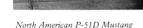

*North American P-51D Mustang*

**NORTH AMERICAN P-51D MUSTANG**
**Role:** Day fighter
**Crew/Accommodation:** One
**Power Plant:** One 1,450 hp Packard/Rolls Royce Merlin V-1650-7 water-cooled inline
**Dimensions:** Span 11.28 m (37 ft); length 9.83 m (32.25 ft); wing area 21.83 m² (235 sq ft)
**Weights:** Empty 3,466 kg (7,635 lb); MTOW 5,493 kg (12,100 lb)
**Performance:** Maximum speed 703 km/h (437 mph) at 7,625 m (25,000 ft); operational ceiling 12,192 m (40,000 ft); range 2,655 km (1,650 miles) with maximum fuel
**Load:** Six .5 inch machine guns, plus up to 907 kg (2,000 lb) of externally carried bombs or fuel tanks

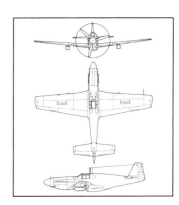

*North American A-36A Apache*

# REPUBLIC P-47 THUNDERBOLT

*P-47D Thunderbolt*

The Thunderbolt was one of a trio of superb American fighters to see extensive service in World War II. The massive fuselage of this heavyweight fighter was dictated by the use of a large turbocharger, which was located in the rear fuselage for balance reasons and therefore had to be connected to the engine by extensive lengths of wide-diameter ducting. The type was clearly related

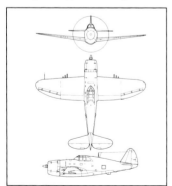

*Republic P-47C Thunderbolt*

to Republic's early portly-fuselage fighters, the P-35 and P-43 Lancer, but was marked by very high performance, high firepower and great structural strength.

The XP-47B prototype flew in May 1941 with the 1380-kW (1,850-hp) XR-2800 radial, later revised to develop 1491 kW (2,000 hp). This formed the basis of the 171 P-47B production aircraft with the R-2800-21 radial, and the 602 P-47Cs with a longer forward fuselage for the same engine or, in later examples, the 1715-kW (2,300-hp) R-2800-59 radial; the type also featured provision for a drop

**REPUBLIC P-47C THUNDERBOLT**
**Role:** Fighter
**Crew/Accommodation:** One
**Power Plant:** One 2,000 hp Pratt & Whitney R-2800-21 Double Wasp air-cooled radial
**Dimensions:** Span 12.42 m (40.75 ft); length 10.99 m (36.08 ft); wing area 27.87 m² (300 sq ft)
**Weights:** Empty 4,491 kg (9,900 lb); MTOW 6,770 kg (14,925 lb)
**Performance:** Maximum speed 697 km/h (433 mph) at 9,144 m (30,000 ft); operational ceiling 12,802 m (42,000 ft); range 722 km (480 miles) with a 227 kg (500 lb) bomb
**Load:** Eight .5 inch machine guns, plus up to 227 kg (500 lb) of bombs

tank or bombs. The P-47D was the main production model, 12,602 being built with the 1715-kW (2,300 hp) R-2800-21W or 1890-kW (2,535-hp) R-2800-59W water-injected radials, as well as a greater load of external stores that could include 1134-kg (2,500-lb) of bombs or ten 127-mm (5-in) rockets in the fighter-bomber role that became an increasingly important part of the Thunderbolt's repertoire. Early aircraft had the original 'razorback' canopy/rear fuselage, but later machines introduced a 360° vision

bubble canopy and a cutdown rear fuselage. P-47G was the designation given to 354 Wright-built P-47Ds. and the only other production models were the 130 P-47M 'sprinters' with the 2088-kW (2,800-hp) R-2800-57(C) radial and the 1,816 P-47N long-range aircraft with a strengthened and longer wing plus the 2088-kW (2,800-hp) R-2800-77 radial. The Thunderbolt was never an effective close-in fighter, but excelled in the high-speed dive-and-zoom attacks useful in long-range escort.

*The Republic P-47D Thunderbolt*

# YAKOVLEV Yak-9 (U.S.S.R.)

*Yak-9D*

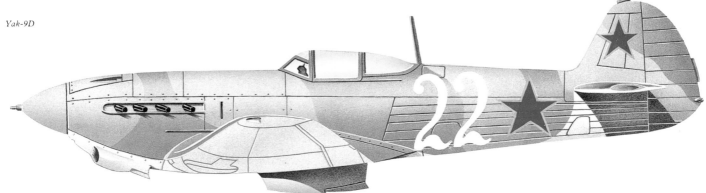

The Yak-9 was one of the finest fighters of World War II, and was the most prolific culmination of the evolutionary design philosophy that started with the Yak-1. The Yak-9 entered combat during the Battle of Stalingrad late in 1942, and was a development of the Yak-7DI that was notable for its mixed wood and metal primary structure.

Production lasted to 1946 and totalled 16,769 aircraft in several important and some lesser variants. These included the original Yak-9 with the 969-kW (1,300-hp) Klimov VK-105PF-1 or 1014-kW (1,360-hp) VK-105PF-3 inline engine plus an armament of one 20-mm cannon and one or two 12.7-mm (0.5-in) machine guns, the Yak-9M with revised armament, the Yak-9D long-range escort fighter with the VK-105PF-3 engine and greater fuel capacity, the Yak-9T anti-tank variant with one 37- or 45-mm cannon and provision for anti-tank bomblets under the wings, the Yak-9K heavy anti-tank fighter with a 45-mm cannon in the nose, the Yak-9B high-speed light bomber with provision for four 100-kg (220-lb) bombs carried internally as part of a 600-kg (1,323-lb) total internal and external warload, the Yak-9MPVO night fighter carrying searchlights for the illumination of its quarry, the Yak-9DD very long-range escort fighter based on the Yak-9D but fitted for drop tanks, the Yak-9U conversion trainer in three subvariants, the YAK-9P post-war interceptor with the 1230-kW (1,650-hp) Klimov VK-107A inline and two fuselage-mounted 20-mm cannon, and the Yak-9R reconnaissance aircraft.

*Yakovlev Yak-9DD long-range fighters*

**YAKOVLEV Yak-9D**
**Role:** Fighter
**Crew/Accommodation:** One
**Power Plant:** One 1,360 hp Klimov VK-105PF-3
**Dimensions:** Span 9.74 m (32.03 ft); length 8.55 m (28.05 ft); wing area 17.1 m² (184.05 sq ft)
**Weights:** Empty 2,770 kg (6,107 lb); MTOW 3,080 kg (6,790 lb)
**Performance:** Maximum speed 602 km/h (374 mph) at 2,000 m (6,560 ft); operational ceiling 10,600 m (34,775 ft); range 1,410 km (876 miles)
**Load:** One 20 mm cannon + one 12.7 mm machine gun

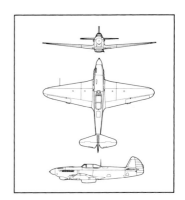

*Yakovlev Yak-9D*

# KAWASAKI Ki-61 HIEN and Ki-100 'TONY' (Japan)

*Ki-61-I-KAIc Hién 'Tong'*

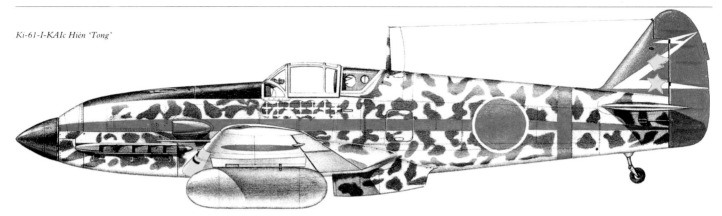

The Ki-61 Hien (Swallow) was the only inline-engined Japanese fighter to see substantial use in World War II, and was developed in parallel with the unsuccessful Ki-60 though using the same Kawasaki Ha-40 engine, a licence-built version of the Daimler-Benz DB 601A. The first Ki-61 prototype flew in December 1941. The Ki-61-I entered combat in April 1943 and soon acquired the Allied reporting name 'Tony'. By the time production ended in January 1945, 2,666 aircraft had been built in variants such as the Ki-61-I with two

7.7-mm (0.303-in) fuselage and two 12.7-mm (0.5-in) wing machine guns, the Ki-61-Ia with two 20-mm wing cannon, the Ki-61-Ib with 12.7-mm (0.5-in) fuselage machine guns, the Ki-61-Ic with a rationalized structure, and the Ki-61-Id with 30-mm wing cannon.

The Ki-61-II had a larger wing and the more powerful Ha-140 engine, but was so delayed in development that only 99 had been produced before United States Air Force bombing destroyed engine production capacity. Variants were the Ki-61-II KAI with

the Ki-61-I's wing, the Ki-61-IIa with the Ki-61-Ic's armament, and the Ki-61-IIb with four 20-mm wing cannon. With the Ha-140 engine unavailable for a comparatively large number of completed Ki-61-II airframes, the Japanese army ordered the type adapted to take the Mitsubishi Ha-112-II radial engine, the 1119-kW (1,500-hp) rating of which was identical to that of the Ha-140. The resulting Ki-100 first flew in 1945 and proved an outstanding interceptor, perhaps Japan's best fighter of World War II, also known to the Allies as 'Tony'. The army ordered completion

of the 272 Ki-61-II airframes as Ki-100-Ia fighters, while new production amounted to 99 Ki-100-Ib aircraft with the cut-down rear fuselage and bubble canopy developed for the proposed Ki-61-III fighter. The designation Ki-100-II was used for three prototypes with the Mitsubishi Ha-112-IIru turbocharged radial for improved high-altitude performance.

*This is a Ki-61-I.*

**KAWASAKI KI-100-II 'TONY'**
**Role:** Fighter
**Crew/Accommodation:** One
**Power Plant:** One 1,500 hp Mitsubishi Ha-112-II air-cooled radial
**Dimensions:** Span 12 m (39.37 ft); length 8.82 m (28.94 ft); wing area 20 m² (215.3 sq ft)
**Weights:** Empty 2,522 kg (5,567 lb); MTOW 3,495 kg (7,705 lb)
**Performance:** Maximum speed 590 km/h (367 mph) at 10,000 m (32,808 ft); operational ceiling 11,500 m (37,500 ft); range 1,800 km (1,118 miles)
**Load:** Two 20 mm cannon and two 12.7 mm machine guns

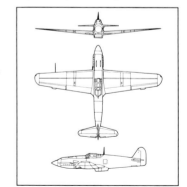

*Kawasaki Ki-61 KAIc*

# FAIREY FIREFLY (United Kingdom)

*Firefly AS.Mk 6*

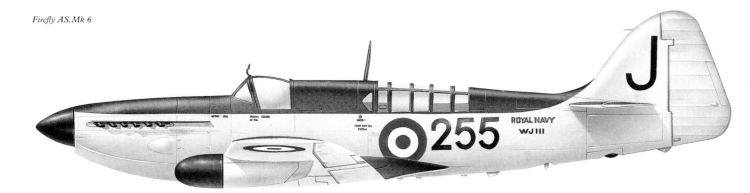

Designed to a requirement for a carrierborne two-seat reconnaissance fighter and first flown in December 1941 as the first of four prototypes powered by the 1290-kW (1,730-hp) Rolls-Royce Griffon IIB inline engine, the Firefly was one of the Royal Navy's most successful warplanes of the 1940s. The type had an all-metal construction, low-set cantilever wings, retractable tailwheel landing gear, and naval features like folding wings and an arrester hook.

The Firefly Mk I initial production series featured wings spanning 13.55 m (44 ft 6 in) and the 1484-kW (1,990-hp) Rolls-Royce Griffon XII with a chin radiator, and was produced in F.Mk I fighter, FR.Mk I fighter reconnaissance, NF.Mk I night-fighter and T.Mk I trainer versions to the extent of 937 aircraft. The 37 Firefly NF.Mk II night fighters had a longer nose and different radar, but were soon converted to Mk I standard.

Post-war conversions of the Mk I were the Firefly T.Mk 1 pilot trainer, T.Mk 2 operational trainer, and T.Mk 3 anti-submarine warfare trainer. The Firefly Mk IV switched to the 1566-kW (2,100-hp) Griffon 61 with root radiators in wings spanning 12.55 m (41 ft 2 in), and was produced in F.Mk IV and FR.Mk 4 versions. The Firefly Mk 5 introduced power-folding wings, and was produced in FR.Mk 5, NF.Mk 5, T.Mk 5 and anti-submarine AS.Mk 5 versions. The AS.Mk 6 was identical to the AS.Mk 5 other than in its use of British rather than American sonobuoys. The last production model, which raised the overall construction total to 1,623 aircraft, was the Firefly AS.Mk 7, which had the original long-span wing and a 1678-kW (2,250-hp) Griffon 59 with a chin radiator. Surplus Fireflies were also converted as remotely controlled target drones for the British surface-to-air missile programme.

*The Fairey Firefly FR.Mk 5 was a two-seat reconnaissance fighter*

**FAIREY FIREFLY FR. Mk 5**
**Role:** Fighter reconnaissance
**Crew/Accommodation:** Two
**Power Plant:** One 2,250 hp Rolls-Royce Griffon 74 water-cooled inline
**Dimensions:** Span 12.55 m (41.17 ft); length 11.56 m (37.91 ft); wing area 30.65 m² (330 sq ft)
**Weights:** Empty 4,389 kg (9,674 lb); MTOW 6,114 kg (13,479 lb)
**Performance:** Maximum speed 618 km/h (386 mph) at 4,270 m (14,000 ft); operational ceiling 8,660m (28,400 ft); range 2,090 km (1,300 miles) with long-range tankage
**Load:** Four 20 mm cannon, plus up to 454 kg (1,000 lb) of externally underslung bombs

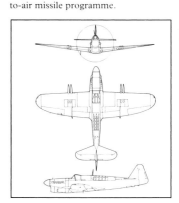

*Fairey Firefly F.Mk I*

# GRUMMAN F6F HELLCAT (U.S.A.)

*F6F-3 Hellcat*

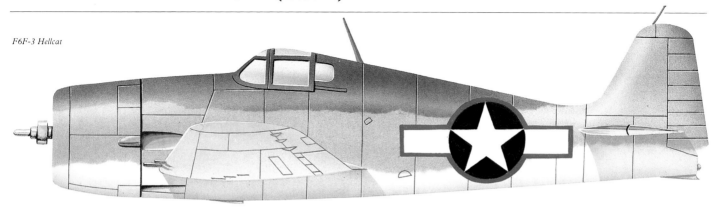

The Hellcat was the logical successor to the Wildcat with more size and power in a generally similar airframe with a low- rather than mid-set wing. A number of operational improvements suggested by Wildcat experience were incorporated in the basic design, and after evaluating this, the U.S. Navy contracted in June 1941 for a total of four XF6F prototypes. These were built with different Wright and Pratt & Whitney engine installations (normally aspirated and turbocharged R-2600 Cyclone and R-2800 Double Wasp units respectively). In June 1942, the

XF6F-1 became the first of these to fly, and the type selected for production was the XF6F-3 powered by the 1491-kW (2,000-hp) R-2800-10 Double Wasp with a two-stage turbocharger. This model entered production as the F6F-3 and reached squadrons in January 1944; the Fleet Air Arm designated the type Gannet Mk I, but later changed the name to Hellcat Mk I. Production lasted to mid-1944, and amounted to 4,423 aircraft including 18 F6F-3E and 205 F6F-3N night fighters with different radar equipments in pods under their starboard wings.

That the Hellcat was in all significant respects 'right' is attested by the relatively few variants emanating from a large production run that saw the delivery of 12,275 aircraft in all. From early 1944, production switched to the F6F-5 (Hellcat Mk II) with aerodynamic refinements including a revised cowling, new ailerons, a strengthened tail unit, and the R-2800-10W radial the suffix of which indicated the water injection system that produced a 10 per cent power boost for take-off and combat. These 6,436 aircraft also

featured provision for underwing bombs or rockets. There were also 1,189 examples of the F6F-5N (Hellcat NF.Mk II) night fighter, and some F6F-5 and F6F-5N fighters were also converted as F6F-5P photo-reconnaissance aircraft. Hellcat pilots claimed 4,947 aircraft shot down in combat, more than 75 per cent of all 'kills' attributed to U.S. Navy pilots in World War II.

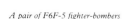

*A pair of F6F-5 fighter-bombers*

**GRUMMAN F6F-5 HELLCAT**
**Role:** Naval carrierborne fighter
**Crew/Accommodation:** One
**Power Plant:** One 2,000 hp Pratt & Whitney R-2800-10W Double Wasp air-cooled radial
**Dimensions:** Span 13.06 m (42.83 ft); length 10.31 m (33.83 ft); wing area 31.03 m² (334 sq ft)
**Weights:** Empty 4,100 kg (9,060 lb); MTOW 5,714 kg (12,598 lb)
**Performance:** Maximum speed 612 km/h (380 mph) at 7,132 m (23,400 ft); operational ceiling 11,369 m (37,300 ft); range 1,521 km (945 miles)
**Load:** Two 20 mm cannon and four .5 inch machine guns, plus up to 975 kg (2,150 lb) of weapons, including one torpedo

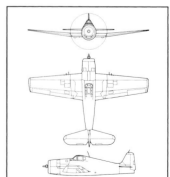

*Grumman F6F-3 Hellcat*

# HAWKER TEMPEST (United Kingdom)

*Tempest F.Mk V Series II*

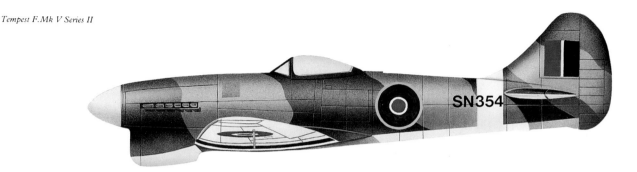

The failure of the Hawker Typhoon in its designed interceptor role left the British short of an advanced interceptor; in 1941 it was suggested the Typhoon be revised with a thinner, elliptical wing with low-drag radiators in the leading edges to replace the Typhoon's chin radiator. In November 1941 two prototypes were ordered with the Napier Sabre inline. Early in 1942, the type was renamed Tempest. The two original prototypes became the Tempest F.Mks I and V with the Sabre IV and II respectively, and another four prototypes were ordered as two Tempest F.Mk IIs with the 1879-kW (2,520-hp) Bristol Centaurus radial and two Tempest F.Mk IIIs with the Rolls-Royce Griffon IIB inline, the latter becoming Tempest F.Mk IVs when fitted with the Griffon 61.

Initial orders were placed for 400 Tempest F.Mk Is, and the first such fighter flew in February 1943. The engine suffered development problems, however, and the variant was abandoned. The first Tempest to fly had been the Tempest F.Mk V in September 1942, and an eventual 800 were built as 100 Tempest F.Mk V Series I and 700 Series II aircraft with long- and short-barrel cannon respectively, some later being converted as Tempest TT.Mk 5 target tugs. The Tempest Mk II materialized with the Centaurus V radial, and production for post-war service amounted to 136 F.Mk II fighters and 338 FB.Mk II fighter-bombers. The only other production model was the Tempest F.Mk VI, of which 142 were produced for tropical service with the 1745-kW (2,340-hp) Sabre V. Some of these were later adapted as Tempest TT.Mk 6s.

*Tempest F.Mk V*

**HAWKER TEMPEST Mk V**
**Role:** Stike fighter
**Crew/Accommodation:** One
**Power Plant:** One 2,180 hp Napier Sabre IIA water-cooled inline
**Dimensions:** Span 12.49 m (41 ft); length 10.26 m (33.67 ft); wing area 28.05 m² (302 sq ft)
**Weights:** Empty 4,196 kg (9,250 lb); MTOW 6,187 kg (13,640 lb)
**Performance:** Maximum speed 700 km/h (435 mph) at 5,180 m (17,000 ft); operational ceiling 11,125 m (36,500 ft); range 1,191 km (740 miles) on internal fuel only
**Load:** Four 20 mm cannon, plus up to 907 kg (2,000 lb) of bombs or rockets

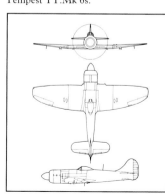

*Hawker Tempest F.Mk II*

# DORNIER Do 335 PFEIL (Germany)

*Do 335A Pfeil*

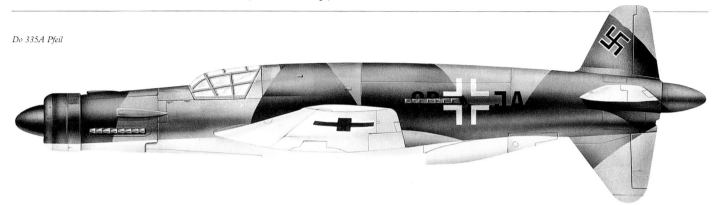

The unusual configuration of the Do 335 Pfeil (Arrow) was designed to allow the installation of two powerful engines in a minimum-drag layout that would also present no single-engined asymmetric thrust problems. Dr Claudius Dornier patented the concept in 1937, and the configuration was successfully evaluated in the Göppingen Gö 9 research aircraft during 1939. Dornier then developed the basic concept as a high-performance fighter, but the Do P.231 type was adopted by the Reichsluftfahrtministerium (German Air Ministry) as a high-speed bomber. Initial work had reached an advanced stage when the complete project was cancelled. There then emerged a German need for a high-performance interceptor, and the wheel turned full circle as Dornier was instructed to revive its design in this role.

The resulting aircraft was of all-metal construction, and in layout was a low-wing monoplane with sturdy retractable tricycle landing gear, cruciform tail surfaces, and two 1342-kW (1,800-hp) Daimler-Benz DB 603 inline engines each driving a three-blade propeller. One engine was mounted in the conventional nose position, and the other in the rear fuselage powering a propeller aft of the tail unit by means of an extension shaft. The first of 14 prototypes flew in September 1943. Considerable development flying was undertaken by these one- and two-seater models, and 10 Do 335A-O pre-production fighter-bombers were evaluated from the late summer of 1944. The first production model was the Do 335A-1, of which 11 were completed. None of these entered full-scale service, though some were allocated to a service test unit in the spring of 1945. The only other aircraft completed were two examples of the Do 335A-12 two-seat trainer. There were also many projected variants.

*Dornier Do 335A-O Pfeil*

**DORNIER Do 335A-O PFEIL**
**Role:** Long range day fighter
**Crew/Accommodation:** One
**Power Plant:** Two 2,250 hp Daimler-Benz DB 603E/MW50 liquid-cooled inlines
**Dimensions:** Span 13.80 m (45.28 ft); length 13.85 m (45.44 ft); wing area 38.50 m² (414.41 sq ft)
**Weights:** Empty 7,400 kg (16,315 lb); MTOW 9,600 kg (21,160 lb)
**Performance:** Maximum speed 768 km/h (477 mph) at 6,890 m (21,000 ft); operational ceiling 11,400 m (37,400 ft); radius 1,397 km (868 miles) at military power
**Load:** One 30 mm and two 15 mm cannons, plus a 500 kg (1,103 lb) bomb

*Dornier Do 335 Pfeil*

# KAWANISHI N1K 'REX' and 'GEORGE' (Japan)

*N1K2-1 'George'*

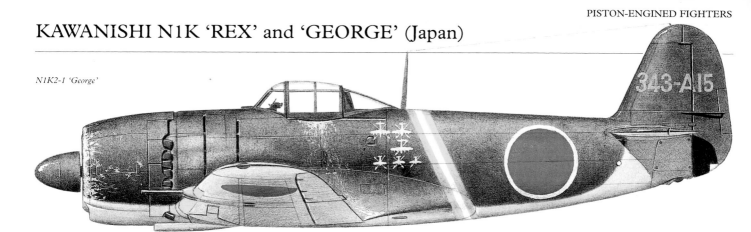

Designed from 1940 as a fighter able to protect and support amphibious landings, the N1K was schemed as a substantial seaplane with single main/ two stabilizing floats and a powerful engine driving contra-rotating propellers that would mitigate torque problems during take-off and landing. The first prototype flew in May 1942 with the 1089-kW (1,460-hp) Mitsubishi MK4D Kasei radial, but

*Kawanishi N1K1 'Rex'*

problems with the contra-rotating propeller unit led to the use of a conventional propeller unit. The type began to enter service in 1943 as the N1K1 Kyofu (Mighty Wind), but the type's *raison d'être* had disappeared by this stage of the war and production was terminated with the 97th machine. The Allied reporting name for the N1K1 was 'Rex'.

The N1K2 with a more powerful engine remained only a project, but in 1942 the company began development of a landplane version as the N1K1-J Shiden (Violet Lightning) with

**KAWANISHI N1K1 'REX'**
**Role:** Fighter floatplane
**Crew/Accommodation:** One
**Power Plant:** One 1,460 hp Mitsubishi Kasei 14 air-cooled radial
**Dimensions:** Span 12 m (39.37 ft); length 10.59 m (34.74 ft); wing area 23.5 m² (252.9 sq ft)
**Weights:** Empty 2,700 kg (5,952 lb); MTOW 3,712 kg (8,184 lb)
**Performance:** Maximum speed 482 km/h (300 mph) at 5,700 m (18,701 ft); operational ceiling 10,560 m (34,646 ft); range 1,690 km (1,050 miles) with full bombload
**Load:** Two 20 mm cannon, two 7.7 mm machine guns, plus up to 60 kg (132 lb) of bombs

retractable tailwheel landing gear and the 1357-kW (1,820-hp) Nakajima NK9H Homare 11 radial. This suffered a number of teething problems, and its need for a large-diameter propeller dictated the design of telescoping main landing gear legs. The new type flew in prototype form during December 1942, but development difficulties delayed the type's service debut to early 1944. N1K1-J production totalled 1,007 in three subvariants known to the Allies

as the 'George'. Yet this had been planned as an interim version pending deliveries of the N1K2-J version with a low- rather than mid-set wing, a longer fuselage, a revised tail unit, and less complicated main landing gear units. Only 423 of this version were produced. The N1K3-J, N1K4-J and N1K5-J prototypes had a longer forward fuselage, the 1491-kW (2,000-hp) Homare 23 engine and the 1641-kW (2,200-hp) Mitsubishi MK9A radial engine respectively.

*The Kawanishi N1K2-J Shiden KAI.*

# de HAVILLAND D.H.103 HORNET (United Kingdom)

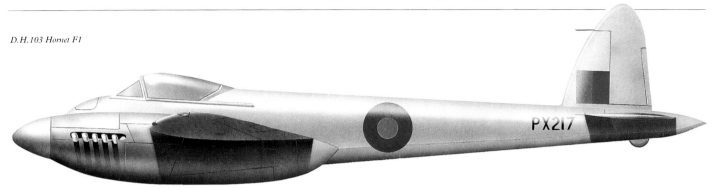

*D.H.103 Hornet F1*

The D.H.103 was designed to provide the British forces fighting the Japanese with a long-range fighter with the advantages of a twin-engined layout. The type was based on the aerodynamics of the Mosquito multi-role warplane, and so impressive were the estimated performance figures that a specification was written round the type in 1943. The D.H.103 retained the Mosquito's plywood/balsa/plywood structure for its single-seat fuselage, but featured new wood and metal wings. Work began in June 1943, and the first prototype flew in July 1944 with two Merlin 130/131 inline engines. Performance and handling were excellent, and initial deliveries were made in April 1945. This first model was the Hornet F.Mk 1, of which 60 were built, but it was too late for service in World War II.

The major variant of this land-based series was the Hornet F.Mk 3 with a dorsal fillet (retrofitted to earlier aircraft), greater internal fuel capacity, and provision for underwing loads of weapons or drop tanks. The last of 120 aircraft were delivered to Hornet FR.Mk 4 reconnaissance fighter standard with the rear fuselage fuel tank deleted to provide accommodation for a single camera. The basic design also appealed to the Fleet Air Arm, which ordered the navalized Sea Hornet series. Deliveries included 78 Sea Hornet F.Mk 20 fighters based on the F.Mk 3 and first flown in August 1946 for a final delivery in June 1951, 79 Sea Hornet NF.Mk 21 two-seat night fighters based on the F.Mk 20 but with radar in a revised nose, and 43 Sea Hornet PR.Mk 23 photo-reconnaissance aircraft based on the F.Mk 20 but with one night or two day cameras. The last Sea Hornets were retired in 1955.

*Hornet F.Mk 3 of No.64 Squadron.*

**de HAVILLAND D.H.103 HORNET F.Mk 1**
**Role:** Long range fighter
**Crew/Accommodation:** One
**Power Plant:** Two 2,070 hp Rolls-Royce Merlin 130/131 liquid-cooled inlines
**Dimensions:** Span 13.72 m (45.00 ft); length 11.18 m (36.66 ft); wing area 33.54 m² (361 sq ft)
**Weights:** Empty 5,671 kg (12,502) lb; MTOW 8,029 kg (17,700 lb)
**Performance:** Maximum speed 760 km/h (472 mph) at 6,706 m (22,000 ft); operational ceiling 11,430 m (37,500 ft); range 4,023 km (2,500 miles)
**Load:** Four 20 mm cannons

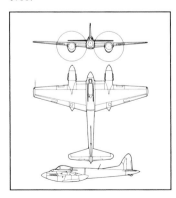

*de Havilland Hornet F.Mk 3*

# HAWKER SEA FURY (United Kingdom)

*Sea Fury FB.Mk 11*

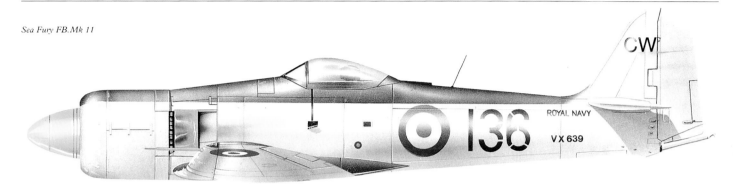

The origins of Hawker's second Fury fighter lay in a 1942 requirement for a smaller and lighter version of the Tempest, and was developed in parallel land-based and naval forms to 1943 specifications. Hawker was responsible for the overall design, with Boulton Paul allocated the task of converting the type for naval use. By December 1943, six prototypes had been ordered, one with the Bristol Centaurus XII radial, two with the Centaurus XXI radial, two with the Rolls-Royce Griffon inline, and one as a test airframe. The first to fly was a Centaurus XII-powered machine that took to the air in September 1944, followed in November by a Griffon-powered machine that was later re-engined with the Napier Sabre inline. Orders were placed for 200 land-based Fury and 100 carrierborne Sea Fury fighters, but the Fury order was cancelled at the end of World War II. The first Sea Fury flew in February 1945 with the Centaurus XII, and development continued after the war to produce the first fully navalized machine with folding wings and the Centaurus XV. This flew in October 1945, and paved the way for the Sea Fury F.Mk X, of which 50 were built.

The first type to enter widespread service was the Sea Fury FB.Mk 11 of which 615 were built including 31 and 35 for the Royal Australian and Royal Canadian Navies respectively. The Fleet Air Arm also took 60 Sea Fury T.Mk 20 trainers, of which 10 were later converted as target tugs for West Germany. Additional operators of new-build aircraft were the Netherlands with 22 Sea Fury F.Mk 50s and FB.Mk 50s, and Pakistan with 93 Sea Fury FB.Mk 60s and five T.Mk 61s. Other buyers were Burma (21 ex-British aircraft), Cuba (17 aircraft) and Iraq (60 aircraft).

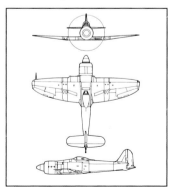

*Hawker Sea Fury FB.Mk 11*

**HAWKER SEA FURY FB.Mk 11**
**Role:** Carrierborne fighter bomber
**Crew/Accommodation:** One
**Power Plant:** One 2,480 hp Bristol Centaurus 18 air-cooled radial
**Dimensions:** Span 11.70 m (38.40 ft); length 10.57 m (34.67 ft); wing area 26.01 m² (280.00 sq ft)
**Weights:** Empty 4,191 kg (9,240 lb); MTOW 5,670 kg (12,500 lb)
**Performance:** Maximum speed 740 km/h (460 mph) at 5,486 m (18,000 ft); operational ceiling 10,912 m (35,800 ft); radius 1,127 km (700 miles) without external fuel tanks
**Load:** Four 20 mm cannons, plus up to 907 kg (2,000 lb) of bombs or twelve 3 inch rocket projectiles

*The Hawker Sea Fury FB.Mk 11.*

# THE ROLE OF
# THE FIGHTER &
# BOMBER

Page 62: Two U.S. Marine Corps F/A-18s
Page 63: Two Dassault Mirage F1s, upgrade
Below: Dassault Mirage 5
Pages 66–67: Boeing B29A Superfortress

# Jet Fighters

Many argue that great progress in combat aircraft performance during World War I came mainly from the development of improved aero engines, with speeds from typically 105 km/h (65 mph) for unarmed reconnaissance aircraft at outbreak of war to over twice that by 1918 for fast fighters and bombers. Yet, by the start of the 1930s, major air forces were taking in new fighters that could only manage 322 km/h (200 mph), although these were followed from 1935 by a new breed of sleek and high-power fighters that raised speed to more than 483 km/h (300 mph). In August 1944 a U.S. Republic XP-47J Thunderbolt proved that a piston-engined fighter could pass the 800 km/h (500 mph) mark. But, by then, RAF and Luftwaffe jets were scoring air victories under combat conditions, proving once again the importance of engine technology in the development of fighters.

To achieve 811 km/h (504 mph) the XP-47J had been specially prepared, even having two guns deleted to save weight. In truth, the fastest operational piston fighters were somewhat slower, making the Luftwaffe's new Me 262 jet the only true over 500 mph fighter in service (with the exception of Germany's equally revolutionary Me 163 Komet rocket-powered interceptor), and thereby a real threat to Allied aircraft involved in continental operations. Fortunately for the Allies, only a small number of the Me 262s built were ever to become fully operational, though if proof was needed of the menace they posed it came with the achievements of unit JV 44, which in just over one month in 1945 managed to destroy some 45 Allied aircraft while keeping only six or so of its many accumulated Me 262s flying at a time. Conversely, many Me 262s were lost in operations, often caught in gunfire as they slowed to attack their heavily defended targets.

Simultaneously, the RAF put its own jet fighter into service, as the Gloster Meteor. Compared with the Me 262, the first Meteors had less engine thrust and offered a much lower speed. But the overall design was very well suited to development and the Mk III version that appeared later in 1944 had more thrust, more fuel and higher performance, while post-war versions approached 965 km/h (600 mph).

Piston fighters generally had their swansong during the Korean War in the early 1950s, the first U.S. air victory coming in June 1950 when a Twin Mustang overcame a North Korean Yak-9, both piston engined. Five months later a U.S.A.F. Lockheed F-80C Shooting Star jet fighter shot down a Chinese MiG-15, thus recording the first ever victory by one jet over another, seemingly sealing the fate of the piston fighters, although it is worth recording that reworked North American F-51D Mustang piston fighters survived in service with a handful of South American countries for counter-insurgency right through the 1970s. But, by the 1950s, the era of the jet fighter had begun in earnest and there was no looking back. The U.S. North American F-100 Super Sabre jet introduced the ability to sustain supersonic flight; in 1958 a Lockheed F-104 Starfighter greatly exceeded 2,000 km/h, and subsequently the Soviet MiG-25 took the speed of a production fighter well beyond 3,000 km/h. The story continues.

*Picture: Boeing F/A-18F Super Hornet during aircraft carrier trials on U.S.S.* John C. Stennis

# MESSERSCHMITT Me 262 SCHWALBE (Germany)

*Me 262A-1a Schwalbe*

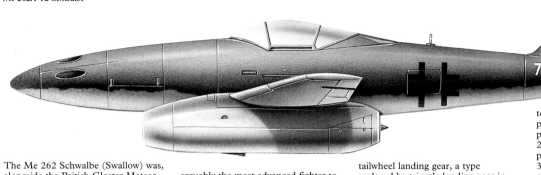

The Me 262 Schwalbe (Swallow) was, alongside the British Gloster Meteor, one of the World's first two operational jet fighters. Because of German indecision whether the Luftwaffe most needed a jet fighter or jet fighter-bomber, and difficulties in engine development, operational deployment was later than might have otherwise been possible; with its clean lines, tricycle landing gear, slightly swept wings and axial-flow turbojets, it was

arguably the most advanced fighter to see service in World War II.

Design work was launched in 1938 to meet a specification that called for a fighter powered by two of the new turbojet engines then under development by BMW, and eventually an order was placed for three prototypes powered by the 600-kg (1,323-lb) thrust BMW P-3302 engines. Work on the airframe proceeded more rapidly than development of the engine, so the Me 262 V1 first flew in April 1941 with a single nose-mounted Junkers Jumo 210G piston engine and retractable

tailwheel landing gear, a type replaced by tricycle landing gear in later prototypes and all production aircraft. The piston engine was later supplemented by two BMW 003 turbojets, but these proved so unreliable that they were replaced by 840-kg (1852-lb) thrust Junkers 004As in a programme that required some redesign as the Junkers engines were larger and heavier than the BMW units. The first all-jet flight

took place on 18 July 1942. The five prototypes were followed by 23 pre-production Me 262A-0s before the Me 262A-1 entered service as the first production variant: the -1a had four 30-mm cannon and the -1b added 24 air-to-air unguided rockets. Operational use of the Schwalbe began in July 1944. Total production of the Me 262 was over 1,400 aircraft, but the majority failed to reach operational status. Variants included the Me 262A-2 Sturmvogel (Stormbird) fighter-bomber, the Me 262A-5 reconnaissance fighter, the Me 262B-1a two-seat conversion trainer and the Me 262B-2 night fighter.

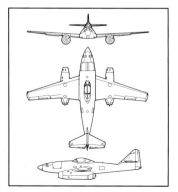

*Me 262A-1a*

**MESSERSCHMITT Me 262A-1a SCHWALBE**
**Role:** Fighter
**Crew/Accommodation:** One
**Power Plant:** Two 990 kgp (1,984 lb s.t.) Junkers Jumo-004B turbojets
**Dimensions:** Span 12.5 m (41.01 ft); length 10.605 m (34.79 ft); wing area 21.68 m² (233.3 sq ft)
**Weights:** Empty 4,000 kg (8,820 lb); MTOW 6,775 kg (14,938 lb)
**Performance:** Maximum speed 868 km/h (536 mph) at 7,000 m (22,800 ft) operational ceiling 11,000 m (36,080 ft); range 845 km (524 miles) at 6,000 mm (19,685 ft) cruise altitude
**Load:** Four 30 mm cannon

*Me 262A-1a fighter in post-war Czech service as the S-92*

# GLOSTER METEOR (United Kingdom)

*Meteor N F.Mk 11*

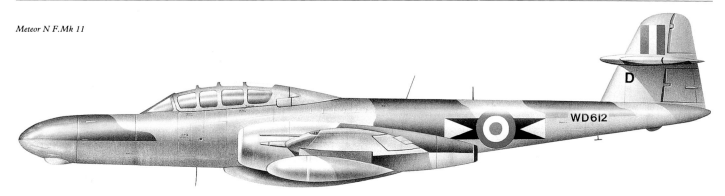

The Meteor was the only Allied jet fighter to see combat in World War II, and just pipped the Germans' Me 262 to the title of becoming the world's first operational jet aircraft. Given its experience with the E.28/39, the research type that had been the first British jet aircraft, Gloster was the logical choice to develop a jet fighter especially as this would leave 'fighter companies' such as Hawker and

Supermarine free to concentrate on their definitive piston-engined fighters. The G.41 design took shape comparatively quickly. The first of eight prototypes started taxiing trials in July 1942 with 454-kg (1,000-lb) thrust Rover W.2B engines, but it was March 1943 before the fifth machine became the first Meteor to fly, in this instance with 680-kg (1,500-lb) thrust de Havilland H.1 engines.

Trials with a number of engine types and variants slowed development of a production variant, but the 20 Meteor F.Mk Is finally entered service in July 1944 with 771-kg (1,700-lb) thrust Rolls-Royce

W.2B/23C Welland I turbojets. The Meteor remained in RAF service until the late 1950s with the Derwent turbojet that was introduced on the second production variant, the Meteor F.Mk III, of which 280 were built, in most cases with the 907-kg (2,000-lb) thrust Rolls-Royce W.2B/37 Derwent I.

The type underwent considerable development in the post-war period when 3,237 were built. The main streams were the Meteor F.Mks 4 and

8 single-seat fighters of which 657 and 1,183 were built with Derwent I and 1633-kg (3,600-lb) thrust Derwent 8s respectively, the Meteor FR.Mk 9 reconnaissance fighter of which 126 were built, the Meteor NF.Mks 11 to 14 radar-equipped night fighters, the Meteor PR.Mk 10 photo-reconnaissance type of which 58 were built, and the Meteor T.Mk 7 two-seat trainer of which 712 were built. Surplus aircraft were often converted into target tugs or target drones.

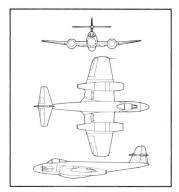

*Gloster Meteor F.Mk 8*

**GLOSTER METEOR F. Mk 8**
**Role:** Fighter
**Crew/Accommodation:** One
**Power Plant:** Two 1,723 kgp (3,800 lb s.t.) Rolls-Royce Derwent 9 turbojets
**Dimensions:** Span 11,33 m (37.16 ft); length 13.59 m (44.58 ft); wing area 32.5 m² (350 sq ft)
**Weights:** Empty 4,846 kg (10,684 lb); MTOW 7,121 kg (15,700 lb)
**Performance:** Maximum speed 962 km/h (598 mph) at 3,048 m (10,000 ft); operational ceiling 13,106 m (43,000 ft); endurance 1.2 hours with ventral and wing fuel tanks
**Load:** Four 20 mm cannon

*Gloster Meteor F.Mk 8 fighter*

# LOCKHEED F-80 SHOOTING STAR and T-33 (U.S.A.)

*F-80C Shooting Star*

The Shooting Star was the best Allied jet fighter to emerge from World War II, though the type was in fact just too late for combat use in that conflict. The design was launched in June 1943 on the basis of a British turbojet, the 1834-kg (2,460-1b) thrust de Havilland (Halford) H. 1B, and the first XP-80 prototype with this engine flew in January 1944 as a sleek, low-wing monoplane with tricycle landing gear and a 360° vision canopy. The two XP-80As switched to the 1746-kg (3,850-lb) thrust General Electric I-40 (later J33) engine, and this powered all subsequent models. The P-80A version began to enter service in January 1945, and just 45 had been delivered before the end of World War II. Production plans for 5,000 aircraft were then savagely cut, but the development of later versions with markedly improved capabilities meant that as many as 5,691 of the series were finally built.

The baseline fighter was redesignated in the F- (fighter) series after World War II, and variants were the 917 F-80As with the J33-GE-11 engine, the 240 improved F-80Bs with an ejector seat and provision for RATO, and the 749 F-80Cs with 2087- or 2449-kg (4,600- or 5,400-lb) thrust J33-GE-23 or -35 engines and provision for underwing rockets in the ground-attack role. The versatility of the design also resulted in 222 F-14 and later RF-80 photo-reconnaissance aircraft, 5,871 TF-80 (later T-33A) air force and TO-1/2 (later TV-1/2) navy flying trainers that were in numerical terms the most important types by far, 150 T2V SeaStar advanced naval flying trainers with the 2767-kg (6,100-lb) thrust J33-A-24 and a boundary-layer control system, many AT-33A weapons trainers for the export and defence aid programmes, and many other variants.

## LOCKHEED F-80B SHOOTING STAR
**Role:** Day fighter
**Crew/Accommodation:** One
**Power Plant:** One 2,041 kgp (4,500 lb s.t.) Allison J33-A-21 turbojet
**Dimensions:** Span 11.81 m (38.75 ft); length 10.49 m (34.42 ft); wing area 22.07 m² (237.6 sq ft)
**Weights:** Empty 3,709 kg (8,176 lb); MTOW 7,257 kg (16,000 lb)
**Performance:** Maximum speed 929 km/h (577 mph) at 1,830 m (6,000 ft); operational ceiling 13,870 m (45,500 ft); range 1,270 km (790 miles) without drop tanks
**Load:** Six .5 inch machine guns

*The P-80B version of the Lockheed Shooting Star*

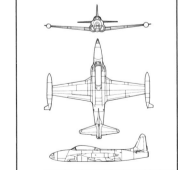

*T-33A Shooting Star*

# de HAVILLAND D.H.100, 113 and 115 VAMPIRES (United Kingdom)

*D.H. 115 Vampire T.Mk 11*

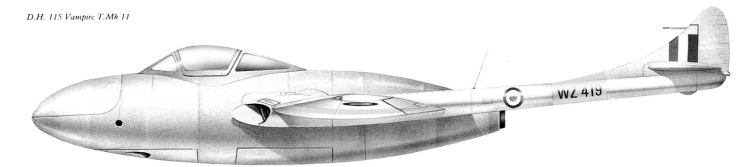

The Vampire, the second turbojet-powered British fighter, was too late for service in World War II. The type, known originally as the Spider Crab, was planned round a portly central nacelle and twin booms to allow the use of a short and therefore less inefficient jetpipe for the de Havilland Goblin engine, which was of the centrifugal-flow type and therefore of greater diameter than axial-flow types.

The first prototype flew in September 1943, a mere 16 months after the start of detail design.

The Vampire F.Mk 1 entered service in 1946 with the 1225-kg (2,700-lb) thrust de Havilland Goblin I turbojet, and was followed by the Vampire F.Mk 3 with provision for underwing stores and modifications to improve longitudinal stability. Next came the Vampire FB.Mk 5 fighter-bomber with a wing of reduced span but greater strength for the carriage of underwing stores, and finally in the single-seat stream the Vampire FB.Mk 9 for tropical service with a cockpit air conditioner. British variants on the Vampire FB.Mk 5 theme were the Sea Vampire FB.Mks 20 and 21 for carrierborne use, while export variants included the generally similar Vampire FB.Mk 6 for Switzerland and a number of Vampire FB.Mk 50 variants with Goblin and Rolls-Royce Nene engines, the latter featuring in the licence-built French version, the Sud-Est S.E.535 Mistral. A side-by-side two-seater for night fighting was also produced as the Vampire NF.Mk 10 (exported as the Vampire NF.Mk 54 to France), and a similar accommodation layout was retained in the Vampire T.Mk 11 and Sea Vampire T.Mk 22 trainers. Australia produced the trainer in Vampire T.Mks 33, 34 and 35 variants, and de Havilland exported the type as the Vampire T.Mk 5.

**de HAVILLAND D.H.100 VAMPIRE FB Mk 5**
**Role:** Strike fighter
**Crew/Accommodation:** One
**Power Plant:** One 1,420 kgp (3,100 lb s.t.) de Havilland Goblin 2 turbojet
**Dimensions:** Span 11.6 m (38 ft); length 9.37 m (30.75 ft); wing area 28.7 m² (266 sq ft)
**Weights:** Empty 3,310 kg (7,253 lb); MTOW 5,600 kg (12,290 lb)
**Performance:** Maximum speed 861 km/h (535 mph) at 5,791 m (19,000 ft); operational ceiling 12,192 m (40,000 ft); range 1,883 km (1,170 miles) with maximum fuel
**Load:** Four 20 mm cannon, plus up to 904 kg (2,000 lb) of ordnance

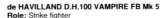

*de Havilland Vampire*

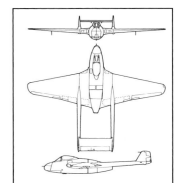

*de Havilland Vampire FB.Mk 5*

# REPUBLIC F-84 Family (U.S.A.)

*F-84F Thunderflash*

The Thunderjet was Republic's first jet-powered fighter, a straight-winged successor to the P-47 Thunderbolt that first flew in February 1946 as the first of three XP-84 prototypes with the 1701-kg (3,750-lb) thrust General Electric J35-GE-7 turbojet. The 25 YP-84A service trial aircraft switched to the 1814-kg (4,000-lb) thrust Allison J35-A-15, the type chosen for the 226 P-84B initial production

aircraft. The 191 P-84C (later F-84C) aircraft had the similarly rated J35-A-13C but a revised electrical system, while the 154 F-84Ds had the 2268-kg (5,000-lb) thrust J35-A-17D engine, revised landing gear and thicker-skinned wings.

Korean War experience resulted in the F-84E, of which 843 were built with a lengthened fuselage, enlarged cockpit and improved systems. The F-84G was similar but powered by the 2540-kg (5,600-lb) thrust J35-A-29, and the 3,025 of this variant were able to deliver nuclear weapons in the tactical strike role. The basic design

was then revised as the Thunderstreak to incorporate swept flying surfaces and the more powerful Wright J65 turbojet for significantly higher performance. Some 2,713 such F-84Fs were built, the first 375 with the J65-W-1 and the others with the more powerful 3275-kg (7,220-lb) thrust J65-W-3.

The final development of this tactically important warplane series was the RF-84F Thunderflash

reconnaissance variant with the 3538-kg (7,800-lb) thrust J65-W-7 aspirated via root inlets, a modification that left the nose clear for the camera installation.

There were a number of experimental and development variants, the most interesting of these being the GRF-84F (later RF-84K) designed to be carried by the Convair B-36 strategic bomber for aerial launch and recovery.

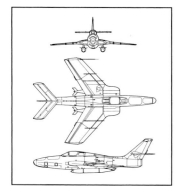

*Republic RF-84F Thunderflash*

**REPUBLIC F-84B THUNDERJET**
**Role:** Fighter bomber
**Crew/Accommodation:** One
**Power Plant:** One 1,814 kgp (4,000 lb s.t.) Allison J35-A-15 turbojet
**Dimensions:** Span 11.1 m (36.42 ft); length 11.41 m (37.42 ft); wing area 24.15 m$^2$ (260 sq ft)
**Weights:** Empty 4,326 kg (9,538 lb); MTOW 8,931 kg (19,689 lb)
**Performance:** Maximum speed 945 km/h (587 mph) at 1,219 m (4,000 ft); operational ceiling 12,421 m (40,750 ft); range 2,063 km (1,282 miles)
**Load:** Six .5 inch machine guns and thirty-two 5 inch rocket projectiles

*Republic RF-84F Thunderflash reconnaissance aircraft*

# MIKOYAN-GUREVICH MiG-15 'FAGOT' Family (U.S.S.R.)

*Mig-17 'Fresco'*

The MiG-15 was the North American F-86 Sabre's main opponent in the Korean War, and was the production version of the I-310 prototype that first flew in late 1947. The MiG-15 was the U.S.S.R.'s first swept-wing fighter to enter large-scale production. The type was powered by the Soviet version of the Rolls-Royce Nene turbojet, which was initially known as the Klimov RD-45 but then in further developed form as the VK-1.

The MiG-15 proved itself a competent fighter, but the type's only major variant, the improved MiG-15bis, could outclimb and out-turn the Sabre in most flight regimes. Many thousands of the series were produced, most of them as standard day fighters, but small numbers as MiG-15P all-weather fighters and MiG-15SB fighter-bombers. The type was given the NATO reporting name 'Fagot', and there was also an

important MiG-15UTI tandem-seat advanced and conversion trainer known as the 'Midget'. Licensed production was undertaken in Czechoslovakia and Poland of the S.102 and LIM variants. The MiG-17 'Fresco' was the production version of the I-330 prototype developed to eliminate the MiG-15's tendency to snap-roll into an uncontrollable spin during a high-speed turn. A new wing of 45° rather than 35° sweep was introduced, together with a longer fuselage, a revised tail unit and more power. Several thousand aircraft were

delivered from 1952 in variants such as the MiG-17 day fighter, MiG-15F improved day fighter with the VK-1F afterburning engine, MiG-17PF limited all-weather fighter, and MiG-17PFU missile-armed fighter. The type was also built in China, Czechoslovakia, and Poland with the designations J-5 (or export F-5), S.104 and LIM-5/6 respectively.

*MiG-15UTI 'Midget' was a two-seat trainer*

**MIKOYAN-GUREVICH MiG-17PF 'FRESCO-D'**
**Role:** Fighter
**Crew/Accommodation:** One
**Power Plant:** One 3,380 kgp (7,452 lb s.t.) Klimov VK/1FA turbojet with reheat
**Dimensions:** Span 9.63 m (31.59 ft); length 11.26 m (36.94 ft); wing area 22.6 m² (243.26 sq ft)
**Weights:** Empty 4,182 kg (9,220 lb); MTOW 6,330 kg (13,955 lb)
**Performance:** Maximum speed 1,074 km/h (667 mph) at 4,000 m (13,123 ft); operational ceiling 15,850 m (52,001 ft); range 360 km (224 miles) with full warload
**Load:** Three 23 mm cannon, plus up to 500 kg (1,102 lb) of bombs or unguided rockets

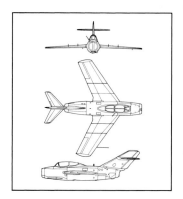

*MiG-15UTI 'Midget'*

# NORTH AMERICAN F-86 SABRE (U.S.A.)

*F-86F Sabre*

The Sabre was the most important American air combat fighter in the Korean War. In 1944 the U.S. Army Air Forces contracted for three XP-86 prototypes for a day fighter that could also double in the escort and ground-attack roles. When the fruits of German aerodynamic research became available to the Americans after World War II, the type was reworked to incorporate swept flying

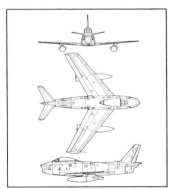

*North American F-86E Sabre*

surfaces, and the first such prototype flew in October 1947 with a 1701-kg (3,750-lb) thrust General Electric TG-180 (later J35-GE-3) axial-flow turbojet. The type was then re-engined with the General Electric J47 turbojet to become the YP-86A, leading to the P-86A (later F-86A) production model with the 2200-kg (4,850-lb) thrust J47-GE-1 engine.

These 554 aircraft with four J47 marks up to a thrust of 2359-kg (5,200-lb) were followed in chronological order by the 456 F-86Es with a slab tailplane and the 3877-kg

### NORTH AMERICAN F-86F SABRE
**Role:** Day fighter
**Crew/Accommodation:** One
**Power Plant:** One 2,708 kgp (5,970 lb s.t.) General Electric J47-GE-27 turbojet
**Dimensions:** Span 11.3 m (37.08 ft); length 11.43 m (37.5 ft); wing area 26.76 m² (288 sq ft)
**Weights:** Empty 4,967 kg (10,950 lb); MTOW 7,711 kg (17,000 lb)
**Performance:** Maximum speed 1,110 km/h (690 mph) at sea level; operational ceiling 15,240 m (50,000 ft); range 1,263 km (785 miles) without external fuel
**Load:** Six .5 inch machine guns, plus up to 907 kg (2,000 lb) of bombs or fuel carried externally

(5,200-lb) thrust J47-GE-27, the 2,540 F-86Fs with the 2708-kg (5,970-lb) thrust J47-GE-27 and, in later aircraft, the '6-3' wing with extended leading edges, the 2,504 F-86D redesigned night and all-weather fighters with the 2517-kg (5,550-lb) thrust J47-GE-33, the 473 F-86H fighter-bombers with the 4037-kg (8,900-lb) thrust J73-GE-3, greater span and a deeper fuselage, the 341 examples of the F-86K simplified

version of the F-86D with the 2461-kg (5,425-lb) J47-GE-17B, and the 981 examples of the F-86L rebuilt version of the F-86D with a larger wing and updated electronics. The Sabre was also built in Australia as the CAC Sabre in Mk 30, 31 and 32 versions with two 30-mm cannon and the Rolls-Royce Avon turbojet, and in Canada as the Canadair Sabre in Mk 2, 4 and 6 versions with the Orenda turbojet.

*F-86F Sabre*

# SAAB 29 (Sweden)

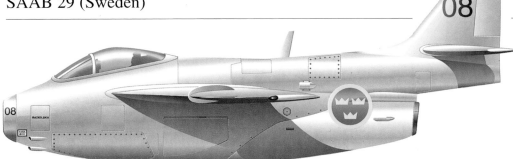

In 1943 SAAB flew its first fighter, the SAAB 21, an unconventional twin-boom pusher type with an ejection seat for the pilot. In 1947 a jet version was first flown as the SAAB 21R, with a British de Havilland Goblin turbojet replacing the earlier piston engine. Although the jet version was put into production and then operated in fighter and attack versions from 1949 to 1955, SAAB by then had much more advanced projects in hand, of which the SAAB 29 became the company's next production jet fighter and, historically, the first European swept-wing fighter to enter operational service.

The Goblin jet engine, then in production in Sweden, also powered Vampire fighters bought direct from Britain to boost Swedish squadrons, and it was logical therefore to design the SAAB 29 around the Goblin. However, with the appearance of the more-powerful 2,268 kg (5,000 lb thrust) de Havilland Ghost engine, the SAAB 29 was revised to use this (as the RM2).

Initial design work on the SAAB 29 had begun as early as 1945, then known as project R 1001. As a completely new design, SAAB chose a 'straight through' fuselage layout, with a nose air intake to feed the jet engine, the latter which exhausted below the narrowing boom-like rear portion of the fuselage and a conventional tail. However, by far the most important design feature was the eventual adoption of wings with 25 degrees of sweepback, original plans to use straight wings having been reviewed after a SAAB engineer had shown foresight to act upon confiscated wartime German technical research material on advanced wing shapes seen during a visit to Switzerland.

The adoption of swept wings followed considerable wind-tunnel testing plus actual flight testing using scaled wings fitted to a Safir lightplane known for research purposes as the SAAB 201.

Featuring also a pressurised cockpit, the first of four prototype SAAB 29s first flew on 1 September 1948 and proved capable of bettering its designed maximum speed of 1,050 km/h (650 mph). Production J 29As were delivered from May 1951, initially to F13 day fighter Wing at Norrköping. Because of its stubby appearance, the fighter gained the nickname Tunnan (Barrel).

After the J 29A came the longer-range SAAB 29B of 1953 appearance, used both as the J 29B fighter and A 29B attack aircraft. The S 29C was a photo reconnaissance variant, which in 1955 established a world closed-circuit speed record of 906 km/h (563 mph). A few J 29Ds followed with Swedish-built afterburners, while the J 29E introduced the 'dog-tooth' wing leading edge to raise the critial Mach number and offer improvements in transonic handling. The final version was the J 29F, with dog-tooth wings, an afterburner to the Ghost 50 (RM2B) engine that raised thrust to 2,800 kg (6,170 lb), and the ability to carry two Sidewinder air-to-air missiles. In total, the Flygvapnet received 661 SAAB 29s, and many Bs were subsequently upgraded to F standard, while Cs later received dog-tooth wings. Austria took in thirty ex-Swedish J 29Fs from 1961. The final flight of a Tunnan was recorded in 1976.

*Two SAAB J 29F in flight*

**SAAB J 29F 'Tunnan'**
**Role**: Fighter and attack
**Crew/Accommodation**: Pilot
**Power Plant**: One 2,800 kgp (6,170 lb s.t.) SFA-built RM2B turbojet with reheat (de Havilland Ghost 50)
**Dimensions**: Span 11.0 m (36.09 ft); length 10.23m (33.56 ft); wing area 24 m$^2$ (258 sq ft)
**Weights**: MTOW typically 8,000 kg (17,637 lb), but 8,375 kg (18,464 lb) possible
**Performance**: Maximum speed 1,060 km/h (658 mph); operational ceiling 15,500 m (50,850 ft); range 1,100 km (683 miles)
**Load**: Four 20 mm cannon plus rockets or two Sidewinder missiles

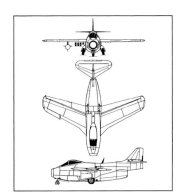

*SAAB J 29F*

# HAWKER HUNTER (United Kingdom)

*Hunter FGA.Mk 58*

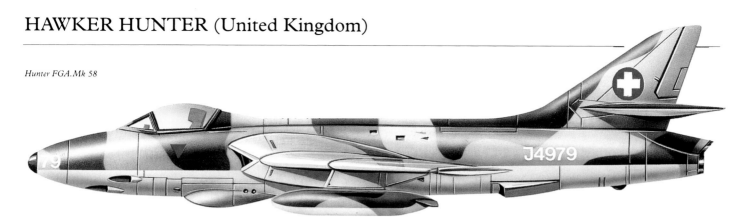

The Hunter was numerically the most successful of British post-World War II fighters, with 1,972 built including 445 manufactured under licence in Belgium and the Netherlands. The type still serves in modest numbers with a few air forces, though not as a fighter. This superb fighter resulted from a British need to replace the obsolescent Gloster Meteor with a more advanced type offering transonic performance and the P.1067 prototype first flew in July 1951, and

was followed just one month later by the first Hunter F.Mk 1 pre-production aircraft.

The first production article flew in May 1953, and the Hunter F.Mk 1 entered squadron service in July 1954. These aircraft were powered by the Rolls-Royce Avon turbojet, but the Hunter F.Mk 2 used the Armstrong Siddeley Sapphire Mk 101 turbojet. Further evolution led to the similar Hunter F.Mks 4 and 5 with more fuel and underwing armament capability,

the former with the Avon Mk 115/121 and the latter with the Sapphire Mk 101. The Hunter F.Mk 6 introduced the Avon Mk 200 series turbojet in its Mk 203/207 forms, greater fuel capacity, along with the underwing armament of the F.Mk 4. The F.Mk 6 was later developed as the Hunter FGA.Mk 9 definitive ground-attack fighter with the dogtoothed leading edges and Avon Mk 207 engine.

There were also tactical reconnaissance variants based on the FGA.Mk 9 and produced in Hunter FR.Mk 10 and FR.Mk 11 forms for the RAF and Fleet Air Arm respectively. Another variant was the

side-by-side two-seat trainer, pioneered in the P.1101 prototype that first flew in mid-1955. This was produced in Hunter T.Mks 7 and 8 forms for the RAF and Fleet Air Arm respectively. Export derivatives of the single- and two-seaters were numerous, and Switzerland continued to acquire large numbers of refurbished Hunters for roles including ground attack.

**HAWKER HUNTER F.Mk 6**
**Role:** Day fighter
**Crew/Accommodation:** One
**Power Plant:** One 4,605 kgp (10,150 lb s.t.) Rolls-Royce Avon Mk 207 turbojet
**Dimensions:** Span 10.25 m (33.33 ft); length 13.97 m (45.83 ft); wing area 32.42 m² (349 sq ft)
**Weights:** Empty 6,505 kg (14,22 lb); MTOW 8,051 kg (17,750 lb)
**Performance:** Maximum speed 1,002 km/h (623 mph) at 10,975 m (36,000 ft); operational ceiling 14,630 m (48,000 ft); range 789 km (490 miles) on internal fuel only
**Load:** Four 30 mm cannon

*A Hawker Hunter F.Mk 1 used as an instructional airframe*

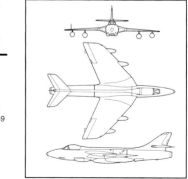

*Hawker Hunter FGA.Mk 9*

# DASSAULT MYSTERE and SUPER MYSTERE (France)

*Mystère IVA*

At the end of World War II, Marcel Bloch was released from a German concentration camp, promptly changed his named to Dassault and started to rebuild his original aircraft company as Avions Marcel Dassault, the premier French manufacturer of warplanes. After gaining experience in the design and construction of jet-powered fighters with the straight-winged M.D. 450 Ouragan fighter-bomber, Dassault turned his attention to a swept-wing design, the Mystère (Mystery). This first flew in the form

of the M.D. 452 Mystère I prototype form during February 1951, and was followed by eight more prototypes each with the Rolls-Royce Tay turbojet: two more Mystère Is, two Mystère IIAs and four Mystère IIBs. Then came 11 pre-production Mystère IICs with the 3000-kg (6,614-lb) thrust SNECMA Atar 101 turbojet, and these paved the way for the Mystère IV production prototype that first flew in September 1952 with the Tay turbojet but thinner and more highly swept wings, a longer oval-

section fuselage, and modified tail surfaces. There followed nine Mystère IVA pre-production aircraft and finally more than 480 production fighters, of which the first 50 retained the Tay but the others used the 3500-kg (7,716-lb) thrust Hispano-Suiza Verdun 350 turbojet.

Further development led to the Mystère IVB prototype with a Rolls-Royce Avon turbojet, a thinner and more highly swept wing, and a revised fuselage of lower drag. The resulting Super Mystère B1 production prototype flew in March 1955 with an

afterburning turbojet as the first genuinely supersonic aircraft of European design, and was followed by 185 examples of the Super Mystère B2 production model with the 4460-kg (9,833-lb) thrust Atar 101G-2/3 afterburning turbojet. Some aircraft were supplied to Israel, which modified a number with the 4218-kg (9,300-lb) thrust Pratt & Whitney J52-P-8A non-afterburning turbojet.

*Dassault Mystère IVA fighters of the French Air Force's EC 8 wing*

**DASSAULT MYSTERE IVA**
**Role:** Strike fighter
**Crew/Accommodation:** One
**Power Plant:** One 3,500 kgp (7,716 lb s.t.) Hispano-Suiza Verdun 350 turbojet
**Dimensions:** Span 11.13 m (36.5 ft); length 12.83 m (42.1 ft); wing area 32 m² (344.5 sq ft)
**Weights:** Empty 5,875 kg (12,950 lb); MTOW 9,096 kg (20,050 lb)
**Performance:** Maximum speed 1,120 km/h (604 knots) at sea level; operational ceiling 13,716 m (45,000 ft); range 460 km (248 naut. miles)
**Load:** Two 30 mm DEFA cannon, plus to up 907 kg (2,000 lb) of externally carried bombs

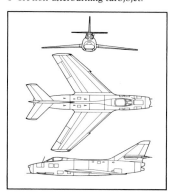

*Dassault Super Mystère BZ*

# CONVAIR F-102 DELTA DAGGER and F-106 DELTA DART (U.S.A.)

*F-106A Delta Dart*

These two delta-winged fighters were designed specifically for air defence of the continental United States and were among the first aircraft in the world designed as part of a complete weapon system integrating airframe, sensors, and weapons. The YF-102 was developed on the basis of data derived from the experimental programme undertaken with the XF-92A, which itself was derived from

American assessment of German research into delta-winged aircraft during World War II. The Model 8 was planned to provide the U.S. Air Force with an 'Ultimate Interceptor' for the defence of North American airspace, and was intended to possess Mach 2+ performance and carry the very advanced MX-1179 Electronic Control System. The resulting Model 8-80 was ordered as a single YF-102 prototype and first flew in October 1952 with a 4400-kg (9,700-lb) thrust

Pratt & Whitney J57-P-11 turbojet. This prototype was soon lost in an accident but had already displayed disappointing performance.

The airframe of the succeeding YF-102A was redesigned with Whitcomb area ruling to reduce drag, and this improved performance to a degree that made feasible the introduction of F-102A single-seat fighter and TF-102A two-seat trainer variants. The MX-1179 ECS had proved too difficult for the technology of the time, so the less advanced MG-3 fire-

control system was adopted for these models, of which 875 and 111 respectively were built.

Greater effort went into the development of the true Mach 2 version, which was developed as the F-102B but then ordered as the F-106 before the first of two YF-106A prototypes flew in December 1956. The F-106A single-seat fighter and F-102B two-seat trainer versions were produced to the extent of 277 and 63 aircraft respectively, and these served into the later 1980s.

*Convair F-106A Delta Dart*

**CONVAIR-F-106A DELTA DART**
**Role:** All-weather interceptor
**Crew/Accommodation:** One
**Power Plant:** One 11,115 kgp (24,500 lb s.t.) Pratt & Whitney J75-P-17 turbojet with reheat
**Dimensions:** Span 11.67 m (38.29 ft); length 21.56 m (70.73 ft); wing area 64.83 m² (697.8 sq ft)
**Weights:** Empty 10,904 kg (24,038 lb); MTOW 17,779 kg (39,195 lb)
**Performance:** Maximum speed 2,135 km/h (1,152 knots) at 10,668 m (35,000 ft); operational ceiling 16,063 m (52,700 ft); radius 789 km (490 miles) on internal fuel only
**Load:** One 20 mm multi-barrel cannon, plus one long-range and four medium-range air-to-air missiles

*A Convair F-106A Delta Dart*

# VOUGHT F-8 CRUSADER (U.S.A.)

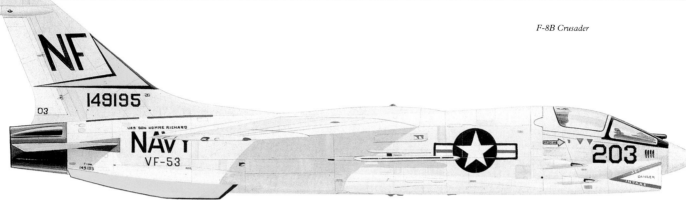

*F-8B Crusader*

A slightly later contemporary of the North American F-100 Super Sabre that used practically the same powerplant, the Crusader carrierborne fighter was an altogether more capable machine despite the additional fixed weight of its naval equipment. The design's most interesting feature was a variable-incidence wing that allowed the fuselage to be kept level during take-off and landing, thereby improving the pilot's fields of vision. The type resulted from a 1952 U.S. Navy requirement for an air-superiority fighter with truly supersonic performance, and from eight submissions the Vought design was selected in May 1953.

The first of two XF8U-1 prototypes flew in March 1955 with the 6713-kg (14,800-lb) thrust Pratt & Whitney J57-P-11 turbojet. Deliveries to operational squadrons began in March 1957 of the F8U-1 with the 7348-kg (16,200-lb) thrust J57-P-4A, four 20-mm cannon, rockets in an underfuselage pack and, as a retrofit, Sidewinder air-to air missiles. Production totalled 318, and from 1962 these aircraft were redesignated F-8A. There followed 30 examples of the F8U-1E (F-8B) with limited all-weather capability, 187 examples of the F8U-2 (F-8C) with the 7666-kg (16,900-lb) thrust J57-P-16, 152 examples of the F8U-2N (F-8D) with the 8,165-kg (18,000-lb) thrust J57-P-20, extra fuel and four Sidewinder missiles, and 286 examples of the F8U-2NE (F-8E) with the 8165-kg (18,000-lb) thrust J57-P-20A, advanced radar and provision for 1,814 kg (4,000 lb) of external stores on four underwing hardpoints. In addition, 42 F-8E (FN)s were built for the French Navy, the only remaining type in service, to be replaced by Rafales. The F-8H to L were rebuilds of older aircraft to an improved standard with a strengthened airframe and blown flaps, and a reconnaissance variant was the F8U-1P (RF-8A); 73 were later rebuilt to RF-8G standard with the J57-P-20A.

*The French Navy's version of the Vought Crusader is the F-8E(FN)*

**VOUGHT F-8E CRUSADER**
**Role:** Naval carrierborne fighter
**Crew/Accommodation:** One
**Power Plant:** One 8,165 kgp (18,000 lb s.t.) Pratt & Whitney J57-P-20 turbojet with reheat
**Dimensions:** Span 10.9 m (35.7 ft); length 16.5 m (54.2 ft); wing area 34.8 m² (375 sq ft)
**Weights:** Empty 8,960 kg (19,750 lb); MTOW 15,420 kg (34,000 lb)
**Performance:** Maximum speed 1,802 km/h (973 knots) Mach 1.7 at 12,192 m (40,000 ft); operational ceiling 17,374 m (57,000 ft); radius 966 km (521 naut. miles)
**Load:** Four 30 mm cannon, plus up to 2,268 kg (5,000 lb) of externally carried weapons, which can include four short-range air-to-air missiles

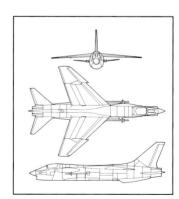

*Vought F8U-2 Crusader*

# SUD-OUEST S.O.4050 VAUTOUR (France)

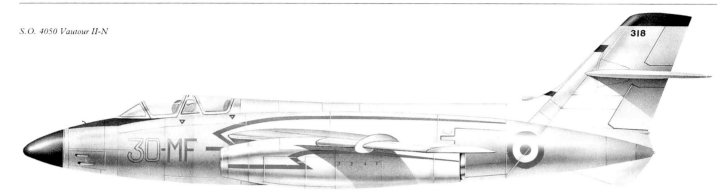

*S.O. 4050 Vautour II-N*

In the late 1940s, Sud-Ouest produced two half-scale research aircraft as the S.O.M.1 air-launched research glider and its powered version, the S.O.M.2 with a Rolls-Royce Derwent turbojet. The company then evolved the S.O.4000 full-scale prototype with two Rolls-Royce Nene turbojets (licence-built by Hispano-Suiza) in the rear fuselage and the unusual landing gear of a single nosewheel and four main wheels, the latter arranged in tandem pairs.

The S.O.4000 first flew in March 1951, and paved the way for the S.O.4050 Vautour (Vulture) prototype with swept flying surfaces and a landing gear arrangement comprising two-twin wheel main units in tandem under the fuselage and single-wheel outriggers under the nacelles of the wing-mounted engines. The first of three prototypes was a two-seat night fighter and flew in October 1952 with 2400-kg (5,291-lb) thrust SNECMA Atar 101B turbojets; the second machine was a single-seat ground-attack type with 2820-kg (6,217-lb) thrust Atar 101Ds; and the third machine was a two-seat bomber with Armstrong Siddeley Sapphire turbojets. There followed six pre-production aircraft before it was decided to procure all three variants with a powerplant standardized as two 3500-kg (7,716-lb) thrust Atar 101Es. Even so, production totalled just 140 aircraft. These comprised 30 single-seat Vautour II-A ground-attack aircraft, 40 two-seat Vautour II-B bombers, and 70 two-seat Vautour II-N night fighters, with equipment and armament optimized for the three types' specific role. The first of these three types flew in April 1956, July 1957 and October 1956 respectively. Some 18 aircraft were later supplied to Israel, and after retrofit with slab tailplanes, the Vautour II-N became the Vautour II-1N.

*Sud-Ouest S.O.4050 Vautour II*

**SUD S.O. 4050 VAUTOUR II-N**
**Role:** All-weather/night fighter
**Crew/Accommodation:** Two
**Power Plant:** Two 3,300 kgp (7,275 lb s.t.) SNECMA Atar 101E-3 turbojets
**Dimensions:** Span 15.1 m (49.54 ft); length 16.5 m (54.13 ft); wing area 45.3 m² (487.6 sq ft)
**Weights:** Empty 9,880 kg (21,782 lb); MTOW 17,000 kg (37,479 lb)
**Performance:** Maximum speed 958 km/h (595 mph) at 12,200 m (40,026 ft); operational ceiling 14,000 m (45, 932 ft); range 2,750 km (1,709 miles) with maximum fuel
**Load:** Four 20 mm cannon

*Sud-Ouest S.O.4050 Vautour*

# LOCKHEED F-104 STARFIGHTER (U.S.A.)

*F-104S Super Starfighter*

The Starfighter resulted from the U.S. Air Force's experiences in the Korean War, where the need for a fast-climbing interceptor became clear. The type was planned by 'Kelly' Johnson with the smallest airframe that would accommodate the most powerful available axial-flow turbojet. This resulted in a fighter possessing a long and basically cylindrical fuselage with unswept and diminutive wings, plus a large T-tail assembly.

The first of two XF-104 prototypes first flew in March 1954 with an interim engine, the 4627-kg (10,200-lb) thrust Wright XJ65-W-6, and four years of troubled development followed with 17 YF-104As before the F-104A entered service with a longer fuselage accommodating the 6713-kg (14,800-lb) thrust J79-GE-3 engine, and an armament of one 20-mm multi-barrel cannon and two AIM-9 Sidewinder air-to-air missiles. The USAF eventually ordered only 296 examples of the Starfighter in variants that included 153 F-104A interceptors, 26 F-104B tandem-seat trainers, 77 F-104C tactical strike fighters with provision for a 907-kg (2,000-lb) external load, and 21 F-104D tandem-seat trainers. The commercial success of the type was then ensured by the adoption of the much-improved F-104G all-weather multi-role type by a NATO consortium. This model had a strengthened airframe, a larger vertical tail, greater power, and more advanced electronics, and itself spawned the F-104J interceptor that was built in Japan. This multi-national programme resulted in the largely licensed production of another 1,986 aircraft up to 1983. The F-104G itself produced TF-104 trainer and RF-104 reconnaissance variants, and Italy developed the special F-104S variant as a dedicated interceptor with better radar and medium-range Sparrow and Aspide air-to-air missiles.

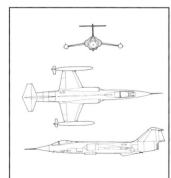

*Lockheed F-104G Starfighter*

*Lockheed F-104G Starfighters of European air forces*

## LOCKHEED F-104A STARFIGHTER
**Role:** Interceptor
**Crew/Accommodation:** One
**Power Plant:** One 6,713 kgp (14,800 lb s.t.) General Electric J79-GE-3B turbojet with reheat
**Dimensions:** Span 6.63 m (21.75 ft); length 16.66 m (54.66 ft); wing area 18.2 m² (196.1 sq ft)
**Weights:** Empty 6,071 kg (13,384 lb); MTOW 11,271 kg (25,840 lb)
**Performance:** Maximum speed 1,669 km/h (1,037 mph) at 15,240 m (50,000 ft) operational ceiling 19,750 m (64,795 ft); range 1,175 km (730 miles) with full warload
**Load:** One 20 mm multi-barrel cannon and two short-range air-to-air missiles

# REPUBLIC F-105 THUNDERCHIEF (U.S.A.)

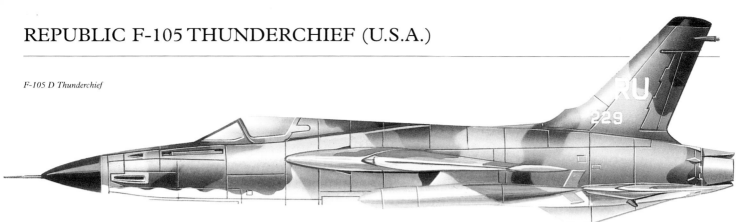

*F-105 D Thunderchief*

The Thunderchief was the final major type to come from the Republic company before its merger into the Fairchild organization, and accorded well with its manufacturer's reputation for massive tactical warplanes. The type was schemed as a successor to the F-84F Thunderstreak and was therefore a strike fighter, but one that offered the advantages of an internal weapons bay able to accommodate 3629-kg (8,000-lb) of stores and fully supersonic performance. This last was provided by the use of a powerful afterburning turbojet in an advanced airframe incorporating the lessons of the area-rule principle.

Two YF-105A prototypes were ordered, and the first of these flew in October 1956 with the 6804-kg (15,000-lb) thrust Pratt & Whitney J57-P-25 turbojet and an 'unwaisted' fuselage. No production followed, for the availability of the new J75 engine and the area-rule theory resulted first in another four prototypes designated YF-105B and powered by 7471-kg (16,470-lb) thrust J75-P-3. Production thus began with 71 F-105B aircraft modelled on the YF-105B and its area-ruled 'waisted' fuselage and forward-swept inlets in the wing roots for the 7802-kg (17,200-lb) thrust J75-P-5 engine. The major variant was the F-105D, of which 610 were built with all-weather avionics, an improved nav/attack system, the 7802-kg (17,200-lb) J75-P-19W turbojet and provision for up to 6350-kg (14,000-lb) of ordnance carried on four underwing hardpoints as well as in the internal load.

The final version was the F-105F tandem two-seat conversion trainer, and of 86 aircraft 60 were later converted to EF-105F (and then F-105G) 'Wild Weasel' defence-suppression aircraft. These were fitted with special radar-detection equipment and anti-radar missiles, and played an important part in American air operations over North Vietnam.

---

**REPUBLIC F-105D THUNDERCHIEF**
**Role:** Fighter
**Crew/Accommodation:** One
**Power Plant:** One 11,113 kgp (24,500 lb s.t.) Pratt & Whitney J75-P-15W turbojet with reheat
**Dimensions:** Span 10.65 m (34.94 ft); length 19.58 m (64.25 ft); wing area 35.76 m² (385 sq ft)
**Weights:** Empty 12,474 kg (27,500 lb); MTOW 23,834 kg (52,546 lb)
**Performance:** Maximum speed 2,369 km/h (1,279 knots) Mach 2.23 at 11,000 m (36,090 ft); operational ceiling 12,802 m (42,000 ft); radius 1,152 km (662 naut. miles)
**Load:** One 20 mm multi-barrel cannon, plus up to 6,350 kg (14,000 lb) of weapons/fuel

*Republic F-105G Thunderchief*

*Republic F-105D single-seaters and, in the foreground, an F-105F two-seater*

# SAAB 35 DRAKEN (Sweden)

*F35 Draken*

An even more remarkable achievement than the Saab 32, the Saab 35 Draken (Dragon) was designed as an interceptor of transonic bombers. This role demanded supersonic speed, a very high rate of climb, better than average range and endurance, and a sizeable weapon load. The tactical philosophy of the Swedish Air Force also dictated that the new type should have STOL capability so that it could operate from lengths of straight road during dispersed operations. The fighter was therefore designed on the basis of a slender circular-section fuselage and a double-delta wing in a combination that provided large lifting area and fuel capacity at minimum profile drag. To achieve much the same performance as the slightly later English Electric Lightning powered by two Rolls-Royce Avon afterburning turbojets, the design team opted for such a single example of the same engine built under licence in Sweden as the Flygmotor RM6. The layout was evaluated successfully in the Saab 210 research aircraft that was in essence a scaled-down Saab 35 and first flew in February 1952 with the 476-kg (1,050-lb) thrust Armstrong Siddeley Adder turbojet.

The first prototype of the Saab 35 flew in October 1955, and the J 35A initial production variant began to enter service in 1958. Production totalled 525 in variants such as the J 35A fighter with the 7000-kg (14,432-lb) thrust RM6B, the J 35B improved fighter with collision-course radar and a data-link system, the Sk 35C tandem-seat operational trainer, the J 35D fighter with the 7830-kg (17,262-lb) thrust RM6C and more advanced electronics, the S 35E tactical reconnaissance aircraft and the J 35F with more advanced radar and Hughes Falcon air-to-air missiles. The type was also exported as the Saab 35X, and surviving J 35Fs have been upgraded to J 35J standard for service into the 1990s.

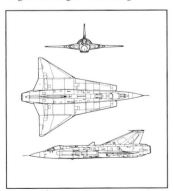

*Saab 35 Draken*

**SAAB 35/J 35 DRAKEN**
**Role:** Interceptor/strike/reconnaissance
**Crew/Accommodation:** One
**Power Plant:** One 7,830 kgp (17,262 lb s.t.) Flygmotor-built Rolls-Royce Avon RM6C turbojet with reheat
**Dimensions:** Span 9.4 m (30.83 ft); length 15.4 m (50.33 ft); wing area 50 m² (538 sq ft)
**Weights:** Empty (not available); MTOW 16,000 kg (35,274 lb)
**Performance:** Maximum/Cruise speed 2,150 km/h (1,160 mph) Mach 2.023 at 11,000 m (36,090 ft); operational ceiling 18,300 m (60,039 ft); range 1,149 km (620 naut. miles) with 2,000 lb warload
**Load:** Two 30 mm cannon, plus up to 4,082 kg (9,000 lb) of bombs

*The J 35F was the definitive interceptor of the Saab Draken family*

# DASSAULT MIRAGE III and IAI KFIR (France and Israel)

*IAI Kfir C-7*

The Mirage was designed to meet a 1954 French requirement for a small all-weather supersonic interceptor, and emerged as the delta-winged M.D.550 Mirage prototype for a first flight in June 1955 with two 980-kg (2,160-lb) thrust Armstrong Siddeley Viper turbojets. The type was too small for any realistic military use, and a slightly larger Mirage II was planned; this was not built, both these initial concepts being abandoned in

favour of the still larger Mirage III that first flew in November 1956 with an Atar 101G-1 afterburning turbojet. Further development led to the Mirage IIIA pre-production type with an Atar 9B of 6,000-kg (13,228-lb) afterburning thrust boosting speed from Mach 1.65 to 2.2 at altitude.

The type went into widespread production for the French forces and for export, and as such was a considerable commercial success for Dassault, especially after Israeli success with the type in the 1967 'Six-Day

War'. The basic variants became the Mirage IIIB two-seat trainer, the Mirage IIIC single-seat interceptor, the Mirage IIIE single-seat strike fighter and the Mirage IIIR reconnaissance aircraft. The Mirage 5 was produced as a clear-weather type, though the miniaturization of electronics in the 1970s and 1980s have allowed the installation or retrofit of avionics that make most Mirage 5 and up-engined Mirage 50 models superior to the baseline Mirage III models. Israel produced a Mirage 5 variant as the IAI Kfir with a General

Electric J79 afterburning turbojet and advanced electronics, and this spawned the impressive Kfir-C2 and later variants with canard foreplanes for much improved field and combat performance. Many surviving Mirages have been modernized to incorporate aerodynamics, avionics and weapon improvements, with newly-named variants including the Chilian ENAER Pantera, Belgian SABCA Elkan (for Chile), and South African Denel Cheetah.

*Dassault Mirage 5*

### DASSUALT MIRAGE IIIE
**Role:** Strike fighter
**Crew/Accommodation:** One
**Power Plant:** One 6,200 kgp (13,670 lb s.t.) SNECMA Atar 9C turbojet, plus provision for one 1,500 kgp (3,307 lb s.t.) SEPR 844 rocket engine
**Dimensions:** Span 8.22 m (27 ft); length 15.03 m (49.26 ft); wing area 34.85 m² (375 sq ft)
**Weights:** Empty 7,050 kg (15,540 lb); MTOW 13,000 kg (29,760 lb)
**Performance:** Maximum speed 2,350 km/h (1,268 knots) Mach 2.21 at 12,000 m (39,375 ft); operational ceiling 17,000 m (55,775 ft); radius 1,200 km (648 naut. miles)
**Load:** Two 30 mm DEFA cannon, plus up to 1,362 kg (3,000 lb) of externally carried ordnance

*A Dassault-Breguet Mirage IIING*

# MIKOYAN MiG-21 'FISHBED' (U.S.S.R.)

*MiG-21 'Fishbed'*

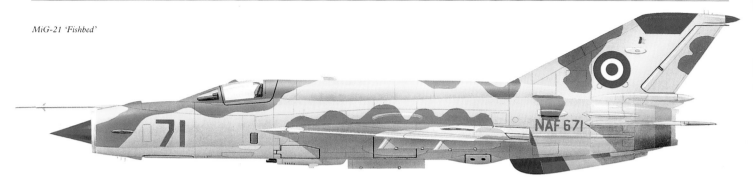

The MiG-21 (NATO name 'Fishbed') was designed, after the U.S.S.R. had digested the implications of the Korean War, to provide a short-range interceptor. The type was analogous to the Lockheed F-104 Starfighter in rationale, but was a radically different aircraft based on a tailed delta configuration, small overall size, and light weight to ensure adequate performance on just one relatively low-powered afterburning turbojet,

the Tumansky R-11, that was only slightly larger and heavier than the RD-9 used in the preceding MiG-19's twin-engined powerplant.

Differently configured Ye-2A and Ye-5 prototypes were flown in 1956, the latter paving the way for the definitive Ye-6 prototype that flew in May 1958. 10,158 MiG-21s were built in the U.S.S.R. (others in India, China as the J-7, and Czechoslovakia) in variants such as the MiG-21 clear-weather interceptor, MiG 21PF limited all-weather fighter with search and track radar, MiG-21 PFS fighter with blown flaps and provision for

RATO units, MiG-21FL export version of the MiG-21PFS but without blown flaps or RATO provision, MiG-21PFM improved version of the MiG-21PFS, MiG-21S/SM second-generation dual-role fighter with a larger dorsal hump and four rather than two underwing hardpoints, MiG-21M export version of the MiG-21S, MiG-21R tactical reconnaissance version, MiG-21MF with the more powerful but lighter R-13-30 engine, MiG-21RF

reconnaissance version of the MiG-21MF, MiG-21SMT aerodynamically refined version of the MiG-21MF with increased fuel and ECM capability and MiG-21bis third generation multi-role fighter. There have also been three MiG-21U 'Mongol' conversion trainer variants. Currently, upgrades are offered by Russia and others, including the MiG-21-93 as chosen by India.

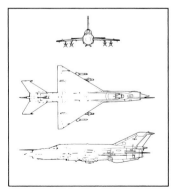

*MiG-21 'Fishbed-K'*

### MIKOYAN-GUREVICH MiG-21SMT 'FISHBED-K'
**Role:** Strike fighter
**Crew/Accommodation:** One
**Power Plant:** One 6,600 kgp (14,550 lb s.t) Tumansky R-13 turbojet with reheat
**Dimensions:** Span 7.15 m (23.46 ft); length 13.46 m (44.16 ft); wing area 23 m² (247.57 sq ft)
**Weights:** Empty 5,450 kg (12,015 lb); MTOW 7,750 kg (17,085 lb)
**Performance:** Maximum speed 2,230 km/h (1,386 mph) Mach 2.1 at 12,000 m (39,370 ft); operational ceiling 18,000 m (59,055 ft); radius 500 km (311 miles) with full warload
**Load:** Two 23 mm cannon, plus up to 1,000 kg (2,205 lb) of air-to-air missiles or bombs depending upon mission

*The Mikoyan-Gurevich MiG-21*

# ENGLISH ELECTRIC LIGHTNING (United Kingdom)

*Lightning F.Mk 6*

The Lightning was the United Kingdom's first supersonic fighter. The type offered superlative speed and climb performance, but was always limited by poor range and indifferent armament. The origins of the type lay in the P.1A, which resulted from a 1947 requirement for a supersonic research aircraft. The first of three prototypes flew in August 1954 and later revealed supersonic performance on two Bristol Siddeley non-afterburning turbojets. It was seen that the type had the makings of an interceptor, and the type was revised as the P.1B that first flew in April 1957 with two superimposed Rolls-Royce Avon turbojets. After a lengthy development with 20 pre-production aircraft, the type began to enter service in 1960 as the Lightning F.Mk 1 with two 30-mm cannon and two Firestreak air-to-air missiles.

Later variants were the Lightning F.Mk 1A with inflight-refuelling capability, the Lightning F.Mk 2 with improved electronics and fully variable afterburners, the Lightning F.Mk 3 with 7420-kg (16,360-lb) thrust Avon Mk 300 series engines, provision for overwing drop tanks, a square-topped vertical tail, improved radar, no guns, and a pair of Red Top air-to-air missiles that offered all-aspect engagement capability in place of the earlier marks' pursuit-course Firestreak missiles.

The final variant was the Lightning F.Mk 6 (originally lightning F.Mk 3A) with a revised wing with cambered and kinked leading edges, and a ventral tank that virtually doubled fuel capacity while also accommodating a pair of 30-mm cannon. There were also two side-by-side trainer models, the Lightning T.Mks 4 and 5; these were based on the F.Mk 1A and F.Mk 3 respectively, and retained full combat capability. For export there was the Lighting Mk 50 series of fighters and trainers.

*An English Electric Lightning F.Mk 53*

**ENGLISH ELECTRIC/BAC LIGHTNING F.Mk 6**

**Role:** Interceptor fighter
**Crew/Accommodation:** One
**Power Plant:** Two 7,420 kgp (16,360 lb s.t.) Rolls-Royce Avon 300 turbojets with reheat
**Dimensions:** Span 10.61 m (34.9 ft); length 16.84 m (55.25 ft); wing area 44.08 m² (474.5 sq ft)
**Weights:** Empty 11,340 kg (25,000 lb); MTOW 18,144 kg (40,000 lb)
**Performance:** Maximum speed 2,230 km/h (1,203 knots) Mach 2.1 at 10,975 m (36,000 ft); operational ceiling 17,375 m (57,000 ft); radius 972 km (604 miles)
**Load:** Two Red Top missiles, plus two 30 mm Aden cannon

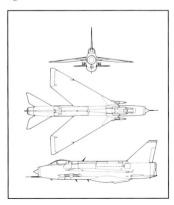

*Lightning F.Mk 6*

# MCDONNELL DOUGLAS F-4 PHANTOM II (U.S.A.)

*IAI F-4 Phantom 2000*

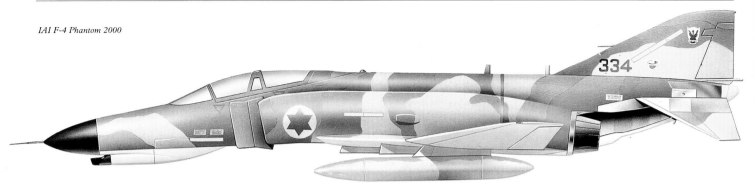

In October 1979, the 5,057th Phantom II was completed, ending the West's largest warplane production programme since World War II. The programme was devoted to an exceptional type that must be numbered in the five most important warplanes of all time. It was planned initially as an all-weather attack aircraft, but then adapted during design into an all-weather fleet-defence and tactical fighter. The first of two XF4H-1 prototypes flew in May 1958 with early examples of the equally classic J79 afterburning turbojet. The 45 F4H-1Fs (later F-4As) were really pre-production types with 7326-kg (16,150-lb) thrust J79-GE-2/2A engines.

True operational capability came with 649 F4H-1 (later F-4B) with 7711-kg (17,000-lb) thrust J79-GE-8 engines, 46 RF-4B reconnaissance aircraft for the U.S. Marine Corps, 635 F-4C (originally F-110A) attack fighters for the U.S. Air Force with 7711-kg (17,000-lb) thrust J79-GE-15 engines, 499 RF-4C USAF tactical reconnaissance aircraft, 773 F-4Ds based on the F-4C but with electronics tailored to USAF rather than U.S. Navy requirements, 1,405 F-4Es for the USAF with 8119-kg (17,900-lb) thrust J79-GE-17 engines, improved radar, leading-edge slats and an internal 20-mm rotary-barrel cannon, 175 F-4F air-superiority fighters for West Germany, 512 F-4Js for the U.S. Navy with 8119-kg (17,900-lb) thrust J79-GE-10 engines, a revised wing and modified tail, 52 F-4Ks based on the F-4J for the Royal Navy with Rolls-Royce Spey turbofans, and 118 F-4Ms based on the F-4K for the Royal Air Force.

There have been several other versions produced by converting older airframes with more advanced electronics as well as other features, such as the similar F-4N and F-4S developments of the F-4B and F-4J for the U.S. Navy, the F-4G for the USAF's 'Wild Weasel' radar-suppression role, and the Super Phantom (or Phantom 2000) rebuild of the F-4E by Israel Aircraft Industries.

**McDONNELL DOUGLAS F-4E PHANTOM II**
**Role:** All-weather strike fighter
**Crew/Accommodation:** Two
**Power Plant:** Two 8,119 kgp (17,900 lb s.t.) General Electric J79-GE-17 turbojets with reheat
**Dimensions:** Span 11.71 m (38.42 ft); length 19.2 m (63 ft); wing area 49.2 m² (530 sq ft)
**Weights:** Empty 13,397 kg (29,535 lb); MTOW 27,965 kg (61,651 lb)
**Performance:** Maximum speed 2,390 km/h (1,290 knots) Mach 2.2 at 12,190 m (40,000 ft); operational ceiling 18,975 m (62,250 ft); radius 960 km (518 naut. miles) typical combat mission
**Load:** One 20 mm multi-barrel cannon and four medium-range air-to-air missiles, plus up to 7,257 kg (16,000 lb) of externally carried weapons or fuel

*The RF-4C is a version of the McDonnell Douglas Phantom II land-based fighter series*

*F-4E Phantom II*

89

# NORTHROP F-5 Family (U.S.A.)

*F-5E Tiger II*

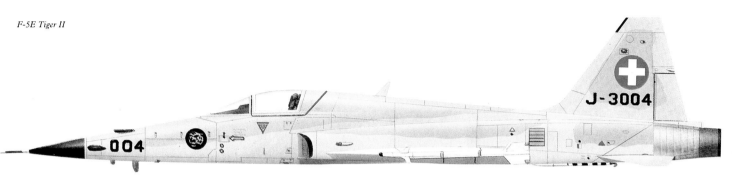

The F-5 Freedom Fighter was developed, using U.S. Government funding, from Northrop's private-venture N-156 design as a modestly supersonic fighter and attack aircraft with the light weight, compact dimensions and simple avionics that would make it suitable for export under the U.S.'s 'Military Assistance Programs', or for sale to other forces requiring an uncomplicated jet. The concept's first concrete expression was the N-156T supersonic trainer that

first flew in April 1959 as the YT-38 with two 953-kg (2,600-lb) thrust General Electric J85-GE-1 non-afterburning turbojets, though the third to sixth prototypes had the 1,633-kg (3,600-lb) afterburning thrust J85-GE-5 engines that paved the way for the 1,746-kg (3,850-lb) thrust J85-GE-5As used in the T-38A Talon version, of which 1,189 were built (including the two prototypes), most going to USAF training establishments; in 1999 many hundreds remain flying and are undergoing upgrade.
The N-156F fighter was developed

in F-5A single-seat and F-5B two-seat variants, and first flew in July 1959 with 1,850-kg (4,850-lb) thrust J85-GE-13 turbojets. Production of the F-5A and F-5B totalled 818 and 290 respectively for various countries in differently designated versions that included the Canadair-built CF-5 for Canada, NF-5 for the Netherlands, F-5G for Norway and the CASA-built SF-5 for Spain. There was also an RF-5A reconnaissance model. The mantle of the Freedom Fighter was then assumed by the more capable Tiger II variant produced in F-5E single-seat and F-5F two-seat forms with an integrated fire-control system as well

as 2,268-kg (5,000-lb) thrust J85-GE-21 engines and aerodynamic refinements for much improved payload and performance.
The F-5E first flew in August 1972 and deliveries of Tiger IIs began in 1973. Large-scale production followed in the U.S.A. and abroad (including Switzerland and Taiwan), and by the close of production Tiger IIs had raised the overall F-5 production total to well over 2,600 aircraft, including a small number of RF-5E TigerEye reconnaissance aircraft.

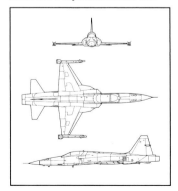

*Northrop F-5E Tiger II*

**NORTHROP F-5E TIGER II**
**Role:** Strike fighter
**Crew/Accommodation:** One
**Power Plant:** Two 2,268 kgp (5,000 lb s.t.) General Electric J85-GE-21 turbojets with reheat
**Dimensions:** Span 8.13 m (26.66 ft); length 14.68 m (48.16 ft); wing area 17.3 m² (186.2 sq ft)
**Weights:** Empty 4,392 kg (9,683 lb); MTOW 11,195 kg (24,680 lb)
**Performance:** Maximum speed 1,730 km/h (934 knots) Mach 1.63 at 11,000 m (36.090 ft); operational ceiling 15,790 m (51,800 ft); radius 222 km (138 miles) with full warload
**Load:** Two 20 mm cannon, plus up to 3,175 kg (7,000 lb) of ordnance, including two short-range air-to-air missiles

*The Northrop F-5F Tiger II became the two-seat version of the F-5E single-seater*

# MIKOYAN MiG-25 'FOXBAT' Series (U.S.S.R.)

*MiG-25 'Foxbat'*

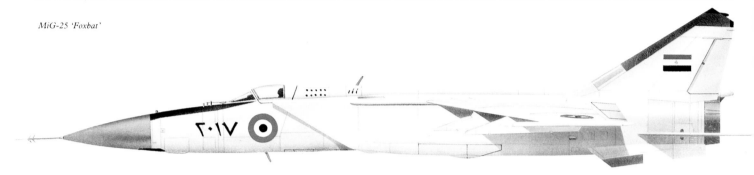

The MiG-25 was designed to provide the Soviets with an interceptor capable of dealing with the United States' North American B-70 Valkyrie Mach 3 high-altitude strategic bomber. When the B-70 was cancelled, the Soviets continued to develop this very high-performance interceptor which first flew as the Ye-266 in 1964. The type is built largely of stainless steel with titanium leading edges to deal with friction-generated heat at Mach 3, but at such a speed is virtually incapable of manoeuvre.

The type entered service in 1972 with valve-technology radar that lacked the sophistication of then current Western equipments but offered very high power, and thus the ability to 'burn through' the defences provided by the enemy's electronic counter-measures. Variants became the 'Foxbat-A' interceptor with four air-to-air missiles, the 'Foxbat-B' operational-level reconnaissance bomber, the 'Foxbat-C' two-seat conversion trainer, and the 'Foxbat-D' improved reconnaissance aircraft.

As 'Foxbat-A' became obsolete, two further combat versions were developed, as 'Foxbat-E', with much-improved radar (both newly built and by conversion of 'Foxbat-A's) and 'Foxbat-F' for an air-defence suppression role with a specialized radar-warning suite and AS-11 'Kilter' anti-radar missiles. Russian interceptors were withdrawn by 1994, although others were used abroad, but reconnaissance versions remain operational. The MiG-31 'Foxhound' entered service in 1983 as a development of the MiG-25 with greater power and the combination of electronically-scanned phased array radar with multi-target capability, improved missiles (mainly to protect against cruise missile attack) and longer range/duration. Maximum speed is Mach 2.83.

*Mikoyan MiG-25 'Foxbat-A'*

**MIKOYAN MIG-25 'FOXBAT-B'**
**Role:** High speed reconnaissance-bomber
**Crew/Accommodation:** One
**Power Plant:** Two 11,200-kgp (24,700-lb s.t.) Soyuz/Tumansky R-15B turbojets with reheat
**Dimensions:** Span 13.38 m (43.9 ft); length 21.55 m (70.7 ft); wing area 61.4 m² (660.9 sq ft)
**Weights:** MTOW 41,200 kg (90,830 lb)
**Performance:** Maximum speed 3,006 km/h (1,868 mph) at 13,000m (42,630 ft); operational ceiling 23,000 m (75,460 ft); range 2,400 km (1,491 miles) with 4 bombs and a drop-tank
**Load:** 5,000 kg (11,023 lb) of bombs

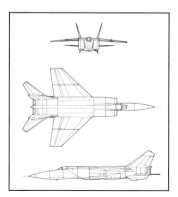

*MiG-25 'Foxbat-A'*

# MIKOYAN MiG-23 and MiG-27 'FLOGGER' Series (U.S.S.R.)

*MiG-27 'Flogger'*

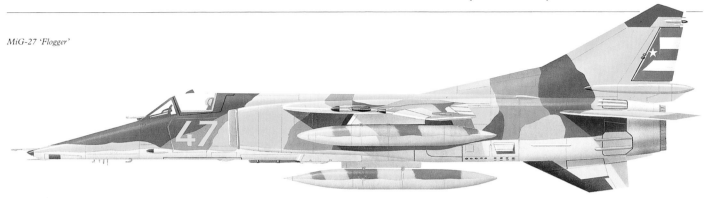

In 1967, the MiG bureau flew its 23-11 swing-wing fighter prototype for evaluation against the 23-01 tailed-delta prototype powered by a single Tumansky R-27-300 turbojet propulsion engine and given V/STOL capability by the incorporation of two Kolesov RD36-35 lift jets in the centre of the fuselage. The 23-11 proved superior, and as the MiG-23 was produced between 1969 and 1985 for Soviet use and export, with 5,047 completed. 'Flogger-A' was given one Tumansky R-27 engine and Sapfir-21 radar, but 'Flogger-B' introduced the R-29 engine and Sapfir-23 'High Lark' radar, plus other improvements and become the standard basic production version. Other versions followed, including 'Flogger-Fard H' as ground-attack variants with Lyulka or Tumansky engines, mainly for export. The final variant was known in the West as 'Flogger-K', an upgrade with vortex generators at the wingroots and nose probe, a radar suited to close-air combat, AA-11 'Archer' missiles and more. The MiG-27 first flew in 1970 as a supersonic dedicated attack derivative of the MiG-23 with a revised forward fuselage offering heavy armour protection and fitted with terrain-avoidance rather than search radar. The MiG-27 also has a less advanced powerplant with fixed inlets and a simple nozzle for its reduced-performance role at low altitude; special target-acquisition and weapon guidance equipment are installed, as are a multi-barrel cannon and additional hardpoints for the larger offensive load. Two variants became the 'Flogger-D' and 'Flogger-J'.

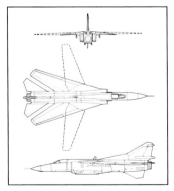

*MiG-23 'Flogger-B'*

**MIKOYAN MIG-27 'FLOGGER-J'**
**Role:** Ground attack with variable geometry wing
**Crew/Accommodation:** One
**Power Plant:** One 11,500-kgp (25,350-lb s.t.) Soyuz R-29B-300 turbofan with reheat
**Dimensions:** Span 13.97 m (45.8 ft), swept 7.78 m (25.5 ft); length 17.08 m (56 ft); wing area 27.26 m² (293.42 sq ft)
**Weights:** Empty 12,100 kg (26,676 lb); MTOW 18,100 kg (39,900 lb)
**Performance:** Maximum speed 1,350 km/h (839 mph) Mach 1.1 at sea level; operational ceiling 13,000+ m (46,650+ ft); radius 540 km (336 miles) with two missiles and three drop-tanks
**Load:** One 30-mm cannon, plus up to 3,000 kg (6,614 lb) of weapons.

*This 'Flogger-D' was given terrain-avoidance radar*

# SAAB 37 VIGGEN (Sweden)

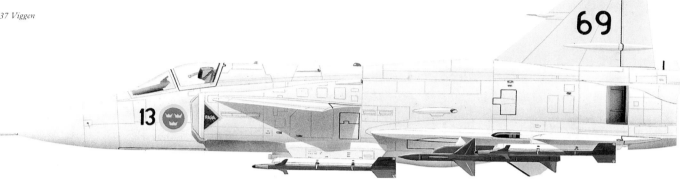

*JA 37 Viggen*

With the Saab 37 Viggen (Thunderbolt), first flown in February 1967, Sweden produced a true multi-role fighter with a thrust-reversible afterburning turbofan and a canard layout for true STOL capability using short lengths of road as emergency airstrips. The type was designed around the integrated weapon system concept pioneered in the United States, with power based on a Swedish licence-built version of the Pratt & Whitney JT8D turbofan but fitted in this application with Swedish-designed afterburning and thrust-reversing units. The advanced electronics include pulse-Doppler radar, a head-up display and other items linked by a digital fire-control system to maximize the type's offensive and defensive capabilities with effective weapons and electronic countermeasures.

Production totalled 329, and the variants have been the AJ 37 attack aircraft with the 11,790-kg (25,992-lb) thrust RM8A, the SF 37 overland reconnaissance aircraft with a modified nose accommodating seven cameras and an infa-red sensor, the SH 37 overwater reconnaissance aircraft with search radar, and the SK 35 tandem two-seat operational trainer with a taller vertical tail. A 'Viggen Mk 2' development became the JA 37 interceptor with the 12,750-kg (28,109-lb) thrust RM8B turbofan, a number of airframe modifications, an underfuselage pack housing the extremely potent Oerlikon-Bührle KCA 30-mm cannon, together with a revised electronic suite with much improved radar. Finally, 75 AJ/SH/SFs were converted between 1993 and 1995 to AJS 37s, given more modern computers and other avionics, plus new reconnaissance equipment and new weapon choices, allowing any aircraft to perform air defence, attack or reconnaissance roles.

*The SH 37 is the overwater reconnaissance variant of the Saab Viggen family*

**SAAB JA 37 VIGGEN**
**Role:** Interceptor
**Crew/Accommodation:** One
**Power Plant:** One 12,750 khp (28,109 lb s.t.) Volvo Flyg motor RM8B turbofan with reheat
**Dimensions:** Span 10.6 m (34.78 ft); length 16.4 m (53.8 ft); wing area 46 m² (495.1 sq ft)
**Weights:** Empty 12,200 kg (26,455 lb); MTOW 20,000 kg (44,090 lb)
**Performance:** Maximum speed 2,231 km/h (1,386 mph) Mach 2.10 at 11,000 m (36.090 ft); operational ceiling 18,000 m (59,050ft); radius 500 km (311 miles)
**Load:** One 30-mm cannon, plus up to 6,000 kg (13,277 lb) of externally-carried weapons/fuel, including two medium-range and four short-range air-to-air missiles

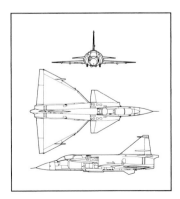

*Saab AJ 37 Viggen*

# GRUMMAN F-14 TOMCAT (U.S.A.)

*F-14 Tomcat*

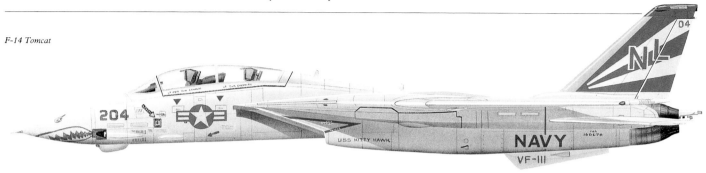

After the cancellation of the F-111B, developed primarily by Grumman as the fleet defence fighter equivalent of the General Dynamics F-111A land-based interdictor, the U.S. Navy issued a requirement for a new fighter. Submissions were received from five companies, but Grumman had a headstart with its G-303 design that made valuable use of the company's experience of variable-geometry wings, and also incorporated the F-111B's TF30 engines, AIM-54 Phoenix long-range air-to-air missiles, and AWG-9 radar fire-control system. In January 1969, the G-303 was selected for development as the F-14, and the first of 12 YF-14A pre-production aircraft flew in December 1970. The Tomcat was aerodynamically more tractable because of its 'glove vanes', small surfaces extending from the leading-edge roots of the main wings' fixed structure as the outer surfaces swept aft, which regulated movement in the centre of pressure to reduce pitch alterations.

The F-14A initial model entered service in October 1972 and immediately proved itself a classic fighter of its type in terms of performance, manoeuvrability, and weapon system capability. Some aircraft have been adapted for the reconnaissance role as the F-14A/TARPS with a ventral equipment pod. The only limitation to the F-14's total success was the powerplant of two 9480-kg (20,900-lb) thrust Pratt & Whitney TF30-P-412-A turbofans, which were not designed for fighter use and therefore lack the flexibility required for this role. For F-14As built after 1984, the TF30-P-414A was introduced, while F-14Bs and Ds produced by manufacture and conversion have 12,247-kg (27,000-lb) thrust General Electric F110-GE-400 turbofans. In addition, many F-14s have been given LANTIRN infra-red pods to permit FAC and strike missions, nicknamed 'Bombats'. Iran also received F-14s

### GRUMMAN F-14A TOMCAT
**Role:** Carrier fighter, attack and reconnaissance
**Crew/Accommodation:** Two
**Power Plant:** Two 9480-kg (20,900 lb) thrust Pratt & Whitney TF30-P-412A turbofans
**Dimensions:** Span unswept 19.6 m (64.1 ft), swept 11.7 m (38.2 ft); length 19.1 m (62.7 ft); wing area 52.5 m² (565 sq ft)
**Weights:** Empty 17,650 kg (38,910 lb); MTOW 33,725 kg (74,350 lb)
**Performance:** Maximum speed 2,498 km/h (1,552 mph), Mach 2.34 at 11.276 m (37,000 ft); operational ceiling 19,500 m (64,000 ft); typical range for air-to-air mission 852 km (530 miles)
**Load:** Up to 6,577 kg (14,500 lb) with typically 4 AIM-54C Phoenix and 2 AIM-9 Sidewinders, plus an internal 6-barrel 20-mm General Electric M61 Vulcan cannon. F-14D can carry AMRAAM AAMs

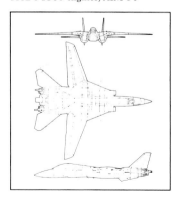

*Grumman F-14A Tomcat*

*A Grumman F-14A Tomcat in the markings of US Naval Aviation*

# DASSAULT MIRAGE F1 (France)

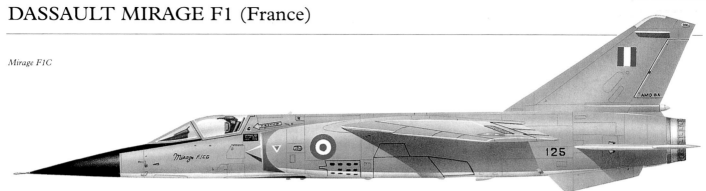

*Mirage F1C*

The Mirage F1 was developed as a successor to the Mirage III/5 family, but is a markedly different aircraft with 'conventional' flying surfaces. The French government originally wanted a two-seat warplane, and such a type was evolved by the company as the Mirage F2, powered by a SNECMA/Pratt & Whitney TF306 turbofan. At the same time the company worked as a private venture on the Mirage F1, a smaller and lighter single-seater sized to the SNECMA Atar turbojet.

The Mirage F2 flew in June 1966, but cost too much for a profitable production contract. The Mirage F1 first flew in December 1966 with the Atar 09K-31 turbojet. After the Mirage F2 programme was cancelled the French government ordered three pre-production examples of the Mirage F1. These displayed excellent performance and overall capabilities as multi-role warplanes, their primary advantages over the Mirage III/5 family being larger warload, easy handling at low altitude, good rate of climb, and 40 per cent greater fuel capacity (through the use of integral rather than bladder tanks) all combined with semi-STOL field performance thanks to the use of droopable leading edges and large trailing-edge flaps on the sharply swept wing, which is mounted in the shoulder position.

The Mirage F1 was ordered into production with the Atar 09K-50 afterburning turbojet. Like the preceding Mirage III/5 series, the Mirage F1 has been a considerable (if not outstanding) commercial success. The main variants have been the Mirage F1A clear-weather ground-attack fighter, the Mirage F1B and D two-seat trainers, the Mirage F1C (and Mirage F1C-200 long-range) multi-role all-weather interceptor with attack capability, the Mirage F1E multi-role export fighter, and the Mirage F1CR-200 long-range reconnaissance aircraft. Some French F1C-200s have been adapted as Mirage F1CTs, basically to F1E standard.

*Dassault Mirage F1 CTs (SIRPA Air)*

### DASSAULT MIRAGE F1CT
**Role:** Strike fighter
**Crew/Accommodation:** One
**Power Plant:** One 7,900 kgp (15,873 lb) SNECMA Atar 09K-50 turbojets with reheat
**Dimensions:** Span 8.4 m (27.55 ft); length 15.3 m (50.2 ft); wing area 25 m² (270 sq ft)
**Weights:** Empty 7,400 kg (16,315 lb); MTOW 16,200 kg (35,700 lb)
**Performance:** Maximum speed 2,335 km/h (1,450 mph) Mach 2.2 at 12.000 m (39,370 ft); operational ceiling 20,000 m (65,600 ft) radius of action 425 km (264 miles) with 3,500 kg attack load
**Load:** Two 30-mm DEFA cannon, plus up to 6,300 kg (13,890 lb) of externally carried weapons

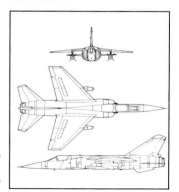

*Dassault Mirage F1C*

# BOEING (McDONNELL DOUGLAS) F-15 EAGLE (U.S.A.)

*F-15C Eagle*

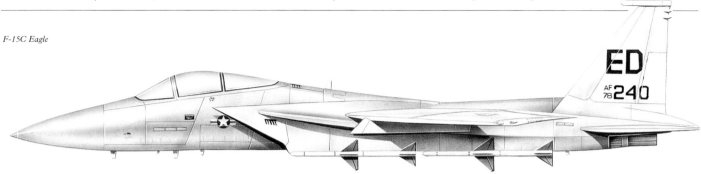

The F-15 was planned as the U.S. Air Force's successor to the F-4 in the air superiority role. After three years of design studies the type was selected for hardware development in December 1969. The first of two YF-15A prototypes emerged for its first flight in July 1972 as a massive aircraft with two 10,809-kg (23,830-lb) thrust Pratt & Whitney F100-P-100 turbofans, sophisticated aerodynamics, advanced electronics including the APG-63 multi-role radar and a pilot's head-up display, and the

world's first production cockpit of the HOTAS (Hands-On-Throttle-And-Stick) type.

The Eagle entered service in November 1974, and has since proved itself a first-class and versatile warplane. Its powerful engines allow the type to carry a large weight of widely assorted weapons in the primary air-to-air and secondary air-to-ground roles, and also generate a thrust-weight ratio in the order of unity for an exceptionally high rate of climb and very good manoeuvrability. The

initial F-15A single-seat model was complemented by the F-15B (originally TF-15A) two-seat combat-capable version.

In 1979 production switched to the F-15C and F-15D respectively. These are powered by 10,637-kg (23,450-lb) thrust F100-P-220 engines, and have more advanced systems, including the improved APG-70 radar from 1985 production onward, as well as provision for external carriage of the so-called FAST (Fuel and Sensor Tactical) packs that provide considerably more fuel and weapons

at a negligible increase in drag and weight. The F-15C and D are built under licence in Japan as the F-15J and F-15DJ. In 1988 the USAF received its first example of the F-15E, airframe (though strengthened) and offering advanced air-to-air capability combined with ground attack. In 1989 the first flight took place of the F-15 SMTD, an experimental vectored-thrust conversion of an F-15B, with two dimensional nozzles and foreplanes.

*F-15E Eagle*

**McDONNELL DOUGLAS F-15E EAGLE**
**Role:** All-weather strike fighter
**Crew/Accommodation:** Two
**Power Plant:** Two 10,782 kgp (23,770 lb s.t.) Pratt & Whitney F100-PW-220 turbofans with reheat
**Dimensions:** Span 13.05 m (42 ft); length 19.45 m (63.79 ft); wing area 56.5 m² (608 sq ft)
**Weights:** Empty 14,515 kg (32,000 lb); MTOW 36,741 kg (81,000 lb)
**Performance:** Maximum speed 2,698 km/h (1,675 mph); operational ceiling 18,300 m (60,000 ft); radius of action 1,271 km (790 miles)
**Load:** Up to 11,113 kg (24,500 lb) of weaponry, and one 20-mm multi-barrel cannon mounted internally

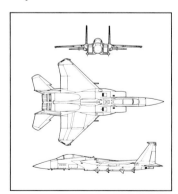

*McDonnell Douglas F-15C Eagle*

# LOCKHEED MARTIN F-16 FIGHTING FALCON (U.S.A.)

*F-16A Fighting Falcon*

During the Vietnam War the United States Air Force discovered that its fighters were in general handicapped by their very large size, weight and Mach 2 performance, all of which were liabilities that seriously eroded reliability and combat agility in the type of turning dogfight that became increasingly common at low and medium altitudes. To help to find a solution to this problem, in 1971 the

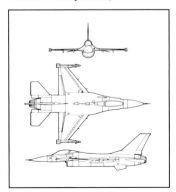

*F-16C Fighting Falcon*

U.S. Air Force instituted a Light-Weight Fighter competition for a low cost day fighter, and General Dynamics produced its Model 401 design.

The first of two YF-16 prototypes flew in January 1974, and 12 months later the type was declared winner of the LWF competition. The basic type was adopted as the U.S. Air Force's Air-Combat Fighter, but its role was greatly expanded to include ground attack and, because of provision for

**LOCKHEED MARTIN F-16C FIGHTING FALCON**
**Role:** Air dominance and ground attack fighter
**Crew/Accommodation:** One
**Power Plant:** One 13,154 kgp (29,000 lb s.t.) General Electric F110-GE-129 or 13,200 kgp (29,100 lb s.t.) Pratt & Whitney F100-PW-229 in current Block 50/52 F-16Cs
**Dimensions:** Span 10 m (32.79 ft); length 15.02 m (49.3 ft); wing area 17.87 m² (300 sq ft)
**Weights:** Empty 8,753 kg (18,900 lb); MTOW 19,187 kg (42,300 lb)
**Performance:** Maximum speed 2,146 km/h (1,335 mph) Mach 2.02 at 12,190 m (40,000 ft); operational ceiling over 15,240 m (50,000 ft); radius of action 1,605 km (997 miles) with four air-to-air missiles and maximum internal fuel and 3,936 litres in drop-tanks
**Load:** One 20-mm cannon, plus up to 7,071–7,225 kg (15,590–15,930 lb) of other weapons

radar and upgraded navigation equipment, all-weather operations. In June 1975 it was announced that the same type had been adopted by a four-nation European consortium. The first production models were the single-seat F-16A and two-seat F-16B, which entered service in January 1979 and received the name Fighting Falcon in 1980. Since then, the type has gone on to become numerically the most important fighter in the Western world, with nearly 4,000 delivered to many countries. The type is based on blended contours and relaxed stability, the latter controlled by a fly-by-wire system. The pilot controls the fighter using a sidestick joystick 'controller', and occupies a 30° reclining ejection seat that assists in helping the pilot withstand high 'g' forces.

Many structural and electronic improvements, including a more capable radar, created the current F-16C single-seat and F-16D two-seat variants, which can again use either General Electric or Pratt & Whitney engines in their most recent and powerful forms. Other variants produced for specific missions or experimental use includes the USAF's F-16HTS (F-16Cs) for SEAD

(suppression of enemy air defenses) and F-16CAS for close air support and battlefield interdiction.

*F-16C Fighting Falcon, formerly a General Dynamics product*

# BOEING F/A-18 HORNET Family (U.S.A.)

*F/A-18A Hornet*

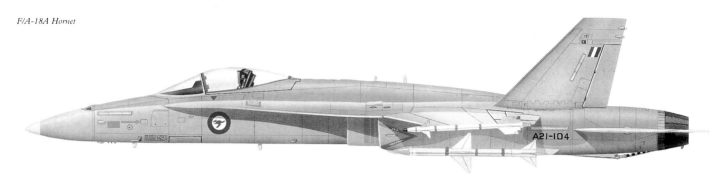

Serving with the U.S. Navy and Marine Corps as replacement for the F-4 and A-7 in the fighter and attack roles respectively, the dual-capability F/A-18 is one of the West's most important carrierborne warplanes, and has also secured useful export orders for land-based use. Originally a McDonnell Douglas product (before the company's merger with Boeing in 1997), the type was derived from the Northrop YF-17 (losing contender to the YF-16 in the USAF's Light-Weight Fighter competition) in order to meet the requirements of the Navy Air Combat Fighter requirement.

In the development programme undertaken by Northrop and McDonnell Douglas, the YF-17 was enlarged, aerodynamically refined, re-engined and fitted with advanced mission electronics. The Hornet prototype first flew in November 1978. Initial plans to procure separate F-18 and A-18 fighter and attack variants had been abandoned when it was realized that different software in the mission computers would allow a single type to be optimized in each role. McDonnell Douglas assumed production leadership, and the F/A-18s entered service late in 1983 as the F/A-18A single-seater and its combat-capable two-seat partner, the F/A-18B, originally designated the TF/A-18A.

The F/A-18A was replaced in production by the F/A-18C in 1987 with a number of electronic and system improvements and the ability to carry more advanced weapons. The two-seat equivalent became the F/A-18D. Night attack capability was added to C/Ds from the 139th aircraft delivered since 1989. Also, 31 USMC F/A-18Ds began entering service as F/A-18D (RC)s in 1999 for reconnaissance. Meanwhile, in November 1995, the F/A-18E Super Hornet prototype first flew, and deliveries to the U.S. Navy have begun of 'E' single-seaters and 'F' two-seaters, offering more power, greater range and payload, improved avionics and more.

*F/A-18A Hornet*

**McDonnell Douglas F/A-18C Hornet**
**Role:** Naval and land-based strike fighter
**Crew/Accommodation:** One
**Power Plant:** Two 7,257 kgp (16,000 lb s.t.) General Electric F404-GE-400 turbofans with reheat, or more powerful GE-402s from 1992
**Dimensions:** Span 11.4 m (36.5 ft); length 17.1 m (56 ft); wing area 37.16 m² (400 sq ft)
**Weights:** Empty 10,810 kg (23,832 lb); MTOW 25,401 kg (56,000 lb)
**Performance:** Maximum speed over Mach 1.8; operational ceiling 15,240 m (50,000 ft); radius 740 km (461miles) with missiles and sinternal fuel only
**Load:** One 20-mm multi-barrel cannon plus up to 7,030 kg (15,500lb of weapons, including up to 10 AMRAAM and two Sidewinder missiles or a mix of AAMS and attack weapons

*F/A-18A Hornet*

# MAPO 'MiG' MiG-29 'FULCRUM' Family (Russia)

*MiG-29 'Fulcrum'*

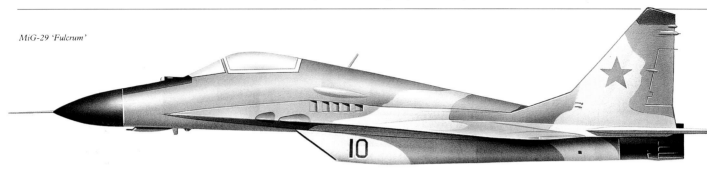

First flown in October 1977 and delivered to the Soviet air force from 1983, the MiG-29 is also known by the NATO reporting name 'Fulcrum' and is a lightweight close-air fighter optimized for air combat but with a secondary attack capability. Despite its use of a conventional mechanical control system in an airframe of very advanced but basically conventional configuration, the type possesses great agility. Moreover, a genuine look-down/shoot-down capability is offered by the combination of a radar that can track up to ten targets simultaneously and engage one or two, and use of AA-10 'Alamo' snap-down air-to-air missiles. The 'Fulcrum-A' has undergone a number of changes since it was first seen, the consensus being that these indicate a number of fixes to bring the design up to the present standard.

The first variant was probably a pre-production model and carried small detachable ventral tail fins reminiscent of those carried by the Sukhoi Su-27 'Flanker'. Later 'Fulcrum-A's introduced extended-chord rudders. The MiG-29UB 'Fulcrum-B' became the two-seat combat-capable conversion and continuation trainer derivative of the 'Fulcrum-A' with the radar removed, though a planned upgrade may restore radar to allow full multi-role capability. The next single-seater became 'Fulcrum-C', distinguishable by its larger dorsal fairing for carriage of an active ECM system and more internal fuel. An improved version of 'C' introduced better Topaz radar and added new AA-12 'Adder' missiles to the weapon choices. MiG-29M 'Fulcrum-E' has been under trial as a new tactical fighter and ground attack model with greatly enhanced capabilities, with export versions including the MiG-33, while MiG-29K has undergone trials as a naval version suited to aircraft carrier operations.

*MiG-29 'Fulcrum-A'*

**MAPO 'MiG' MiG-29 'FULCRUM'**
**Role:** Fighter
**Crew/Accommodation:** One
**Power Plant:** Two 8,300 kgp (18,300 lb s.t.) Klimov RD-33 turbofans with reheat
**Dimensions:** Span 11.36 m (37.27 ft); length 17.32 m (56.83 ft); wing area 38.1 m² (410 sq ft)
**Weights:** Empty 10,900 kg (24,030 lb); MTOW 18,480 kg (40,740 lb)
**Performance:** Maximum speed 2,440 km/h (1,516 mph Mach 2.3 at 11,000 m (36.090 ft); operational ceiling 17,500 m (57,400 ft); range 2,100 km (1,305 miles) maximum
**Load:** One 30-mm cannon plus about 4,000 kg (8,818 lb) of external weapons, typically 2 medium-range AA-10s and 4 AA-11 or AA-8 short-range missiles

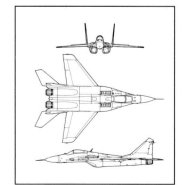

*MiG-29 'Fulcrum-A'*

# SUKHOI Su-27 'FLANKER' Family (Russia)

*Su-27 'Flanker-A'*

Developed during the 1970s as a long-range air-superiority fighter to match the U.S. Air Force's McDonnell Douglas F-15 Eagle, the Su-27 drew on similar aerodynamic research that assisted the MiG-29, but was designed to be inherently unstable because of the adoption of an analog fly-by-wire control system. First flown in May 1977, initial operational capability was achieved in December 1984. The first version became known to NATO as

the 'Flanker-A', though referring to four prototypes and five pre-production aircraft with the vertical tail surfaces located centrally above the engine installations, rounded wingtips and mostly AL-21F3 engines.

The basic full-production version became the 'Flanker-B' with squared-off wingtips, plus a number of refinements such as leading edge slats and vertical tail surfaces located farther outboard. 'Flanker-B' has been built in Su-27S tactical and Su-27P air defence models.

Su-27UB 'Flanker-C' is a tandem two-seat combat trainer variant, first

flown in production form in 1986. Although adding a second cockpit forced a reduction in fuel load, it retains full combat capability and has all the necessary radar and weapon systems.

From Su-27 has been developed a wide family of related warplanes. These include the Su-30 two-seat long-range multi-role interceptor that has extra avionics to lead a group of Su-27 fighters; Su-32FN with side-by-side seating for maritime strike and related Su-27IB/Su-34 for tactical interdiction; Su-33/Su-27K

carrierborne fighter and anti-ship single-seater, known to NATO as 'Flanker-D' (also two-seat version); and Su-35 and Su-37 (or Su-27M) as fighter and ground attack aircraft, the Su-37 with thrust-vectoring nozzles.

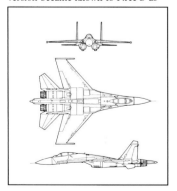

*Sukhoi Su-27 'Flanker-B'*

**SUKHOI Su-27 'FLANKER B'**
**Role:** Interceptor
**Crew/Accommodation:** One
**Power Plant:** Two 12,500 kgp (27,560 lb s.t.) Saturn AL-31F turbofans with reheat
**Dimensions:** Span 14.7 m (48.25 ft); length 21.94 m (72 ft); wing area 62.04 m² (667.8 sq ft)
**Weights:** Empty 16,380 kg (36,112 lb); MTOW 28,300 kg (62,390 lb)
**Performance:** Maximum speed 2,300 km/h (1,429 mph) Mach 2.17; operational ceiling 18,500 m (60,700 ft); range 2,800 km (1,740 miles)
**Load:** One 30-mm multi-barrel cannon plus up to 8,000 kg (17,636 lb) of weapons, including 10 air-to-air missiles ( up to six AA-10 'Alamos'

*A Sukhoi Su-27 'Flanker-B'*

# DASSAULT MIRAGE 2000 (France)

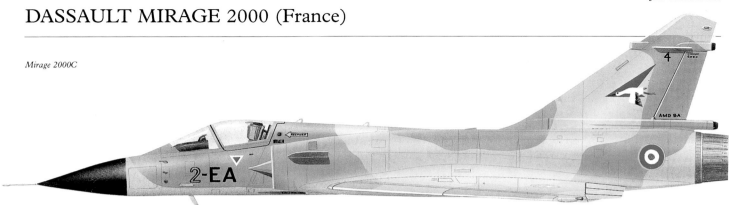

*Mirage 2000C*

With the Mirage 2000 the manufacturer reverted to the delta-wing planform but, in this instance, of the relaxed-stability type with an electronic 'fly-by-wire' control system to avoid many of the low-level handling and tactical limitations suffered by the aerodynamically similar Mirage III/5 family. In the early and mid-1970s, Dassault was working on a prototype to meet the French air force's ACF (Avion de Combat Futur) requirement, but this was cancelled in 1975 when the service decided that a warplane powered by two SNECMA M53-3 turbofans was too large. In December 1975, therefore, the French government authorized the design and development of a smaller single-engined machine. This emerged as the Mirage 2000 with the 9,000-kg (19,840-lb) thrust SNECMA M53-5 turbofan in the smallest and lightest possible airframe for a high power/weight ratio.

The first of five prototypes flew during March 1978 and the prototypes soon demonstrated the Mirage 2000's complete superiority to the Mirage III in all flight regimes. The type remains in production, and the primary variants have been the Mirage 2000B two-seat operational trainer with a lengthened fuselage, the Mirage 2000C single-seat interceptor and multi-role fighter (now with the 9,700-kg (21,384-lb) thrust M53-P2 turbofan and RDI pulse Doppler radar in place of the original RDM multi-mode radar), the Mirage 2000N two-seat nuclear-capable strike fighter based on the airframe of the Mirage 2000B and optimized for low-level penetration, the Mirage 2000D based on 'N' and for all-weather attack, the Mirage 2000R single-seat reconnaissance fighter, the Mirage 2000E single-seat multi-role export derivative of the Mirage 2000C with RDM radar, the Mirage 2000ED training version of 'E' and the Mirage 2000-5 latest advanced multi-role combat aircraft for export and as some modified Mirage 2000Cs for French operation, with RDY radar capable of tracking up to 24 targets.

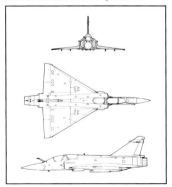

*Mirage 2000-5*

**DASSAULT MIRAGE 2000C**
**Role:** air superiority fighter
**Crew/Accommodation:** One
**Power Plant:** One 9,700 kgp (21,385 lb s.ts) SNECMA M53-P2 turbofan with reheat
**Dimensions:** Span 9.13 m (29.95 ft); length 14.36 m (47.1 ft); wing area 41 m² (441.3 sq ft)
**Weights:** Empty 7,500 kg (16,534 lb); MTOW 17,000 kg (37,480 lb)
**Performance:** Maximum speed 2,335 kn/h (1,450 mph) Mach 2.2 at 11,000m (36,000 ft); operational ceiling 18,000 m (60,000 ft); range 3,335 km (2,072 miles) with external fuel and four 250 kg bombs
**Load:** Two 30-mm DEFA cannon plus up to 6,300 kg (13,890 lb) of weapons including two Matra Magic 2 and two Matra Super 530D missiles

*Mirage 2000C*

# SAAB AB GRIPEN JAS 39 (SWEDEN)

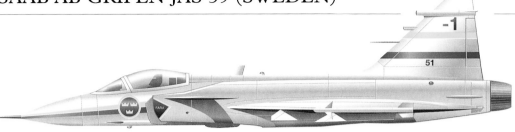

The Gripen is Sweden's very latest multi-role warplane, and is generally acknowledged to be the world's first production combat aircraft of the new fourth generation. It was developed and is being built by a Swedish industrial group in which SAAB is the largest partner in terms of programme value. Such is the potential of the aircraft that British Aerospace became a partner for joint marketing, adapting and supporting the Gripen on the export market.

Although a fairly small nation, Sweden has never compromised on its military aircraft, deciding its needs and building accordingly, even without

the backing of export orders, though Gripen may well prove internationally successful. Another Swedish tradition has been to produce a single aircraft capable of fulfilling many roles through the adoption of specifically-equipped variants, while Swedish aircraft also have the ability to disperse to and operate from short sections of the nation's main road network in an emergency. With Gripen, the concept has been taken a stage further by having advanced computer systems so that each single Gripen can fully perform in any of the required fighter, attack and reconnaissance roles with the same pilot at any time, merely by

selecting the system function and thereby the characteristics required to undertake that mission.

As a lightweight combat aircraft intended to eventually replace Viggens and Drakens in Swedish service, development of Gripen began in 1980 with a project definition phase. Full development started in June 1982, with the signing of a contract for five test aircraft and the first thirty production aircraft (Batch 1). The first flight of a test aircraft was achieved on 9 December 1988 and the Gripen joined the Air Force in 1996, first going to F7 Wing. The final Gripen of Batch 1 (30 aircraft) was delivered in December 1996, when deliveries of

Batch 2 aircraft (including JAS 39B two-seat operational trainers) began to the Swedish Defence Material Administration. Batch 2 covered 96 single-seaters and 14 two-seaters, equipped with upgraded avionics software and new flight control system hardware, while in 1997 a third batch was ordered (64 aircraft). Eventually, twelve of the Air Force's thirteen squadrons will operate Gripens.

Gripen has rear-mounted delta wings and close-coupled all-moving canards, and uses a flight-by-wire flight control system. Strong but light carbonfibre has been used in the construction of about a third of the airframe. Remarkably, Gripen can be refuelled, rearmed, and essential servicing and inspections made in a turnaround time of under ten minutes by a technician and five conscripts under combat conditions

*Gripen in F7 Wing markings, carrying wingtip Sidewinders, two underwing AGM-65 Maverick missiles and a drop tank*

## JAS 39A GRIPEN

**Role:** Multi-role fighter, attack, maritime attack and reconnaissance
**Crew/Accommodation:** One
**Power Plant:** One 8,212 kgp (18.105 lb s.t.) Volvo RM12 with reheat
**Dimensions:** Span 8.4 m (27.56 ft); length 14.1 m (46.26 ft);
**Weights:** Empty 6,620 kg (14,600 lb); MTOW 14,000 kg (30,865 lb)
**Performance:** Supersonic at all heights; radius of action 800 km (497 miles)
**Load:** One 27-mm Mauser cannon. Pylons on each wingtip (two), under the wings (four), under the air intakes (two) and under the fuselage (one) for a selection of weapons and stores that can include Sidewinder, AMRAAM or operational Mica air-to-air missiles, anti-ship, air-to-surface or other missiles, cluster weapons, rockets or other types.

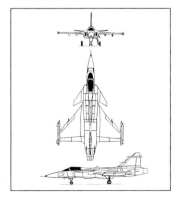

*JAS 39 Gripen*

# LOCKHEED MARTIN F-22 RAPTOR (U.S.A.)

*YF-22A Raptor*

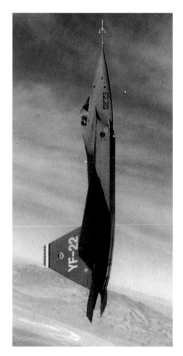

*First F-22 Raptor EMD test aircraft*

In late April 1991 the U.S. Air Force Secretary announced the selection of the Lockheed/Boeing/General Dynamics team to develop the Advanced Tactical Fighter (ATF) as the replacement for the F-15 Eagle.

The ATF was conceived in the first year of President Reagan's administration. In June 1981, a specification was issued whilst the F-15 and F-16 were quite new. At the time, however, there was a shortage of low-level, all-weather strike and

### LOCKHEED MARTIN F-22A

**Role:** Advanced Tactical Fighter (ATF)

**Crew/Accommodation:** One (in 360° tear-drop pressurized cockpit)

**Power Plant:** Two 15,875 kgp (35,000 lb s.t.) Pratt & Whitney F119-PW-100 turbofans with reheat

**Dimensions:** Span 13.56 m (44.5 ft); length 18.92 m (62.08 ft); wing area 78.04 m² (840 sq ft)

**Weights:** Empty 14,515 kg (32,000 lb); MTOW 24,950 kg (55,000 lb)

**Performance:** Maximum speed Mach 2+, also quoted as Mach 1.8+; Mach 1.58 supercruise, also quoted as Mach 1.4+; operational ceiling 15,240 m+ (50,000 ft+); range 3,200 km+ (2,000 miles+)

**Load:** One M61A-2 20-mm cannon; two side bays with AIM-9M Sidewinder air-to-air missiles (one in each) and one main bay with up to six AIM-120C AMRAAM missiles. 8 AMRAAMs can be carried under the wings. Attack weapons can be carried in main bay

interdiction aircraft. The Air Force set certain requirements and limits for the project. These subsequently included the ability to fly at supersonic speed without afterburner (known as supercruise), have enough fuel for mission radius, have unrestricted manoeuvrability with the use of two-dimensional engine nozzles, incorporate stealth technology and other systems to provide high survivability, internal weapons carriage in air-superiority role, conform to specific weight and cost requirements, have a cruise speed of Mach 1.5 with a combat radius of 800 miles, and more.

Two prototypes were ordered, one powered by Pratt & Whitney F119 engines, the other with General Electric F-120s. Boeing would build the wings and aft fuselage, General Dynamics the centre fuselage and empennage and Lockheed the cockpit and nose section.

Boeing provided a 757 for flight testing the complete avionics system, the first with active matrix liquid crystal displays instead of cathode ray tubes.

In 1987 radical redesign was undertaken because of weight problems; consequently, the contract was extended by six months.

The first YF-22 flew on 29 September 1990 and in 1991 the F-22/F119 engine combination was selected over the rival Northrop/McDonnell Douglas YF-23. A further 9 test aircraft (EMDs) followed, the first flying in September 1997, and it is expected that the USAF will receive 339 F-22As, with deliveries from the year 2002.

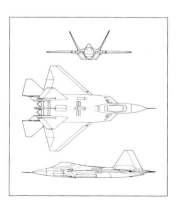

*Lockheed Martin YF-22A Raptor*

# Heavy Bombers

Strategic bombing began at the very start of World War I, when in November 1914 three tiny Avro 504 biplanes of the Royal Naval Air Service set out to destroy the German Zeppelin sheds at Friedrichshafen. Each aircraft carried just four 20 lb bombs but still managed to damage Zeppelin LZ32 and blow up the adjacent gasworks.

Such tiny aircraft could hardly be termed strategic bombers, despite the nature of their historic mission, but in February 1915 giant four-engined Russian Sikorsky Ilya Mourometzs began their wartime raids with an attack on a target in Poland. It fell to Italy to begin the first sustained strategic bombing offensive when, from August 1915, triple-engined Caproni Ca 32s and other types began

striking targets in Austria-Hungary. Ca 32s also recorded the first Italian night bombing raids.

Already, by January 1915, German Navy Zeppelin airships had begun bombing attacks on Great Britain, with London hit for the first time that May. Such attacks lasted until April 1918, the 51 Zeppelin raids on Britain dropping 199 tonnes of bombs and causing 557 fatalities. However, from 1917 Germany put greater faith in new Gotha and other heavy bombing aeroplanes to undertake strategic attacks, with the first mass raid by 21 Gothas recorded on 25 May. Despite some earlier success in bringing down Zeppelins, the British RFC and RNAS found the bombers a different matter and on that first raid no contacts with the enemy were made during 77 defence sorties. Night attacks by Gothas started in

September 1917, the same month that Germany introduced even larger Zeppelin Staaken R VI bombers capable of dropping 1,000 kg bombs, the largest of the war.

In retaliation for German bombing of civilians, and to meet public outcry, in 1916 Britain fielded the Handley Page O/100, a twin-engined heavy bomber built to the Admiralty's call for a 'bloody paralyser'. It was followed by the high-powered O/400, but other heavy bombers such as the Vickers Vimy had hardly reached service status by the Armistice and so saw most service post-war. Indeed, the Vimy will always be remembered in the annals of aviation for carrying Alcock and Brown on the first-ever non-stop flight across the Atlantic in 1919.

The heavy bomber was, by the start of the 1920s, standard equipment for all major air

forces and by the 1930s huge monoplanes began the slow process of superseding biplanes, with the Soviet Union establishing the world's most potent heavy bomber force with its Tupolev TB series of metal low-wing monoplanes. The stage was set for the development of the bombers used in World War II, as detailed in the following pages.

*Picture: Zeppelin Staaken R VI represented Germany's largest bomber of World War I, some versions having six engines.*

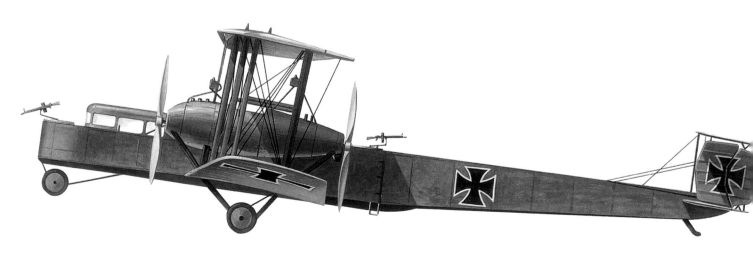

# BOEING B-17 FLYING FORTRESS (U.S.A.)

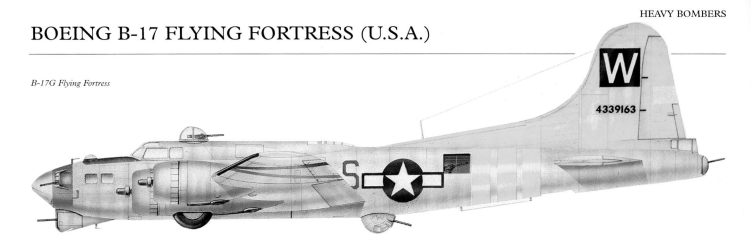

*B-17G Flying Fortress*

The Flying Fortress was one of the United States' most important warplanes of World War II, and resulted from a 1934 requirement for a multi-engined bomber with the ability to carry a 907-kg (2,000-lb) bomb load over minimum and maximum ranges of 1640 and 3540 km (1,020 and 2,200 miles) at speeds between 322 and 402 km/h (200 and 250 mph). Boeing began work on its Model 299 design in June 1934, and the prototype flew in July 1935 with four 599-kW (750-hp) Pratt & Whitney R-1680-E Radials.

Although it crashed during a take-off in October 1935 as a result of locked controls, the prototype had demonstrated sufficiently impressive performance for the U.S. Army Air Corps to order 14 YB-17 (later Y1B-17) pre-production aircraft including the static test airframe brought up to flight standard. Twelve of these aircraft were powered by 694-kW (930-hp) Wright GR-1820-39 radials, while the thirteenth was completed as the Y1B-17A with 746-kW (1,000-hp) GR-1820-51 radials, each fitted with a turbocharger for improved high-altitude performance. The early production models were development variants and included 39 B-17Bs, 38 B-17Cs with 895-kW (1,200-hp) R-1820-65 engines, and 42 B-17Ds with self-sealing tanks and better armour. The tail was redesigned with a large dorsal fillet, which led to the first of the definitive Fortresses, the B-17E and B-17F, of which 512 and 3,405 were built, the latter with improved defensive armament.

The ultimate bomber variant was the B-17G with a chin turret and improved turbochargers for better ceiling, and this accounted for 8,680 of the 12,731 Flying Fortresses built. The type was discarded almost immediately after World War II, only a few special-purpose variants remaining in service. In addition, there were a number of experimental and navy models.

**BOEING B-17G FLYING FORTRESS**
**Role:** Long-range day bomber
**Crew/Accommodation:** Ten
**Power Plant:** Four 1,200 hp Wright R-1820-97 Cyclone air-cooled radials
**Dimensions:** Span 31.62 m (103.75 ft); length 22.66 m (74.33 ft); wing area 131.92 m² (1,420 sq ft)
**Weights:** Empty 16,391 kg (36,135 lb); MTOW 29,484 kg (65,000 lb)
**Performance:** Maximum speed 462 km/h (287 mph) at 7,620 m (25,000 ft); operational ceiling 10,851 m (35,600 ft); range 5,472 km (3,400 miles)
**Load:** Twelve .5-inch machine guns, plus up to 2,722 kg (6,000 lb) of bombs

*The definitive B-17G version of the Boeing B-17 Flying Fortress*

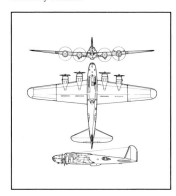

*B-17C Flying Fortress*

105

# CONSOLIDATED B-24 LIBERATOR (U.S.A.)

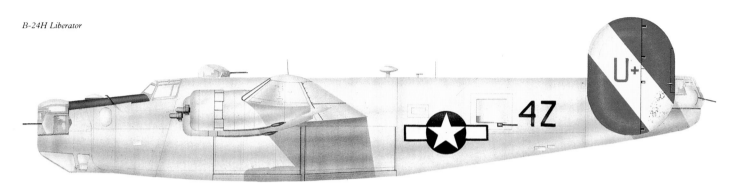

*B-24H Liberator*

The Liberator was a remarkably versatile aircraft, and was built in greater numbers than any other U.S. warplane of World War II. The Model 32 was designed to a U.S. Army Air Corps request of January 1939 for a successor to machines such as the Boeing XB-15 and Douglas XB-19, neither of which entered production, and offering higher performance than the Boeing B-17.

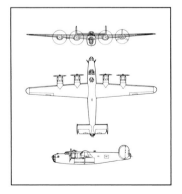

*Consolidated B-24D Liberator*

The design was based on the exceptional wing of the Model 31 flying boat, the high aspect ratio of which offered low drag and thus the possibility of high speed and great range. The XB-24 prototype flew in December 1939 with 895-kW (1,200-hp) R-1830-33 radial engines, and the seven YB-24 pre-production machines were followed by nine B-24As with two 7.62-mm (0.3-in) tail guns and six 12.7-mm (0.5-in) guns in nose, ventral, dorsal and waist positions, and nine B-24Cs with turbocharged R-1830-41 engines and eight 12.7-

### CONSOLIDATED B-24J LIBERATOR
**Role:** Long-range day bomber
**Crew/Accommodation:** Ten
**Power Plant:** Four 1,200 hp Pratt & Whitney R.1830-65 Twin Wasp air-cooled radials
**Dimensions:** Span 33.53 m (110 ft); length 20.47 m (67.16 ft); wing area 97.36 m² (1,048 sq ft)
**Weights:** Empty 16,556 kg (36,500 lb); MTOW 29,484 kg (65,000 lb)
**Performance:** Maximum speed 467 km/h (290 mph) at 7,620 m (25,000 ft); operational ceiling 8,534 m (28,000 ft); range 3,379 km (2,100 miles) with full bombload
**Load:** Ten .5 inch machine guns, plus up to 3,992 kg (8,800 lb) of internally carried bombs

mm guns in single-gun nose, ventral, and twin waist positions, and twin-gun dorsal and tail turrets. These paved the way for the first major model, the B-24D based on the B-24C but with R-1830-43 engines, self-sealing tanks and, in later aircraft, a ventral ball turret together with two 12.7-mm guns.

These 2,381 aircraft were followed by 801 B-24Es with modified propellers. Then came 430 B-24Gs with R-1830-43 engines and a power-operated nose turret carrying twin 12.7-mm guns, and 3,100 improved B-24Hs with a longer nose. The most important variant was the slightly

modified B-24J, of which 6,678 were built with R-1830-65 engines, an autopilot and an improved bombsight. The 1,667 B-24Ls were similar to the B-24Js but had hand-operated tail guns, as did the 2,593 B-24Ms in a lighter mounting. There were also a number of experimental bomber variants, while other roles included transport (LB-30, air force C-87 and navy RY variants), fuel tanking (C-109), photographic reconnaissance (F-7), patrol bombing (PB4Y-1 and specially developed PB4Y-2 with a single vertical tail surface) and maritime reconnaissance (British Liberator GR models).

*A Consolidated B-24D Liberator in USAAF markings*

# HANDLEY PAGE HALIFAX (United Kingdom)

*Halifax B.Mk II*

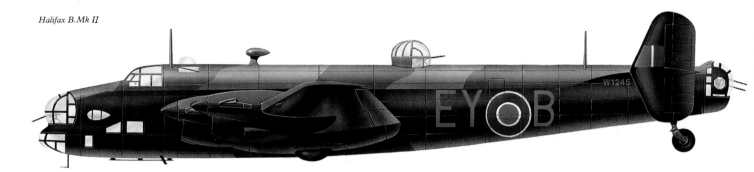

The Halifax was one of the RAF's trio of four-engined night bombers in World War II, and while not as important in this role as the Lancaster, it was more important in secondary roles such as maritime reconnaissance transport, and airborne forces' support. The type originated from a 1936 requirement for a medium/heavy bomber powered by two Rolls-Royce Vulture inline engines, and the resulting H.P.56 design was ordered

in prototype form. The company had doubts about the Vulture, and began to plan an alternative H.P.57 with four Rolls-Royce Merlin inlines. In September 1937, two H.P.57 prototypes were ordered. The first flew in October 1939.

The type entered service as the Halifax B.Mk I with 954-kW (1,280-hp) Merlin Xs, and these 84 aircraft were produced in three series as the initial Series I, the higher-weight

Series II, and the increased-tankage Series III. Later bombers were the 1,977 Halifax B.Mk IIs with Merlin XXs or 22s and a two-gun dorsal turret, the 2,091 Halifax B.Mk IIIs with 1204-kW (1,615-hp) Bristol Hercules VI or XVI radials, the 904 Halifax B.Mk Vs based on the Mk II with revised landing gear, the 467 Halifax B.Mk VIs based on the Mk III but with 1249-kW (1,675-hp) Hercules 100s, and the 35 Halifax B.Mk VIIs that reverted to Hercules XVIs; there were also bomber subvariants with important

modifications. The other variants retained the same mark number as the relevant bomber variant, and in the transport type these were the C.Mks II, VI and VII, in the maritime role GR.Mks II, V and VI, and in the airborne support role the A.Mks II, V and VII. Post-war development produced the C.Mk 8 and A.Mk 9 as well as the Halton civil transport, and total production was 6,178 aircraft.

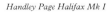

*Handley Page Halifax Mk I*

**HANDLEY PAGE HALIFAX B.Mk III**
**Role:** Heavy night bomber
**Crew/Accommodation:** Seven
**Power Plant:** Four 1,615 hp Bristol Hercules XVI air-cooled radials
**Dimensions:** Span 30.12 m (98.83 ft); length 21.82 m (71.58 ft); wing area 116.3 m² (1,250 sq ft)
**Weights:** Empty 17,346 kg (38,240 lb); MTOW 29,484 kg (65,000 lb)
**Performance:** Maximum speed 454 km/h (282 mph) at 4,115 m (13,500 ft); operational ceiling 7,315 m (24,000 ft); range 2,030 km (1,260 miles) with full warload
**Load:** Nine .303 inch machine guns, plus up to 5,897 kg (13,000 lb) of internally-stowed bombload

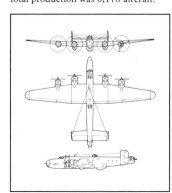

*Handley Page Halifax B.Mk III*

107

# AVRO LANCASTER (United Kingdom)

*Lancaster B.Mk III*

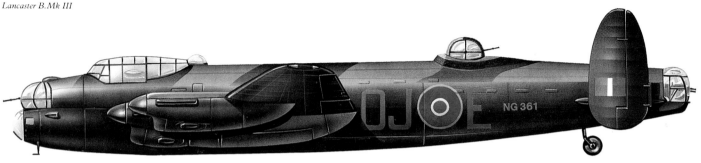

Certainly the best night bomber of World War II, the Lancaster was conceived as a four-engined development of the twin-engined Type 679 Manchester, which failed because of the unreliability of its Rolls-Royce Vulture engines. The first Lancaster flew in January 1941 with 854-kW (1,145-hp) Rolls-Royce Merlin Xs and the same triple vertical tail surfaces as the Manchester, though these were later replaced by the larger endplate surfaces that became a Lancaster hallmark. The type was ordered into large-scale production as the Lancaster Mk I (later B.Mk I), of which 3,435 were produced. Defensive armament was eight 7.7-mm (0.303-in) machine-guns in three powered turrets: twin-gun nose and dorsal units, and a four-gun tail unit.

The first aircraft had 954-kW (1,280-hp) Merlin XXs or XXIIs, but later machines used the 1208-kW (1,620-hp) Merlin XXIVs. A feared shortage of Merlin inline engines led to the development of the Lancaster Mk II with 1294-kW (1,735-hp) Bristol Hercules VI or XVI radial engines, but only 301 of this model were built as performance was degraded and Merlins were in abundant supply. The Lancaster Mk I was soon supplemented by the Lancaster B.Mk III and Canadian-built Lancaster B.Mk X, both powered by Packard-built Merlins.

Production of the Mk III and Mk X totalled 3,039 and 430 respectively. The final production version was the Lancaster B.Mk VIII with an American dorsal turret containing two 12.7-mm (0.5-in) heavy machine guns, and deliveries totalled 180 bringing overall Lancaster production to 7,377. After the war Lancasters were modified to perform a number of other roles.

*Avro Lancaster Mk I*

**AVRO LANCASTER Mk I**
**Role:** Heavy night bomber
**Crew/Accommodation:** Seven
**Power Plant:** Four 1,640 hp Rolls-Royce Merlin 24 water-cooled inlines
**Dimensions:** Span 31.09 m (102 ft); length 21.18 m (69.5 ft); wing area 120.49 m² (1,297 sq ft)
**Weights:** Empty 16,780 kg (37,000 lb); MTOW 29,408 kg (65,000 lb)
**Performance:** Maximum speed 394 km/h (245 mph) at sea level; operational ceiling 6,706 m (22,000 ft); range 3,589 km (2,230 miles) with 3,182 kg (7,000 lb) bombload
**Load:** Eight .303 inch machine guns, plus up to 8,165 kg (18,000 lb) of bombs

*This is the RAF's preserved Avro Lancaster B.Mk I*

# BOEING B-29 and B-50 SUPERFORTRESS (U.S.A.)

*B-29A Superfortress*

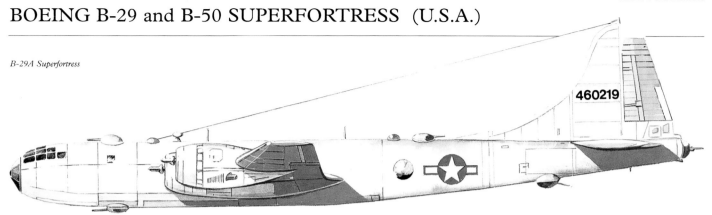

The B-29 was the world's first genuinely effective long-range strategic bomber, and was designed from January 1940 as the Model 345 to meet the U.S. Army Air Corps' extremely ambitious plan for a 'hemisphere defense' bomber. The type was an extremely advanced design with pressurized accommodation, remotely controlled defensive armament, a formidable offensive load, and very high performance including great ceiling and range. The first of three XB-29 prototypes flew in September 1942 with four Wright R-3550 twin-row radials; each fitted with two turbochargers. By this time, Boeing already had contracts for more than 1,500 production bombers. The XB-29s were followed by 14 YB-29 preproduction aircraft, of which the first flew in June 1943.

A prodigious effort was made to bring the Superfortress into full service, and a wide-ranging programme of subcontracting delivered components to four assembly plants. The type entered full service in time to make a major contribution to the war against Japan in World War II, which it ended with the A-bombings of Hiroshima and Nagasaki in August 1945.

Some 2,848 B-29s were complemented by 1,122 B-29As with slightly greater span and revised defensive armament, and by 311 B-29Bs with no defensive armament but a radar-directed tail barbette. The type was also developed for reconnaissance and experimental roles, and was then revised with a sturdier structure and Pratt & Whitney R-4360 engines as the B-29D, which entered production as the B-50A. This was followed by its own series of bomber, reconnaissance and tanker aircraft.

*B-29 Superfortress heavy bomber*

**BOEING B-29A SUPERFORTRESS**
**Role:** Long-range, high altitude day bomber
**Crew/Accommodation:** Ten
**Power Plant:** Four 2,200 hp Wright R-3350-23 Cyclone Eighteen air-cooled radials
**Dimensions:** Span 43.05 m (141.25 ft); length 30.18 m (99 ft); wing area 161.56 m² (1,739 sq ft)
**Weights:** Empty 32,369 kg (71,360 lb); MTOW 62,823 kg (138,500 lb)
**Performance:** Maximum speed 576 km/h (358 mph) at 7,620 m (25,000 ft); operational ceiling 9,708 m (31,850 ft); range 6,598 km (4,100 miles) with 7,258 kg (16,000 lb) bombload
**Load:** One 20 mm cannon and twelve .5 inch machine guns, plus up to 9,072 kg (20,000 lb) of bombs

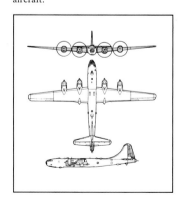

*Boeing B-29 Superfortress*

# CONVAIR B-36 'PEACEMAKER' (U.S.A.)

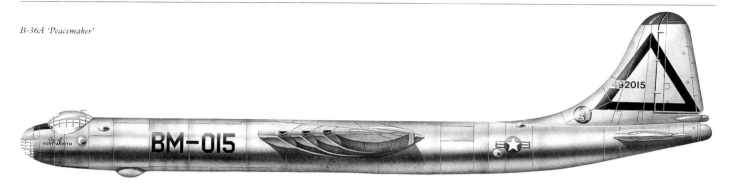

*B-36A 'Peacemaker'*

Designed as the Model 36 while the company was still Consolidated but built after it had become Convair, this extraordinary machine was the world's first genuinely intercontinental strategic bomber. The type resulted from an April 1941 requirement of the U.S. Army Air Corps for a machine able to carry a maximum bomb load of 32,659 kg (72,000 lb) but more realistically to deliver 4536 kg (10,000 lb) of bombs on European targets from bases in the United States. From four competing designs, the Model 36 was selected by the U.S. Army Air Forces for construction as the XB-36 prototype. This first flew in August 1946 and featured a pressurized fuselage and pusher propellers on the six 2237-kW (3,000-hp) R-4360-25 radial engines buried in the trailing edges of wings sufficiently deep to afford inflight access to the engines. The service trials model was the YB-36 with a raised cockpit roof, and this was subsequently modified as the YB-36A with four- rather than single-wheel main landing gear units. These were features of the first production model, the B-36A unarmed crew trainer of which 22 were built without armament. The 104 B-36Bs introduced 2610-kW (3,500-hp) R-4360-41 engines and a defensive armament of 16 20-mm cannon in nose, tail and six fuselage barbettes. Some 64 were later revised as B-36D strategic reconnaissance aircraft with greater weights and performance through the addition of four 2359-kg (5,200-lb) thrust General Electric J47-GE-19 turbojets in podded pairs under the outer wing, and in this role they complemented 22 aircraft which were built as such.

Later bombers with greater power and improved electronics were the 34 B-36Fs with 2833-kW (3,800-hp) R-04360-53s and J47-GE-19s, 83 B-36Hs with an improved flight deck, and 33 B-36Js with strengthened landing gear. There were also RB-36D, E, F and H reconnaissance versions, and even the GRB-36F with an embarked fighter for protection over the target area. Plans for jet- and even nuclear-powered versions resulted in no production variants.

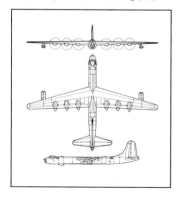

*Convair B-36H*

**CONSOLIDATED/CONVAIR B-36D**
**Role:** Long-range heavy bomber
**Crew/Accommodation:** Fifteen, including four relief crew members
**Power Plant:** Six 3,500 hp Pratt & Whitney R-4360-41 air-cooled radials, plus four 2,359 kgp (5,200 lb s.t.) General Electric J47-GE-19 turbojets
**Dimensions:** Span 70.1 m (230 ft); length 49.4 m (162.08 ft); wing area 443 m² (4,772 sq ft)
**Weights:** Empty 72,051 kg (158,843 lb); MTOW 162,161 kg (357,500 lb)
**Performance:** Maximum speed 706 km/h (439 mph) at 9,790 m (32,120 ft); operational ceiling 13,777 m (45,200 ft); range 12,070 km (7,500 miles) with 4,535 kg (10,000 lb bombload)
**Load:** Twelve 20 mm cannon, plus up to 39,009 kg (86,000 lb) of bombs

*A Convair B-36B in its original form*

# BOEING B-47 STRATOJET (U.S.A.)

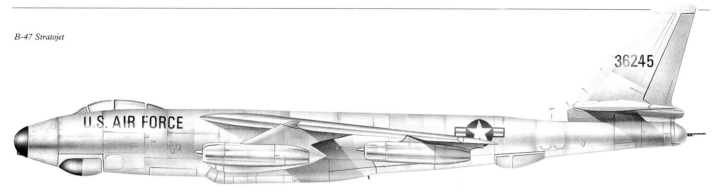

*B-47 Stratojet*

The B-47 was a great achievement, and as a swept-wing strategic bomber in the medium-range bracket it formed the main strength of the U.S. Strategic Air Command in the early 1950s. The U.S. Army Air Forces first considered a jet-powered bomber as early as 1944; at that time four companies were involved in producing preliminary designs for such a type. The Model 424 failed to attract real interest, but the later Model 432 was thought more acceptable and initial contracts were let. The company then recast the design as the Model 448 with the swept flying surfaces that captured German research data had shown to be desirable, but the USAAF was unimpressed. The design was finalized as the Model 450 with the six engines relocated from the fuselage to two twin-unit and two single-unit underwing nacelles.

In the spring of 1946, the USAAF ordered two Model 450 prototypes with the designation XB-47 and the first of these flew in December 1947. The type was notable for many of its features including the 'bicycle' type landing gear the twin main units of which retracted into the fuselage. The 10 B-47As were essentially development aircraft, and the first true service variant was the 399 B-47Bs, followed by 1,591 B-47Es with a host of operational improvements including greater power, inflight refuelling capability, and ejector seats. The B-47B and B-47E were both strengthened structurally later in their lives, leading to the designations B-47B-II and B-47E-II. There were also RB-47 reconnaissance together with several special-purpose and experimental variants.

*Boeing B-47E bomber*

**BOEING B-47E STRATOJET**
**Role:** Heavy bomber
**Crew/Accommodation:** Three
**Power Plant:** Six 3,266 kgp (7,200 lb s.t.) General Electric J47-GE-25 turbojets, plus a 16,329 kgp (36,000 lb s.t.) rocket pack for Jet Assisted Take-Off (JATO)
**Dimensions:** Span 35.36 m (116 ft); length 32.92 m (108 ft); wing area 132.67 m² (1,428 sq ft)
**Weights:** Empty 36.631 kg (80,756 lb); MTOW 93,759 kg (206,700 lb) with JATO rocket assistance
**Performance:** Maximum speed 975 km/h (606 mph) at 4,968 m (16,300 ft); operational ceiling 12,344 m (40,500 ft); range 6,228 km (3,870 miles) with 4,536 kg (10,000 lb) bombload
**Load:** Two rear-firing 20 mm cannon, plus up to 9,979 kg (22,000 lb) of bombs

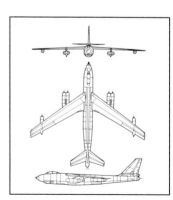

*Boeing B-47E Stratojet*

# VICKERS VALIANT (UNITED KINGDOM)

*Valiant B(K).Mk 1*

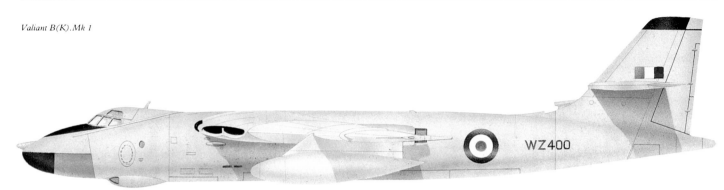

The Valiant was the first of the U.K.'s trio of strategic V-bombers to enter service and, though not as advanced or capable as the later Avro Vulcan and Handley Page Victor, it was nonetheless a worthy warplane. The Type 667 was originated in response to a 1948 requirement for a high-altitude bomber to carry the British free-fall nuclear bomb that would be dropped with the aid of a radar bombing system. The type was based on modestly swept flying surfaces that included a shoulder-set cantilever wing with compound-sweep leading edges, a circular-section fuselage accommodating the five-man crew in its pressurized forward section, retractable tricycle landing gear, and, in addition, four turbojets buried in the wing roots.

The prototype first flew in May 1951 with 2948-kg (6,500-lb) Rolls-Royce Avon RA.3 turbojets, improved to 3402-kg (7,500-lb) thrust Avon RA.7s in the second prototype that took over the flight test programme after the first had been destroyed by fire. The first five of 36 Valiant B.Mk 1 bombers served as pre-production aircraft, and this type began to enter squadron service in 1955. The type was used operationally as a conventional bomber in the Suez campaign of 1956, and was also used to drop the first British atomic and hydrogen bombs in October 1956 and May 1957 respectively. Production for the RAF totalled 104 aircraft in the form of 36 Valiant B.Mk 1 bombers, 11 Valiant B(PR).Mk. 1 strategic reconnaissace aircraft, 13 Valiant B(PR).Mk 1 multi-role aircraft usable in the bomber, reconnaissance and inflight refuelling tanker tasks, and 44 Valiant B(K).Mk 1 bomber and tanker aircraft. The Valiant B.Mk 2 did not pass the prototype stage, and all surviving aircraft were retired in 1965 as a result of fatigue problems.

## VICKERS VALIANT B.Mk 1
**Role:** Strategic bomber
**Crew/Accommodation:** Five
**Power Plant:** Four 4,536 kgp (10,000 lb s.t.) Rolls-Royce Avon 28 turbojets
**Dimensions:** Span 34.85 m (114.33 ft); length 32.99 m (108.25 ft); wing area 219.4 m² (2,362 sq ft)
**Weights:** Empty 34,419 kg (75,881 lb); MTOW 63,503 kg (140,000 lb)
**Performance:** Maximum speed 912 km/h (492 knots) at 9,144 m (30,000 ft); operational ceiling 16,459 m (54,000 ft); range 7,242 km (3,908 naut. miles) with maximum fuel
**Load:** No defensive armament, but internal stowage for up to 9,525 kg (21,000 lb) of bombs

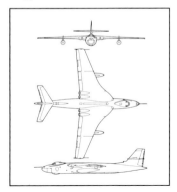

*Vickers Valiant B(K).Mk 1*

*Vickers Valiant B.Mk 1 bomber*

# BOEING B-52 STRATOFORTRESS (U.S.A.)

*B-52G Stratofortress in early form*

In numerical terms, the B-52 is still the most important bomber in the U.S. Strategic Air Command inventory. It offers an excellent combination of great range and very large payload, though the type's radar signature is large and its operational capabilities are ensured only by constantly updated offensive and defensive electronic systems.

The Stratofortress was first planned as a turboprop-powered successor to the B-50, but was then recast as a turbojet-powered type using eight 3402-kg (7,500-lb) thrust Pratt & Whitney J57s podded in four pairs under the swept wings. The B-52 employs the same type of 'bicycle' landing gear as the B-47, and after design as the Model 464 the XB-52 prototype first flew in April 1952 with a high-set cockpit that seated the two pilots in tandem. The current cockpit was adopted in the B-52A, of which three were built as development aircraft. The 50 B-52Bs introduced the standard nav/attack system, and the 35 B-52Cs had improved equipment and performance. These were in reality development models, and the first true service version was the B-52D, of which 170 were built with revised tail armament. This model was followed by 100 B-52Es with improved navigation and weapon systems, 89 B-52Fs with greater power, 193 B-52Gs with a shorter fin, remotely controlled tail armament, integral fuel tankage and underwing pylons for two AGM-28 Hound Dog stand-off nuclear missiles, and 102 B-52Hs, with Pratt & Whitney TF33 turbofans, a rotary-barrel cannon as tail armament, and structural strengthening for the low-altitude role.

The only version currently in service is the B-52H, capable of carrying more than a 22,680-kg (50,000-lb) load. Apart from conventional weapons such as bombs, B-52H has an anti-shipping capability using Harpoon missiles, while for a nuclear mission it can carry up to twenty air-launched cruise missiles or a mix of these and gravity bombs. Other new missiles are also coming on stream for B-52H.

**BOEING B-52H STRATOFORTRESS**
**Role:** Long-range bomber
**Crew/Accommodation:** Six
**Power Plant:** Eight 7,718 kgp (17,000 lb s.t.) Pratt & Whitney TF33-P-3 turbofans.
**Dimensions:** Span 56.42 m (185 ft); length 49.04 m (160 ft); wing area 371.6 m² (4,000 sq ft)
**Weights:** Empty 78,355 kg (172,740 lb); MTOW 221,350 kg (488,000 lb)
**Performance:** Maximum speed 958 km/h (595 mph) at high altitude; operational ceiling 16,750 m (55,000 ft); range 16,090 km (10,000 miles)
**Load:** More than 22,680 kg (50,000 lb) of bombs or missiles

*A Boeing B-52G Stratofortress*

113

# AVRO VULCAN (United Kingdom)

*Vulcan B.Mk 2*

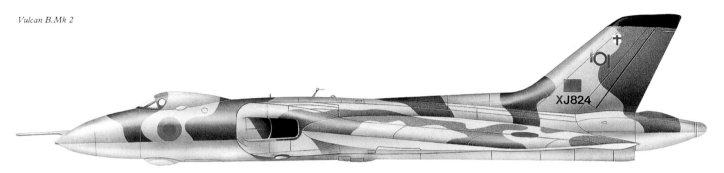

The Type 698 was a massively impressive delta-winged bomber, and by any standards was an extraordinary aerodynamic feat that, with the Handley Page Victor and Vickers Valiant, was one of the U.K.'s trio of nuclear 'V-bombers' from the 1950s. The type was planned as a high-altitude bomber able to deliver the British free-fall nuclear bomb over

long ranges. The first of two Type 698 prototypes flew in August 1952 with four 2,948-kg (6,500-lb) thrust Rolls-Royce Avon RA.3 turbojets, later replaced by 3,629-kg (8,000-lb) thrust Armstrong Siddeley Sapphire turbojets. The initial production model, the Vulcan B.Mk 1, had Olympus turbojet in variants increased in thrust from 4,990 to

6,123-kg (11,000 to     13,500-lb).

In 1961 existing  aircraft were modified to Vulcan B.Mk 1A standard with a bulged tail containing electronic counter-measures gear. The definitive model was the Vulcan B.Mk 2 with provision for the Avro Blue Steel stand-off nuclear missile, a turbofan powerplant offering considerably greater fuel economy as well as more power, and a much-modified wing characterized by a cranked leading edge and offering greater area as well as elevons in place of the Mk 1's separated elevators and ailerons. The type was later modified

as the Vulcan B.Mk 2A for the low-level role with conventional bombs and ECM equipment, and the Vulcan SR.Mk 2 was a strategic reconnaissance derivative.

Soon after the outbreak of the 1982 Falklands War, an RAF Vulcan attacked Port Stanley airfield; the flight from its Ascension Island base was then the largest ever operational sortie. Final retirement followed soon after.

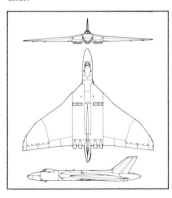

*Avro Vulcan B.Mk 2A*

**AVRO VULCAN B.Mk 2**
**Role:** Long-range bomber
**Crew/Accommodation:** Five
**Power Plant:** Four 9,072 kgp (20,000 lb s.t.) Bristol Siddeley Olympus 301 turbojets
**Dimensions:** Span 33.83 m (111 ft); length 30.45 m (99.92 ft); wing area 368.29 m² (3,964 sq ft)
**Weights:** Empty 48,081 kg (106,000 lb); MTOW 98,800 kg (200,180 lb)
**Performance:** Maximum speed 1,041 km/h (562 knots) Mach 0.98 at 12,192 m (40,000 ft); operational ceiling 19,912 m (65,000 ft); radius 3,701 km (2,300 miles) at altitude with missile
**Load:** Up to 9,525 kg (21,000 lb) of bombs, or one Blue Steel Mk 1 stand-off missile

*An Avro Vulcan B.Mk 2*

# TUPOLEV Tu-95 and Tu-142 'BEAR' (U.S.S.R.)

*Tu-95 'Bear'.*

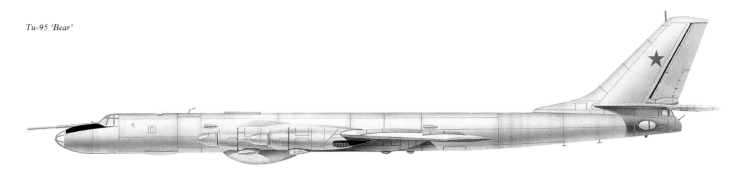

The Tu-95 prototype first flew in November 1952 and the type entered service in 1957. An extraordinary feature of this giant bomber was the adoption of massive turboprop engines, despite the official requirement for a speed of 900–950 km/h and a range of 14,000–15,000 km with a nuclear bomb. 'Bear-A' and 'Bear-B' were the original versions, the latter carrying the AS-3 'Kangaroo' missile semi-recessed

under the fuselage, while retrofits later added inflight refuelling and, in some aircraft, strategic reconnaissance capabilities. Introduced in about 1963, the 'Bear-C' carried photographic and electronic reconnaissance equipment. 'Bear-D' appeared in 1962 as a multi-sensor maritime reconnaissance and sea target acquisition version for the Soviet navy. It was followed by 'Bear-E' for photographic reconnaissance and, from the mid-1970s, by 'Bear-G' to carry AS-4 'Kitchen' missiles but

was also used for electronic intelligence. All of these versions are now out of service. The 'Bear-H' first flew in 1979 and remains operational, armed with AS-15 'Kent' cruise missiles.

The TU-142 designation was applied to a long-range anti-submarine version of the Tu-95 for the Soviet navy, first flown in 1968 and which remained in production until 1994. The ASW 'Bear-F' entered service in 1972 and remains operational with Russia and India. A communications

relay variant became known to NATO as 'Bear-J' and continues in its role of providing an emergency link between the government and its nuclear submarines.

*Tupolev Tu-95 'Bear-H'*

### TUPOLEV Tu142 'BEAR-F'
**Role:** Long-range anti-submarine warfare
**Crew/Accommodation:** Eleven to thirteen (mission dependent)
**Power Plant:** Four 15,000 eshp Kuznetsov NK-P 12M turboprops driving contra-rotating propellers
**Dimensions:** Span 50.04 m (164.17 ft); length 53.07 m (174.08 ft); wing area 289.9 m² (3,121 sq ft)
**Weights:** Empty 91,800 kg (202,384 lb); MTOW 185,000 kg (407,885 lb)
**Performance:** Maximum speed 855 km/h (531 mph); operational ceiling 11,000 m (36,000 ft); range 12,000 km (7,456 miles)
**Load:** Two 23-mm cannons and up to 9,000 kg (19,842 lb) of weaponry

*A variant of the Tupolev Tu-95 family, a 'Bear-D'*

# HANDLEY PAGE VICTOR (United Kingdom)

*Victor SR.Mk 2*

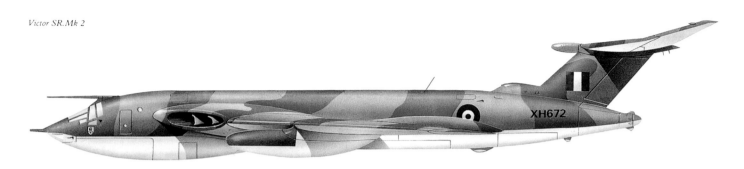

The last of the United Kingdom's trio of nuclear 'V-bombers' to enter service, it is now the only one still in service, albeit as a tanker. The type was planned against the requirements of a 1946 specification for a bomber able to carry a free-fall nuclear bomb over long range at a speed and altitude too high for interception by the fighters of the day. The H.P.80 was based on what was in effect a pod-and-boom fuselage that supported crescent-shaped flying surfaces. For its time it was a very advanced type. The

first of two prototypes flew in December 1952.

After considerable development, the type entered squadron service in November 1957 with 5012-kg (11,050-lb) thrust Armstrong Siddeley Sapphire ASSa.7 Mk 202 turbojets. Production totalled just 50 aircraft that were formally designated Victor B.Mk 1H with better equipment and electronic counter-measures than the basic Victor B.Mk 1 that had originally been planned; soon after delivery, 24 aircraft were modified to

Victor B.Mk 1A standard with improved defensive electronics. Though planned with Sapphire ASSa.9 engines in a wing increased in span to 34.05 m (115 ft 0 in), the radically improved Victor B.Mk 2 was delivered with Rolls-Royce Conway turbofans, initially 7824-kg (17,250-lb) thrust RCo.11 Mk 200s, but then in definitive form 9344-kg (20,600-lb) thrust Conway Mk 201s. Production totalled 34 aircraft, and of these 21 were modified to Victor B.Mk 2R standard with provision for the Avro Blue Steel stand-off nuclear missile that allowed the Victor to avoid flight

over heavily defended targets. Soon after this, the Victor was retasked to the low-level role as Soviet defensive capability was thought to have made high-altitude overflights little more than suicidal. Later conversions were the nine Victor B(SR).Mk 2 maritime reconnaissance and the tanker models that included 11 Victor K.Mk 1s, six Victor B.Mk 1A(K2P)s, 14 Victor K.Mk 1As and 24 Victor K.Mk 2s.

## HANDLEY PAGE VICTOR K.Mk 2
**Role:** Air-to-air refueller
**Crew/Accommodation:** Five
**Power Plant:** Four 9,344 kgp (20,600 lb s.t.) Rolls-Royce Conway Mk.201 turbo fans
**Dimensions:** Span 35.69 m (117 ft); length 35.02 m (114.92 ft); wing area 204.38 m² (2,200 sq ft)
**Weights:** Empty 33,550 kg (110,000 lb); MTOW 101,150 kg (223,000 lb)
**Performance:** Maximum speed 1,020 km/h (550 knots) Mach 0.96 at 11,000 m (36,090 ft); operational ceiling 15,850 m (52,000 ft); range 7,403 km (3,995 naut. miles) unrefuelled
**Load:** Up to 15,876 kg (35,000 lb)

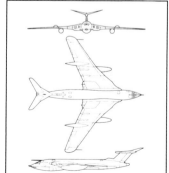

*Handley Page Victor B.Mk 2*

*A Handley Page Victor B.Mk 2*

# CONVAIR B-58 HUSTLER (U.S.A.)

*B-58A Hustler*

The B-58 Hustler resulted from a 1949 U.S. Air Force requirement for a supersonic medium strategic bomber and was a stupendous technical achievement. In 1952 the Convair Model 4 was selected for development as an initial 18 aircraft. Convair's own experience in delta-winged aircraft, themselves based on German data captured at the end of World War II, was used in the far-sighted concept. The smallest possible airframe required advances in aerodynamics,

structures, and materials, and was designed on Whitcomb area ruling principles with a long but slender fuselage that carried only a tall vertical tail and a small delta wing. This latter supported the nacelles for the four afterburning turbojets. The airframe was too small to accommodate sufficient fuel for both the outbound and return legs of the Hustler's mission, so the tricycle landing gear had very tall legs that raised the fuselage high enough off the ground to

accommodate a large underfuselage pod 18.90 m (62 ft 0 in) long. This pod contained the Hustler's nuclear bombload and also the fuel for the outward leg, and was dropped over the target. The crew of three was seated in tandem escape capsules.

In July 1954 the order was reduced to two XB-58 prototypes, 11 YB-58A pre-production aircraft, and 31 pods. The first XB-58 flew in November 1956, and proved tricky to fly. Extensive development was undertaken with the aid of another 17

YB-58As ordered in February 1958 together with 35 pods; the last 17 YB-58As were later converted to RB-58A standard with ventral reconnaissance pods. The type became operational in 1960, but as the high-altitude bomber was clearly obsolescent, full production amounted to only 86 B-58As plus 10 upgraded YB-58As. Training was carried out in eight TB-58A conversions of YB-58As.

*The Convair B-58A Hustler*

**CONVAIR B-58A HUSTLER**
**Role:** Supersonic bomber
**Crew/Accommodation:** Three
**Power Plant:** Four 7,076 kgp (15,600 lb s.t.) General Electric J79-GE-3B turbojets with reheat
**Dimensions:** Span 17.32 m (56.83 ft); length 29.49 m (96.75 ft); wing area 143.26 m² (1,542 sq ft)
**Weights:** Empty 25,202 kg (55,560 lb); MTOW 73,936 kg (163,000 lb)
**Performance:** Maximum speed 2,126 km/h (1,147 knots) Mach 2.1 at 12,192 m (40,000 ft); operational ceiling 19,202 m (63,000 ft); range 8,247 km (4,450 naut. miles) unrefuelled
**Load:** One 20 mm multi-barrel cannon, plus up to 8,820 kg (19,450 lb) of stores and fuel carrier in mission pod

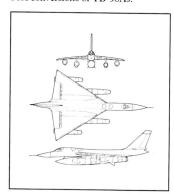

*Convair B-58A Hustler*

117

# ROCKWELL B-1B LANCER (U.S.A.)

*B-1A*

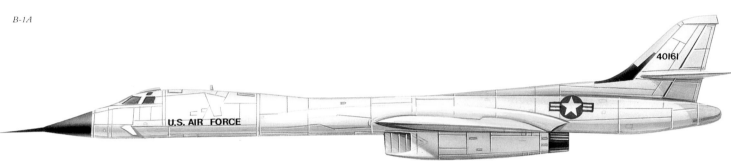

40161

U.S. AIR FORCE

Entering service from July 1985 to supersede the Boeing B-52 in the penetration bomber role, the B-1B resulted from a protracted development history that began in 1965 when the U.S. Air Force issued a requirement for an Advanced Manned Strategic Bomber. This was expected to have a dash capability of Mach 2.2+ for delivery of free-fall and stand-off weapons. The U.S. Department of Defense issued a request for proposals in 1969 and the Rockwell submission was accepted as

the B-1 in 1970, and the full-scale development was soon under way as a complex variable-geometry type with General Electric F101 turbofans and variable inlets.

The prototype first flew in December 1974 and the flight test programme moved ahead without undue delay. In June 1977, however, President Carter made the decision to scrap the programme in favour of cruise missiles, but the administration of President Reagan reactivated the

programme in 1981 to procure just 100 B-1B bombers in the revised very low-level penetration role, using an automatic terrain following system. Other features included fixed inlets and modified nacelles (reducing speed to Mach 1.25) and a strengthened airframe and landing gear for operation at higher weights. Further changes were concerned with reduction of the type's already low radar signature, including some use of radar absorbent materials. The second and fourth B-1s were used from March 1983 to flight-test features of the B-1B, which itself first flew in October 1984 with the advanced offensive and defensive electronic

systems. The second B-1B flew in May 1985 and became the first to join the Air Force, in July 1985. From the ninth aircraft the type was built with revised weapons bays, the forward bay having a movable bulkhead allowing the carriage of 12 AGM-86B ALCMs internally, as well as additional fuel tanks and SRAMs. The final B-1B was delivered in April 1988, and currently some 77 are in the active inventory. Since 1993 emphasis has also been placed on giving the B-1B a conventional weapon capability, though remaining a nuclear bomber. Upgrading for new weapons continues.

### ROCKWELL B-1B
**Role:** Long-range low-level variable-geometry stand-off, strategic and conventional bomber
**Crew/Accommodation:** Four
**Power Plant:** Four 13,960 kpg (30,780 lb s.t.) General Electric F101-GE-102 turbofans with reheat
**Dimensions:** Span 41.66 m (136.68 ft); swept 23.84 m (78.23 ft); length 44.43 m (145.75 ft); wing area 181.2 m² (1,950 sq ft)
**Weights:** Empty 87,090 kg (192, 000 lb); MTOW 213,367 kg (477,000 lb)
**Performance:** Maximum speed 966 km/h (600 mph) at low level or Mach 1.2 at altitude; operational ceiling 15,240+ m (50,000+ ft); range 12,070 km (7,500 miles)
**Load:** Up to 56,699 kg (125,000 lb) of weapons as absolute maximum, including up to 24 nuclear bombs, 84 x 500 lb conventional bombs, sea mines, JDAM missiles or other weapons

*Rockwell B-1B*

*Rockwell B-1B Lancer*

# NORTHROP GRUMMAN B-2A SPIRIT (U.S.A.)

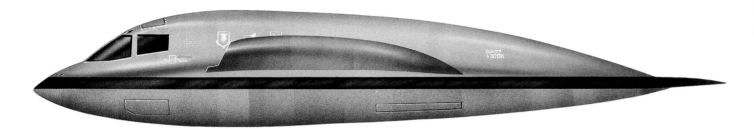

Developed at enormous cost during the late 1970s and 1980s, and first revealed in November 1988 for an initial flight in July 1989, the B-2 was designed as successor to the Rockwell B-1B in the penetration bomber role, although now intended to supplement it due partly to the tiny number built. Unlike the low-altitude B-1B, however, the B-2 is designed for penetration of enemy airspace at medium and high altitudes, relying on its stealth design, composite structure and defensive avionics suite to evade detection by an enemy until it has closed to within a few miles of its target, where attack accuracy is enhanced by use of the APQ-181 low-probability-of-intercept radar. Thereby, B-2A can strike at maximum defended and moving targets, allowing follow-up raids by non-stealth aircraft.

The B-2 is a design of the relaxed-stability type, and is a flying wing with highly swept leading edges and W-shaped trailing edges featuring all-horizontal flight-control surfaces (2-section elevons functioning as elevators and ailerons, and 2-section outer surfaces performing as drag rudders, spoilers and airbrakes) operated by a fly-by-wire control system. The design emphasis was placed on completely smooth surfaces with blended flightdeck and nacelle bulges. Radar reflectivity is very low because of the use of radiation-absorbent materials and a carefully optimized shape (including shielded upper-surface inlets), and the head-on radar cross-section is only about one-tenth of that of the B-1B.

Production of 132 B-2s was originally planned, but this total was progressively lowered until just 21 were completed for service, a figure including all six development aircraft raised to operational standard. The final B-2A was delivered in 1998 and full operational capability was achieved in 1999.

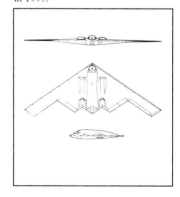

**NORTHROP B-2A**
**Role:** Long-range subsonic stealth bomber
**Crew/Accommodation:** Two/three
**Power Plant:** Four 8,620 kgp (19,000 lb s.t.) General Electric F118-GE-100 turbofans
**Dimensions:** Span 52.43 m (172 ft); length 21.03 m (69 ft); wing area about 477.5 m (5,140 sq ft)
**Weights:** Empty 56,700 kg (125,000 lb); MTOW 170,550 kg (376,000 lb)
**Performance:** Maximum speed Mach 0.8; operational ceiling 15,240 m (50,000 ft); range 11,100 km (6,900 miles) with a 14,515 kg (32,000 lb) load.
**Load:** Up to 18,145 kg (40,000 lb) in two bays

*B-2A is a costly but potentially decisive warplane*

*B-2A Spirit*

119

# MILITARY
# AIRCRAFT

Page 120: Tornado GR4 development aircraft
Page 121: Dassault Mirage IVP refuelling
Right: Sea Harrier F/A2
Pages 124–125: Grumman F-14D

# Light/Medium Bombers

The light bomber is arguably the oldest recorded form of combat aircraft. The first known illustration of an aerial attacker dates from 1326, as a bomb-carrying pennon kite, and thereby easily predates depictions in art of bomb-carrying balloons. Interestingly, more than a decade before the American Wright brothers achieved the world's first recognized manned and powered aeroplane flight, the first-ever contract to build a military heavier-than-air aeroplane had been issued to France's famed pioneer, Clément Ader, in 1892. Ader's aeroplane was to be a two-seater capable of carrying 75 kg (165 lb) of bombs; but the machine proved unable to fly during trials in 1897 and so the contract was not completed.

In one of the first demonstrations of how aeroplanes could be used offensively in war, in January 1910 American Lt. Paul Beck dropped sandbags over Los Angeles from an aeroplane piloted by Louis Paulhan. More significantly, American pioneer Glenn Curtiss dropped dummy bombs over Lake Keuka in June that year, using buoys to indicate the outline of a battleship to be attacked from low level. Then, in January 1911, Lt. Myron Crissy and Philip Parmalee released explosive bombs from their Wright biplane during live trials over San Francisco.

Italy was the first to take aeroplanes to war, in 1911, and that November Second Lt. Giulio Gavotti piloted an aeroplane from which Cipelli grenades were thrown by hand onto Turkish forces at Taguira Oasis and Ain Zara (Libya), the first-ever recorded bombing raid by aeroplane. Fighting in Mexico provided the backdrop for the first aeroplane bombing of a warship when Didier Masson, supporting the forces of General Alvarado Obregon, attacked Mexican gunships in Guaymas Bay. During this conflict, Mexican generals often used the services of foreign pilots, and it is curious to note that in Mexico in November 1913 the very first aerial combat took place between aircraft, yet neither pilot exchanged pistol fire was Mexican!

With the outbreak of World War I, tiny aircraft immediately undertook both nuisance and strategic bombing raids on the enemy, but in essence were the lightest of bombers. From a tactical standpoint, the first missions of real significance came on May 1915, when British aircraft attacked the railway system bringing up German reinforcements during the Neuve Chapelle offensive, thereby working in direct support of British ground forces. Areas around Courtrai and Menin were raided, plus the stations at Don, Douai and Lille, while for good measure three other aircraft bombed the German Divisional Headquarters at Fournes. The light bomber had established its importance as a tactical weapon and, despite the appearance of the much larger bombing aeroplanes possessing greater range and warload, the light bomber in developed forms remained an essential part of air forces from this time forward.

Post World War I, the medium bomber bridged the gap between light and heavy types, although the definition became blurred as some air forces used payload carried as the defining factor, while others used range. Some difficulty in pinning down an exact definition continued until after World War II, when new light bomber jets such as the RAF's Canberra that could carry a nuclear weapon to the U.S.S.R. caused further erosion of reasonable definitions.

Today, only a few air forces field heavy bombers, and it is probably true to say that the only truly modern medium bomber currently operational is the Russian Tu-22M *Backfire*, although even this is more often referred to as an intermediate-range bomber. Instead, many forces rely on smaller high-speed or subsonic jet attack aircraft armed with free-fall or precision-guided weapons. These, after all, can often carry a bomb load in excess of those managed by heavy bombers during World War II. 'Interdiction', 'strike', 'ground attack' and 'close air support' are all modern-day terms for the varied traditional roles of the smaller bomber, and many (such as Tornado, Mirage 2000N and Sukhoi Su-24/Su-34) could, if called upon, carry out strategic as well as tactical attacks if the target was not too distant. Smaller jets have often been used at the outset of regional conflicts to deliver crippling blows against enemy forces, their size better suiting pinpoint attacks against high-value or critical targets. Indeed, air power in all forms has proven to be decisive in modern campaigns.

*Picture: Italy and Brazil collaborated on development of the AMX International AMX close air support and interdiction jet, entering service from 1989 and capable of delivering 3,800 kg (8,378 lb) of free-fall and guided weapons*

# BREGUET 14 (France)

Bre.14B2

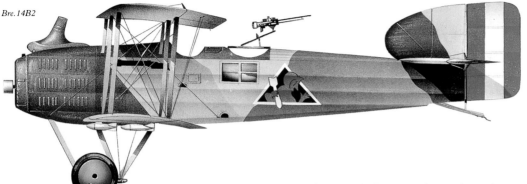

The Breguet Bre. 14 was France's single most important and successful warplane of World War I, and perhaps the best known French combat plane until the advent of the Dassault Mirage III series. The type began to take shape on the drawing boards of the company's designers during the summer of 1916, and the first AV Type XIV flew in November 1916 with the AV (Avant, or forward) signifying that the plane was of the tractor type. Though not notable for its aesthetic qualities, the machine that soon became the Type 14 and later

the Bre. 14 was immensely sturdy as a result of its steel, duralumin and wooden construction covered in fabric and light alloy panels and supported on strong landing gear of the spreader type. The pilot and gunner were located close together in the optimum tactical location, and the front

mounted Renault in line engine proved both powerful and reliable.

An initial 150 aircraft were ordered in the A.2 two-seat artillery observation category during April 1917, and by the end of that year orders had been placed for 2,650 aircraft to be produced by Breguet and five licensees in two-seat A.2 artillery and B.2 bomber variants, the latter with wings of increased span and flaps on the trailing edges of the lower wing. Other World War I variants were the Bre. 14B.1 single-seat bomber and Bre. 14S ambulance. Production up to the end of World War I totalled 5,300 aircraft with a variety of engine types, and more than 2,500 additional aircraft were built before production ended in 1928. Many of the post-war aircraft were of the Bre. 14 TOE type for use in France's colonial possessions. The Bre. 14 was finally phased out of French service only in 1932. Substantial exports were also made.

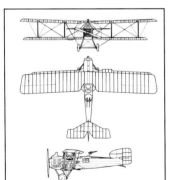

Breguet Bre.14

**BREGUET Bre.14B2**
**Role:** Fast day bomber/reconnaissance
**Crew/Accommodation:** Two
**Power Plant:** One 300 hp Renault 12 Fcy water-cooled inline
**Dimensions:** Span 14.91 m (48.92 ft); length 8.87 m (29.10 ft); wing area 51.1 m² (550 sq ft)
**Weights:** Empty 1,035 kg (2,282 lb); MTOW 1,580 kg (3,483 lb)
**Performance:** Maximum speed 195 km/h (121 mph) at sea level; operational ceiling 4,265 m (13,993 ft); range 485 km (301 miles) with full warload
**Load:** Two/three .303 inch machine guns, plus up to 260 kg (573 lb) of externally-carried bombs

*A Breguet Bre.14 in Portuguese service*

# AIRCO (de HAVILLAND) D.H.9 and D.H.9A (United Kingdom)

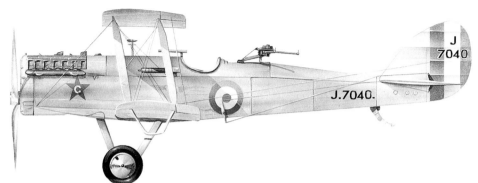

*D.H.9A*

The D.H.9 was planned as a longer-range successor to the D.H.4. To speed production, the D.H.4's flying surfaces and landing gear were combined with a new fuselage that located the pilot and gunner close together and provided better streamlining for the engine, in this instance a 171.5-kW (230-hp) Galloway-built BHP engine. The type first flew in July 1917, and proved so successful that outstanding D.H.4 contracts were converted to the D.H.9, which therefore entered large-scale production with the 224-kW (300-hp) lightweight version of the BHP developed by Siddeley-Deasy and known as the Puma. The engine was unreliable and generally derated to 171.5 kW (230 hp), which gave the D.H.9 performance inferior to that of the D.H.4. As a result, the D.H.9 suffered quite heavy losses when it entered service during April 1918 over the Western Front, though it fared better in poorer defended areas, such as Macedonia and Palestine. Some 3,200 D.H.9s were built by Airco and 12 subcontractors.

Given the fact that the D.H.9's failing was its engine, it was hoped that use of the excellent 280-kW (375-hp) Rolls-Royce Eagle VIII would remedy the situation, but demands on this motor were so great that an American engine, the 298-kW (400-hp) Packard Liberty 12, was used instead to create the D.H.9A, which was perhaps the best strategic bomber of World War I. British production of 885 aircraft was complemented by 1,415 American-built Engineering Division USD-9 aircraft.

**AIRCO D.H.9**
**Role:** Light day bomber
**Crew/Accommodation:** Two
**Power Plant:** One 230 hp Siddeley-Deasy B.H.P. water-cooled inline
**Dimensions:** Span 12.92 m (42.4 ft); length 9.28 m (30.46 ft); wing area 40.32 m² (430 sq ft)
**Weights:** Empty 1,012 kg (2,230 lb); MTOW 1,508 kg (3,325 lb)
**Performance:** Maximum speed 177 km/h (110 mph) at 3,048 m (10,000 ft); operational ceiling 4.724 m (15,500 ft); endurance 4.5 hours
**Load:** Two .303 inch machine guns, plus up to 412 kg (908 lb) bombload

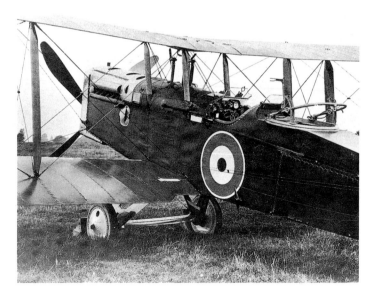

*Airco D.H.9A*

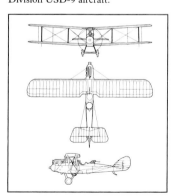

*Airco (de Havilland) D.H.9*

# BREGUET 19 (France)

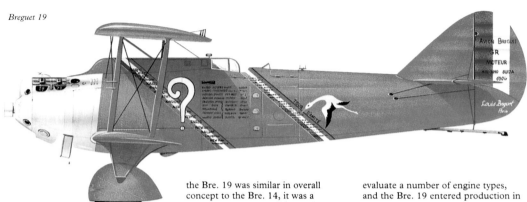

First flown in March 1922 with a 336-kW (450-hp) Renault 12Kb inline engine, the Bre. 19 was planned as successor to the Bre. 14 but was produced in parallel with its predecessor for service with units based in metropolitan France. Though

the Bre. 19 was similar in overall concept to the Bre. 14, it was a considerably more pleasing and aerodynamically refined design with unequal- rather than almost-equal span wings with single outward sloping I-type interplane struts, a circular-section rather than slab-sided fuselage, and a much cleaner landing gear arrangement with a spreader-type main unit. The structure was primarily of duralumin with fabric covering, though the forward fuselage as far aft as the gunner's cockpit was covered with duralumin sheet.

The prototype was followed by 11 development aircraft that were used to

evaluate a number of engine types, and the Bre. 19 entered production in 1923. By 1927 some 2,000 aircraft had been delivered, half each in the

B.2 bomber and A.2 spotter/reconnaissance roles. Most aircraft in French service were powered by the Renault 12K or Lorraine-Dietrich 12D/E engines, and with each type gave invaluable service mainly at home but also in France's colonial wars of the 1920s in Morocco and Syria. The Bre. 19 soldiered on into obsolescence, and late in its career equipped four night fighter squadrons before being relegated to the reserve and training roles during 1934. The type also secured considerable export success (direct sales and licensed production) mainly of the Bre. 19GR long-range variant. The Bre. 19 was also developed in Bidon (petrol can) and Super Bidon variants for a number of classic record-breaking distance flights.

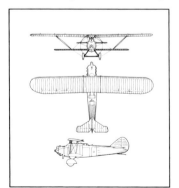

*Breguet 19*

**BREGUET Bre. 19 B2**
**Role:** Light day bomber
**Crew/Accommodation:** Two
**Power Plant:** One 550 hp Renault 12Kc water-cooled inline
**Dimensions:** Span 14.8 m (48.5 ft); length 8.89 m (29.16 ft); wing area 50 m² (538.4 sq ft)
**Weights:** Empty 1,485 kg (3,273 lb); MTOW 2,301 kg (5,093 lb)
**Performance:** Maximum speed 240 km/h (149 mph) at sea level; operational ceiling 7,800 m (25,590 ft); range 800 km (497 miles) with full warload
**Load:** Three/four .303 inch machine guns, plus up to 700 kg (1,543 lb) of bombs

*Breguet 19TR*

# JUNKERS Ju 87 (Germany)

*Ju 87B-1*

The Ju 87 was planned as a dedicated dive-bomber, a type known to the Germans as the *Sturzkampfflugzeug* or Stuka, and proved a decisive weapon in the opening campaigns of World War II. The type delivered its weapons with great accuracy, and came to be feared so highly that the appearance of its inverted gull wings and the sound of the 'Jericho trumpet' sirens on its landing gear legs often caused panic.

The first of four prototypes flew late in 1935 as the Ju 87 V1 with the 477-kW (640-hp) Rolls-Royce Kestrel V inline engine and endplate vertical surfaces. The next two prototypes had single vertical tail surfaces and were powered by the 455-kW (610-hp) Junkers Jumo 210Aa inline, while the last prototype introduced a larger

vertical tail. The type entered service in the spring of 1937 as the Ju 87A with the 477-kW (640-hp) Jumo 210C, and production of this variant totalled 210 aircraft.

Later variants included the Ju 87B with the 895-kW (1,200-hp) Jumo 211D, a larger canopy, and the wheel fairings replaced by spats, the Ju 87D dive-bomber and ground-attack type with the 1051-kW (1,410-hp) Jumo 211J, in a revised cowling, a redesigned canopy, a still larger vertical tail, simplified landing gear, and upgraded offensive and defensive features, the Ju 87G anti-tank model with two 37-mm underwing cannon, the Ju 87H conversion of the Ju 87D as a dual-control trainer, and the Ju 87R version of the Ju 87B in the long-range anti-ship role. From 1941 the Ju 87's limitations in the face of effective anti-aircraft and fighter defences were fully evident, but Germany lacked a replacement and the type had to remain in service as increasingly specialized ground-attack and anti-tank aircraft. Production of the series totalled 5,709 aircraft.

**JUNKERS Ju 87B**
**Role:** Dive bomber
**Crew/Accommodation:** Two
**Power Plant:** One 1,200 hp Junkers Jumo 211 Da water-cooled inline
**Dimensions:** Span 13.8 m (45.3 ft); length 11 m (36.83 ft); wing are a 31.9 m² (343.3 sq ft)
**Weights:** Empty 2,750 kg (6,063 lb); MTOW 4,250 kg (9,321 lb)
**Performance:** Maximum speed 380 km/h (237 mph) at 4,000 m (13,124 ft); operational ceiling 8,100 m (26,575 ft); range 600 km (372 miles) with full warload
**Load:** Three 7.9 mm machine guns, plus 1,000 kg (2,205 lb) bombload

*A pair of Ju 87B aircraft*

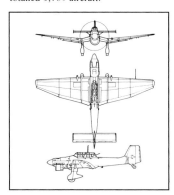

*Junkers Ju 87B-2*

# HEINKEL He 111 (Germany)

*He 111H-5*

The He 111 was Germany's most important bomber of World War II, and was built to the extent of 7,300 or more aircraft. The type was designed supposedly as an airliner, and in its first form it was basically an enlarged He 70 with two 492-kW (660-hp) BMW VI 6,0Z inline engines mounted on the wings. The first prototype flew in February 1935, and considerable development was necessary in another prototype, 10 pre-production aircraft and finally another prototype before the He 111B began to enter military

service with 746-kW (1,000-hp) Daimler-Benz DB 600 inlines, which were also used for the six He 111C 10-passenger airliners. The DB 600 was in short supply, so the He 111E used the 746-kW (1,000-hp) Junkers Jumo 211A and was developed in five subvariants to a total of about 190 aircraft.

The 70 He 111Fs combined the wing of the He 111G with Jumo 211A-3 engines, and at the same time the eight He 111Gs introduced a wing of straight rather than curved taper and was built in variants with BMW 132 radial or DB 600 inline engines. The He 111H was based on the He 111P and became the most

extensively built model, some 6,150 aircraft being produced in many important subvariants, both built and converted, up to the He 111H-23 with increasingly powerful engines (including the Jumo 211 and 213), heavier armament and sophisticated equipment. The He 111J was a torpedo bomber, and about 90 were delivered. Despite its late designation, the He 111P was

introduced in 1939 and pioneered the asymmetric and extensively glazed forward fuselage in place of the original stepped design, and about 40 aircraft were built in subvariants up to the He 111P-6.

The oddest variant was the He 111Z heavy glider tug, which was two He 111H-6 bombers joined by a revised wing section incorporating a fifth Jumo 211F engine.

*Heinkel He 111D-1*

**HEINKEL HE 111H-16**
**Role:** Bomber
**Crew/Accommodation:** Five
**Power Plant:** Two 1,350 hp Junkers Jumo 211F-2 water-cooled inlines
**Dimensions:** Span 22.6 m (74.15 ft); length 16.4 m (53.81 ft); wing area 86.5 m² (931 sq ft)
**Weights:** Empty 8,680 kg (19,136 lb); MTOW 14,000 kg (30,865 lb)
**Performance:** Maximum speed 435 km/h (270 mph) at 6,000 m (19,685 ft); operational ceiling 6,700 m (21,982 ft); range 1,950 km (1,212 miles) with maximum bombload
**Load:** Two 20 mm cannon and five 13 mm machine guns, plus up to 3,600 kg (7,937 lb) of bombs

*Heinkel He 111H bombers*

# DORNIER Do 17 Family (Germany)

*Do 217K*

The origins of this important German bomber lie with a 1933 Deutsche Lufthansa requirement for a six-passenger mailplane, though this requirement was also responsible for the narrow 'pencil' fuselage that was one of the main hindrances to the type's later development as a warplane. The Do 17 first flew in the autumn of 1934, and its performance suggested a military development with the single vertical tail surface replaced by endplate surfaces to increase the dorsal gunner's field of fire. Six military prototypes were followed by two pre-production types, the Do 17E-1 bomber with a shortened but glazed nose and 500-kg (1,102-lb) bomb load, and the Do 17F-1 photographic reconnaissance type, both powered by 559-kW (750-hp) BMW VI inlines.

There followed a number of experimental and limited-production variants before the advent of the Do 17Z definitive bomber built in several subvariants with the 746-kW (1,000-hp) BMW-Bramo 323 Fafnir radials in 1939 and 1940. Do 17 production was perhaps 1,200 aircraft, and from this basic type was developed the Do 215, of which 112 were produced with Daimler-Benz DB 601A inline engines. The two main models were the Do 215B-4 reconnaissance type and the Do 215B-5 night fighter. The Do 217 that first flew in September 1938 was essentially a Do 17 with 802-kW (1,075-hp) DB 601A engines, a larger fuselage, and a revised empennage.

Production was 1,750 aircraft in three basic series: the Do 217E heavy bomber and anti-ship type with stepped forward fuselage and 1178-kW (1,580-hp) BMW 801 radial engines, the Do 217K and Do 217M heavy night bomber and missile-armed anti-ship types with unstepped forward fuselage plus 1268-kW (1,700-hp) BMW 801 radials and 1305-kW (1,750-hp) DB 603A inline engines, and the Do 217N night fighter and intruder types with radar, specialist weapon fit, and 1379-kW (1,850-hp) DB 603A inline engines.

### DORNIER Do 17Z-2
**Role:** Medium bomber
**Crew/Accommodation:** Five
**Power Plant:** Two 1,000 hp BMW Bramo 323P Fafnir air-cooled radials
**Dimensions:** Span 18 m (59.06 ft); length 15.8 m (51.84 ft); wing area 55 m² (592 sq ft)
**Weights:** Empty 5,210 kg (11,488 lb); MTOW 8,590 kg (18,940 lb)
**Performance:** Maximum speed 410 km/h (255 mph) at 4,000 m (13,124 ft); operational ceiling 8,200 m (26,904 ft); radius 330 km (205 miles) with full bombload
**Load:** Eight 7.9 mm machine guns, plus up to 1,000 kg (2,205 lb) of bombs

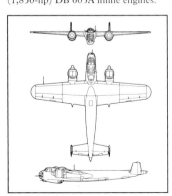

*Dornier Do 217E-2*

*The Do 217P, the final development of the Dornier Do 217 series*

133

# BRISTOL BLENHEIM (United Kingdom)

*Blenheim Mk IF*

In 1934 Lord Rothermere commissioned Bristol to produce a fast and capacious light personal transport. This appeared as the Type 142 that first flew in April 1935 with two 485-kW (650-hp) Bristol Mercury VIS radials. The aircraft caused a

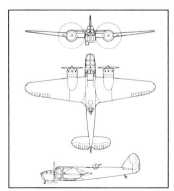

*Bristol Blenheim Mk IV*

great stir as it was 48 km/h (30 mph) faster than the U.K.'s latest fighter, and it was presented to the nation by the air-minded Rothermere after the Air Ministry asked for permission to evaluate the machine as a light bomber. As a result, Bristol developed the Type 142M bomber prototype that first flew in June 1936. The type offered higher performance than current light bombers, and was ordered in large numbers for service from 1937 onwards.

**BRISTOL BLENHEIM Mk I**
**Role:** Medium bomber
**Crew/Accommodation:** Three
**Power Plant:** Two 840 hp Bristol Mercury VIII air-cooled radials
**Dimensions:** Span 17.17 m (56.33 ft); length 12.11 m (39.75 ft); wing area 43.57 m² (469 sq ft)
**Weights:** Empty 3,674 kg (8,100 lb); MTOW 5,670 kg (12,500 lb)
**Performance:** Maximum speed 459 km/h (285 mph) at 4,572 m (15,000 ft); operational ceiling 8,315 m (27,280 ft); range 1,810 km (1,125 miles) with full bombload
**Load:** Two .303 inch machine guns, plus up to 454 kg (1,000 lb) of bombs

The main variants were the original Blenheim Mk I of which 1,365 were built in the U.K. and 61 under licence (45 in Finland and 16 in Yugoslavia) with 626-kW (840-hp) Mercury VIII radials, the Blenheim Mk IF interim night fighter of which about 200 were produced as conversions with radar and a ventral pack of four machine guns, the generally improved Blenheim Mk IV of which 3,297 were built in the U.K. and another 10 under licence in Finland with 686-kW (920-hp) Mercury XV engines, more fuel and a lengthened nose, the Blenheim Mk IVF extemporized night fighter, the Blenheim Mk IVF fighter conversion, and the Blenheim Mk V of which 945 were built with 708-kW (950-hp) Mercury 25 or 30 engines and a solid nose housing four machine-guns in Mk VA bomber, Mk VB close support, Mk VC operational trainer and Mk VD tropicalized bomber subvariants. The Blenheim Mk IV was built in Canada as the Bolingbroke coastal reconnaissance

and light bomber aircraft, of which 676 were built as Mk Is with Mercury VIIIs, Mk IVs with Mercury XVs and MK IV Ws with Pratt & Whitney R-1830 Wasp radials.

*Bristol Blenheim Mk IV*

# SAVOIA-MARCHETTI SM. 79 SPARVIERO (Italy)

*SM. 79 Sparviero*

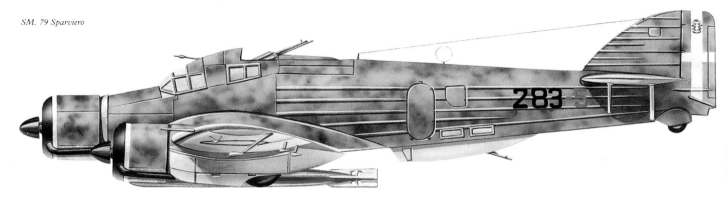

The SM. 79 Sparviero (Sparrowhawk) was Italy's most important bomber of World War II and, in its specialist anti-ship version, the best torpedo bomber of the war. The type was evolved from the company's earlier tri-motor types, and first flew in late 1934 as the SM. 79P prototype of a planned eight-passenger civil transport, and in this form was powered by three 455-kW (610-hp) Piaggio Stella radials. The type was a cantilever low-wing monoplane of mixed construction with retractable tailwheel landing gear, and its considerable capabilities soon

prompted the adoption of a more warlike role with a revised cockpit, a vental gondola, provision for offensive and defensive armament, and 582-kW (780-hp) Alfa Romeo 125 RC 35/126 RC 34 radial engines.

Production of the series totalled about 1,370 for Italy and for export, and the initial variant was the SM. 79-I bomber with 582-kW (780-hp) Alfa-Romeo 126 RC 34 radials and no windows in the fuselage sides. This type was successfully evaluated in the Spanish Civil War in both the level bomber and the torpedo bomber roles,

and proved so admirable in the latter that a specialized variant was then ordered as the SM. 79-II torpedo bomber with 746-kW (1,000-hp) Piaggio P.XI RC 40 or 768-kW (1,030-hp) Fiat A.80 RC 41 radials and provision for two 450-mm (17.7-in) torpedoes. The SM. 79-III was an improved version of the SM. 79-II without the ventral gondola and with heavier defensive armament. Production of the SM. 79-I, II and III totalled 1,230. Other variants were the SM. 79B twin-engined export version

of the SM. 79-I with a variety of radials, the SM.79C (and SM. 79T long-range) prestige conversion of the SM. 79-I without dorsal and ventral protusions, the SM. 79JR model for Romania with two Junkers Jumo 211Da inline engines, the SM.79K version of the SM. 79-I for Yugoslavia, and the SM. 83 civil transport version.

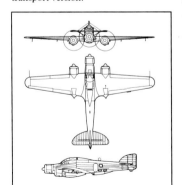

*SM. 79-II Sparviero*

**SAVOIA-MARCHETTI SM.79 SPARVIERO**
**Role:** Bomber
**Crew/Accommodation:** Four
**Power Plant:** Three 780 hp Alfa Romeo 126 RC34 air-cooled radials
**Dimensions:** Span 21 m (69.55 ft); length 15.62 m (51.25 ft); wing area 61.7 m² (664.2 sq ft)
**Weights:** Empty 6,800 kg (14,991 lb); MTOW 10,500 kg (23,148 lb)
**Performance:** Maximum speed 430 km/h (267 mph) at 4,000 m (13,125 ft); operational ceiling 6,500 m (21,325 ft); range 1,900 km (1,180 miles) with full bombload
**Load:** Three 12.7 mm and two 7.7 mm machine guns, plus up to 1,250 kg (2,756 lb) of bombs or one torpedo

*Savoia-Marchetti SM. 79C*

# JUNKERS Ju 88 Family (Germany)

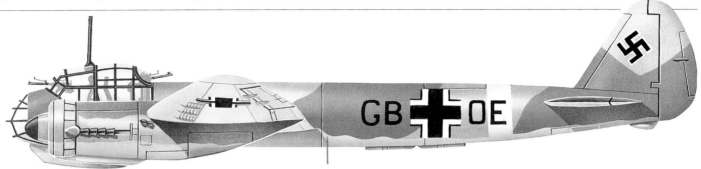

*Ju 88A-4*

The Ju 88 can be considered Germany's equivalent to the British Mosquito and with that type was certainly the most versatile warplane of World War II. Production of the Ju 88 family totalled about 15,000 aircraft. The type was schemed as a high-speed bomber and first flew in December 1936 with 746-kW (1,000-hp) Daimler-Benz DB 600A inlines, subsequently changed to Junkers Jumo 211s of the same rating, a low/mid-set wing and, in the standard German fashion, the crew grouped closely together in an extensively glazed nose section that proved comparatively vulnerable despite steadily heavier defensive armament. With the Jumo 211, the Ju 88A entered widespread service, being built in variants up to the Ju 88A-17. Six manufacturers produced about 7,000 of this series alone.

The next operational bomber was the Ju 88S in three subvariants with the 1268-kW (1,700-hp) BMW 801G radial, smoother nose contours, and reduced bomb load to improve performance; companion reconnaissance models were the two variants of the Ju 88T and the three variants of the longer-range Ju 88H. Production of the Ju 88H/S/T series totalled some 550 aircraft. From the Ju 88A was developed the Ju 88C heavy fighter; this had BMW 801A radials and a 'solid' nose for the heavy gun armament, together with radar in a few night fighter variants. The definitive night fighter series with steadily improving radar and effective armament was the Ju 88G, together with the improved Ju 88R version of the Ju 88C. Other series were the Ju 88D long-range reconnaissance and Ju 88P anti-tank aircraft. Development of the same concept yielded the high-performance Ju 188 and high-altitude Ju 388 series.

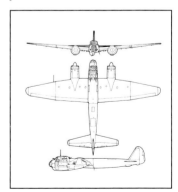

*Junkers Ju 88A-4*

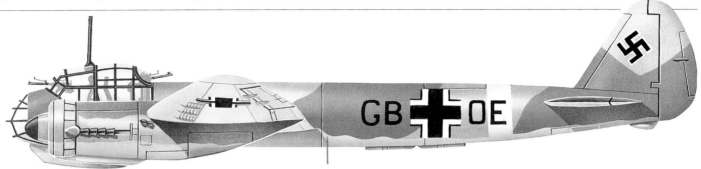

*Junkers Ju 88A-4 bombers*

**JUNKERS Ju 88A-4**
**Role:** Light fast bomber
**Crew/Accommodation:** Four
**Power Plant:** Two 1,340 hp Junkers Jumo 211J-1 water-cooled inlines
**Dimensions:** Span 20 m (65.63 ft); length 14.4 m (47.23 ft); wing area 54.5 m² (586.6 sq ft)
**Weights:** Empty 9,860 kg (21,737 lb); MTOW 14,000 kg (30,870 lb)
**Performance:** Maximum speed 470 km/h (292 mph) at 5,300 m (17,390 ft); operational ceiling 8,200 m (26,900 ft); range, 1,790 km (1,112 miles) with full bombload
**Load:** Two 13 mm and three 7.9 mm machine guns, plus up to 2,000 kg (4,409 lb) bombload

# VICKERS WELLINGTON (United Kingdom)

*Wellington B.Mk III*

The Wellington was the most important British medium bomber of World War II, and indeed during the early stages of the war was perhaps the only truly effective night bomber after the type was switched to this role in the aftermath of some disastrously heavy losses in early daylight raids. A Wellington of No. 149 Squadron was responsible for dropping the RAF's first 4,000-lb 'block buster' bomb during an attack on Emden in April 1941, and on the first RAF 'thousand bomber' raid on Germany (Cologne) in May 1942, no fewer than 599 of the 1,046 bombers used were Wellingtons.

Designed to meet a 1932 requirement, the prototype first flew in June 1936 with 682-kW (915-hp) Bristol Pegasus X radials. The type used the geodetic lattice-work form of airframe construction pioneered in the Vickers Wellesley by inventor Barnes Wallis, and was thus immensely strong. When production ceased in October 1945, no fewer than 11,461 Wellingtons had been produced in versions with the 746-kW (1,000-hp) Pegasus XVIII radial (the Wellington B.Mks I, IA and IC with steadily improved defensive capability, and the Wellington GR.Mk VIII with searchlight and provision for anti-submarine weapons), the 1,119-kW (1,500-hp) Bristol Hercules radial (the Wellington B.Mk III with the Hercules XI and B.Mk X with the Hercules VI or XVI, and the Wellington GR.Mks XI, XII, XIII and XIV with the Hercules VI or XVI and steadily improved anti-submarine

equipment), the 783-kW (1,050-hp) Pratt & Whitney Twin Wasp radial (the Wellington B.Mk IV) and the 854-kW (1,145-hp) Rolls-Royce Merlin X inline (the Wellington B.Mks II and VI). Wellingtons were extensively converted later in the type's career into alternative roles such as freighting and training. Several aircraft were also used as engine test-beds, and the basic concept was developed considerably further in the Type 294 Warwick that was designed as a heavy bomber but actually matured as a maritime reconnaissance aircraft.

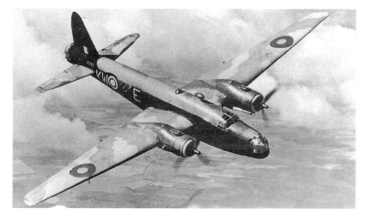

*Vickers Wellington Mk III*

**VICKERS WELLINGTON B.Mk IC**
**Role:** Heavy bomber
**Crew/Accommodation:** Five/six
**Power Plant:** Two 1,050 hp Bristol Pegasus XVIII air-cooled radials
**Dimensions:** Span 26.27 m (86.18 ft); length 19.69 m (64.6 ft); wing area 78 m² (848 sq ft)
**Weights:** Empty 8,709 kg (19,200 lb); MTOW 12,927 kg (28,500 lb)
**Performance:** Maximum speed 378 km/h (235 mph) at 1,440 m (4,724 ft); operational ceiling 5,486 m (18,000 ft); range 2,575 km (1,600 miles) with 925 kg (2,040 lb) bombload
**Load:** Six .303 inch machine guns, plus up to 2,041 kg (4,500 lb) internally stowed bombload

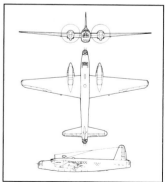

*Vickers Wellington Mk II*

# AICHI D3A 'VAL' (Japan)

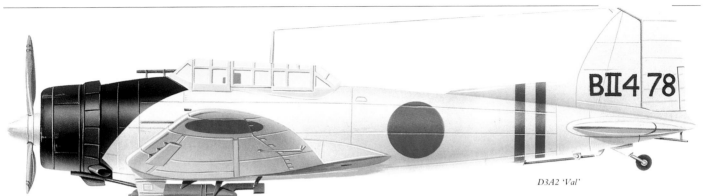

D3A2 'Val'

Designed as successor to the same company's D1A and first flown in 1938 with the 544-kW (730-hp) Kinsei 3 radial engine, the D3A was

Japan's most important naval dive-bomber at the beginning of World War II, and played a major part in the Pearl Harbor attack. Known to the Allies as the 'Val', the D3A played a decisive part in Japan's expansionist campaign in South-East Asia and the South-West Pacific, but was eclipsed by American carrierborne fighters from mid-1942 onward.

The type's elliptical flying surfaces were aerodynamically elegant, and the combination of a lightweight structure and fixed but spatted landing gear provided good performance. Production aircraft were based on the second prototype, but with slightly reduced span and also a long dorsal fin to improve directional stability. Total construction was 1,495 aircraft, and the main variants were the D3A1 and D3A2, which totalled 476 and 1,007 respectively.

The D3A1 entered service in 1940 with the 746-kW (1,000-hp) Kinsei 43

that was altered later in the production run to the 1,070-hp (798-kW) Kinsei 44 radial. The D3A2 was fitted with a propeller spinner and a modified rear cockpit canopy, and was powered by the 969-kW (1,300-hp) Kinsei 54 that could draw on greater fuel capacity for better performance and range. The D3A2-K was a trainer conversion of the earlier models. From late 1942 the type was relegated to the land-based attack role, and then to second-line tasks such as training before final use as kamikaze attack aircraft.

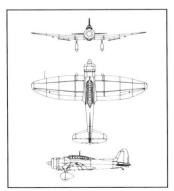

Aichi D3A2 'Val'

**AICHI D3A2 'VAL'**
**Role:** Naval carrierborne dive bomber
**Crew/Accommodation:** Two
**Power Plant:** One 1,300-hp Mitsubishi Kinsei 54 air-cooled radial
**Dimensions:** Span 14.37 m (47.1 ft); length 10.23 m (33.6 ft); wing area 23.6 m² (254 sq ft)
**Weights:** Empty 2,618 kg (5,722 lb); MTOW 4,122 kg (9,087 lb)
**Performance:** Maximum speed 430 km/h (267 mph) at 9,225 m (20,340 ft); operational ceiling 10,888 m (35,720 ft); range 1,561 km (970 miles)
**Load:** Three 7.7-mm machine guns, plus up to 370 kg (816 lb) of bombs

The Aichi D3A2

# DOUGLAS SBD DAUNTLESS (U.S.A.)

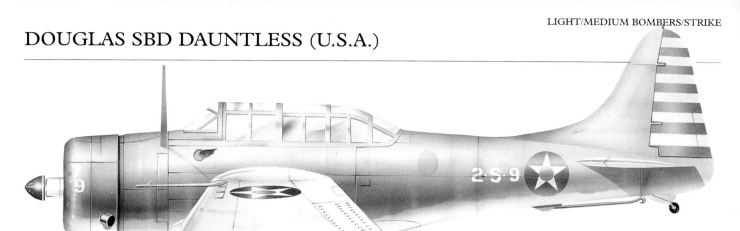

*SBD-3 Dauntless*

The SBD Dauntless was the most successful dive-bomber produced by the Americans during World War II, and assumed historical importance as one of the weapons that checked the tide of Japanese expansion in the Battles of the Coral Sea and Midway during 1942. The type began life as a development of the 1938 Northrop

BT-1 after Northrop's acquisition by Douglas. The Douglas development was first flown in July 1938 as the XBT-2 low-wing, monoplane with the 746-kW (1,000-hp) Wright R-1820-32 Cyclone radial engine, perforated split trailing-edge flaps that also served as airbrakes, and the main bomb carried under the fuselage on a crutch that swung it clear of the propeller before it was released in a steep dive.

### DOUGLAS SBD-5 DAUNTLESS
**Role:** Naval carrierborne dive bomber
**Crew/Accommodation:** Two
**Power Plant:** One 1,200 hp Wright R-1820-60 Cyclone air-cooled radial
**Dimensions:** Span 12.66 m (41.54 ft); length 10.09 m (33.1 ft); wing area 30.19 m² (325 sq ft)
**Weights:** Empty 2,905 kg (6,404 lb); MTOW 4,853 kg (10,700 lb)
**Performance:** Maximum speed 410 km/h (255 mph) at 4,265 m (14,000 ft); operational ceiling 7,780 m (25,530 ft); range 1,795 km (1,115 miles) with 726 kg (1,600 lb) bombload
**Load:** Two .5 inch and two .303 inch machine guns, plus up to 1,021 kg (2,250 lb) of bombs

The type began to enter U.S. Navy carrierborne and U.S. Marine Corps land-based service as the SBD-1, of which 57 were built with one trainable and two fixed 7.62-mm (0.3-in) machine guns. The 87 SBD-2s had greater fuel capacity and revised offensive armament. Next came the 584 SBD-3s which introduced the R-1820-52 engine, a bulletproof windscreen, armour protection, self-sealing fuel tanks of greater capacity, and the definitive machine gun armament of two 12.7-mm (0.5-in) fixed guns and two 7.62-mm (0.3-in) trainable guns. The 780 SBD-4s had a revised electrical system. The 3,025

SBD-5s had the 895-kW (1,200-hp) R-1820-60 engine and greater ammunition capacity. The 451 examples of the final SBD-6 had the yet more powerful R-1820-66 engine and increased fuel capacity.

Subvariants of this series were the SBD-1P, SBD-2P and SBD-3P photo-reconnaissance aircraft. The U.S. Army ordered an A-24 version of the SBD-3, further contracts specifying A-24A (SBD-4) and A-24B (SBD-5) aircraft, but these were not successful. The Fleet Air Arm received nine SBD-5s that were designated Dauntless DB.Mk I but not used operationally.

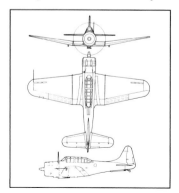

*SBD-5 Dauntless*

*Douglas SBD Dauntless*

# NORTH AMERICAN B-25 MITCHELL (U.S.A.)

*B-25J Mitchell*

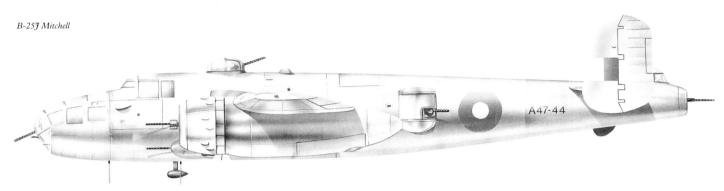

Immortalized as the mount of Doolittle's Tokyo Raiders when flown off the deck of USS *Hornet* in April 1942, the NA-40 was designed to meet a U.S. Army requirement for a twin-engined attack bomber, and emerged for its first flight in January 1939 as a shoulder-wing monoplane with tricycle landing gear and 820-kW (1,100-hp) Pratt & Whitney R-1830-S6C3-G radials that were soon replaced by 969-kW (1,300-hp) Wright GR-2600-A71 radials. The R-2600 was retained throughout the rest of the type's 9,816-aircraft production run. Further development produced the NA-62 design with the wing lowered to the mid-position, the fuselage widened for side-by-side pilot seating, the crew increased from three to five, greater offensive and defensive armament, and 1268-kW (1,700-hp) R-2600-9 engines. In this form the type entered production as the B-25, and the first of 24 such aircraft flew in August 1940.

Development models produced in small numbers were the B-25A (40 with armour and self-sealing fuel tanks) and B-25B (119 with power-operated dorsal and ventral turrets but with the tail gun position removed). The major production models began with the B-25C; 1,625 of this improved version were built with an autopilot, provision for an underfuselage torpedo, underwing racks for eight 113-kg (250-lb) bombs and, in some aircraft, four 12.7-mm (0.5-in) machine guns on the fuselage sides to fire directly forward. The 2,290 B-25Ds were similar but from a different production line. A few experimental versions intervened, and the next series-built models were the B-25G (405 with a 75-mm/2.95-in nose gun) and similar B-25H (1,000 with the 75-mm gun and between 14 and 18 12.7-mm machine-guns).

The final production version was the B-25J (4,390 with R-2600-92 radials and 12 12.7-mm machine-guns). Other variants included in the total were the F-10 reconnaissance, the AT-25 and TB-25 trainers, together with the PBJ versions, the last provided for the U.S. Navy.

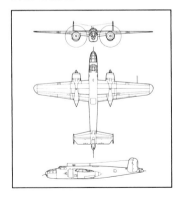

*North American B-25A Mitchell*

---

### NORTH AMERICAN B-25C MITCHELL
**Role:** Medium bomber
**Crew/Accommodation:** Five/six
**Power Plant:** Two 1,700-hp Wright R-2600-19 Cyclone air-cooled radials
**Dimensions:** Span 20.6 m (67.58 ft); length 16.13 m (52.92 ft); wing area 56.67 m² (610 sq ft)
**Weights:** Empty 9,208 kg (20,300 lb); MTOW 15,422 kg (34,000 lb)
**Performance:** Maximum speed 457 km/h (284 mph) at 4,572 m (15,000 ft); operational ceiling 6,041 m (21,200 ft); range 2,414 km (1,500 miles) with full bombload
**Load:** Four .5-inch machine guns, plus up to 1,361 kg (3,000 lb) of bombs

*North American B-25J Mitchell*

# DOUGLAS DB-7/A-20 HAVOC Series (U.S.A.)

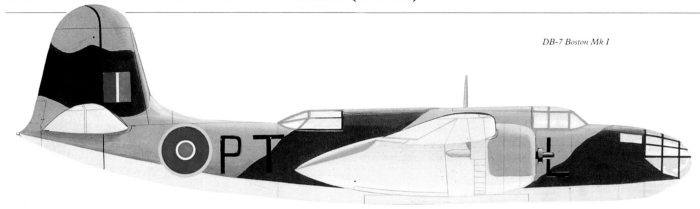

*DB-7 Boston Mk I*

The Model 7 was a basic twin-engined light bomber design that was evolved as a private venture and then went through a number of important forms during the course of an extensive production programme that saw the delivery of 7,478 aircraft in World War II up to September 1944. The type originated as a possible replacement for the U.S. Army's current generation of single-engined attack aircraft, and first flew as the Model 7B in October 1938 with 820-kW (1,100-hp) Pratt & Whitney R-1830 radials in place of the 336-kW (450-hp) engines of the originally

proposed Model 7A. Initial orders came from France for a Douglas Bomber 7 (DB-7) variant with 895-kW (1,200-hp) R-1830-S3C4-G engines and a deeper fuselage, followed by the improved DB-7A with 1119-kW (1,500-hp) Wright R-2600-A5B engines.

Most of these aircraft were delivered to the U.K. after the fall of France, and were placed in service with the name Boston Mks I and II, though several were converted to Havoc radar-equipped night-fighters. A redesigned DB-7B bomber variant with larger vertical tail surfaces and

British equipment became the Boston Mk III, and the same basic type was ordered by the U.S. Army as the A-20 Havoc. The latter were used mainly as reconnaissance aircraft, though a batch was converted to P-70 night fighter configuration. Thereafter the U.S. Army accepted large numbers of the A-20A and subsequent variants up to the A-20K with more power, heavier armament, and improved equipment. Many of these passed to the RAF and other British Commonwealth Air Forces in variants

up to the Boston Mk V. The steady increases in engine power maintained the performance of these types despite their greater weights and warloads. In addition to the Western Allies, the U.S.S.R. operated comparatively large numbers of the series received under Lend-Lease and often fitted with locally modified armament.

A A-20G of the US Army Air Force

**DOUGLAS A-20B HAVOC**
**Role:** Light day bomber
**Crew/Accommodation:** Three
**Power Plant:** Two 1,600 hp Wright R-2600-11 Double Cyclone air-cooled radials
**Dimensions:** Span 18.69 m (61.33 ft); length 14.48 m (47.5 ft); wing area 43.1 m² (464 sq ft)
**Weights:** Empty 6,727 kg (14,830 lb); MTOW 10,796 kg (23,800 lb)
**Performance:** Maximum speed 563 km/h (350 mph) at 3,658 (12,000 ft); operational ceiling 8,717 m (28,600 ft); range 1,328 km (825 miles) with 454 kg (1,000 lb) of bombs
**Load:** Three .5 inch and one or three .303 inch machine guns, plus to 1,089 kg (2,400 lb) of bombs

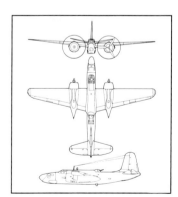

*Douglas A-20J Havoc*

141

# PETLYAKOV Pe-2 (U.S.S.R.)

*Petlyakov Pe-2*

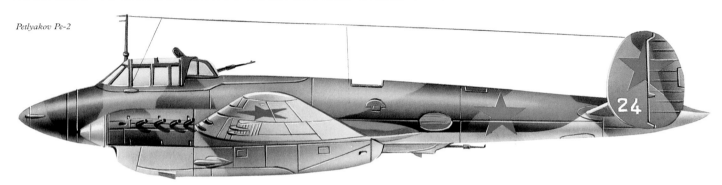

The Pe-2 was one of the U.S.S.R.'s most important tactical aircraft of World War II, and resulted from the VI-100 high-altitude fighter prototype with the 783-kW (1,050-hp) Klimov M-105 inlines. The planned role was then changed to dive-bombing, resulting in the PB-100 design for a dive-bomber with a crew of three rather than two, dive-brakes and other modifications including provision of a bomb aimer's position and elimination of the pressure cabin. The type was of all-metal construction and a thoroughly modern concept with a cantilever low-set wing, endplate vertical tail surfaces, a circular-section fuselage, and retractable tailwheel landing gear. The aircraft entered service in November 1940 as the Pe-2 with two 902-kW (1,210-hp) VK-105RF engines, and when production ended early in 1945 some 11,427 aircraft of the series had been built.

The versatility of the type is attested by the development and production of variants intended for the bombing, reconnaissance, bomber destroyer, night fighter and conversion trainer roles. In addition to the baseline Pe-2, the main variants were the Pe-2R photo-reconnaissance type with cameras and greater fuel capacity, the Pe-2UT dual-control trainer with a revised cockpit enclosure over tandem seats, and the Pe-3 multi-role fighter, of which some 500 were built as 200 Pe-3 bomber destroyers and 300 Pe-3bis night fighters; the Pe-3 had the fixed nose armament of two 20-mm cannon, two 12.7-mm (0.5-in) and two 7.62-mm (0.3-in) machine guns plus one 12.7-mm gun in the dorsal turret, while the Pe-3bis entered production with a nose armament of one 20-mm cannon, one 12.7-mm machine gun and three 7.62-mm machine guns but ended with two 20-mm cannon, two 12.7-mm guns and two 7.62-mm guns.

**PETLYAKOV Pe-2**
**Role:** Dive bomber
**Crew/Accommodation:** Three/four
**Power Plant:** Two 1,100 hp Klimov M-105R water-cooled inlines
**Dimensions:** Span 17.16 m (56.23 ft); length 12.66 m (41,54 ft); wing area 40.5 m² (435.9 sq ft)
**Weights:** Empty 5,876 kg (12,954 lb); MTOW 8,496 kg (18,730 lb)
**Performance:** Maximum speed 540 km/h (336 mph) at 5,000 m (16,404 ft); operational ceiling 8,800 m (28,871 ft); range 1,500 km (932 miles)
**Load:** One 12.7 mm and two 7.62 mm machine guns, plus up to 1,200 kg (2,646 lb) of bombs

*Petlyakov Pe-2*

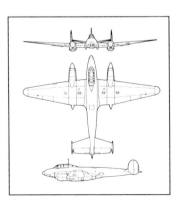

*Petlyakov Pe-2*

# de HAVILLAND D.H.98 MOSQUITO (United Kingdom)

*Mosquito B.Mk VI*

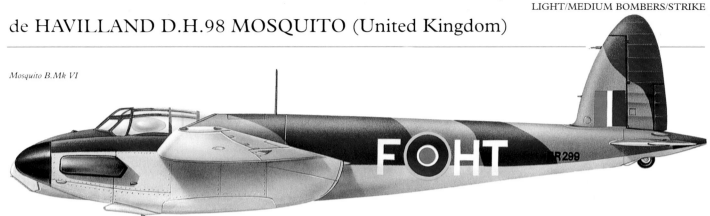

Perhaps the most versatile warplane of World War II and certainly one of the classic warplanes of all time, the 7,785 Mosquitoes began from a private venture based on the company's composite plywood/balsa construction principal. It was planned as a high-performance but unarmed light bomber. The Mk I prototype flew in November 1940. Photographic reconnaissance, fighter, trainer and bomber variants followed.

The PR versions were the Mosquito PR.Mk IV with four cameras, PR.Mk VIII with two-stage Merlins, PR.Mk IX with greater fuel capacity, PR.Mk XVI with cockpit pressurization, PR.Mk 32 based on the NF.Mk XV, PR.Mk 34 with extra fuel in a bomb bay 'bulge', PR.Mk 40 Australian development of the FB.Mk 40, and PR.Mk 41 version of the PR.Mk 40 with two-stage engines.

The fighters were the Mosquito NF.Mk II night fighter, FB.Mk VI fighter-bomber with bombs and underwing rockets, NF.Mk XII and XIII with improved radar, NF. Mk XV conversion of the B. Mk IV for high-altitude interception, NF.Mk XVII conversion of the NF.Mk II with U.S. radar, FB.Mk XVIII anti-ship conversion or the FB.Mk VI with a 57-mm gun and rockets, NF.Mk XIX with British or U.S. radar, FB.Mk 21 Canadian-built FB.Mk VI, FB.Mk 26 version of the FB.Mk 21 with Packard-built Merlin engines, NF.Mk 30 high-altitude model with two-stage Merlins, TR.Mk 33 naval torpedo fighter, NF.Mk 36 higher-altitude equivalent to the NF.Mk 30, TR.Mk 37 version of the TR.Mk 33 with British radar, and FB.Mk 40 Australian-built equivalent of the FB.Mk VI.

The trainer versions were the Mosquito T.Mk III, T.Mk 22 Canadian-built equivalent to the T.Mk III, T.Mk 27 version of the T.Mk 22 with Packard-built engines, T.Mk 29 conversion of the FB.Mk 26, and T.Mk 43 Australian-built equivalent to the T.Mk III.

The bomber versions were the basic Mosquito B.Mk IV, B.Mk VII Canadian-built type with underwing hardpoints, B.Mk IX high-altitude type with a single 1814-kg (4,000-lb) bomb, B.Mk XVI development of the B.Mk IX with pressurized cockpit, B.Mk 20 B.Mk 25 version of the B.Mk 20 and B.Mk 35 long-range high-altitude model.

*This is a de Havilland Mosquito T.Mk III trainer of the Royal Air Force*

## de HAVILLAND D.H.98 MOSQUITO NF. Mk 36

**Role:** Night/all-weather fighter
**Crew/Accommodation:** Two
**Power Plant:** Two 1,690 hp Rolls-Royce Merlin 113 water-cooled inlines
**Dimensions:** Span 16.51 m (54.17 ft); length 12.34 m (40.5 ft); wing area 42.18 m² (454 sq ft)
**Weights:** Empty 7,257 kg (16,000 lb); MTOW 9,707 kg (21,400 lb)
**Performance:** Maximum speed 650 km/h (404 mph) at 8,717 m (28,600 ft); operational ceiling 10,972 m (36,000 ft); range 2,704 km (1,680 miles)
**Load:** Four 20 mm cannon (interception guided by AI Mk 10 radar)

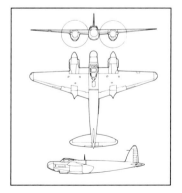

*Mosquito NF.Mk 36*

143

# ILYUSHIN Il-2 (U.S.S.R.)

*Ilyushin Il-2*

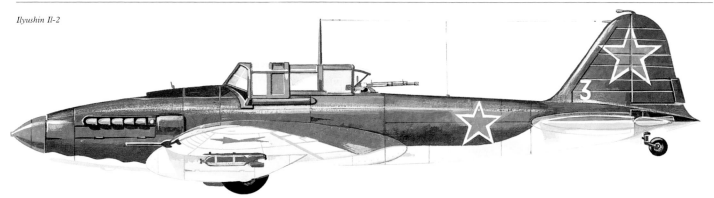

The Il-2 was probably the finest ground-attack aircraft of World War II and was built to the extent of some 36,165 aircraft. The type began life as the TsKB-55 (alternatively BSh-2 or DBSh) two-seat prototype that first flew in December 1939 with the 1007-kW (1,350-hp) Mikulin AM-35 inline engine. Flight tests indicated that the type was too heavy because of its massive armour 'bath' structural core,

so the basic design was developed into the single-seat TsKB-57 that flew in October 1940 with a 1268-kW (1,700-hp) Mikulin AM-38 inline. This entered production as the single-seat BSh-2, a designation that was altered to Il-2 during April 1941, and by August production had risen to some 300 aircraft per month.

Early operations confirmed the design bureau's initial objections to the removal of the TsKB-55's rear gunner, for the Il-2 was found to be especially vulnerable to rear attack. The Il-2 was therefore refined as the

Il-2M with the cockpit extended aft for a rear gunner equipped with a 12.7-mm (0.5-in) machine gun but separated from the pilot by a fuel tank. The original two wing-mounted 20-mm cannon were replaced by 23-mm weapons offering greater armour-penetration capability, and provision was made for the eight 82-mm (3.2-in) rockets to be replaced by four 132-mm (5.2-in) weapons. Later the type was also produced in the aerodynamically improved Il-2 Type 3 version with a 1320-kW (1,770-hp) engine, a refined canopy and faster-

acting doors for the bomb cells in the wings that carried 200 2.5-kg (5.51-lb) anti-tank bomblets. There was also an Il-2 Type 3M variant with further aerodynamic refinement, and a fixed forward-firing armament of two 37-mm cannon complemented by up to 32 82-mm (1 in) rockets on a two-stage zero-length installation. Other Il-2 versions were the Il-2T torpedo bomber with one 533-mm (21-in) torpedo under the fuselage and the I1-2U tandem-seat trainer. Production ended in late 1944 to allow for the much improved Il-10.

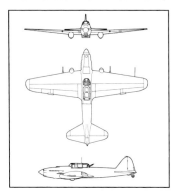

**ILYUSIHN Il-2M**
**Role:** Strike/close air support
**Crew/Accommodation:** Two
**Power Plant:** One 1,700 hp AM-38F water-cooled inline
**Dimensions:** Span 14.6 m (47.9 ft); length 11.6 m (38.06 ft); wing area 38.5 m² (414.41 sq ft)
**Weights:** Empty 4,525 kg (9,976 lb); MTOW 6,360 kg (14,021 lb)
**Performance:** Maximum speed 404 km/h (251 mph) at 1,500 m (4,921 ft); operational ceiling 6,000 m (19,685 ft); range 765 km (475 miles) with full warload
**Load:** Two 23 mm cannon and two 7.62 mm machine guns, plus up to 600 kg (1,321 lb) of bombs or anti-armour rockets

*Ilyushin Il-2 Type 3M*

# MARTIN B-26 MARAUDER (U.S.A.)

*B-26F Marauder*

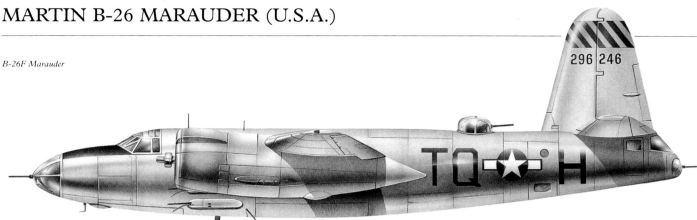

The Marauder was designed to meet a particularly difficult specification issued in 1939 by the U.S. Army Air Corps for a high-performance medium bomber, and was ordered 'off the drawing board' straight into production without any prototype or even pre-production aircraft. The first B-26 flew in November 1940 with two 1380-kW (1,850-hp) Pratt & Whitney R-2800-5 radials as a highly streamlined mid-wing monoplane with tricycle landing gear. The type was able to deliver the required performance, but because of the high wing loading low-speed handling was poor, resulting in a spate of accidents.

Total production was 4,708 aircraft, and in addition to the 201 B-26s the main variants were the B-26A (139 aircraft) with 1380-kW (1,850-hp) R-2800-9 or -39 engines, greater fuel capacity and provision for an underfuselage torpedo, the B-26C (1,883) with 1491-kW (2,000-hp) R-2800-41 engines and, from the 642nd aircraft, a wing increased in span by 1.83 m (6 ft 0 in) as a means of reducing wing loading, though this was negated by inevitably increased weight, the B-26C (1,210) generally similar to the B-26B but from a different production line, the B-26F (300) which introduced a higher wing incidence angle to improve field performance, and the B-26G (893) generally similar to the B-26F. There were two target tug-gunnery trainer variants produced by converting bombers as 208 AT-23As (later TB-26Bs) and 375 AT-23Bs (later TB-26Cs); 225 of the latter were transferred to the U.S. Navy as JM-1s. There was also the new-build TB-26G crew trainer, and 47 of these 57 aircraft were transferred to the U.S. Navy as JM-2s. Comparatively large numbers of several models were used by the British and, to a lesser extent, the French and South Africans.

**MARTIN B-26B MARAUDER**
**Role:** Medium bomber
**Crew/Accommodation:** Seven
**Power Plant:** Two 2,000 hp Pratt & Whitney R-2800-41 Double Wasp air-cooled radials
**Dimensions:** Span 21.64 m (71 ft); length 17.75 m (58.25 ft); wing area 61.13 m² (658 sq ft)
**Weights:** Empty 10,660 kg (23,500 lb); MTOW 17,328 kg (38,200 lb)
**Performance:** Maximum speed 454 km/h (282 mph) at 4,572 m (15,000 ft); operational ceiling 4,572+ m (15,000+ ft); range 1,086 km (675 miles) with maximum bombload
**Load:** Twelve .5 inch machine guns, plus up to 1,815 kg (4,000 lb) of internally carried bombs, or one externally carried torpedo

*This Martin B-26B Marauder shows evidence of protracted services*

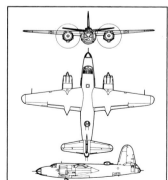

*Martin B-26G Marauder*

145

# CURTISS SB2C HELLDIVER (U.S.A.)

*SB2C-1 Helldiver*

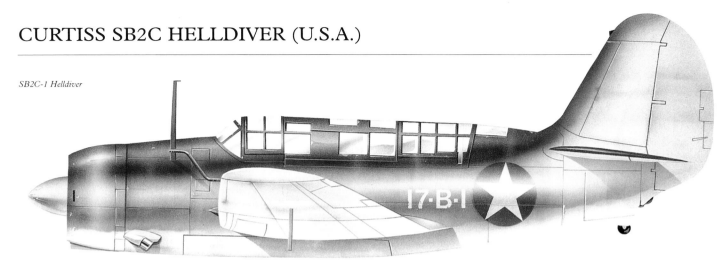

The SB2C was the third Curtiss design to bear the name Helldiver, the first two having been the F8C/O2C biplanes of the early 1930s and SBC biplane of the late 1930s. The Model 84 (or SB2C) monoplane was designed in competition to the Brewster XSB2A Buccaneer as successor to the Model 77 (or SBC) biplane in the carrierborne scout

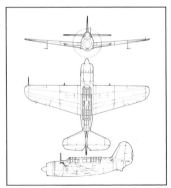

*SB2C-1C Helldiver*

bomber/dive bomber role. The type was designed as a substantial all-metal monoplane of the low-wing variety with retractable tailwheel landing gear (complete with arrester hook), a substantial tail unit, and a deep oval-section fuselage characterized by extensive glazing over the rear compartment. The X2B2C-1 prototype flew in December 1940 but was lost in an accident only a short time later. The U.S. Navy had considerable faith in the type,

## CURTISS SB2C-5 HELLDIVER
**Role:** Naval carrierborne bomber/reconnaissance
**Crew/Accommodation:** Two
**Power Plant:** One 1,900-hp Wright R-2600-20 Double Cyclone air-cooled radial
**Dimensions:** Span 15.15 m (49.75 ft); length 11.17 m (36.66 ft); wing area 39.2 m² (422 sq ft)
**Weights:** Empty 4,799 kg (10,580 lb); MTOW 7,388 kg (16,287 lb)
**Performance:** Maximum speed 418 km/h (260 mph) at 4,907 m (16,100 ft); operational ceiling 8,047 m (26,400 ft); range 1,875 km (1,165 miles) with 454 kg (1,000 lb) bombload
**Load:** Two 20-mm cannon and two .303-inch machine guns, plus up to 907 kg (2,000 lb) of bombs

however, and large-scale production had already been authorized to launch a programme that saw the eventual delivery of 7,200 aircraft. But because of the need to co-develop an A-25A version for the U.S. Army, the first SB2C-1 production aeroplane with the 1268-kW (1,700-hp) Wright R-2600-8 Cyclone 14 radial did not emerge until June 1942. The A-25A in fact entered only the most limited of army service, and the majority of the army's aircraft were reassigned to the U.S. Marine Corps in the land-based

role with the designation SB2C-1A.

Other variants were the SB2C-1C with the four wing-mounted 12.7-mm (0.5-in) machine guns replaced by two 20-mm cannon, the SB2C-3 with the 1417-kW (1,900-hp) R-2600-20 engine, the SB2C-4 with underwing bomb/rocket racks, the radar-fitted SB2C-4E, and the SB2C-5 with greater fuel capacity. Similar versions were built by Fairchild and Canadian Car & Foundry with the basic designation SBF and SBW respectively.

*Curtiss SB2C Helldiver*

# GRUMMAN TBF AVENGER (U.S.A.)

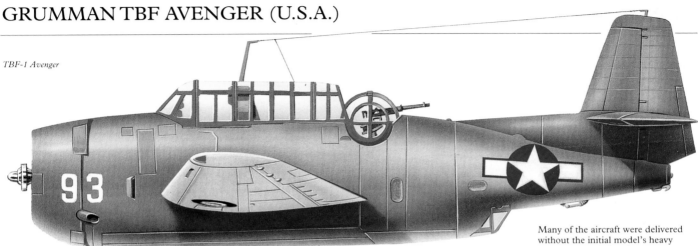

*TBF-1 Avenger*

Despite a disastrous combat debut in which five out of six aircraft were lost, the TBF Avenger was a decisive warplane of World War II, and may rightly be regarded as the Allies' premier carrierborne torpedo bomber. The TBF resulted from a 1940 requirement for a successor to the Douglas TBD Devastator. Orders were placed for two Vought XTBU-1 prototype in addition to the two XTBF-1s, and the Grumman type first flew in August 1941 on the power of the 1268-kW (1,700-hp) Wright R-

2600-8 Cyclone radial. The type was of typical Grumman design and construction, and despite the fact that it was the company's first essay in the field of carrierborne torpedo bombers, the Avenger proved itself a thoroughbred and immensely strong.

The type was ordered into production as the TBF-1 or, with two additional heavy machine-guns in the wings plus provision for drop tanks, TBF-1C; production totalled 2,291 aircraft. The Royal Navy also received the type as the Tarpon Mk I, later

changed to Avenger Mk I. The Eastern Aircraft Division of General Motors was also brought into the programme to produce similar models as 550 TBM-1s and 2,336 TBM-1Cs (Avenger Mk IIs), and the only major development was the TBM-3. Eastern produced 4,657 of this model, which had been pioneered as the XTBF-3 with the 1417-kW (1,900-hp) R-2600-219 engine and strengthened wings for the carriage of drop tanks or rockets.

Many of the aircraft were delivered without the initial model's heavy power-operated dorsal turret.

Late in World War II and after the war, the series was diversified into a host of other roles, each indicated by a special suffix, such as photo-reconnaissance, early warning, electronic warfare, anti-submarine search/attack, transport, and target towing. Total production was 9,839 aircraft.

*A version of the Grumman TBF Avenger, the TBM, built by General Motors*

**GRUMMAN TBF-1 AVENGER**
**Role:** Naval carrierborne strike
**Crew/Accommodation:** Three
**Power Plant:** One 1,700 hp Wright R-2600-8 Double Cyclone air-cooled radial
**Dimensions:** Span 16.51 m (54.16 ft); length 12.23 m (40.125 ft); wing area 45.52 m² (490 sq ft)
**Weights:** Empty 4,572 kg (10,080 lb); MTOW 7,214 kg (15,905 lb)
**Performance:** Maximum speed 436 km/h (271 mph) at 3,658 m (12,000 ft); operational ceiling 6,828 m (22,400 ft); range 1,955 km (1,215 miles) with torpedo
**Load:** One .5 inch and two .303 inch machine guns, plus up to 726 kg (1,600 lb) of internally-stowed torpedo or bombs

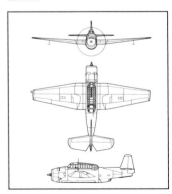

*Grumman TBF-1 Avenger*

# MITSUBISHI Ki-67 HIRYU 'PEGGY' (Japan)

*Ki-67-I Type 4 'Peggy'*

In February 1941, Mitsubishi received instructions from the Imperial Japanese Army Air Force to design a tactical heavy bomber, and the company responded with a type that secured good performance and agility through the typically Japanese defects of minimal protection (armour and self-sealing fuel tanks) combined with a lightweight structure that was little suited to sustain battle damage.

The first of 19 Ki-67 prototypes and pre-production aircraft flew in December 1942 with two 1417-kW (1,900-hp) Mitsubishi Ha-104 radials. Production was delayed as the Japanese army considered a whole range of derivatives based on this high-performance basic aircraft, but in December 1943, the army belatedly decided to concentrate on just a single heavy bomber type capable of the level and torpedo bombing roles. The type entered production with the company designation Ki-67-I and entered

service as the Army Type 4 Heavy Bomber Model 1 Hiryu (Flying Dragon). Only 679 of these effective aircraft were built, all but the first 159 having provision for an underfuselage rack carrying one torpedo to give the type an anti-ship capability. Many were converted as three-seat Ki-67-I KAI *kamikaze* aircraft with the defensive gun turrets removed and provision made for two 800-kg (1,764-lb) bombs or 2900 kg (6,393 lb) of explosives. Further production

was to have been of the Ki-67-II version with two 1789-kW (2,400-hp) Mitsubishi Ha-214 radials, however, the only other production was in fact of the Ki-109 heavy fighter variant. This type was armed with a 75-mm (2.95-in) nose gun in the bomber destroyer role, and production totalled just 22 aircraft before the end of World War II. The Ki-67 was known to the Allies as the 'Peggy', however the Ki-109 received no reporting name.

**MITSUBISHI Ki-67-1 OTSU HIRYU 'PEGGY'**
**Role:** Bomber
**Crew/Accommodation:** Eight
**Power Plant:** Two 1,900-hp Mitsubishi Ha-104 air-cooled radials
**Dimensions:** Span 22.5 m (73.82 ft); length 18.7 m (61.35 ft); wing area 65.85 m² (708.8 sq ft)
**Weights:** Empty 8,649 kg (19,068 lb); MTOW 13,765 kg (30,347 lb)
**Performance:** Maximum speed 537 km/h (334 mph) at 6,090 m (19,980 ft); operational ceiling 9,470 m (31,070 ft); range 2,800 km (1,740 miles) with 500 kg (1,102 lb) bombload
**Load:** One 20-mm cannon and four 12.7-mm machine guns, plus up to 1,080 kg (2,359 lb) of ordnance, including one heavyweight torpedo

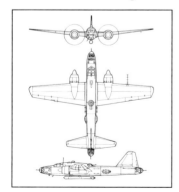

*Mitsubishi Ki-67-I Hiryu*

*Mitsubishi Ki-67-iB*

# DOUGLAS A-1 SKYRAIDER (U.S.A.)

*A-1B Skyraider*

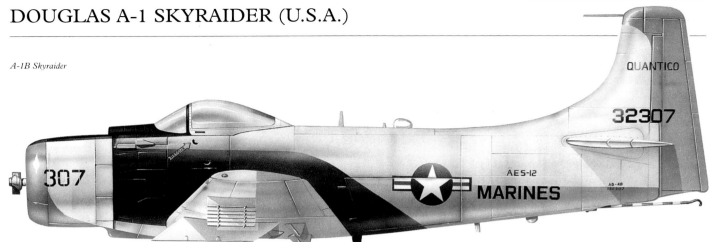

The massive single-seat Skyraider was designed as a carrierborne dive- and torpedo-bomber, and the first of 25 XBT2D-1 Destroyer II prototype and service test aircraft flew in March 1945. The capabilities of the new aircraft were so impressive that large-scale production was ordered and it proved an invaluable U.S. tool in the Korean and Vietnam Wars.

The type went through a number of major marks, the most significant being the 242 AD-1s with the 1864-kW (2,500-hp) R-3350-24W radial and an armament of two 20-mm cannon plus 3629 kg (8,000 lb) of disposable stores, the 156 improved AD-2s with greater fuel capacity and other modifications, the 125 AD-3s with a redesigned canopy and longer-stroke landing gear as well as other improvements, the 372 AD-4s with the 2014-kW (2,700-hp) R-3350-26WA and an autopilot, the 165 nuclear-capable AD-4Bs with four 20-mm cannon, the 212 AD-5 anti-submarine search and attack aircraft with a widened fuselage for a side-by-side crew of two, the 713 examples of the AD-6 improved version of the AD-4B with equipment for highly accurate low-level bombing, and the 72 examples of the AD-7 version of the AD-6 with the R-3350-26WB engine and strengthened structure.

From 1962 all surviving aircraft were redesignated in the A-1 sequence. The Skyraider's large fuselage and greater load-carrying capability also commended the type for adaptation to other roles, and these roles were generally indicated by a letter suffix to the final number of the designation; E indicated anti-submarine search with radar under the port wing, N three-seat night attack, Q two-seat electronic counter-measures, S anti-submarine attack in concert with an E type, and W three/four-seat airborne early warning with radar in an underfuselage radome. Total production was 3,180 aircraft up to 1957, and from 1962 the series was redesignated in the A-1 series.

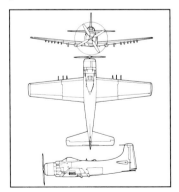

*Douglas A-1J Skyraider*

**DOUGLAS AD-1 SKYRAIDER**
**Role:** Naval carrierborne strike
**Crew/Accommodation:** One
**Power Plant:** One 2,500 hp Wright R-3350-24W air-cooled radial
**Dimensions:** Span 15.24 m (50.02 ft); length 12 m (39.35 ft); wing area 37.19 m² (400.3 sq ft)
**Weights:** Empty 4,749 kg (10,470 lb); MTOW 8,178 kg (18,030 lb)
**Performance:** Maximum speed 517 km/h (321 mph) at 5,580 m (18,300 ft); operational ceiling 7,925 m (26,000 ft); range 2,500 km (1,554 miles)
**Load:** Two 20 mm cannon, plus up to 2,722 kg (6,000 lb) of weapons

*A Douglas A-1H Skyraider with the markings of the South Vietnamese Air Force*

# ENGLISH ELECTRIC CANBERRA AND MARTIN B-57 (United Kingdom)

*Canberra B(I).Mk 6*

The Canberra was planned as a nuclear-capable medium bomber with turbojet engines, and as a high-altitude type it was designed round a large wing and a crew of two using a radar bombing system. It matured as a medium/high-altitude type with optical bomb aiming by a third crew member and first flew in May 1949. Canberra was the first jet bomber produced in Britain, the RAF's first jet bomber, and the first aircraft in history to cross the Atlantic twice in a single day (1952). Its great development potential ensured that the type enjoyed a long first-line

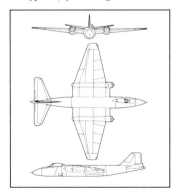

*Canberra PR.Mk 9*

career as well as diversification into other roles. The main bomber stream began with the Canberra B.Mk 2 powered by 2,948-kg (6,500-lb) Avon RA.3 Mk 101 turbojets, and then advanced to the B.Mk 6 with greater fuel capacity and 3,357-kg (7,400-lb) thrust Avon Mk 109s, the B.Mk 15 conversion of the B.Mk 6 with underwing hardpoints, the B.Mk 16 improved B.Mk 15, and the B.Mk 20 Australian-built B.Mk 6; there were also many export versions. The intruder/interdictor series began with the Canberra B(I).Mk 6 version of the B.Mk 6 with underwing bombs and a ventral cannon pack, and continued with the B(I).Mk 8 multi-role version; there were also several export versions. The reconnaissance models began with the Canberra

## ENGLISH ELECTRIC CANBERRA B.Mk 2
**Role:** Bomber reconnaissance
**Crew/Accommodation:** Two
**Power Plant:** Two 2,948 kgp (6,500 lb s.t.) Rolls-Royce Avon RA.3 Mk 101 turbojets
**Dimensions:** Span 19.49 m (63.96 ft); length 19.96 m (65.5 ft); wing area 89.2 m² (960 sq ft)
**Weights:** Empty 10,070 kg (22,200 lb); MTOW 20,865 kg (46,000 lb)
**Performance:** Maximum speed 917 km/h (570 mph) at 12,192 m (40,000 ft); operational ceiling 14,630 m (48,000 ft); range 4,281 km (2,660 miles)
**Load:** Up to 2,722 kg (6,000 lb) of ordnance all carried internally

PR.Mk 3 based on the B.Mk 2, and then moved through variants including the PR.Mk 7 equivalent of the B.Mk 6, and the PR.Mk 9 high-altitude model with increased span, extended centre-section chord, and 4,990-kg (11,000-lb) thrust Avon Mk 206s; there were also a few export models. Other streams included trainer, target tug and remotely controlled target drone models. The last surviving Canberras were mostly of reconnaissance and electronic warfare types, but not exclusively. The importance of the Canberra is also attested by the fact that it became the first non-U.S. type to be manufactured under licence in the U.S. after World War II. This variant was the Martin B-57, the first version of which was the B-57A with Wright J65-W-1 (licence-built Armstrong Siddeley Sapphire) turbojets.

The main production model was the B-57B, an extensively adapted night intruder with two seats in tandem and a fixed armament of four 20-mm cannon plus eight 12.7-mm (0.5-in) machine-guns as well as the standard bomb bay and underwing loads. Other variants were the B-57C dual-control version of the B-57B, and the B-57E target-tug version of the B-57B. The aircraft were also extensively converted as RB-57 photo-reconnaissance and EB-57 electronic warfare platforms, the most radical such version being the General Dynamics-produced RB-57F with span increased to 37.19 m (122 ft 0 in) for ultra-high flight with two 8,165-kg (18,000-lb) thrust Pratt & Whitney TF33-P-11 turbofans and, in underwing nacelles, two 1,497-kg (3,300-lb) thrust Pratt & Whitney J60-P-9 turbojets.

*This Argentine bomber is a English Electric Canberra B.Mk 62*

150

# TUPOLEV Tu-16 'BADGER' (U.S.S.R.)

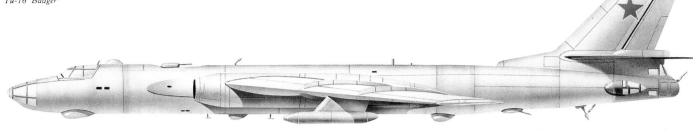

*Tu-16 'Badger'*

A great technical achievement in the fields of aerodynamics and structures by the Tupolev design bureau, the Tu-16 twin-jet intermediate-range strategic bomber first flew as the type 88 prototype in April 1952, with production at Kazan beginning in 1953 and later at Kuibyshev. In May 1954 nine bombers flew over Red Square and later that year the Tu-16KS missile carrier flew for the first time. By 1963, all 1,500 or thereabouts production aircraft had been delivered, although other versions followed by conversion of existing models.

The baseline 'Badger-A' bomber was originally equipped with free-fall weapons while the 'Badger-B' was developed as a launcher for anti-ship missiles, but later became a free-fall bomber. The 'Badger-C' was an anti-ship type carrying either one AS-2 'Kipper' under the fuselage or two AS-6 'Kingfish' missiles under the wings. The 'Badger-D' was an electronic and/or maritime reconnaissance platform while 'Badger-E' first appeared in 1955 as a photo-reconnaissance and electronic intelligence version. The 'Badger-F' was a conversion of 'Badger-A' for sea reconnaissance. The 'Badger-G' became a very important anti-ship and anti-radar missile carrier with two AS-5 'Kelt' or, in its 'Badger-G (Modified)' form with AS-6 'Kingfish' missiles under its wings. The 'Badger-H', 'J', 'K', and 'L' were all developed as air force or naval electronic warfare aircraft optimized for the escort and/or stand-off, locator jamming, revised locator jamming, and electronic intelligence/jamming roles respectively. Many of the older aircraft were finally converted into either of two types of in-flight refuelling tanker. By 1998, the Tu-16 was out of service in Russia. However, the same basic type is produced in China as the Xi'an H-6 bomber and anti-ship missile carrier, after receipt of a licence in 1957.

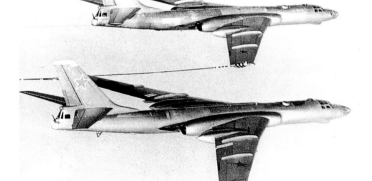

*Tupolev Tu-16 tanker and bomber*

**TUPOLEV Tu-16 'BADGER-G'**
**Role:** Missile-carrying bomber, reconnaissance, electronic warfare
**Crew/Accommodation:** Six to nine dependent on mission
**Power Plant:** Two 8,750-kgp (19,290-lb s.t.) Mikulin AM-3M turbojets
**Dimensions:** Span 32.93 m (108 ft); length 34.8 m (114.2 ft); wing area 164.65 m² (1,772 sq ft)
**Weights:** Empty 40,000 kg (88,185 lb); MTOW 77,000 kg (169,756 lb)
**Performance:** Maximum speed 941 km/h (585 mph) at 11,000 m (36,090 ft); operational ceiling 12,200 m (40,026 ft); radius 2,895 km (1,800 miles) unrefuelled with full warload
**Load:** Three 23-mm cannon, plus up to 9,000 kg (19,842 lb) of bombs

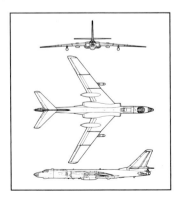

*Tupolev Tu-16 'Badger-A'*

# McDONNELL DOUGLAS A-4 SKYHAWK (U.S.A.)

*A-4S Super Skyhawk*

Nicknamed 'Heinemann's Hot Rod' after its designer, the Skyhawk was conceived as a private-venture successor to the AD Skyraider. At this time the U.S. Navy envisaged a turboprop-powered machine in the role, but Douglas produced its design to offer all the specified payload/range capability in an airframe that promised higher-than-specified performance and about half the planned maximum take-off weight. The concept was sufficiently attractive for the service to order two XA4D-1 prototypes, and the first of these flew in June 1954 as a low-wing delta monoplane with integral fuel tankage

and the 3,266-kg (7,200-lb) Wright J65-W-2 version of a British turbojet, the Armstrong Siddeley Sapphire. Production deliveries began in October 1956 and continued to February 1979 for a total of 2,960 aircraft.

The first version was the A4D-1 (A-4A from 1962), of which just 19 were delivered with the 3,493-kg (7,700-lb) thrust Wright J65-W-4 and an armament of two 20-mm cannon and 2,268 kg (5,000 lb) of disposable stores. The main successor

variants were the 542 A4D-2s (A-4Bs) with more power and inflight-refuelling capability, the 638 A4D-2Ns (A-4Cs) with terrain-following radar and more power, the 494 A4D-5s (A-4Es) with the 3,856-kg (8,500-lb) thrust Pratt & Whitney J52-P-6 turbojet and two additional hardpoints for a 3,719-kg (8,200-lb) disposable load, the 146 A-4Fs with a dorsal hump for more advanced electronics, the 90 examples of the A-4H based on the A-4E for Israel with 30-mm cannon and upgraded

electronics, the 162 A-4Ms with an enlarged dorsal hump and more power, and the 117 examples of the A-4N development of the A-4M for Israel. There were a number of TA-4 trainer models, and other suffixes were used to indicate aircraft built or rebuilt for export. There is currently a considerable boom in upgraded aircraft, some (such as Argentina's refurbished A-4AR Fightinghawks) only now going back into service.

*A McDonnell Douglas A-4M Skyhawk II of the VMA-324 squadron*

**McDONNELL DOUGLAS A-4E SKYHAWK**
**Role:** Naval carrierborne strike
**Crew/Accommodation:** One
**Power Plant:** One 3,856-kgp (8,500-lb s.t.) Pratt & Whitney J52-P-6A turbojet
**Dimensions:** Span 8.38 m (27.5 ft); length 12.23 m (40.125 ft); wing area 24.16 m² (260 sq ft)
**Weights:** Empty 4,469 kg (9,853 lb); MTOW 11,113 kg (24,500 lb)
**Performance:** Maximum speed 1,083 km/h (673 mph) at sea level; operational ceiling 11,460 m (37,600 ft); range 1,865 km (1,160 miles) with 1,451-kg (3,200- lb) bombload
**Load:** Two 20-mm cannon, plus up to 3,719 kg (8,200 lb) of weapons

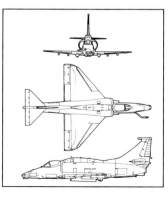

*A-4N Skyhawk II*

# SUKHOI Su-7 'FITTER' Family (U.S.S.R.)

*Su-7B 'Fitter'*

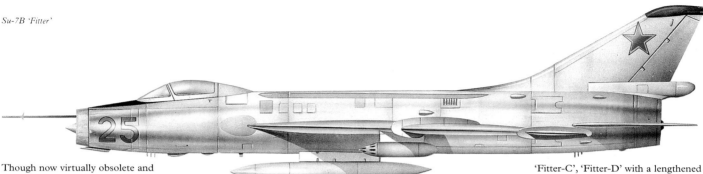

Though now virtually obsolete and no longer in Russian service, in its time the Su-7 had a superb reputation as a ground-attack fighter able to absorb practically any amount of combat damage yet still deliver its ordnance with accuracy. On the other side of the coin, however, the type was given an engine so prodigiously thirsty that at least two hardpoints were used for drop tanks rather than ordnance.

Various S-1 and S-2 prototypes flew in the mid-1950s, the latter introducing a slab tailplane, and during 1958 the Su-7 was ordered with the 9,000-kg (19,841-lb) thrust Lyulka AL-7F turbojet as the service version of the S-22 pre-production derivative of the S-2 with an area-ruled fuselage. The type was developed in steadily improved Su-7 variants, known to NATO by the reporting name 'Fitter-A', with greater power, soft-field capability and six rather than four hardpoints. This effective yet short-ranged type was then transformed into the far more potent Su-17 with variable-geometry outer wing panels. The Su-71G prototype of 1966 confirmed that field performance and range were markedly improved. With the 10,000-kg (22,046-lb) AL7F-1 turbojet in early aircraft and the 11,200-kg (24,691-lb) thrust AL-21F-3/F-3A in later aircraft, the variable-geometry type was extensively built up to 1990 for Soviet, Warsaw Pact and allied use.

The main Soviet and Warsaw Pact models were delivered as Su-17 variants known to NATO as the 'Fitter-C', 'Fitter-D' with a lengthened nose, 'Fitter-H' with a new weapon system, and 'Fitter-K' as the most advanced version and having ten weapon pylons. The main export variant was the Su-20 with inferior electronics to the Soviet 'Fitter-C', while the Su-22 became a Third-World export model with the 11,500-kg (25,353-lb) Tumansky R-29BS-300 or later AL-21F3 turbojet and inferior electronics. The final models in Russian service were for reconnaissance, but many remain flying with other air forces.

**SUKHOI Su-7BMK 'FITTER A'**
**Role:** Strike-fighter
**Crew/Accommodation:** One
**Power Plant:** One 9,600 kgp (21,164 lb s.t.) Lyulka AL-7F-1 turbojet with reheat
**Dimensions:** Span 8.77 m (28.77 ft); length 16.8 m (55.12 ft); wing area 34.5 m² (371.4 sq ft)
**Weights:** Empty 8,616 kg (18,995 lb); MTOW 13,500 kg (29,762 lb)
**Performance:** Maximum speed 1,160 km/h (720 mph) Mach 0.95 at 305 m (1,000 ft); operational ceiling 13,000+ m (42,650 ft); radius 460 km (285 miles) with 1,500 kg (3,307 lb) warload
**Load:** Two 3 mm cannon, plus up to 2,500 kg (5,512 lb) of weapons/fuel carried externally

*Sukhoi Su-7B 'Fitter-A'*

*Sukhoi Su-7 'Fitter'*

# NORTH AMERICAN A-5 VIGILANTE (U.S.A.)

*RA-5C Vigilante*

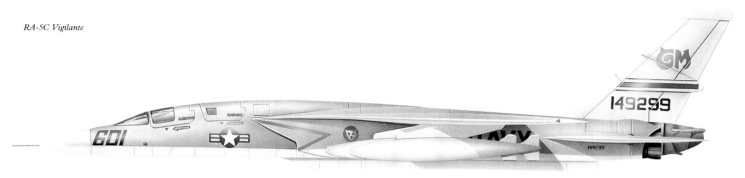

The Vigilante was designed as a Mach 2 all-weather strike aircraft to provide the U.S. Navy with a carrierborne type able to deliver strategic nuclear weapons, and the design known as the North American General Purpose Attack Weapon was ordered in the form of two YA3J-1 prototypes. The first of these flew in August 1958 with two 7326-kg (16,150-lb) thrust General Electric J79-GE-2

afterburning turbojets aspirated via the first variable-geometry inlets fitted on any operational warplane. The overall design was of great sophistication, and included wing spoilers for roll control in conjunction with differentially operating slab tailplane halves that worked in concert for pitch control. Considerable problems were caused by the design's weapon bay, which was a longitudinal tunnel that contained fuel cells as well as the nuclear weapon in a package that was ejected to the rear as the Vigilante flew

over the target.

The A3J-1 began to enter service in June 1961 with the 7711-kg (17,000-lb) thrust J79-GE-8, and just over a year later the type was redesignated A-5A. These 57 aircraft were followed by the A-5B long-range version with additional fuel in a large dorsal hump, wider-span flaps, blown leading-edge flaps, and four underwing hardpoints. Only six of this variant were built as a change in the U.S. Navy's strategic

nuclear role led to the Vigilante's adaptation for the reconnaissance role with additional tankage and cameras in the weapon bay and side-looking airborne radar in a ventral canoe fairing. Production of this RA-5C model totalled 55 with 8101-kg (17,860-lb) thrust J79-GE-10 engines and revised inlets, in addition, extra capability was provided by 59 conversions (53 A-5As and the six A-5Bs).

**NORTH AMERICAN A-5A VIGILANTE**
**Role:** Naval carrierborne nuclear bomber
**Crew/Accommodation:** Two
**Power Plant:** Two 7,324 kgp (16,150 lb s.t.) General Electric J79-GE-2/4/8 turbojets with reheat
**Dimensions:** Span 16.15 m (53 ft); length 23.11 m (75.83 ft); wing area 71.45 m² (769 sq ft)
**Weights:** Empty 17,009 kg (37,498 lb); MTOW 36.287 kg (80,000 lb)
**Performance:** Maximum speed 2,229 km/h (1,203 knots) Mach 2.1 at 12.192 m (40,000 ft); operational ceiling 14,326 m (47,000 ft); range 3,862 km (2,084 naut. miles) with nuclear weapons
**Load:** One multi-megaton warhead class nuclear weapon

*RA-5C Vigilante*

*The North American RA-5C Vigilante*

# BLACKBURN BUCCANEER (United Kingdom)

*Buccaneer S.Mk 2B*

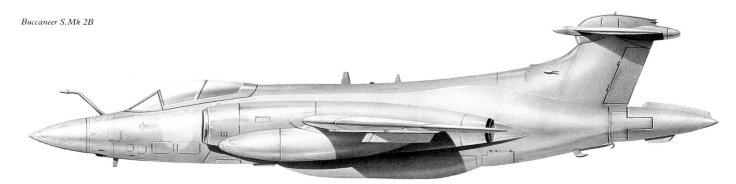

This superb aircraft was planned as a B-103 to meet the NA.39 requirement for a carrierborne low-level transonic strike warplane, and was designed with a boundary layer control system for the wings and tailplane, an area-ruled fuselage, a sizeable weapon bay with a rotary door carrying the main weapons, and a vertically split tail cone that could be opened into larger-area air brakes. The prototype was the first of 20 pre-production aircraft, and first flew in April 1958 with two 3,175-kg (7,000-lb) thrust de Havilland Gyron Junior DGJ. 1 turbojets.

Forty Buccaneer S.Mk 1s were ordered with the 3,221-kg (7,100-lb) thrust Gyron Junior 101, and these began to enter service in July 1962. To overcome the S.Mk 1's lack of power, the 84 Buccaneer S.Mk 2s were powered by the 5,105-kg (11,200-lb) thrust Rolls-Royce Spey Mk 101 turbofan, and with this engine displayed an all-round improvement in performance. The Royal Navy received its first aircraft in October 1965. The type had greater range than the S.Mk 1, but was also equipped for inflight refuelling. The similar Buccaneer S.Mk 50 was procured by South Africa, this model also having a 3,629-kg (8,000-lb) thrust Bristol Siddeley Stentor rocket motor for improved 'hot and high' take-off.

With the demise of the Navy's large carriers, some 70 S.Mk 2s were reallocated to the RAF from 1969 Buccaneer S.Mk 2As. Updated aircraft with provision for the Martel ASM became Buccaneer S.Mk 2Bs, and another 43 new aircraft were ordered to this standard. Further upgrades were made to RAF aircraft to extend their service career.

**BLACKBURN BUCCANEER S.Mk 2**
**Role:** Low-level strike
**Crew/Accommodation:** Two
**Power Plant:** Two 5,035 kgp (11,100 lb s.t.) Rolls-Royce Spey Mk 101 turbofans
**Dimensions:** Span 13.41 m (44 ft); length 19.33 m (63.42 ft); wing area 47.82 m² (514.7 sq ft)
**Weights:** Empty 13,517 kg (29,800 lb); MTOW 28,123 kg (62,000 lb)
**Performance:** Maximum speed 1,040 km/h (561 knots) Mach 0.85 at 76 m (250 ft); operational ceiling 12,192 m (40,000+ ft); radius 1,738 km (938 naut. miles) with full warload
**Load:** Up to 3,175 kg (7,000 lb) of ordnance, including up to 1,815 kg (4,000 lb) internally, the remainder typically Martel or Sea Eagle anti-ship missiles, being carried externally under the wings

*Buccaneer S.Mk 2B*

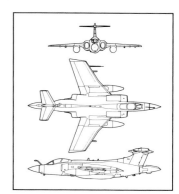

*Buccaneer S.Mk 2B*

# DASSAULT ETENDARD Family (France)

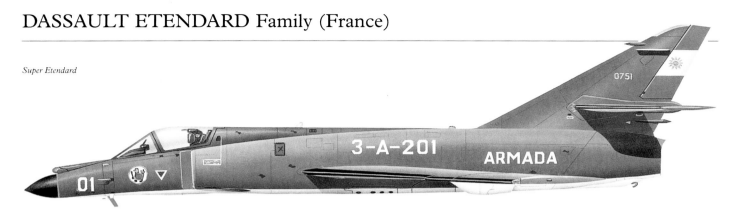

*Super Etendard*

By the middle of the 1950s the growing complexity of modern warplanes was beginning to dictate types of such size, weight, cost and lengthy gestation that considerable thought was given to lightweight attack fighters that could be developed comparatively quickly and cheaply for use on small airfields or even semi-prepared airstrips that would remove the need to build the large and costly air bases that were becoming increasingly vulnerable.

NATO formulated the requirement, and one of several contenders was the Etendard (Standard). Three prototypes were built, one of them with company funding, and the first of these flew in July 1956 as the Etendard II with two 1,100-kg (2,425-lb) thrust Turboméca Gabizo turbojets; the second prototypes had the 2,200-kg (4,850-lb) thrust Bristol Siddeley Orpheus BOr. 3 turbojet. The competition was won by the Fiat G91, but the company's own Etendard IV prototype, the Etendard IVM, larger than its half-brothers and designed to accommodate more

powerful engines, first flew in July 1956 and soon attracted naval interest as a carrierborne attack fighter.

One prototype and six pre-production aircraft validated revisions such as folding wingtips, naval equipment, a large rudder, beefed-up landing gear, and the 4,400-kg (9,700-lb) thrust SNECMA Atar 8B turbojet. Production totalled 90 aircraft, including 21 of the Etendard IVP reconnaissance/tanker variant. From 1970 Dassault revised the basic type as the Super Etendard, and the

first of two prototype conversions flew in October 1974. This model was given aerodynamic and structural revisions for transonic performance, and a modern nav/attack system including Agave multi-role radar for targeting of the AM.39 Exocet anti-ship missile. Seventy Super Etendards were delivered to the French navy from 1978, plus 12 to Argentina, with many French aircraft being modified to have the ability to carry ASMP nuclear stand-off missiles.

*Dassault Super Etendard*

**DASSAULT SUPER ETENDARD**
**Role:** Carrierborne strike fighter
**Crew/Accommodation:** One
**Power Plant:** One 5,000-kgp (11,023-lb s.t.) SNECMA Atar 8K50 turbojet with reheat
**Dimensions:** Span 9.60 m (31.50 ft); length 14.31 m (46.90 ft); wing area 28.40 m² (307.00 sq ft)
**Weights:** Empty 6,300 kg (14,330 lb); MTOW 12,000 kg (26,455 lb)
**Performance:** Maximum speed 1,200 km/h (746 mph) at sea level; operational ceiling 13,700 m (45,000 ft); radius of action 880 km (547 miles) with one Exocet
**Load:** Two 30-mm cannon, plus up to 2,087 kg (4,600 lb) of externally carried weapons/missiles/fuel

*Dassault Super Etendard strike fighter*

*Dassault Super Etendards with two Etendard IVPs nearest the camera (Dassault)*

# GRUMMAN A-6 INTRUDER (U.S.A.)

*A-6E Intruder*

After the Korean War, the U.S. Navy wanted a jet-powered attacker able to undertake the pinpoint delivery of large warloads over long ranges and under all weather conditions. The resulting specification attracted 11 design submissions from eight companies, and at the very end of 1957 the G-128 design was selected for development as the A2F. Eight

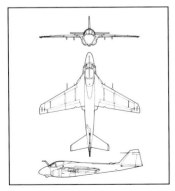

*Grumman A-6E/TRAM Intruder*

YA2F-1 development aircraft were ordered, and the first of these flew in April 1960 with two 3,856-kg (8,500-lb) thrust Pratt & Whitney J52-P-6 turbojets. In 1962 the type was designated A-6, and in February 1963 the first of 482 A-6A production aircraft were delivered with 4,218-kg (9,300-lb) thrust J52-P-8A/B engines, a larger rudder, and the world's first digital nav/attack system. The Intruder had high maintenance requirements, but proved itself a superb attack platform during the Vietnam War.

## GRUMMAN A-6E/TRAM INTRUDER
**Role:** Naval carrierborne all-weather heavy strike (bomber)
**Crew/Accommodation:** Two
**Power Plant:** Two 4,218-kgp (9,300-lb s.t.) Pratt & Whitney J52-P-8B turbojets
**Dimensions:** Span 16.15 m (53 ft); length 16.69 m (54.75 ft); wing area 49.15 m² (529 sq ft)
**Weights:** Empty 12,525 kg (27,613 lb); MTOW 26,580 kg (58,600 lb) for carrier use
**Performance:** Maximum speed 1,036 km/h (644 mph) Mach 0.85 at sea level; operational ceiling 13,600 m (44,600 ft); range 1,738 km (1,080 miles) with full load
**Load:** Up to 8,165 kg (18,000 lb) of weapons – all externally carried

The next three models were conversions, and comprised 19 A-6B day interdictors with simplified avionics and capability for the AGM-78 Standard anti-radar missile, 12 A-6C night attack aircraft with forward-looking infra-red and low-light-level TV sensors in an underfuselage turret, and 58 KA-6D 'buddy' refuelling tankers with a hose and drogue unit in the rear fuselage. This paved the way for the definitive A-6E attack model with J52-P-8B or -408 engines and

an improved nav/attack system based on solid-state electronics for greater reliability and reduced servicing requirements. Large numbers of A-6As were converted to this standard, with 205 A-6Es and A-6E/TRAM also newly built before all production ended in February 1992; TRAM aircraft featured the Target Recognition and Attack Multisensor package in a small undernose turret. The Intruder has now been withdrawn from service.

*A Grumman A-6A Intruder*

# BRITISH AIRCRAFT CORPORATION TSR-2 (United Kingdom)

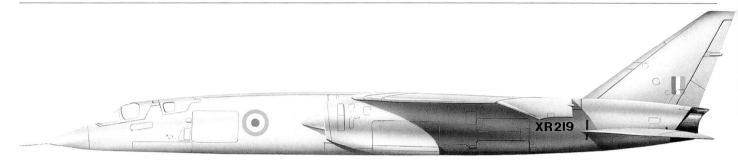

This is one of history's great 'aircraft that might have been'. The TSR-2 resulted from attempts, started as early as the 1950s, to produce a successor to the English Electric Canberra for long-range interdiction and reconnaissance. There were considerable difficulties in defining the type of aircraft required, and in envisaging the appropriate technology. Eventually it was announced in 1959 that the concept offered by the partnership of English Electric and Vickers-Armstrong was

to be developed as the TSR-2 weapons system providing the capability for supersonic penetration of enemy airspace at very low level for the accurate delivery of conventional and/or nuclear weapons. In configuration the TSR-2 was a high-wing monoplane with tandem seating for the crew of two, highly swept wings with downturned tips and wide-span blown trailing-edge flaps to provide STOL performance, and a swept tail unit, the surfaces of which provided

control in all three planes. The onboard electronic suite included an air-data system, inertial navigation system, forward-looking radar, and side-looking radar the data of which were integrated via an advanced computer to provide terrain-following capability and, on the pilot's head-up display and navigator's head-down displays, navigation cues and information relevant to weapon arming and release.

The result was an advanced but potentially formidable warplane that first flew in September 1964. As was

only to be expected in so complex a machine, there were a number of problems. These were in the process of being solved when rising costs and political antipathy persuaded the Labour government to cancel the project in April 1965. Only the first of four completed aircraft had flown, and this had accumulated only 13 hours 14 minutes of flying time during 24 flights.

**BRITISH AIRCRAFT CORPORATION TSR-2**
**Role:** Long range, low-level strike and reconnaissance
**Crew/Accommodation:** Two
**Power Plant:** Two 13,800 kgp (30,600 lb s.t) Bristol-Siddeley Olympus B.01.22R turbojets with reheat
**Dimensions:** Span 11.32 m (37.14 ft) length 27.14 m (89.04 ft); wing area 65.30 m² (702.90 sq ft)
**Weights:** Empty 24,834 kg (54,750 lb) MTOW 46,357 kg (102,200 lb)
**Performance:** Maximum speed 1,344+ km/h (725+ knots) Mach 1.1+ at sea level; operational ceiling 17,374+ m (57,000+ ft): radius 1,853 km (1,000 naut. miles)
**Load:** Up to 4,536 kg (10,000 lb) of weaponry/fuel

*British Aircraft Corporation TSR-2*

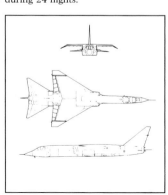

*British Aircraft Corporation TSR-2*

159

*Dassault Mirage IVPs taking fuel from a C-135FR tanker (SIRPA 'AIR')*

# DASSAULT MIRAGE IV (FRANCE)

*Mirage IVA*

Requiring a supersonic delivery platform for the atomic bomb that was then the French nuclear deterrent weapon, the French air force in 1954 issued a requirement for a bomber offering long-range as well as high speed. Dassault headed a consortium that looked first at the development of the Sud-Ouest S.O. 4050 Vautour but from 1956 turned its attentions to the potential of an earlier aborted Dassault twin-engined night fighter design. This resulted in the design of the Mirage

IV of what was in essence a scaled-up Mirage III with two engines and provision for a 60-kiloton AN22 free-fall bomb semi-recessed under the fuselage.

The prototype first flew in June 1959 on the power of two 6,000-kg (13,228-lb) thrust SNECMA Atar 9 turbojets, and soon demonstrated its ability to maintain Mach 2 speed at high altitude. There followed three pre-production aircraft with slightly larger overall dimensions and two 6,400-kg (14,110-lb) thrust Atar 9C

turbojets. The first of these flew in October 1961, and was more representative of the Mirage IVA production model with a circular radome under the fuselage for the antenna of the bombing radar. The last of these three aircraft was fully representative in its Atar 9K engines, inflight refuelling probe and definitive nav/attack system. Mirage IVA production totalled 62 aircraft. Twelve aircraft were later converted as Mirage IVR strategic reconnaissance platforms with the CT52 mission package in the erstwhile bomb station, and from 1983 another 18 aircraft were converted as Mirage IVP missile

carriers (plus one more later because of attrition loss). These were given a new nav/attack system and upgraded electronic defences, and were designed for low-level penetration of enemy airspace as the launchers for the ASMP nuclear-tipped stand-off missile. The strategic/tactical bomber role was finally ended in 1996, leaving only a single squadron of reconnaissance aircraft.

*The fourth Dassault Mirage IVA prototype*

**DASSAULT MIRAGE IVA**
**Role:** Supersonic strategic bomber
**Crew/Accommodation:** Two
**Power Plant:** Two 7,000 kgp (15,432 lb s.t.) SNECMA Atar 09K turbojets with reheat
**Dimensions:** Span 11.85 m (38.88 ft); length 23.50 m (77.08 ft); wing area 78.00 m² (839.58 sq ft)
**Weights:** Empty 14,500 kg (31,965 lb); MTOW 31,600 kg (69,665 lb)
**Performance:** Maximum speed 2,124 km/h (1,146 knots) Mach 2.2 at 11,000 m (36,088 ft); operational ceiling 20,000 m (65,616 ft); radius 1,600+ km (994+ miles) unrefuelled
**Load:** One megaton range nuclear bomb carried semi-recessed beneath fuselage

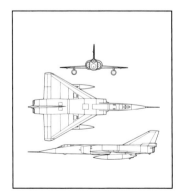

*Dassault Mirage IVA*

# GENERAL DYNAMICS F-111 'Aardvark' (U.S.A.)

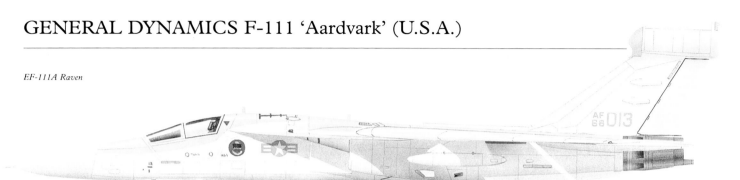

*EF-111A Raven*

The F-111 was the world's first operational 'swing-wing' aircraft and remained in service as the U.S. Air Force's most potent all-weather long-range interdiction platform until July 1997, when it was belatedly named Aardvark. However, it remained operational with the Australian Air Force. The type originated from a 1960 requirement for a strike platform with the variable-geometry wings, the positions of which at minimum sweep would provide semi-STOL field performance at very high weights, at intermediate sweep long

cruising range at high subsonic speed, and at maximum sweep very high dash performance. So versatile a tactical warplane suggested to the Department of Defense's civilian leadership the economic advantages of cheaper development and production costs if this land-based type could also be used as a basis for a new fleet defence fighter. Despite technical objections, the Tactical Fighter Experimental requirement was drawn up and orders placed for 23 pre-production aircraft (18 F-111As and five F-111Bs). The first of these flew in December 1964, but weight and performance problems led to the July 1968 cancellation of the F111B. The F111A also had problems before and after its March

1968 operational service debut in Vietnam, but despite an indifferent powerplant it matured into an exceptional combat aircraft. The most important tactical models were 158 F-111As with 8,391-kg (18,500-lb) thrust TF30-P-3 engines, 24 F-111Cs for Australia with the FB-111A's longer-span wings, 96 F-111Ds with 8,890-kg (19,600-lb) thrust TF30-P-9s, 94 F-111Es with 8,890-kg (19,600-lb) thrust TF30-P-103s, and 106 F-111Fs with 11,385-kg (25,100-lb) thrust TF30-P-111s and improved electronics; 42 of the F-111As were

modified into EF-111A Raven electronic platforms for service from 1981; Ravens were retired in 1998. There is also a strategic model in the form of 76 FB-111As with wings of 2.13 m (7 ft 0 in) greater span, two extra wing hardpoints, 9,185-kg (20,150-lb) thrust TF30-P-7 engines, and revised electronics; many of these were later converted into F-111G tactical aircraft for use in the European theatre by the USAF as conventionally armed aircraft (now retired), with some also going to the RAAF.

### GENERAL DYNAMICS F-111F
**Role:** Long-range, low-level variable-geometry strike
**Crew/Accommodation:** Two
**Power Plant:** Two 11,385-kgp (25,100-lb s.t.) Pratt & Whitney TF30-P-111 turbofans with reheat
**Dimensions:** Span 19.2 m (63.00 ft), swept 9.73 m (31.95 ft); length 22.4 m (73.5 ft); wing area 48.77 m² (525 sq ft)
**Weights:** Empty 21,700 kg (47,840 lb); MTOW 45,360 kg (100,000 lb)
**Performance:** Maximum speed Mach 2.5 at altitude or 1,471 km/h (914 mph) Mach 1.2 at sea level; operational ceiling 17,650 m (57,900 ft); range over 4,667 km (2,900 miles)
**Load:** One 22-mm multi-barrel cannon, plus up to 11,340 kg (25,000 lb) of ordnance/fuel

*General Dynamics F-111*

*A General Dynamics F-111 in flight with its wings extended*

# VOUGHT A-7 CORSAIR II (U.S.A.)

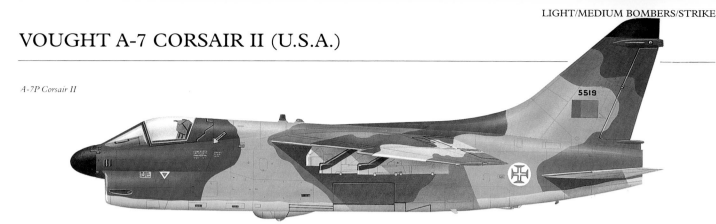

*A-7P Corsair II*

The A-7 was developed with great speed on the aerodynamic basis of the F-8 Crusader to provide the U.S. Navy with a medium-weight replacement for the light-weight Douglas A-4 Skyhawk in the carrierborne attack role, and in March 1964 the navy ordered three YA-7A prototypes. The first of these flew in September 1965 with the 5148-kg (11,350-lb) thrust Pratt & Whitney

TF30-P-6 non-afterburning turbofan, and the flight test programme moved ahead with great speed. This allowed the Corsair II to enter service during February 1967 in the form of the A-7A with the same engine as the YA-7A. Production totalled 199 aircraft of this initial model, and was followed by 196 examples of the A-7B with the 5534-kg (12,200-lb) thrust TF30-P-8 that was later upgraded to -408

standard, and by 67 examples of the A-7C with the 6078-kg (13,400-lb) thrust TF309-P-408 and the armament/avionics suite of the later A-7E variant.

In December 1965 the U.S. Air Force decided to adopt a version with a different engine, the Rolls-Royce Spey turbofan in its licence-built form as the Allison TF41. The USAF series was now named Corsair II, and the first model was the A-7D, of which 459 were built with the 6577-kg (14,500-lb) thrust TF41-A-1, a 20-mm six-barrel rotary cannon in place of the Corsair II's two 20-mm single-barrel cannon, a much improved nav/attack package and, as a retrofit,

manoeuvring flaps and the 'Pave Penny' laser tracker. This model was mirrored by the Navy's A-7E, of which 551 were built with the 6804-kg (15,000-lb) thrust TF41-A-2 and, as a retrofit, a forward-looking infra-red sensor. There have been some two-seat versions and limited exports, but nothing came of the A-7 Plus radical development that was evaluated as the YA-7F with advanced electronics and the combination of more power and a revised airframe for supersonic performance.

*A Vought A-7E Corsair II*

**VOUGHT A-7E CORSAIR II**
**Role:** Naval carrierborne strike
**Crew/Accommodation:** One
**Power Plant:** One 6,804 kgp (15,000 lb s.t.) Allison/Rolls-Royce TF41-A-1 turbofan
**Dimensions:** Span 11.8 m (38.75 ft); length 14.06 m (46.13 ft); wing area 34.83 m² (375 sq ft)
**Weights:** Empty 8,592 kg (18,942 lb); MTOW 19,051 kg (42,000 lb)
**Performance:** Maximum speed 1,060 km/h (572 knots) at sea level; operational ceiling 13,106 m (43,000 ft); range 908 km (489 naut. miles) with 2,722 kg (6,000 lb) bombload
**Load:** One 6-barrel 20 mm cannon, plus up to 6,804 kg (15,000 lb) of weapons

*Vought A-7E Corsair II*

# BRITISH AEROSPACE HARRIER Family (United Kingdom)

*Harrier GR.Mk 3*

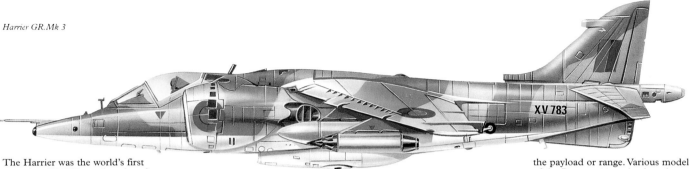

XV 783

The Harrier was the world's first operational VTOL combat aircraft, and at its core is the remarkable Rolls-Royce (Bristol Siddeley) Pegasus vectored-thrust turbofan. The type was pioneered in the form of six P. 1127 prototypes. The first of these made its initial hovering flights, in tethered mode, during October 1960, and the first transition flights between direct-thrust hovering and wingborne forward flight followed during September 1961. Such was the potential of this experimental type that nine Kestrel F(GA).Mk 1

evaluation aircraft were built for a combined British, U.S. and West German trials squadron.

The Harrier became the operational version, and the main types were the Harrier GR.Mk 1 with the 8,618-kg (19,000-lb) thrust Pegasus Mk 101, the GR.Mk 1A with the 9,072-kg (20,000-lb) thrust Pegasus Mk 102, and the GR.Mk 3 with the 9,752-kg (21,000-lb) thrust Pegasus Mk 103 and revised nose accommodating a laser ranger and marked-target seeker. Combat-capable two-seat trainers were also

built. The U.S. Marine Corps used the Harrier as the AV-8A single-seater (of which many were upgraded to AV-8C standard) and TAV-8A two-seater examples were exported to Spain with the local name Matador.

A much improved variant of Harrier was developed by McDonnell Douglas and BAe as the Harrier II, first flown in 1981 and featuring a larger wing of composite construction with leading-edge root extensions, other aerodynamic improvements, better avionics and more engine power, allowing twice

the payload or range. Various models of the Pegasus 11 engine have been fitted, the most powerful being the 10,795-kg (23,800-lb) thrust Pegasus 11-61 in late U.S. Marine Corps aircraft (designated F402-RR-408A), as also used in Spanish Matador IIs and Italian trainers.

U.S. Marine Corps Harrier IIs are designated AV-8B, while the current RAF version is the GR.Mk 7, upgraded from GR. Mk 5/5As to permit night attack. The companies have also developed the Harrier II Plus with APG-65 radar for expanded roles. Naval versions of Harrier became Sea Harrier, now in its latest F/A Mk 2 form for the Royal Navy.

**BRITISH AEROSPACE HARRIER GR. Mk 7**
**Role:** Close air support and interdiction
**Crew/Accommodation:** One
**Power Plant:** One 9,775-kgp (21,550-lb s.t.) Rolls-Royce Pegasus 11 Mk 105 vectored-thrust turbofan
**Dimensions:** Span 9.25 m (30.33 ft); length 14.53 m (47.66 ft); wing area 21.37 m² (230 sq ft)
**Weights:** Empty 6,831–7,123 kg (15,060–15,705 lb); MTOW 14,515 kg (32,000 lb)
**Performance:** Maximum speed Mach 0.98; radius of action 1,111 km (691 miles) with two 1,000-lb bombs, three BL 755s and two drop tanks
**Load:** Two 25-mm externally mounted cannon, plus up to 4,900 kg (10,800 lb) of ordnance/fuel

*Harrier GR.Mk 3*

*Harrier GR.Mk 7*

# SEPECAT JAGUAR (France/United Kingdom)

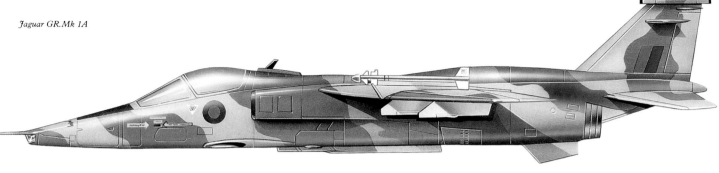

*Jaguar GR.Mk 1A*

In the early 1960s, the British and French air forces each showed interest in a dual-role supersonic warplane able to function as a tandem-seat operational trainer and single-seat attack aircraft. The similarity of the two requirements suggested a collaborative design, development and production programme, and in May 1965 the British and French governments signed an agreement for such a programme. Several British and French designs were studied before the Breguet Br.121 concept was selected as the basis for the new warplane, the development of which

was undertaken by the Société Européenne de Production de l'Avion Ecole de Combat at d'Appui Tactique (SEPECAT) formed by the British Aircraft Corporation and Breguet. An equivalent engine grouping combined Rolls-Royce and Turboméca for the selected Adour afterburning turbofan.

The Jaguar first flew in September 1968 as a conventional monoplane with swept flying surfaces and retractable tricycle landing gear, a shoulder-set wing being selected as this provided good ground clearance for the wide assortment of disposable stores carried on four underwing

hardpoints in addition to a centreline hardpoint under the fuselage.

Such were the capabilities of the aircraft that major production was initiated, with variants as the Jaguar A and S single-seat attack aircraft (160 and 165 aircraft respectively for the French and British air forces, of which the latter has considerably upgraded its aircraft with greater power and a more advanced nav/attack system, and in GR. Mk 3 form) plus Jaguar E and Jaguar B trainers (40 and 38 aircraft respectively for the French and

British air forces). There has also been the Jaguar International for the export market, with overwing hardpoints for air-to-air missiles as standard, uprated engines and, in Indian aircraft, an improved nav/attack system including radar in some aircraft. Customers were Ecuador, Nigeria, Oman and India, plus others built in India by HAL as Shamshers (Indian total of 131 aircraft).

*A SEPECAT Jaguar GR.Mk 1 of the RAF's No. 6 Squadron*

**SEPECAT JAGUAR INTERNATIONAL**
**Role:** Low-level strike fighter and maritime strike
**Crew/Accommodation:** One
**Power Plant:** Two 3,811-kgp (8,400-lb s.t.) Rolls-Royce/Turboméca Adour Mk 811 turbofans with reheat
**Dimensions:** Span 8.69 m (28.5 ft); length 15.52 m (50.92 ft) as single-seater, without probe; wing area 24 m² (258.33 sq ft)
**Weights:** Empty 7,000 kg (15,432 lb); MTOW 15,700 kg (34,613 lb)
**Performance:** Maximum speed 1,350 km/h (839 mph) Mach 1.1 at sea level; radius of action 852 km (529 miles) with 3,629 kg (8,000 lb) warload
**Load:** Two 30-mm cannon, plus up to 4,536 kg (10,000 lb) of weapons, including bombs, rockets or air-to-surface missiles, plus two short-range air-to-air missiles

*SEPECAT Jaguar GR.Mk 1A*

# TUPOLEV Tu-22M 'BACKFIRE' (U.S.S.R.)

*Tu-22M 'Backfire'*

Known to NATO as the 'Backfire', the Tu-22M is the world's only modern medium bomber, and was conceived to make nuclear or conventional strikes against targets in Western Europe and China, plus attack aircraft carriers and other large ships in a maritime role. It was specified to require a 2,000 km/h dash speed and Mach 0.9 low-level penetration speed while armed with

AS-4 'Kitchen' missiles. It was to be a supersonic 'swing-wing' successor to the Tu-16 'Badger' via the interim supersonic Tu-22 'Blinder'.

The new bomber first flew in August 1969 and 'Backfire-A' pre-series aircraft appeared from 1971. Tu-22M2 'Backfire-B' initial large-scale production aircraft joined the Soviet air force from 1975, fitted with new avionics and two cannon

in the tail, but most importantly offering a range of 2,753 nautical miles and speed of 972 knots.

The Tu-22M3 'Backfire-C' entered service in 1983 and introduced uprated NK-25 engines, modified forward fuselage with larger wedge air inlets and other improvements, making it over twice as combat-capable as the Tu-22M2. Since 1992, M3s have been further

upgraded to M5s, with changes including those to the radar and missiles carried. Tu-22MP and Tu-22MR are electronic warfare and reconnaissance versions respectively.

Tu-22 operators are the Russian air force and navy plus Ukraine.

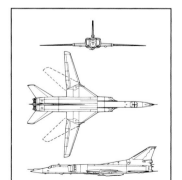

*Tupolev Tu-22M 'Backfire-C'*

**TUPOLEV Tu-22M 'BACKFIRE-C'**
**Role:** Bomber/reconnaissance with variable-geometry wing
**Crew/Accommodation:** Four
**Power Plant:** Two 25,000-kgp (55,115 s.t.) Samara NK-25 turbofans with reheat
**Dimensions:** Span 34.28 m (112.5 ft), swept 23.3 m (76.4 ft); length 42.46 m (139.33 ft); wing area 183.58 m² (1,976 sq ft)
**Weights:** MTOW 124,000 kg (273,373 lb) without JATO rockets
**Performance:** Maximum speed 2,000 km/h (1,243 mph) Mach 1.8 at high altitude; operational ceiling 14,000 m (45,925 ft); radius of action 2,200 km (1,367 miles) with one 'Kitchen' missile and unrefuelled
**Load:** two 23-mm cannon, plus 24,000 kg (52,910 lb) of weapons, including three AS-4 'Kitchen' missiles or a mix with AS-16 'Kick-back' short-range missiles on a rotary launcher, nuclear or conventional bombs, mines, etc.

*Tupolev Tu-22M 'Backfire-B'*

# YAKOVLEV Yak-38 'FORGER' (U.S.S.R.)

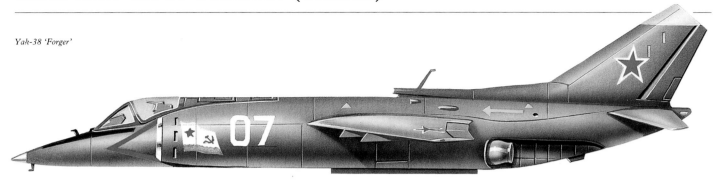

*Yak-38 'Forger'*

The Yak-38 (or Yak-36M for prototype) was the first-ever and so far only Soviet operational vertical take-off (VSTOL) combat aeroplane, of which 231 were built for the navy, but was withdrawn from service in the early 1990s. Supersonic replacements to be used as carrierborne interceptors, the Yakovlev Yak-41 and Yak-43 (the former known to NATO as

'Freestyle' and first flown in 1987) were subsequently abandoned before reaching service status.

The 'Forger' prototype first flew in January 1971, with the thrust-vectoring turbojet in the rear fuselage complemented by two small liftjets in the forward fuselage and mounted almost vertically to exhaust downward. A fully automatic control system was employed during take-off/landing, to ensure correct use of engines and jet reaction

nozzles/aerodynamic controls used in association with devices on board ship. Subsequently, short take-offs became more common than vertical, using similar methods of control.

The 'Forger-A' was a single-seat type designed principally to provide Soviet naval forces with experience in the operation of such aircraft. The type is therefore limited in terms of performance, warload and electronics, but still provided Soviet aircraft

carriers/cruiser carriers with useful interception and attack capabilities in areas too distant for the involvement of land-based air defences. The original production 'Forger-A' had less powerful liftjets than the improved Yak-38M 'Forger-A' of 1984 onwards service. The Yak-38UV was known to NATO as 'Forger-B' and was the tandem two-seat conversion trainer variant with the fuselage lengthened to accommodate the second cockpit.

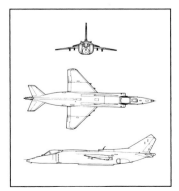

*Yak-38 'Forger-A'*

**YAKOVLEV Yak-38M 'FORGER-A'**
**Role:** Vertical take-off and landing naval strike fighter
**Crew/Accommodation:** One
**Power Plant:** One 6,700-kgp (14,770-lb s.t.) Soyuz R-28V-300 vectored-thrust turbojet plus two 3,250 kgp (7,165 lb s.t.) Rybinsk RD-36 lift turbojets
**Dimensions:** Span 7.3 m (24 ft); length 15.5 m (51 ft); wing area 18.5 m² (199 sq ft)
**Weights:** MTOW 11,700 kg (25,794 lb)
**Performance:** Maximum speed 1,164 km/h (723 mph) Mach 0.95 at sea level; operational ceiling 12,000 m (39,370 ft); radius of action 371 km (230 miles)
**Load:** Up to 2,000 kg (4,409 lb) of externally carried weapons, including two AA-8 'Aphid' air-to-air missiles

*Yak-38 'Forger-As'*

167

# FAIRCHILD REPUBLIC A-10 THUNDERBOLT II (U.S.A.)

*A-10A Thunderbolt II*

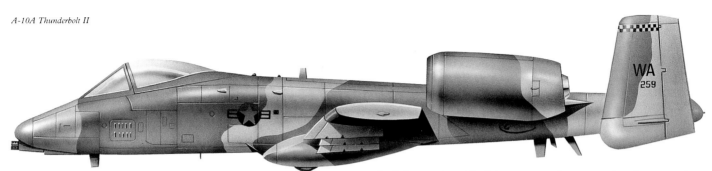

First flown in May 1972 as the YA-10A after Republic Aviation had become a division of Fairchild, the Thunderbolt II was developed to meet the U.S. Air Force's Attack Experimental requirement of 1967. The two YA-10A prototypes were competitively evaluated against the two YA-9s produced by Northrop, and the Fairchild Republic design was declared winner of the competition in January 1973. The requirement called for a specialist close-support and anti-tank aircraft offering high rates of survival from ground fire, a high-subsonic speed combined with good low-speed manoeuvrability, and a heavy weapon load.

The particular nature of its role dictated the Thunderbolt II's peculiar configuration with two turbofan engines located high on the fuselage sides between the wings and tailplane, and straight flying surfaces that restrict outright performance but enhance take-off performance and agility at very low level. To reduce the effect of anti-aircraft fire, all major systems are duplicated, extensive armour is carried, and vulnerable systems such as the engines are both duplicated and shielded as much as possible from ground detection and thus from ground fire. The first of 713 production aircraft were delivered in 1975, and though the type remains in valuable service in both A-10A attack and OA-10A lightly-armed forward air control variants, many have been passed to U.S. Air National Guard and Air Force Reserve units.

The core of the A-10A is the massive GAU-8/A Avenger seven-barrel cannon that occupies most of the forward fuselage and carries 1,174 rounds of 30-mm anti-tank ammunition delivering a pyrophoric penetrator of depleted uranium. A large load of other weapons, both 'smart' and 'dumb', can be carried on no fewer than 11 hardpoints.

*A Fairchild Republic A-10A Thunderbolt II*

**FAIRCHILD REPUBLIC A-10A THUNDERBOLT II**
**Role:** Close air support
**Crew/Accommodation:** One
**Power Plant:** Two 4,112-kgp (9,065-lb s.t.) General Electric TF34-GE-100 turbofans
**Dimensions:** Span 17.53 m (57.5 ft); length 16.25 m (53.33 ft); wing area 47.01m² (506 sq ft)
**Weights:** Empty 12,700 kg (28,000 lb); MTOW 23,586 kg (52,000 lb)
**Performance:** Maximum speed 707 km/h (439 mph) without external weapons; operational ceiling 10,575 m (34,700 ft); radius of action 763 km (474 miles)
**Load:** One 30-mm multi-barrel cannon, plus up to 7,250 kg (16,000 lb) of externally carried weapons

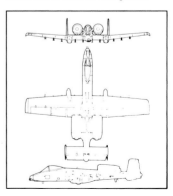

*A-10A Thunderbolt II*

# PANAVIA TORNADO (Italy/United Kingdom/ West Germany)

*Tornado F.Mk 3*

Currently one of the NATO alliance's premier front-line aircraft types, the Tornado was planned from the late 1960s as a multi-role combat aircraft able to operate from and into short or damaged runways for long-range interdiction missions at high speed and very low level. The keys to the mission are variable-geometry wings able to sweep from 25° spread to 67° fully swept and carrying an extensive array of high-lift devices on their leading edges and trailing edges,

advanced high by-pass turbofan engines that offer low fuel burn at cruise speed and high afterburning thrust, and an advanced sensor and electronic suite. This suite is based on a capable nav/attack system that includes attack and terrain-following radars, an inertial navigation system, and a triplex fly-by-wire control system.

The first of the Tornado prototypes flew in August 1974, and after a protracted development

the first production Tornados for the RAF and Luftwaffe were handed over in June 1979, followed eventually by the first for Italy (in 1981). The three main variants are the Tornado IDS baseline interdiction and strike warplane, the Tornado ADV air-defence fighter with different radar and weapons (including four semi-recessed Sky Flash air-to-air missiles) in a longer fuselage, and the Tornado ECR electronic combat and reconnaissance type. The British RAF version of the

IDS was delivered as the Tornado GR.Mk 1, while Tornado GR.Mk 1A became the reconnaissance derivative and GR.Mk 1B a maritime attack model carrying two Sea Eagle missiles; GR.Mk 4/4As are current upgrades of Mk 1/1As. The air defence variant interceptor for the RAF is currently flown in F.Mk 3 version, while Italy is leasing 24 pending Eurofighter deliveries. Including exports of IDS/ADVs to Saudi Arabia, total Tornado production amounted to 781 IDS/ECRs and 194 ADVs.

### PANAVIA TORNADO IDS

**Role:** All-weather, low-level strike and reconnaissance
**Crew/Accommodation:** Two
**Power Plant:** Two 7,257-kgp (16,000-lb s.t.) Turbo-Union RB199 Mk 103 turbofans with reheat
**Dimensions:** Span 13.9m (45.6 ft), swept 8.6 m (28.2 ft); length 16.7 m (54.8 ft); wing area 26.6 m² (286.3 sq ft)
**Weights:** Empty 14,000 kg (30,864 lb); MTOW 28,000 kg (61,729 lb)
**Performance:** Maximum speed Mach 2.2 clean or 1,483 km/h (921 mph), Mach 1.2 at 152 m (500 ft); operational ceiling 15,240+ m (50,000+ ft); radius of action typically 1,482 km (921 miles) with four 1,000-lb bombs, two Sidewinders and two drop tanks
**Load:** Two 27-mm cannon, plus up to 9,000 kg (19,842 lb) of externally carried weaponry and fuel

*Panavia Tornado IDSs of the German navy's Marinefliegergeschwader 1*

*Panavia Tornado F.Mk 3*

169

# LOCKHEED MARTIN F-117 NIGHTHAWK (U.S.A.)

*F-117A*

The world's first fully 'stealth' aircraft to reach operational status, the F-117 was developed to penetrate dense threat environments during the hours of darkness, and destroy critical or high-value enemy targets with amazing accuracy. Its strange shape and secret nature comes from its ability to counter radar, infra-red, visual, contrails, engine smoke, acoustic and electromagnetic signatures.

Development began with two small XST Have Blue technology demonstrators, the first flown in December 1977, and five FSD flight test aircraft (first flown in January 1981). Delivery of 59 F-117As to the USAF started in August 1982 and initial operational capability was achieved in October 1983. The public did not hear of the aircraft until 1988. Its first combat use came in December 1989 when two aircraft dropped laser-guided bombs on barracks in Panama during Operation Just Cause, while during the 1991 Gulf War 42 flew 1,271 missions.

The F-117A's airframe is of the 'lifting body' type, with the outer faceted skin formed from flat surfaces arranged at angles to overcome enemy radars. All aspects of the design were carefully considered, including the air intakes which have heated grids to block radar energy, while the engine nozzles are horizontal slots that produce a thin exhaust plume that is mixed with cold air and quickly dispersed. No radar is carried, the pilot instead relying on sophisticated navigation and attack systems, automated mission planning, and forward/downward-looking infra-red devices.

**LOCKHEED MARTIN F-117A**
**Role:** Low-observability strike
**Crew/Accommodation:** One
**Power Plant:** Two 4,899-kgp (10,800-lb s.t.) General Electric F404-GE-F1D2 non-reheated turbofans
**Dimensions:** Span 13.20 m (43.44 ft); length 20.09 m (65.92 ft); wing area 84.82 m² (913 sq ft)
**Weights:** MTOW 23,814 kg (52,500 lb)
**Performance:** Maximum speed 1,040 km/h (646 mph); radius of action 1,111 km (691 miles) with full weapon load, unrefuelled
**Load:** Two laser-guided 2,000-lb bombs in the bay, or other weapons up to 2,268 kg (5,000 lb)

*Lockheed Martin F-117A Nighthawk*

*U.S.A.F. Lockheed Martin F-117A Nighthawk*

*USAF Lockheed Martin F-117A Nighthawk*

# Maritime Patrol

Few people fully appreciate the importance of maritime aircraft in the annals of aviation. Two years before the Wright brothers flew for the first time in their powered *Flyer*, Austrian Wilhelm Kress 'hopped' his tandem-wing powered seaplane from the Tullnerbach reservoir (in 1901), experiments which preceded even the famous Potomac River trials by American Samuel Pierpoint Langley.

Maritime aircraft were widely used during World War I, both in floatplane form and as flying-boats. The German navy made particular use of floatplanes as naval station defence fighters and for reconnaissance patrol and fighter escort, while Claude Dornier became responsible for several giant flying-boats from 1915 that were produced as Zeppelin-Lindau Rs type prototypes under the patronage of Count von Zeppelin of airship fame. Although these Dornier-designed aircraft were not significant to the German war effort, it gave the young designer the means to go on and conceive some of the finest flying-boats of the inter-war period.

Other fighting nations also produced maritime aircraft, not least the truly beautifully-styled small Italian Macchi flying-boat fighters and maritime patrol aircraft that were operational from 1917. Overall, though, it was Britain that led the world in the development and use of large flying-boats, aircraft which performed brilliantly in combatting both German U-boat submarines and Zeppelin airships. Interestingly, the best of these was without question the R.N.A.S.'s Felixstowe F.2A/F.3, developed by Sqdn. Cdr. John C. Porte from the earlier and less successful American Curtiss H.12 Large America which could trace its ancestry to an original pre-war flying-boat intended to attempt a transatlantic flight. Despite its bulk and weight, the Felixstowe had the added virtue of being highly manoeuvrable, and on 4 June 1918 this was put to the test when three F.2As defended a fourth aircraft (which had alighted due to a fuel blockage) from 14 attacking enemy seaplanes, shooting down six in the process. Indeed, as testimony to the Felixstowe design, Curtiss went on to produce a version as the F-5L for the U.S. Navy, as an American-built example of a British-improved flying-boat of Curtiss original design!

Flying-boats were ideally suited to long over-water flights, and post-war were highly developed for both military and commercial use. They remained much prized during World War II for an expanded number of roles, including spotter-reconnaissance and air-sea rescue, the latter often by small craft launched from ships at sea as well as from land and coastal waters. But it was the large flying-boats that made such an impact on anti-submarine warfare and convoy escort. The RAF Short Sunderland, for example, proved so successful that the aircraft were not retired by the RAF until 1959, having first become operational in 1938, while the American Consolidated PBY Catalina was used from 1941 in a whole gamut of roles and became the most-produced flying-boat of all time.

Germany, as others, built fine flying-boats, among the best remembered being the unorthodox Blohm und Voss Bv 138 for reconnaissance and some giant types from the same company. The sleek Dornier Do 24, despite its capability to carry bombs, is thought never to have been employed on any offensive mission. Instead, Germany placed its faith partly in the Focke-Wulf Fw 200 Condor landplane for long-range maritime reconnaissance and maritime bomber duties, as one of the few German four-engined bombers of that war. This proved extremely successful in its combined operations with German U-boats against Allied convoys, until confronted by fighters from new escort carriers or catapult-launched from merchant ships. It may be said, therefore, that Condor led the way to post-war preferences towards landplanes and, since the 1950s, most of the world's purpose-built maritime patrol aircraft have been of landplane design.

*Picture: The Dassault Atlantique 2 has been developed from the original Atlantic of 1961 first appearance, which was originally conceived to offer NATO forces a standardized long-range maritime patrol and anti-submarine landplane. Atlantic was the first European landplane specifically designed for anti-submarine and anti-surface vessel use*

# CONSOLIDATED PBY CATALINA (U.S.A.)

*PBY-1 Catalina*

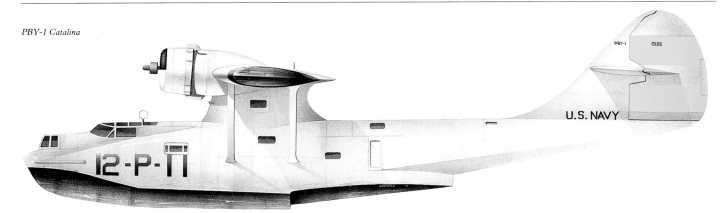

In the early 1930s, the U.S. Navy issued a requirement for a patrol flying boat that offered greater range and payload than the Consolidated P2Y and Martin P3M then in service. Design proposals were received from Consolidated and Douglas, and single prototypes of each were ordered. The Douglas

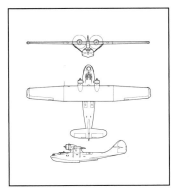

*Consolidated PBY Catalina*

type was restricted to a single XP3D-1 prototype, but the Consolidated Model 28 became one of the most important flying-boats ever developed. The XP3Y-1 prototype first flew in March 1935 and was a large machine with a wide two-step hull, a strut-braced parasol wing mounted on top of a massive pylon that accommodated the flight engineer, and stabilizing

**CONSOLIDATED PBY-5 (RAF CATALINA Mk IV)**
**Role:** Long-range maritime patrol bomber flying boat
**Crew/Accommodation:** Nine
**Power Plant:** Two, 1,200 hp Pratt & Whitney R-1830-92 Twin Wasp air-cooled radials
**Dimensions:** Span 37.10 m (104 ft); length 19.47 m (63.88 ft); wing area 130.1 m² (1,400 sq ft)
**Weights:** Empty 7,809 kg (17,200 lb); MTOW 15,436 kg (34,000 lb)
**Performance:** Cruise speed 182 km/h (113 mph) at sea level; operational ceiling 5,517 m (18,100 ft); range 4,812 km (2,990 miles) with full warload
**Load:** Two .5 inch and two .303 inch machine guns, plus up to 1,816 kg (4,000 lb) of torpedoes, depth charges or bombs carried externally

floats that retracted in flight to become the wingtips and so reduce drag.

The type clearly possessed considerable potential and after being reworked as a patrol bomber was ordered into production as the PBY-1, of which 60 were built with 671-kW (900-hp) R-1830-64 radial engines. The following PBY-2 had equipment improvements, and production totalled 50. Next came 66 PBY-3s with 746-kW (1,000-hp) R-1830-66 engines and 33 PBY-4s with 783-kW (1,050-hp) R-1830-72 engines. The generally improved PBY-5 with 895-kW (1,200-lb) R-1830-82 or -92 engines was the definitive flying-boat model and many hundreds were built, complemented by many PYB-5A and 5B amphibians, including those for lend-lease to Britain. The Naval Aircraft Factory produced 156 of a PBN-1 Nomad version of the PBY-5 with aerodynamic and hydrodynamic improvements, and 235 of a comparable amphibian model were built by Consolidated

as the PBY-6A for the U.S. Navy, USAAF and Russia, making 2,398 Catalinas built by Consolidated. The basic type was also produced in Canada by Canadian Vickers and Boeing, plus in the U.S.S.R. as the GST, while the U.K. adopted the aircraft in several variants with the name Catalina that has since been generally adopted for all PBY models.

*The Consolidated PBY-6A Catalina*

# SHORT SUNDERLAND Family (United Kingdom)

*Sunderland Mk I*

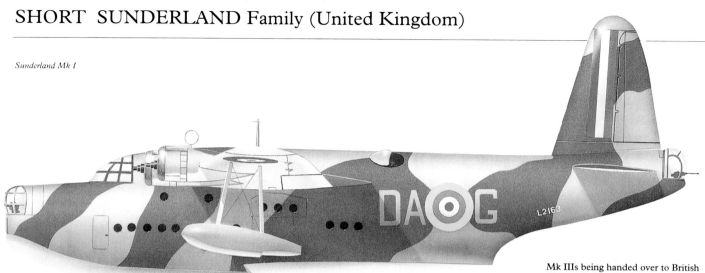

The Sunderland was the U.K.'s premier maritime reconnaissance flying boat of World War II, and derived ultimately from the S.23 class of civil 'Empire' flying boats. The prototype flew in October 1937 with 753-kW (1,010-hp) Bristol Pegasus XXII radials, and was the first British flying boat to have power-operated defensive gun turrets. The prototype proved most satisfactory, and production of this variant totalled 90

*Sunderland Mk II*

174

before it was overtaken on the lines by the Sunderland Mk II with 794-kW (1,065-hp) Pegasus XVIII radials and a power-operated dorsal turret in place of the Mk I's two 7.7-mm (0.303-in) beam guns in manually operated waist positions.

These 43 'boats were in turn succeeded by the Sunderland Mk III, which was the most extensively built variant with 456 being built. This variant had a hull revised with a faired step, and some 'boats were to the Sunderland Mk IIIA standard with ASV. Mk III surface-search radar. The Sunderland Mk IV was developed for Pacific operations and became the S.45 Seaford, of which a mere 10 examples (three prototypes and seven production 'boats) were built with 1253- and 1283-kW (1,680- and 1,720-hp) Bristol Hercules XVII and XIX radials respectively. The last Sunderland variant was the Mk V, of which 150 were built with 895-kW

(1,200-hp) Pratt & Whitney R-1830-90B radials and ASV. Mk VIC radar under the wingtips; the more powerful engines allowed the type to operate at cruising rather than maximum engine revolutions, which improved engine life and aided economical running.

Sunderlands were also used for civil transport, the first of 24 Sunderland

## SHORT SUNDERLAND Mk V
**Role:** Anti-submarine/maritime patrol
**Crew/Accommodation:** Seven
**Power Plant:** Four 1,200 hp Pratt & Whitney R-1830-90B Twin Wasp air-cooled radials
**Dimensions:** Span 34.39 m (112.77 ft); length 26 m (85.33 ft); wing area 156.6 m² (1,687 sq ft)
**Weights:** Empty 16,783 kg (37,000 lb); MTOW 27,250 kg (60,000 lb)
**Performance:** Maximum speed 343 km/h (213 mph) at 1,525 m (5,000 ft); operational ceiling 5,455 m (17,900 ft); range 4,300 km (2,690 miles) with maximum fuel
**Load:** Six .5 inch machine guns and eight .303 inch machine guns, plus up to 908 kg (2,000 lb) of bombs/depth charges

Mk IIIs being handed over to British Airways in March 1943. The 'boats were later brought up to more comfortable standard as Hythes, and were then revised as Sandringham with R-1830-92 radials and, in addition, neat aerodynamic fairings over the erstwhile nose and tail turret positions.

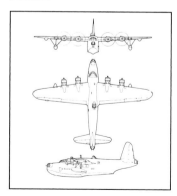

*Sunderland Mk V*

# ARADO Ar 196 (Germany)

*Ar 196A-3*

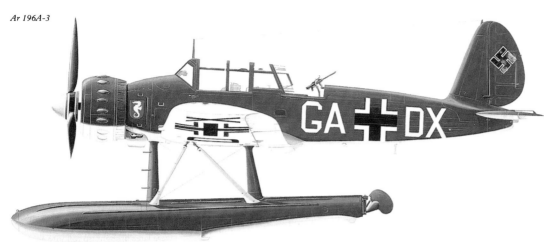

The Ar 196 was designed to meet a 1936 requirement for a floatplane reconnaissance aircraft to succeed the same company's Ar 95 biplane, and was intended for catapult-launched use from German major surface warships, though a secondary coastal patrol capability was also envisaged. The type clearly had more than a passing kinship with the Ar 95, but was an all-metal monoplane and was designed for use on either twin floats or a combination of one main and two outrigger floats. Several proposals had been received in response to the requirement, and orders were placed for Arado monoplane and Focke-Wulf biplane prototypes.

Initial evaluation in the summer of 1937 removed the Focke-Wulf contender from the running and, after testing of the two alighting gear arrangements, the Arado type was ordered into production as the Ar 196A with twin floats. Total construction was 546 aircraft, including machines built in Dutch and French factories under German control.

The type was built in two main streams for shipboard and coastal use. The shipboard stream comprised 20 Ar 196A-1s with two wing-mounted 7.92-mm (0.312-in) machine guns and 24 strengthened Ar 196A-4s based on the Ar 196A-3. The coastal stream comprised 391 examples of the Ar 196A-2 with two 20-mm wing-mounted cannon and the strengthened Ar 196A-3 with a variable-pitch propeller, and 69 examples of the Ar 196A-5 with better radio and a twin rather than single machine-gun installation for the radio-operator/gunner. The Ar 196 was used in most of the German theatres during World War II.

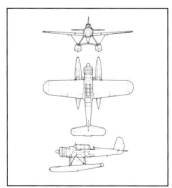

*Arado Ar 196A-3*

**ARADO Ar 196A-3**
**Role:** Shipborne reconnaissance floatplane
**Crew/Accommodation:** Two
**Power Plant:** One 960 hp BMW 132K air-cooled radial
**Dimensions:** Span 12.4 m (40.68 ft); length 11 m (36.09 ft); wing area 28.4 m² (305.6 sq ft)
**Weights:** Empty 2,990 kg (6,593 lb); MTOW 3,730 kg (8,225 lb)
**Performance:** Maximum speed 310 km/h (193 mph) at 4,000 m (13,120 ft); operational ceiling 7,000 m (22,960 ft); range 1,070 km (665 miles)
**Load:** Two 20 mm cannon and two 7.9 mm machine guns, plus 100 kg (210 lb) of bombs

*The Arado Ar 196A floatplane*

# VOUGHT OS2U KINGFISHER (U.S.A.)

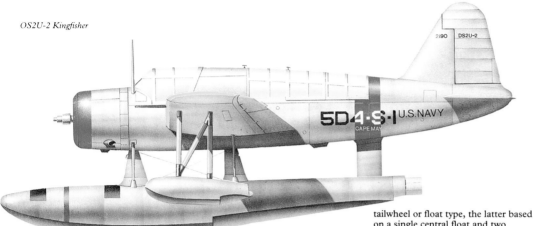

*OS2U-2 Kingfisher*

To replace its O3U Corsair biplane operated by the U.S. Navy in the scouting role, Vought produced its VS.310 design with a cantilever monoplane wing in the low/mid-position, a portly fuselage with extensive glazing, and provision for fixed landing gear that could be of the tailwheel or float type, the latter based on a single central float and two stabilizing floats under the wings.

The U.S. Navy ordered a single XOS2U-1 prototype, and this first flew in March 1938 in landplane configuration with the 336-kW (450-hp) Pratt & Whitney R-985-4 Wasp Junior radial; in May of the same year the type was first flown in floatplane form. The trial programme was completed successfully, and the type was ordered into production as the OS2U-1 with the R-985-48 engine.

Production totalled 54 aircraft, and in August 1940 these became the first catapult-launched observation/scout aircraft to serve on American capital ships. Further production embraced 158 examples of the OS2U-2 with the R-985-50 engine and modified equipment, and 1,006 examples of the OS2U-3 with the R-985-AN-2 engine, self-sealing fuel tanks, armour protection, and armament comprising two 7.7-mm (0.303-in) machine guns (one fixed and the other trainable) and two 147-kg (325-lb) depth charges. The type was also operated by inshore patrol squadrons in the anti-submarine air air-sea rescue roles, proving an invaluable asset. Some aircraft were supplied to Central and South American nations, and 100 were transferred to the Royal Navy as Kingfisher Mk I trainers and catapult-launched spotters. Nothing came of the planned OS2U-4 version with a more powerful engine and revised flying surfaces that included a straight-tapered tailplane and narrow-chord wings with full-span flaps and square cut tips.

*A Vought OS2U-2 Kingfisher floatplane*

**VOUGHT-SIKORSKY 0S2U-3 KINGFISHER**
**Role:** Shipborne (catapult-launched) reconnaissance
**Crew/Accommodation:** Two
**Power Plant:** One 450 hp Pratt & Whitney R-985-AN-2 or -8 air-cooled radial
**Dimensions:** Span 10.95 m (35.91 ft); length 10.31 m (33.83 ft); wing area 24.34 m² (262.00 sq ft)
**Weights:** Empty 1,870 kg (4,123 lb); MTOW 2,722 kg (6,000 lb)
**Performance:** Maximum speed 264 km/h (164 mph) at 1,676 m (5,500 ft); operational ceiling 3,962 m (13,000 ft); radius 1,296 km (805 miles)
**Load:** Two 0.3 in machine guns, plus up to 295 kg (650 lb) bombload

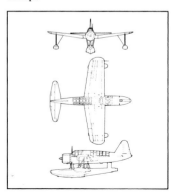

*Vought OS2U Kingfisher*

# AVRO SHACKLETON (United Kingdom)

*Shackleton AEW.Mk 2*

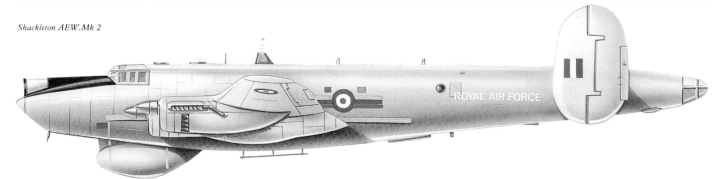

To give the Lancaster a long-range capability at high altitude, Avro planned the Lancaster Mk IV, but this Type 694 emerged as so different an aeroplane that it was given the name Lincoln. The prototype flew in June 1944 and, although plans were laid for 2,254 aircraft, British postwar production amounted to only 72 Lincoln B.Mk1s and 465 Lincoln B.Mk 2s. Canada completed one

Lincoln B.Mk XV, but Australia built 43 Lincoln B.Mk 30s and 30 Lincoln B.Mk 30As, and 20 of these were later modified to Lincoln B.Mk 31 standard together with a longer nose accommodating search radar and two operators.

Meanwhile, experience with the Lancaster in the maritime role after World War II made the British decide to develop a specialized aeroplane as

the Lincoln GR.Mk III with the wing and landing gear of the bomber married to a new fuselage, revised empennage, and Rolls-Royce Griffon engines, each driving a contra-rotating propeller unit. Later renamed Shackleton, the first example of the new type flew in March 1949, leading to production of the Shackleton GR.Mk 1 (later MR.Mk 1) with two Griffon 57As and two Griffon 57s, and the Shackleton MR.Mk 1A with four Griffon 57As. The Shackleton MR.Mk 2 had revised armament and search radar with its antenna in a retractable 'dustbin' rather than a chin radome, while the definitive

Shackleton MR.Mk 3 was considerably updated, lost the dorsal turret but gained underwing hardpoints, and changed to tricycle landing gear. Eight MR.Mk3s also went to the South African air force. Twelve MR.Mk 2s were converted in the 1970s into Shackleton AEW.Mk 2 airborne early-warning aircraft for the RAF, especially equipped with specialist radar, remaining in service until the arrival of Boeing E-3s.

---

**AVRO SHACKLETON AEW.Mk 2**
**Role:** Airborne early warning
**Crew/Accommodation:** Ten
**Power Plant:** Four 2,456 hp Rolls-Royce Griffon 57A water-cooled inlines
**Dimensions:** Span 36.52 m (119.83 ft); length 28.19 m (92.5 ft); wing area 135.45 m² (1,458 sq ft)
**Weights:** Empty 25,583 kg (56,400 lb); MTOW 44,452 kg (98,000 lb)
**Performance:** Cruise speed 322 km/h (200 mph) at 3,050 m (10,000 ft); operational ceiling 5,852 m (19,200 ft); endurance 16 hours
**Load:** None, other than APS 20 long-range search radar

*Avro Shackleton MR.Mk 3*

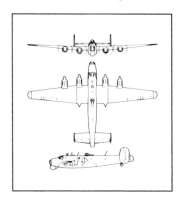

*Avro Shackleton MR.Mk 1*

# LOCKHEED MARTIN P-3 ORION (U.S.A.)

*P-3C Orion*

In 1957 the U.S. Navy required a maritime patrol type to supplant the piston-engined Lockheed P2V Neptune, and stressed the urgency of the programme by agreeing to the development of the type on the basis of an existing civil airframe. Lockheed's Model 85 proposal was therefore based on the airframe/powerplant combination of the relatively unsuccessful Model 188 Electra turboprop-powered airliner, though with the fuselage shortened by 2.24 m (7 ft 4 in) as well as modified to include a weapons bay in the lower fuselage.

The YP3V-1 prototype first flew in November 1959, and while the initial production variant was delivered from August 1962 with the designation P3V-1, it was redesignated P-3A in 1962. By the end of U.S. Orion production in 1996, 649 had been delivered to the U.S. Navy and forces abroad while others continued to be built by Kawasaki in Japan. The original 157 P-3As were powered by 3,356-kW (4,500-shp) Allison T56-A-10W turboprops and, though the initial aircraft had the same tactical system as the P2V-7, the 109th and later aircraft had the more advanced Deltic system that was then retrofitted to the earlier machines. The 145 P-3Bs were given the same Deltic system, but were powered by 3,661-kW (4,910-shp) T56-A-14 engines and were delivered with provision for the launch of AGM-12 Bullpup air-to-surface missiles. The final version was the P-3C, which retain the airframe/powerplant combination of the P-3B but was given the A-NEW ASW avionics system with new sensors and controls. In 1975 the first of a series of Update models was introduced, aimed to increase operational effectiveness, the last being Update III, in 1984. There were also several export models including the CP-140 Aurora for Canada that combined the P-3C's airframe and powerplant with the electronics of the Lockheed S-3 Viking carrierborne anti-submarine platform; the related Canadian CP-140A Arcturus has no ASW equipment and is used for surveillance. The U.S. Navy also took in electronic surveillance models as EP-3 Aries IIs, plus various transport, trainer and the research models RP-3, while an airborne early warning version P-3AEW went to U.S. Customs.

*Lockheed Martin P-3C in Australian service as the AP-3C*

**LOCKHEED ORION P-3C Update III ORION**
**Role:** Long-range maritime patrol and anti-submarine
**Crew/Accommodation:** Ten
**Power Plant:** Four 4,910-shp Allison T56-A-14 turboprops
**Dimensions:** Span 30.38 m (99.66 ft); length 35.6 m (116.8 ft); wing area 120.8 m² (1,300 sq ft)
**Weights:** Empty 27,892 kg (61,491 lb); MTOW 64,410 kg (142,000 lb)
**Performance:** Maximum speed 761 km/h (466 mph) at 4,572 m (15,000 ft); operational ceiling 10,485 m (34,400 ft); radius of action 3,836 km (2,384 miles)
**Load:** Up to 9,072 kg (20,000 lb) of weapons and sonobuoys

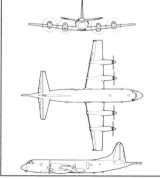

*Lockheed Martin P-3C Orion*

# BRITISH AEROSPACE NIMROD (United Kingdom)

*Nimrod MR.Mk 2*

The Nimrod was developed on the aerodynamic and structural basis of the Comet 4 airliner as a jet-powered maritime patroller to replace the piston-engined Avro Shackleton. The Nimrod looks remarkably similar to the Comet 4, but features a fuselage shortened by 1.98 m (6 ft 6 in) and deepened to allow the incorporation of a weapons bay 14.78 m (48 ft 6 in) long below the wide tactical compartment, a turbofan

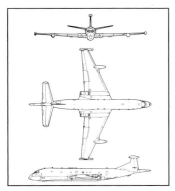

*Nimrod MR.Mk 1*

powerplant for much improved reliability and range (especially in the patrol regime with two engines shut down), and highly advanced mission electronics including radar, MAD and an acoustic data-processing system using dropped sonobuoys. Wings, tailplane and landing were similar to those of Comet 4C, though the landing gear was strengthened, and the first prototype flew in May 1967 as a conversion of a Comet 4C. Successful trials led to production of 46 Nimrod MR.Mk 1s with EMI ASV-21D search radar and

**BRITISH AEROSPACE NIMROD MR.Mk 2P**
**Role:** Long-range maritime reconnaissance/anti-submarine
**Crew/Accommodation:** Twelve
**Power Plant:** Four 5,440-kgp (11,995-lb s.t.) Rolls-Royce Spey Mk 250 turbofans
**Dimensions:** Span 35 m (114.83 ft); length 39.32 m (129 ft); wing area 197 m² (2,121 sq ft)
**Weights:** Empty 39,000 kg (86.000 lb); MTOW 87,090 kg (192,000 lb)
**Performance:** Maximum speed 926 km/h (576 mph) at 610 m (2,000 ft); operational ceiling 12,802 m (42,000 ft); endurance 12 hours
**Load:** Up to 6,120 kg (13,500 lb) including up to nine Stingray lightweight anti-submarine torpedoes, Harpoon missiles, depth charges, mines and/or cluster bombs

Emerson ASQ-10A magnetic anomaly detector in a tail 'sting'.

A variant of this baseline version became the Nimrod R.Mk 1, a special electronic intelligence variant of which three were produced. Further development in the electronic field led to the improved Nimrod MR.Mk 2, of which 35 were produced by conversion of MR.Mk 1 airframes with EMI Searchwater radar, Loral ESM in wingtip pods (to complement the original Thomson-CSF ESM system in a fintop fairing), and a thoroughly upgraded

*Nimrod MR.Mk 1*

tactical suite with a Marconi ASQ-901 acoustic data-processing and display system allowing use of many active and passive sonobuoy types. Redelivery of Mk 2s began in 1979, the addition of inflight refuelling later adding a 'P' to the designation.

Under current development is the Nimrod 2000 or MRA.Mk 4, initially for the RAF from 2003 and 21 are being produced by major rework of existing aircraft, having new mission systems, a 2-man cockpit with modern LCD screen displays, new wings and other components, BMW Rolls-Royce BR710 turbofans, Searchwater 2000 radar, other advanced avionics and more.

179

# CIVIL
# AIRCRAFT

# Civil Piston-Engined Transports

The 'stick and string' aeroplanes that pioneered flying in the early years of the 20th century had enough difficulty keeping the pilot aloft without the added complication of a commercially viable payload. And yet, hardly had the Wright brothers recovered from the exhilaration of their first-ever powered flights than a letter arrived from a businessman, enquiring whether they could transport minerals by air over a 26-km (16-mile) hop in West Virginia, for which they would be paid $10 per ton. Politely, the offer was turned down for practical reasons.

However, a much developed Wright Model B biplane was used in November 1910 to carry the first-ever air freight, this time 542 yards of silk transported between Dayton and Columbus. The cost of the flight to the Morehouse-Martens Company was a staggering $5,000, yet the flight generated such interest in the company's Home Dry Goods Store that, by cutting some silk into small pieces for sale as souvenirs attached to postcards, Morehouse-Martens showed an overall profit from the venture of over $1,000.

This and similar high-publicity flights were little more than advertising stunts, but already in 1910 the first-ever commercial passenger airline had begun operating in Germany, carrying over 34,000 passengers without injury until November 1913. Known as Delag, the airline had been founded by Count von Zeppelin and consequently operated giant airships. At the start of the following year, in 1914, the first-ever scheduled airline services using an aeroplane (Benoist flying-boat) began in Florida, but these lasted only a few months.

Even while World War I raged at its bloodiest, British and German civil airline companies were registered for post-war activities, allowing operations to start in 1919. Progress in aeroplane development had by then, made commercial operations viable. Very little time passed before other airlines began to appear, able to call upon cheap ex-military aircraft that could be crudely converted for their new peacetime roles, while the first purpose-designed commercial transports were but a step away.

*Picture: The piston-engined Lockheed Constellation had been designed for commercial use but first served with the U.S.A.A.F as the C-69 wartime military transport. To expand MATS post-war long-range transport capacity, Super Constellations followed as C-121s*

# JUNKERS F 13 (Germany)

*Junkers F 13*

From its DI single-seat fighter and CLI two-seat escort fighter and close-support warplane of 1918, both all-metal monoplanes that saw limited service in World War I, Junkers developed Europe's single most important transport of the 1920s, the classic F 13 low-wing monoplane with a single nose-mounted engine and fixed tail wheel landing gear. This used the metal construction patented by Dr Hugo Junkers in 1910 for thick-section cantilever monoplane wings and was the world's first all-metal purpose-designed commercial transport.

The F 13 first flew in June 1919, and was based on nine spars braced with welded duralumin tubes and covered in streamwise corrugated duralumin skinning to create an immensely strong and durable structure. The accommodation comprised an open cockpit for two pilots and an enclosed cabin for four passengers. The cockpit was later enclosed, and the engine of the first machine was a 119-kW (160-hp) Mercedes D.IIIa inline, which was superseded in early production aircraft by the 138-kW (185-hp) BMW IIIa inline that offered much superior performance. Production continued to 1932, and amounted to at least 320 and probably 350 aircraft in more than 60 variants with a host of modifications and different engines, the most frequent being the 156-kW (210-hp) Junkers L-5 inline.

The main operator of the type was Junkers Luftverkehr, which operated more than 60 aircraft in a period between 1921 and 1926, in the process flying some 15,000,000 km (9,300,000 miles) and carrying nearly 282,000 passengers. The airline then became part of Deutsche Luft-Hansa (later Deutsche Lufthansa) which still had 43 such aircraft in service in 1931. The other F 13s were used by civil and military operators in most parts of the world. The fact that the type was immensely strong, needed little maintenance, and could operate from wheel, ski or float landing gear, made the F 13 especially popular with operators in remoter areas.

*The Junkers F 13 was a light but enduring light transport*

**JUNKERS F 13**
**Role:** Light passenger transport
**Crew/Accommodation:** One, plus up to four passengers
**Power Plant:** One 185 hp BMW III A water-cooled inline
**Dimensions:** Span 14.47 m (47.74 ft) length 9.6 m (31.5 ft); wing area 39 m² (419.8 sq ft)
**Weights:** Empty 1,150 kg (2,535 lb); MTOW 1,650 kg (3,638 lb)
**Performance:** Cruise speed 140 km/h (75.5 mph) at sea level; operational ceiling 3,000 m (9,843 ft); range 725 km (450 miles)
**Load:** Up to 320 kg (705 lb) payload

*Junkers F 13*

# FOKKER F.VII-3m (Netherlands)

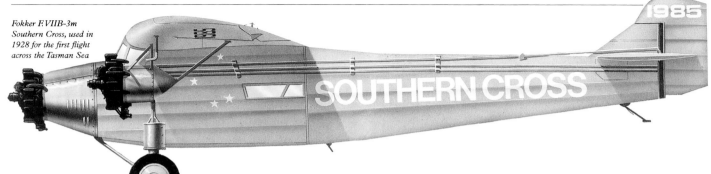

*Fokker F.VIIB-3m Southern Cross, used in 1928 for the first flight across the Tasman Sea*

In 1924-25, Fokker built five examples of its F.VII powered by the 268-kW (360-hp) Rolls-Royce Eagle inline engine, and then evolved the eight-passenger F.VIIA that first flew in March 1925 with a 298-kW (400-hp) Packard Liberty 12 engine and a number of aerodynamic refinements and simple three-strut rather than multi-strut main landing gear units. The type undertook a successful demonstration tour of the United States, and orders were received there and in Europe for 42 aircraft with inline or radial engines in the class between 261 and 391 kW (350 and 525 hp); licensed production was also undertaken in several countries. The type was a typical Fokker construction, with a welded steel-tube fuselage and tail unit covered in fabric, and a high-set cantilever wing of thick section and wooden construction. For the Ford Reliability Tour of the United States, Fokker produced the first F.VIIA-3m with a powerplant of three 179-kW (240-hp) Wright Whirlwind radials mounted one on the nose and the others on the main landing gear struts below the wing.

All subsequent production was of the three-engined type, and many F.VIIAs were converted. The F.VIIA-3m spanned 19.30 m (63 ft 3.75 in), but to meet the requirement of Sir Hubert Wilkins for a long-range polar exploration type, a version was produced as the F.VIIB-3m with wings spanning 21.70 m (71 ft 2.5 in). This also became a production type. Dutch construction of the two F. VII-3m models was 116 aircraft, and large numbers were built under licence in seven countries. The British and American models were the Avro Ten and Atlantic F.7. The type was also adopted by the U.S. Army Air Corps and U.S. Navy as the C-2 and RA respectively. The F.VII-3m was of great importance in the development of European and third-world transport for passengers and freight, and was also used extensively for route-proving and record-breaking flights.

## FOKKER F.VIIB-3m

**Role:** Passenger Transport
**Crew/Accommodation:** Two, plus up to 8 passengers
**Power Plant:** Three 240 hp Gnome-Rhone Titan air-cooled radials (the aircraft was equipped with various makes/powers of European and U.S. radials)
**Dimensions:** Span 21.70 m (71.19 ft); length 14.20 m (46.56 ft); wing area 71.20 m² (722 sq ft)
**Weights:** Empty 3,050 kg (6,724 lb); MTOW 5,250 kg (11,574 lb)
**Performance:** Maximum speed 185 km/h (115 mph) at sea level; operational ceiling 4,875 m (15,994 ft); range 837 km (520 miles) with full payload
**Load:** Up to 1,280 kg (2,822 lb)

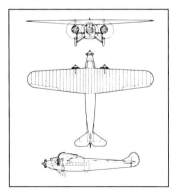

*Fokker F.VIIB-3m*

*Fokker F.VIIA-3m Josephine Ford, used by American Lt. Cdr. Richard Byrd for the first*

# FORD TRI-MOTOR (U.S.A.)

The much loved Ford Tri-Motor was the result of Henry Ford purchasing the Stout Metal Airplane Company in 1925, which had developed the Pullman 6-passenger monoplane, and progressing on to the larger design. Remembered for its corrugated all-metal construction, it gained the nickname 'Tin Goose'. From his 2-AT Pullman powered by a single 298-kW (400-hp) Packard Liberty inline engine, William B. Stout had evolved the 3-AT with three uncowled radial engines mounted two on the wings and one low on the nose. This was unsuccessful, but paved the way for th 4-AT that first flew in June 1926 with three 149-kW (200-hp) Wright Whirlwind J-4 radials located two under the wings in strut-braced nacelles and one in a neat nose installation. The 4-AT accommodated two pilots in an open cockpit and eight passengers in an enclosed cabin.

The type was produced in variants that ranged from the initial 4-AT-A to the 4-AT-E with 224-kW (300-hp) Whirlwind J-6-9 radials and provision for 12 passengers. Production totalled 81 aircraft, and was complemented from 1928 by the 5-AT with 13 passengers, span increased by 1.17 m (3 ft 10 in), and three 313-kW (420-hp) Pratt and Whitney Wasp radials. Production continued up to 1932, and these 117 aircraft included variants up to the 5-AT-D with 17 passengers in a cabin given greater headroom by raising the wing 0.203 m (8 in). Other variants were four 6-ATs based on the 5-AT but with Whirlwind J-6-9 engines, one 7-AT conversion of a 6-AT with a 313-kW Wasp, one 8-AT conversion of a 5-AT with only the nose engine, one 9-AT conversion of a 4-AT with 224-kW Pratt and Whitney Wasp Junior radials, one 11-AT conversion of a 4-AT with three 168-kW (225-hp) Packard diesel engines. Army and Navy versions were the C-3, C-4 and C-9, and the JR and RR respectively.

*The legendary Ford 5-AT 'Tin Goose'*

## FORD 4-AT-E TRI-MOTOR

**Role:** Passenger transport
**Crew/Accommodation:** Two, plus up to 11 passengers
**Power Plant:** Three 300 hp Wright J-6 air-cooled radials
**Dimensions:** Span 22.56 m (74 ft); length 15.19 m (49.83 ft); wing area 72.93 m² (785 sq ft)
**Weights:** Empty 2,948 kg (6,500 lb); MTOW 4,595 kg (10,130 lb)
**Performance:** Cruise speed 172 km/h (107 mph) at sea level; operational ceiling 5,029 m (16,500 ft); range 917 km (570 miles)
**Load:** Up to 782 kg (1,725 lb)

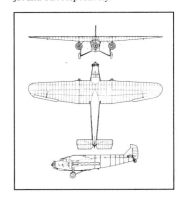

*Ford 5-AT Tri-Motor*

# JUNKERS Ju 52/3 (Germany)

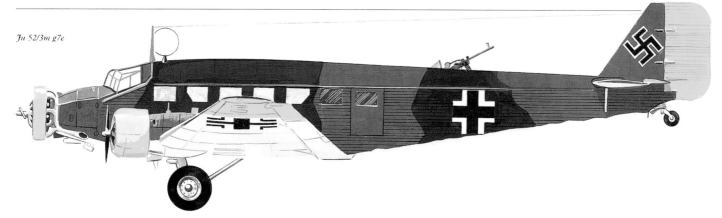

*Ju 52/3m g7e*

First flown in October 1930 with a single 541-kW (725-hp) BMW VII engine, the Ju 52 was produced to the extent of just six aircraft as civil transports with various engines. The type was of typical Junkers concept for the period, with corrugated alloy skinning on an angular airframe, fixed but faired tailwheel landing gear, and a low-set wing trailed by typical

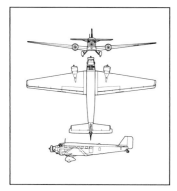

*Junkers Ju 52/3m*

Junkers full-span slotted ailerons/flaps. The Ju 52 would clearly benefit from greater power, and the company therefore developed the Ju 52/3m ce tri-motor version that first flew in April 1931 with 410-kW (550-hp) Pratt & Whitney Hornet radials. The type was produced in Ju 52/3m ce, de, fe and ge civil variants, the last with accommodation for 17 passengers on the power of three 492-kW (660-hp) BMW 132A-1 radials. Development then veered to German military needs, resulting in the Ju 52/3m g3e interim

bomber-transport pending the arrival of purpose-designed aircraft. Then the type was built as Germany's main transport and airborne forces aircraft of World War II.

The main variants in an overall production total of about 4,850 aircraft were the Ju 52/3m g4e bomber-transport with a heavier payload and a tailwheel in place of the original skid, the Ju 52/3m g5e with 619-kW (830-hp) BMW 132T-2 radials, the Ju 52/3m g6e improved transport, the Ju 52/3m g7e with an

autopilot and a larger loading hatch, Ju 52/3m g8e multi-role transport with conversion kits for specialized roles, Ju 52/3m g9e airborne forces version with a glider-tow attachment and BMW 132Z radials, Ju 52/3m g12e civil and military transport with 596-kW (800-hp) BMW 132L radials, and Ju 52/3m g14e final transport version with improved armament and armour protection. There were also small numbers of the later Ju 252 and Ju 352 developments with more power and retractable landing gear.

**JUNKERS Ju 52/3m g4e**
**Role:** Military transport (land or water-based)
**Crew/Accommodation:** Three, plus up to 18 troops
**Power Plant:** Three 830 hp BMW 132T-2 air-cooled radials
**Dimensions:** Span 29.25 m (95.97 ft); length 18.9 m (62 ft); wing area 110.5 m² (1,189.4 sq ft)
**Weights:** Empty 6,510 kg (14,354 lb); MTOW 10,500 kg (23,157 lb)
**Performance:** Cruise speed 200 km/h (124 mph) at sea level; operational ceiling 5,000 m (18,046 ft); range 915 km (568 miles) with full payload
**Load:** Three 7.9 mm machine guns and up to 2,000 kg (4,409 lb) payload

*Junkers Ju 52/3m floatplane in Swedish use*

# BOEING MODEL 247 (U.S.A.)

*Boeing Model 247D*

The Model 247 was the logical development of the other pioneering Boeing aircraft, most notably the Model 200 Monomail and Model 215. The Model 200 was a mailplane with limited passenger capacity, and introduced the cantilever monoplane wing, semi-monocoque fuselage, and retractable landing gear. The Model 215 was an extrapolation of the Model 200's concept into the bomber category, and introduced larger size and a twin-engined powerplant. The Model 247 was slightly smaller and lighter than the Model 215, and has many claims to the title of world's first 'modern' air transport as it had features such as all-metal construction, cantilever wings, pneumatic de-icing of the flying surfaces, a semi-monocoque fuselage, retractable landing gear, and fully enclosed accommodation for two pilots, a stewardess, and a planned 14 passengers. Passenger capacity was in fact limited to 10, but with this load the Model 247 could in fact both climb and maintain cruising altitude on just one engine.

The type first flew in February 1933 but, despite its undoubted technical merits, was not a great commercial success. The reasons for this were two-fold: firstly it was not available soon enough for all the airlines wishing to purchase such a modern design; and secondly the aircraft was sized to the requirement of Boeing Air Transport and therefore lacked the larger capacity needed by some potential purchasers. Thus the 60 United Air Lines examples (formed from BAT in 1931) were completed by only 15 more aircraft for companies or individuals. A Model 247 ordered by Roscoe Turner and Clyde Pangbourne for the 1934 England to Australia 'MacRobertson' air race introduced drag-reducing NACA engine cowlings and controllable-pitch propellers, and these features proved so successful that they were retrofitted to most aircraft, which became the Model 247Ds.

*Model 247 of United Air Lines*

**BOEING 247D**
**Role:** Passenger transport
**Crew/Accommodation:** Two crew, one cabin crew, plus up to ten passengers
**Power Plant:** Two 550 hp Pratt & Whitney Wasp S1H1G air-cooled radials
**Dimensions:** Span 22.56 m (74 ft); length 15.72 m (51.58 ft); wing area 77.67 m² (836 sq ft)
**Weights:** Empty 4,148 kg (9,144 lb); MTOW 6,192 kg (13,650 lb)
**Performance:** Cruise speed 304 km/h (189 mph); operational ceiling 7,742 m (25,400 ft); range 1,199 km (745 miles)
**Load:** Up to 998 kg (2,200 lb)

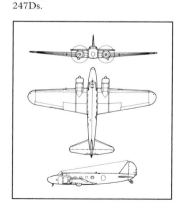

*Boeing Model 247D*

# LOCKHEED L10 ELECTRA (U.S.A.)

*XR20-1*

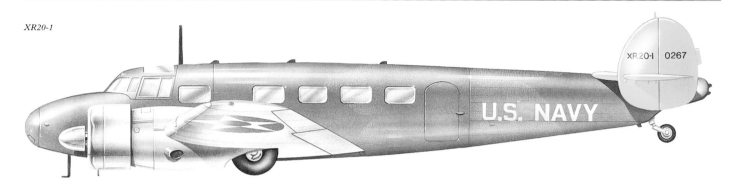

After cutting its teeth on a series of single-engined light transports that also achieved many record long-distance flights, Lockheed decided to move a step up into the potentially more lucrative twin-engined transport market with the Model 10 Electra that offered lower capacity but higher performance than contemporary Boeing and Douglas aircraft. The Electra was an advanced type of all-metal construction with endplate vertical tail surfaces, retractable tailwheel landing gear and other advanced features. The first machine flew in February 1934 with a pair of Pratt & Whitney Wasp Junior SB radials and, though the type's 10-passenger capacity was thought by many to be too small for airline operators, production totalled 148 aircraft in major variants such as 101 Electra 10-As with 336-kW (450-hp) Wasp Juniors and accommodation for 10 passengers, 18 Electra 10-Bs with 328-kW (440-hp) Wright R-975-E3 Whirlwinds, eight Electra 10-Cs with Wasp SC1s, and 15 Electra 10-Es with 447-kW (600-hp) Wasp S3H1s.

Nothing came of the projected Electra 10-D military transport, but 26 civil Electras were later impressed with the designation C-36A to C to supplement the single XC-36 high-altitude research type, three C-36s with 10-seat accommodation and the single C-37 used by the Militia Bureau. The XR2O and XR3O were single U.S. Navy and U.S. Coast Guard aircraft. The L-12 Electra Junior was a scaled-down version intended mainly for feederlines and business operators, and first flew in June 1936. Some 114 were built in Model 12 and improved Model 12-A forms with accommodation for five passengers, and many of the 73 civil aircraft were later impressed for military service. Here they shared the C-40 designation with the machines built for the U.S. Army Air Corps.

## LOCKHEED L10-A ELECTRA

**Role:** Passenger transport
**Crew/Accommodation:** Two, plus up to ten passengers
**Power Plant:** Two 450 hp Pratt & Whitney R-1340 Wasp Junior SB air-cooled radials
**Dimensions:** Span 16.76 m (55 ft); length 11.76 m (38.58 ft); wing area 42.59 m² (458.5 sq ft)
**Weights:** Empty 2,927 kg (6,454 lb); MTOW 4,672 kg (10,300 lb)
**Performance:** Maximum speed 306 km/h (190 mph) at 1,525 m (5,000 ft); operational ceiling 5,915 m (19,400 ft); range 1,305 km (810 miles)
**Load:** Up to 816 kg (1,800 lb)

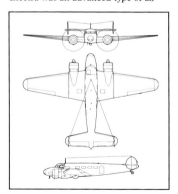

*Lockheed L-10A Electra*

*Lockheed L-10A Electra*

# SIKORSKY S-42 (U.S.A.)

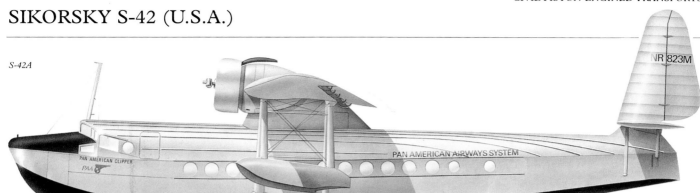

*S-42A*

In August 1931, Pan American Airways issued a requirement for a new type of flying boat. This was needed for the transatlantic service that the airline intended to inaugurate, and called for a type carrying a crew of four and at least 12 passengers over a range of 4023 km (2,500 miles) at a cruising speed of 233 km/h (145 mph). At the end of 1932, the airline contracted with Martin for its M-130 and with Sikorsky for its S-42. The latter was related to the S-40 amphibian to be used on Pan American's routes across the Caribbean and South America.

The S-40 had been based on the S-38 and retained the earlier design's combination of a central pod for 40 passengers and a crew of six, with a twin-boom tail and a parasol wing braced to a 'lower wing' that also supported the stabilizing floats. The larger and more powerful S-42 was a parasol-winged flying boat with a wholly conventional boat hull, a high-set braced tailplane with twin vertical surfaces, the wing braced directly to the hull and supporting the two stabilizing floats as well as four radial engines on the leading edges. The first S-42 was delivered in August 1934, and the type flew its first service during that month between Miami and Rio de Janeiro. The type was used mainly on the airline's South American and transpacific routes (including pioneering flights across the South Pacific to New Zealand). Total production was 10 'boats including three S-42s with the 522-kW (700-hp) Pratt & Whitney Hornet S5D1G, three-S-42A 'boats with 559-kW (750-hp) Hornet S1EG radials and longer-span wings, and four S-42B 'boats with further refinements and Hamilton Standard constant-speed propellers permitting 907-kg (2,000-lb) increase in maximum take-off weight.

*The Sikorsky S-42 was based on a substantial hull*

### SIKORSKY S-42B
**Role:** Intermediate/short-range passenger transport flying boat
**Crew/Accommodation:** Four and two cabin crew, plus up to 32 passengers
**Power Plant:** Four 800 hp Pratt & Whitney R-1690 Hornet air-cooled radials
**Dimensions:** Span 35.97 m (118.33 ft); length 20.93 m (68.66 ft); wing area 124.5 m² (1,340 sq ft)
**Weights:** Empty 9,491 kg (20,924 lb); MTOW 19,504 kg (43,000 lb)
**Performance:** Cruise speed 225 km/h (140 mph) at 610 m (2,000 ft); operational ceiling 4,878 m (16,000 ft); range 1,207 km (750 miles) with full payload
**Load:** Up to 3,626 kg (7,995 lb)

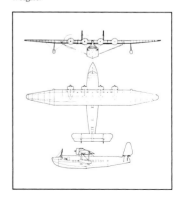

*Sikorsky S-42*

# DOUGLAS DC3 and Military Derivatives (U.S.A.)

*DC-3*

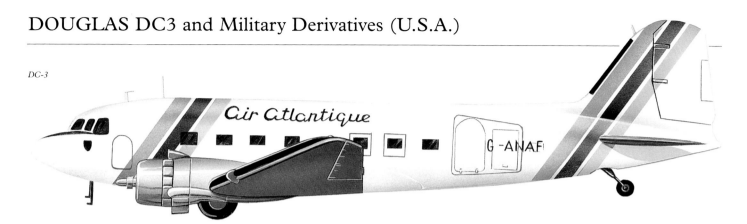

The DC-3 can truly be said to have changed history, for this type opened the era of 'modern' air travel in the mid-1930s, and became the mainstay of the Allies' air transport effort in World War II. Production of 10,349 aircraft was completed in the United States; at least another 2,000 were produced under licence in the U.S.S.R. as the Lisunov Li-2, and 485 were built in Japan as the Showa

(Nakajima) L2D.

The series began with the DC-1 that first flew in July 1933 as a cantilever low-wing monoplane of all-metal construction (except fabric-covered control surfaces) with enclosed accommodation and features such as retractable landing gear and trailing-edge flaps. From this prototype was developed the 14-passenger DC-2 production model, which was built in modest numbers but paved the way for the Douglas Sleeper Transport that first flew in December 1935 as an airliner for

transcontinental night flights with 16 passengers in sleeper berths. From this was evolved the 24-passenger DC-3. This latter was produced in five series with either the Wright SGR-1820 Cyclone or Pratt & Whitney R-1830 Twin Wasp radial as the standard engine. The type was ordered for the U.S. military as the C-47 Skytrain (U.S. Army) and R4D (U.S. Navy), while the British adopted the name Dakota for aircraft supplied under the terms of the Lend-Lease Act.

The type was produced in a vast number of variants within the new-build C-47, C-53, C-117 and R4D series for transport, paratrooping, and glider-towing duties, while impressed aircraft swelled numbers and also designations to a bewildering degree. After the war, large quantities of these monumentally reliable aircraft were released cheaply to civil operators, and the series can be credited with the development of air transport in most of the world's remoter regions.

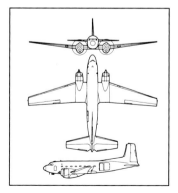

*Douglas R4D-8*

**DOUGLAS DC-3A**
**Role:** Passenger transport
**Crew/Accommodation:** Three, plus two cabin crew and up to 28 passengers
**Power Plant:** Two 1,200 hp Pratt & Whitney Twin Wasp S1C3-G air cooled radials
**Dimensions:** Span 28.96 m (95 ft); length 19.65 m (64.47 ft); wing area 91.7 m² (987 sq ft)
**Weights:** Empty 7,650 g (16,865 lb); MTOW 11,431 kg (25,200 lb)
**Performance:** Maximum speed 370 km/h (230 mph) at 2,590 m (8,500 sq ft); operational ceiling 7,070 m (23,200 ft); range 3,420 km (2,125 miles)
**Load:** Up to 2,350 kg (5,180 lb)

*A Douglas DC-3 in service with East African Airways*

# FOCKE-WULF Fw 200 CONDOR (Germany)

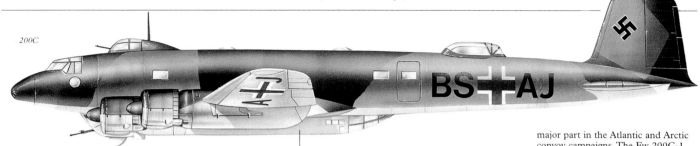

*200C*

The Fw 200 was developed as a transatlantic passenger and mail aircraft that might appeal to Deutsche Lufthansa. The first of three prototypes flew during July 1937 with 652-kW (750-hp) Pratt and Whitney Hornet radials and room for a maximum of 26 passengers in two cabins; the next two aircraft had 537-kW (720-hp) BMW 132G-1 radials. Eight Fw 200A pre-production transports were delivered to Lufthansa and single examples to Brazilian and Danish airliners. Four Fw 200B airliners with 619-kW (830-hp) BMW 132H engines followed. Some of these later became the personal transports of Nazi VIPs.

The Condor's real claim to fame rests with its Fw 200C series, Germany's most important maritime reconnaissance bomber of World War II. This was pioneered by a maritime reconnaissance prototype ordered by Japan but never delivered. Ten Fw 200C-0 pre-production aircraft were delivered as six maritime reconnaissance and four transport aircraft, and there followed a steadily more diverse sequence of specialized aircraft that were hampered by a structural weakness in the fuselage aft of the wing but nevertheless played a major part in the Atlantic and Arctic convoy campaigns. The Fw 200C-1 was a reconnaissance bomber with a 1750-kg (3,757-lb) bomb load, and the Fw 200C-2 was an aerodynamically refined variant. The Fw 200C-3 had 895-kW (1,200-hp) BMW-Bramo 323R-2 Fafnir radials, structural strengthening, and improved defensive and offensive armament in four subvariants. The main model was the Fw 200C-4 with radar, and there were two 11- and 14-passenger transport derivatives of this. The Fw 200C-6 was the C-3 modified as launcher for two Henschel Hs 293 anti-ship missiles, while the Fw 200C-8 was another missile carrier with improved radar. Total production was 276 aircraft.

### FOCKE-WULF Fw 200C-3 CONDOR

**Role:** Long-range maritime reconnaisance bomber

**Crew:** Accommodation: Seven

**Power Plant:** Four 1,200-hp BMW Bramo 323 R-2 Fafnir air-cooled radials

**Dimensions:** Span 32.84 m (107.74 ft); length 23.85 m (78.25 ft); wing area 118m² (1,290 sq ft)

**Weights:** Empty 17,000 kg (37,485 lb); MTOW 22,700 kg (50,045 lb)

**Performance:** Cruise speed 335 km/h (208 mph) at 4,000 m (13,124 ft); operational ceiling 6,000 m (19,685 ft); range 3,560 km (2,211 miles)

**Load:** One 20-mm cannon, three 13-mm and two 7.9-mm machine guns, plus up to 2,100 kg (4,630 lb) of bombs

*The Fw 200 V5*

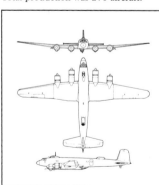

*Focke-Wulf Fw 200C-1 Condor*

# DORNIER Do 26 (Germany)

*Dornier Do 26*

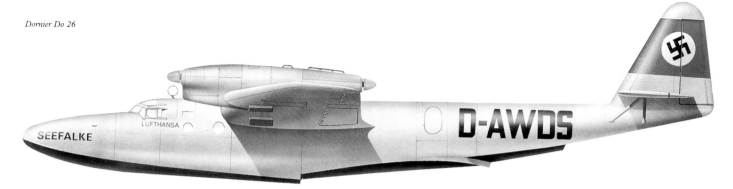

Dornier built many types of flying boat, but the type that offered the cleanest aerodynamics and the most pleasing lines was, without doubt, the Do 26. The type had its origins in the transatlantic mail services developed in the 1930s, and was designed to carry a flight crew of four and 500 kg (1,102 lb) of mail between Lisbon and New York. The all-metal design was based on a slender two-step hull carrying a shoulder-mounted gull wing

and a simple tail unit with braced tailplane halves. The four engines were located in the angles of the gull wings as push/pull tandem pairs in single nacelles that offered minimum resistance. Junkers Jumo 205C/D diesel engines each delivering 447-kW (600-hp) were chosen for their reliability and low specific fuel consumption, and the two pusher engines were installed on mountings that allowed them to be tilted up at

10° at take-off so that the three-blade propeller units were clear of the spray from the hull.

The flying boats were stressed for catapult launches from support ships, and Deutsche Lufthansa ordered three aircraft during 1937. The first of these flew in May 1938, and the two machines completed before the outbreak of World War II were delivered to the airline with the designation Do 26A. These were never used for their intended North Atlantic route, and completed just 18 crossings of the South Atlantic. The third machine was to have been the

Do 26B with provision for four passengers, but was completed as the first of an eventual four Do 26D military flying boats in the long-range reconnaissance and transport roles. These were powered by 522-kW (700-hp) Jumo 205Ea engines, and carried a bow turret armed with a single 20-mm cannon in addition to three 7.92-mm (0.312-in) machine guns in one dorsal and two waist positions.

*In the air, the Dornier Do 26 had very clean lines*

**DORNIER Do 26A**
**Role:** Long-range mail transport
**Crew/Accommodation:** Four
**Power Plant:** Four 700 hp Junkers Jumo 205C liquid-cooled diesels
**Dimensions:** Span 30.00 m (98.42 ft); length 24.60 m (80.71 ft); wing area 120 m² (1,291.67 sq ft)
**Weights:** Empty 10,700 kg (23,594 lb); MTOW 20,000 kg (44,100 lb)
**Performance:** Maximum speed 335 km/h (208 mph) at sea level; operational ceiling 4,800 m (15,748 ft); range 9,000 km (5,592 miles) with full payload
**Load:** Up to 500 kg (1,103 lb)

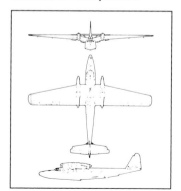

*Dornier Do 26 V4*

# BOEING 314 (U.S.A.)

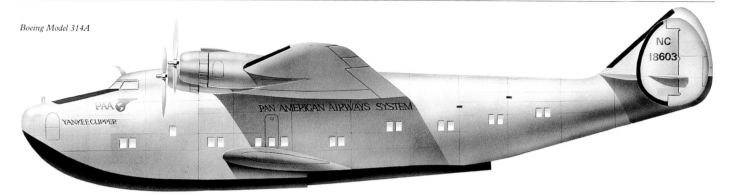

*Boeing Model 314A*

The Model 314 was the greatest flying boat ever built for the civil air transport role. It was designed to the requirement of Pan American Airways for the transatlantic service which the airline had requested from the U.S. Bureau of Air Commerce as early as January 1935. The airline already operated the Martin M-130 and Sikorsky S-42 flying boat airliners, but wanted a 'state-of-the-art' type for this new prestige route. Boeing designed its Model 314 on the basis of the wings and modified tailplane of the Model 294 (XB-15) experimental bomber married to a fuselage accommodating a maximum of 74 passengers in four cabins. The engines were a quartet of 1119-kW (1,500-hp) Wright GR-2600 Double Cyclone radials with fuel for a range of 5633 km (3,500 miles). Some of the fuel was stored in the two lateral sponsons that stabilized the machine on the water and also served as loading platforms.

The first aeroplane flew in June 1938, and the original single vertical tail was soon replaced by twin endplate surfaces that were then supplemented by a central fin based on the original vertical surface but without a movable rudder. The Model 314 entered service in May 1939 as a mailplane, and the first passengers were carried in June of the same year. The six Model 314s were later joined by six Model 314As (including three for the British Overseas Airways Corporation) with more fuel and 1193-kW (1,600-hp) engines driving larger-diameter propellers. Six of the aircraft were used in World War II by the American military in the form of C-98s and B-314s.

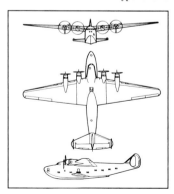

*Boeing Model 314*

### BOEING 314A
**Role:** Long-range passenger flying boat
**Crew/Accommodation:** Three, plus seven cabin crew and up to 74 passengers
**Power Plant:** Four 1,600 hp Wright GR-2600 Double Cyclone air-cooled radials
**Dimensions:** Span 46.33 m (152 ft); length 32.31 m (106 ft); wing area 266.35 m² (2,867 sq ft)
**Weights:** Empty 22,801 kg (50,268 lb); MTOW 37,422 kg (82,500 lb)
**Performance:** Cruise speed 295 km/h (183 mph) at sea level; operational ceiling 4,084 m (13,400 ft); range 5,632 km (3,500 miles)
**Load:** Up to 6,713 kg (14,800 lb)

*The Boeing Model 314 was undoubtedly the finest flying boat airliner ever built*

# LOCKHEED CONSTELLATION Family (U.S.A.)

*EC-121K*

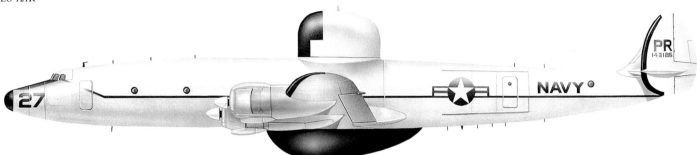

This was surely one of the classic aircraft of all time, developed as an elegant yet efficient airliner but also of great military importance as the basis of the world's first long-range airborne early warning and electronic warfare aircraft. The design was originated in 1939 to provide Pan American Airways and Transcontinental and Western Air with an advanced airliner for use on long-range domestic routes.

The Lockheed design was centred on refined aerodynamics, pressurized accommodation and high power for sustained high-altitude cruising at high speed, and tricycle landing gear was incorporated for optimum field performance and passenger comfort on the ground.

The type first flew in January 1943, and civil production was overtaken by the needs of the military during World War II; the L-49 thus became the U.S. Army's C-69, of which 22 were completed before Japan's capitulation

and the cancellation of military orders. Some aircraft then on the production line were completed as 60-seat L-049 airliners, but the first true civil version was the 81-seat L-649 with 1864-kW (2,500-hp) Wright 749C-18BD-1 radials. Further airliners were the L-749 with additional fuel, the L-1049 Super Constellation with the fuselage lengthened by 5.59 m (18 in 4 in) for the accommodation of 109 passengers, and the L-1649 Starliner with a new, longer-span wing and 2535-kW (3,500-hp) Wright 988TC-

18EA-2 radials fed from increased fuel tankage for true intercontinental range. Production of the series totalled 856 including military variants that included the C-121 transport version of the L-749, the R7O naval transport version of the L-1049, and the PO-1 and VW-2 Warning Star airborne early warning aircraft. These R7O, PO-1 and VW-2 aircraft were later redesignated in the C-121 series that expanded to include a large number of EC-121 electronic warfare aircraft.

*Lockheed L-749 Constellation*

**LOCKHEED L749 CONSTELLATION**
**Role:** Long-range passenger transport
**Crew/Accommodation:** Four and two cabin crew, plus up to 81 passengers
**Power Plant:** Four 2,500 hp Wright 749C-18BD-1 Double Cyclone air-cooled radials
**Dimensions:** Span 37.49 m (123 ft); length 29.03 m (95.25 ft); wing area 153.3 m² (1,650 sq ft)
**Weights:** Empty 27,648 kg (60,954 lb); MTOW 47,627 (105,000 lb)
**Performance:** Cruise speed 557 km/h (346 mph) at 9,072 m (20,000 ft); operational ceiling 10,886 m (24,000 ft); range 3,219 km/h (2,000 miles) with 6,124 (13,500 lb) payload plus reserves
**Load:** Up to 6,690 kg (14,750 lb) with 6,124 kg (13,500 lb)

*This is an L-049E named Baltimore*

# CONVAIR CONVAIRLINER Series (U.S.A.)

*Convair 440*

The CV-240 series was developed in the hope of producing a successor to the legendary Douglas DC-3, and though the type was in every respect good, with features such as pressurized accommodation and tricycle landing gear that kept the fuselage level on the ground, it failed to make a decisive impression on a market saturated by the vast number of C-47s released on to the civil market when they became surplus to military requirements. The spur for the type's original design was a specification issued in 1945 by American Airlines for a modern airliner to supersede the DC-3 and offer superior operating economics.

The CV-110 prototype first flew in July 1946 with 1566-kW (2,100-hp) Pratt & Whitney R-2800-S1C3-G radial engines and pressurized accommodation for 30 passengers. Even before this prototype flew, however, American Airlines had revised its specification and now demanded greater capacity. It proved a comparatively straightforward task to increase capacity to 40 passengers by lengthening the fuselage by 1.12 m (3 ft 8 in), and in this form the airliner became the CV-240. No prototype was built, the company flying its first production example in March 1947. The CV-240 entered service in June 1948, and 176 were built as airliners. There followed the 44-passenger CV-340 with 1864-kW (2,500-hp) R-2800-CB-16 or 17 engines and a fuselage stretch of 1.37 m (4 ft 6 in), and finally the similar CV-440 with aerodynamic refinements and high-density seating for 52 passengers. Turboprop conversions were later made to produce the CV-540, 580, 600 and 640 series. Variants for the military were the T-29 USAF crew trainer, the C-131 air ambulance and transport for the USAF, and the R4Y transport for the U.S. Navy.

## CONVAIR 440 CONVAIRLINER

**Role:** Short-range passenger transport
**Crew/Accommodation:** Two, plus up to 52 passengers
**Power Plant:** Two 2,500 hp Pratt & Whitney R-2800-CB16/17 Double Wasp air-cooled radials
**Dimensions:** Span 31.10 m (105. 33 ft); length 24.84 m (81.5 ft); wing area 85.47 m² (920 sq ft)
**Weights:** Empty 15,111 kg (33,314 lb); MTOW 22,544 kg (49.700 lb)
**Performance:** Cruise speed 465 km/h (289 mph) at 6,096 m (20,000 ft); operational ceiling 7,590 m (24,900 ft); range 459 km (285 miles) with maximum payload
**Load:** Up to 5,820 kg (12,836 lb)

*CV-440 Metropolitan*

*Convair CV-580*

199

# AIRSPEED AMBASSADOR (United Kingdom)

*AS.57 Ambassador*

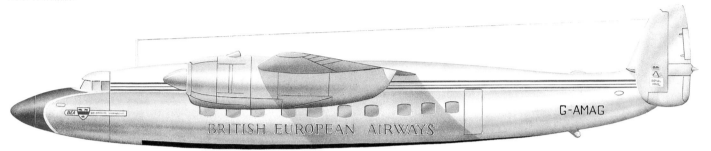

The Ambassador was one of the most elegant aircraft ever built, and resulted from the Brabazon Committee's 1943 recommendation for a 30-seat short/medium-range airliner to be built after World War II within the context of reviving the U.K.'s airline network and civil aircraft production capability. The AS.57 was designed in the closing stages of the war with a high aspect ratio wing set high on the circular-section pressurized fuselage, which ended in an upswept tail unit with triple vertical surfaces; the main units of the tricycle landing gear retracted into the rear part of the two engine nacelles slung under the inner portions of the wing.

The first Ambassador flew in July 1947 and, with two Bristol Centaurus radials, had very promising performance. Just over one year later, an order for 20 aircraft was received from BEA, but the programme was then beset by a number of technical problems during its development. This delayed the Ambassador's service entry until March 1952, and meant that the initial 20-aircraft order was the only one fulfilled as this piston-engined type had been overtaken in performance and operating economics by the turboprop-powered Vickers Viscount. Even so, the 'Elizabethan' class served BEA with great popularity for six years, and the aircraft were then acquired by five other operators. The second and third prototypes went on to important subsidiary careers as test beds for turboprops, such as the Bristol Proteus, the Napier Eland, and the Rolls-Royce Dart and Tyne.

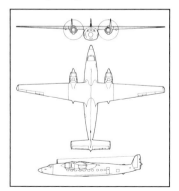

*Airspeed AS.57 Ambassador*

## AIRSPEED AMBASSADOR
**Role:** Short range passenger transport
**Crew/Accommodation:** Three, plus three cabin crew and 47/49 passengers
**Power Plant:** Two 2,700 hp Bristol Centaurus 661 air-cooled radials
**Dimensions:** Span 35.05 m (115 ft); length 24.69 m (81 ft); wing area 111.48 m² (1,200 sq ft)
**Weights:** Empty 16,277 kg (35,884 lb); MTOW 23,590 kg (52,000 lb)
**Performance:** Cruise speed 483 km/h (300 mph) at 6,096 m (20,000 ft); range 1,159 km (720 miles) with maximum payload
**Load:** Up to 5,285 kg (11,650 lb)

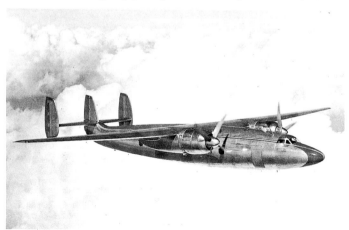

*The Airspeed Ambassador was a design of aerodynamic elegance*

# BOEING STRATOCRUISER and C-97 Series (U.S.A.)

*Stratocruiser*

The Model 377 was a commercial transport developed from the C-97 military transport, which itself evolved as the Model 367 to combine the wings, engines, tail unit, landing gear and lower fuselage of the B-29 bomber with a new upper fuselage lobe of considerably larger radius and so create a pressurized 'double-bubble' fuselage. This provided considerable volume, and also provided the Model 377 with its distinctive two-deck layout. The Model 377-10-9 prototype was based on the YC-97A with Pratt & Whitney R-4360 radial engines, and first flew in July 1947.

The aircraft was later delivered to Pan American Airways, which soon became the world's largest operator of the Stratocruiser, with 27 of the 55 aircraft built. Ten of them were fitted with additional fuel tankage as Super Stratocruisers, and these were suitable for the transatlantic route. At a later date, all Pan Am's aircraft were modified with a General Electric CH-10 turbocharger on each engine for an additional 37.3 kW (50 hp) of power for high-altitude cruise. The other major operator of the type was BOAC, which bought six new aircraft and then found this particular type so useful that is secured another 11 from other operators.

The Stratocruiser was available in Model 377-10-26, -28, -29, -30 and -32 variants with interior arrangements that catered for anything between 58 and 112 day passengers, or alternatively 33 night passengers accommodated in five seats as well as 28 upper- and lower-deck berths. The standard accommodation was on the upper deck, with access to the 14-person cocktail lounge on the lower deck via a spiral staircase.

Strange derivatives of the C-97/Stratocruiser became the Guppy series of 'outsized' transports developed by Aero Spacelines, starting with the Pregnant Guppy in 1962. Each featured a huge fuselage extension to allow carriage of very bulky freight.

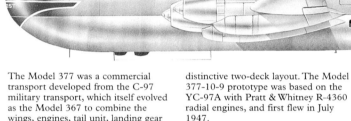

*The Aero Spacelines Guppy-201*

**BOEING 377 STRATOCRUISER**
**Role:** Long range passenger transport
**Crew/Accommodation:** Five and five cabin crew, plus up to 95 passengers
**Power Plant:** Four 3,500 hp Pratt & Whitney R-4360B3 Double Wasp air-cooled radials
**Dimensions:** 43.03 m (141.19 ft); length 33.63 m (110.33 ft); wing area 159.79 m² (1,720 sq ft)
**Weights:** Empty 35,797 kg (78,920 lb); MTOW 67,131 kg (148,000 lb)
**Performance:** Maximum speed 603 km/h (375 mph) at 7,625 m (25,000 ft); operational ceiling 9,754 m (32,000 ft); range 7,360 km (4,600 miles) with full fuel
**Load:** Up to 13,608 kg (30,000 lb)

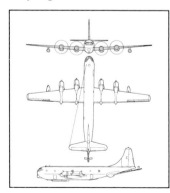

*KC-97G Stratofreighter*

# de HAVILLAND CANADA DHC-2 BEAVER (Canada)

*DHC-2 Beaver*

The DHC-2 Beaver was designed from 1946 specifically to meet a specification issued by the Ontario Department of Lands and Forests, and resulted in a superb aircraft that fully met the overall Canadian need for a bushplane to replace pre-World

*de Havilland Canada DHC-2 Beaver*

War II types such as the Noorduyn Norseman and various Fairchild aircraft. Key features of the design were the rugged reliability of the airframe and single radial engine, STOL performance, operational versatility, and the ability to carry wheels, skis, or floats on the main units of its tailwheel landing gear, whose wide track gave the type exceptional stability on the ground, snow, or water. The DHC-2 was designed round the readily available

**de HAVILLAND CANADA DHC-2 BEAVER I**
**Role:** Light utility transport
**Crew/Accommodation:** One, plus up to six passengers
**Power Plant:** One 450 hp Pratt & Whitney R-985AN-6B Wasp Junior air-cooled radial
**Dimensions:** 14.62 m (48.00 ft); length 9.23 m (30.25 ft); wing area 23.20 m² (250.00 sq ft)
**Weights:** Empty 1,294 kg (2,850 lb); MTOW 2,313 kg (5,100 lb)
**Performance:** Maximum speed 257 km/h (160 mph) at 1,524 m (5,000 ft); operational ceiling 5,486 m (18,000 ft); range 756 km (470 miles) with full payload
**Load:** Up to 613 kg (1,350 lb)

and thoroughly reliable Pratt & Whitney R-985 Wasp Junior engine, and emerged for its first flight in August 1947 as a braced high-wing monoplane together with sturdy fixed landing gear.

The only model to achieve mass production was the Beaver I, of which 1,657 were produced with the ability to carry the pilot and a basic payload of seven passengers or 680 kg (1,500 lb) of freight. No fewer than 980 of these Beaver Is were bought by the U.S. Army and U.S. Air Force with the basic designation L-20 (from 1962 U-6); six were YL-20 service test aircraft, 968 were L-20A production aircraft, and six were L-20B production aircraft with different equipment. One Beaver II was produced with the 410-kW (550-hp) Alvis Leonides radial, and there were also a few Turbo-Beaver IIIs with the 431-kW (578-ehp) Pratt & Whitney Canada PT6A-6/20 turboprop and provision for 10 passengers. Production of this classic type ended in the mid-1960s as de Havilland Canada concentrated on more ambitious aircraft.

*The de Havilland Canada DHC-2 Beaver*

# DOUGLAS DC-7 (U.S.A.)

*Douglas DC-7C*

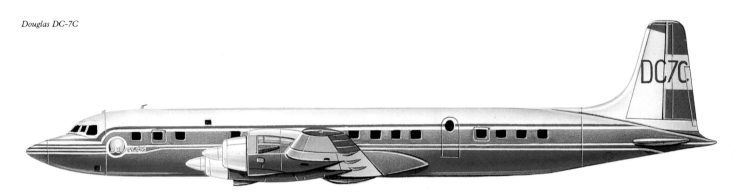

In its C-54 military guise, the DC-4 proved an invaluable long-range transport in World War II. The type's reliability is attested by the fact that only three aircraft were lost in the course of 80,000 or more oceanic crossings. Capacity was limited, however, and Douglas developed to army order the similar but pressurized XC-112A with a longer fuselage. This first flew in February 1946 and was thus too late for the war. With no military orders forthcoming, Douglas marketed the type as the civil DC-6 that later spawned a military C-118 Liftmaster derivative. And from the DC-6B passenger transport, the company developed the DC-7 to meet an American Airlines' requirement for an airliner to compete with TWA's Lockheed Super Constellation. The DC-7 had a lengthened fuselage, beefed-up landing gear and the same 2424-kW (3,250-hp) Wright R-3350 Turbo-Compound engines as the Super Constellation.

The type first flew in May 1953 and entered production as the DC-6 transcontinental transport, of which 105 were built. To provide transatlantic range, Douglas developed the DC-7B with additional fuel capacity in longer engine nacelles. Production of this variant totalled 112 aircraft, but the model proved to possess only marginally adequate capability in its intended role, and was therefore superseded by the DC-7C, often called the Seven Seas. This became one of the definitive piston-engined airliners, and production totalled 120. The type had 2535-kW (3,400-hp) R-3350-18EA-1 engines, a fuselage lengthened by 1.02 m (3 ft 4 in) to allow the carriage of 105 passengers and, most importantly, increased fuel capacity in parallel-chord inboard wing extensions that also possessed the additional benefit of moving the engines farther from the fuselage and so reducing cabin noise.

*This was the thirtieth Douglas DC-7 to be built*

## DOUGLAS DC-7C

**Role:** Long-range passenger transport
**Crew/Accommodation:** Four and four/five cabin crew, plus up to 105 passengers
**Power Plant:** Four 3,400 hp Wright R-3350-18EA-1 Turbo-Compound air-cooled radials
**Dimensions:** Span 38.86 m (127.5 ft); length 34.21 m (112.25 ft); wing area 152.08 m² (1,637 sq ft)
**Weights:** Empty 33,005 kg (72,763 lb); MTOW 64,864 kg (143,000 lb)
**Performance:** Cruise speed 571 km/h (355 mph) at 5,791 m (19,000 ft); operational ceiling 6,615 m (21,700 ft); range 7,410 km (4,605 miles) with maximum payload
**Load:** Up to 10,591 kg (23,350 lb)

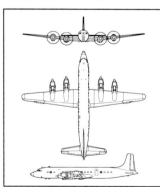

*Douglas DC-7C*

# BRITTEN-NORMAN BN2 ISLANDER Family (United Kingdom)

*BN2A Islander*

The Islander was designed as a simple feederliner for operators in remoter areas, and was schemed as a low-maintenance type of all-metal construction with fixed tricycle landing gear, a high-set wing mounting the two reliable piston engines, and a slab-sided fuselage with 'wall-to-wall' seating accessed by one door on the starboard side and two on the port side. The first Islander flew in June 1965 with two 157-kW (210-hp) Continental IO-360-B engines. The type was underpowered and had too high a wing loading. This meant the adoption of a wing spanning 1.22 m (4 ft 0 in) more, and a power plant of two 194-kW (260-hp) Lycoming O-540-E engines. The result was the BN2 model that entered service in August 1967.

Later variants became the refined BN2A and the heavier BN2B with an interior of proved design and smaller-diameter propellers for lower cabin noise levels. Options have included an extended nose providing additional baggage volume. The current piston-engined models are the BN2B-26 and the BN2B-20, the latter with more powerful engines. The type has also been produced in Defender and other militarized models with underwing hardpoints, and options for weapons and/or sensors that can optimize the aircraft for a number of important roles in the electronic warfare arena. Turbine power became an increasingly attractive alternative during the Islander's early production career, and the result was the BN2T with two 239-kW (320-shp) Allison 250-B17C turboprops, which remains available. The largest derivative became the Trislander with a third engine added at the junction of the enlarged vertical tail and the mid-set tailplane. The Trislander was given a lengthened fuselage for 17 passengers.

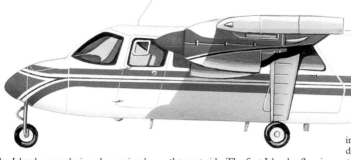

*BN2A Islander*

**BRITTEN-NORMAN BN2B-20**
**Role:** Light short-field utility/passenger transport
**Crew/Accommodation:** One, plus up to nine passengers
**Power Plant:** Two 260 hp Lycoming O-540-E4C5 air-cooled flat-opposed
**Dimensions:** Span 14.94 m (49 ft); length 10.97 m (36 ft); wing area 30.2 m² (325 sq ft)
**Weights:** Empty 1,866 kg (4,114 lb); MTOW 2,993 kg (6,600 lb)
**Performance:** Cruise speed 263 km/h (164 mph) at 2,440 m (8,000 ft); operational ceiling 3,444 m (11,300 ft); range 1,763 km (1,096 miles) with optional wingtip tanks for IFR flying
**Load:** Up to 1,082 kg (2,386 lb) disposable load

*The triple-engined Britten-Norman Trislander*

*Britten-Norman BN2B Islander, operated by British Airways Express*

# Civil Turboprop-Engined Transports

It was as long ago as 1926 that British Dr A.A. Griffith first suggested that a turbine engine could be used to produce not only jet exhaust but the power needed to turn a propeller via a reduction gear. During World War II Rolls-Royce developed its Derwent turbojet engine and, from this, conceived a turboprop derivative as the Trent, which drove a five-blade propeller. Incredibly, an early Gloster Meteor fighter prototype was used to flight-test the Trent, in September 1945, and thereby became the first aeroplane in history to fly on turboprop power alone.

The wartime Brabazon Committee recommended that a turboprop-powered short/medium-range airliner should be developed among other types, and what was originally named the Brabazon IIB eventually appeared in 1948 as the Vickers Viscount, the world's first turbine-powered airliner of either turboprop or turbojet varieties. The Dart engines chosen provided the required mix of high performance and fuel economy and, although virtually all large commercial jetliners were eventually to adopt turbojets for greatest performance gains from turbine power, turboprops remained the favoured engine type for many of the smaller airliners to this day. Of course, it should not be overlooked that some of the world's largest aircraft have also used turboprop power, including giant Soviet and Ukrainian types, while another historic first for

turboprop power came in December 1957 when a BOAC Bristol Britannia 312 flew from London to New York and was thereby the first-ever turbine airliner to undertake a transatlantic passenger service.

*Bringing older aircraft up to required modern standards of performance has included DC-3s being re-engined with turboprops. Here a Balser Turbo-67 (DC-3 type) has a lengthened fuselage, twin Pratt & Whitney Canada PT6A turboprops and other updates, thereby offering 76 per cent more productivity than a standard piston-engined DC-3 plus many other benefits.*

# VICKERS VISCOUNT (United Kingdom)

*Viscount 800*

The Type 630 Viscount was the world's first turbine-powered airliner to enter service. The aircraft was developed as the Vickers VC2 (originally the Brabazon IIB) to meet a requirement for a 24-seat short/medium-range airliner with a turboprop powerplant. The specification was issued during World War II by the Brabazon Committee that was charged with assessing the U.K.'s post-war civil air transport needs, and the prototype

Type 630 was designed as a 32-passenger airliner of attractive design and orthodox construction based on a cantilever low-wing monoplane layout with retractable tricycle landing gear.

The first example flew in July 1948 with four 738-kW (990-shp) Rolls-Royce Dart RDa.1 Mk 502 turboprops in slim wing-mounted nacelles. The type had too low a capacity to attract any real commercial interest, but was then revised in

accordance with the requirement of British European Airways for an airliner with pressurized accommodation for between 40 and 59 passengers. This Type 700 became the first production version with a powerplant of four 1044-kW (1,400-shp) Dart Mk 506s or, in the Type 700D, four 1193-kW (1,600-shp) Dart Mk 510s. These latter engines also powered the Type 800 with a lengthened fuselage for between 65 and 71 passengers. The Type 810 was structurally strengthened for operation at higher weights, and was powered by 1566-kW (2,100-shp) Dart RDa.7/1

Mk 525s. Total production was eventually 444 aircraft, and the type made the world's first turbine-powered commercial airline flight on 29 July 1950 at the beginning of a two-week experimental service between London and Paris. The Viscount was sold in many parts of the world, and made good though not decisive inroads into the lucrative American market.

*A Vickers Viscount 785 of Alitalia*

**VICKERS VISCOUNT 810**
**Role:** Short-range passenger transport
**Crew/Accommodation:** Three and two cabin crew, plus up to 71 passengers
**Power Plant:** Four 2,100 shp Rolls-Royce Dart R.Da 7/1 Mk. 525 turboprops
**Dimensions:** Span 28.5 m (93.76 ft); length 26.11 m (85.66 ft); wing area 89.46 m² (963 sq ft)
**Weights:** Empty 18,753 kg (41,565 lb); MTOW 32,886 kg (72,500 lb)
**Performance:** Maximum speed 563 km/h (350 mph) at 6,100 m (20,000 ft); operational ceiling 7,620 m (25,000 ft); range 2,775 km (1,725 miles) with maximum payload
**Load:** Up to 6.577 kg (14.500 lb)

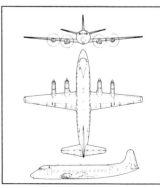

*Vickers Viscount 800*

207

# BRISTOL BRITANNIA (United Kingdom)

*Britannia*

Probably the finest turboprop airliner ever built, the Britannia was so delayed by engine problems that it was overtaken by jet-powered airliners and thus failed to fulfil its great commercial promise. The type was one of eight types proposed by five companies to meet a BOAC requirement shortly after the end of World War II for a Medium-Range Empire airliner with pressurized accommodation for 36 passengers. The Type 175's proposed powerplant of four Bristol Centaurus radials was more than adequate for the specified load, so the design was enlarged to 48-passenger capacity. The Ministry of Supply ordered three prototypes, but the design was further amended and, when the first machine flew in August 1952, it had provision for 90 passengers on the power of four 2088-kW (2,800-ehp) Bristol Proteus turboprops. This paved the way for the first production model, the Britannia Series 100 which entered service in 1957 with 2819-kW (3,780-ehp) Proteus 705s; 15 of these were built for BOAC.

There followed eight Britannia Series 300s with the fuselage lengthened by 3.12 m (10 ft 3 in) for a maximum of 133 passengers carried over transatlantic routes, and 32 Britannia Series 310s with 3072-kW (4,120-ehp) Proteus 755s and greater fuel capacity. Only two were built of the final Britannia Series 320 with 3318-kW (4,450-ehp) Proteus 765s, while production of the Britannia for the civil market in total numbered just 60 aircraft. The last variant was the Britannia Series 250 modelled on the Series 310 but intended for RAF use as 20 Britannia C.Mk 1s and three C.Mk 2s. Exactly the same basic airframe was used by Canadair as the core of two aircraft, the CL-28 Argus maritime patroller with 2535-kW (3,400-hp) Wright R-3350-EA1 Turbo-Compound piston engines, together with the CL-44 long-range transport with 4273-kW (5,730-ehp) Rolls-Royce Tyne 515 Mk 10 turboprops.

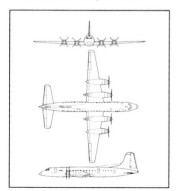

*Bristol Britannia 320*

**BRISTOL BRITANNIA 310 Series**
**Role:** Long-range passenger transport
**Crew/Accommodation:** Four, four cabin crew and up to 139 passengers
**Power Plant:** Four 4,120 ehp Bristol Siddeley Proteus 755 turboprops
**Dimensions:** Span 43.37 m (142.29 ft); length 37.87 m (124.25 ft); wing area 192.78 m² (2,075 sq ft)
**Weights:** Empty 37,438 kg (82,537 lb); MTOW 83,915 kg (185,000 lb)
**Performance:** Cruise speed 660 km/h (410 mph) at 6,401 m (21,000 ft); operational ceiling 9,200+ m (30,184 ft); range 6,869 km (4,268 miles) with maximum payload
**Load:** Up to 15,830 kg (34,900 lb)

*A Bristol Britannia 253F*

# FOKKER F.27 FRIENDSHIP and 50 (Netherlands)

*F.27 Mk 200 Friendship*

After World War II Fokker sought to recapture a slice of the airliner market with a type matching the best of its classic interwar airliners. After long deliberation, the company fixed on a short/medium-range type powered by two Rolls-Royce Dart turboprops on the high-set wing. The first of two prototypes flew in November 1955. The Friendship entered service in December 1958 as the F.27 Mk 100 with two 1279-kW (1,715-shp) Dart RDa. 6 Mk 514-7 engines for the carriage of between 40 and 52 passengers, and was followed by successively upgraded models such as the F.27 Mk 200 with 1529-kW (2,050-shp) Dart RDa. 7 Mk 532-7 engines, the F.27 Mks 300 and 400 Combiplane derivatives of the Mks 100 and 200 with reinforced cabin floors and a large cargo door on the port side of the forward fuselage. The F.27 Mk 500 introduced a fuselage lengthened by 1.50 m (4ft 11 in) for between 52 and 60 passengers. The last variant was the F.27 Mk 600 convertible variant of the Mk 400 without the reinforced floor.

Military variants became the F.27 Mks 400M and 500M Troopship, and specialized maritime reconnaissance models were the unarmed F.27 Maritime and armed F.27 Maritime Enforcer. F.27 production ended with the 579th aircraft, which was delivered in 1987. The basic Mks 100, 200 and 300 were licence-built in the United States as the Fairchild F-27A, B and C to the extent of 128 aircraft, and the same company also produced a variant with its fuselage stretched by 1.83m (6 ft 0 in) as the FH-227, of which 79 were produced.

The durability of the Friendship's basic design was attested by the follow-up development of the Fokker 50, a thoroughly updated 58-passenger version with Pratt & Whitney Canada PW125B or PW127B turboprops driving six-blade propellers. The first Fokker 50 was delivered in August 1987.

*A Fokker F.27 Mk 600R Friendship*

**FOKKER 50**
**Role:** Short-range passenger transport
**Crew/Accommodation:** Two and two cabin crew, plus up to 58 passengers
**Power Plant:** Two 2,250 shp Pratt & Whitney PW 125B turboprops
**Dimensions:** Span 29 m (95.15 ft); length 25.25 m (82.83 ft); wing area 70 m² (754 sq ft)
**Weights:** Empty 12,741 kg (28,090 lb); MTOW 18,990 kg (41,865 lb)
**Performance:** Cruise speed 500 km/h (270 knots) at 6,096 m (20,000 ft); operational ceiling 7,620 m (25,000 ft); range 1,125 km (607 naut. miles) with 50 passengers
**Load:** Up to 5,262 kg (11,600 lb)

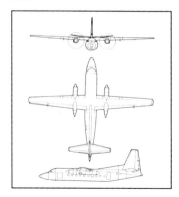

*F.27 Mk 200 Friendship*

# ANTONOV An-22 ANTHEUS 'COCK' (U.S.S.R.)

*AN-22 'Cock'*

In its time the An-22 Antei (Antheus) was the world's largest aircraft although now beaten by the turbofan and 73.3 m (240.5 ft) span An-124 and 88.4 m (290 ft) An-225. An-22 was designed for the twin tasks of military heavy transport and support for the resources exploitation industry in Siberia (flying typically in civil Aeroflot markings). The specification for the type was issued in 1962, and the first example flew in February 1965. The type was first revealed in the West, where it had the NATO reporting name 'Cock' during the Paris air show of June 1965. At that time it was reported that the design could also be developed as a 724-passenger airliner, but this proposal came to nothing. Given the type's highly specialized role and size, it is not surprising that production was limited to only about 60 aircraft, all completed by 1974 and many still flying.

Keynotes of the design are four potent turboprops driving immense contra-rotating propeller units, and an upswept tail unit with twin vertical surfaces at about three-fifths span. The 14-wheel landing gear allows operations into and out of semi-prepared airstrips, and comprises a twin-wheel nose unit and two six-wheel units as main units; the latter are three twin-wheel units in each of the two lateral sponson fairings that provide an unobstructed hold. The upswept tail allows in the rear-fuselage a hydraulically operated ramp/door arrangement for the straight-in loading of items as large as tanks or complete missiles. The hold is 32.7 m (107 ft 3 in) long and 4.4 m (14 ft 5 in) wide and high, and has four overhead travelling gantries as well as two 2500-kg (5,511-lb) capacity winches for the loading of freight.

## ANTONOV An-22 ANTHEUS 'COCK'
**Role:** Long-range freight transport
**Crew/Accommodation:** Five, plus up to 29 passengers/troops in upper cabin
**Power Plant:** Four 14,805 shp Kuznetsov NK 12MA turboprops
**Dimensions:** Span 64.4 .m (211.29 ft); length 57.31 m (188 ft); wing area 345 m² (3,713.6 sq ft)
**Weights:** Empty 118,727 kg (261,748 lb); MTOW 225,000 kg (496,040 lb)
**Performance:** Cruise speed 580 km/h (360 mph); operational ceiling 10,000 m (32,808 ft); range 5,000 km (2,698 naut. miles) with maximum payload
**Load:** Up to 60,000 kg (132,340 lb)

*Antonov An-22 'Cock'*

*An Antonov An-22 of the Soviet civil operator Aeroflot*

# EMBRAER EMB-110 BANDEIRANTE Family (Brazil)

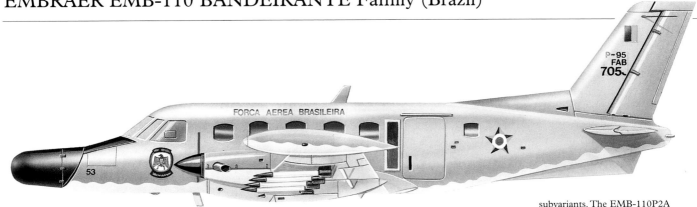

The Empresa Brasileira de Aeronáutica SA was created in 1969 to promote the development of an indigenous Brazilian aircraft industry, and began operation in January 1970. The company has had astonishing international success, particularly with a number of interesting light transports that most recently include the ERJ 135 and 145 regional turbofan jets. Early success came with the EMB-110 Bandeirante (pioneer), whose design origins lie in the period before EMBRAER's creation. The EMB-110 was evolved under the leadership of Max Holste as a utility light transport to meet the multi-role requirements of the Brazilian ministry of aeronautics, and first flew in October 1968 in the form of a YC-95 prototype.

The Bandeirante is of all-metal construction and of typical light transport configuration with low-set cantilever wings, a conventional fuselage and tail unit, retractable tricycle landing gear, and two wing-mounted Pratt & Whitney Canada PT6A turboprop engines. The accommodation varies with model and role, but the EMB-110P2 is typical of the series with seating for 18–19 passengers. The type has been produced in a number of civil variants such as the 15-passenger EMB-110C feederliner, 7-passenger executive EMB-110E, all-cargo EMB-110K1, 18-passenger EMB-110P export model, a higher-capacity model with a fuselage stretch of 0.85 m (2 ft 9.5 in) in EMB-110P1 mixed or all-cargo and EMB-110P2 passenger subvariants, and the EMB-110P/41 higher-weight model in EMB-110P1/41 quick-change and EMB-110P2/41 passenger subvariants. The EMB-110P2A accommodates 21 passengers. Large-scale production for the Brazilian Air Force resulted in a number of C-95 utility transport, R-95 survey and SC-95 transport and search-and-rescue models. Also produced was the EMB-111 Patrulha coastal patrol version operated as the P-95 with search radar, a tactical navigation system, wingtip tanks and provision for underwing weapons. Bandeirante production ended in 1994.

*EMBRAER EMB-111 Patrulha*

**EMBRAER EMB-110P1A BANDEIRANTE**
**Role:** Short-range passenger/cargo transport
**Crew/Accommodation:** Two, plus up to 19 passengers
**Power Plant:** Two 750 shp Pratt & Whitney PT6A-34 turboprops
**Dimensions:** Span 15.32 m (50.26 ft); length 15.08 m (49.47 ft); wing area 29.1 m² (313 sq ft)
**Weights:** Empty 3,630 kg (8,010 lb); MTOW 5,900 kg (13,010 lb)
**Performance:** Cruise speed 417 km/h (259 mph); operational ceiling up to 6,860 m (22,500 ft); range 1,898 km (1,179 miles)
**Load:** Up to 1,565 kg (3,450 lb) passenger version, or 1,724 kg (3,800 lb) cargo-carrier

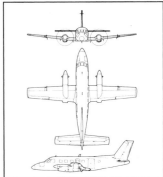

*EMB-110 Bandeirante*

# CASA C-212 AVIOCAR (Spain)

*C-212 Aviocar*

This simple yet effective light transport aircraft was developed to replace the Spanish Air Force's miscellany of obsolete transports. CASA conceived the type with the civil as well as military markets in mind, and thus schemed the type with STOL capability, highly cost-effective operation, great reliability, and simple maintenance. The resulting Aviocar is of all-metal construction and of typical airlifter configuration with an upswept tail unit above a rear ramp/door that provides straight-in access to the rectangular-section cabin; in the latest C-212 Series 300/400 forms, the cabin is 7.275 m (23.88 ft) long in passenger layout and 6.55 m (21.5 ft) in cargo layout, with a width at the floor of 2.1 m (6.92 ft) and 1.87 m (6.17 ft) respectively, and 1.8m (5.92 ft high.

The tricycle landing gear is fixed, and the attachment of the main units to external fairings leaves the hold entirely unobstructed.

The first C-212 first flew in March 1971, and it soon became clear that CASA had designed the right type as orders arrived from third-world civil operators as well as air forces. Spanish production has been complemented by Indonesian construction by IPTN.

More than 460 have been ordered of all versions, going to over 50 civil operators plus military/government agencies in 24 countries. Until recently the Series 300 Aviocar was the current production version, the last with all electro-mechanical instrumentation. For the latest Series 400, first flown in 1997, display screens provided a 'glass cockpit' environment. The military version is designated C-212M, while specialized variants for maritime patrol, anti-submarine, counter-insurgency, search and rescue, electronic warfare and other missions carry the designations 'MP', 'ASW' and 'DE Patrullero'.

**CASA C-212 AVIOCAR Series 400, unless stated**
**Role:** Short, rough field-going utility transport
**Crew/Accommodation:** Two, plus up to 2–6 passengers
**Power Plant:** Two 900 shp AlliedSignal TPE331-10R-513C turboprops for Series 300 and two 925 shp TPE331-12JR-701Cs for Series 400
**Dimensions:** Span 20.275 m (66.5 ft); length 16.154 m (53 ft); wing area 41 m² (441.3 sq ft)
**Weights:** Empty 3,780 kg (8.333 lb) for Series 300; MTOW 8,100 kg (17,857 lb)
**Performance:** Cruise speed 361 km/h (225 mph) at 3,050 m (10,000 ft); operational ceiling 7,925 m (26,000 ft); range 1,594 km (990miles)
**Load:** Up to 2,320 kg (5,115 lb) of passengers or 2,800 kg (6,172 lb) of cargo for Series 300, 2,950 kg (6,504 lb) for Series 400

*C-212 Aviocar*

*CASA C-212M Aviocar in military form with Angola*

# SHORTS 360 (United Kingdom)

*Shorts 360*

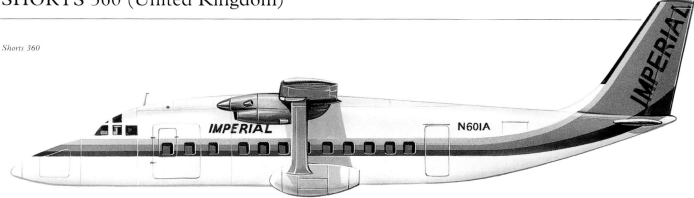

After the success of its SC.7 Skyvan series, Shorts decided to produce a larger and more refined derivative as the SD3-30 that then became the Shorts 330 with retractable tricycle landing gear and accommodation for 30 passengers. The type entered service in August 1976, and has proved most successful. Even so, the company appreciated that a larger-capacity type would broaden the series' market appeal, and the result

was the Shorts 360. Market research indicated that capacity 20 per cent greater than that of the Shorts 330 was really desirable, and it was in 36-passenger configuration that the first Shorts 360 flew in June 1981 on the power of two 990-kW (1,327-shp) Pratt & Whitney Canada PT6A-65R turboprops.

The Shorts 360 is similar to its predecessor in being a high-wing monoplane with aerofoil-section lifting

struts that brace the high aspect ratio wing to the sponsons that accommodate the main units of the retractable tricycle landing gear, but differs in having a single vertical tail in place of twin endplate surfaces, the lengthening of the forward fuselage by 0.91 m (3 ft 0 in) to allow the incorporation of an extra three-seat passenger row, and revision of the rear fuselage to improve aerodynamic form and permit the addition of another extra three-seat passenger row.

The Shorts 360 entered service in December 1982, and the type's only major improvement to date has been the introduction from 1986 of 1063-kW (1,424-shp) PT6A-65AR engines to produce the Shorts 360 Advanced. The maximum passenger payload is 3184 kg (7,020 lb), but in the type's alternative freight configuration the payload is somewhat increased to 3765 kg (8,300 lb).

---

**SHORTS 360-300**

**Role:** Short range passenger transport/ freighter

**Crew/Accommodation:** Two and two cabin crew, plus up to 37 passengers

**Power Plant:** Two 1,424 shp Pratt & Whitney Canada PT6A-67R turboprops

**Dimensions:** Span 22.80 m (74.79 ft); length 21.58 m (70.94 ft); wing area 42.18 m² (454.00 sq ft)

**Weights:** Empty 7,870 kg (17,350 lb); MTOW 12,292 kg (27,100 lb)

**Performance:** Maximum speed 401 km/h (216 knots) at 3,048 m (10,000 ft); operational ceiling 3,930 m (12,900 ft); range 1,178 km (732 miles) with 36 passengers

**Load:** Up to 4,536 kg (10,000 lb) for freighter version.

Note: operational ceiling artificially restricted for passenger comfort

*Shorts 360*

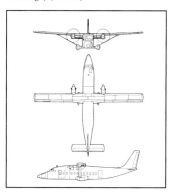

*A Shorts 360-300*

# CESSNA CARAVAN Series (U.S.A.)

*Caravan I*

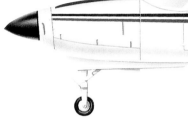

The Model 208 Caravan can be considered as Cessna's replacement for the elderly Model 185 Skywagon in the light utility transport role. The Model 208 offers its operators considerably greater capacity and performance, combined with more advanced features such as tricycle landing gear and the turboprop powerplant that runs off fuel that can be obtained anywhere in the world and also offers great reliability and better operating economics.

The first Model 208 flew in December 1982, and the first deliveries of production aircraft followed in 1985. The type can operate on sturdy wheeled or float landing gear, and is otherwise a conventional high-wing monoplane with a fuselage of slightly odd appearance because it has been optimized for the freight role in its long parallel upper and lower lines and large loading door in the side at easy loading/unloading height.

Current versions are the basic Caravan with a PT6A-114 engine, a cabin volume of 7.19 m³ (254 cu ft) plus optional 2.37 m³ (82.7 cu ft) external cargo pod, and with maximum seating for 14 persons; Caravan Floatplane, without external cargo pod but with baggage capacity in floats; the large Grand Caravan with a 675 shp PT6A-114A engine and cabin volume of 9.63 m³ (340 cu ft) plus a 3.16 m³ (111.5 cu ft) cargo pod; and Super Cargomaster, a cargo version of Grand Caravan. There is also a U-27A military version for U.S. foreign military sales programme.

## CESNA GRAND CARAVAN

**Role:** Commercial and military short field-capable utility transport
**Crew/Accommodation:** One, plus up to 14 passengers
**Power Plant:** One 675 shp Pratt & Whitney Canada PT6A-114A turboprop
**Dimensions:** Span 15.88 m (52.08 ft); length 12.67 m (41.58 ft); wing area 25.96 m² (279.4 sq ft)
**Weights:** Empty 2,064 kg (4,550 lb); MTOW 3,856 kg (8,500 lb)
**Performance:** Cruise speed 324 km/h (202 mph) at 3,050 m (10,000 ft); operational ceiling 8,780 m (28,800 ft); range 1,783 km (1,109 miles)
**Load:** 1,921 kg (4,235 lb) useful load

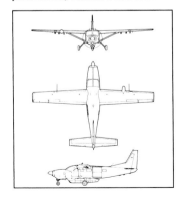

*Cessna Caravan I*

*A Cessna Caravan I of the small-package carrier Federal Express*

# SAAB 340 and 2000 (Sweden)

*Saab 340*

In January 1980, Saab and Fairchild agreed to undertake the collaborative design and development of a turboprop-powered small transport for the civil market. This was initially known as the Saab-Fairchild SF-340 and planned in the form of a low-wing monoplane featuring a wing of high aspect ratio with long-span slotted flaps and retractable tricycle landing gear with twin wheels on each unit. Construction is of the all-metal type, with selective use of composite materials in some areas, and while Saab was responsible for the fuselage, assembly and flight testing, Fairchild built the wings, tail unit and nacelles. The type was planned as a passenger transport with provision for 34 passengers in addition to a flight crew of two or three plus one flight attendant, but the cabin was schemed from the beginning for easy completion in the passenger/freight or alternative 16-passenger executive/corporate transport roles.

The first machine flew in January 1983 with 1215-kW (1,630-hp) General Electric CT7-5A turboprops, and the certification programme was undertaken by the first production machine in addition to the two prototypes. Certification was achieved in May 1984, and the type entered service in the following month. In November 1985, Fairchild indicated its unwillingness to continue with the programme, which thereupon became a Saab responsibility. Fairchild continued as a subcontractor until 1987, giving Saab time to complete additional construction facilities in Sweden. Early aircraft were limited to a maximum take-off weight of 11,794 kg (26,000 lb). Later machines were given CT7-5A2 turboprops driving larger-diameter propellers, and were cleared for higher weights. Since 1994 the standard version has been the 340B Plus (replacing the 340B of 1989–94 deliveries, which in turn had replaced the 340A). Production was expected to end in 1999, along with production of the 50–58-seat Saab 2000 (first flown in 1992).

*A Saab 340 of the American operator Northwest Airlines*

### SAAB 340B Plus
**Role:** Regional passenger transport
**Crew/Accommodation:** Two and one cabin crew, plus up to 37 passengers
**Power Plant:** Two 1,870 shp General Electric CT7-9B turboprops
**Dimensions:** Span 21.44 m (70.33 ft); length 19.73 m (64.75 ft); wing area 41.81 m² (450.00 sq ft)
**Weights:** Empty 8,255 kg (18,135 lb); MTOW 13,155 kg (29,000 lb)
**Performance:** Typical cruise speed 528 km/h (328 mph); operational ceiling 7,620 m (25,000 ft); range 1,551 km (964 miles) with 35 passengers
**Load:** Up to 3,795 kg (8,366) lb

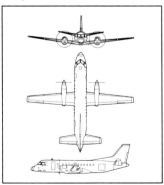

*Saab 340*

# BOMBARDIER de HAVILLAND DASH 8Q (Canada)

*Bombardier de Havilland Dash 8Q Series 100*

The DHC-8 was developed to the same basic operating philosophy as the 50-passenger DHC-7, but was sized for 40 passengers in the commuterliner role. As with other de Havilland Canada transports, STOL capability was a primary consideration, and the type was made attractive to potential operators by its fuel-economical turboprop engines driving propellers of large diameter, which turn slowly and so generate considerably less noise than fast-turning propellers of smaller diameter. Other features include a large cargo-loading door in the port side of the fuselage aft of the wing, retractable tricycle landing gear with twin-wheel main units, and a T-tail keeping the tailplane well clear of the disturbed airflow behind the wings and propellers.

The first of four pre-production aircraft flew in June 1983. The type entered revenue-earning service in December 1984. The baseline variant is now the Dash 8Q Series 100A with 2,000-shp Pratt & Whitney Canada PW120A turboprops. In its basic commuterliner layout, this carries a crew of three (two flight crew and one cabin attendant) and between 37–39 passengers. The same seating capacities apply to the Series 100B (PW121 engines) and Series 200A and B (PW123 series engines), all engines being of 2,150 shp rating. Seating jumps to 50–56 for the Series 300A, B and E, whose PW123 series engines are rated at 2,380 shp, 2,500 shp and 2,380 shp respectively. With these versions, the fuselage length increases to 25.68 m (84,25 ft). The largest versions are the Series 400A and B with 5,071 shp PW150A engines, 32.84 m (107.75 ft) length fuselages and seating for 70 and 72–78 passengers respectively.

*Bombardier de Havilland Dash 8Q*

**de HAVILLAND CANADA DASH 8Q Series 100A**
**Role:** Short field-capable passenger transport
**Crew/Accommodation:** Two, plus up to 39 passengers
**Power Plant:** Two 2,000 shp Pratt & Whitney Canada PW120A turboprops
**Dimensions:** Span 25.91 m (85 ft); length 22.25 m (73 ft); wing area 54.4 m² (585 sq ft)
**Weights:** Empty 10,310 kg (22,730 lb); MTOW 15,649 kg (34,500 lb)
**Performance:** Cruise speed 491 km/h (303 mph); operational ceiling 7,620 m (25,000 ft); range 1,365 km (848 miles)
**Load:** Up to 3,887 kg (8,570 lb)

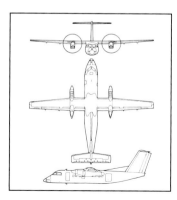

*Bombardier de Havilland Dash 8Q*

# EMBRAER EMB-120 BRASILIA (Brazil)

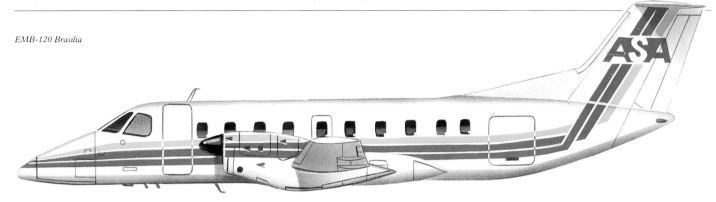

*EMB-120 Brasilia*

The Brazilian government and EMBRAER were both highly encouraged by the EMB-110's penetration of the world market for commuterliners and feederliners. From this success, there emerged plans for an EMB-12X series of three pressurized types sharing a fuselage of common diameter but different lengths. Of these only the EMB-121 Xingu business transport actually entered production. In September 1979 EMBRAER decided to move a step further up the size ladder with a pressurized 30-seat regional airliner, and this retained the overall configuration of the earlier 20-passenger EMB-120 Araguaia.

The type was designated EMB-120 and later named Brasilia, and metal was cut for the first aircraft in May 1981. Six aircraft were produced for the test and certification programmes, and the first machine flew in July 1983 as a low-wing monoplane with a circular-section fuselage, a T-tail, retractable tricycle landing gear, and a powerplant of two wing-mounted 1118-kW (1,500-shp) Pratt & Whitney Canada PW115 turboprop engines. Though designed as a regional airliner with 30 seats, the Brasilia has a large cargo door in the port side of the rear fuselage, and is also available in freight and mixed-traffic versions, the former offering a payload of 3470-kg (7,650-lb) and the latter the capacity for 26 passengers and 900-kg (1,984-lb) of cargo. The Brasilia has an airstair door on the port side of the forward fuselage to reduce demand on external support at small airports, and for the same reason is also offered with a Garrett auxiliary power unit in the tail cone as an option. Later aircraft are powered by a pair of 1343-kW (1,800-shp) PW118 turboprops for improved performance at higher weights.

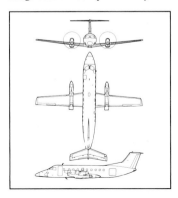

*EMB-120 Brasilia*

**EMBRAER EMB-120 BRASILIA**
**Role:** Short range passenger transport
**Crew/Accommodation:** Two and one cabin crew, plus up to 30 passengers
**Power Plant:** Two 1,600 shp Pratt & Whitney PW115 turboprops
**Dimensions:** Span 19.78 m (64.90 ft); length 20.00 m (65.62 ft); wing area 39.43 m² (424.42 sq ft)
**Weights:** Empty 6,878 kg (15,163 lb); MTOW 11,500 kg (25,353 lb)
**Performance:** Maximum speed 556 km/h (300 knots) at 7,620 m (25,000 ft); operational ceiling 9,083 m (29,800 ft ); range 1,751 km (945 naut. miles) with 30 passengers
**Load:** Up to 3,470 kg (7,650 lb)

*An EMBRAER EMB-120 Brasilia of the German carrier DLT*

217

# Civil Jet-Engined Transports

The turboprop, turbojet and turbofan are related in that all are turbine engines and therefore 'jets'. Because of this, it is slightly misleading to title only this section as 'Jet'-engined transports, having separated out the propeller-driven aircraft. Yet, in the common usage of the term 'jet', most people think only of an engine without a propeller.

By the early years of World War II, several British companies were engaged in jet propulsion research, as were others abroad. In 1941 de Havilland began the design of what ultimately became the Goblin engine, used successfully on its Vampire fighter. The company also required a larger turbojet engine to power a proposed jet airliner, the engine and airliner eventually becoming the Ghost and Comet respectively. The Ghost adopted the same simple form of the smaller Goblin and Ghost 50 form was the first turbojet engine to obtain civil Type Approval. With Ghost 50s buried neatly into its wing roots, the de Havilland Comet first flew in 1949, gained it certificate of airworthiness in 1952 and entered commercial service later that year.

What was a British triumph soon turned to tragedy, however, when in March 1953 a Comet 1 on its delivery flight in stages to Australia crashed on take-off in Pakistan. Then, in May, a BOAC Comet 1 was lost near Calcutta, the first fatal accident for a turbojet airliner while on a scheduled service. British and foreign jetliner manufacturers learned from the tragedies.

While de Havilland developed and produced superior models of the Comet that later performed well in commercial use, Boeing had meantime flown the prototype of a jet which it had developed as a private venture against the perceived needs of the U.S.A.F. for a tanker/transport able to service present and future high-speed combat aircraft, while suiting commercial applications. This was known as the Model 367-80 and, in 1954, was ordered for the U.S.A.F. as the KC-135. Importantly, in July 1955 Boeing gained the necessary official clearance to permit production of the commercial variant as the Model 707, to be built simultaneously with the military KC-135. Backed by vast military orders and with many potential worldwide customers for its jetliner,

Boeing never looked back. Indeed, the last 707-based airframe did not leave the production line until 1992, although for the final decade production was at a low rate to satisfy only the need to provide airframes for specialized military aircraft. By then, of course, a wide range of Boeing jetliners had been created.

Despite early setbacks, Britain still managed to claim the first transatlantic passenger services using a turbojet airliner when BOAC inaugurated Comet 4 flights between London and New York in October 1958. However, the Boeing 707 was in a class of its own and in 1959 was used for the first trans-Pacific jetliner service and, in the hands of Pan-American World Airways, the first round-the-world passenger jetliner service. Turbojet airliners from France, the Soviet Union and elsewhere soon got in on the act, and it was the combined talent of France and Britain that a decade later went on to win the battle to produce a viable supersonic airliner against strong competition from the Soviet Union and to a lesser extent the U.S.A.

Today, in 1999, the vast majority of the world's larger airliners are built by just two companies, Boeing of the U.S.A. and the rival European Airbus Industrie. Boeing, having taken over McDonnell Douglas, has a very extensive range that spans from the smallest Model 717 to the huge Model 747 and includes the extremely important C-17 Globemaster III military transport, whereas Airbus will soon add the new A3XX to its list of highly successful products, to be the world's first ultra-large, full double-deck, long-range airliner.

*RIGHT*
*Impression of the Airbus A3XX ultra-large airliner for service in the 21st century*

# de HAVILLAND D.H.106 COMET (United Kingdom)

*D.H.106 Comet 4*

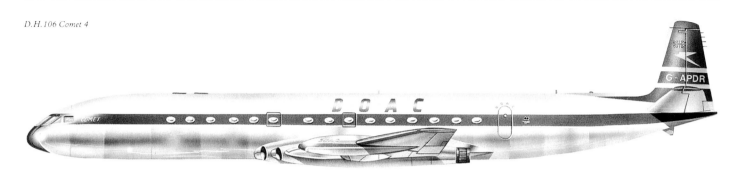

The Comet was the world's first turbojet-powered airliner, but failed to secure the financial advantages of this potentially world-beating lead because of technical problems. The type was planned from 1944 in response to the far-sighted Type IV specification resulting from the Brabazon Committee's wartime deliberations into the shape of British air transport needs after the end of World War II. It

first flew in July 1949 with four de Havilland Ghost 50 centrifugal-flow turbojets. The type entered service in January 1952 as the Comet 1 with multi-wheel bogies rather than the two prototypes' single wheels on the main landing gear units. The Comet 1 was used initially as a freighter, and only later as a passenger-carrying airliner, and deliveries to the British Overseas Airways Corporation totalled nine between January 1951 and September 1952; there followed 10 Comet 1As with greater fuel capacity.

One crash in 1953 and two in 1954 resulted in the type's grounding, and it

was then established that fatigue failures at the corners of the rectangular window frames were to blame. Rounded windows were introduced on the 44-passenger Comet 2, of which 12 were built with a 0.91-m (3-ft) fuselage stretch and axial-flow Rolls-Royce Avon 503 engines, but these BOAC aircraft were diverted to the RAF as 70-passenger Comet C.Mk 2s. The Comet 3 was precursor to a transatlantic version

that entered service as the 78-seat Comet 4 with Avon 524 engines in May 1958, when the conceptually more advanced Boeing Model 707 and Douglas DC-8 were already coming to the fore of the market. Some 27 were built. Derivatives were the 18 shorter-range Comet 4Bs with a shorter wing but longer fuselage for 99 passengers, and the 29 Comet 4Cs combining the wing of the Comet 4 with the Comet 4B's fuselage.

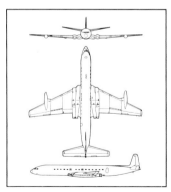

*de Havilland D.H.106 Comet 4*

---

**de HAVILLAND D.H. 106 COMET 4**
**Role:** Intermediate range passenger transport
**Crew/Accommodation:** Three, plus four cabin crew and up to 78 passengers
**Power Plant:** Four 4,649 kgp (10,250 lb s.t.) Rolls-Royce Avon RA29 turbojets
**Dimensions:** Span 35 m (114.83 ft); length 33.99 m (111.5 ft); wing area 197 m² (2,121 sq ft)
**Weights:** Empty 34,200 kg (75,400 lb); MTOW 72,575 kg (160,000 lb)
**Performance:** Cruise speed 809 km/h (503 mph) at 12,802 m (42,000 ft); operational ceiling 13,411+ m (44,000+ ft); range 5,190 km (3,225 miles) with full load
**Load:** Up to 9,206 kg (20,286 lb)

*This is a Comet 4B of British European Airways*

# BOEING 707 and 720 (U.S.A.)

*Boeing 707-300C*

Though preceded into service by the de Havilland Comet, the Model 707 must rightly be regarded as the world's first effective long-range jet transport. In an exceptionally bold technical and commercial move, Boeing decided during August 1952 to develop, as a private venture, the prototype of an advanced transport with military as well as civil applications. This Model 367-80 prototype first flew in July 1954 with 4309-kg (9,500-lb) thrust Pratt &

Whitney JT3P turbojets, and in October of the same year the company's faith in its capabilities was rewarded by the first of many orders for the KC-135A inflight refuelling tanker derived from the 'Dash 80'. Once the U.S. Air Force had given clearance, the company then started marketing the type as the 707 civil transport with a slightly wider fuselage, and in October 1955 Pan American took the bold step of ordering the 707 for its long-haul domestic network in the United States.

A total of 1,010 707s and closely related 720s was built, in the last decade (1982–92), however, only as airframes for military special versions, while U.S.A.F. KC-135s and C-135/137s were delivered during 1957-66 (808 aircraft) plus 12 to France. The major commercial variants were the Model 707-120 transcontinental airliner with 6123-kg (13,500-lb) thrust Pratt & Whitney JT3C turbojets, the Model 707-120B with JT3D turbofans, the Model 707-220 with 7938-kg (17,500-lb) thrust JT4A turbojets, the Model 707-320 intercontinental airliner with longer wing and fuselage plus 7938-kg

(17,500-lb thrust JT4A turbojets, the Model 707-320B with aerodynamic refinements and turbofans, the Model 707-320C convertible or freighter variants with turbofans, and the Model 707-420 with 7983-kg (17,600-lb) thrust Rolls-Royce Conway turbofans. The model 720 was aerodynamically similar to the Model 707-120 but had a shorter fuselage plus a new and lighter structure optimized for the intermediate-range role. There was also a Model 720B turbofan-powered variant.

## BOEING 707-320C

**Role:** Long-range passenger/cargo transport
**Crew/Accommodation:** Three, plus five/six cabin crew, plus up to 189 passengers
**Power Plant:** Four 8,618 kgp (19,000 lb s.t.) Pratt & Whitney JT3D-7 turbofans
**Dimensions:** Span 44.42 m (145.71 ft); length 45.6 m (152.92 ft); wing area 283.4 m² (3050 sq ft)
**Weights:** Empty 66,224 kg (146,000 lb); MTOW 151,315 kg (333,600 lb)
**Performance:** Cruise speed 886 km/h (550 mph) at 8,534 m (28,000 ft); operational ceiling 11,885 m (39,000 ft); range 6,920 km (4,300 miles) with maximum payload
**Load:** Up to 41,453 kg (91,390 lb)

*A Boeing 707-320 of Air India*

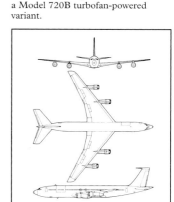

*Boeing 707-300C*

# SUD-EST CARAVELLE (France)

*Caravelle VI-N*

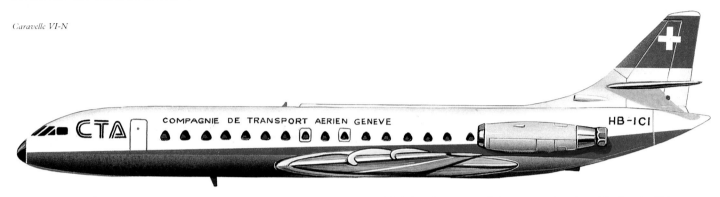

The Caravelle was France's first jet-powered airliner, the world's first short/medium-range jet airliner, and also the world's first airliner with its engines pod-mounted on the sides of the rear fuselage. The type resulted from a 1951 French civil aviation ministry requirement, and out of submissions from six manufacturers the S.E.210 was selected for hardware development in the form of two

prototypes. The first of these flew in May 1955 with two 4536-kg (10,000-lb) thrust Rolls-Royce Avon RA.26 turbojets and had accommodation for 52 passengers.

Successful evaluation paved the way for the Caravelle I with its fuselage lengthened by 1.41 m (4 ft 7.5 in) for 64 passengers. The 19 Caravelle Is had 4763-kg (10,500-lb) Avon RA. 29 Mk 522s, while the 13 Caravelle IAs had Avon RA.29/1 Mk 526s. Next came 78 Caravelle IIIs with 5307-kg (11,700-lb) thrust Avon RA.29/3 Mk 527s, and all but one of

the Mk I aircraft were upgraded to this standard. The Caravelle VI followed in two forms: the 53 VI-Ns had 5534-kg (12,200-lb) Avon RA.29/6 Mk 531s and the 56 VI-Rs had thrust-reversing 5715-kg (12,600-lb) thrust Avon Mk 532R or 533R engines.

Considerable refinement went into the Super Caravelle 10B, of which 22 were built. This first flew in March 1964 with extended wing roots, double-slotted flaps, a larger tailplane,

a lengthened fuselage for 104 passengers, and 6350-kg (14,000-lb) thrust Pratt & Whitney JT8D-7 turbofans. The 20 Super Caravelle 10Rs used the Mk VI airframe with JT8D-7 engines, and 20 were built. The final models were the six Caravelle IIRs for mixed freight and passenger operations, and the 12 Caravelle 12s lengthened for 140-passenger accommodation and powered by 6577-kg (14,500-lb) thrust JT8D-9s.

**AEROSPATIALE (SUD AVIATION) CARAVELLE 12**
**Role:** Short-range passenger transport
**Crew/Accommodation:** Two, four cabin crew, plus up to 140 passengers
**Power Plant:** Two 6,577 kgp (14,500 lb s.t.) Pratt & Whitney JT8D-9 turbofans
**Dimensions:** Span 34.30 m (112.5 ft); length 36.24 m (118.75 ft); wing area 146.7 m² (1,579 sq ft)
**Weights:** Empty 31,800 kg (70,107 lb); MTOW 56,699 kg (125,000 lb)
**Performance:** Maximum speed 785 km/h (424 knots) at 7,620 m (25,000 ft); operational ceiling 12,192 m (40,000+ ft); range 1,870 km (1,162 miles) with full payload
**Load:** Up to 13,200 kg (29,101 lb)

*Caravelle*

*Caravelle VI-N*

# DOUGLAS DC-8 (U.S.A.)

*Douglas DC-8-50*

After planning the DC-7D with four 4273-kW (5,730-shp) Rolls-Royce Tyne turboprop engines, Douglas decided instead to challenge the Boeing Model 707 in the market for turbojet-powered airliners. The result was the DC-8, a worthy type that nevertheless trailed the Model 707 because of its later start and the availability of only a single fuselage length. In an effort to catch up with the Model 707, Douglas produced nine test aircraft with three different types of engine, and the first of these

flew in May 1958. Total production of the initial five series was 294 built over a period of nine years. These series were the DC-8-10 domestic model with 6123-kg (13,500-lb) thrust Pratt & Whitney JT3C-6 turbojets, the similar DC-8-20 with uprated engines for 'hot-and-high' routes, the DC-8-30 intercontinental model typically with 7620-kg (16,800-lb) thrust JT4A-9 turbojets, the similar DC-8-40 with 7938-kg (17,500-lb) thrust Rolls-Royce Conway Mk 509 turbofans, and the DC-8-50 with Pratt &

Whitney JT3D turbofans and a rearranged cabin for 189 passengers. The DC-8F Jet Trader was based on the DC-8-50 but available in all-freight or convertible freight/passenger layouts.

From 1967 production was of the JT3D-powered Super Sixty series, of which 262 were produced. This series comprised the DC-8 Super 61 with the fuselage stretched by 11.18 m (36 ft 8 in) for 259 passengers, the DC-8 Super 62 with span increased by 1.83 m (6 ft 0 in) and length by 2.03 m (6 ft 8 in) for 189 passengers carried over very long range, and the DC-8 Super

63 combining the Super 61's fuselage and Super 62's wing. These models could be delivered in all-passenger, all-freight, or convertible freight/passenger configurations. Finally came the Super Seventy series, which comprised Super 61, 62, and 63 aircraft converted with General Electric/SNECMA CFM56 turbofans with the designations DC-8 Super 71, 72, and 73 respectively.

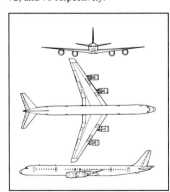

**DOUGLAS DC-8-63**
**Role:** Long-range passenger transport
**Crew/Accommodation:** Four and four cabin crew, plus up to 251 passengers
**Power Plant:** Four 8,618 kgp (19,000 lb s.t.) Pratt & Whitney JT3D-7 turbofans
**Dimensions:** Span 45.24 m (148.42 ft); length 57.1 m (187 ft); wing area 271.93 m² (2,927 sq ft)
**Weights:** Empty 71,401 kg (157,409 lb); MTOW 158,760 kg (350,000 lb)
**Performance:** Cruise speed 959 km/h (517 knots) at 10,973 m (36,000 ft); operational ceiling 12,802 m (42,000 ft); range 6,301 km (3,400 naut. miles) with full payload
**Load:** Up to 30,126 kg (55,415 lb)

*A Douglas DC-8-50 of Japan Air Lines*

*Douglas DC-8 Series 70*

# VICKERS VC10 (United Kingdom)

*Vickers VC10*

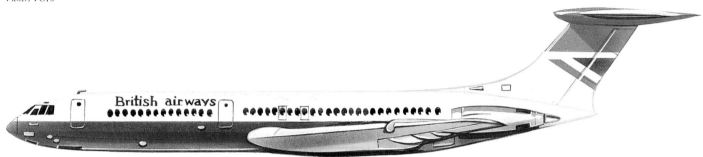

In 1957, the British Overseas Airways Corporation issued a requirement for an airliner able to carry a 15,422-kg (34,000-lb) payload over a range of 6437 km (4,000 miles) on the operator's Commonwealth routes. Vickers responded with its Type 1100 design. This was optimized for BOAC's route network, which included many 'hot-and-high' airports with short runways, with a large wing left uncluttered for its primary lifting task by the location of the four engines in paired pods on the sides of the rear fuselage below the tall T-tail. Other features were the retractable tricycle landing gear and six-abreast seating in the pressurized circular-section fuselage.

The first VC10 flew in July 1962, and the type entered service with BOAC in April 1964 with 9525-kg (21,000-lb) Rolls-Royce Conway RCo. 42 turbofans, a crew of 10 and a payload of between 115 and 135 passengers. BOAC took 12 such aircraft, and other customers were Ghana Airways (two), British United Airways (three), and the Royal Air Force (14 VC10 C.Mk 1s with a revised wing, greater fuel capacity and Conway RCo.43 engines). The prototype was also revised to production standard and was then sold to Laker Airways.

Development evolved the Type 1150 that entered production as the Super VC10 with Conway RCo.43 engines, greater fuel capacity and a fuselage lengthened by 3.96 m (13 ft 0 in). BOAC took 17 such aircraft and East African Airways another five. Because of its large wing, the VC10 had inferior operating economics to the Boeing Model 707, and most airports upgraded their facilities to cater for the Model 707 and Douglas DC-8.

The RAF bought from airlines VC10s and Super VC10s for conversion as VC10 K.Mks 2, 3 and 4 inflight refuelling tankers (14 aircraft). Many VC10 C.Mk 1s were also adapted as two-point tanker transports with the designation VC10 C.Mk1(K).

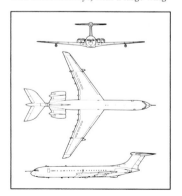

*Vickers VC10 K.Mk 3*

**VICKERS/BRITISH AIRCRAFT CORPORATION SUPER VC-10**
**Role:** Long range passenger transport
**Crew/Accommodation:** Five and seven cabin crew, plus up to 180 passengers
**Power Plant:** Four 9,888 kgp (21,800 lb) Rolls-Royce Conway RCo.43D Mk 550 turbofans
**Dimensions:** Span 44.55 m (146.17 ft); length 52.32 m (171.66 ft); wing area 272.40 m² (2,932 sq ft)
**Weights:** Empty 71,940 kg (158,594 lb); MTOW 151,950 kg (335,000 lb)
**Performance:** Maximum speed 935 km/h (505 knots) at 9,449 m (31,000 ft); operational ceiling 11,582 m (38,000 ft); range 7,596 km (4,720 miles) with full payload
**Load:** Up to 27,360 kg (60,321 lb)

*A Vickers Super VC10 of East African Airways*

# BOEING 727 (U.S.A.)

*Boeing Model 727-100*

The Model 727 was conceived as a short/medium-range partner to the Model 707, with the primary task of bringing passengers to the larger airports used by the long-range type. The type was designed for as much construction commonality as possible with the Model 707, and among other features was designed to use the same fuselage cross-section. The design team considered 70 concepts before finalizing its concept for the Model

727 as a fairly radical type able to meet the apparently conflicting requirements for high cruising speed at the lowest possible altitude and minimum seat/mile costs. Other factors that had to be taken into account were frequent take-off/landing cycles, the need for fast 'turn-round' time, and the need for low take-off noise so that the type could use airports close to urban areas. The Model 727 emerged with three rear-

mounted engines, a T-tail and an uncluttered wing with triple-slotted flaps along its trailing edges. Independence of airport services was ensured by an auxiliary power unit and a ventral airstair/door.

The Model 727 first flew in February 1963, and production has reached 1,831 in two main variants. The basic variant is the Model 727-100, which was also produced in convertible and quick-change convertible derivatives. Then came the Model 727-200 lengthened by 6.1 m (20 ft) and featuring the structural modifications required for operation

at higher weights; the latest version is the Advanced 727-200 with a performance data computer system to improve operating economy and safety. Also operational in smaller numbers is the Model 727F, which was produced to the special order of small-package operator Federal Express; this variant has no fuselage windows and can carry 26,649-kg (58,750-lb) of freight.

**BOEING 727-200**
**Role:** Intermediate-range passenger transport
**Crew/Accommodation:** Three and four cabin crew, plus up to 189 passengers
**Power Plant:** Three 7,257 kgp (16,000 lb s.t.) Pratt & Whitney JT8D-17 turbofans
**Dimensions:** Span 32.9 m (108 ft); length 46.7 m (153.17 ft); wing area 153.3 m² (1,650 sq ft)
**Weights:** Empty 46,164 kg (101,773 lb); MTOW 95,028 kg (209,500 lb)
**Performance:** Cruise speed 982 km/h (530 knots) at 7,620 m (25,000 ft); operational ceiling 11,582+ m (38,000+ ft); range 5,371 km (2,900 naut. miles)
**Load:** Up to 18,597 kg (41,000 lb)

*A Boeing 727-200 of Pan American World Airways*

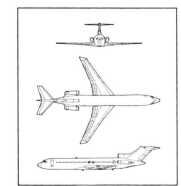

*Boeing Model 727-200*

# BRITISH AIRCRAFT CORPORATION ONE-ELEVEN (United Kingdom)

*BAC One-Eleven 500*

This pioneering airliner was conceived as the Hunting H.107 short-range airliner with accommodation for 59 passengers, and to provide the type with excellent field performance and low cabin noise levels it was decided to use aft-mounted engines; this left the wing uncluttered and therefore better able to perform its primary function, and dictated the use of a T-tail to lift the tailplane well clear of the jet exhausts. Hunting was bought by

BAC and the H.107 became the BAC 107. There was little airline enthusiasm for an airliner with so small a passenger payload, and the basic concept was therefore enlarged to provide 79-passenger capacity. This was redesignated the BAC 111, and later the One-Eleven. The design was finalized with a circular-section pressurized fuselage with a ventral airstair let into the underside of the fuselage under the tail unit, a low-set wing of modest sweep with Fowler trailing-edge flaps, and a variable-incidence tailplane at the very top of the vertical tail surfaces.

The prototype flew in August 1963 with two 4722-kg (10,410-lb) thrust Rolls-Royce Spey Mk 506 turbofans, and was lost in a fatal crash some two months later as a result of a 'deep stall' occasioned by the aft engine/T-tail configuration. After this problem had been cured, useful sales were secured for the basic One-Eleven Series 200 with Spey Mk 506s, the One-Eleven Mk 300 with 5171-kg (11,400-lb) thrust Spey Mk 511s, the generally similar but higher-weight

One-Eleven Mk 400 for U.S. airlines, the stretched One-Eleven Series 500 for 119 passengers, and the 'hot and high' One-Eleven Series 475 with the fuselage of the Series 400 plus the wings and powerplant of the Series 500. The One-Eleven production line was bought by Romaero in Romania where nine One-Elevens were built for a short time, the first Romaero 1-11 flying in 1982.

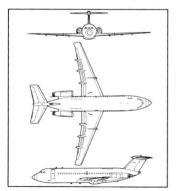

*British Aircraft Corporation One-Eleven 675*

**BRITISH AIRCRAFT CORPORATION ONE-ELEVEN 500**
**Role:** Short-range passenger transport
**Crew/Accommodation:** Two and three/four cabin crew, plus up to 119 passengers
**Power Plant:** Two 5,692 kgp (12,500 lb s.t.) Rolls-Royce Spey 512-DW turbofans
**Dimensions:** Span 28.5 m (92.5 ft); length 32.61 m (107 ft); wing area 95.78 m² (1,031 sq ft)
**Weights:** Empty 24,758 kg (54,582 lb); MTOW 47,000 kg (104,500 lb)
**Performance:** Maximum speed 871 km /h (470 knots) at 6,400 m (21,000 ft); range 2,380 km (1,480 miles) with full passenger load
**Load:** Up to 11,983 kg (26,418 lb) including belly cargo

*The BAC One-Eleven pioneered the aft engine/T-tail combination*

# ILYUSHIN Il-62 (U.S.S.R.)

*Il-62M*

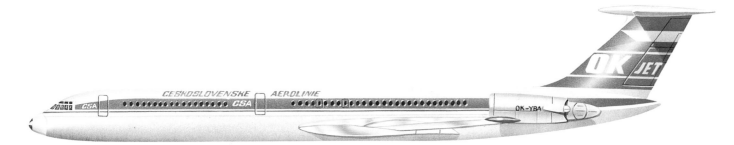

The Il-62 (known to NATO as 'Classic') was developed as a long-range airliner to complement and then to supplant the Tupolev Tu-114 on domestic and international routes. The Soviets specified high levels of comfort and performance in the hope that this would result in a type that would gain a measure of the export success that had eluded earlier Soviet airliners. The first Il-62 flew in January 1963 with four 7,500-kg (16,535-lb) thrust Lyulka AL-7 turbojets as the planned 10,500-kg (23,150-lb) thrust Kuznetsov NK-8-4

turbofans were not yet ready for flight. Clearly the design had been influenced by that of the Vickers VC10 in its configuration with a large wing, a T-tail, rear-mounted engines, and retractable tricycle landing gear. This similarity was also carried over into the flight test programme for, like the VC10, the Il-62 required lengthy development for the problem of its deep-stall tendency to be overcome. The NK-4 turbofans were introduced later in the test programme, which involved two prototypes and three pre-production aircraft.

The initial Il-62 production version entered service in September 1967 with accommodation for between 168 and 186 passengers, and cascade-type thrust reversers were fitted only on the outer engines. In 1971 there appeared the Il-62M with 11,000-kg (24,250-lb) thrust Soloviev D-30KU turbofans with clamshell-type thrust reversers, and the improved specific fuel consumption of this more advanced engine type combined with additional fuel capacity (a fuel tank in the fin) to improve the payload/range performance to a marked degree over

that of the Il-62. Other improvements were a revised flight deck, new avionics, and wing spoilers that could be operated differentially for roll control. The Il-62MK of 1978 introduced structure, landing gear and control system modifications to permit operations at higher weights. All production ended in the mid-1990s.

*An Ilyushin Il-62 long-range airliner of Aeroflot*

### ILYUSHIN Il-62M 'CLASSIC'

**Role:** Long-range passenger transport
**Crew/Accommodation:** Five, four cabin crew, plus up to 186 passengers
**Power Plant:** Four 11,500 kgp (25,350 lb s.t.) Soloviev D-30KU turbofans
**Dimensions:** Span 43.2 m (141.75 ft); length 53.12 m (174.28 ft); wing area 279.6 m² (3,010 sq ft)
**Weights:** Empty 69,400 kg (153,000 lb); MTOW 165,000 kg (363,760 lb)
**Performance:** Cruise speed 900 km/h (485 knots) at 12,000 m (39,370 ft); operational ceiling 13,000+ m (42,650+ ft); range 8,000 km (4,317 naut. miles) with full payload
**Load:** Up to 23,000 kg (50,700 lb)

*Ilyushin Il-62M*

227

# DOUGLAS DC-9 and McDONNELL DOUGLAS (now BOEING) MD-80/90 Series (U.S.A.)

*McDonnell Douglas MD-80*

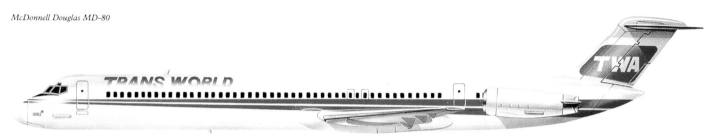

Planned as a medium-range partner to the DC-8, the DC-9 was then recast as a short-range type to compete with the BAC One-Eleven. Having learned the sales disadvantages of a single-length fuselage with the DC-8, Douglas planned the DC-9 with length options, and decided to optimize the efficiency of the wing by pod-mounting engines on the fuselage sides under a T-tail. The type first flew in February 1965 and built up an excellent sales record based on low operating costs and fuselage length tailored to customer requirements. The success of the type

also demanded so high a level of production investment, however, that Douglas was forced to merge with McDonnell.

The variants of the initial production series were the DC-9-10 with Pratt & Whitney JT8D turbofans and 90 passengers, the DC-9-15 with uprated engines, the DC-9-20 for 'hot-and-high' operations with more power and span increased by 1.22 m (4 ft 0 in), the DC-9-30 with the fuselage stretched by 4.54 m (14 ft 10.75 in) for 119 passengers, the DC-9-40 with a further stretch of 1.92 m (6 ft 3.5 in) for 132 passengers, and the DC-9-50 with more power and a further stretch of 2.44 m (8 ft 0 in) for 139 passengers. Developments for the military were the C-9A Nightingale aeromedical

transport based on the DC-9-30, and the C-9B Skytrain II fleet logistic transport combining features of the DC-9-30 and -40. Production totalled 976, and from 1975 McDonnell Douglas offered the DC-9 Super Eighty series with a longer fuselage and the refanned JT8D (-200 series) turbofan. This first flew in October 1979, and variants became the DC-9 Super 81 (now MD-81) with JT8D-209s and a fuselage stretched by 4.34 m (14ft 3 in) for 172 passengers, the DC-9 Super 82 (now MD-82) with JT8D-217s, the DC-9 Super 83 (now MD-83) with JT8D-219s and extra fuel, the DC-9 Super 87 (now MD-87) with JT8D-217Bs and a

fuselage shortened by 5.0 m (16 ft 5 in), and the DC-9 Super 88 (now MD-88) development of the MD-82 with JT8D-217Cs and an electronic flight instruments system combined with a flight-management computer and inertial navigation system. McDonnell also produced the MD-90 series, based on the MD-8C but with electronic engine controls, modernized flight deck, a fuselage lengthened to 46.51 m (152.6 ft), Internation Aero Engines turbofans and many other improvements. First flown in 1993, it is now also a Boeing type since the merger of Boeing and McDonnell Douglas.

*McDonnell Douglas DC-9 Super 80*

### DOUGLAS DC-9-10
**Role:** Short-range passenger transport
**Crew/Accommodation:** Two and three cabin crew, plus up to 90 passengers
**Power Plant:** Two 6,580 kgp (14,500 lb s.t.) Pratt & Whitney JT8D-9 turbofans
**Dimensions:** Span 27.2 m (89.42 ft); length 31.8 m (104.42 ft); wing area 86.8 m² (934.3 sq ft)
**Weights:** Empty 23,060 kg (50,848 lb); MTOW 41,142 kg (90,700 lb)
**Performance:** Cruise speed 874 km/h (471 knots) at 9,144 m (30,000 ft); operational ceiling 12,497 m (41,000 ft); range 2,038 km (1,100 naut. miles) with maximum payload
**Load:** Up to 8,707 kg (19,200 lb)

*A McDonnell Douglas MD-83*

# BOEING 737 (U.S.A.)

*Boeing 737-200*

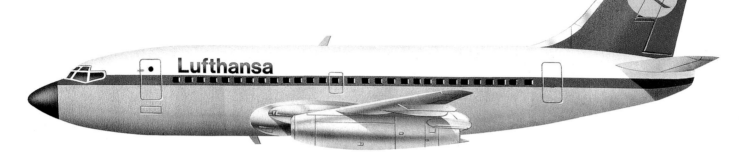

The short/medium range Model 737 became the small brother to the 707 and 727, and completed the Boeing family of airliners covering the full spectrum of commercial operations at the time of the company's November 1964 decision to design such a type. The Model 737 is currently the world's best-selling airliner, with more than 4,000 ordered. Originally intended for short sectors, the Model 737 first flew in April 1967. Despite the somewhat different appearance of

the two aircraft, Boeing managed about 60 per cent commonality of structure and systems between the Models 727 and 737.

The initial variant was the Model 737-100 for 100 passengers, but only a few were built before production switched to the larger 737-200 for 130 passengers, offering also convertible, quick-change convertible, and advanced derivatives. In 1984 came the 737-300 with an advanced technology flight deck, 9072-kg (20,000-lb) thrust

CFM56-3 turbofans (instead of the previous Pratt & Whitney JT8Ds) and further lengthening for 128–149 passengers, while in February 1988 the 737-400 flew offering up to 168 passengers in a 3.05-m (10-ft) longer fuselage, with the basic engine option of 9,980-kg (22,000-lb) CFM 56-35. The 737-500 for 108–132 passengers flew in June 1989, the basic engines derated to 8,391-kg (18,500-lb) thrust. Next generation versions are

the 108–140-passenger 737-600, 128–149-passenger 737-700, 162–189-passenger 737-800 and largest 737-900, offering CFM56-7B engines on larger wings. The 737-700 and -800 first flew in 1997.

**BOEING 737-300**
**Role:** Short/medium-range passenger transport
**Crew/Accommodation:** Two and four cabin crew, plus 149 passengers
**Power Plant:** Two 9,072 kgp (20,000 lb s.t.) CFM International CFM56-3B or 3C1 turbofans
**Dimensions:** Span 28.9 m (94.75 ft); length 33.4 m (109.58 ft); wing area 105.44 m² (1,135 sq ft)
**Weights:** Empty 32,704 kg (72,100 lb); MTOW 56,472 kg (124,500 lb)
**Performance:** Cruise speed 908 km/h (564 mph) at 7,925 m (26,000 ft); operational ceiling 11,278 m (37,000 ft); range 4,184 km (2,600 miles) with 124 passengers
**Load:** 16,030 kg (35,270 lb)

*Boeing 737-300s*

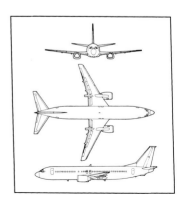

*Boeing 737-400*

# FOKKER F.28 FELLOWSHIP and 100 (Netherlands)

*F.28 Fellowship Mk 1000*

The F.28 Fellowship was designed as a complement to the turboprop-powered F.27 with slightly higher passenger capacity and considerably improved performance through the use of a twin-turbofan powerplant. Initial design work began in 1960, and Fokker opted for a T-tail configuration and rear-mounted Rolls-Royce Spey engines to provide an uncluttered wing. The first of three F.28 prototypes flew in May 1967,

and the certification and delivery of the initial production machines were achieved at the same time in February 1969.

The first production version was the F.28 Mk 1000 for 65 passengers on two 4468-kg (9,850-lb) thrust Spey Mk 555-15s, and a subvariant was the F.28 MK 1000C with a large cargo door on the port side of the forward fuselage for all-freight or mixed freight/passenger services. Subsequent models have been the

F.28 Mk 2000 with its fuselage stretched by 2.21 m (7 ft 3 in) for 79 passengers, and the F.28 Mks 3000 and 4000 with the fuselages of the Mks 1000 and 2000 respectively, span increased by 1.57 m (6 ft 11.5 in), and two 4491-kg (9,900-lb) thrust Spey Mk 555-15Ps.

In order to keep the type matched to current airline demands, in November 1983 Fokker announced an updated and stretched Fokker 100 version. This was given a revised wing of greater efficiency and spanning

3.00 m (9 ft 9.5 in) more than that of the F.28, a larger tailplane, a fuselage stretched by 5.74 m (18 ft 10in) by plugs forward and aft of the wing to increase capacity to 107 passengers, and Rolls-Royce Tay 620-15 or Tay 650 turbofans. At the same time, the interior was completely remodelled, composite materials were introduced, and an electronic flight instrument system was introduced. The first Fokker 100 flew in November 1986, and 278 were delivered before production was brought to an end in 1997 following the company's bankruptcy.

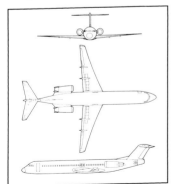

*Fokker 100*

**FOKKER 100**
**Role:** Short-range jet passenger transport
**Crew/Accommodation:** Two and four cabin crew, plus up to 109 passengers
**Power Plant:** Two 6,282 kgp (13,850 lb s.t.) Rolls-Royce Tay 620-15 or 6,850 kgp (15,100 lb s.t.) Tay 650 turbofans
**Dimensions:** Span 28.08 m (92.13 ft); length 35.53 m (116.57 ft); wing area 93.5 m² (1,006.5 sq ft)
**Weights:** Empty 24,593 kg (54,218 lb) with Tay 620s; MTOW 43,090 kg (95,000 lb) standard
**Performance:** Cruise speed 765 km/h (475 mph) at 8,534 m (28,000 ft); operational ceiling 10,668 m (35,000 ft); range 2,389 km (1,485 miles) at standard MTOW with 107 passengers and Tay 520 engines
**Load:** 11,242–12,147 kg (24,784–26,780 lb) with Tay 620s

*A Fokker 100 of Swissair*

# BOEING 747 (U.S.A.)

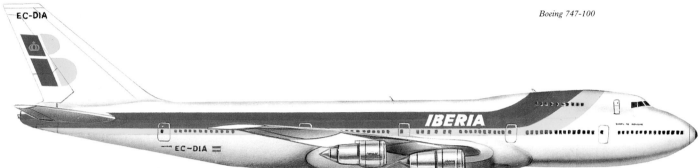

*Boeing 747-100*

Known universally as the 'Jumbo Jet', the Model 747 introduced the 'wide-body' airliner concept. It is the world's largest airliner, and is the mainstay of the Western world's long-range high-capacity routes. After failing to win the U.S. Air Force's CX-HLS competition for a long-range logistic freighter, Boeing decided to capitalize on its work by developing the basic concept into a civil transport. Initial thoughts centred on a 430-seat type with a 'double bubble' fuselage configuration in which each lobe would be about 4.57m (15 ft) wide. This failed to secure major airline interest, so Boeing finally opted for a 'big brother' to the Model 707 using

basically the same layout but with a fuselage large enough to accommodate a cabin 6.13 m (20 ft 1.5 in) wide and 56.39 m (185 ft 0 in) long. The type first flew in February 1969 and, with more than 1,300 aircraft ordered, the Model 747 is still in development and production with a choice of General Electric, Pratt & Whitney and Rolls-Royce turbofan engines.

The main variants have been the initial Model 747-100 with a maximum weight of 322,051 kg (710,000 lb) and strengthened Model 747-100B, the Model 747-200 (also offered in convertible and freighter

versions) with further structural strengthening, greater fuel capacity and uprated engines for a maximum weight of 377,842 kg (833,000 lb), the Model 747SP long-range version with the fuselage reduced in length by 14.35 m (47 ft 1 in) for a maximum of 440 passengers, the Model 747SR short-range version of the Model 747-100B with features to cater for the higher frequency of take-off/landing cycles, the Model 747-300 with a

stretched upper deck increasing this area's accommodation from 16 first-class to 69 economy-class passengers, and the current Model 747-400 with structural improvements to reduce weight, a two-crew flight deck with the latest cockpit displays and instrumentation, extended wings with drag-reducing winglets on the international versions, lean-burn turbofans, and extra fuel for longer range.

*Boeing 747-400*

## BOEING 747-400
**Role:** Long-range passenger/cargo transport
**Crew/Accommodation:** Two, plus 420 passengers in a 3-class configuration or other layouts up to 568 passengers.
**Power Plant:** Four 26,263 kgp (57,900 lb s.t.) General Electric CF6-80C2B or 25,741 kgp (56,750 lb s.t.) Pratt & Whitney PW 4000 series or 26,308 kgp (58,000 lb s.t.) Rolls-Royce RB211-524G or higher rated H turbofans.
**Dimensions:** Span 64.44 m (211.4 ft); length 70.66 m (231.83 ft); wing area 520.25 m² (5,600 sq ft)
**Weights:** Empty 182,256 kg (402,400 lb) typically; MTOW up to 394,625 kg (870,000 lb)
**Performance:** Cruise speed 939 km/h (507 knots) at 10.670 m (35,000 ft); cruise altitude 12,500 m (41,000 ft); design range up to13,418 km (8,342 miles)
**Load:** Up to 65,230 kg (143,800 lb) with cargo

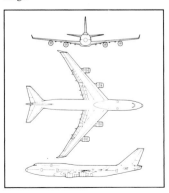

*Boeing 747-400*

# AEROSPATIALE/BAC CONCORDE (France/United Kingdom)

*Concorde*

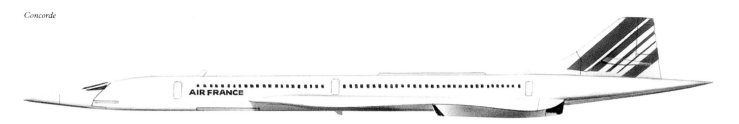

Currently the world's only supersonic air transport, the Concorde originated from separate French and British projects which were considered too expensive for single-nation development. The two efforts were therefore amalgamated in 1962 by an inter-governmental agreement. The French and British airframe contractors were Sud-Aviation and the British Aircraft Corporation, which eventually became parts of Aérospatiale and British Aerospace respectively. The project matured as a medium-sized type with a delta wing and a slender fuselage; the wing has an ogival leading edge, and the aerodynamically clean forward section of the fuselage has a 'droop snoot' arrangement to provide the crew with an adequate field of vision for take-off and landing.

The French were responsible for the wings, the rear cabin section, the flying controls, and the air-conditioning, hydraulic, navigation and radio systems; the British were tasked with the three forward fuselage sections, the rear fuselage and vertical tail, the engine nacelles and ducts, the engine installation, the electrical, fuel and oxygen systems, and the noise and thermal insulation. A similar collaborative arrangement was organized between Rolls-Royce and SNECMA for the design and construction of the engines.

The first of two prototypes, one from each country, flew in March 1969, and these two machines had slightly shorter nose and tail sections than later aircraft. The type has proved an outstanding technical success, but political and environmental opposition meant that only two pre-production and 14 production aircraft were built.

**AEROSPATIALE/BAC CONCORD**
**Role**: Supersonic passenger transport
**Crew/Accommodation**: Three and four cabin crew, plus up to 144 passengers
**Power Plant**: Four 17,260-kgp (38,050-lb s.t.) Rolls-Royce/SNECMA Olympus 593 Mk610 turbojets with reheat
**Dimensions**: Span 25.6 m (84 ft): Length 67.17 m (203.96 ft); wing area 358.25 m² (3,856 sq ft)
**Weights**: Empty 77,110 kg (170,000 lb); MTOW 181,400 kg (400,000 lb)
**Performance**: Maximum speed 2,333 km/h (1,450 knots) Mach 2.05 at 16,600 m (54,500 ft); operational ceiling 18,288 m (60,000 ft); range 7,215 km (4,483 miles)
**Load**: Typically 11,340 kg (25,000 lb)

*Concorde*

*A British Aerospace/Aerospatiale Concorde of British Airways*

# McDONNELL DOUGLAS and BOEING (McDONNELL DOUGLAS) MD-11 (U.S.A.)

*DC-10-10*

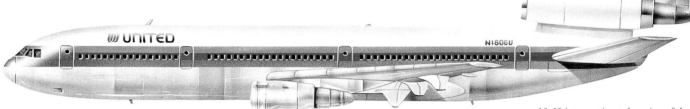

Douglas began work on the design of the DC-10 in 1966 in response to a requirement of American Airlines for a wide-body airliner offering the same sort of range as the Boeing Model 747 with a smaller payload. With orders for 55 aircraft and options for another 55 received, Douglas launched production in April 1968. The design matured as a basically conventional low-wing monoplane with swept flying surfaces, tricycle landing gear and three turbofan engines (one under

each wing and the third on a vertical pylon above the rear fuselage with the vertical tail above it).

The first example flew in August 1970, by which time Douglas had amalgamated with McDonnell. A total of 386 commercial and 60 military DC-10s were ordered, the last (a KC-10A) delivered in April 1990. These included the DC-10-10 with 18,144-kg (40,000-lb thrust General Electric CF-

6 turbofans for 380 passengers and which first entered service in August 1971, the DC-10-10CF convertible freight passenger transport, the DC-10-15 with 21,092-kg (46,500-lb) thrust CF6-50 engines and higher weights, the DC-10-30 intercontinental transport with the span increased by 3.05 m (10 ft 0 in), 22,226-kg (49,000-lb thrust CF6-50A/C engines, extra fuel and a two-wheel additional main landing gear unit between the standard units, the DC-10-30F freighter and DC-10-30CF convertible freighter, the DC-

10-40 intercontinental version of the 30 with 22,407-kg (49,400-lb) thrust and later 24,040-kg (53,000-lb) thrust Pratt & Whitney JT9D turbofans, and 60 KC-10A Extender transport/tankers for the U.S. Air Force. The MD-11 is an updated version that first flew in January 1990. A total 192 had been ordered in airliner, freighter and combi forms, but production is expected to end in the year 2000. MD-11 features include drag-reducing winglets, on extended wings, a lengthened fuselage for up to 410 passengers, advanced avionics and a choice of modern high-thrust General Electric or Pratt & Whitney engines.

**MCDONNELL DOUGLAS MD-11 airliner**
**Role:** Long/intermediate-range passenger/cargo transport
**Crew/Accommodation:** Two, eight cabin crew and 250–410 passengers
**Power Plant:** Three 27,896 kgp (61,500 lb s.t.) General Electric CF6-80C2D1F or 27,215–28,123 kgp (60,000–62,000 lb s.t.) Pratt & Whitney PW 4460/4462 turbofans
**Dimensions:** Span 51.7 m (169.5 ft); length 61.62 m (202.17 ft) with G.E. engines; wing area 338.91 m² (3,648 sq ft)
**Weights:** Empty (operating) 130,165 kg (286,965 lb); MTOW 273,314 kg–285,990 kg (602,555–630,500 lb)
**Performance:** Maximum speed 946 km/h (588 mph) at 9,450 m (31,000 ft); operational ceiling 12,800 m (42,000 ft); range 12,668 km (7,871 miles) with 298 passengers, no auxiliary tanks
**Load:** Typically 51,272 kg (113,035 lb) or up to 90,787 kg (200,151 lb) for freighter (including tare weight)

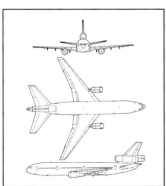

*McDonnell Douglas DC-10-30*

*A McDonnell Douglas DC-10-30*

# LOCKHEED L-1011 TRISTAR (U.S.A.)

*L-1011-1 TriStar*

The TriStar was planned to meet an Eastern Airlines' requirement for a wide-body airliner optimized for short- and medium-range operations with a large number of passengers, and was planned in parallel with its engine, the Rolls-Royce RB.211 turbofan initially offered at a 19,051-kg (42,000-lb) thrust rating. Development problems with the engine broke Rolls-Royce and nearly broke Lockheed, both companies having to be rescued by their respective governments. Construction began in 1968, and the first TriStar flew in November 1970.

Certification was delayed until April 1972 by the two companies' financial problems, and the L-1101-1 variant entered service in the same month with RB.211-22B engines and provision for up to 400 passengers at a maximum take-off weight of 195,045-kg (430,000-lb). The L-1011-100, which was the same basic airliner with RB.211-22B engines but with the fuel capacity and weights of the L-1011-200, which first flew in 1976 with 21,772-kg (48,000-lb) thrust RB.211-524 engines and a maximum take-off weight of up to 216,363-kg (477,000-lb) depending on the fuel load. The final production model was the L-1011-500 for very long-range operations, with 22,680-kg (50,000-lb) thrust RB.211-524B engines, increased fuel capacity, the fuselage shortened by 4.11 m (13 ft 6 in) for the accommodation of between 246 and 330 passengers, and the wings increased in span by 2.74 m (9 ft 0 in) as part of the new active control system that also saw a reduction in tailplane size. Sales failed to match Lockheed's marketing forecasts, and production ended in 1984 with the 250th aircraft. TriStars modified with the L-1011-500's engines and given a strengthened airframe and landing gear for higher gross weights (including more fuel for extended range) became L-1011-250s. Other conversions included several ex-airline aircraft converted as TriStar K.Mk 1 tankers and KC.Mk 1 tanker/freighters for the RAF.

*A Lockheed L-1011-1 TriStar of Air Canada*

**LOCKHEED L-1011 TRISTAR**
**Role:** Intermediate-range passenger transport
**Crew/Accommodation:** Three, six cabin crew, plus up to 400 passengers (charter)
**Power Plant:** Three 19,051 kgp (42,000 lb s.t.) Rolls-Royce RB211-22 turbofans
**Dimensions:** Span 47.35 m (155,33 ft); length 54.46 m (178.66 ft); wing area 321.1m² (3,456 sq ft)
**Weights:** Empty 106,265 kg (234,275 lb); MTOW 195,045 kg (430,000 lb)
**Performance:** Cruise speed 796 km/h (495 mph) at 9,140 m (30,000 ft); operational ceiling 12,800 m (42,000 ft); range 4,635 km (2,880 miles) with maximum payload
**Load:** Up to 41,152 kg (90,725 lb)

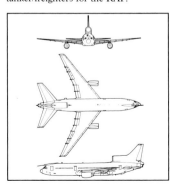

*Lockheed TriStar K.Mk 1*

# AIRBUS INDUSTRIE A300 (France/Germany/Spain/U.K.)

*Airbus Industrie A300 B4*

The Airbus consortium was founded in 1970 to manage this European challenge to the American 'big three' of airliner production – Boeing, Lockheed and McDonnell Douglas. A number of national designs had already been studied before the consortium was created to design, develop and build a 250-seat airliner powered by two British or American turbofans. The political and economic difficulties as the programme got underway were considerable, and the two sponsoring and largest shareholding countries became France and West Germany joined by the United Kingdom and Spain that have smaller shareholdings. All became industrial participants, joined as associate members by Belgium and the Netherlands.

The first A300B1 flew in October 1972, and this was lengthened by 2.65 m (8ft 8 in) to create the basic production model, the A300B2-100 with General Electric CF6-50 engines; variants became the A300B2-200 with leading-edge flaps, the A300B2-220 with Pratt & Whitney JT9D-59A turbofans, and the A300B2-300 with higher take-off and landing weights. Then came the A300B4-100 long-range version offered with CF6 or JT91 engines, the strengthened A300B4-200 with still higher weights and the A300B4-200FF with a two-crew cockpit. The A300C4 first flew in 1979 as a convertible freighter based on the A300B4, while an all-freight model became F4. In July 1983 the first flight took place of the A300-600, the only version currently available as new, itself available in passenger, extended range (R), convertible (C) and freighter (F) variants. Total A300 sales are well over 500 aircraft

*An Airbus Industrie A300-600R*

### AIRBUS A300-600

**Role:** Long/intermediate-range passenger transport
**Crew/Accommodation:** Two and six cabin crew plus up to 361 passengers
**Power Plant:** Two 25,400-kgp (56,000-lb s.t.) Pratt & Whitney PW4156 or 26,310-kgp (58,000-lb s.t.) PW4158 turbofans, or General Electric CF6-80C2As of 26,762–27,895 kgp (59,000–61,500 lb s.t.)
**Dimensions:** Span 44.84 m (147.1 ft); length 54.08 m (177.4 ft); wing area 260 m² (2,799 sq ft)
**Weights:** Empty 90,100 kg (198,636 lb); MTOW 165,000 kg (363,760 lb) typically
**Performance:** Maximum speed 891 km/h (554 mph) at 9,450 m (31,000 ft); operational ceiling 12,200 m (40,000 ft); range 6,852 km (4,260 miles) with G E engines and 266 passengers

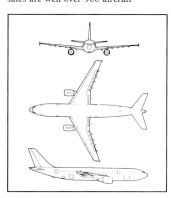

*Airbus Industrie A300-600*

235

# BOEING 767 and 777 (U.S.A.)

*767-200*

Planned in concert with the Model 757, the Model 767 is a wide-body transport with a cabin width of 4.72 m (15.5 ft), compared with 3.53 m (11.58 ft) for the Model 757. Even so, the Models 757 and 767 have so much in common that pilots can secure a single rating for both types. Drafting was undertaken with the aid of computer-aided design techniques. The type was schemed as a high-capacity airliner for medium-range routes, and present versions offer accommodation for 181 and 350 passengers, plus a choice of General Electric CF6-80C2B, Pratt & Whitney PW4052/4056/4060/4062, or Rolls-Royce RB211-524G4 or H turbofans. The Model 767 also differs from the Model 757 in having larger wings of increased sweep, but similar features are the tail unit, landing gear and engine pods.

The first Model 767 flew in September 1981 and, with the cancellation of the planned Model 767-100 with a shorter fuselage for the carriage of a maximum of 180 passengers, the Model 767-200 became the basic variant, with a typical maximum take-off weight of 136,077 kg (300,000 lb) and range of 8,465 km (5,260 miles). The extended- range Model 767-200ER has additional fuel in a second centre section tank for greater range, while the Model 767-300 provides greater capacity, and has its length stretched from 48.51 m (159.17 ft) to 54.94 m (180.25 ft). Variants include the extended range 767-300ER and 767-300F freighter. Latest version is the 767-400, launched in 1997 and offering accommodation for 303 passengers in 2-class layout and a range of 10,460 km (6,500 miles). Well over 800 767s have been ordered. The model 777 first flew in June 1994 as a long-range wide-body airliner of increased size, for up to 550 passengers

**BOEING 767-300**
**Role:** Intermediate-range passenger transport
**Crew/Accommodation:** Two/three, six cabin crew plus up to 290 passengers
**Power Plant:** Two General Electric CF6-80C2B or Pratt & Whitney PW4050/4060 series turbofans, ranging from 23,814–28,123 kgp (52,500–62,000 lb s.t.)
**Dimensions:** Span 47.57 m (156.08 ft); length 54.94 m (180.25 ft); wing area 283.35 m² (3,050 sq ft)
**Weights:** Empty 86,954 kg (191,700 lb); MTOW 159,211 kg (351,000 lb)
**Performance:** Maximum speed 906 km/h (563 mph) at 11,887 m (39,000 ft); operational ceiling 13,000+ m (42,650+ ft); range 6,920 km (4,300 miles)
**Load:** Up to 39,145 kg (86,300 lb)

*Boeing 767-300*

*A Boeing 767-200*

# BOEING 757 (U.S.A.)

*Boeing 757-200*

G·BKRM

In the later part of 1978, Boeing announced its intention of developing a new generation of advanced-technology airliners. The two definitive members of this family were the Models 757 and 767, while the Model 777 was less certain. The Model 757 retained the same narrow fuselage cross-section as the Model 727, and could be regarded as the Model 727's successor in the carriage of between 150 and 239 passengers over short- and medium-range routes, while the latest 757-300 (launched 1996) can carry up to 289 persons. Where Boeing offered considerable improvement, however, was in a new standard of fuel efficiency expected to offer 45 per cent fuel savings per passenger/mile by comparison with contemporary types. The Model 757 was therefore first offered with Rolls-Royce RB211-535 or General Electric CF6-32C1 turbofans in underwing pods; General Electric then dropped the CF6-32 engine, and Pratt & Whitney entered the lists with the PW2037.

The type was originally planned in Model 757-100 short-fuselage and Model 757-200 long-fuselage variants; launch customers all opted for the latter with RB211 engines, and the shorter variant was then dropped. The Model 757-200 first flew in February 1982.

Freighter, PF Package Freighter and M combi models are also available, the PF and M each having a large main-deck cargo door. For delivery to customers from 1999, the latest 757-300 is a stretched version for 240–289 passengers, with strengthened wings and landing gear and maximum take-off weight increased to 122,470-kg (270,000-lb).

*A Boeing 757-200*

**BOEING 757-200**
**Role:** Intermediate-range passenger transport
**Crew/Accommodation:** Two, four cabin crew plus up to 239 passengers
**Power Plant:** Two 18,189-kgp (40,100-lb s.t.) Rolls-Royce RB211-535E4 or 17,350-kgp (38,250-lb s.t.) Pratt & Whitney PW2037 or other turbofans
**Dimensions:** Span 38.05 m (124.83 ft); length 47.32 m (155.25 ft); wing area 185.25 m² (1,994 sq ft)
**Weights:** Empty from 57,970 kg (127,800 lb); MTOW 115,666 kg (255,000 lb)
**Performance:** Cruise speed 950 km/h (590 mph) at 8,230 m (27,000 ft); operational ceiling 13,000+ m (42,650+ ft); range 7,278 km (4,525 miles) with PW2037 engines and maximum payload

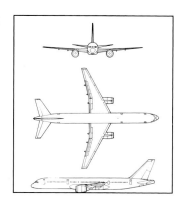

*Boeing 757-200*

237

# AIRBUS INDUSTRIE A310 (France/Germany/Spain/U.K.)

A major problem facing the design team of the Airbus family of airliners was the lack of clear signals from potential purchasers both in Europe and elsewhere in the world. The A310 resulted from an Airbus programme designed to produce a large-capacity airliner for the short-haul market. At one time, the programme encompassed no fewer than 11 proposals designed to attract the widest possible spectrum of potential buyers. The final A310 was designed to satisfy the emerging market for a 200-seater offering the same type of fuel economy as the A300, and was indeed designed for the highest possible commonality with the A300. Thus the A310 may be regarded as a short-fuselage derivative of the A300, with other features including aerodynamically clean outer wing areas without vortex generators, offering a lift coefficient usefully higher than that of the A300.

The type was first flown in April 1982, entering service in 1983. It was proposed in A310-100 short-range and A310-200 medium-range versions, but the former was dropped in favour of different-weight versions of the A310-200 optimized for the two roles. The A310-300 is a longer range version with drag-reducing wingtip fences (retrospectively applied to the A310-200) and a tailplane trim tank, available in the weight options for the A310-200. Convertible and freight versions are designated A310C and A310F.

*Airbus Industrie A310*

### AIRBUS A310-300
**Role:** Intermediate-range passenger transport
**Crew/Accommodation:** Two flight and six cabin crew, plus up to 280 passengers
**Power Plant:** Two 23,586-kgp (52,000-lb s.t.) Pratt & Whitney PW4152 or 4156A or 24,267-kgp (53,500-lb s.t.) General Electric CF6-80C2A2 or more powerful CF6-80C2A8 turbofans
**Dimensions:** Span 43.9 m (144.0 ft); length 44.66 m (153.08 ft); wing area 219 m² (2,357 sq ft)
**Weights:** Empty 80,800 kg (178,113 lb); MTOW 164,000 kg (361,558 lb)
**Performance:** Maximum speed 903 km/h (561 mph) at 10,670 m (35,000 ft); operational ceiling 13,000+ m (42,650 ft); range up to 9,630 km (5,988 miles) with P & W engines and 220 passengers
**Load:** Maximum for A310C is 41,500 kg (91,490 lb), structural

*An Airbus Industrie A310-300*

# AIRBUS INDUSTRIE A340 (France/Germany/Spain/U.K.)

*Airbus Industrie A340-300*

The A340 was launched as a project on 5 June 1987. At the time it was the largest aircraft to achieve production status in Europe. A340-200 is the reduced capacity version with a length of 59.39 m (194.83 ft), while the A340-300 is the standard length model for up to 440 passengers. Singapore Airlines was the first operator (in 1996) to receive an ultra-long-range and higher weight A340-300E. Further versions are the A340-400E as a variant of A340-300 but with a 6.4m (21.0 ft) fuselage stretch and CFM56-5C4 engines, the A340-500 short-fuselage and longer-range variant of the A340-600 with engine options including Rolls-Royce Trents, the stretched A340-600 with more engine power for 378 passengers in 3-class layout (enlarged and improved wings), and the proposed A340-800 for up to 400 passengers (MTOW 275,000 kg/606,270 lb). First flight of the -200 was October 1991.

First customer for the A340 was Lufthansa, as a replacement for DC-10s and entering service in March 1993.

In June 1993 the A340-200 prototype set several international distance records in its class by flying non-stop from Paris to New Zealand.

Another first for the A340 series was their being fitted with toilet facilities especially for handicapped passengers, plus a collapsible wheelchair for in-flight use.

The Airbus A330 is a twin-engined variant, first flown in November 1992 and corresponds in size to the A340-300.

*Airbus Industrie A340-300*

**AIRBUS A340-300**
**Role:** Long-range passenger transport
**Crew/Accommodation:** Two pilots and cabin crew plus up to 440 passengers
**Power Plant:** Four 14,152-kgp (31,200-lb s.t.) CFM International CFM56-5C2 turbofans initially, with 14,742 kgp (32,500 lb s.t.), -5C3 and 15,442 kgp (34,000lb s.t.), -5C4s optional
**Dimensions:** Span 60.3 m (197.83 ft); length 63.69 m (208.92 ft); wing area 363.1 m² (3,908.37 sq ft)
**Weights:** Empty 126,870 kg (279,700 lb); MTOW 257,000 kg (566,587 lb)
**Performance:** Cruise speed 890 km/h (553 mph); range 12,225 km (7,600 miles); operational ceiling 12,200m (40,000 ft);
**Load:** About 47,690 kg (105,139 lb)

*Airbus Industrie A340-300*

*Airbus Industrie A340-300*

239

*Airbus A330 is the twin-engined variant of A340-300, with similar advanced aerofoil sections, high-lift devices, extended fly-by-wire and computer flight control system, and more*

# SATIC A300-600ST SUPER TRANSPORTER 'BELUGA' (France/Germany)

*SATIC A300-600ST 'Beluga'*

From 1971, the Airbus Industrie Consortium transported major assemblies of aircraft sections between their various manufacturing and assembly plants using a fleet of four converted Boeing Stratocruisers. These, known as 'Super Guppies', had proved successful but were in need of replacement. They were finally retired in October 1997.

There being no suitable replacement available with a huge open fuselage cross-section for outsized cargo, the consortium developed its own outsize transporter.

The result is the SATIC A300-600ST 'Beluga' Airbus Super Transporter which flew for the first time on 13 September 1994. SATIC (Special Aircraft Transport International Company) was formed jointly by Deutsche Aerospace Airbus and Aérospatiale in 1991 to build the aircraft. The 600ST has 80 per cent of spares in common with the basic aircraft, the A300-600R Airbus, with corresponding low maintenance costs.

The design employs five major conversions or modifications over the original A300 airframe. These are: an increase from 5.3 m (17.4 ft) to 7.4 m (24.3 ft) in the fuselage diameter, the lowering of the cockpit to below and forward of the freight floor level, reinforcement of the cargo floor, installation of an upper deck cargo door, and the redesigning and reinforcement of the tail plane surfaces.

The cockpit layout is identical to the A300-600R. Payloads are inserted through the main forward freight door, the largest ever fitted to an aircraft, which opens upwards above the cockpit. The aircraft can be loaded or unloaded by two men within 45 minutes turn-round schedule, compared with two hours, by 8 to 10 men for the Super Guppy. Maximum payload has increased to 45.5 tonnes, held in a cargo compartment of 1,400 cubic metres volume.

Four Belugas had been delivered by 1998, with the fifth and last expected in 2001.

Airbus became aware that other industries could require 'super transport' availability, including the European Space Agency, and in 1996 Airbus Transport International was formed to offer charter services using any spare Beluga capacity from the main Airbus activities.

*The first SATIC A300-600ST 'Beluga' (still in primer) takes off for its maiden flight 13 September 1994*

### SATIC A300-600ST 'BELUGA'
**Role:** Heavy lift freighter
**Crew/Accommodation:** Pilot and co-pilot plus 2 handlers with folding seats in the cockpit
**Power Plant:** Two 26,762-kgp (59,000- lb s.t.) General Electric CF-6-80C2A8 turbofans
**Dimensions:** Span 44.84 m (147.083 ft); length 56.16 m (184.25 ft); wing area 260 m² (2,798.6 sq ft)
**Weights:** MTOW 150,000 kg (330,693 lb)
**Performance:** Cruise speed 778 km/h (484 mph); range 1,666 km (1,035 miles)
**Load:** Up to 45,500 kg (100,310 lb)

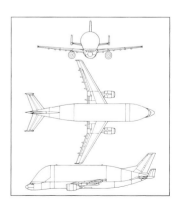

*SATIC A300-600ST 'Beluga'*

# SPECIALIZED
# AIRCRAFT

Page 242: High-altitude reconnaissance
Page 243: BAe Hawk Mk. 208 and 108
Right: Citation Excel
Pages 246–247: Northrop N-1M

# Special Mission Aircraft

'Special mission' can signify a complete range of tasks, not all military, the common factor often being the application of electronic sensors or emitters in one form or another. Intelligence gathering, communications relay or jamming, airborne early warning and surveillance are typical military roles, undertaken by uniquely equipped variants of existing large transport aircraft or by purpose-designed types, while survey, remote sensing and pollution control are among non-military roles for aircraft often based on small commercial transports or civil lightplanes.

It was during World War II that 'special missions' aircraft began to ply their trade, with early examples including RAF Vickers Wellington bombers fitted with huge 14.6 m (48 ft) diameter degaussing rings to fly over and explode German magnetic mines. But it was during the Vietnam War that 'special missions' really got underway, typified by the U.S.'s need to jam enemy radars during raids on the North, to prevent surface-to-air missiles and radar-guided guns from claiming so many of its aircraft. Such electronic warfare aircraft, used to escort the fighter-bombers, greatly reduced losses.

The three aircraft chosen to represent 'special mission' types are all U.S., although such aircraft have been produced in many countries. Interestingly, one of the most incredible 'special mission' aircraft to appear recently has been the Scaled Composites Proteus, a uniquely-configured sensor platform suited to both military and civil uses, including communications relay, earth and ocean resources monitoring and much else besides, with an early application expected to be for telecommunications and data relay. Missions are greatly assisted by an on-station endurance of up to 18 hours.

*Picture: Operators crewing a Northrop Grumman E-8C Joint STARS surveillance target attack radar system aircraft which can provide real-time battle management information to commanders, by distinguishing moving and fixed targets from other types of objects on the ground*

# NORTHROP GRUMMAN E-2 HAWKEYE (U.S.A.)

*E-2C Hawkeye*

Grumman developed its G-89 concept as the world's first purpose-designed airborne early warning platform to meet a U.S. Navy requirement for the aerial component of the Naval Tactical Data System. The Grumman design was selected in March 1957. Interestingly, it had been preceded by the Grumman E-1B Tracer for aircraft carrier operations in this role, but Tracer was based on the Tracker ASW aircraft and so, despite

its over-fuselage radome, was not a purpose design. The first W2F-1 aerodynamic prototype flew in October 1960, while the second machine, which flew in April 1961, introduced the original APS-96 surveillance radar (with its antenna in a large-diameter rotodome) and the advanced data-processing system that allowed the three-man tactical crew to watch and control all air activity within a large radius. The first aircraft were delivered with the designation W2F-1, but these 62 aircraft entered service from January 1964 as E-2As. This model was limited to overwater operations, but from

1969 most aircraft were modified to the E-2B standard adding overland capability. This resulted from the combination of APS-120 radar and a new central computer; other improvements were inflight refuelling capability and larger vertical tail surfaces.

In January 1971 Grumman flew the prototype of the E-2C that entered service in November 1973 with the more capable and digital APS-125 radar able to detect air targets out to a range of 370 km (230 miles) even in ground clutter and also able to track more than 250 air and surface targets simultaneously, allowing the tactical crew to control 30 or more interceptions at the same

time. Later aircraft were given the APS-138 radar for the tracking of 600 targets to a range of 483 km (300 miles) and enhanced electronic support measures capability. From 1988 the APS-139 radar added the capability to track even stationary targets. A total of 166 E-2Cs was built up to 1995, with 139 going to the U.S. Navy and most of the remainder exported. Production has since been restarted to provided the U.S.N with 36 new Hawkeye 2000s, featuring AN/APS-145 radar able to track over 2,000 targets and guide interceptors to 40 enemy targets simultaneously.

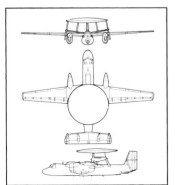

*Northrop Grumman E-2C Hawkeye*

### NORTHROP GRUMMAN E-2C HAWKEYE
**Role:** Naval carrierborne airborne early warning and control
**Crew/Accommodation:** Five
**Power Plant:** Two 5,100 hp Allison T56-A-427 turboprops
**Dimensions:** Span 24.6 m (80.6 ft); length 17.6 m (57.7 ft); wing area 65.03 m² (700 sq ft)
**Weights:** Empty 18,363 kg (40,484 lb); MTOW 24,687 kg (54,426 lb)
**Performance:** Maximum speed 626 km/h (389 mph); operational ceiling 11,278 m (37,000 ft); endurance 5.3 hours at 200 naut. miles from base
**Load:** None, other than special-to-task onboard equipment

*Northrop Grumman E-2B of the U.S. Navy*

# NORTHROP GRUMMAN EA-6 PROWLER (U.S.A.)

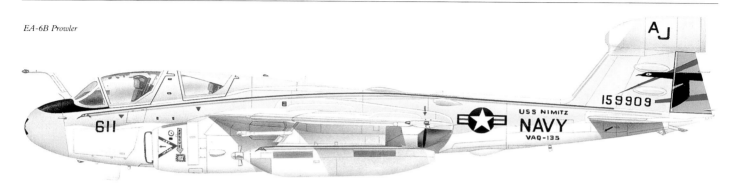

*EA-6B Prowler*

From early in the programme to develop the A2F Intruder strike aircraft, the U.S. Navy realized the importance of producing a support version fitted with the specialized electronic systems that could aid passage through enemy airspace. The result was the development of the EA-6A (initially the A2F-1Q) as an electronic support variant that also retained partial attack capability. The first example of this variant flew in 1963 as a conversion from YA-6A (initially YA2F-1) standard, and was followed by another two YA-6A and

four A-6A conversions, and by 21 new-build aircraft. The variant became distinguishable by its revised vertical tail surfaces, which were surmounted by the large fairing that accommodated the receiver antennae for the electronic warfare system, which had internal and external jammers.

In 1966, the U.S. Navy called for a dedicated electronic warfare variant, and this appeared as the EA-6B Prowler with its fuselage lengthened by 1.37 m (4 ft 6 in) to allow the insertion of a stretched cockpit

accommodating, in addition to the standard two crew, two specialist operators for the ALQ-99 system to detect, localize and analyse enemy radar emissions before finding the right jamming set-on frequency for any of the five jammer pods carried under the fuselage and wings. Since entering service in 1971 the EA-6B has undergone enormous electronic development in the form of steadily more comprehensive and wide-ranging standards known as the Expanded Capability, Improved Capability,

Improved Capability 2, Defensive Electronic Counter-Measures, and Advanced Capability, together with aerodynamic and powerplant enhancements. Some 127 Prowlers remained in service in 1998/99 with the U.S. Navy and Marines and, with the 1998 retirement of USAF EF-111A Ravens, Prowlers now provide the stand-off jamming requirements of the three services.

*Northrop Grumman EA-6B in U.S. Marines markings*

**NORTHROP GRUMMAN EA-6B PROWLER**
**Role:** Naval carrierborne, all-weather electronic warfare
**Crew/Accommodation:** Four
**Power Plant:** Two 5,080 kgp (11,200 lb s.t.) Pratt & Whitney J52-P-408 or 5,443 kgp (12,000 lb s.t.) J52-P-409s
**Dimensions:** Span 16.16 m (53 ft); length 18.24 m (59.83 ft); wing area 49.15 m² (529 sq ft)
**Weights:** Empty 14,320 kg (31,572 lb); MTOW 29,480 kg (65,000 lb)
**Performance:** Maximum speed 1,047 km/h (651 mph); operational ceiling 12,560 m (41,200 ft); range 1,770 km (1,100 miles)
**Load:** Up to in excess of 11,340 kg (25,000 lb) of electronic broad-band jammers and other specialized electronic warfare systems within the AN/ALQ-99F tactical jamming system, and HARM missiles

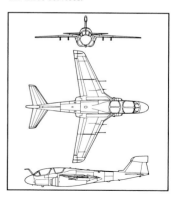

*Northrop Grumman EA-6B Prowler*

# BOEING E-3 SENTRY (U.S.A.)

*E-3A Sentry*

One of the most expensive but important current military aircraft, the Sentry is a highly capable Airborne Warning And Control System type designed for three-dimensional surveillance of a massive volume of air and the direction of aerial operations within that volume as a force multiplier. The type is based on the Model 707-300B airliner, and two EC-137D prototypes were used to evaluate the Westinghouse APY-1 and Hughes APY-2 radars. The former was chosen for the 34 E-3A production aircraft, which were delivered between 1977 and 1984. The first 24 aircraft for the USAF were Core E-3As with only an overland capability, CC-1 computer, nine situation display consoles and two auxiliary display units, while the last 10 were Standard E-3As with additional overwater sensor capability, a faster CC-2 computer, secure voice communications, and Joint Tactical Information Distribution System.

The Standard E-3A type (though with improved APY-2 radar and provision for self-defence AAMs) was ordered for the multi-national NATO early warning force, and these 18 aircraft were delivered between January 1982 and April 1985. Another five were delivered to Saudi Arabia as E-3A/Saudi aircraft with slightly less capable electronics and four 9,979-kg (22,000-lb) thrust CFM56-A2-2 turbofans. The Core E-3As (and two EC-137Ds) were later raised to E-3B standard with the CC-2 computer, 14 display consoles, JTIDS, improved ECM capability, and limited overwater sensor capability, while the Standard E-3As were raised to E-3C standard with five extra situation display consoles and the 'Have Quick-A' communications system. The type also has the capability to carry small underwing pylons, which could carry AIM-9 Sidewinder AAMs for modest self-defence facility. Comparable aircraft for the RAF and French air force are seven E-3Ds (that is, Sentry AEW.Mk 1s) and four E-3Fs with CEM56 engines.

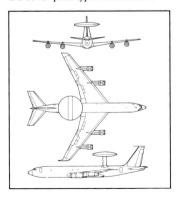

*Grumman E-3 Sentry*

### BOEING E-3D SENTRY
**Role:** Airborne early warning and command
**Crew/Accommodation:** Four, plus 17 AWACS specialists
**Power Plant:** Four 10,886 kgp (24,000 lb s.t.) CFM International CFM56-2A-2 or -3 turbofans
**Dimensions:** Span 44,43 m (145.75 ft); length 46.62 m (152 ft); wing area 284.40 m² (3,050 sq ft)
**Weights:** Empty 77,238 kg (170,277 lb); MTOW 151,995 kg (335,000 lb)
**Performance:** Maximum speed 805 km/h (500 mph) at 8,839 m (29,000 ft); operational ceiling 11,430 m (37,500 ft); range 9,250 km (5,760 miles)
**Load:** Nil

*A Boeing E-3D Sentry in RAF markings as a Sentry AEW.Mk 1*

# Trainers and Light Strike

At the birth of powered aeroplane flight there were few, if any, restrictive rules to govern the conduct of the intrepid aviators, although the Fédération Aéronautique Internationale (FAI) had been founded in 1905 and became the ruling body over official world performance records. By 1909, however, flying was becoming sufficiently regular that authority had to be established for various activities, and the first 'official' aeroplane meetings were organized to cater for widespread public interest. More importantly, the Aéro Club de France and British Aero Club, formed in 1898 and 1901 respectively (the latter becoming the Royal Aero Club in 1910), began issuing proper Pilot's Certificates, with the first in Britain being awarded to a civilian in March 1910, the 15th to a Royal Navy officer in June and the 17th to a British Army officer that July. Also in March 1910, France certified its first military pilot as its 33rd qualified aviator and the world's first woman pilot as that nation's 36th. A German officer received a flying certificate in 1910, and during February 1911 France awarded its first military flying certificate.

The first aircraft used as trainers were generally two-seat versions of existing 'stick and string' aeroplanes, but already thought had been given to proper means of instruction and Short Brothers, for example, produced its S.32 in 1911 as a purpose-designed trainer with dual controls and was used to instruct members of the British Territorials over that winter. In America, birth-place of powered aeroplane flying, the third and fourth aeroplanes purchased by the Army (Wright Model Bs) were for training, though each had only one set of shared controls, while the U.S. Navy received an early Curtiss type as a dual-control trainer.

After war broke out in 1914, aeroplanes that were no longer suited to first-line duties were often given over to training. However, one of the greatest trainers of all time, the British Avro 504, which had begun the war as a reconnaissance and light bombing biplane, became so successful in its new role from 1915 that it remained in production until 1933, from 1931 providing many pilots with their first taste of instrument 'blind' flying. The equivalent U.S. aircraft was the Curtiss JN 'Jenny', the last examples being retired from the National Guard in 1927.

The RAF's main trainer in 1939 at elementary and reserve flying training schools was the de Havilland Tiger Moth, which was a direct descendent of the original D.H.60 Moth of 1925 appearance. The Moth is perhaps the most important civil trainer of all time, chosen to equip all the flying clubs formed under a British Air Ministry scheme and widely recognized as the aircraft that kick-started the civil flying club movement.

Modern day basic and advanced training syllabuses are often shared between turboprop- and turbofan-powered types, the former typified by the incredibly successful Brazilian Embraer Tucano, while the U.S. forces are currently receiving huge numbers of the Swiss Pilatus PC-9 Mk II built by Raytheon/Beech in the U.S.A. as the T-6A Texan II. But turbofan trainers normally permit a more capable secondary light attack role, with weapon loads in the 1,000–3,000-kg range, some even spawning single-seat combat-dedicated variants.

*Picture: An example of a two-seat turbofan trainer spawning a single-seater is the British Aerospace Hawk, seen here as a Malaysian Mk 108 (rear) and Mk 208*

# AVRO 504 (United Kingdom)

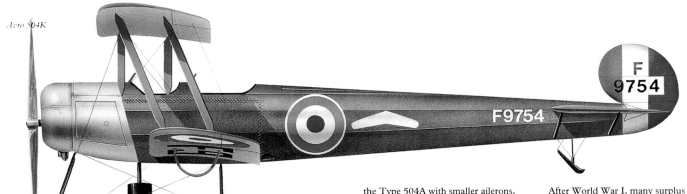

*Avro 504K*

One of the most remarkable aircraft of all time, the Type 504 was developed from the Type 500 basic trainer, and first flew in July 1913 with a 60-kW (80-hp) Gnome rotary that in fact yielded only about 46-kW (62-hp). In the summer of 1913 the British army and navy ordered the Type 504 as a general-purpose aeroplane. After a limited amount of front-line service, which included the successful bombing of the Zeppelin sheds at Friedrichshafen in November 1914, the Type 504 was relegated to second-line duties. Here it found its métier as a trainer.

The main variants were Type 504, the Type 504A with smaller ailerons, the Type 504B with a larger fin, the Type 504C anti-Zeppelin single-seater, and the Type 504D, all powered by the 60-kW (80-hp) Gnome Monosoupape rotary engine. Trainer and civil variants were the Type 504E with less wing stagger, the classic Type 504J of 1916 with the same 75-kW (100-hp) Gnome Monosoupape as the Type 504E, the Type 504K standard trainer with a universal engine mounting able to accommodate a variety of inline, radial and rotary engines, the Type 504L floatplane and the Type 504M cabin transport.

After World War I, many surplus Type 504 models were converted to improved Type 504N standard with a number of structural revisions, revised landing gear that eliminated the central skid of earlier models, and a 134-kW (180-hp) Armstrong Siddeley Lynx IV radial engine. Well over 8,000 Type 504s were built in World War I, and post-war conversions were supplemented by 598 Type 504Ns built between 1925 and 1932.

**AVRO 504K**
**Role:** Reconnaissance/trainer
**Crew/Accommodation:** Two
**Power Plant:** One 130 hp Clerget air-cooled rotary
**Dimensions:** Span 10.97 m (36 ft); length 7.75 m (25.42 ft); wing area 30.66 m² (330 sq ft)
**Weights:** Empty 558 kg (1,231 lb); MTOW 830 kg (1,829 lb)
**Performance:** Maximum speed 153 km/h (95 mph) at sea level; operational ceiling 5,486 m (18,000 ft); endurance 3 hours
**Load:** A number of 504s were converted into home defence single-seat fighters with one .303 inch machine gun, plus stowage for hand-released small bombs

*Avro Type 504K*

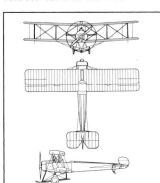

*Avro Type 504K*

# CURTISS JN 'JENNY' (U.S.A.)

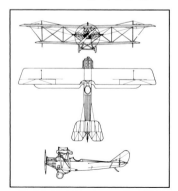

*Curtiss JN-4N*

Generally known as the 'Jenny', this celebrated trainer resulted from the Model J. This had a 67-kW (90-hp) Curtiss O inline engine and unequal-span biplane wings with upper-wing ailerons operated by the obsolete Deperdussin-type control system. The contemporary Model N had the 75-kW (100-hp) Curtiss OXX inline and interplane ailerons. Features of both types were included in the JN-2 that appeared in 1915 with equal-span biplane wings each carrying an aileron, and powered by a 67-kW (90-hp) Curtiss OX engine. The succeeding JN-3 was essentially an interim type and had unequal-span wings with ailerons only on the upper surfaces, but these control surfaces were operated by a wheel on the joystick

**CURTISS JN-4D**
**Role:** Primary trainer
**Crew/Accommodation:** Two
**Power Plant:** One 90 hp Curtiss OX-5 water-cooled inline
**Dimensions:** Span 13.29 m (43.6 ft); length 8.33 m (27.33 ft); wing area 32.7 m² (352 sq ft)
**Weights:** Empty 630.5 kg (1,390 lb); MTOW 871 kg (1,920 lb)
**Performance:** Cruise speed 97 km/h (60 mph) at sea level; operational ceiling 1,981 m (6,500 ft); range 402 km (250 miles)
**Load:** None

*JN-4H 'Jenny'*

rather than a shoulder-yoke. In July 1916 there appeared the definitive JN-4, and this was built in large numbers for useful service well into the 1920s. As first delivered, the JN-4 had unequal-span wings of the two-bay type, and spreader-bar landing gear, so the definitive form of the

JN-4 appeared later in the production run.

The JN-4A had a larger tailplane and engine downthrust; the slightly earlier JN-4B introduced the larger tailplane and used the OX-2 engine; the JN-4C was an experimental model of which just two were produced, the JN-4 Can (generally known as the Canuck) was a development by the Curtiss company's Canadian associate and was a very successful evolution of the JN-3; the JN-4D combined features of the JN-4A and the JN-4 Can to become the nearest there was to a standard variant; the JN-4H was the JH-4D re-engined with the 112-kW (150-hp) Wright-built Hispano-Suiza inline. JHN-4H variants were the JN-4HT, JN-4HB and JN-4HG dual-control trainer, bombing and gunnery trainers. A variant of the JN family produced in smaller but still useful numbers was the JN-6, which evolved via the JN-5 with a stronger aileron structure and was developed in several subvariants.

*This 'Jenny' is a Curtiss JN-4D*

# de HAVILLAND D.H.82 TIGER MOTH (United Kingdom)

*D.H.82 Tiger Moth*

The incredible success of its Cirrus-engined D.H.60 Moth for civil flying clubs (see introduction) and the acceptance of the more powerful Gipsy-engined Gipsy Moth into RAF service as an elementary trainer and communications aircraft, convinced de Havilland that there was a large market for more military trainers. Although the original Moth and some early versions of the Gipsy Moth (D.H.60G) had wooden structures, in 1929 the company introduced the D.H.60M version with a metal structure (as for RAF Gipsy Moths) from which it evolved its first all-military Moth version as the D.H.60T Moth Trainer with a strengthened airframe and the 89-kW (120-hp) de Havilland Gipsy II engine. From this latter the company derived the D.H.82 Tiger Moth for the military market with a sturdier airframe for operation at higher weights with equipment such as a camera gun or practice bombs.

Eight pre-production aircraft were built with the same D.H.60T designation as the Moth Trainer, and these also retained the straight lower wing and dihedralled upper wing of the Moth Trainer; stagger was increased as the upper-wing centre section was moved forward to ease movement into and out of the front cockpit. The aircraft were powered by the 89-kW (120-hp) Gipsy III engine in a cowling, the sloping upper line of which improved the pilot's field of vision, and the lower wing was given dihedral for improved ground clearance. The definitive form was reached in the D.H.82 prototype that first flew in October 1931 with increased lower-wing dihedral and sweepback. Large-scale production followed, and of the 8,280 aircraft all but a few were of the Tiger Moth Mk II (D.H.82A) variant in which the ridged stringer/fabric rear decking of the Tiger Moth Mk I was replaced by a smooth plywood decking. The D.H.82B was the Queen Bee remotely controlled target drone, and the D.H.82C was a winterized variant built by de Havilland Canada. Surplus military aircraft found a ready civilian market, and the well loved Tiger Moth is even today flying in fairly large numbers.

## de HAVILLAND D.H.82A TIGER MOTH

**Role:** Trainer/tourer
**Crew/Accommodation:** Two
**Power Plant:** One 130 hp de Havilland Gipsy Major I air-cooled inline
**Dimensions:** Span 8.94 m (29.3 ft); length 7.3 m (23.95 ft); wing area 22.2 m² (239 sq ft)
**Weights:** Empty 506 kg (1,115 lb); MTOW 828 kg (1,825 lb)
**Performance:** Maximum speed 167 km/h (104 mph) at sea level; operational ceiling 4,267 m (14,000 ft); range 483 km (300 miles)
**Load:** 81.6 kg (180 lb)

*The de Havilland D.H.82A Tiger Moth was a first-class elementary trainer*

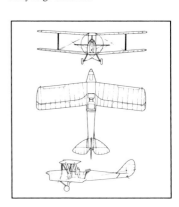

*D.H.82 Tiger Moth*

# BOEING/STEARMAN MODEL 75/PT-13 and PT-17 (U.S.A.)

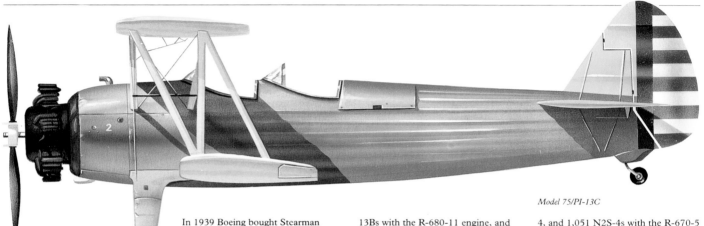

*Model 75/PI-13C*

In 1939 Boeing bought Stearman Aircraft, and as a result acquired the excellent Model 75 developed by Stearman from the X-70 first flown in December 1933. The U.S. Navy had taken 61 of the Model 73 production type with the designation NS-1, and development had then led to the Model 75 accepted by the U.S. Army as the PT-13 with the 160-kW (215-hp) Lycoming R-680-5 radial.

These 26 aircraft were just the beginning of a major development and production programme. Further evolution led to 92 PT-13As with the 164-kW (220-hp) R-680-7 engine and improved instrumentation, 255 PT-

13Bs with the R-680-11 engine, and six PT-13Cs with night-flying instrumentation. A change was then made to the 164-kW Continental R-670-5 radial for the PT-17, of which 3,510 were built in 1940. Specialist versions were the 18 blind-flying PT-17As and three pest-control PT-17Bs. The navy also operated the Model 75 as the N2S, and this series included 250 N2S-1s with the R-670-14 engine, 125 N2S-2s with the R-680-8 engine, 1,875 N2S-3s with the R-670-

4, and 1,051 N2S-4s with the R-670-5 engine. Then came a common army/navy model produced as 318 PT-13Ds and 1,450 N2S-5s with the R-680-17 engine. Variants with Jacobs R-755-7 radials were designated PT-18 and, in the blind-flying role, PT-18A.

Some 300 aircraft supplied to Canada were designated PT-27 by the U.S.A. but were called Kaydet in the receiving country. This name is usually given to all Model 75 variants.

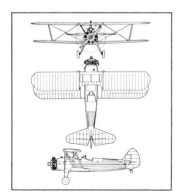

*Boeing Stearman PT-13D*

**BOEING/STEARMAN PT-17A**
**Role:** Basic trainer
**Crew/Accommodation:** Two
**Power Plant:** One 220 hp Continental R-670-5 air-cooled radial
**Dimensions:** Span 9.8 m (32.16 ft); length 7.32 m (24.02 ft); wing area 27.63 m² (297.4 sq ft)
**Weights:** Empty 878 kg (1,936 lb); MTOW 1,232 kg (2,717 lb)
**Performance:** Maximum speed 200 km/h (124 mph) at sea level; operational ceiling 3,414 m (11,200 ft); range 813 km (505 miles)
**Load:** None

*A Boeing (Stearman) Kaydet*

# NORTH AMERICAN T-6/SNJ TEXAN and FOREBEARS (U.S.A.)

*T-6G Texan*

This series comprised the Western Alliance's most important trainers of World War II, and production was in the order of 17,000 or more aircraft. The series was pioneered by the NA-16 prototype that flew in April 1935 as an all-metal cantilever low-wing monoplane with two open cockpits, fixed landing gear and the 298-kW (400-hp) Wright R-975 radial. The type was then ordered in a form with a glazed enclosure over the cockpits as the BT-9 and NJ series for the U.S. Army and U.S. Navy respectively.

Additional aircraft were produced for export to several countries including Canada, where the aircraft was known as the Yale.

This NA-18 version was then developed further with the 447-kW (600-hp) Pratt & Whitney R-1340 radial, equipment comparable with that of contemporary combat aircraft, and retractable tailwheel landing gear to serve as a combat trainer. This NA-26 variant was first ordered as the AT-6 Texan (initially BC-1) and SNJ series for the U.S. Army and Navy

respectively. Production was undertaken in many improved and specialized models up to the T-6F and SNJ-6. The USAAF's most numerous models were the AT-6C and AT-6D (2,970 and 4,388)·with a revised structure that made fewer demands on strategically important light alloys, while the U.S. Navy's equivalents were the 2,400 SNJ-4s and 1,357 SNJ-5s. The British and their Commonwealth allies also operated the type in comparatively large numbers under the basic designation Harvard, which were delivered from

American and licensed Canadian production in variants up to the Harvard Mk 4. From 1949 some 2,086 American aircraft were rebuilt as T-6G multi-role trainers with the R-1340-AN-1 engine, increased fuel capacity, an improved cockpit layout, a steerable tailwheel together with many other modifications.

*The Harvard Mk IIB*

**NORTH AMERICAN T-6D TEXAN (RAF HARVARD)**
**Role:** Advanced trainer
**Crew/Accommodation:** Two
**Power Plant:** One 550 hp Pratt & Whitney R-1340-AN1 Wasp air-cooled radial
**Dimensions:** Span 12.81 m (42.02 ft); length 8.84 m (28.99 ft); wing area 23.57 m² (253.72 sq ft)
**Weights:** Empty 1,886 kg (4,158 lb); MTOW 2,722 kg (6,000 lb)
**Performance:** Maximum speed 330 km/h (205 mph) at 1,524 (5,000 ft); operational ceiling 6,553 m (21,500 ft); range 1,207 km (750 miles)
**Load:** Two .303 inch machine guns

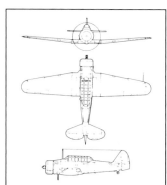

*North American BC-1*

# MILES MAGISTER (United Kingdom)

*Magister Mk I*

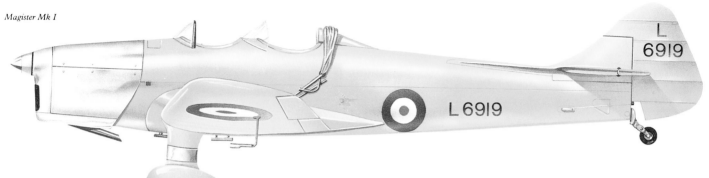

The Magister was the Royal Air Force's most important elementary trainer in the opening stages of World War II, and was also of historical importance as the service's first monoplane trainer. The type was developed to meet a 1936 requirement for a monoplane trainer

*Magister elementary trainer*

to complement the monoplane combat aircraft entering Royal Air Force service in this period. It was derived as the M.14 from the Hawk Trainer, of which 25 had been built within the context of the M.2 Hawk series. Modifications from the Hawk Trainer included larger cockpits and blind-flying equipment, the latter including a hood that could be erected over the rear cockpit.

The type was a low-wing monoplane with fixed but nicely faired tailwheel landing gear and open

**MILES MAGISTER Mk II**
**Role:** Elementary trainer
**Crew/Accommodation:** Two
**Power Plant:** One 130 hp de Havilland Gipsy Major air-cooled inline
**Dimensions:** Span 10.31 m (33.83 ft); length 7.51 m (24.63 ft); wing area 16.35 m² (176 sq ft)
**Weights:** Empty 583 kg (1,286 lb); MTOW 862 kg (1,900 lb)
**Performance:** Maximum speed 225 km/h (140 mph) at sea level; operational ceiling 5,029 m (16,500 ft); range 591 km (367 miles)
**Load:** Up to 109 kg (240 lb) including student pilot

tandem cockpits, and was unusual in reverting to the type of all-wood construction that the RAF had eschewed from the early 1920s. In addition to its monoplane configuration, trailing-edge flaps and full aerobatic capability, the Magister also offered to the pilots who trained on it the advantage of higher overall performance without any significant increase in landing speed. Production began in May 1937, and deliveries of the initial Magister Mk I to the Central Flying School started in October of the same year. The type was generally operated without its

main landing gear fairings, and to improve spin recovery the Magister Mk II of 1938 introduced a slightly larger rudder.

Production lasted to 1941 and comprised 1,293 aircraft in the U.K. and another 100 licence-built in Turkey. After the end of World War II, many surplus Magisters were sold on to the civil market, and large numbers of these were adopted by civil flying schools with the designation Hawk Trainer Mk III. The Royal Air Force retired its last Magisters in 1948.

*The Miles Magister was a simple yet highly effective trainer*

# BEECH T-34 MENTOR (U.S.A.)

*T-34C Turbo*

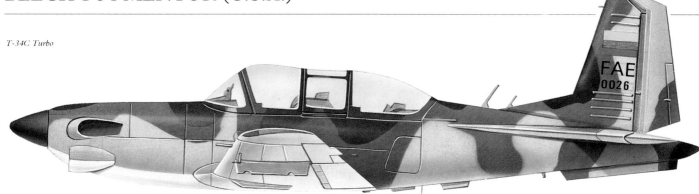

The T-34 resulted from Beech's 1948 decision to develop a trainer derived from the Model 33 Bonanza with a conventional tail and accommodation for the pupil and instructor in tandem. The first example of the Model 45 Mentor flew in December 1948. At this time the U.S. Air Force was looking for a new primary trainer, and in 1950 evaluated three Model 45s under the designation YT-34 with two types of Continental flat-six piston engine. In March 1953 the Model 45 was selected for USAF service, and 450 T-34As were ordered with the

168-kW (225-hp) Continental O-470-13 engine. In June 1954, the U.S. Navy followed this lead with an order for 290 out of an eventual 423 T-34B trainers with the identically rated O-470-4 engine.

The basic soundness of the design is attested by further development of the airframe in the early 1970s. By this time the turboprop was seen as the better powerplant, offering engine reliability, considerable fuel economies, and the use of turbine engines right through the pupil pilot's training. Two T-34Bs were therefore

converted to YT-34C standard with the Pratt & Whitney Canada PT6A-25, and the first of these flew in September 1973. The engine is provided with a torque limiter that restricts power output to some 56 per cent of the maximum, and this ensures constant performance over a wide range of altitude and temperature conditions. Successful evaluation led to orders for the T-34C Turbo-Mentor production model with a strengthened airframe. Between November 1977 and April 1984 the U.S. Navy received 334 newly built T-34Cs, followed by 19 more in

1989–90. For the export market, Beech developed the T-34C-1 with four underwing hardpoints for a 544-kg (1,200-lb) warload in the weapon training role, with counter-insurgency and light attack as possible operational tasks. The export civil version without hardpoints became the Turbine Mentor 34C.

*Beech T-34C-1s*

## BEECH T-34C TURBO-MENTOR
**Role:** Basic trainer/light strike
**Crew/Accommodation:** Two
**Power Plant:** One 550*shp Pratt & Whitney Canada PT6A-25 turboprop (*400 shp in torque-limited form used by the U.S. Navy)
**Dimensions:** Span 10.16 m (33.33 ft); length 8.75 m (28.71 ft); wing area 16.70 m² (179.6 sq ft)
**Weights:** Empty 1,343 kg (2,960 lb); MTOW 2,495 kg (5,500 lb)
**Performance:** Maximum speed 396 km/h (246 mph); operational ceiling 9,144 m (30,000 ft); range up to 1,310 km (814 miles)
**Load:** Up to 544 kg (1,200 lb) of external weapons/fuel for T-34C-1

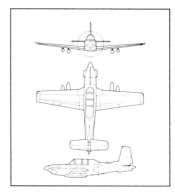

*Beech T-34C Mentor*

# FOUGA CM.170 MAGISTER (France)

*CM.170 Magister*

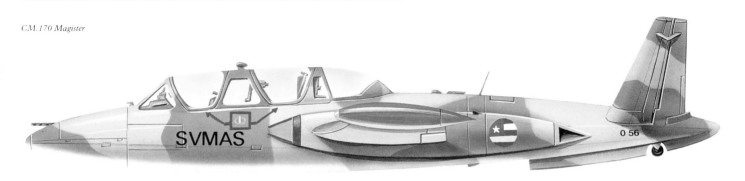

The Magister was designed as the CM.170 and placed in production by Air Fouga, which later became part of the Potez corporation that was then absorbed in the Aerospatiale group. The CM.170 was evolved to meet a French Air Force requirement for a purpose-designed jet basic trainer, and in its time was one of the world's most widely used trainers and light attack aircraft. The type's characteristic features are a high cockpit enclosure over the tandem seats, a V-tail, and mid-set wings with the two small turbojets installed in their roots. The type flew in prototype form during July 1952, and in the following year a pre-production batch of 10 aircraft was ordered for evaluation purposes. The French Air Force ordered an initial 95 aircraft in 1954, and the first of these CM.170-1 aircraft was delivered in February 1956 in a programme that eventually witnessed the delivery of 437 Magisters to the French Air Force.

The CM.170-1 is exclusively a land-based variant powered by two 400-kg (882-lb) Turboméca Marboré IIA turbojets, and overall production was 916 aircraft including major exports to West Germany, and licensed construction in both Finland and Israel. Variants produced in substantially smaller numbers were the CM.170-2 Super Magister and CM.175 Zephyr. The 137 Super Magisters are land-based aircraft powered by two 480-kg (1,058-lb) thrust Marboré VI turbojets, while the 32 Zephyrs are naval trainers fitted with arrester hooks and powered by Marboré IIA engines. The basic type has a useful light attack capability, and this is improved in the AMIT Fouga, otherwise the Tzukit (Thrush), an upgraded version developed by Israel Aircraft Industries with Marbore VI engines in a strengthened airframe and fitted with modern avionics.

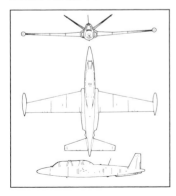

*Fouga CM.170 Magister*

**FOUGA CM. 170 MAGISTER**
**Role:** Basic/advanced trainer
**Crew/Accommodation:** Two
**Power Plant:** Two 440 kgp (880 lb s.t.) Turboméca Maboré IIa turbojets
**Dimensions:** Span 12.15 m (39. 83 ft); length 10.06 m (33 ft); wing area 17.3 m² (186.1 sq ft)
**Weights:** Empty 2,150 kg (4,740 lb); MTOW 3,200 kg (7,055 lb)
**Performance:** Maximum speed 700 km/h (435 knots) at sea level; operational ceiling 13,500 m (44,291 ft); range 1,250 km (775 miles)
**Load:** Two 7.62 mm machine guns

*Fouga Magister trainers of the French Air Force*

# CESSNA T-37 TWEET and A-37 DRAGONFLY (U.S.A.)

*A-37B Dragonfly*

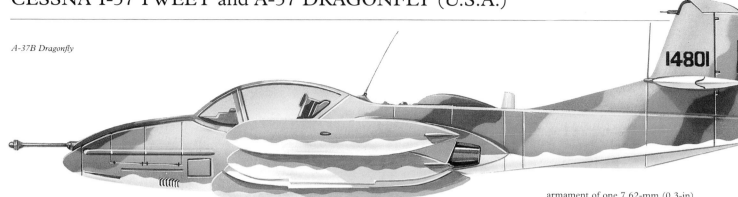

In the early 1950s, the U.S. Air Force adopted a programme of all-through training using jet-powered aircraft, and issued a requirement for a new basic trainer with turbojet propulsion as its first purpose-built jet trainer. Several companies responded with design proposals; in 1953 Cessna was declared winner with its Model 318. Two XT-37 prototypes were ordered. The first of these flew in October 1954 with two Turboméca Marboré turbojets licence-built in the United States as 417-kg (920-lb) thrust

Continental YJ69-T-9s. The type was ordered into production as the T-37A. Powered by J69-T-9 turbojets, hundreds of these aircraft entered service but only from 1957 as changes were found to be necessary, most notably in the layout of the cockpit.

These aircraft were followed by examples of the T-37B with 465-kg (1,025-lb) thrust J69-T-25 engines and improved avionics, bringing total production to 985 aircraft. All surviving T-37As were later brought

up to T-37B standard. The last trainer was the T-37C, which offered light armament capability on underwing hardpoints, together with the option of wingtip fuel tanks. Production totalled 198 aircraft for delivery in aid packages to eight countries. A special counter-insurgency and light attack version for use in Vietnam was developed as the YAT-37D with 1089-kg (2,400-lb) thrust General Electric J85-GE-5 turbojets. Some 39 of the type were produced as T-37B conversions, and these were evaluated from 1967. Their success with an

armament of one 7.62-mm (0.3-in) Minigun multi-barrel machine gun and disposable stores on eight underwing hardpoints led to development of the beefed-up Model 318E, which was ordered into production as the A-37B with 1293-kg (2,850-lb) thrust J85-GE-17A engines, inflight refuelling capability, and the ability to carry a warload of more than 2268 kg (5,000 lb). Many hundreds were built. Tweets are now being replaced in USAF service by T-6A Texan IIs.

*A Cessna T-37B Tweet with the marking of the Greek Air Force*

**CESSNA A-37B DRAGONFLY**
**Role:** Light strike
**Crew/Accommodation:** Two
**Power Plant:** Two, 1,293 kgp (2,850 lb s.t.) General Electric J85-GE-17A turbojets
**Dimensions:** Span 11.71 m (38.42 ft); length 9.69 m (31.83 ft); wing area 17.09 m² (183.9 sq ft)
**Weights:** Empty 1,845 kg (4,067 lb); MTOW 6,350 kg (14,000 lb)
**Performance:** Maximum speed 771 km/h (479 mph) at 4,724 m (15,500 ft); operational ceiling 7,620 m (25,000 ft); radius 380 km (236 miles) with 843 kg (1,858 lb) bombload
**Load:** One 7.62 mm multi-barrel machine gun, plus up to 2,576 kg (5,680 lb) of bombs or air-to-ground rockets carried on underwing pylons

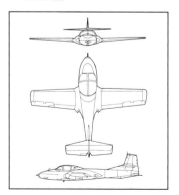

*Cessna T-37B*

261

# AERO L-39 ALBATROS and derivatives (Czech Republic)

*L-39ZA Albatros*

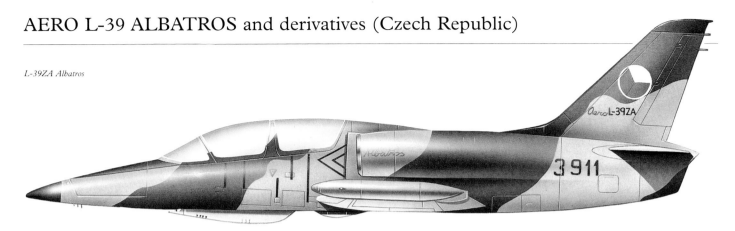

The L-39 is an attractive and effective trainer that was developed to succeed the same company's L-29 Delfin.

The first of three prototypes flew in November 1968, and the only major problem was integration of the Soviet turbofan into the Czech airframe. The original L-39C basic training version entered service in 1974 and became the standard jet trainer of most Communist air arms. The unswept

*Aero L-39 Albatross*

flying surfaces curtail outright performance, but in addition to the fuel-economical turbofan engine and height-staggered seating, positive features are the type's tractable handling, reliability, and easy maintenance.

Variants are the L-39C with two underwing hardpoints for up to 284 kg (626 lb) of stores, the L-39ZO weapons trainer with four hardpoints on strengthened wings, the L39ZA attack/reconnaissance type with four hardpoints and a detachable underfuselage pack containing one 23-mm twin-barrel cannon, the L-39ZA/MP multi-purpose variant with

### AERO L-39ZA ALBATROS
**Role:** Light strike/reconnaissance/training
**Crew/Accommodation:** Two
**Power Plant:** One 1,720 kgp (3,792 lb s.t.) Ivchenko PROGRESS AI-25TL turbofan
**Dimensions:** Span 9.46 m (31 ft); length 12.13 m (39.76 ft); wing area 18.80 m² (202.4 sq ft)
**Weights:** Empty 3,565 kg (7,859 lb); MTOW 5,600 kg (12,346 lb)
**Performance:** Maximum speed 755 km/h (469 mph); operational ceiling 11,000 m (36,090 ft); range 1,350 km (839 miles) at 4,470 kg all-up weight on internal fuel only
**Load:** One 23-mm cannon, plus up to 1,290 kg (2,844 lb) of externally underslung ordnance

Western avionics and a head-up display (as used by Thailand), and the L-39V target-tug. All versions with four hardpoints can carry a 1,290-kg (2,844-lb) load. Well over 2,200 L-39s have been delivered to date to many countries. The L-39MS became the more powerful and more capable L-59, delivered from 1991, while

subsequent developments have been the more advanced L-139 Albatros 2000 (flown 1993) and single/two-seat L-159 ALCA multi-role combat aircraft (flown 1997).

*The Aero L-39 Albatros has straight flying surfaces and turbofan power*

# BRITISH AEROSPACE HAWK Family (United Kingdom)

*Hawk 200*

The Hawk was developed to replace the Hawker Siddeley (Folland) Gnat in the training role, and first flew during August 1974 as the P. 1182 prototype. The RAF received 176 as Hawk T.Mk1s of which 88 were later converted to permit a secondary air-defence role as Hawk T.Mk 1As with provision for AIM-9L Sidewinder air-to-air missiles on four rather than two hardpoints under the wings. They use the 2,376-kg (5,240-lb) thrust Adour 151 engine. There have also been several export models. The Hawk Mk 50 series is based on the T.Mk 1, but with a similarly-rated Adour Mk 851, and the Hawk Mk 60 has a slightly lengthened fuselage and usually the 2,590-kg (5,710-lb) thrust Adour Mk 861 turbofan for improved field performance, acceleration, climb and turn rates, and payload/range. Other and more radically developed variants are the Hawk 100 two-seat dual-role trainer and light ground-attack aircraft, and the Hawk 200 single-seat attack model.

The 100 is based on the Mk 60 but has the 2,600-kg (5,730-lb) thrust Adour Mk 871 and an advanced nav/attack system based on a digital databus and including a head-up display, weapon-aiming computer and radar-warning receiver. Most importantly, it used a new wing with leading-edge droop to enhance manoeuvrability and manual combat flaps, and has the option of FLIR/laser ranging in the extended nose. The 200 is also based on the Mk 60 but has a single-seat cockpit, Adour Mk 871 engine, Mk 100 wings and Mk 100 advanced electronics; it also introduced APG-66H multi-mode radar and provision for state-of-the-art weaponry.

The Hawk's basic design was adapted by McDonnell Douglas (now Boeing) as the T-45 Goshawk carrier-capable trainer for the U.S. Navy. This has a revised cockpit, strengthened landing gear (including long-stroke main units and a twin-wheel nose unit), an arrester hook, ventral finlets, larger tail surfaces, a revised wing, and the 2651-kg (5,845-lb) thrust F405-RR-401 version of the Adour Mk 871 turbofan.

**BRITISH AEROSPACE HAWK 60 Series**
**Role:** Light strike/trainer
**Crew/Accommodation:** Two
**Power Plant:** One 2,590 kgp (5,710 lb s.t.) Rolls-Royce Turboméca Adour 861 turbofan
**Dimensions:** Span 9.4 m (30.83 ft); length 12.42 m (40.75 ft); wing area 16.69 m² (179.64 sq ft)
**Weights:** Empty 4,012 kg (8,845 lb); MTOW 9,100 kg (20,062 lb)
**Performance:** Maximum speed 1,037 km/h (560 knots) Mach 0.81 at sea level; operational ceiling 14,000 m (46,000 ft); radius 842 kn (524 miles) with two rocket pods and two drop tanks
**Load:** Up to 3,000 kg (6,000 lb) of weapons/fuel carried externally

*British Aerospace Hawk 60*

*A British Aerospace Hawk 100*

# Reconnaissance and Communications

In practical terms, aerial warfare has its origins in 1794, when Captain Coutelle of the French Republican Army carried out an aerial reconnaissance from a tethered balloon at Maubeuge in Belgium during the Battle of Fleurus. Another balloonist became the first-ever pilot to be shot down in war when, in 1898, American Sgt. Ivy Baldwin of the Army Signal Corps was brought down (virtually unharmed) by Spanish ground fire during the Battle of Santiago. These two unrelated events involving balloonists a century apart, were portents of aerial warfare in the 20th century, with the need for reconnaissance being later countered by a requirement to prevent an enemy using that information or gaining a similar advantage.

A Blériot monoplane, accompanied by a Royal Aircraft Factory B.E.2a, made the first RFC reconnaissance flight over German lines during the 1914–18 war, on 19 August 1914. Just days later aerial reconnaissance was instrumental in bringing victory to German forces at the Battle of Tannenberg, when 120,000 Russian soldiers and 500 guns were captured, and from that time to this reconnaissance has been a vital part of tactical and strategic planning, though modern-day commanders can also call upon satellites.

Communications has been a less glamorous military role, yet of importance in peace and war. Normally undertaken by off-the-shelf light aircraft or small transports, such types have traditionally provided the means for VIPs to be air-lifted on urgent non-regular business, either for connecting bases or flying to other destinations. An advantage of the lightplane has been its ability to operate from unprepared airstrips, and the Fieseler Storch that had incredible short take-off capability was not only the favoured transport of wartime Generalfeldmarschall Erwin Rommel in North Africa but a captured example was used by his opponent, Field Marshal Bernard Montgomery.

Examples of important communications work are numerous: one worthy of recounting came during the 1939–45 war when RAF de Havilland Dominie biplanes co-operated with Air Transport Auxiliary in vital aircraft ferrying work, returning pilots after they had delivered combat aircraft to base. Occasionally, even combat aircraft have found their way to communications units, and it should be remembered that, as one example of many, a Fairey IIIF general-purpose biplane, set aside for such duties, took Lord Londonderry to the 1932 Disarmament Conferences in Geneva. Even fighters have been used by commanders as personal mounts to flit between bases, and in America a Boeing F4B-1A biplane of the early 1930s was used for communications flights by the Assistant Secretary of the U.S. Navy, while in recent times even a Russian Mach 2 Sukhoi Su-27 allegedly became the 'personal' transport of a test pilot.

*Picture: The most famous strategic and tactical reconnaissance aircraft of all time was to be the Lockheed U-2 Dragon Lady, developed in secrecy for the USAF at the Lockheed 'Skunk Works' and first flown in August 1955. Possessing the ability to operate at 24,400 m (80,000 ft), the USAF still has some 35 in service in modernized U-2S form carrying sensors and cameras (Eric Schulzinger)*

# BLERIOT MONOPLANES (France)

*Bleriot XI*

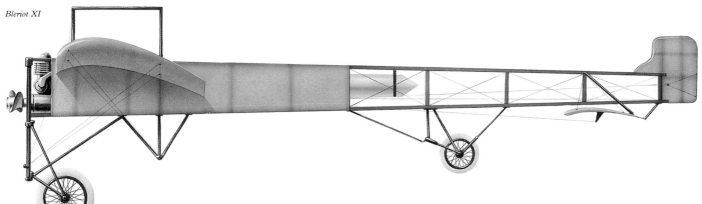

Louis Blériot was one of the true pioneers of aviation, and secured his place in history during 1909 as the first man to fly a heavier-than-air craft across the English Channel. The

*Bleriot XI*

machine involved in this epoch-making flight was a Blériot XI with an 18.7-kW (25-hp) Anzani engine, the culmination of a series of monoplanes that had started with the unsuccessful Blériot V of 1906. The V was Blériot's first design after he had ended his association with Gabriel Voisin, and was a canard type that made a few hopping flights, then crashed and was scrapped. Next came the tandem-wing Blériot VI that achieved a few hops during 1907. The Blériot VII was a modestly successful tractor monoplane, and this layout was used in the fabric-covered Blériot VIII that was later rebuilt as the Blériot BIIIbis

with flap-type ailerons and Blériot VIIIter with pivoting wingtip ailerons. The Blériot XI had paper-covered wings of short span and a fuselage partially covered in fabric, but never flew, while the Blériot X pusher biplane was never completed.

The Blériot XI was initially powered by a 21-kW (28-hp) R.E.P. engine, but its lack of success with this engine led to its modification as

the Blériot XI (Mod) with the 18.7-kW (25-hp) Anzani. The Blériot XI (Mod)'s cross-Channel triumph secured a comparative flood of orders for his aircraft, which was steadily upgraded with more powerful engines. The type was also developed for the military as a reconnaissance machine in Blériot XI-2 and -3 two- and three-seat forms. (See introduction for early military missions.)

**BLERIOT XI-2**
**Role:** Reconnaissance/training
**Crew/Accommodation:** Two
**Power Plant:** One 80 hp Gnome air-cooled rotary
**Dimensions:** Span 10.35 m (33.96 ft); length 8.4 m (27.56 ft); wing area 19 m² (205 sq ft)
**Weights:** Empty 335 kg (786 lb); MTOW 585 kg (1,290 lb)
**Performance:** Maximum speed 120 km/h (75 mph) at sea level; endurance 3.5 hours
**Load:** None other than crew

*The Bleriot XI monoplane was highly successful*

# FIESELER Fi 156 STORCH (Germany)

*Fi 156C Storch*

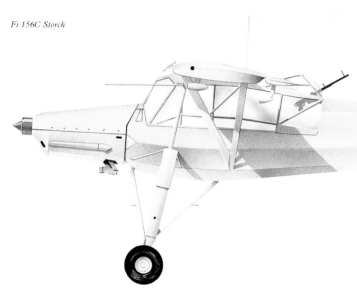

The Fi 156 Storch (Stork) was Germany's most important army co-operation and battlefield reconnaissance aircraft of World War II, and the first of four prototypes flew in the early part of 1936. The Fi 156 was a braced high-wing monoplane with an extensively glazed cockpit offering very good fields of vision and fixed tailwheel landing gear, the main units of which were of the long-stroke type to absorb landing forces at high sink rates. The prototype displayed exceptional STOL capabilities because of its wing, which combined good aerodynamic qualities with the advantages offered by fixed slats and slotted ailerons/flaps over the entire leading and trailing edges respectively. The prototypes showed that the Storch could take off in as little at

60 m ( 200 ft) in a light head wind, and also land in about one-third of that same distance.

The type was adopted for a wide assortment of army co-operation and associated duties in its Fi 156A-1

*The Fieseler Fi 156 Vi*

initial production form. The civil Fi 156B remained only a project, so the next variant was the military Fi 156C. This had improved radio equipment and a raised rear section of the cabin glazing allowing a 7.92-mm (0.312-in) machine gun to be mounted. Fi 156C variants were the Fi 156C-1 for liaison, two-seat Fi 156C-2 for tactical reconnaissance or casualty evacuation with a litter in the rear cockpit, Fi 156C-3 for light transport, and Fi 156C-5 with a ventral tank for extended range. The last production

model was the Fi 156D-1 ambulance powered by an Argus AS 10P engine and with provision for one litter loaded through a larger hatch. Production totalled about 2,900 aircraft built in Germany and, under German control, Czechoslovakia and France. Mraz and Morane-Saulnier continued production in these two countries after the war.

## FIESELER Fi 156 C-1 STORCH
**Role:** Army co-operation/observation and communications
**Crew/Accommodation:** Two or one, plus one litter-carried casualty
**Power Plant:** One 240 hp Argus As 10C air-cooled inline
**Dimensions:** Span 14.25 m (46.75 ft); length 9.9 m (32.48 ft); wing area 26 m² (279.9 sq ft)
**Weights:** Empty 930 kg (2,051 lb); MTOW 1,320 kg (2,911 lb)
**Performance:** Maximum speed 145 km/h (90 mph) at sea level; operational ceiling 4,600 m (15,092 ft); range 385 km (239 miles)
**Load:** One 7.9 mm machine gun, plus provision to evacuate one litterborne casualty

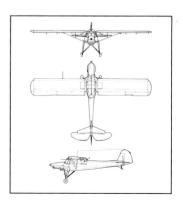

*Fieseler Fi 156C-0*

# WESTLAND LYSANDER (United Kingdom)

*Lysander Mk III*

The Lysander resulted from a 1934 British Air Ministry requirement for a two-seat army co-operation aircraft. Key features of the requirements were good fields of vision and STOL performance, and for this reason the design team opted for an extensively glazed cockpit supporting the roots of the unusually shaped high-set wing, the outer portions of which were braced by V-struts to the cantilever main legs of the fixed tailwheel landing gear. These legs were also fitted with small stub wings which could carry up to 227-kg (500-lb) of light bombs or other types of stores.

The first of two prototypes flew in June 1936 with the 664-kW (890-hp) Bristol Mercury XII radial, and after successful trials the type was ordered into production as the Lysander Mk I, of which 169 were built for service from June 1938. Further development of this aircraft resulted in the Lysander Mk II, of which 517 were built with the 675-kW (905-hp) Bristol Perseus XII radial, the Lysander Mk III of which 517 were built with the 649-kW (870-hp) Mercury XX, and the Lysander Mk IIIA of which 347 were built with the Mercury 30. Early operations in France revealed that the Lysander was too vulnerable for its designed role in the presence of modern fighters and anti-aircraft defences, and though the type saw further limited first-line service in the Middle East and the Far East, most aircraft were relegated to second-line duties such as target towing, air-sea rescue, radar calibration and special agent infiltration and extraction. Some 14 Mk I conversions to Lysander TT.Mk I standard validated the target tug version, and a similar process provided five TT.Mk IIs, 51 T.Mk IIIs and 100 TT.Mk IIIA aircraft.

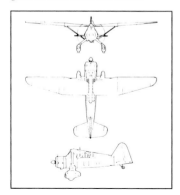

*Westland Lysander Mk III*

**WESTLAND LYSANDER Mk III**
**Role:** Communications/tactical reconnaissance
**Crew/Accommodation:** Two
**Power Plant:** One 890 hp Bristol Mercury XX air-cooled radial
**Dimensions:** Span 15.24 m (50.00 ft); length 9.29 m (30.50 ft); wing area 24.15 m² (260.00 sq ft)
**Weights:** Empty 1,980 kg (4,365 lb); MTOW 2,865 kg (6,318 lb)
**Performance:** Maximum speed 336 km/h (209 mph) at 1,524 m (5,000 ft); operational ceiling 6,553 m (21,500 ft); range 966 km (600 miles)
**Load:** Four .303 in machine guns, plus up to 227 kg (500 lb) of bombs

*The Westland Lysander had excellent STOL performance*

# ARADO Ar 234 BLITZ (Germany)

*Ar 234B-2 Blitz*

The Ar 234 Blitz (Lightning) was the world's first purpose-designed jet reconnaissance aircraft and bomber. As first flown in June 1943, the all-metal Ar 234A had straight flying surfaces with two Junkers Jumo 004B turbojets in nacelles slung under the shoulder-mounted wings, and a fuselage too slender to accommodate retractable wheeled landing gear. As a result, the first prototypes were designed to take off from a jettisonable trolley and land on retractable skids. Some 18 prototypes were trialled with twin Jumo 004B or quadruple BMW 003A turbojets. The trolley/skid arrangement proved workable but was hardly effective, so the 20 pre-production aircraft featured a wider fuselage to make possible the installation of retractable tricycle landing gear.

These paved the way for the 210 examples of the Ar 234B production model with two engines but no pressurization or ejector seat; this series included the Ar 234B-1 reconnaissance and Ar 234B-2 bomber variants. Another 12 prototypes were used to develop the multi-role Ar 234C model, which had four engines, cabin pressurization and an ejector sea; only 14 of this late-war model were built, and the series included the Ar 234C-1 reconnaissance and Ar 234C-4 multi-role bomber and ground attack variants. The Ar 234C-4 bomber and Ar 234C-2 armed reconnaissance variants remained projects, as did several other variants. The Ar 234 first entered service in the summer of 1944 in the form of two evaluation prototypes operated by 1 Staffel for reconnaissance, followed that September by Ar 234B-1s going to Sonderkommando Götz. From 24 December, Ar 234B-2 jet bombers went into action, initially with II/KG 76 during the Ardennes offensive. Night operations by KG 76 began on the last night of 1944, against targets in Brussels and Liège.

*Arado Ar 234B Blitz*

**ARADO Ar 234B-2 BLITZ**
**Role:** High speed bomber
**Crew/Accommodation:** One
**Power Plant:** Two 900 kgp (1,980 lb s.t.) Junkers 004B Orkan turbojets
**Dimensions:** Span 14.44 m (47.38 ft); length 12.64 m (41.47 ft); wing area 27.3 m² (284.2 sq ft)
**Weights:** Empty 5,200 kg (11,464 lb); MTOW 9,800 kg (21,715 lb)
**Performance:** Maximum speed 742 km/h (461 mph) at 6,000 m (19,685 ft); operational ceiling 10,000 m (32,810 ft); range 1,556 km (967 miles) with 500 kg (1,102 lb) payload
**Load:** Two rear-firing 20 mm cannon, plus up to 2,000 kg (4,410 lb) of bombs

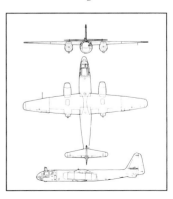

*Arado Ar 234B-2 Blitz*

# LOCKHEED SR-71 (U.S.A.)

*SR-71*

Until its first retirement at the end of 1989, and then the planned reactivation of two in the mid 1990s but followed by the announcement of continuing full retirement in April 1998, the SR-71 was the world's fastest and highest-flying 'conventional' aircraft. It was a truly extraordinary machine, designed for the strategic reconnaissance role with a mass of sensors including ASARs-1 (advanced synthetic aperture radar system) or the Itek camera that could scan to the horizon on each side of the flightpath, and two pre-programmable high-resolution cameras. The 'stealthy' airframe was designed for a crew of two (pilot and systems operator) and minimum drag, and was therefore evolved with a very slender fuselage and thin wings of delta planform blended into the fuselage by large chines that generated additional lift, prevented the pitching down of the nose at higher speeds, and provided additional volume for sensors and fuel. The airframe was built largely of titanium and stainless steel to deal with the high temperatures created by air friction at the SR-71's Mach 3+ cruising speed at heights over 21,335 m (70,000 ft). Power was provided by the two special continuous-bleed turbojets which at high speed provided only a small part of the motive power in the form of direct jet thrust from the nozzles (18%), the greater part of the power being provided by inlet suction (54%) and thrust from the special outlets at the rear of the multiple-flow nacelles (28%). Nicknamed 'Blackbird' for its special overall colour scheme that helped dissipate heat and absorb enemy radar emissions, the SR-71 was developed via three YF-121-A interceptors which reached only the experimental stage, from 15 A-12 (including one trainer) Mach 3.6 reconnaissance aircraft ordered for the CIA (and, in the case of two A-12 (M)s, as launching platforms for D-21 hypersonic cruise reconnaissance drones) and first flown from Groom Lake in March 1962. The SR-71A entered service in 1966 and 30 aircraft were built, while training was carried out on a conversion type comprising one SR-71B and one similar SR-71C converted from SR-71 standard.

### LOCKHEED SR-71A

**Role:** Long-range high supersonic reconnaissance

**Crew/Accommodation:** Two

**Power Plant:** Two 14,742 kgp (32,500 lb s.t.) Pratt & Whitney J58 turbo-ramjets

**Dimensions:** Span 16.94 m (55.58 ft); length 32.74 m (107.41 ft); wing area 149.1m² (1,605 sq ft)

**Weights:** Empty 30,618 kg (67,500 lb); MTOW 78,020 kg (172,000 lb)

**Performance:** Cruise speed 3,661 km/h (1,976 knots) Mach 3.35 at 24,385 m (80,000 ft); operational ceiling 25,908 m (85,000 ft); range 5,230 km (2.822 naut. miles) unrefuelled

**Load:** Up to around 9,072 kg (20,000 lb) of specialized sensors

*A dramatic view of a Lockheed SR-71A taking on fuel*

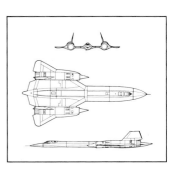

*Lockheed SR-14A 'Blackbird'*

# Transports

By the time the Great War ended in 1918, aeroplanes had firmly established themselves as vital to any nation possessing fighting forces. Their influence extended not only far beyond the skies, but also to the very deployment and use of traditional land armies and naval ships, as all were within reach of 'spying' and armed aeroplanes. However, there was one form of aeroplane that had been largely overlooked due to the nature of warfare on the Western Front and elsewhere – that of the military transport.

Post-war, the RAF found itself much diminished in size but still tasked with new and hitherto untested roles such as policing the vast areas of Iraq under the so-called 'air control' duties, whereby it was hoped that a small number of RAF squadrons could enforce law and order from the air, thus replacing large army garrisons. To the initial four squadrons of de Havilland (Airco) D.H.9As, one of Bristol Fighters and one of Sopwith Snipe fighters were added and from 1922 two squadrons of new Vickers Vernons, the first-ever purpose-built troop-carrying transports. Based on the Vimy bomber but given a rotund fuselage to provide internal accommodation for twelve troops, the newly-built Vernons joined just two

squadrons in the Middle East, where their duties were varied; on one day in 1922, the year air control operations in Iraq began, Vernons evacuated sick British troops from Northern Iraq to a Baghdad hospital, while other duties included mail carrying. The 22-troop Vickers Victoria began replacing the Vernons from 1926, based on the Virginia bomber, such had been the success of the first troop carriers, and these remained in use for nearly a decade.

So with the Vernon began a new venture for the aeroplane, that of military transport. In the United States a Martin GMB bomber had been completed in 1919 with the fuselage height raised and windows added for carrying ten passengers, and was followed by six so-modified MB-1 bombers for use by the Postal Service. These were later transferred to the U.S. Army Air Corps, thus becoming the first Army aircraft to use the original 'T' for transport designation. Two T-2s followed and were imported Dutch Fokker F-IVs, one later becoming the A-2 ambulance aircraft, while the first aircraft of the new Army 'C' serial designation (for transports) system introduced in 1925 was the Douglas C-1 eight-passenger transport.

By the 1930s the production of new commercial transports provided also military equivalents for the armed forces, with the Luftwaffe taking in huge numbers of Junkers Ju 52/3ms, for example, and the important wartime Allied C-47 was based on the Douglas DC-3 airliner. But, once peace had again been restored, military needs for freighting vast numbers of troops or heavy loads of military equipment, such as tanks and guns, meant that giant transports began to appear as specialized military types to meet Cold War demands, a tradition of original design that continues today with the latest Boeing C-17A Globemaster III for the USAF. Interestingly, the Lockheed Martin C-130 Hercules that first joined the service in 1956 as a turboprop-powered tactical transport in original C-130A form, continues in production today in latest C-130J form, and is well set to become the first aeroplane in history to complete over half a century of production by its original company and possibly the first to complete (by 2056) a full century of service!

*Picture: USAF Boeing C-17A Globemaster IIIs of the 437th Airlift Wing being readied at a base in Germany for flights into Hungary and Bosnia as part of Operation Joint Endeavour*

# DOUGLAS DC-4 and C-54 SKYMASTER (U.S.A.)

*Douglas DC-4*

Even before the DC-3 had flown, Douglas was planning a longer-range air transport with four engines, retractable tricycle landing gear, and greater capacity. The DC-4 (later DC-4E) pressurized prototype first flew in June 1938, but was too advanced for its time and therefore suffered a number of technical problems. The DC-4E's performance and operating economics were also below specification, and the company therefore dropped the type. As a replacement, Douglas turned to the unpressurized and otherwise simplified DC-4 with a lighter structure, a new high aspect ratio wing, and a tail unit with a single central vertical surface in place of the DC-4E's twin endplate surfaces. The type was committed to production with 1081-kW (1,450-hp) Pratt & Whitney R-2000-2SD1-G Twin Wasp radial engines even before the first example had flown.

With the United States caught up into World War II during December 1941, the type was swept into military service as the C-54 (Army) and R5D (Navy) long-range military transport, and the first aircraft flew during February 1942 in U.S. Army Air Forces markings. The main military versions were the 24 impressed C-54s with R-2000-3 radials for 26 passengers, the 207 fully militarized C54As and R5D-1s with R-2000-7s for 50 passengers, the 220 C-54Bs and R5D-2s with integral wing tanks, the 380 C-54Ds and R5D-3s with R-2000-11s, the 125 C-54E and R5D-4 convertible freight/passenger models with revised fuel tankage, and the 162 C-54G and R5D-5 troop carriers with R-2000-9s. After military service many of these aircraft found their way on to the civil register and performed excellently in the long-range passenger and freight roles. Two civil models were produced after World War II; total production was 1,122 aircraft.

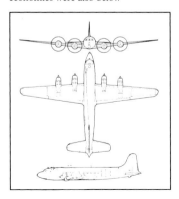

*Douglas C-54D Skymaster*

**DOUGLAS DC-4 and C-54 SKYMASTER**
**Role:** Long-range passenger transport
**Crew/Accommodation:** Four, plus three/four cabin crew, plus up to 86 passengers
**Power Plant:** Four 1,450 hp Pratt & Whitney R.2000 Twin Wasp air-cooled radials
**Dimensions:** Span 35.81 m (117.5 ft); length 28.6 m (93.83 ft); wing area 135.35 m² (1,457 sq ft)
**Weights:** Empty 16,783 kg (37,000 lb); MTOW 33,113 kg (73,000 lb)
**Performance:** Cruise speed 309 km/h (192 mph) at 3,050 m (10,000 ft); operational ceiling 6,705 m (22,000 ft) ; range 3,220 km (2,000 miles) with 9,979 kg (22,000 lb) payload
**Load:** Up to 14,515 kg (32,500 lb)

*The Douglas R5D series was the naval counterpart of the C-54 Skymaster*

# CURTISS-WRIGHT C-46 COMMANDO (U.S.A.)

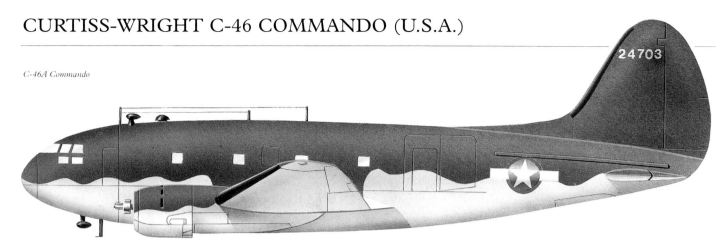

*C-46A Commando*

The aircraft that entered widespread production as the C-46 Commando troop and freight transport was conceived as a civil type to pick up where the Douglas DC-3 left off by offering such advantages as longer range, higher cruising speed, cabin pressurization, and a larger payload in the form of 36 passengers carried in a smooth-nosed fuselage of the double-lobe type. The twin-finned CW-20T prototype flew in March 1940 with 1268-kW (1,700-hp) Wright R-2600

radials, but soon afterwards was converted into the CW-20A with a revised tail unit featuring a single vertical surface and flat rather than dihedralled tailplane halves.

Such were the needs of the growing U.S. military establishment, however, that subsequent development was geared to the requirements of the U.S. Army Air Corps (later U.S. Army Air Forces), which evaluated the CW-20A as the C-55 and then ordered the type as the militarized CW-20B. This

version became the C-46 with 1491-kW (2,000-hp) Pratt & Whitney R-2800-51 radials and accommodation for 45 troops. Some 25 of the original C-46 troop transports entered service from July 1942 as the USAAF's largest and heaviest twin-engined aircraft. The series was used almost exclusively in the Pacific theatre during World War II.

There were several variants after the C-46, including 1,493 C-46As as the first definitive model with R-2800-51 engines and a strengthened fuselage floor that could take up to 50 troops or freight loaded through large

port-side cargo doors. Later variants such as the 1,410 C-46D troop and 234 C-46F utility transports were comparable to the C-46A apart from minor modifications and adaptations. The type was also used by the United States Navy with the designation R5C, and after the war many ex-military machines were released on to the civil market where some remain to the present.

*A Curtiss-Wright C-46 Commando*

**CURTISS-WRIGHT C-46A COMMANDO**
**Role:** Long-range transport
**Crew/Accommodation:** Four, plus up to 50 troops
**Power Plant:** Two, 2,000 hp Pratt & Whitney R-2800-51 Double Wasp air-cooled radials
**Dimensions:** Span 32.91 m (108 ft); length 23.26 m (76.33 ft); wing area 126.34 m² (1,360 sq ft)
**Weights:** Empty 13,608 kg (30,000 lb); MTOW 25,401 kg (56,000 lb)
**Performance:** Cruise speed 278 km/h (173 mph) at 4,572 m (15,000 ft); operational ceiling 7,468 m (24,500 ft); range 1,931 km (1,200 miles) with full payload
**Load:** Up to 6,804 kg (15,000 lb)

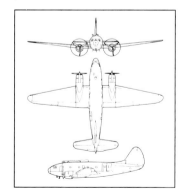

*Curtiss-Wright C-46A Commando*

# FAIRCHILD C-82 AND C-119 Family (U.S.A.)

*C-119C*

In 1941, Fairchild began work on its F-78 design to meet a U.S. Army Air Forces' requirement for a military freighter. The XC-82 prototype first flew in September 1944 as a high-wing monoplane with twin booms extending from the engine nacelles angles of the inverted gull wing to support the empennage so that clamshell rear doors could provide access to the central payload nacelle.

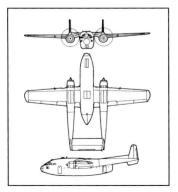

*Fairchild C-119G Flying Boxcar*

The payload could comprise 78 troops, or 42 paratroops, or 34 litters, or freight. The only production version was the C-82A Packet with 1566-kW (2,100-hp) Pratt & Whitney R-2800-34 radials, and delivery of 220 such aircraft was completed.

The basic concept was further developed into the C-119 Flying Boxcar with 1976-kW (2,650-hp) Pratt & Whitney R-4360-4 radial engines and the cockpit relocated into the nose of the nacelle. The XC-82B prototype of 1947 led to production of the C-119B with 2610-kW (3,500-hp) R-4360-20 engines, structural

### FAIRCHILD C-119C FLYING BOXCAR

**Role:** Military bulk freight/paratroop transport
**Crew/Accommodation:** Four, plus up to 42 paratroops
**Power Plant:** Two 3,500 hp Pratt & Whitney R-4360-20 Wasp Major air-cooled radials
**Dimensions:** Span 33.32 m (109.25 ft); length 26.37 m (86.5 ft); wing area 134.4 m² (1,447 sq ft)
**Weights:** Empty 18,053 kg (39,800 lb); MTOW 33,566 kg (74,000 lb)
**Performance:** Maximum speed 452 km/h (281 mph) at 5,486 (18,000 ft); operational ceiling 7,285 m (23,900 ft); range 805 km (500 miles) with maximum load
**Load:** Up to 8,346 kg (18,400 lb)

strengthening, and the fuselage widened by 0.36 m (1 ft 2 in) for the carriage of a heavier payload that could include 62 paratroops or freight. The 55 examples of this initial model were followed by 303 C-119Cs with R-4360-20WA engines, dorsal fin extensions, and no tailplane outboard of the vertical tail surfaces, 212 examples of the C-119F with ventral fins and other detail modifications, and 480 examples of the C-119G with different propellers and equipment

changes. The 26 AC-119G aircraft were gunship conversions of C-119Gs and were later upgraded to AC-119K standard, the 62 C-119Js were C-119F/G transports revised with a flight-openable door in the rear of the central pod, the five C-119Js were C-119Gs modified with two 1293-kg (2,850-lb) thrust General Electric J85-GE-17 booster turbojets in underwing nacelles, and the 22 C-119Ls were C-119Gs updated and fitted with new propellers.

*The C-119G was built in large numbers*

# ANTONOV An-2 and An-3 'COLT' (U.S.S.R.)

*An-2 'Colt'*

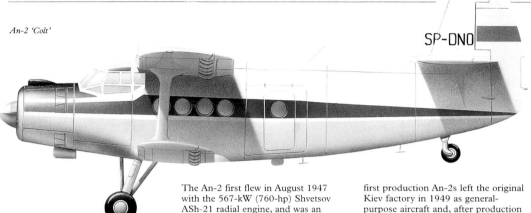

SP-DNO

The An-2 first flew in August 1947 with the 567-kW (760-hp) Shvetsov ASh-21 radial engine, and was an anachronism for being a large biplane with I-type interplane struts, fixed but exceptionally robust tailwheel landing gear, and a strut-braced tailplane. The first production An-2s left the original Kiev factory in 1949 as general-purpose aircraft and, after production of 3,167 up to 1962, Dolgoprudnyi became the Russian source of 429 An-2Ms during 1964–65. The type became known to NATO as 'Colt'.

An all-metal but unpressurized type with fabric covering on the tailplane and rear portions of the wings, the An-2 is exceptionally rugged, and has admirable field performance thanks to its combination of automatic leading-edge slats, slotted trailing-edge flaps, drooping ailerons on the upper wings, and full-span slotted trailing-edge flaps on the lower wings. The type entered service with the 746-kW (1,000-hp)

ASz-62IR radial, and though designed primarily for agricultural use, it was and still is produced in a number of variants suited to a variety of other roles. Typically, these are for use as transport (12 passengers and two children or 1,240-kg/2,733-lb of freight), float-equipped transport, paradropping, ambulance work, fire-fighting, meteorological research, geophysical research, photogrametric survey and TV relay.

Well over 16,000 examples of the An-2 have been built, about 10,600 of them in Poland since 1960. This total also includes many hundreds of examples of the licensed Chinese model, the Shijiazhuang Y5, although the original Chinese source was Nanchang (727 built between 1957 and 1968). The An-3 was developed as a turboprop-powered version using a 701-kW (940-shp) Glushenkov TVD-10B, to offer 40 per cent more payload.

*The Antonov An-2 is a modern oddity*

**An-2TD 'COLT' by PZL-Mielec in Poland**
**Role:** Utility transport/agricultural spraying
**Crew/Accommodation:** Two, plus up to 12 passengers
**Power Plant:** One 967-hp WSK-Kalisz ASz-62IR air-cooled radial
**Dimensions:** Span 18.18 m (59.65 ft); length 12.74m (41.8 ft); wing area 71.5 m² (770 sq ft)
**Weights:** Empty 3,445 kg (7,959 lb); MTOW 5,500 kg (112,125 lb)
**Performance:** Cruise speed 190 km/h (118 mph) at 800m (2,625 ft); operational ceiling 4,160 m (13,650 ft); range 1,390 km (863 miles)
**Load:** Up to 1,500 kg (3,307 lb)

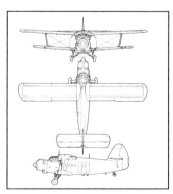

*Antonov An-2*

# LOCKHEED MARTIN C-130 HERCULES (U.S.A.)

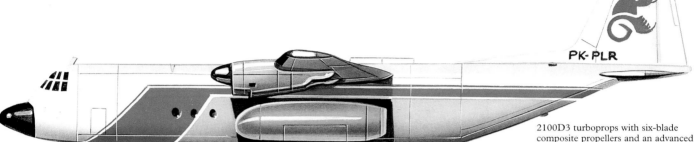

*L-100-30 Hercules*

The Hercules is the airlifter against which all other turboprop tactical transports are measured. It was the type that pioneered the modern airlifter layout with a high-set wing, a capacious fuselage with a rectangular-section hold terminating at its rear in an integral ramp/door that allows the straight-in loading/unloading of bulky items under the upswept tail, and multi-wheel landing gear with its main units accommodated in external fairings. No demands are made on hold area and volume, leaving the hold floor and opened ramp at truckbed height to help loading and unloading.

The type was designed in response to a 1951 requirement for STOL transport, and first flew in YC-130 prototype form during August 1954 with 2,796-kW (3,750-shp) Allison T56-A-1A turboprops driving three-blade propellers. Over 2,200 aircraft have been delivered and the type remains in both development and production, having been evolved in major variants, from its initial C-130A form to the C-130B with more fuel and a higher maximum weight; the C-130E with 3,020-kW (4,050-shp) T56-A7a turboprops driving four-blade propellers, greater internal fuel capacity and provision for external fuel tanks; the C-130H with airframe and system improvements as well as 3,362-kW (4,508-shp) T56-A-15 turboprops, and the C-130H-30 with a lengthened fuselage for the accommodation of bulkier payloads. The latest versions are the C-130J and lengthened C-130J-30, the latter first flown in April 1996 and first joining the RAF's No. 24 Squadron in 1998. The 'J' introduces 3,424 kW (4,591-shp) Allison AE 2100D3 turboprops with six-blade composite propellers and an advanced 2-pilot flight deck with multi-function displays and digital avionics, among other changes. There has also been a host of variants for tasks as diverse as Arctic operations, drone and spacecraft recovery, special forces insertion and extraction, airborne command post operations, and communication with submerged submarines. It has also been produced in L-100 civil form that has secured modest sales, with the new L-100J representing a commercial version of the C-130J-30.

**LOCKHEED C-130H HERCULES**
**Role:** Land-based, rough field capable tactical transport
**Crew/Accommodation:** Four crew with up to 92 troops or 74 stretchers
**Power Plant:** Four 4,508 shp Allison T56-A-15LFE turboprops
**Dimensions:** Span 40.4 m (132.6 ft); length 29.8 m (97.75 ft); wing area 162.1 m² (1,745 sq ft)
**Weights:** Empty 34,702 kg (76,505 lb); MTOW 79,380 kg (175,505 lb)
**Performance:** Maximum cruise speed 621 km/h (335 knots), at 3,658 m (12,000 ft); operational ceiling 10,060 m (33,000 ft); range 3,600 km (2,240 miles) with 18,143 kg (40,000 lb payload
**Load:** 19,340 kg (42,637 lb)

*The special mission EC-130H 'Compass Call'*

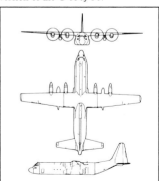

*Lockheed C-130H-30 Hercules*

# BOEING KC-135 STRATOTANKER (U.S.A.)

*KC-135A Stratotanker*

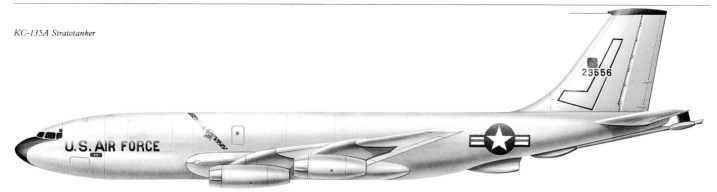

One of the provisions of Boeing's Model 367-80 prototype was for the company's patented 'flying boom' inflight refuelling system, and after this had been proved in trials, the U.S. Air Force announced in August 1954 that it was to procure the KC-135A inflight refuelling tanker based on the 'Dash 80'. The first of these flew in August 1956. Such was the priority allocated to this essential support for the United States' strategic bombers

that production built up very rapidly, and eventually 732 KC-135 Stratotankers were produced with 6,237-kg (13,750-lb) thrust Pratt & Whitney J57-P-59W turbojets; later aircraft were built with the taller vertical tail surfaces that were retrofitted to the earlier machines. In addition, 48 Stratolifter long-range transports were completed as 18 turbojet-powered C-135A and 30 C-135B turbofan-powered transports; but as the role was better performed by the Lockheed C-130 Hercules and C-141 StarLifter, the aircraft were later converted into special-purpose machines to complement a number of

KC-135As also adapted as EC-135 command post and communication relay platforms, or as RC-135 photographic/electronic reconnaissance platforms.

The type remains so important that most are being upgraded for continued service. A total of 163 KC-135As operated by the Air Force Reserve and Air National Guard are being improved to KC-135E standard with reskinned wing undersurfaces, new brakes and anti-skid units, and 8,165-kg (18,000-lb) thrust Pratt & Whitney

JT3D turbofans (complete with their pylons and nacelles and redesignated TF33-PW-102s) plus the tail units from surplus civil Model 707 transports. A similar but more extensive upgrade is being undertaken to improve USAF KC-135As to KC-135R standard with better systems, a larger tailplane, greater fuel capacity, and 10,000-kg (22,050-lb) thrust CFM International F108-CF-100 turbofans. The KC-135T is similar to the 'R' but could refuel the SR-71 (when in service).

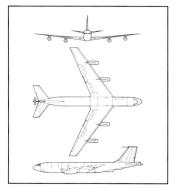

*Boeing KC-135A Stratotanker*

**BOEING KC-135A STRATOTANKER**
**Role:** Military tanker-transport
**Crew/Accommodation:** Four, including fuel boom operator
**Power Plant:** Four 6,237 kgp (13,750 lb s.t.) Pratt & Whitney J57P-59W turbojets
**Dimensions:** Span 39.88 m (130.83 ft); length 41.53 m (136.25 ft); wing area 226.03 m² (2,433 sq ft)
**Weights:** Empty 44,664 kg (98,466 lb); MTOW 134,718 kg (297,000 lb)
**Performance:** Cruise speed 888 km/h (552 mph) at 9,144 m (30,000 ft); operational ceiling 15,240 m (50,000 ft); range 1,850 m (1,150 miles) with maximum payload
**Load:** Up to 54,432 kg (120,000 lb)

*A Boeing KC-135A Stratotanker*

# LOCKHEED MARTIN C-5 GALAXY (U.S.A.)

*C-5A Galaxy*

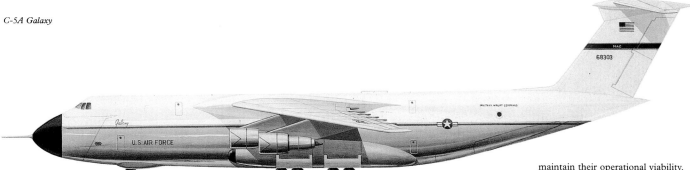

The Galaxy was produced to meet a U.S. Air Force requirement – ultimately shown to be considerably over-ambitious in its payload/range requirements – of the early 1960s for a long-range strategic airlifter to complement the Lockheed C-141 StarLifter logistic freighter. As such, it was to be capable of operating into and out of tactical airstrips close to the front line, through use of its 28-wheel landing gear that keeps ground pressure to the low figure that makes it possible for the Galaxy to use even

unpaved strips. The C-5A first flew in June 1968, and the type has many similarities to the C-141, though it is very much larger and possesses a lower deck 36.91 m (121 ft 1 in) long and 5.79 m (19 ft 0 in) wide. This hold can accommodate up to 120,204-kg (256,000-lb) of freight, and is accessed not only by the standard type of power-operated rear ramp/door arrangement but also by a visor-type nose that hinges upward and so makes possible straight-through loading and unloading for minimum turn-round time.

Production comprised 81 aircraft with 18,597-kg (41,000-lb) thrust General Electric TF39-GE-1 turbofans, and the first operational aircraft were delivered in December 1969 as the first equipment for an eventual four squadrons. Service use revealed that the wing structure had been made too light in an effort to improve payload/range performance, so the 77 surviving aircraft were rewinged and fitted with 19,504-kg (43,000-lb) thrust TF39-GE-1C engines to

maintain their operational viability. This process also allowed an increase in maximum take-off weight from 348,809-kg (768,980-lb) to 379,633-kg (837,000-lb), allowing the carriage of a maximum 124,740-kg (275,000-lb) payload. Another 50 aircraft were later built to this standard as C-5Bs with improved systems. The first C-5B flew in September 1985 and deliveries took place between January 1986 and February 1989. Two C-5As were also modified for outsized space cargo operations as C-5Cs.

**LOCKHEED MARTIN C-5 GALAXY**
**Role:** Military long-range, heavy cargo transport
**Crew/Accommodation:** Five with provision for relief crew and up to 75 troops on upper decks as well as 340 troops on main deck in place of cargo
**Power Plant:** Four 18,643 kgp (41,100 lb s.t.) General Electric TF-39-GE-1C turbofans
**Dimensions:** Span 67.89 m (222.75 ft); length 75.54 m (247.83 ft); wing area 576 m² (6,200 sq ft)
**Weights:** Empty 169,643 kg (374,000 lb); MTOW 348,812 kg (769,000 lb)
**Performance:** Maximum speed 919 km/h (571 mph) at 7,620 m (25,000 ft); operational ceiling 14,540 m (47,700 ft); range 5,526 km (3,434 miles) with maximum payload
**Load:** up to 120,200 kg (265,000 lb)

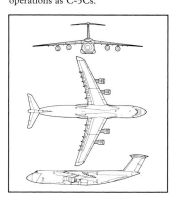

*Lockheed C-5B Galaxy*

*Lockheed C-5B Galaxy*

# Research Aircraft

It is strange, but nonetheless true, that all aircraft produced during the so-called 'pioneering period' of aeroplane flight were research types. Arguably, the pioneers themselves who went on to establish production companies were among the best of the few, as designers were frequently also the test pilots and those who survived their own inventions had thereby demonstrated the ability to construct aeroplanes of sufficient strength and competence to keep themselves safe.

When considering research aircraft, it is important to keep firm demarcation between a research type and a prototype, as they are quite different. The most simple demarcation is, perhaps, to understand that the first is built solely to gain knowledge, while the latter is intended to be a direct forerunner of a production model.

Rocket motors have powered many important research aircraft that can be said to have originated with the German *Ente* powered sailplane which, in 1938, flew for approximately one minute on the power of two slow-burning rocket motors. Though aeroplane applications for rocket motors were extensively researched, the only operational production aircraft to properly benefit from this form of powerplant has been the German Messerschmitt Me 163 Komet interceptor that entered brief service in 1944–45, although rocket motors were fundamental in providing the necessary thrust for some of the most historically important aircraft every built, including the U.S. Bell X-1 that first flew supersonically in 1947. Also, around this time, rocket power and turbojet engines were sometimes brought together in an attempt to merge the benefits of the long-endurance turbojet and the high thrust rocket motor. The Douglas Skyrocket that first flew in 1948 was one such mixed application, built to investigate sweptback wings and was the first manned aircraft to exceed twice the speed of sound, while another was the French Sud-Ouest SO 9000 Trident of 1953 appearance that was expected to provide data for a mixed-power interceptor.

Early British and German turbojet engines had been flight tested on research airframes, and it was during World War II that Germany investigated so many advanced concepts that assisted the victorious Allies in the early post-war period to develop sweptback wings, tail-less aircraft, variable-geometry, ramjet aircraft, delta wings, vertical aeroplane flight, ballistic missiles and more besides. But, while Germany is particularly remembered for its wartime research, it should not be overlooked that during this conflict others too conducted important work for the future, with the U.S.A. making particular strides into the development of flying-wing aircraft which, half a century later, finally came to fruition with the B-2 bomber, while Britain eventually became the conqueror of practical vertical aeroplane flight, though a great many weird and wonderful aircraft from many countries had earlier tried and failed.

But, perhaps one aircraft above all others encompasses the ideals of research. The rocket-powered North American X-15 had been ordered in 1955 for manned flight at up to seven times the speed of sound, to investigate heating, control and stability at hypersonic speed and the problems associated with re-entry into the earth's atmosphere, occasionally taking its pilot so high that he became an astronaut. Though, at that time, the first supersonic fighters were only just appearing, it was not an impossible dream for, in 1961, the X-15 exceeded Mach 6 and some years later almost reached its Mach 7 goal.

*Picture: Northrop N-1M research demonstrator in 1940, intended to provide data for a large flying-wing transport. It was then the most successful flying-wing aircraft ever tested and eventually accumulated over 200 flights*

# WRIGHT FLYER (U.S.A.)

*Flyer I*

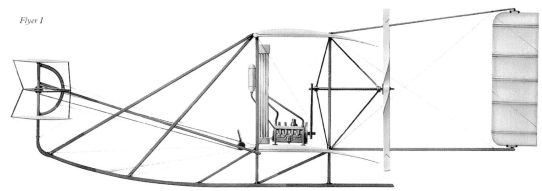

With the Flyer (or Flyer I), Orville Wright made the world's first powered, sustained and controlled flights in a heavier-than-air craft in 1903 at Kill Devil Hills, Kitty Hawk, North Carolina. The machine was a canard biplane powered by a 9-kW (12-hp) Wright engine driving two pusher propellers that turned in opposite directions as the drive chain to one was crossed, and take-off was effected with the aid of a two-wheel trolley that carried the Flyer on a 18.3-m (60-ft) wooden rail.

On that historic day, 17 December 1903, the Flyer achieved four flights: the first covered 36.6 m (120 ft) in 12 seconds, and the last achieved 260 m (852 ft) in 59 seconds. The improved Flyer II of 1904 was of the same basic configuration and dimensions as its predecessor, but its wings had revised camber and the engine was an 11-kW (15-hp) type. Take-off was aided by the use of a trolley that was boosted by a weight that was dropped from a derrick to pull the tow rope connected to the trolley.

The Flyer II took off about 100 times and achieved some 80 flights as the brothers perfected the task of piloting this inherently unstable aircraft. The flights totalled about 45 minutes in the air, and the longest covered about 4.43 km (2.75 miles) in 5 minutes 4 seconds.

The machine was broken up in 1905, the year in which the brothers produced the world's first really practical aircraft as the Flyer III, with improved controls but with the engine and twin propellers of the Flyer II. This machine made more than 40 flights, and as they were now able to control the type with considerable skill, the emphasis was placed on endurance and range. Many long flights were achieved, the best of them covering some 38.6 km (24 miles) in 38 minutes 3 seconds.

*Wright Flyer III*

**WRIGHT FLYER I**
**Role:** Powered flight demonstrator
**Crew/Accommodation:** One
**Power Plant:** One 12 hp Wright Brothers' water-cooled inline
**Dimensions:** Span 12.29 m (40.33 ft); length 6.41 m (21.03 ft); wing area 47.38 m² (510 sq ft)
**Weights:** Empty 256.3 kg (565 lb); MTOW 340.2 kg (750 lb)
**Performance:** Cruise speed 48 km/h (30 mph) at sea level; operational ceiling 9.14 m (30 ft); range 259.7 m (852 ft)
**Load:** None
Note: the range quoted here was the longest of four flights made by the Wright Brothers on 17 December, 1903

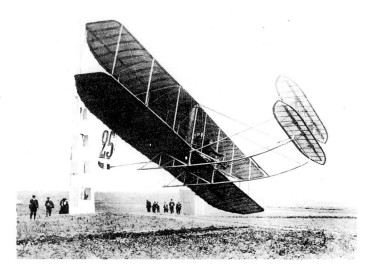

*Wilbur Wright piloting the Wright Type A*

# BELL X-1 (U.S.A.)

*Bell X-1A*

The X-1 has a distinct place in aviation history as the first aircraft to break the 'sound barrier' and achieve supersonic speed in level flight. The origins of the type lay in the February 1945 decision of the U.S. Army Air Forces and National Advisory Committee for Aeronautics for the joint funding of an advanced research aircraft to provide data on kinetic heating at supersonic speeds. Bell had the choice of turbojet or liquid-propellant rocket power, and opted for the latter in a very purposeful design with an unstepped cockpit, mid-set wings that were unswept but very thin, unswept tail surfaces, and tricycle landing gear, the units of which all retracted into the circular fuselage. This girth of body provided the capacity for the rocket fuel and oxidizer.

The type was designed for air launch from a converted Boeing B-29 bomber, and the first of three aircraft was dropped for its first gliding flight in January 1946. The first powered flight followed in December of the same year, and on 14 October 1947 Captain Charles 'Chuck' Yeager achieved history's first supersonic flight with a speed of Mach 1.015 at 12,800 m (42,000 ft) altitude. The third X-1 was lost in an accident on the ground, but in total the X-1s flew 156 times. Three more airframes were ordered for the type's immensely important research programme, and these were delivered as one X-1A with a stepped cockpit and a fuselage lengthened by 1.40 m (4 ft 7 in) for the greater fuel capacity that made possible a maximum speed of Mach 2.435 in December 1953 and an altitude of more than 27,430 m (90,000 ft) in June 1954, one X-1B, which was used for thermal research, and one X-1D variant of the X-1B that was lost when it was jettisoned after a pre-launch explosion. The X-1E was the second X-1 that had been modified to have wings of 4% thickness/chord ratio, instead of 10%, a distinctive stepped knife-edge canopy and ballistic control rockets; it was flown 26 times.

*The first Bell X-1 in flight*

**BELL X-1**
**Role:** Trans-sonic research
**Crew/Accommodation:** One
**Power Plant:** One 2,721 kgp (6,000 ll s.t.) Reaction Motors E6000-C4 (Thiokol XLR-11) four barrel liquid fuel rocket
**Dimensions:** Span 8.54 m (28,00 ft); length 9.45 m (31.00 ft); wing area 12.08 m² (130.00 sq ft)
**Weights:** Empty 3,674 kg (8,100 lb); MTOW 6,078 kg (13,400 lb)
**Performance:** Maximum speed 1,556 km/h (967 mph) Mach 1.46 at 21.379 m (70,140 ft); operational ceiling 24,384 m (80,000 ft); endurance 2.5 minutes at full power
**Load:** Nil, other than specific-to-mission test equipment

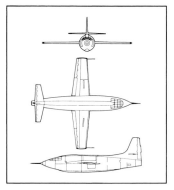

*Bell X-1*

# DOUGLAS D-558-1 SKYSTREAK and D-558-2 SKYROCKET (U.S.A.)

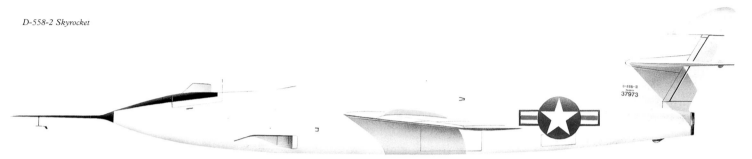

*D-558-2 Skyrocket*

In 1945, the U.S. Navy's Bureau of Aeronautics and the National Advisory Committee for Aeronautics issued a joint requirement for a research aircraft able to generate the type of high-subsonic, air-load measurements data that was unobtainable in current wind tunnels. The resulting D-558-1 Skystreak was kept as simple as possible, and was based on a circular-section fuselage and straight flying surfaces. The type was powered by one

1,814-kg (4,000-lb) thrust Allison J35-A-23 turbojet, and the first of three aircraft flew in May 1947; later a 2,268-kg (5,000-lb) thrust J35-A-11 engine was fitted. The type secured two world speed records, and also a mass of invaluable data using a pressure recording system with attachments to 400 points on the airframe and strain gauges attached to key positions on the wings and tail unit.

Soon after the Skystreak programme began, the official requirement was altered to also encompass investigation of sweptback

wings. To provide higher thrust, a rocket booster was needed and the Skystreak concept was thus modified into a new type with swept flying surfaces. This materialized as the D-588-2 Skyrocket, which had not only the mixed powerplant and swept flying surfaces, but also a larger-diameter fuselage incorporating a pointed nose as the D-558-1's nose inlet was replaced by two lateral inlets. Three aircraft were again ordered, and the first of these flew in February 1948.

The original flush canopy offered the pilot wholly inadequate fields of vision, and was soon replaced by a more conventional raised enclosure. The Skyrocket flight programme proved successful in the extreme before it finished in December 1956, and included such milestones as an altitude of 25, 370 m (83,235 ft) in August 1953 and the first 'breaking' of the Mach 2 barrier in November 1953 with a speed of Mach 2.005.

**DOUGLAS D-558-2 SKYROCKET**
**Role:** Swept wing research
**Crew/Accommodation:** One
**Power Plant:** One 2,721 kgp (6,000 lb s.t.) Reaction Motors XLR-8 rocket plus one 1,360 kgp (3,000 lb s.t.) Westinghouse J34-WE-22 Turbojet
**Dimensions:** Span 7.62 m (25.00 ft); length 13.79 m (45.25 ft); wing area 16.26 m² (175,00 sq ft)
**Weights:** MTOW 7,161 kg (15,787 lb) from airborne launch
**Performance:** Maximum speed 2,078 km/h (1,291 mph) Mach 2.005 at 18,900 m (62,000 ft); operational ceiling 25,370 m (83,235 ft)
**Load:** Nil, other than specific mission test equipment

*Douglas D-558-2 Skyrocket*

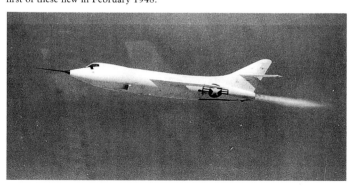

*Douglas D-558-2 Skyrocket*

# FAIREY DELTA 2 (United Kingdom)

*Fairey Delta 2*

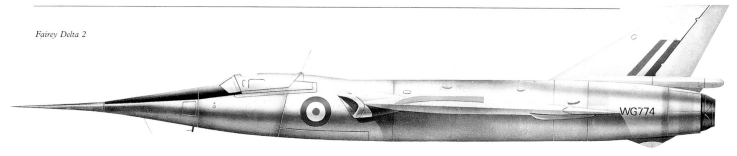

After a number of experiments in 1947 with vertically launched models, which confirmed the basic feasibility of the delta-winged planform, Fairey was asked to consider the possibility of supersonic delta-winged models. The company anticipated that this would eventually lead to a piloted supersonic research aircraft, and started initial work in advance of any officially promulgated requirement. When a requirement was eventually announced for a research aircraft able to investigate flight and control characteristics at transonic and supersonic speeds, English Electric and Fairey each secured a contract for two prototypes. The English Electric type was the P.1 that led finally to the swept-wing Lightning fighter and the Fairey design was the droop-snoot-nosed Fairey Delta 2. This was designed only as a supersonic research aircraft, and was based on a pure delta wing and a slender fuselage sized to the Rolls-Royce Avon turbojet.

Greater priority was given to the company's Gannet carrierborne anti-submarine warplane, so construction of the first F.D.2 began only in late 1952.

The machine first flew in October 1954, and after a delay occasioned by the need to repair damage suffered in a forced landing after engine failure, the type went supersonic for the first time in October 1955. The world absolute speed record was then held by the North American F-100A Super Sabre at 1,323 km/h (822 mph), and the capabilities of the F.D.2. were revealed

when it raised the speed record to 1,822 km/h (1,132 mph) in March 1956, the first-ever over-1,000-mph world speed record. The second F.D.2 joined the programme in February 1956, and the two aircraft undertook a mass of varied and most valuable research work. The first F.D.2 was later revised as the BAC 221 with an ogival wing for test before its use on the Concorde supersonic airliner.

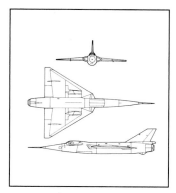

*The first of two Fairey Delta 2 research aircraft*

**FAIREY DELTA 2**
**Role:** Supersonic research
**Crew/Accommodation:** One
**Power Plant:** One 4,309 kgp (9,500 lb s.t.) Rolls-Royce Avon RA14R turbojet with reheat, the use of which was limited, but gave 5,386 kgp (11,875 lb s.t.) at 11,580 m (38,000 ft)
**Dimensions:** Span 8.18 m (26.83 ft); length 15.74 m (51.62 ft); wing area 38.4 m² (360 sq ft)
**Weights:** Empty 5,000 kg (11,000 lb); MTOW 6,298 kg (13,884 lb)
**Performance:** Maximum speed 1,846 km/h 1,147 mph; operational ceiling 14,021 m (46,000 ft); range 1,335 km (830 miles) without reheat
**Load:** Confined to specialized test equipment

*Fairey Delta 2*

283

# NORTH AMERICAN X-15 (U.S.A.)

*North American X-15*

The X-15 was designed to meet a U.S. Air Force and U.S. Navy requirement for an aircraft able to reach an altitude of 80,500 m (264,000 ft) and a speed of Mach 7 after air-launch from a modified Boeing B-52 bomber. Though funded by the two services, the programme was overseen at the technical level by NASA's predecessor, the National Advisory Committee on Aeronautics. In December 1954 a request for proposals was issued to 12 airframe manufacturers, and in February 1955 four companies were invited to tender

for the planned machine's rocket propulsion system. Contracts eventually went to North American for the NA-240 aircraft and Reaction Motors for the XLR99 rocket engine.

The X-15 was made mainly of titanium and stainless steel, with an armoured skin of Inconel X nickel alloy steel to permit extreme temperatures of -300°F to +1,200°F, and comprised a long cylindrical fuselage with lateral fairings to accommodate control systems and fuel tanks, small thin wings of 5% section, an all-moving tailplane, and wedge-shaped dorsal and ventral fins; control at very high altitudes was by twelve rocket nozzles in the wingtips and nose. The lower fin was jettisoned before landing to provide ground

clearance for the retractable twin skids that, with a nosewheel unit, formed the landing gear. The first of three X-15As was powered by two 3,629-kg (8,000-lb) thrust LR11-RM-5 rockets, as the XLR99 was not ready, and made its initial unpowered free flight in June 1959, followed by the first powered flight in September 1959. The second X-15A, also initially with the LR11s, made its first powered flight in November 1960. The X-15As made 199 flights, including those of the second machine that made very important

contributions after being rebuilt as the X-15A-2 with Emersion Electric T-500 ablative material as a heat-resistant surface treatment, a fuselage lengthened by 0.74 m (2 ft 5 in) and external auxiliary fuel tanks. In this form the machine reached 107,960 m (354,200 ft) and 7,297 km/h (4,534 mph) or Mach 6.72.

*North American X-15*

**NORTH AMERICAN X-15A-2**
**Role:** Hypersonic research
**Crew/Accommodation:** One
**Power Plant:** One 25,855 kgp (57,000 lb s.t.) Thiokol XLR99-RM-2 rocket motor
**Dimensions:** Span 6.81 m (22.33 ft); length 15.98 m (52.42 ft ); wing area 18.58 m² (200 sq ft)
**Weights:** Empty 6,804 kg (15,000 lb); MTOW 23,095 kg (50.914 lb) air-launched
**Performance:** Maximum speed 7,297 km/h (3,937 knots) Mach 6.72 at 31,120 m (102,100 ft); operational ceiling 107,960 m (354,200 ft); radius 443 km (275 miles)
**Load:** Nil, other than dedicated mission test equipment

*The X-15A-2 had great endurance and high speed*

# Trainers/Tourers/Executive Aircraft

An earlier section of this book describes various military trainers, and also details how the de Havilland Moth biplane brought about huge interest in civil flying clubs and private flying after its appearance in 1925. Understanding that inexpensive and economical-to-operate aeroplanes were needed to kick-start club flying had, however, already been recognized and in 1923 the first lightplane competition in Britain had been organized at Lympne in Kent by the Royal Aero Club, with the intention of encouraging construction of extremely light single-seaters. One prize, partly sponsored by the *Daily Mail* newspaper, was for the longest flight on one gallon of petrol by an aeroplane with an engine of 750 cc or less, which in the event, was shared by two aircraft managing 141 km (87.5 miles).

The success of the competition was not really matched by the useful worth of the entries, and in 1924 the Royal Aero Club organized a similar competition for two-seaters, with the Air Ministry offering a £3,000 prize. Here, the winning entry was the Beardmore Wee Bee with a 32-hp engine, but this too was not a particularly practical design. Then, in 1925, came the Moth, as a scaled down D.H.51 with a 120-hp engine cut in half to produce 60 hp!

Public interest in lightplanes was greatly heightened by highly-publicized long-distance flights, such as that from London to Karachi made in stages by Stack and Leete in a Moth between November 1926 and January 1927, and from London to Cape Town (South Africa) by Lt. R. Bentley in another Moth in 1927. England to Australia was accomplished in an Avro Avian lightplane in 1928, while a similar aircraft was flown to England from South Africa that same year by Lady Heath, marking the first time the journey had been flown by a woman. In 1930, Amy Johnson became world-famous for flying a Gipsy Moth solo from England to Australia, and many other lightplane flights brought about a new awareness in flying. Of course, a certain gentleman named Charles Lindbergh had played his part in May 1927, when he had flown alone from New York to Paris across the North Atlantic in a single-engined Ryan monoplane named *Spirit of St. Louis*, taking over 33 hours to cover 5,810 km (3,610 miles).

For most private pilots, of course, long distance flying meant touring in lightplanes. A great industry grew to satisfy this requirement, many of the aircraft being equally suited to training, while for business companies that needed larger transports to communicate between facilities, highly appointed executive aircraft were eventually evolved and, with the advent of turbine power, purpose-designed executive jets.

*Picture: First flown in December 1945, the Raytheon/Beech Bonanza lightplane and trainer celebrated its 50th anniversary at the EAA Convention in 1995*

# BELLANCA PACEMAKER (U.S.A.)

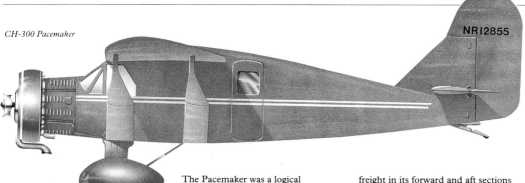

*CH-300 Pacemaker*

NR12855

The Pacemaker was a logical development of the CH-300 utility transport, and the first model was the PM-300 Pacemaker Freighter. This was certificated in September 1929, and the cabin was laid out for four passengers and 386 kg (850 lb) of freight in its forward and aft sections respectively; three of the seats could be removed to allow a 714-kg (1,575-lb) freight load. For its time the Pacemaker was a remarkable transport, for on the power of a single 224-kW (300-hp) Wright J-6 it could carry a payload greater than its own empty weight. The type could be used on wheels, skis or floats, and though not many Pacemaker Freighters were built, some CH-300s were in fact modified to this standard. In May 1931 a Pacemaker Freighter with a 168-kW (225-hp) Packard diesel engine set a world unrefuelled endurance record of 84 hours 33 minutes.

The basic Pacemaker design was refined during its six-year production life. The Model E Senior Pacemaker of 1932 had a 246-kW (330-hp) Wright engine that was soon replaced by the 313-kW (425-hp) Wright R-975-E2. In concert with a larger wing and spatted landing gear, this offered improved performance with a payload of six passengers; this model also had chair-pack parachutes that formed part of the upholstery until needed. Another variant was the Senior Pacemaker Series 8, which was a pure freighter that could carry a 907-kg (2,000-lb) payload over a range of 805 km (500 miles) in wheeled configuration, or a 811-kg (1,787-lb) payload over the same range in floatplane configuration. As an alternative to the R-975, Bellanca offered the Pacemaker with the Pratt & Whitney Wasp Junior radial of the same power. While the only known U.S. military Pacemaker was a single JE-1 operated by the U.S. Navy as a nine-seat communications type, the Royal Canadian Air Force used 13 CH-300 in all, the type being operated by the RCAF between 1929 and 1940.

**BELLANCA CH-300 PACEMAKER**
**Role:** Utility transport
**Crew/Accommodation:** One, plus up to five passengers
**Power Plant:** One 300 hp Wright J-6E Whirlwind air-cooled radial
**Dimensions:** 14.12 m (46.33 ft); length 8.46 m (27.75 ft); wing area 25.36 m² (273 sq ft)
**Weights:** Empty 1,201 kg (2,647 lb); MTOW 1,952 kg (4,300 lb)
**Performance:** Maximum speed 230 km/h (143 mph) at sea level; operational ceiling 5,181 m (17,000 ft); radius 2,189 km (1,360 miles with full fuel)
**Load:** Up to 408 kg (900 kg)

*A Bellanca Senior Skyrocket*

*Bellanca Skyrocket*

# PIPER J-3 CUB and L-4 GRASSHOPPER (U.S.A.)

*L-4 Grasshopper*

In 1929, C. Gilbert·Taylor and his brother created the Taylor Brothers Aircraft Corporation, reorganized as the Taylor Aircraft Company in 1931.

*A Piper L-4 Grasshopper*

When the company ran into financial problems, the rights to the Taylor Cub were bought by W.T. Piper Snr, the company's secretary and treasurer. In 1937, Piper bought out the Taylor brothers and renamed the company the Piper Aircraft Corporation in order to continue production of the Cub, which had first flown in September 1930.

The Cub was a classic braced high-wing monoplane of mixed construction with fabric covering, and could be powered by any of several types of flat-four piston engine. The initial J-3 Cub was powered by the 30-kW (40-hp) Continental A40-4, but production soon switched to the J-3C-50 with the 37-kW (50-hp) A50-4, the suffix to the aircraft's basic designation

indicating the make of engine and its horsepower. Further development produced the Continental-engined J-3C-65 and then variants with Franklin and Lycoming engines as the J-3F-50 and F-65 and the J-3L-50 and L-65, while a radial-engined model was the J-3P-50 with the Lenape Papoose. Some 14,125 Cubs were built in these series for the civil market, and another 5,703 military liaison and observation aircraft expanded this number. The U.S. Army evaluated several types of civil lightplane in these roles during 1941, and the four J-3Cs evaluated as YO-59s with the 48-kW (65-hp) Continental O-170-3 paved the way for 140 O-59s and 948 O-59As that were later redesignated L-4 and L-4A in a sequence that ran to L-4J and included training gliders; the U.S. Marine Corps also adopted the type as the NE. Such has been the abiding popularity of the type that it was reinstated in production during 1988 with a number of more refined features that, however, fail to obscure the essentially simple nature of the basic aircraft.

**PIPER L-4 GRASSHOPPER**
**Role:** Observation/communications
**Crew/Accommodation:** Two
**Power Plant:** One 65 hp Continental 0-170-3 air-cooled flat-opposed
**Dimensions:** Span 10.47 m (32.25 ft); length 6.71 m (22 ft); wing area 16.63 m² (179 sq ft)
**Weights:** Empty 331 kg (730 lb); MTOW 553 kg (1,220 lb)
**Performance:** Maximum speed 137 km/h (85 mph) at sea level; operational ceiling 2,835 m (9,300 ft); range 306 km (190 miles)
**Load:** Up to 86 kg (190 lb)

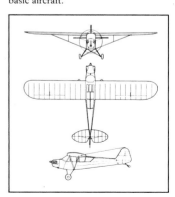

*Piper L-4A Grasshopper*

# FAIRCHILD 24 (U.S.A.)

*Fairchild 24R*

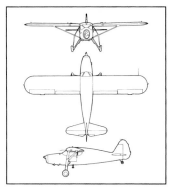

*Fairchild 24*

In 1931, Sherman Fairchild bought the American Aviation Corporation's Kreider-Reisner subsidiary, and with this new Fairchild Aircraft Corporation came the rights to a two-seat sport and training aircraft of braced parasol-wing layout. This was marketed as the Fairchild 22 Model

C7 that survived slow initial sales to become a commercially successful and popular type. The success of the Model C7A variant persuaded Fairchild to produce a version with enclosed accommodation for two seated side-by-side in a higher fuselage that turned the parasol-wing Model C7A into the high-wing Fairchild 24 Model C8. The type was certificated in April 1932 with the 71-kW (95-hp) A.C.E. Cirrus Hi-Ace inline engine and though only 10 of this variant were produced, the type paved the

way for extensive development and production.

The main developments (with approximate production total) were the Model C8A (25) with the 93-kW (125-hp) Warner Scarab radial, the Model C8C (130) with slightly greater size and the 108-kW (145-hp) Warner

**FAIRCHILD MODEL 24W-9**
**Role:** Touring
**Crew/Accommodation:** One, plus up to three passengers
**Power Plant:** One 165 hp Warner Super Scarab 175 air-cooled radial
**Dimensions:** Span 11.07 m (36.33 ft); length 8.79 m (25.85 ft); wing area 17.96 m² (193.30 sq ft)
**Weights:** Empty 732 kg (1,613 lb); MTOW 1,162 kg (2,562 lb)
**Performance:** Maximum speed 212 km/h (132 mph) at sea level ; operational ceiling 4,267 m (14,000 ft); range 1,028 km (639 miles)
**Load:** Up to 245 kg (540 lb)

Super Scarab, the Model C8D (14) with three seats and the 108-kW Ranger 6-390B inline, the Model C8E (50) version of the Model C8C with improved equipment, and the Model C8F (40) version of the Model C8D with improved equipment. The designation then changed to Model 24, and this series ran to some 200 aircraft in four Model 24-G to Model 24-K three/four-seat variants. The final civil models were the two Model 24R (60) and four Model 24W (165) variants with Ranger inline and Warner radial engines. Another 981 inline- and radial-engined aircraft were built to military order as the U.S. Army Air Forces' UC-61 Forwarder, including large numbers supplied to the Royal Air Force with the name Argus. Additional aircraft were impressed for the American forces, the U.S. Navy and U.S. Coast Guard models being the GK and J2K.

*The Fairchild Model 24*

# BÜCKER Bü 131 JUNGMANN and Bü 133 JUNGMEISTER (Germany)

*Bü 133 Jungmeister*

Bü 131B spanned 7.40 m (24 ft 3.25 in) and had a maximum take-off weight of 680 kg (1,499 lb).

To meet production for its Bü 131, Bücker opened a second factory and here the company's design team evolved for the advanced training role the basically similar Jungmeister (Young Champion). This had smaller dimensions than the Bü 131, had single-seat accommodation, and was stressed for full aerobatic capability. The first example flew with the 101-kW (135-hp) HM 6 inline engine and revealed excellent performance. The type was ordered in large numbers by the German air force, and the major variants were the Bü 133A with the 101-kW (135-hp) HM 6 inline, the Bü 133B with the 119-kW (160-hp) HM 506 inline and the Bü 133C main production model with the 119-kW Siemens Sh 14 radial.

The Jungmann (Young Man, or Youth) was the first product of Bücker Flugzeugbau, and first flew in April 1934 as a compact trainer of the classic single-bay biplane formula with tandem open cockpits in a fabric-covered airframe comprising wooden wings and a steel-tube fuselage and empennage. The type entered production as the Bü 131A with the same 60-kW (80-hp) Hirth HM 60R air-cooled inline engine that had powered the prototype, while the improved Bü 131B had the 78-kW (105-hp) HM 504A-2. The type was built in Japan as the Watanabe Ki-86 and K9W, of which more than 1,250 were produced, and was also widely exported by the parent factory. The

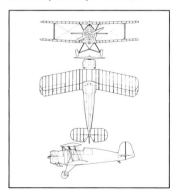

*Bücker Bü 133 Jungmeister*

**BÜCKER BÜ 131B JUNGMANN**
**Role:** Trainer
**Crew/Accommodation:** Two
**Power Plant:** One 105 hp Hirth HM 504A-2 air-cooled inline
**Dimensions:** Span 7.4 m (24.28 ft); length 6.62 m (21.72 ft); wing area 13.5 m² (145.3 sq ft)
**Weights:** Empty 390 kg (860 lb); MTOW 680 kg (1,500 lb)
**Performance:** Maximum speed 183 km/h (114 mph) at sea level; operational ceiling 3,000 m (9,843 ft); range 650 km (404 miles)
**Load:** None

*This is a Bücker Bü 131*

# BEECH 18 (U.S.A.)

*Beech C-45G*

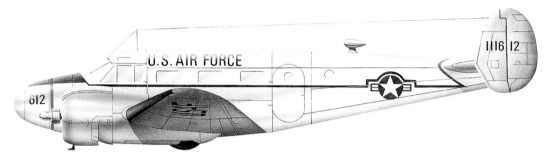

In 1935, Beech began the development of an advanced light transport of monoplane layout to supersede its Model 17 biplane transport, whose reverse-staggered wings had earned the soubriquet 'Staggerwing'. The Model 18A was an all-metal type with a semi-monocoque fuselage, cantilever wings, electrically retracted tailwheel landing gear, and endplate vertical tail surfaces. The first example of this celebrated aeroplane flew in January 1937 with two 239-kW (320-hp) Wright R-760-E2 radial engines, and the type then entered manufacture for 32 years.

The initial civil models were powered by a number of radial engine types, and reached an early peak as the Model 18D of 1939, which was powered by two 246-kW (330-hp) Jacobs L-6 engines that combined the Model 18A's economy of operation with higher performance. The American military acquired an interest in the type during 1940, and during World War II the type was produced to the extent of 4,000 or more aircraft in various roles. The staff transport in several variants had the American designations C-45 (army) and JRB (navy), and the British name Expediter. In 1941 Beech introduced the AT-7 Navigator and AT-11 Kansan (or naval SNB) navigation and bombing/gunnery trainers.

After the war improved civil models appeared. From 1953 the Super 18 appeared as the definitive civil model with drag-reducing features, cross-wind landing gear, and a separate flightdeck, and from 1963 retractable tricycle landing gear was an option. Substantial numbers were converted to turboprop power by several specialist companies, these variants including the Volpar Turbo 18 and Turboliner, the Dumod Liner, the PAC Turbo Tradewind, and the Hamilton Westwind.

*The Model 18 was a superlative light transport*

**BEECH D18S**
**Role:** Light passenger/executive transport
**Crew/Accommodation:** Two/one, plus up to seven passengers
**Power Plant:** Two 450 hp Pratt & Whitney R.985-AN14B Wasp Junior air-cooled radials
**Dimensions:** Span 14.50 m (47.58 ft); length 10.35 m (33.96 ft); wing area 32.4 m² (349 sq ft)
**Weights:** Empty 2,558 kg (5,635 lb); MTOW 3,980 kg (8,750 lb)
**Performance:** Cruise speed 338 km/h (211 mph) at 3,050 m (10,000 ft); operational ceiling 6,250 m (20,500 ft); range 1,200 km (750 miles)
**Load:** Up to 587 kg (1,295 lb)

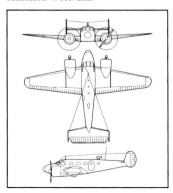

*Beech Model 18*

# RAYTHEON/BEECH BONANZA (U.S.A.)

*V35B Bonanza*

Another long-lived Beech design, the four/five-seat Bonanza first flew in December 1945 as the V-tailed Model 35 with the 138-kW (185-hp) Continental E-185-1 piston engine, though later aircraft have the 213-kW (285-hp) Continental I0-520 flat-six engine. The type was an immediate success, for, even before the first production Bonanza had been delivered, the company had orders for some 1,500 aircraft, many of them for pilots who had learned to fly with the ever-expanding military forces during World War II. Large-scale production of the Bonanza was undertaken in a number of forms with normally aspirated or turbocharged engines, the use of the latter being indicated by the suffix TC after the model number. From the beginning, the Model 35 had retractable tricycle landing gear, but from 1949 the original castoring nosewheel was replaced by a steerable unit to create the model A35.

In 1959 the company introduced the Beech 33 Debonair with a conventional tail and lower-powered engine for those worried about the 'gimmickry' of the V-tail. The lower-powered engine dictated that passenger accommodation was reduced from four to three, and in 1967 this variant was taken into the designation mainstream as the Model E33 Bonanza.

The third Bonanza type is the Model 36 Bonanza. This was intoduced in 1968 as a utility six-seater. This is based on the Model V35B with its fuselage lengthened by 0.25 m (10 in), and fitted with the tail unit of the Model 33 as well as the strengthened landing gear of the Model 55 Baron. The fuselage is accessed by double doors so that the type can double as a light freight transport. Many variants were in fact produced.

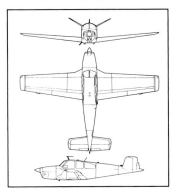

*Beech Bonanza V35*

**BEECH BONANZA**
**Role:** Tourer
**Crew/Accommodation:** One, plus up to three passengers
**Power Plant:** One 196 hp Continental E185-8 air-cooled flat-opposed
**Dimensions:** Span 10.01 m (32.83 ft); length 7.67 m (25.16 ft); wing area 16.49 m² (177.6 sq ft)
**Weights:** Empty 715 kg (1,575 lb); MTOW 1,203 kg (2,650 lb)
**Performance:** Cruise speed 272 km/h (170 mph) at 2,440 m (8,000 ft); operational ceiling 5,485 m (17,100 ft); range 1,207 km (750 miles)
**Load:** Up to 373 kg (822 lb)

*Beech Bonanza V35A*

# de HAVILLAND CANADA DHC-1 CHIPMUNK (Canada)

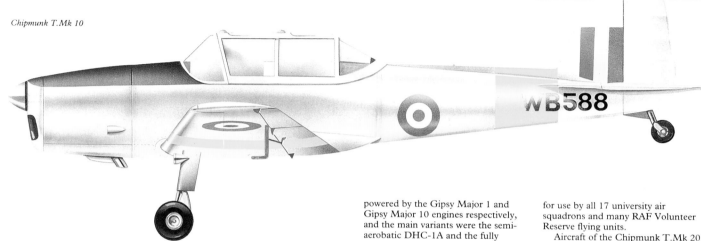

*Chipmunk T.Mk 10*

The DHC-1 Chipmunk was the first aircraft designed by de Havilland's Canadian subsidiary, and was evolved as a successor to the legendary D.H.82 Tiger Moth, of which a special version had been built in Canada. The type was therefore designed as a primary trainer, and despite its low performance and fixed tailwheel landing gear, the DHC-1 was a thoroughly modern type with enclosed tandem accommodation, stressed-skin construction of light alloy, a low-set wing with trailing-edge flaps, and attractive lines highlighted by the typically de Havilland tail unit. The first example flew in May 1946 with a 108-kW (145-hp) de Havilland Gipsy Major 1C inline engine. Production of the Chipmunk in Canada lasted to 1951 and accounted for 218 aircraft, most of which had a bubble canopy.

Aircraft suffixed -1 and -2 were powered by the Gipsy Major 1 and Gipsy Major 10 engines respectively, and the main variants were the semi-aerobatic DHC-1A and the fully aerobatic DHC-1B in a total of nine subvariants including the Royal Canadian Air Force's DHC-1A-1 and DHC-1B-2-S3 used as the Chipmunk T.Mk 1 and T.Mk 2 respectively, the latter for refresher training at civil clubs. In its fully aerobatic form, the type also found favour with the Royal Air Force, and this resulted in British manufacture of 1,014 Chipmunks, of which 735 Gipsy Major 8-powered examples went to the RAF as Chipmunk T.Mk 10 *ab initio* trainers for use by all 17 university air squadrons and many RAF Volunteer Reserve flying units.

Aircraft of the Chipmunk T.Mk 20 were produced for the military export market (217 Chipmunk T.Mk 20s with the Gipsy Major 10-2) and for the civil market (28 basically similar Chipmunk T.Mk 21s). Another 60 Chipmunks were built under licence in Portugal by OGMA.

**de HAVILLAND CANADA DHC-1 CHIPMUNK T.MK 10**
**Role:** Primary trainer
**Crew/Accommodation:** Two
**Power Plant:** One 145 hp de Havilland Major 8 air-cooled inline
**Dimensions:** Span 10.46 m (34.33 ft); length 7.82 m (25.66 ft); wing area 15.98 m² (172.00 sq ft)
**Weights:** Empty 643 kg (1,417 lb); MTOW 908 kg (2,000 lb)
**Performance:** Maximum speed 223 km/h (138 mph) at sea level; operational ceiling 4,876 m (16,000 ft); radius 483 km (300 miles)
**Load:** Nil

*de Havilland Chipmunk T.Mk 10*

*de Havilland Canada DHC-1 Chipmunk*

# CESSNA 170, 172, 175 and 182 Series (U.S.A.)

*Cessna 172 Skyhawk*

This series enjoys the distinction of being the most successful lightplane of all time. The Model 170 first flew in 1948 as the two-seat Model 120 with the 108-kW (145-hp) Continental C-145-2 engine and its fuselage re-engineered to four-seat configuration. Good sales were later boosted by the advent of the Model 170B with improved field performance as a result of the Fowler slotted trailing-edge flaps, a type pioneered in the Cessna range by the Model 305. In 1955, the company introduced the Model 172, which was basically the Model 170B with the original fixed tailwheel landing gear replaced by fixed tricycle landing gear.

In 1958, Cessna placed into production the Model 175, which was in essence the Model 172 with a number of refinements (including a free-blown windscreen and speed fairings), as well as the more powerful 131-kW (175-hp) GO-300-C geared engine driving a constant-speed propeller. This short-lived variant also appeared in upgraded Model 175A and de luxe Skylark forms.

A comparable de luxe version of the Model 172 was also produced as the Skyhawk, and this was later revised with a swept vertical tail of the type which market research had shown to be desirable as a means of keeping the model's appearance fully up to date. From 1980, a new and slimmer rear fuselage with rear windows was introduced on the Skylark II and Skyhawk II. The Model 182 of 1956 introduced more power in the form of the 172-kW (230-hp) Continental O-470-S engine, and was also produced in upgraded Skylane versions.

Further development of the Models 172 and 182 has produced a host of versions with improved furnishing, better instrumentation, retractable landing gear, and turbocharged engines. The Model 172 has additionally been produced in T-41 Mescalero trainer form.

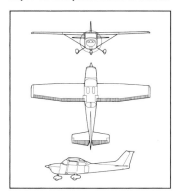

*Cessna Model 172*

**CESSNA 172 SKYHAWK (T-41A)**
**Role:** Light touring (and military basic trainer)
**Crew/Accommodation:** One, plus up to three passengers
**Power Plant:** One 160 hp Lycoming 0-320 air-cooled flat-opposed
**Dimensions:** Span 10.92 m (35.83 ft); length 8.20 m (26 ft); wing area 16.16 m² (174 sq ft)
**Weights:** Empty 636 kg (1,402 lb); MTOW 1,043 kg (2,300 lb)
**Performance:** Cruise speed 226 km/h (122 knots) at 2,438 m (8,000 ft); operational ceiling 4,328 m (14,200 ft); range 1,065 km (575 naut. miles) with full payload
**Load:** Up to 299 kg (660 lb)

*A Cessna Model 172*

# PIPER CHEROKEE (U.S.A.)

*Cherokee 140*

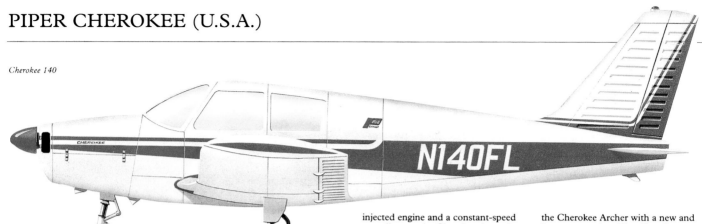

N140FL

First flown in prototype form during January 1960, the four-seat Cherokee and its successors have been a remarkable success story for Piper. This all-metal cantilever low-wing type has gone through a large number of developments and variants with engine horsepower indicated by the numerical suffix appended to the basic

designation; thus the initial PA-28-150 with the 112-kW (150-hp) Lycoming O-320 engine and fixed tricycle landing gear was followed in chronological sequence by the PA-28-160, PA-28-180, PA-28-235, and PA-28-140. An upgraded series introduced in June 1967 with retractable landing gear, a fuel-

injected engine and a constant-speed propeller was the Cherokee Arrow in PA-28-180R and PA-28-200R forms. The first series was then redesignated, the PA-29-140 becoming the Cherokee Flite Liner and, in de luxe form, the Cherokee Cruiser 2 Plus 2, the PA-28-180 becoming the Cherokee Challenger with a slightly lengthened fuselage and increased-span wings, and the PA-28-235 becoming the Cherokee Charger. In 1974 further changes in name were made: the Cherokee 2 Plus 2 became the Cherokee Cruiser, the Cherokee Challenger became the Cherokee Archer, and the Cherokee Charger became the Cherokee Pathfinder.

A new type introduced was the PA-28-151 Cherokee Warrior based on

the Cherokee Archer with a new and longer-span wing. The Cherokee Cruiser and Cherokee Pathfinder went out of production in 1977, when the PA-28-236 Dakota was introduced with the longer-span wing and the 175-kW (235-hp) O-540 engine. In 1978 there appeared the PA-28-201T Turbo Dakota that went out of production in 1980 to leave in production aircraft now designated PA-28-161 Warrior II, PA-28-181 Archer II and PA-28RT-201T Turbo Arrow IV.

**PIPER PA 28-161 CHEROKEE WARRIOR II**
**Role:** Tourer
**Crew/Accommodation:** One, plus up to three passengers
**Power Plant:** One 150 hp Lycoming 0-320-E3D air-cooled flat-opposed
**Dimensions:** Span 10.65 m (35 ft); length 7.2 m (23.8 ft); wing area 15.8 m² (170 sq ft)
**Weights:** Empty 590 kg (1,301 lb); MTOW 1,065 kg (2,325 lb)
**Performance:** Cruise speed 213 km/h (133 mph) at 2,438 m (8,000 ft); operational ceiling 3,930 m (12,700 ft); range 1,660 km (720 miles) with full payload
**Load:** Up to 342 kg (775 lb)

*A Piper Cherokee Six*

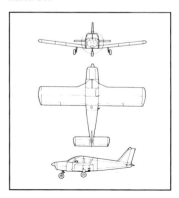

*Piper PA-28 Cherokee*

# BEECH STARSHIP (U.S.A.)

*Starship 1*

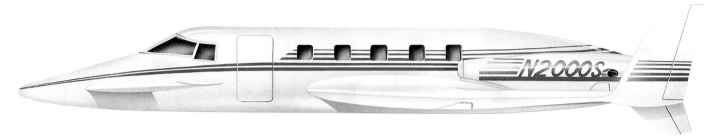

The Starship marks a radical departure from previous aircraft in the Beech line, being a futuristic canard design with swept flying surfaces and two turboprops located in the rear-mounted wing to drive pusher propellers. The engines are located as close to the rear fuselage as possible to reduce thrust asymmetry problems in the event of an engine failure. The type is also notable for the high percentage of composite materials used in the airframe: this offers an extremely attractive combination of low weight with great strength. The Starship's wings are monocoque structures with composite wingtip stabilizers, and terminate in endplate surfaces that provide directional stability as well as serving as drag-reducing winglets. The foreplanes are of the variable-geometry design that contribute to the Starship's good field performance before being swept back to improve maximum cruise speed.

In overall terms, the Starship reflects the design concepts of the adventurous Burt Rutan, and the type was first flown during August 1983 in the form of an 85 per cent scale version developed by Rutan's Scaled Composites Inc. Full-scale flight trials began in February 1986 with the first of six pre-production Starships. The type received Federal Aviation Administration certification in 1989, with deliveries beginning later in the same year, despite the fact that payload/range performance is lower than guaranteed because of unexpected drag and weight problems. A number of fixes are being developed, and it is expected that these shortfalls will be eliminated in the early 1990s.

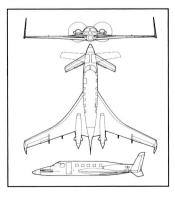

*Beech Starship*

**BEECH STARSHIP 1**
**Role:** Executive transport
**Crew/Accommodation:** Two, plus up to ten passengers
**Power Plant:** Two 1,100 shp Pratt & Whitney Canada PT6A-67 turboprops
**Dimensions:** Span 16.46 m (54 ft); length 14.05 m (46.08 ft); wing area 26.09 m² (280.9 sq ft)
**Weights:** Empty 4,044 kg (8,916 lb); MTOW 6,350 kg (14,000 lb)
**Performance:** Cruise speed 652 km/h (405 mph) at 7,620 m (25,000 ft); operational ceiling 12,495 m (41,000 ft); range 2,089 km (1,298 miles) with maximum payload
**Load:** Up to 1,264 kg (2,884 lb)

*The Starship and the Model 17 'Staggerwing'*

# RAYTHEON/BEECH KING AIR and SUPER KING AIR (U.S.A.)

*C-12A*

The King Air was developed as a turboprop-powered derivative of the Model 65 Queen Air, and first flew in 1963 as the Model 65-80 conversion with two 373-kW (500-shp) Pratt & Whitney Canada PT6A engines. The type entered production as the unpressurized Model 65-90T King Air to meet initial orders from the military for what became the U-21 Ute utility and special mission series, the first examples of which were delivered in 1967. This family was in fact preceded into service by the initial civil version, the pressurized Model A90.

The type went through many variants and in 1994 deliveries started of the C90SE, a lower cost and reduced specification model of King Air, to accompany the standard 7/8-seat King Air C90B.

Delivered from August 1969, the Model 100 King Air introduced a reduced-span wing based on that of the Model 99 Airliner, larger elevator and rudder areas, and a fuselage lengthened for 15 persons (including the pilot) rather than the 10 carried by the Model 90. Powered by 507-kW (680-shp) PT6A-28 turboprops, the Model 100 was followed in 1971 by the improved Model A100 (military U-21F), and from 1975 by the Model B100 with 533-kW (715-shp) Garrett TPE331-6-252B turboprops. In October 1972 the company flew the first Model 200 Super King Air with a T-tail, an increased-span wing, and greater fuel capacity for its more powerful PT6A-41 turboprops.

The type is used by the U.S. military as the C-12 Huron communications and special mission series, while civil models include the Model B200 with PT6A-42 engines for improved cruise performance. This can also be delivered in freighter or maritime surveillance configurations, and has itself formed the basis of the RC-12 Guardrail and Guardian Common Sensor intelligence and communications intercept/direction-finding military versions. The Model 350 Super Air King was introduced in 1988, also offered in RC-350 Guardian form.

### BEECH SUPER KING AIR 350
**Role:** Pressurized executive transport
**Crew/Accommodation:** Two plus up to 15 passengers
**Power Plant:** Two 1,050 shp Pratt & Whitney Canada PT6A-60A turboprops
**Dimensions:** Span 17.65 m (57.92 ft); length 14.22 m (46.66 ft); wing area 28.8 m² (310 sq ft)
**Weights:** Empty 4,110 kg (9,062 lb); MTOW 6,804 kg (15,000 lb)
**Performance:** Maximum speed 583 km/h (363 mph); operational ceiling 10,670 m (35,000 ft); range 3,507 km (2,180 miles) at 10,670 m (35,000 ft)
**Load:** Up to 1,660 kg (3,600 lb)

*Beech Model 200 Super King Air*

*A Beech King Air 100*

# CESSNA CITATION (U.S.A.)

*Citation I*

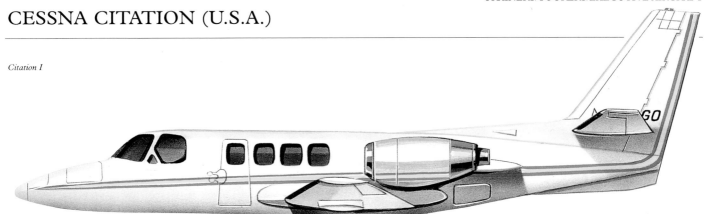

With its Citation family, Cessna moved into the market for high-performance 'bizjets' offering its purchasers the combination of performance and fuel economy they wanted for commercial reasons, together with the low noise 'footprint' that avoided the vociferous complaints of the growing environmental lobby. The company's investment in the project was very considerable, and when the prototype, at that time called the Fanjet 500, first flew in September 1969, it became clear that Cessna had a type that offered serious competition to market leaders such as the BAe HS 125, Dassault Falcon 20, and Gates Learjet. The type was typical of Cessna twin-engined aircraft in many features other than its aft-mounted podded engines, and was renamed Citation shortly after its first flight. Test flights revealed the need for several important modifications before certification could be secured, so this straight-winged type entered service only in 1971 with Pratt & Whitney Canada JT15D-1 turbofans.

Later developments have been the Citation I of 1976 with greater span, the Citation I/SP for single-pilot operation, the Citation II of 1978 with greater span, a lengthened fuselage and 1134-kg (2,500-lb) thrust JT15D-4 engines, the single-pilot Citation II/SP, the completely revised Citation III of 1982 with swept wings of supercritical section, a lengthened fuselage for two crew and 13 passengers, a T-tail and 1656-kg (3,650-lb) thrust Garrett TFE731-3B-100S turbofans, and the most recent Citation V, which combines the short-field performance of the Citation II with a larger cabin and the speed and cruising altitude of the Citation III.

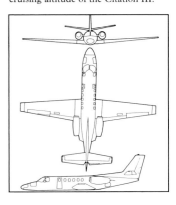

*Cessna Citation II*

**CESSNA CITATION S/II (T-47A)**
**Role:** Executive transport and military trainer
**Crew/Accommodation:** Two, plus up to eight passengers
**Power Plant:** Two, 1,134 kgp (2,500 lb s.t.) Pratt & Whitney JT15D-4B turbofans
**Dimensions:** Span 15.90 m (52.21 ft); length 14.39 m (47.21 ft); wing area 31.83 m² (342.6 sq ft)
**Weights:** Empty 3,655 kg (8,059 lb); MTOW 6,849 kg (15,100 lb)
**Performance:** Cruise speed 746 km/h (403 knots) Mach 0.70 at 10,670 m (35,000 ft); operational ceiling 13,105 m (43,000 ft); range 3,223 km (1,739 naut. miles) with four passengers
**Load:** Up to 871 kg (1,920 lb)

*The Citation II/SP*

# Racing/Sportplanes

Racing has long been accepted as a means of speeding development in aviation, in addition to providing public spectacle. The very first international air race was held in Paris, France in September 1906, as a balloon meeting for the Gordon Bennett Trophy. At this time few people in France has any idea that proper powered aeroplane flights had already taken place years earlier in the U.S.A., and so this balloon event was seen as state-of-the-art flying. Therefore, when in November that same year Alberto Santos-Dumont lifted off the ground in a tail-first biplane for just 220 metres (772 ft), many thought this to be the world's first flight by a powered aeroplane.

With flights in the U.S.A. and France, and some progress in Germany and elsewhere by 1908, it began to look as though Britain was lagging behind in aeroplane development. *The Daily Mail* newspaper, having awarded a cash prize for a model aeroplane competion in 1907 that had been won by the young Alliot Verdon Roe (of later Avro fame), decided to offer further large cash prizes for aviation achievements. In July 1909 a £1,000 prize went to Frenchman Louis Blériot for making the first aeroplane crossing of the English Channel, while that October a similar prize went to J.T.C. Moore-Brabazon as the first Briton to fly a mile in a British aeroplane. Other *Daily Mail* prizes followed which greatly encouraged progress. By then, however, the first international aeroplane meeting in the world had been staged at Reims in France, during August 1909, which only served to show the dominance of French and U.S. types.

Also in France, in 1912, Jacques Schneider had been concerned at the slow rate of progress in developing seaplanes, believing that such craft were best suited to expanding air transportation. In response he established

La Coupe d'Aviation Maritime Jacques Schneider, better remembered as the Schneider Trophy Contest, with the first event gaining only seven entries at one race at the April 1913 international Hydro-Aeroplane Meeting in Monaco. Although the start was modest, it later became an event of international prestige, attracting many nationally sponsored teams that fielded purpose-developed and streamlined racers. The final contest was won by Britain in 1931 with the Supermarine S.6B, which soon after became the first-ever aeroplane to exceed 400 mph (640 km/h) and was an early inspiration for the Spitfire fighter.

In America, the first Pulitzer Trophy Race took place in 1920, while many other important races culminated (pre-World War II) in the first trans-World air race in 1934, known as the MacRobertson Race. Flown from England to Australia, it was sponsored by MacRobertson Confectionery of Melbourne to commemorate the centenary of the founding of the State of Victoria.

Aerobatics had begun by error, when pilots entered unintentional spins. It was a fatal manoeuvre until 1912 when a Royal Navy pilot managed to recover his Avro by correct stick and rudder movement. The first loop was performed in Russia in 1913 and the first sustained inverted flight in France the same year. It was just the beginning, and even now new manoeuvres are being devised, such as Pugachev's Cobra performed by a Russian Sukhoi Su-27 jet fighter at Paris in 1989 and the Kulbit or somersault displayed by an Su-37 fighter in 1996, the latter involving rapid deceleration with a 360-degree tight loop.

*Picture: German-built Extra 300 aerobatic aircraft in vertical display flight.*

# MACCHI MC.72 (Italy)

*Macchi MC.72*

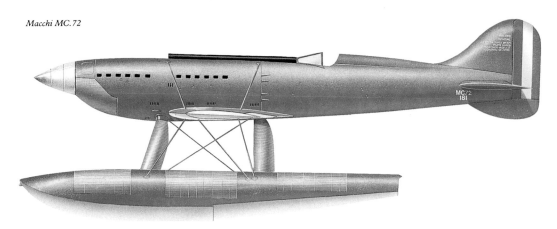

The MC.72 was the culmination of a long series of racing floatplanes designed by Mario Castoldi for the Schneider Trophy races, and despite the fact that it never won such a race, the MC.72 was without doubt the finest machine of its type ever produced. The starting point for this family was the M.39, which pioneered the twin-float layout with a low-set wing wire-braced to the floats and the upper part of a slim fuselage tailored to the frontal area of the inline engine.

The first of six M.39s flew in July 1926 as a trainer with the 447-kW (600-hp) Fiat AS.2 engine, and a racer powered by a 597-kW (800-hp) version of the same engine won the 1926 race; the type also raised the world speed record to 416.68 km/h (258.875 mph). For the 1927 race, the company produced three examples of the M.52 with slightly smaller dimensions but powered by the 746-kW (1,000-hp) AS.3. Technical problems knocked all three out of the race, but one machine later raised the speed record to 479.29 km/h (297.818 mph) and another was fitted with a smaller wing to become the M.52R that raised the record to 512.776 km/h (318.625 mph).

For the 1929 race, Castoldi designed the M.69 of which three were built with the 1342-kW (1,800-hp) Isotta-Fraschini 2-800 with coolant radiators on the wing surfaces, underside of the nose, sides of the rear fuselage, float legs, and upper sides of the floats! Neither of the entered aircraft finished the race.

The MC.72 was designed for the 1931 race, and was powered by a Fiat AS.6 engine (two 1119-kW/1,500-hp AS.5 units mounted front to back and driving contra-rotating propellers). Five aircraft were built, but problems prevented any of them from taking part in this last Schneider Trophy race. Two of the machines later set world speed records, the latter at 709.209 km/h (440.683 mph).

## MACCHI MC.72
**Role:** Racing
**Crew/Accommodation:** One
**Power Plant:** One 3,100 hp Fiat AS.6 liquid-cooled inline
**Dimensions:** Span 9.48 m (31.10 ft); length 8.32 m (27.29 ft) wing area 15.00 m² (161.46 sq ft)
**Weights:** Empty 2,500 kg (5,511 lb) MTOW 2,907 kg (6,409 lb)
**Performance:** Maximum speed 709.209 km/h (440.681 mph) at 500 m (1,640 ft)
**Load:** Nil

*The Macchi MC.72 drove contra-rotating propeller units*

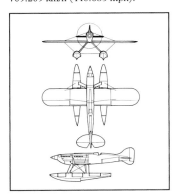

*Macchi MC.72*

# GEE BEE SPORTSTER (U.S.A.)

*Sportster R-1*

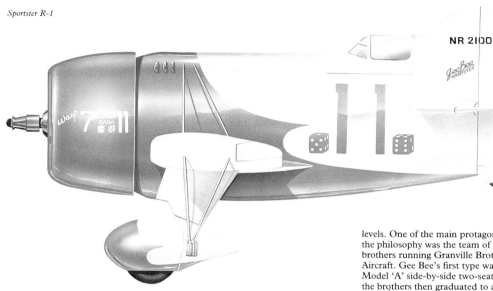

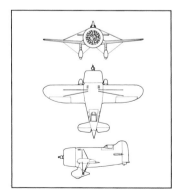

*Super Sportster Model R-1*

The period between 1925 and 1935 saw the development of many fascinating aircraft specifically for racing, especially in the United States, where the philosophy of cramming maximum engine into minimum airframe approached extraordinary

levels. One of the main protagonists of the philosophy was the team of five brothers running Granville Brothers Aircraft. Gee Bee's first type was the Model 'A' side-by-side two-seater, but the brothers then graduated to a low-cost sporting machine, the Model 'X' Sportster single-seater of 1930, that developed into the Model 'Y' Senior Sportster two-seater.

A number of racing successes

followed, so the brothers decided to produce a pure racer as the Model 'Z' Super Sportster that introduced the distinctive barrel-shaped fuselage tailored to the diameter of its 399-kW (535-hp) Pratt & Whitney Wasp Junior, and featured a diminutive vertical surface that projected only marginally above the enclosed cockpit, a wire-braced low/mid-set monoplane wing, and fixed but nicely faired tailwheel landing gear. The type enjoyed some racing success, but broke up in an attempt on the world air speed record in December 1931.

For the 1932 season there followed two Model 'R' Super Sporters: the Model R-1 with a 597-kW (800-hp) Pratt & Whitney Wasp and the Model R-2 with a 410-kW (550-hp) Wasp Junior. The first flew in August 1932, and won the Thomson Trophy race as well as setting a landplane record of 476.815 km/h (296.287 mph). Both aircraft were entered for the 1933 Bendix Trophy race, the Model R-1 with a 671-kW (900-hp) Pratt & Whitney Hornet and the Model R-2 with the R-1's original Wasp. The R-1 was later damaged and the R-2 virtually destroyed, but components of both were used to create the Model R-1/R-2.

### GEE BEE SUPER SPORTSTER R-1
**Role:** Racing
**Crew/Accommodation:** One
**Power Plant:** One 730 hp Pratt & Whitney Wasp TD3-1 air-cooled radial
**Dimensions:** Span 7.62 m (25.00 ft); length 5.41 m (17.66 ft); wing area 9.29 m² (100.00 sq ft)
**Weights:** Empty 835 kg (1,840 lb); MTOW 1,095 kg (2,415 kg)
**Performance:** Maximum speed 473.82 km/h (294.418 mph) at sea level
**Load:** Nil

*Gee Bee Super Sportster Model R-1/R-2 hybrid*

# PERCIVAL P.6 MEW GULL (United Kingdom)

*Mew Gull*

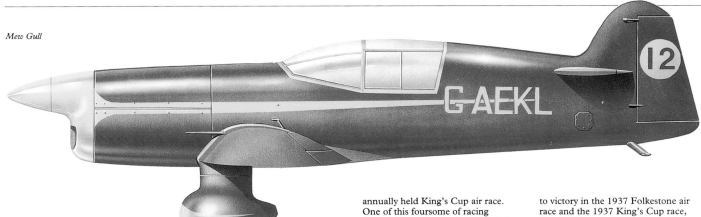

First flown in March 1934, the P.2 prototype was of angular and somewhat austere appearance that gave little hint of the beautiful P.6 Mew Gull to follow. Altogether, five examples of the P.6 were to be built,

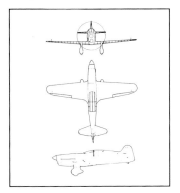

*Percival Type E Mew Gull*

including the converted P.2 and these subsequently dominated the British air racing scene during the three years prior to September 1939 and the outset of World War II. Of exceptionally well-proportioned shape, the P.6 Mew Gulls were constantly in the headlines, frequently being flown by the aircraft's designer/pilot Captain Edgar Percival in such events as the

**PERCIVAL P.6 MEW GULL**
**Role:** Racer
**Crew/Accommodation:** One
**Power Plant:** One 205 hp de Havilland Gipsy Six Series II air-cooled inline
**Dimensions:** Span 7.54 m (24.75 ft); length 6.88 m (21.92 ft); wing area 8.18 m² (88 sq ft)
**Weights:** Empty 562 kg (1,240 lb); MTOW 1,066 kg (2,350 lb)
**Performance:** Maximum speed 398 km/h (247 mph) at sea level; range 3,219 km (2,000 miles) with 3,861l (85 Imp gal) tankage
**Note:** figures are for Alex Henshaw's modified G-AEXF as configured for his February 1939, record-breaking England-Cape Town return flight

annually held King's Cup air race. One of this foursome of racing thoroughbreds has had a particularly long and illustrious career, remaining airworthy into the 1990s. Initially built for the South African pilot A. H. Miller and carrying the appropriate ZS-AHM registration, this machine took part in the September 1936 Schlesinger England-South Africa air race, having to retire at Athens as a result of a fuel-feed problem. Shortly thereafter, this machine passed into the hands of Alex Henshaw, receiving the British registration G-AEXF. Initially acquired by the extremely youthful, but capable Henshaw, G-AEXF was powered by a DH Gipsy Six I, in which form Henshaw flew it

to victory in the 1937 Folkestone air race and the 1937 King's Cup race, from which he retired with contaminated fuel. Prior to the start of the 1938 racing season, Henshaw had his aircraft re-engined with the higher-powered Gipsy Six R, simultaneously fitting a Ratier variable pitch propeller to better utilize the extra 30 hp (23 kW) engine output. In this form, G-AEXF achieved 398.3 kph (247.5 mph) in both the Hatfield-Isle of Man and Manx Air Derby races of 1938. Later that year, by now sporting a new DH propeller, Henshaw romped home to win the King's Cup with a record-setting speed of 380 kph (236 mph).

*This is the fifth of the six Percival Mew Gulls built*

# de HAVILLAND D.H.88 COMET (United Kingdom)

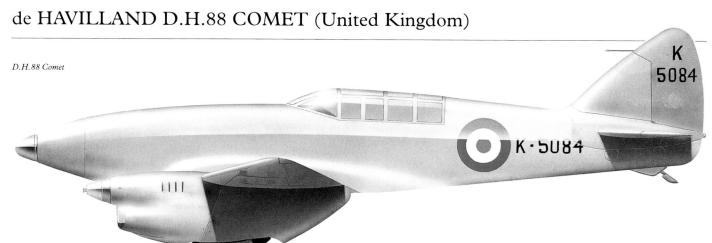

*D.H.88 Comet*

The Comet was planned specifically as a competitor for the October 1934 Victorian Centenary Air Race between Mildenhall in England and Melbourne in the Australian state of Victoria. Prize money was donated by Sir MacPherson Robertson, and de Havilland received three orders before the expiry of its February 1934 deadline. The design was very clean by the aerodynamic standards of the day, and based on an all-wood structure as a low-wing monoplane with two wing-mounted engines. The fuselage accommodated three large fuel tanks in the nose immediately ahead of the two crew members, who were seated in tandem under a canopy faired into the tail unit by a dorsal decking. The engines were 172-kW (230-hp) de Havilland Gipsy Six R inlines driving two-position propellers which used the air pressure of 240-km/h (150-mph) speed for the shift from take-off fine pitch to cruising coarse pitch. Other notable features were split trailing-edge flaps and manually retractable main units for the tailwheel landing gear. The first Comet flew in September 1934, and all three machines had received their required certificates of airworthiness before the start of the race on 20 October. The speed section of the race was won by *Grosvenor House* in 70 hours 54 minutes, and is now preserved at the Shuttleworth Trust. *Black Magic* was forced to retire at Baghdad, and G-ACSR finished fourth but then set an out-and-back record of 13.5 days when it came straight back to England with film and mail. Two other Comets were later built, one as a mailplane to French government order and the other for two unsuccessful attempts on the London to Cape Town record.

**de HAVILLAND D.H.88 COMET**
**Role:** Long range racing
**Crew/Accommodation:** Two
**Power Plant:** Two 230 hp de Havilland Gipsy Six R air-cooled inlines
**Dimensions:** Span 13.41 m (44.00 ft); length 8.84 m (29.00 ft); wing area 19.74 m² (212·50 sq ft)
**Weights:** Empty 1,329 kg (2,930 lb); MTOW 2,517 kg (5,550 lb)
**Performance:** Maximum speed 381 km/h (237 mph) at sea level; operational ceiling 5,791 m (19,000 ft); range 4,707 km (2,925 miles)
**Load:** Nil

*The D.H. 88 Comet was an elegant high-speed monoplane*

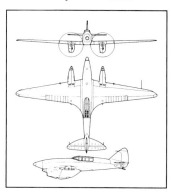

*de Havilland D.H.88 Comet*

# PITTS SPECIAL (U.S.A.)

*S-1 Special*

*Pitts Special S-1*

Designed and built by Curtis Pitts for the celebrated aerobatic display pilot Betty Skelton, the Pitts 190 Special first flew in September 1944 with a 67-kW (90-hp) Continental engine and single-seat accommodation in an open cockpit. The type was of mixed construction, with a covering of fabric over the wooden wings and the steel-tube fuselage and tail unit. The result was a diminutive braced biplane with fixed tailwheel landing gear, and from the very beginning the design revealed exceptional aerobatic capabilities. Pitts then developed the design for homebuilders as the Special Biplane with engines in a range between 48 and 71 kW (65 and 90 hp) and

ailerons on the lower wings only. The type's aerobatic qualities meant that an increasing number were built for competition purposes with airframes stressed to higher levels, ailerons on the upper as well as lower wings, and engines of up to 134 kW (180 hp).

In the mid-1960s Pitts developed a two-seat model, and this first flew in 1967 as the S-2 Special to complement what now became the S-1 Special. The S-2 was somewhat larger than the S-1 and powered by the 134-kW (180 hp) Lycoming O-360-A1A, while aerodynamic refinements made it stable in rough air and also enhanced manoeuvrability. This model reintroduced factory production with Pitts Aviation

Enterprises (later Pitts Aerobatic Company), and definitive models were the S-1S with the 134-kW (180 hp) IO-360-B4A engine, the S-1T with the 149-kW (200-hp) AEIO-360-A1E driving a constant speed propeller, the S-2A with the same engine, and the S-2B with the 194-kW (260-hp) AEIO-540-D4A5.

In 1983 Christen Industries bought Pitts, continuing production of current models and introducing the S-2S single-seat version of the S-2B.

## PITTS S-1 SPECIAL
**Role:** Aerobatic sportsplane
**Crew/Accommodation:** One
**Power Plant:** One 180 hp Lycoming 10-360-B4A air-cooled flat-opposed
**Dimensions:** Span 5.28 m (17.33 ft); length 4.72 m (15.5 ft); wing area 9.15 m² (98.5 sq ft)
**Weights:** Empty 327 kg (720 lb); MTOW 522 kg (1,150 lb)
**Performance:** Maximum speed 285 km/h (177 mph) at sea level; operational ceiling 6,795 m (22,300 ft); range 507 km (315 miles)
**Load:** None

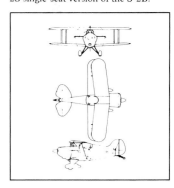

*Pitts S Special*

# THE CHRONOLOGY
# OF FLIGHT

c. 843 B.C.–2001

# Introduction

As we approach the millennium, with all the wonders of modern life about us, it becomes increasingly difficult to appreciate that the science of aviation has a lineage almost as old as recorded history itself. True, ascending flight without tether to the ground was only achieved by a manned balloon in 1783 and it took until 1903 for a controllable and powered aeroplane to fly; but it should not be overlooked that in the time of the ancient civilizations of Rome, Greece and China attempts had been made to fly using artificial wings and some important discoveries were then made.

China is attributed with the invention and practical application of kites from the second century B.C. although another 15 centuries would pass before the outside world would hear of tethered man carrying kites through the stories of that remarkable European traveller and trader, Marco Polo. By then, China had forged still further ahead in matters aeronautical, having fought off armies using gunpowder rockets and been host to the first-ever parachute jumps.

A Chronology, with historic milestones detailed in order of occurrence, is perhaps the best way of presenting these events. It offers a silent commentary on human ingenuity, a fascinating insight into the creative minds of would-be aviators. Neither the fear of death, nor of failure and ridicule, stopped the march of discovery, albeit slowly at the beginning. Each tiny advance disentangled part of the mystery of mechanical flight that has led to today's stealth fighter and supersonic airliners. For, while man cannot ever hope to match the birds and bats of the natural world for pure muscle-related flying ability, a flair for inventiveness has allowed only humans to venture beyond the Earth's atmosphere and onto another planetary body.

As with many discoveries, the knowledge of 'how to fly' proved to be a mixed blessing. Like a muzzled dog released from its confinement, snapping in all directions and at first unsure of what to do with itself, aviation (once mastered) took many divergent paths. Flying for sport and pleasure was one avenue, warfare another. And, while an eminent Victorian historian commented that inventions which abridge distance did most for civilization by tending to remove national and provincial antipathies, in 1917 Orville Wright reportedly said 'When my brother and I built and flew the first man-carrying flying machine, we thought that we were introducing into the world an invention which would make further wars practically impossible – what a dream it was; what a nightmare it has become'.

Aviation, now so much a part of our everyday life, has brought each nation of the world within easy reach of holidaymakers and relief agencies. It has also brought every nation within the striking power of heavily armed forces. A mixed blessing, certainly. As to the future, many of the new aircraft for operation in the first part of the 21st century are already designed. Manufacturers have the ability to produce airliners for 600 or more passengers, to build aerospace craft capable of flying at hypersonic speed, and much more besides. One thing is certain: the challenge to be the first, fastest, greatest and so on continues, and even as this book was being prepared the latest attempt to make the first non-stop around-the-world flight by balloon had only just ended. Funny to think that balloons can still generate historical firsts.

*Among the many individuals and organizationa that helped in the production of this chronology, special thanks go to my good friend David Morley for writing sections of the text for the original 1983 edition.*

*1794: Captain Coutelle observes from* Entreprenant. *(Courtesy Royal Aeronautical Society)*

## c. 843 B.C.

King Bladud, the ninth ruler of Britain, becomes the first recorded aviation fatality after attempting to fly from the Temple of Apollo in Trinavantum (London) using wings of feathers. He had come to the throne in 863 B.C.

## 470–391 B.C.

Chinese philosopher Mo Ti, better known as Mo Tzo, lives in China. An exponent of universal love, he is believed to have invented and built the first wooden kite for pleasure.

## c. 400–345 B.C.

Archytas of Tarentum, a Greek-born mathematician, philosopher and scientist, lives in Italy before drowning in the Adriatic. Among his scientific achievements had been the construction of a 'flying' wooden bird (shaped as a dove or pigeon), which was attached to a well-balanced whirling arm. It is thought that the bird had been capable of 'lift' when propelled by a 'hidden and enclosed air', probably hot or compressed air, steam or another force requiring fire.

## c. 169 B.C.

Chinese General Han Hsin uses kites in warfare to measure distances between his forces and the enemy.

## c. 6th Century

Kites are used in China for signalling military instructions by semaphore.

## c. 1020

An English Benedictine monk, known as Oliver of Malmesbury, 'The Flying Monk', attempts to fly from Malmesbury Abbey using wings. He breaks his legs in the attempt.

## 1042

Tseng Kung Liang of China tells of the use of rockets in war. These early projectiles are fuelled with gunpowder.

## 12th–14th Century

The first model helicopters are flown as string-pull toys. One is illustrated in a Flemish manuscript of c. 1325, while a painting of 1460 depicts a toy helicopter. (q.v. April 28, 1784)

## 1250

Roger Bacon, an English Franciscan monk, completes a book entitled *Secrets of Art and Nature*. In it he makes the first known reference to a flying machine with 'artificiall Wings made to beat the Aire', known today as an ornithopter. It is not published until 1542.

## 14th Century

Marco Polo, his father and an uncle witness man-carrying kites being flown by sailors in Cathay (China).

## 1306

Quasi-parachute jumps are made in China during the coronation of Emperor Fo-Kin.

## 1326

Bomb-carrying pennon-type kites are first illustrated in Europe, in an illuminated manuscript by Walter de Milemete. The kite carries a fire-bomb over a fortified city, controlled by three soldiers using a rope and pulley.

## c. 1420

Italian Joanes Fontana designs the first rocket-powered aeroplane, configured as a model bird. This is illustrated in a manuscript in the state library at Munich.

## 1452–1519

The Italian artist and inventor Leonardo da Vinci produces several designs for aviation-related machines during his lifetime. Between 1483 and 1497 he designs a parachute, ornithopter, helicopter and powered aeroplane.

## 1507

John Damian, Abbot of Tungland in Galloway, breaks his thigh bone after attempting to fly from a wall at Stirling Castle, Scotland, to France using feather-covered wings. His failure is blamed on using the feathers of dunghill fowls instead of eagles alone.

## c. 1595

The first published design for a parachute is seen in the Venetian *Machinae Novae*, by Fausto Veranzio.

## 1647

Italian Titus Livio Burattini, who resides at the Polish court of King Wladyslaw IV, makes and flies a model aeroplane. It has four sets of wings, two sets beating as those of an ornithopter.

## 1655

Englishman Robert Hooke builds and flies a model ornithopter.

## 1670

Jesuit priest Francesco de Lana-Terzi completes the first full design for a lighter-than-air machine. This is basically a boat hull fitted with a mast and sail, lifted by four rope-tethered 20ft (6.1m) diameter copper spheres from which the air would be extracted using an air pump (as invented by Otto von Guericke in 1654). However, Lana-Terzi realizes that the spheres cannot be made thin enough for lightness, yet strong enough to prevent crushing by outside air pressure, and abandons the concept.

## 1678

French locksmith Besnier attempts to fly at Sablé using two paddle-like wings hand-held across his shoulders, driven up and down in flapping motion by rods attached between his ankles and one end of each wing. Two pairs of hinged surfaces on a pole make up each wing, these surfaces spreading during the downward motion and folding during the upward. Details of the trials are published on September 12 that year, in which claims of actual flights are made over neighbouring houses. One set of Besnier wings is later sold to a M. Guibre, who is said to achieve some success. (Any flights by Besnier or Guibre could at best be uncontrolled glides.)

## 1680

The Italian Giovanni Borelli outlines his theories of why man cannot achieve flight without mechanical aid in a book entitled *De Motu Animalium*.

## 1694

**September** Father Vassou, a missionary in

Canton, China, writes home that he has seen documentary evidence that a balloon ascent had been made at the coronation of Emperor Fo-Kin. (q.v. 1306).

## c. 17th Century

Hezarfen Celebi of Turkey attempts to fly from a tower in Galata. He is said to have glided some distance.

## 1709

**August 8** Father Bartolomeu de Gusmão demonstrates a small model hot-air balloon in the Ambassador's drawing room at the Casa da India, Lisbon, to King John V of Portugal and other dignitaries. The balloon lifts to a height of 12ft (3.5m) before setting the curtains on fire. He later constructs a model glider.

## 1742

The Marquis de Bacqueville attempts to fly across the river Seine from the roof of a Paris hotel using multi-wings. Some gliding flight is achieved.

## 1754

Russian Michael Vasilyevitch Lomonosov flies a model helicopter powered by clockwork.

## 1763

**July** Melchior Bauer of Germany designs a heavier-than-air craft intended as a military bomber. His aircraft is named *Sky Wagon* and is intended to carry a pilot plus approximately 100lb (45kg) of weapons. Power is provided by the pilot flapping two wings, while the main fixed wing is a lightweight structure of silk-covered pinewood with brass wire strengthening. Expected to be constructed on a mountain top for the convenience of flight testing, it was probably never built.

## 1766

Henry Cavendish isolates hydrogen and refers to it as Phlogiston. He informs the Royal Society that Phlogiston is much lighter than atmospheric air.

## 1780

Hyder Ali of Mysore, India, repels British forces at Guntur with iron-cased artillery rockets.

Brother Cyprian, an east-European monk, claims to have achieved gliding flight from a mountain.

## 1781

In Austria, Karl Friedrich Meerwein designs and builds an advanced form of glider, for which a proper area of wing has been calculated for manned flight. It is said to have flown on at least two occasions. Some propulsion is claimed by an up-and-down movement of the oval wing.

## 1782

The French Montgolfier brothers demonstrate a model hot-air balloon.

## 1783

Frenchman Louis-Sébastien le Normand jumps from the height of a first storey building at Montpellier grasping a 30in (76cm) diameter conical parachute.

**April 25** A full-size but unmanned Montgolfier hot-air balloon rises to an altitude of about 1,000ft (300m).

**June 4** At Annonay, in public, the Montgolfier brothers demonstrate a small hot-air balloon of 36ft (11m) diameter

**August 27** Jacques Alexandre César Charles releases a 12ft (3.5m) diameter unmanned hydrogen balloon from the Champ-de-Mars, Paris, which makes a 45-minute flight to Gonesse. On landing it is attacked and destroyed by villagers who believe it to be a monster, the evil smell coming from its punctured envelope adding credence to this theory.

**September 19** A sheep, cock and duck ascend in a 41ft (13m) Montgolfier hot-air balloon at the Court of Versailles. Reaching an altitude of 1,700ft (520m) and flying for eight minutes, it comes to rest 2 miles (3.2km) away in the Forest of Vaucresson.

**October 15** François Pilâtre de Rozier ascends in a tethered Montgolfier hot-air balloon to become the first aeronaut in history. He rises to an altitude of about 84ft (26m), restrained by retaining ropes.

**November 21** Francois Pilâtre de Rozier and the Marquis d'Arlandes make the first free flight by balloon (Montgolfier), from the Château la Muette to the Butte-aux-Cailles, remaining airborne for 25 minutes. They become the world's first pilot and passenger and the first men to make a journey by air.

**December 1** Jacques Alexandre César Charles and M. Robert become the first men to make a free flight in a hydrogen balloon, flying 27 miles (43km) from the gardens of Les Tuileries, Paris, to Nesles.

## 1784

Frenchman Lt. Jean-Baptiste Marie Meusnier shows his design for a dirigible.

**February 4** Irishman Riddick releases an unmanned hot-air balloon from the Rotunda Gardens, Dublin.

**February 25** The first balloon ascent (Montgolfier) is made in Italy by the Chevalier Paulo Andreani, Charles Gerli and Augustin Gerli.

**April 15** Irishman Rosseau and a small boy make a flight in a balloon lasting two hours. This is the first manned flight in Ireland.

**April 28** Frenchmen Launoy and Bienvenu demonstrate the first known self-propelled model helicopter. It uses a two-blade propeller at each end of a stick, powered by a bowdrill system. (q.v. 1796)

**May 20** The Marchioness de Montalembert and three others become the first women to fly, ascending from the Faubourg-Saint-Antoine, Paris, in a tethered Montgolfier hot-air balloon.

**June 4** Madame Thible makes the first free flight by a woman in a hot-air balloon, from Lyon, France.

**August 25** James Tytler makes a flight at Edinburgh in a Montgolfier-type hot-air balloon. Tytler had previously flown on August 7 from the Comely Gardens, Edinburgh.

**September 15** The first journey of significance in a hydrogen balloon is made by Vincenzo Lunardi of Lucca, who makes a flight in England from the Honourable Artillery Company's Moorfields ground to Standon Green End, Hertfordshire.

**October 4** James Sadler becomes the first English aeronaut, going aloft in a Montgolfier-type hot-air balloon in Oxford.

**October 16** Jean-Pierre Blanchard attempts to propel his balloon by hand-turning a six-blade propeller fitted to the basket.

## 1785

**January 7** Jean-Pierre Blanchard and American Dr. John Jeffries fly across the English Channel in a hydrogen balloon from Dover, England, to the Forêt de Felmores, France, the journey taking about two and a half hours.

**January 19** Irishman Richard Crosbie attempts the first aerial crossing of the Irish Sea by hydrogen balloon. But, once airborne, he decides that a night crossing might be too dangerous and lands again.

**May 12** A second attempt by Richard Crosbie to cross the Irish Sea fails when the hydrogen balloon proves to be insufficient to lift him. A volunteer from the onlookers, Richard

McGwire, takes his place (as a lighter man) but alights in the sea some 10 miles (16km) from Howth.

**June 15** François Pilâtre de Rozier and Jules Romain are killed while trying to fly across the English Channel in a composite hot-air and hydrogen balloon.

**July 19** Richard Crosbie makes a third attempt at an aerial crossing of the Irish Sea. His journey is full of incident and he is eventually rescued by the barge *Captain Walmitt* as he heads away from the Welsh coast during a storm.

## 1785–9

Jean-Pierre Blanchard undertakes balloon flights throughout Europe, including first flights in Belgium, Germany and Switzerland.

## 1790

French chemist Lavoisier refers to Cavendish's 'inflammable air' as hydrogen. (q.v 1766)

## 1791

**August 2** Blanchard drops animals by parachute from a balloon flying over Vienna.

## 1793

Blanchard makes a parachute descent at Basle but breaks a leg. This followed an earlier experiment in which he released a dog from a balloon flying at a height of 6,000ft (1,830m) over Strasbourg. The dog landed without injury. (q.v. August 2, 1791)

**January 9** Blanchard makes the first balloon ascent in the United States of America, flying in a hydrogen balloon from the Walnut Street Prison, Philadelphia, to Gloucester County, New Jersey. The journey lasts 46 minutes.

An Aerostatic Corps of the French Republican Army is established at Meudon, France, under the command of Captain Coutelle. With 50 recruits, it starts with a single 33ft (10m) diameter training balloon, which can be winched out to 500ft (150m) with two persons on board. Hydrogen gas is generated by equipment devised by chemist Guyton de Morveau.

## 1794

June 26 Captain Coutelle of the French Republican Army ascends in a tethered hydrogen balloon at Maubeuge, during the Battle of Fleurus. The balloon named *Entreprenant*, appropriated to the army of the north, is the first balloon used in war.

## 1796

George Cayley builds a bowdrill-powered model helicopter similar to that of Launoy and Bienvenu in France. It uses four-blade rotors made from bird feathers.

## 1797

**October 22** André Jacques Garnerin makes the first parachute jump from a balloon at considerable height (about 2,230ft/680m), at Parc Monceau, Paris. Garnerin eventually loses his life during a descent in France. (q.v. September 21, 1802)

## 1798

**November 10** Mademoiselle Labrosse and Mademoiselle Henry ascend in a balloon at Paris. Mademoiselle Labrosse later becomes Madame Garnerin.

## 1799

George (later Sir George) Cayley produces the first known design for an aeroplane incorporating fixed wings, a cruciform tail unit, and a propulsion system (paddles). The design is engraved on a silver disc.

## 1802

**September 21** André Jacques Garnerin makes the first parachute descent in England, but is injured when one of the straps attaching the parachute to the basket gives way.

## 1804

George Cayley constructs his first monoplane model glider. It incorporates such modern features as a monoplane wing of large area, mounted about a third of the way along the single-rod fuselage, and small cruciform horizontal and vertical tail surfaces.

## 1805

British Colonel William Congreve first tests his developed artillery rocket at the Royal Laboratory, Woolwich.

## 1806

**October 8** The Royal Navy fleet sailing for Boulogne during the Napoleonic Wars includes 24 ships carrying Congreve rockets. These rockets do great damage to Boulogne and French naval vessels.

**1807**

Some 25,000 Congreve rockets are fired against Copenhagen by the Royal Navy, each with a range of up to 2 miles (3.2km).

**1808**

July 24 R. Jordarki Kuparanto becomes the first man to bale out of a damaged aircraft with a parachute when his Montgolfier hot-air balloon catches fire over Warsaw.

**1809**

George Cayley completes his first full-size glider and launches it without a pilot.

Jacob Degen of Switzerland makes hop flights using an ornithopter fitted with a fairly small hydrogen balloon for extra lift. By itself the ornithopter would be unsuccessful.

**March 7** Jean-Pierre Blanchard dies of a heart attack while aloft in a balloon.

**1811**

German Albrecht Berblinger attempts to fly across the river Danube using an ornithopter based on a design by Jacob Degen. The attempt is unsuccessful.

**1812**

**October 1** James Sadler attempts to make the first air crossing of the Irish Sea. He leaves Dublin in a hydrogen balloon and successfully flies to Anglesey, but is blown out to sea again. He is later rescued. (q.v. July 22, 1817)

**1815**

A Rocket Brigade of the British Army is used during the Battle of Waterloo.

**September** Eliza Garnerin, André Jacques Garnerin's niece, ascends in a balloon at Paris and then makes the first parachute descent by a woman.

**1816**

Jacob Degen builds a clockwork model helicopter with contra-rotating rotors.

**1817**

**July 22** Windham Sadler, son of James Sadler, makes the first aerial crossing of the Irish Sea, flying in a balloon from Portobello Barracks to Holyhead, Wales.

**1819**

**July 7** Madame Blanchard becomes the first woman to die in a flying accident when her hydrogen balloon catches fire during a firework party in Paris.

**August 2** Charles Guille makes the first parachute jump from a balloon in the United States, descending from a height of 8,000ft (2,440m) over New Bushwick, Long Island, NY.

**1825**

A school teacher from Bristol, England, named George Pocock, is said to have lifted his daughter Martha off the ground using a kite of his own design.

**1827**

George Pocock demonstrates the effectiveness of his kites by tying one to a carriage. With this arrangement Pocock is pulled from Bristol to Marlborough at speed.

**1828**

Englishman Mayer builds a full-size man-powered helicopter. It is unsuccessful.

**1832**

**May 14** Probably the first aeronaut to reach a century of flights is Charles Green, who on this day takes off for his 100th flight from the Mermaid Tavern, Hackney, England.

**1836**

**August** The *Royal Vauxhall Balloon*, later renamed the *Great Nassau Balloon*, is flown for the first time.

**November 7–8** Charles Green, Robert Holland and Monck Mason ascend from Vauxhall Gardens, London in the *Royal Vauxhall Balloon* and travel 480 miles (772km) to a location close to Weilberg, Duchy of Nassau – prompting the name change. (q.v. August, 1836)

**1837**

**July 24** Briton Robert Cocking attempts to make a descent from the *Great Nassau Balloon* using a parachute of his own design. Its main feature is the new canopy, which is turned upside down in order to prevent the oscillations of earlier parachutes. At an altitude of about 6,600ft (2,000m), the parachute is released from under the balloon. After steady descent, the upper rim of the parachute collapses and Cocking is killed.

**1842**

Englishman W.H. Phillips builds a powered model helicopter which flies. It is powered

by a steam pressure-jet system through the rotor-tips.

**1843**

Englishman William Samuel Henson patents the design of his passenger-carrying steam-powered aeroplane known successively as the *Aerial Steam Carriage* and the *Ariel*.

Sir George Cayley designs the first convertiplane as the *Aerial Carriage*, with four circular wings and two pusher propellers for horizontal flight, the wings being capable of opening into eight-blade rotors for vertical flight.

**March** An Aerial Transit Bill is read before the British Parliament, its purpose being to propose the establishment of a public company to operate aeroplanes in all regions of the world.

**1844**

Henson's model of the *Aerial Steam Carriage*, with a span of 20ft (6m) and driven by a steam engine, is built. During flight trials at Bala Down in Chard, Somerset, in 1845-47, a launching ramp is eventually used to help gather speed prior to take-off; but the *Carriage* is incapable of sustaining flight. (q.v. 1843)

**1848**

John Stringfellow, who in 1842 had been asked by Henson to build a steam engine for the *Aerial Steam Carriage*, attempts to fly a model aeroplane with tapered wings and a steam engine at Chard, launched from a suspended wire. It is unsuccessful, as are later models.

**1849**

A young boy makes a tethered flight of several yards in a glider designed and constructed by Sir George Cayley, to become the first person to fly in a heavier-than-air aircraft.

**August 22** Austrian pilotless hot-air balloons are launched against defending forces in Venice. Each balloon carries a light bomb and fuse.

**October 7** M.F. Farban makes the first balloon flight over the Alps, travelling from Marseille to Turin.

**1852**

**September 24** Henri Giffard makes the first powered flight in a dirigible, flying from the Hippodrome in Paris to Trappes (a distance of about 17 miles/27km). Power is provided by a 3hp (2.24kw) steam engine driving a large three-blade propeller.

**1853**

**June** Sir George Cayley's coachman flies in a Cayley glider at Brompton Hall, Scarborough, England. On landing he offers his notice, having been hired to drive, not fly.

**1854**

**June 27** Frenchman Louis Charles Letur is fatally injured in a parachuting accident in England. He had previously made several successful descents using his controllable parachute.

**1856**

Frenchman L.P. Mouillard, author of *L'Empire de l'Air*, attempts to fly a model glider. It is a

failure. Other model gliders follow, but are equally unsuccessful.

**1857**

J.M. le Bris completes a short free flight in a glider launched from a moving horse-drawn cart.

**December 15** Sir George Cayley, the so-called 'father' of heavier-than-air aviation, dies.

**1857–58**

Félix du Temple de la Croix flies a model aeroplane over a distance (tractor monoplane) powered first by a clockwork motor and later by a steam engine. (q.v. 1874).

**1858**

Frenchman Félix Tournachon (Nadar) takes the earliest known aerial photograph, depicting part of Paris, from a tethered balloon.

**March 29** The first ascent by a hydrogen balloon in Australia made from the Cremorne Gardens, Melbourne.

**1859**

**July 2** John O. Wise, O. Gager and John La Mountain fly 1,120 miles (1,800km) from St. Louis, Missouri, to Henderson, York, in a hydrogen balloon. (q.v. 1873).

E. Cordner flies a man-carrying sea rescue kite in Ireland.

**1860**

Frenchman Etienne Lenoir invents the gas engine.

**1861**

**June 18** American Thaddeus Sobieski Constantine Lowe pilots the balloon *Enterprise*, from which the first aerial telegraph message is transmitted.

**October 1** The American Army Balloon Corps is formed comprising five balloons and 50 men.

**November** The *George Washington Parke Custis*, a converted coal barge, becomes the world's first operational aircraft carrier (carrying balloons) when it enters service with General McClellan's Army of the Potomac during the American Civil War.

**1862**

**May 31–June 1** The hydrogen balloon *Intrepid* is used for observation duties during the Battle of Fair Oaks in the American Civil War.

**December 11** A balloon of the American Army Balloon Corps is used during the crossing of the river Rappahannock.

**1863**

**April 3–May 5** The Battle of Chancellorsville is fought during the American Civil War, with balloons being used for observation and artillery direction.

The American Balloon Corps is disbanded.

**1864–70**

Manned balloons are first used in a South American war, when forces from Argentina, Brazil and Uruguay go to war against

Paraguay. The joint air operations are made by the Brazilian Marquis de Caxias.

**1865**

Frenchman Charles de Louvrie produces the first design for a jet-propelled aeroplane (the *Aéronave*). This uses a canopy-type wing above a four-wheel cart supporting the motor.

**1865–72**

Austrian Paul Hänlein produces a gas-driven internal combustion engine with four horizontally-opposed cylinders, intended for motive power.

**1866**

**January 12** The Aeronautical Society of Great Britain is founded. (q.v. June 1868 and June 25, 1918)

**1867**

Englishmen J.W. Butler and E. Edwards patent the design of a delta-winged powered aeroplane.

**1868**

**June** The Aeronautical Society of Great Britain holds the first aeronautical exhibition at the Crystal Palace, England.

**1870**

Gustave Trouvé successfully flies a model ornithopter which uses revolver parts to beat the wings up and down.

The Prussian Army forms two Luftschiffer detachments to operate lighter-than-air craft during the Franco-Prussian War. These are organized by Englishman Henry Coxwell, but soon disband.

**September 23** Jules Durouf ascends from Paris in a balloon following the surrounding of the city by the Prussian Army during the Franco-Prussian War. He lands in Evreux. Five other balloons are available within the city, and a balloon construction programme is soon begun in railway stations and other buildings. Using gas from the Villette gasworks, by January 28, 1871 some 66 balloon flights have been made, carrying 155 persons, nearly 3 million letters, carrier pigeons and other cargo out of Paris. Of the 66 flights, seven go off course and two may have sustained damage from Prussian gunfire. (q.v. October 1870)

**October** The chemist Barreswill invents microfilm to allow messages to be carried back into Paris by carrier pigeon (see above).

## 1870–76

During 1870–71, Alphonse Pénaud demonstrates several model helicopters with rotors driven by twisted rubber. He also flies a model aeroplane with built-in stability. In 1876 he designs the first amphibian, becoming second only to Sir George Cayley in the development of early aeronautics.

## 1871

In Britain, Francis H. Wenham and John Browning build the first wind tunnel. Frenchman Charles Renard flies a multi-wing model glider. It features movable winglets for stability in flight.

## 1872

Austrian Paul Hänlein demonstrates his dirigible, 164ft (50m) in length, with a number of tethered flights. Power is provided by a single 5hp (3.7kW) Lenoir engine, fuelled by hydrogen from the envelope.

## 1873

John Wise pilots a very large hydrogen balloon on the first attempted transatlantic air crossing. Financed by the New York *Daily Graphic*, the balloon crashes after only 41 miles (66km) have been flown.

## 1874

French Navy officer Félix du Temple de la Croix makes a 'hop' flight at Brest in his bird-like aeroplane, having used a ramp to gather pace.

## 1875

**June** Thomas Moy's unmanned powered aeroplane *Aerial Steamer* lifts itself off the ground at the Crystal Palace, England.

## 1876

Nikolaus Otto of Germany patents a four-stroke cycle gas-fuelled engine. (q.v. 1877)

## 1877

Nikolaus Otto invents the four-stroke petrol-fuelled internal combustion engine. Director of the Otto engine factory is Gottlieb Daimler who, in 1884, designs the first petrol-fuelled internal combustion engine to be put to practical use. A single-cylinder engine, it is used by Karl-Friedrich Benz to power the first motorcycle proper of 1885. (q.v. October 1901)

The French Établissement Aérostatique Militaire is set up at Meudon.

## 1878

The first British government funding of aircraft takes place with the allocation of £150 for the construction of a hydrogen balloon. The resulting coal-gas balloon costs £71 and is named *Pioneer*. (q.v. June 24, 1880)

## 1879

In France, Victor Tatin flies a model aeroplane powered by a compressed air motor. It is of advanced concept, with monoplane wings, a tailplane and two four-blade tractor-mounted propellers.

The dirigible hangar completed at Chalais-Meudon for an exhibition of 1878 is officially taken over as hangar Y. The French State Airship Factory is operated at Chalais-Meudon from the 1880s until 1940.

## 1880

**June 1** Russian Alexander Fedorovich Mozhaiski patents his original 'flying machine' powered by a steam engine. (q.v. 1884)

Dr. Karl Wölfert and Herr Baumgarten of Germany ascend in a dirigible fitted with a small engine. Poor load distribution causes it to crash. Baumgarten leaves the project.

**June 24** A balloon detachment of the British Army takes part in manoeuvres for the first time, at Aldershot.

## 1882

**March 5** Dr. Karl Wölfert of Germany tries to propel an airship with a hand-turned propeller at Charlottenburg. The attempt is unsuccessful.

## 1883

**October 8** Frenchman Gaston Tissandier becomes the first to fit an electric motor (Siemens) to an airship, powered by 24 bichromate of potash batteries.

## 1884

Alexander Fedorovich Mozhaiski completes his 74ft 10in (22.8m) wing span and 46ft 7in (14.2m) chord monoplane, powered by 20hp (15kW) and 10hp (7.5kW) steam engines. Piloted by I.N. Golubev, during one test at Krasnoye Selo, it is believed to have made a 'hop' flight of nearly 100ft (30m) after a slope launch.

**August 9** Capt. Charles Renard and Lt. Arthur Krebs, French Corps of Engineers, fly the dirigible *La France* from and back to Chalais-Meudon, the journey taking 23 minutes and covering 5 miles (8km). *La France*, powered by a 9hp (6.7kW) Gramme electric motor, thus becomes the first fully controllable dirigible to fly.

**November 26** A balloon detachment of the British Army leaves Britain to accompany the infantry to Cape Town during the expedition to Bechuanaland. It arrives on December 19.

## 1885

**February 15** A balloon detachment of the British Army leaves Britain to accompany the infantry as part of the expeditionary force to the Sudan.

The Prussian Airship Arm is made into a permanent air arm with the founding of the Preussische Luftschiffer-Abteilung. Based at Berlin-Schöneburg, it operates tethered balloons for four years.

## 1888

**August 12** Dr. Wölfert flies a balloon fitted with a 2hp (1.5kW) Daimler petrol engine at Seelberg, Germany.

## 1889

German engineer Otto Lilienthal has *Der Vogelflug als Grundlage der Fliegekunst* (The Flight of Birds as the Basis of the Art of Flying) published.

## 1890

Königliche Bayerisehe Luftschiffer-Abteilung is formed as a separate force to Preussische Luftschiffer-Abteilung, remaining active until 1919.

**May** The Balloon Section of the Royal Engineers is formed as part of the British Army.

**October 9** Frenchman Clément Ader makes the world's first powered 'hop' from level ground in his bat-like steam-powered *Éole* monoplane at Château Pereire, Armainvilliers. A distance of about 165ft (50m) is covered.

## 1891

Sir Hiram Maxim begins fabrication of components for his huge 4,000sq ft (371.61m²) wing area biplane test-rig.

American physicist Samuel Pierpont Langley begins designing and building model aeroplanes with steam engines. Each is later launched from a catapult mounted on the roof of a houseboat on the Potomac River, Washington D.C. The aeroplanes are known under the collective name *Aerodrome*. (q.v. May 6, 1896)

## 1892

Austria's first air section is formed as the K.u.K. Militäräronautische Anstalt.

**February 3** The French Minister of War contracts Clément Ader to build and supply a military aeroplane. It has to be a two-seater capable of carrying 165lb (75kg) of bombs. Known as the *Avion III*, it is tested at Satorg on October 12 and 14, but only high-speed taxiing is managed on the circular track.

## 1893

Australian Lawrence Hargrave originates the box-kite structure.

**May** Horatio Phillips is said to have flown (unmanned) an early Multiplane aeroplane at Harrow, England. A 72lb (33kg) weight represented the pilot. The Multiplane has 41 narrow-chord wings.

## 1894

French-born American railroad engineer Octave Chanute has *Progress in Flying Machines* published.

August von Parseval and Premierleutnant Bartsch von Sigsfeld demonstrate the first German kite balloons. (q.v. 1897)

Czeslaw Tanski flies a model aeroplane. This is the first successful Polish heavier-than-air aircraft. From 1896 he flight-tests various fall-size hang gliders.

Count Ferdinand von Zeppelin's first passenger-carrying airship design is rejected by the German Government's technical commission.

**July 31** Sir Hiram Maxim's huge biplane test rig, powered by two 180hp (134kW) steam engines and with 4,000 sq ft (371.6m²) of wing area, lifts off the ground during a test run. The 'flight' is restricted to a height of about 2ft (0.61m) by restraining guard rails positioned above the launching rails. One guard rail is smashed by the impact of the lifting biplane.

## 1895

British marine engineer Percy S. Pilcher completes his *Bat* monoplane glider. The *Bat* is subsequently fitted with a tail unit, following his visit to Germany at the invitation of Otto Lilienthal.

Count Ferdinand von Zeppelin is granted the first patent for his method of rigid airship construction.

Irishman Professor George Francis Fitzgerald attempts to fly at College Park, Dublin, using towed gliders. His experiments are unsuccessful despite the modern appearance of his aircraft which look similar to those flown successfully by Lilienthal in Germany.

## 1896

The last of Percy Pilcher's four gliders is completed as the *Hawk*. This has a twin-wheel forward landing gear with shock absorbers. *Hawk* proves very successful.

Count Ferdinand von Zeppelin raises 800,000 Reichsmarks for the 'Joint Stock Company for the Promotion of Airship Flight'.

Octave Chanute begins designing and constructing gliders, eventually producing the classic constant-chord biplane configuration.

**May 6** American Samuel Pierpont Langley flies the first model *Aerodrome* from a houseboat on the Potomac River. This model is steam-powered.

**August 10** Otto Lilienthal dies of his injuries caused by a crash in one of his gliders on the Rhinower Hills the previous day. Since 1891, Lilienthal had flown two biplane and five monoplane gliders with outstanding success.

## 1897

The tethered Drachen or kite-balloon is first used in manoeuvres with the German Army, devised by August von Parseval and Premierleutnant Bartsch von Sigsfeld to offer great stability.

**June 14** The first deaths in a dirigible accident are recorded when Wölfert and his mechanic

Herr Knabe are killed in Germany. The engine vaporizer on *Deutschland* sets fire to the dirigible's envelope, causing the gas to explode.

**July 11** Salomon August Andrée, Nils Strindberg and Knut Fraenkel of Sweden start off from Danes Island, Spitzbergen, on the first attempt to fly over the North Pole by balloon. The attempt ends three days later when the balloon descends and all three men eventually die. (q.v. August 6, 1930)

**October 12 and 14** Clément Ader's *Avion III* is tested at Satorg, France, but only high-speed taxiing is managed on the circular track. Official backing is withdrawn. (q.v. February 3, 1892)

## 1898

A carved wooden bird made of sycamore, dating from the 3rd or 4th century B.C. and weighing 1½ oz (40g), is found at Saqqara in Egypt. This has many features of a model glider, including a thin and tapering body, straight wings and a horizontal tail.

The Aéro Club de France is established.

Langley receives a $50,000 subsidy from the U.S. Government to continue his experiments with *Aerodromes*, but now in full-size form.

Sergeant Ivy Baldwin of the U.S. Army Signal Corps becomes the first-ever American airman to be shot down, his balloon being hit by groundfire during the Battle of Santiago between forces of America and Spain contesting Cuba. He survived.

## 1899

**August** The brothers Orville and Wilbur Wright, bicycle makers, use a biplane kite with a span of 5ft (l.5m) to test control by wing warping.

American-born Samuel Franklin Cody begins his experiments with man-lifting kites.

Work begins on an airship hangar for Count Ferdinand von Zeppelin, which will be anchored on Lake Constance and resting on 95 floats.

**September 30** Percy Pilcher crashes at the home of Lord Braye at Market Harborough when a bamboo strut in the tail unit of the *Hawk* breaks while airborne. He dies two days later, the first Briton to die in a heavier-than-air aircraft accident.

## 1900

The Wright brothers produce their No. 1 glider, of 17ft (5.18m) span. Tested at Kitty Hawk, North Carolina, the biplane is successfully flown as an unmanned kite, piloted kite and free-flying piloted glider but is considered to have too little span.

Three Balloon Sections of the Royal Engineers are operated in South Africa during the Boer War.

**July 2** Count Ferdinand von Zeppelin takes up five other people on the initial flight of his first airship, the LZ 1. The flight, from the airship's floating hangar on Lake Constance, lasts about 20 minutes.

## 1901

**Summer** The Wright brothers produce their No. 2 glider, with wings of much greater span that also feature camber and anhedral, plus a foot-activated wing-warping system. Tests at Kill Devil Hills prove disappointing.

**June** Langley flies a petrol-engined quarter-scale model of his projected full-size *Aerodrome*. This is the first aeroplane with a petrol engine to achieve level flight. It flies three times in June. (q.v. August 8, 1903)

**October** Austrian Wilhelm Kress begins trials with his tandem three-winged seaplane. It eventually achieves the first 'hop' from water before capsizing. Fitted with a 30hp (22.4kW) Daimler engine, it is the first-ever piloted aeroplane to use a petrol internal combustion engine.

**October 19** Brazilian Alberto Santos-Dumont wins a cash prize by flying his No. 6 airship around the Eiffel Tower.

**October 29** The Aero Club is established in Britain. (q.v. February 15, 1910)

## 1902

**January 17** Gustav Whitehead reportedly flies the world's first flying-boat (as opposed to a seaplane), covering a distance of approximately 7 miles (11km) and alighting on water. Produced from components stripped from his earlier landplane, it uses two engines and is fully controllable. This flight, and those that follow, are not officially recognized, possibly through lack of publicity.

**September–October** The Wright brothers flight test their No. 3 glider of 32ft (9.75m) span, the design of which has been based not on previously published technical material but on original research of their own. It also features twin rear fins. During these months No. 3 is flown on nearly 1,000 occasions and proves very successful, especially after the fins are replaced by a single steerable rudder to prevent the aircraft wanting to spin.

## 1903

**March 23** The Wright brothers file a patent for an aeroplane based on the No. 3 glider.

**August 8** Langley flies his petrol-engined quarter-scale *Aerodrome* fully successfully for the first time (q.v. June 1901)

**August 18** German Carl Jatho 'hops' his aeroplane for a distance of 59ft (18m). It is powered by a 9hp (6.7kW) petrol engine.

**October 7** Langley's full-size *Aerodrome* of 48ft (14.6m) span, piloted by Charles M. Manly (creator of the 52hp/39kW Manly-Balzer petrol engine that powers the aircraft) attempts a flight from the houseboat launcher. The *Aerodrome* fouls the launcher on take-off and drops into the river below.

**November 12** The Lebaudy brothers fly their airship between Moisson and the Champ-de-Mars, Paris, a distance of 37 miles (60km).

**December 8** The second attempted launch of the *Aerodrome* takes place, again with Manly at the controls. Its rear wing fouls the launcher and the *Aerodrome* is badly damaged as it falls tail-first into the river. Official support for the project is withdrawn.

**December 14** Wilbur Wright fails in his attempt to make a sustained flight with the powered *Flyer* and the aircraft is slightly damaged after stalling three and a half seconds after take-off.

**December 17** At 10.35 am at Kill Devil Hills, Kitty Hawk, North Carolina, Orville Wright pilots the Wright *Flyer* on a 120ft (36.5m) flight lasting 12 seconds, achieving the world's first manned, powered, sustained and controlled flight by a heavier-than-air aircraft. Three further flights are made this day, the longest lasting nearly a minute and covering 852ft (260m).

**1904**

**May 26** The Wright brothers make the first of 105 flights with *Flyer No. II.*

**September 20** Wilbur Wright makes the first-ever circuit flight in an aeroplane.

**October** Frenchman Robert Esnault-Pelterie flies a glider with ailerons for control. This is the first full-scale aeroplane to feature this innovation. He later becomes famous for his REP powered monoplanes, the most important of which is the REP 2 *bis* (flown in 1909).

**November 9** Wilbur Wright flies 2¼ miles (4.43km) at Dayton, recording the first aeroplane flight of more than five minutes.

**1905**

**January 18** Initial discussions for the purchase of an aeroplane are conducted between the Wright brothers and the U.S. Government (q.v. December 23, 1907).

**June 6** Gabriel Voisin lifts off from the river Seine in his 'box-kite' glider, which is towed by a motorboat.

**June 23** The first flight of the Wright *Flyer III* is made, the first practical version of the *Flyer*. It is fully controllable.

**October 5** Wilbur Wright pilots the *Flyer III* during a flight covering nearly 24.2 miles (39km) and lasting 38 minutes.

**October 14** The Fédération Aéronautique Internationale (FAI) is established in France.

**October 16** The Wright brothers make their last flight for nearly three years. (q.v. May 6, 1908)

**November 30** An attempt to launch Zeppelin LZ 2 from Lake Constance results in damage to the airship before flight is achieved.

The Aero Club of America is founded.

**1906**

**January 17** Zeppelin LZ 2 is launched successfully but has to land at Kisslegg due to fuel system problems. It is destroyed in a gale while moored at Kisslegg the next day.

**February 27** In the U.S., Samuel Pierpont Langley dies at Aiken, South Carolina.

**March 18** Romanian Trajan Vuia hops his No. 1 monoplane for the first time. It features a tractor-mounted engine, variable-incidence wing and an undercarriage with pneumatic tyres.

**July 7** The first officially-recognized balloon race in Britain begins at Barn Elms, London.

**August 11** Mrs C.J. Miller becomes the first American woman passenger in a dirigible.

**August 16** Jacob C.H. Ellehammer of Denmark hops his semi-biplane at Lindholm. (q.v. below)

**September 12** Ellehammer makes a tethered hop of about 140ft (43m) in his semi-biplane, which is powered by a 20hp (15kW) engine of his own design. It rises about 18 inches (50cm) above the 985ft (300m) circular track. (q.v. above and June 28, 1908).

**September 13** Alberto Santos-Dumont's 14-*bis* biplane 'hops' for a distance of 23ft (7m).

**September 30** The first international balloon race starts at Les Tuileries, Paris, and 16 entrants compete for the Gordon Bennett Trophy. It is won by Lt. Frank P. Lahm, U.S. Army, who flies the balloon *United States* 402 miles (647km) to Fylingdales Moor, England.

**October 9** The Zeppelin LZ 3 flies. It subsequently becomes the first military Zeppelin, as Army Z1. (q.v. November 7, 1908 and June 20, 1909)

**October 23** Alberto Santos-Dumont flies his biplane 14-*bis* nearly 197ft (60m) to win the 3,000-franc Archdeacon Prize for a flight more than 82ft (25m).

**November 12** Alberto Santos-Dumont makes the first officially recognized sustained flight by a piloted and powered aeroplane in Europe,

flying his tail-first biplane 14-*bis* 722ft (220m) in just over 21 seconds. This becomes the first internationally-ratified world distance record for aeroplanes.

**1907**

Horatio Phillips flies his latest Multiplane aircraft for about 500ft (152m) at Streatham. Although this is the first flight of a piloted and powered aeroplane in Great Britain, it is not officially accredited as such. The Multiplane has some 160 very narrow-chord wings.

**March 16–April 13** The French brothers Charles and Gabriel Voisin produce a biplane for Léon Delagrange, which performs six flights at Bagatelle between these dates, the best of 197ft (60m). The Voisin-Delagrange No. 1 is destroyed on November 3, following a period as a floatplane.

**April 5** Louis Blériot makes a brief flight in his tail-first pusher-engined Type V monoplane.

**April 6** The *Daily Mail* newspaper sponsors a model aircraft exhibition at the Agricultural Hall, London. The best flying models are taken for a 'fly-off' competition at Alexandra Palace. This is won by Alliot Verdon Roe, who wins a reduced prize of £75. With this Roe partly finances his first full-size aeroplane. This is the first of many *Daily Mail* newspaper prizes for air achievements. (q.v. June 8, 1908)

**July 11** Louis Blériot's tandem-wing Type VI Libellule flies about 80ft (25m). It features the first cantilever wings to be tested and wingtip-type ailerons. During July and August it makes

11 take-offs, six of the flights covering more than 328ft (100m).

**August 1** The Aeronautical Division, U.S. Signal Corps, is formed.

**September 10** The British Army Dirigible No. 1 *Nulli Secundus* flies for the first time at Farnborough. With a length of 122ft (37m), it is manned by Col. Capper of the Royal Engineers as pilot, Capt W.A.C. King of the British Army Balloon School and Samuel Cody who is in charge of the engine.

**September 29** The Bréguet-Richet helicopter lifts into the air at Douai, France, but has to be steadied by ground crew with poles. Power comes from a 50hp (37kW) Antoinette engine.

**September 30** The first flight takes place of the Voisin-Farman I biplane. Between this date and November 23 this aircraft performs about 20 flights at Issy-les-Moulineaux, the one on November 9 of 3,379ft (1,030m) lasting 1 minute 14 seconds. (q.v. January 13, 1908)

**October 10** *Nulli Secundus* has to be split at its temporary mooring at Crystal Palace, to prevent it tearing away in the wind. It later reappears as *Nulli Secundus II*.

**October 12–13** A.F. Gaudron and two crew members make the first crossing of the North Sea by air in the *Mammoth* hydrogen balloon, travelling about 721 miles (1,160km) from Crystal Palace, England, to Lake Väner, Sweden.

**October 26** Henry Farman sets an officially recognized distance record in the Voisin-Farman I, of 2,530ft (771m).

**November 10** Louis Blériot makes a first flight in his Type VII monoplane. This is the ancestor of the modern tractor monoplane, and is followed by the Type VIII and eventually the highly successful Type XI.

**November 13** Paul Cornu makes the first free flight in a helicopter at Lisieux, France. This twin rotor machine is powered by a 24hp (18kW) Antoinette engine. The flight lasts 20 seconds, at a height of 1ft (0.30m).

**November 16** The Frenchman Robert Esnault-Pelterie flies 1,968ft (600m) in his REP 1 monoplane.

**November 30** Glenn Curtiss forms the first aeroplane company in the United States of America.

**December 23** Brigadier-General James Allen, Chief Signal Officer, U.S. Army, produces the first specification for a U.S. military aeroplane. Tenders are requested. This is the first specification ever for a military aeroplane issued for commercial tender, but not the first official military aeroplane specification. (q.v. February 3, 1892)

## 1908

The Lebaudy *République* is the first dirigible to be used by the French Army on manoeuvres.

The first Gnome rotary aero-engine appears in France, giving an output of 50hp (37.25kW). However, the rotary engine had been invented as long ago as the 1880s.

**January 13** Henry Farman wins the Deutsch-Archdeacon Prize of 50,000 francs for the first officially observed circular flight of 1km in Europe.

**February 6** The U.S. Army accepts tenders from the Wright brothers, A. Herring and J. Scott for military aeroplanes. Only the Wrights eventually deliver an aeroplane. (q.v. December 23, 1907)

**February 10** The U.S. Army signs a contract for the construction of a Wright Model A biplane as its first military aeroplane. This is just one of three contracts signed. (q.v. December 23, 1907, and February 6, 1908)

**February 15** Capt. Thomas Baldwin submits a tender for the first U.S. Army dirigible.

**March 12** The Aerial Experiment Association's first aeroplane to fly successfully is the *Red Wing*, designed by Lt. Thomas Selfridge. (q.v. September 17, 1908)

**April 11** Lt. Frank P. Lahm becomes head of the Aeronautical Division, U.S. Signal Corps.

**May** Frenchman Léon Delagrange makes the first aeroplane flight in Italy.

Henry Farman makes the first aeroplane flight in Belgium.

**May 6** The Wright brothers begin flying again after nearly three years. They have now lost their technical lead over other pioneers and never regain it.

**May 14** Charles W. Furnas becomes the first passenger to fly in an aeroplane when he is taken up by Wilbur Wright for a 29-second flight.

**May 29** Ernest Archdeacon becomes the first aeroplane passenger in Europe when he is taken up by Henry Farman in France.

**May 30** The first British-held international balloon race attracts 30 starters.

**June 8** A.V. Roe makes a 'hop' flight in his full-size Roe 1 biplane (24hp /18kW Antoinette engine) at Brooklands, England.

**June 10** The first U.S. Aeronautical Society is established in New York.

**June 20** Glenn Curtiss follows the much earlier success of the Wright brothers by flying his biplane *June Bug*, so becoming America's third aviation pioneer. *June Bug* is the Aerial Experiment Association's third aeroplane.

Zeppelin LZ 4 flies for the first time. It begins Army trials on August 4 but after flying for 20 hours makes an emergency landing at Echterdingen.

**June 28** Dane J.C.H. Ellehammer makes the first aeroplane flight in Germany, at Kiel.

**July 4** Glenn Curtiss wins the Scientific American Trophy by flying nearly 1 mile (1.6 km) in his biplane *June Bug*.

**July 8** Frenchwoman Madame Thérèse Peltier becomes the first woman to fly as passenger in an aeroplane when she is taken up by Frenchman Léon Delagrange in a Voisin biplane.

**July 23** Thomas Baldwin delivers a dirigible and gas plant to the U.S. Army at Fort Myer. (q.v. February 15, 1908)

**August 4** Flight trials of Baldwin's U.S. Army Signal Corps' No. 1 dirigible begin at Fort Myer.

**August 5** Zeppelin LZ 4 is destroyed by fire after striking electrical wires while anchored during trials for the Army. The subsequent 'Zeppelin Donation Fund' raises over 6,000,000 Reichsmarks in voluntary contributions and allows Count von Zeppelin to continue his work.

**August 8** Wilbur Wright flies at Le Mans, France, in the new two-seat Model A.

**August 29** The Curtiss *Golden Flyer* wins the Coupe Gordon Bennett speed prize, attaining 47mph (75.5km/h).

**September 3** Flight trials of the Wright brothers' military aeroplane begin at Fort Myer. (q.v. February 10, 1908)

**September 5** The French Goupy I flies for the first time. It is the first full-size triplane to fly.

**September 6** Frenchman Léon Delagrange flies for 29 minutes 53 seconds at Issy-les-Moulineaux, covering a distance of more than

15 miles (24km). This is the first half-hour flight in Europe.

**September 17** Lt. Thomas Etholen Selfridge, U.S. Army Signal Corps, becomes the first person to be killed in a powered aeroplane when the Wright military biplane in which he is a passenger crashes at Fort Myer; Virginia. The pilot, Orville Wright, is badly injured.

**September 21** The first significant endurance flight is performed by Wilbur Wright, remaining airborne in France over a distance of 41.3 miles (66.5km).

**October** Hans Grade becomes the first German pilot. (q.v. January 12, 1909)

**October 8** Griffith Brewer becomes the first Briton to fly as a passenger in an aeroplane when he is taken up by Wilbur Wright in France.

**October 16** American-born Samuel Franklin Cody makes the first officially recognized aeroplane flight in Great Britain, piloting the British Army Aeroplane No. 1 during a flight of 1,390ft (424m) at Farnborough, England.

**October 30** Henry Farman makes the first cross-country flight in Europe, flying about 16 miles (26km) from Châlons to Reims in a Voisin.

**November 7** Zeppelin LZ 3 flies to Donaueschingen with the German Crown Prince on board.

**December 4** Briton J.T.C. Moore-Brabazon makes a flight of 1,350ft (410m) in a Voisin

while taking flying instruction at Issy-les-Moulineaux.

**December 31** Wilbur Wright wins the Michelin prize with a flight of 77 miles (124km) at Camp d'Auvours, France.

**1909**
Yakov M. Gakkel flies the first successful Russian-built aircraft, the Gakkel-3 of his own design.

**January 12** Hans Grade flies his triplane, the first successful German aeroplane.

**January 23** The Blériot Type XI makes its first flight, powered by a 30hp (21.5kW) REP engine.

**February** Shellbeach, Isle of Sheppey, becomes Britain's first aerodrome proper.

Eustace Short concludes an agreement with Wilbur Wright to build six Wright biplanes under licence in Britain. The Short brothers become, therefore, the first to manufacture aeroplanes in series.

**February 23** J.A.D. McCurdy flies the Aerial Experiment Association's *Silver Dart* over Baddeck Bay in Nova Scotia, covering a distance of 4 miles (6.5km). This records the first aeroplane flight in Canada and the first sustained flight in the British Empire.

**March 9** The French Goupy II flies for the first time. It is the first fully successful tractor-engined biplane.

**April** Frenchman Legagneux makes the first aeroplane flight in Austria.

**April 24** Wilbur Wright pilots a Wright biplane at Centocelle, Italy, from which the first aerial cinematograph film is taken.

**April 30** J.T.C. Moore-Brabazon makes the first accredited flight by an Englishman in England, flying his Voisin biplane over a distance of about 450ft (137m) at Leysdown, Isle of Sheppey.

**May 14** Samuel Cody flies for a distance of more than one mile from Laffan's Plain, Hampshire, in the British Army Aeroplane No. 1.

**May 20** Frenchman Paul Tissandier makes the first one-hour flight in France, in a Wright biplane. Paul Tissandier was the second pupil to be taught in France in 1908 by Wilbur Wright.

Paul Tissandier sets the first officially recognized (by the FAI) world speed record for aeroplanes in a Wright biplane, achieving 34.03mph (54.77km/h).

**May 26** Zeppelin LZ 6 is launched and flies successfully.

**June 5** John Berry and Paul McCullough win the first National Balloon Race in America, covering about 378 miles (608km).

**June 12** The Blériot XII becomes the first aeroplane to fly with two passengers (Santos-Dumont and Fournier) at Issy-les-Moulineaux.

**June 20** Zeppelin LZ 3 is delivered to the German Army.

**July 13** Alliot Verdon Roe becomes the first Briton to make a recognized flight in a British aeroplane, covering 100ft (30m) in his paper-covered triplane at Lea Marshes, Essex.

**July 19** Wireless telegraphy is used to relay information to Dover on the French weather situation prior to Latham's flight (see below).

Englishman Hubert Latham attempts to be the first man to cross the English Channel by aeroplane, but ditches his Antoinette IV following engine trouble.

**July 23** A.V. Roe flies 900ft (274m) in his triplane at Lea Marshes, Essex, England.

**July 25** Frenchman Louis Blériot becomes the first man to fly across the English Channel by aeroplane (Blériot XI monoplane), taking off from Les Baraques, near Calais, at 4.41 am and landing at Northfall Meadow by Dover Castle, 36½ minutes later. Blériot wins the £1,000 prize offered by the *Daily Mail*.

**July 27** Latham makes a second attempt to fly the Channel from Cap Blanc Nez to Dover, but ditches in the sea 1 mile (1.6km) from the English coast.

The first flight takes place of the French Antoinette VII monoplane.

**July 29** Frenchman Legagneux makes the first aeroplane flight in Sweden.

**July–October** The first International Airship Exhibition (I.L.A.) is held at Frankfurt/Main. Count Ferdinand von Zeppelin lands his LZ 5 in the grounds.

**August 2** The American Government buys its first aeroplane, a Wright Model A biplane later named *Miss Columbia*. The cost of the aeroplane is $25,000, not including a $5,000 bonus paid because it exceeds the official specification,

**August 22** The first international meeting for aeroplanes is held at Reims, France. Twenty-three aircraft compete for cash prizes in speed, distance and duration competitions.

**August 23** Glenn Curtiss flies the *Golden Flyer* at the Reims International Meeting, setting a record for speed at 43.385mph (69.821km/h).

**August 24** Louis Blériot flies at Reims in his Type XI at a speed of 46.179mph (74.318km/h).

**August 26** Hubert Latham gains a distance in a closed circuit record at Bétheny of 96.076 miles (154.620km), flying an Antoinette IV.

**August 27** Henry Farman makes the first aeroplane flight of more than 100 miles, covering 111.847 miles (180km) in a closed circuit during the Reims International Meeting.

**August 29** Glenn Curtiss wins the speed prize at the Reims International Meeting with a flight at 47mph (75.7km/h) in the *Golden Flyer*. He also wins the Coupe Gordon Bennett.

**September** Delagrange makes the first officially recognized aeroplane flight in Denmark.

**September 7** Eugène Lefebvre crashes his Wright Model A at Port Aviation Juvisy and is killed, becoming the first pilot to die while flying.

**September 8** Cody makes the first flight in Great Britain of more than one hour's duration.

**September 22** Capt. Ferdinand Ferber is killed at Boulogne while attempting to take off in a Voisin. He is the second pilot to be killed in a powered aeroplane.

**September 25** Four people are killed when the gasbag of the French dirigible *République* is pierced at an altitude of 400ft (122m) over Avrilly, France.

**October 15–23** The first aviation meeting proper in Britain begins at Doncaster, though it is not officially recognized by the Aero Club of Great Britain. Of the 12 aeroplanes assembled, five fly.

**October 16** Count Ferdinand von Zeppelin forms Delag (Die Deutsche Luftschiffahrt Aktiengesellschaft) as the world's first commercial airline company. Using airships, Delag carries more than 34,000 passengers from 1910 to November 1913 between German cities, 19,100 of them flown from March 1912. Although the services are without injury, only three of the original six airships survive to the end.

**October 18–23** The first officially recognized (by the Aero Club of Great Britain) aviation meeting in Britain takes place at Squires Gate,

Blackpool. Of the 12 aircraft assembled, seven fly.

**October 27** Mrs Ralph H. van Deman becomes the first American woman passenger in an aeroplane, being taken aloft by Wilbur Wright.

**October 30** Moore-Brabazon wins the *Daily Mail* prize of £1,000 as the first Briton to fly for one mile in a British aeroplane (Short No. 2 biplane).

**November** The first flight takes place of the *Etrich Taube*, the first Austrian-designed and built aeroplane to be flown in Austria. A bird-like monoplane, versions became early military aircraft in Austria and Germany.

**December** Frenchman Meurisse takes still photographs from an Antoinette monoplane, showing areas of Mourmelon and Châlons.

**December 9** Colin Defries makes the first aeroplane flight in Australia.

**December 31** Harry Ferguson makes the first aeroplane flight in Ireland, in a machine of his own design.

## 1910

The Imperial Russian Flying Corps is founded.

The *Golub* (Pigeon), the first Russian-designed non-rigid airship, joins the Russian army at Lida.

**January 7** Hubert Latham makes the first flight at an altitude of 3,281ft (1,000m) at Châlons, France, in an Antoinette VII.

**January 10** The first aeroplane meeting in the U.S.A. is held at the Dominguez Field, Los Angeles, under the control of the Aero Club of California. During the event, the first great American barnstormer, Charles F. Willard, wins the spot landing competition.

**January 19** Lt. Paul Beck drops dummy bombs (sandbags) over Los Angeles from an aeroplane piloted by Louis Paulhan.

**February 15** The Aero Club of Great Britain becomes the Royal Aero Club.

**March 8** Moore-Brabazon is given the first Aviator Certificate by the Royal Aero Club of Great Britain.

Madame la Baronne de Laroche becomes the first certificated woman pilot and the 36th French pilot.

**March 10** Frenchman Émil Aubrun makes night flights in a Blériot monoplane at Villalugano, Buenos Aires, Argentina.

**March 13** Capt. Engelhardt makes the first aeroplane flight in Switzerland.

**March 28** Frenchman Henri Fabre performs the first recognized take-off from water in a powered seaplane, the *Hydravion*, at La Mède harbour, Martigues, France.

**April** The French Service Aéronautique is formed as part of the Army.

**April 27/28** Claude Grahame-White makes the first night flight in the U.K., performed during the *Daily Mail* £10,000 London to Manchester race. However, the race is eventually won by Louis Paulhan, who is the first to comply with the rules to fly from a point near the newspaper's London office to a point near its Manchester office.

**June 2** The Hon. C.S. Rolls flies a Wright biplane across the English Channel and back, dropping a letter for the Aéro Club de France just before the return journey.

**June 3** The British Army dirigible *Beta I* flies for the first time. Actually the lengthened *Baby*, which had followed *Nulli Secundus*, *Beta I* was the first British airship to be installed with WT and the first non-rigid airship anywhere to be moored by mast.

**June 9** A Henry Farman, piloted by Lt. Féquant, undertakes the first French photographic reconnaissance flight.

**June 13** The *New York Times'* $10,000 prize for a return flight between New York and Philadelphia is won by Charles Hamilton.

**June 17** First flight of the *Vlaicu I* parasol monoplane designed by Aurel Vlaicu in Romania. This date is still celebrated as National Aviation Day in Romania.

Zeppelin LZ 7 *Deutschland*, operated by the airline Delag, begins passenger services between Frankfurt, Baden-Baden and Düsseldorf.

**June 24** A.V. Roe flies his *Roe III*. This represents an advanced triplane design. Four are built; three are powered by 35hp (26kW) Green engines and all introduce trailing-edge ailerons, tail unit elevators and large-area rudders.

LZ 7 *Deutschland* makes a commercial return flight between Essen, Bochum and Dortmund, carrying 32 passengers.

**June 28** LZ 7 *Deutschland* is wrecked in a gale at Teutoburger Wald but all 20 passengers survive.

**June 30** American Glenn Hammond Curtiss drops dummy bombs on the shape of a battleship marked out on Lake Keuka.

**July 10** Walter Brookins becomes the first pilot to fly at an altitude of more than one mile. His flight at Indianapolis, U.S.A., is in a Wright biplane. The actual height achieved is 6,234ft (1,900m).

**July 13** Five people die when a German Erbslön non-rigid dirigible explodes near Opladen. It was powered by a 28hp (21kW) Benz engine.

**July 24** German August Euler patents an aeroplane/fixed machine-gun armament arrangement, which he later demonstrates on his biplane *Gelber Hund*. (Prior to the start of the First World War another German named Franz Schneider produces the first synchronized gun arrangement for an aeroplane.)

**July 31** The Bristol Boxkite flies for the first time.

**August** Harry Ferguson carries a woman passenger (Rita Marr) in his aeroplane, the first passenger flight performed in Ireland.

**August 10** Claude Grahame-White attempts to carry mail in his Blériot monoplane from Squires Gate, Blackpool, to Southport, but lands short.

**August 17** Franco-American John Moisant's mechanic becomes the first passenger to fly across the English Channel (Blériot monoplane).

**August 20** Lt. Jacob Earl Fickel, U.S. Army, fires his Springfield rifle from the passenger seat of a Curtiss biplane at a target at Sheepshead Bay, New York State.

**August 27** American James McCurdy transmits and receives radio messages between his Curtiss biplane and the ground.

**September 2** Blanche Scott becomes the first American woman pilot to fly solo.

**September 8** The first recorded air collision takes place between aircraft flown by two brothers named Warchalovski in Austria.

**September 11** Robert Loraine flies a Farman biplane from Holyhead to the coast of Howth, making the first recognized aeroplane flight across the Irish Sea. During the flight his engine cut out on six occasions and he actually failed to reach the Irish coast by a few hundred metres.

**September 14** Zeppelin LZ 6 is destroyed by fire at its hangar at Boden-Oos.

**September 23** Peruvian Georges Chavez flies a Blériot monoplane over the Alps from Brig to Domodossola but is killed when he crash-lands.

**October 2** The first properly recorded mid-air collision between two aeroplanes happens at Milan when a Henry Farman biplane piloted by Englishman Capt. Bertram Dickson is struck by an Antoinette flown by H. Thomas. Both pilots survive the accident. Dickson is also remembered as the first to fly an aeroplane with a passenger for two hours, on June 6, 1910.

**October 22** The Aéronautique Militaire is formed from the French Service Aéronautique.

**October 28** M. Tabuteau, flying a Maurice Farman biplane at Étampes, France, sets up a distance in a closed circuit record of 289.38 miles (465.72km). The supremacy in performance of the Wright biplanes is at an end.

**October 29** Claude Grahame-White wins the first Gordon Bennett international air race.

**November 4** Briton E.T. Willows makes the first airship flight from England to France in his *Willows III*.

**November 7** Philip O. Parmalee pilots a Wright Model B biplane on the world's first freight-carrying flight, transporting 542yds (495m) of silk between Dayton and Columbus, Ohio, for the Morehouse-Martens Company. The flight costs the company $5,000.

**November 14** American Eugene B. Ely becomes the first man to fly an aeroplane from a ship when he takes off in his Curtiss Hudson Flier from the 83ft (25m) platform constructed over the bows of the anchored U.S. Navy cruiser U.S.S. *Birmingham*.

**December 10** Romanian Henri Coanda 'hops' the world's first jet-powered aeroplane. It is powered by a 50hp (27.25kW) Clerget piston engine driving a centrifugal air compressor.

**December 18** Thomas O.M. Sopwith makes a flight of 177m (285km) to win the Baron de Forest Prize of £4,000. His flight is from Eastchurch, England to Beaumont, Belgium, the longest straight-line flight into Europe by a British pilot in a British aeroplane in 1910. His aircraft is a modified Howard Wright biplane.

**1911**

**January 7** Lt. Myron S. Crissy, U.S. Army, drops a live bomb on a target in San Francisco from a Wright biplane piloted by Philip Parmalee.

**January 18** Eugene B. Ely becomes the first man to land an aeroplane on a ship when he lands his Curtiss pusher on the 119ft (36m) platform constructed on the stern of the anchored cruiser U.S.S. *Pennsylvania*.

**January 26** Glenn Curtiss takes off in his hydroaeroplane and then alights on the water of San Diego Harbor, performs taxi manoeuvres and takes off again. (q.v. February 17, 1911)

**February 5** Vivian Walsh makes the first aeroplane flight in New Zealand.

**February 7** The first French military flying certificate is awarded to Lt. de Rose.

**February 17** Glenn Curtiss flies his seaplane to U.S.S. *Pennsylvania* in San Diego Bay, taxis alongside and is hoisted on board by crane. He is subsequently returned to the water and flies back to land.

**February 18** Henri Pequet flies his Humber biplane from Allahabad to Naini Junction, India, on the first official airmail flight.

**February 22** Pequet and Captain W.G. Windham begin a regular airmail service between Allahabad and Naini Junction to coincide with the Universal Postal Exhibition being held in Allahabad. The special envelopes carried are marked First Aerial Post.

**March 2** Four Royal Navy officers begin flying training at Eastchurch, Isle of Sheppey, Kent, England.

**March 3** Philip Parmalee and passenger Lt. B. Foulois fly from Laredo on the Mexico/Texas border to Eagle Pass, Texas. During the course of the flight they receive radio messages and drop written messages to Army units.

**March 17** The Curtiss D pusher-engined biplane with a tricycle landing gear is demonstrated to the U.S. Army. It subsequently becomes the Army Aeroplane No. 2.

**March 23** Louis Bréguet carries 11 passengers for a distance of 3.1 miles (5km) in a huge parasol-winged monoplane of his own design.

**March 24** Roger Sommer carries 12 passengers on a flight covering 2,625ft (800m) in an aircraft of his own design.

**April 12** Pierre Prier flies his Blériot monoplane from Hendon, London, to Issy-les-Moulineaux, Paris, non-stop in 3 hrs 56 mins.

**May** The British Army receives a Bristol Boxkite for army co-operation duties, following trials during manoeuvres.

**May 16** Delag passenger-carrying airship Zeppelin LZ 8 *Ersatz Deutschland* is wrecked while docking but there are no casualties. (LZ 8 had entered service in March 1911.)

**June 18** The Circuit of Europe air race begins. It is won on July 7 by Lt. de Vaisseau Conneau in a Blériot monoplane. The race starts and finishes in Paris.

**July 1** The first U.S. Navy aeroplane, a Curtiss A-1 Triad hydroaeroplane, is flown.

**July 4** Horatio Barber is paid £100 by the General Electric Company to carry a box of Osram lamps in his Valkyrie monoplane from Shoreham to Hove and thus completes the first air cargo flight in the U.K.

**July 22** The *Daily Mail* newspaper £10,000, five-day 'Round Britain' air race starts at Brooklands. It is eventually won by Lt. de

Vaisseau Conneau, French Navy, flying a Blériot XI monoplane.

**August 2** Harriet Quimby gains her licence to become the first American woman pilot.

**August 3** A Voisin biplane takes off from the airfield at Issy-les-Moulineaux and alights on the river Seine using the aircraft's amphibious landing gear, thereafter returning to Issy.

**August 18** The Royal Aircraft Factory F.E.2 pusher-engined biplane flies for the first time. Designed by Geoffrey de Havilland, this forms the general configuration for the wartime F.E.2a/b/c/d fighters and bombers.

**September 9** British-born Gustav Hamel, flying a Blériot XI monoplane, makes the initial flight of the first official airmail service in Great Britain, from Hendon to Windsor, under the auspices of the Blériot and Grahame-White flying schools. The service lasts until September 26.

**September 17–November 5** The first coast-to-coast flight across the U.S.A. is made by Calbraith P. Rodgers in a Burgess-Wright aeroplane, between New York and Pasadena.

**September 19** The first Italian airmail service starts between Bologna, Venice and Rimini.

**September 23** Earle L. Ovington carries the first official consignment of airmail in the U.S.A., flying in a Blériot-type monoplane (known as a Queen monoplane) from Nassau Boulevard, Mineola, Long Island. He is made Air Mail Pilot No. 1 by Postmaster-General Hitchcock.

**September 24** Britain's first rigid airship, the R1 *Mayfly*, is destroyed in an accident before making a flight.

**September 26** Britain's first airmail service is suspended.

**October 22** Capitano Piazza, Italian Air Flotilla, flies a Blériot monoplane from Tripoli to Azizia to make a reconnaissance of the Turkish forces. This is the first use of an aeroplane in war.

**November 1** 2nd Lt. Giulio Gavotti, Italian Air Flotilla, drops Cipelli grenades on Turkish forces at Taguira Oasis and Ain Zara. This is the first time that bombs have been dropped from an aeroplane in war.

**November 18** Cmdr. Oliver Schwann performs the first take-off from water in Britain.

**December** A naval flying school is formed at Eastchurch, Kent, England.

**December 27** The Royal Aircraft Factory B.E.1 two-seater flies for the first time. From it is developed the wartime B.E.2 reconnaissance biplane.

**1912**

The U.S. Army purchases six Burgess Model H biplane trainers. These are its first aeroplanes with tractor-mounted engines. Burgess also builds under licence (four years later) two British Dunne swept-wing and tailless seaplanes for the U.S. Navy on which

that service carries out its initial air-gunnery experiments.

Frenchmen Ponche and Primard fly the world's first all-metal aeroplane, the Tubavion monoplane.

**January 10** Lt. Charles Rumney Samson takes off in the Short S.38 from a specially-built wooden platform on board the battleship H.M.S. *Africa*.

Glenn Curtiss makes a flight in the first flying-boat proper, a converted Curtiss A-2.

**February 17** French military aircraft make their first flights in Algeria.

**March** The German Aviation Experimental Establishment (DVL) is founded at Berlin-Adlershof.

The first competition for seaplanes is held at Monaco.

The French government orders Blériot monoplanes to be grounded while investigations are made into the structural failures of several machines. Louis Blériot instigates the inquiry, which boosts his reputation. The ban lasts just two weeks.

**March 1** Capt. Albert Berry makes the first parachute jump from an aeroplane (Benoist) in the U.S.A., descending over Jefferson Barracks, St. Louis.

**March 12** The French Service de L'Aéronautique de la Marine is formed.

**March 15** The newly-formed Turkish Army Aviation Section receives its first two French-built aircraft at Yesilköy.

**April 16** American Harriet Quimby flies the English Channel in a Blériot monoplane, taking off from Deal and landing at Cap Gris-Nez.

**April 22** Englishman Denys Corbett Wilson flies the St. Georges Channel, recording the first aeroplane crossing between England (London) and Ireland (Co. Wexford). (q.v. September 11, 1910)

**May 1** A.V. Roe flies the Avro Type F, the first monoplane with a fully-enclosed cabin for the pilot.

**May 9** Cmdr. Samson of the Royal Navy becomes the first man to take off from a moving ship when he flies a Short pusher amphibian from the battleship H.M.S. *Hibernia* during the Naval Review off Portland.

**May 13** The Royal Flying Corps is officially inaugurated in Great Britain, initially comprising one airship and man-carrying kite squadron and two aeroplane squadrons.

**May 30** Pioneer aviator Wilbur Wright dies of typhoid fever.

**June** The new Royal Aircraft Factory B.E.2 two-seat observation biplane sets up a British altitude record of 10,560ft (3,219m) over Salisbury Plain.

**June 7** Capt. Charles de Forest Chandler, U.S. Army Signal Corps, fires a Lewis machine-gun from a Wright Model B biplane being piloted by Lt. Thomas de Witt Milling, the first occasion a gun had been fired from an aeroplane.

**June 10** Airships *Schwaben* and *Gelber Hund* are used to carry the first German airmail between Darmstadt and Frankffurt/Main. The experimental service lasts just 12 days.

**June 19** The Central Flying School is established at Upavon, England.

**June 21** Tina Broadwick becomes the first American woman to make a parachute descent in the U.S.A.

**June 27** The Italian Aviation Service is formed from the Battaglione Aviatori.

**June 28** Delag passenger-carrying airship Zeppelin LZ 10 *Schwaben* is destroyed by fire while in its shed.

**July 31** Lt. T.G. Ellyson is catapult-launched in an aeroplane from a wall platform at Annapolis, U.S.A. This follows an earlier launch in September 1911 from a ground platform.

**August** The first British military aeroplane trials are held. The prize in the speed competition (considered the most important) is won by Cody in his primitive but highly powered *Cathedral*, although more advanced aircraft are displayed.

**August 10** F.K. McClean flies under the Thames bridges in London in a Short S.33 pusher biplane.

U.S. Army Signal Corps aeroplanes fly during Army manoeuvres for the first time

**August 25** Lt. Wilfred Parke, Royal Navy, makes the first recorded recovery from a spin while flying an Avro biplane.

**September** The Australian Army Aviation Corps is formed.

**September 19** Zeppelin LZ 13 *Hansa*, operated by Delag, starts the world's first international commercial service by an airship, flying between Hamburg, Copenhagen and Malmö.

**October 1** The Military Aviation Service is formed in Germany. It is disbanded in 1919.

**October 26** American Lt. John H. Towers begins trials to determine the aeroplane's capability for anti-submarine warfare. (q.v. May 8, 1919)

**November 12** A Curtiss A-l Triad hydroaeroplane, piloted by Lt. T. Ellyson, becomes the first aeroplane to be successfully catapult-launched from an anchored ship, at Washington Navy Yard.

**November 19** The Italian Servizio d'Aviazione Coloniale is formed.

The British Admiralty awards Vickers a contract to design and build a prototype fighting aeroplane, which becomes the E.F.B.I. (q.v. February 1913)

**November 27** A Curtiss F two-seat biplane becomes the U.S. Army Signal Corps' first flying boat. The Army eventually purchases three, and others are built for the Navy and private pilots.

**November 28** Flotta Aerea d'Italia is formed.

**December 5** Frenchman Jacques Schneider announces his intention to sponsor an international competition to encourage the development of seaplanes.

## 1913

The Serbian Military Air Service is formed.

Americans Lawrence Sperry and Lt. Bellinger demonstrate the world's first gyroscopic automatic stabilizer in a Curtiss F flying-boat.

A German engineer named Schneider submits a patent application for his original synchronization mechanism for a fixed machine-gun installation.

The Oberursel engine works in Germany acquires a licence to build French Gnome rotary aero engines.

The first armed aircraft to be built in Russia flies as the Dux 1. This pusher-engined biplane carries a machine-gun in the nose for ground attack.

**January** The Australian Flying Corps is formed.

**February** Vickers Ltd. displays the Destroyer E.F.B.I. armed biplane fighter at the Olympia Air Show, England.

**March** Russian-born Igor Sikorsky produces his twin-engined *Bolshoi Bal'tisky* (The Great Baltic) or Grand RBVZ, which makes its first flight early this month.

**March 5** The 1st Aero Squadron, U.S. Army, is formed.

**April 16** Compagnie des Aviateurs is formed in Belgium from the previous Balloon Company.

The first Schneider Trophy race, contested over 28 10-km circuits, is held at the Monaco seaplane meeting. It is won by Maurice Prévost in a Deperdussin, at an average speed of 45.75mph (73.63km/h).

**April 16–17** Lt. R. Cholmondeley of No. 3 Squadron, makes the first night flight by a pilot of the R.F.C.

**April 17** Gustav Hamel makes the first non-stop flight by aeroplane from England to Germany, taking 4 hrs 18 mins to fly his Blériot XI from Dover to Cologne.

**May 10** Didier Masson, supporter of General Alvarado Obregon, drops bombs from an aeroplane on Mexican Government gunships in Guaymas Bay.

**May 13** Igor Sikorsky makes the first flight in the world's first four-engined aeroplane, *Le Grand* (*Russky Vityaz* or Russian Knight). This was not merely the Bolshoi Bal'tisky with two extra engines, as sometimes thought, but a new aircraft with four engines in tandem pairs. The first flight lasts less than ten minutes.

However, the engine arrangement does not prove satisfactory and in June *Le Grand* is modified to have all four engines mounted in tractor configuration.

**May 17** Domingo Rosillo flies a French Morane-Saulnier monoplane from Key West, Florida, to Havana, Cuba.

**June 21** Georgia Broadwick becomes the first woman to descend by parachute from an aeroplane when she jumps over Los Angeles.

**August 2** The Sikorsky *Le Grand* (*Russky Vityaz*) makes a flight of 1 hr 54 mins with eight passengers on board.

**August 7** One of Britain's most famous pioneer aviators, Samuel Cody, is killed in a crash on Laffan's Plain, Farnborough, England.

**August 16** The *Daily Mail* Hydro-Aeroplane Trial for seaplanes begins, the competitors setting out to fly 1,540 miles (2,478km) around the United Kingdom. Only Harry Hawker starts the journey, which has to be completed by August 30 and flown in a British aeroplane, but crashes near Dublin. He receives a consolation prize of £1,000.

**August 27** Lt. Nesterov, Imperial Russian Army, flying a Nieuport Type IV monoplane over Kiev, performs the first loop.

**September 2** Four aircraft of No. 2 Squadron make the first sea crossing by the Royal Flying Corps, when they fly to the Rathbane Camp, County Limerick, for manoeuvres.

**September 9** Zeppelin LZ 14 (L 1), the first German Navy airship, crashes into the North Sea off Heligoland and most of the crew of 20 are killed.

**September 18** The prototype Avro 504 reconnaissance biplane flies for the first time. It competes in the 1913 Aerial Derby two days later.

**September 21** Adolphe Pégoud deliberately flies his Blériot monoplane upside down, so making the first sustained inverted flight.

**September 23** Roland Garros makes the first crossing of the Mediterranean by air, flying his Morane-Saulnier monoplane from Saint-Raphaël to Bizerte, Tunisia.

**September 29** Flying the Deperdussin 'monocoque' (1913) at Reims, Maurice Prévost manages to set the first over 200km/h speed record. He achieves 203.850km/h (126.666mph), the last speed record before the First World War.

**October 13** Seguin and Farman (France) fly 634 miles (1,021km), establishing the last international distance record before the First World War.

**October 17** Zeppelin LZ 18 (L 2) burns while airborne at Johannisthal and there are no survivors from a crew of 28.

**November** Mexico becomes the scene of the first-ever aerial combat, when an aeroplane flown by Dean Ivan Lamb for the army of Venustiano Carranza exchanges handgun shots with an aeroplane flown by Phillip Rader for General Huerta.

**November 29–December 29** Frenchman Jules Védrines makes the first flight from France to Egypt. His aeroplane is a Blériot monoplane.

**December 28** Georges Legagneux sets the first altitude record for aeroplanes of more than 20,000ft, attaining 20,079ft (6,120m) in a Nieuport Type IIN at St. Raphaël, France.

## 1914

The second Schneider Trophy contest is flown at Monaco. It is won by Briton C. Howard Pixton flying a modified Sopwith Tabloid at an average speed of 86.75mph (139.66km/h).

**January** The first U.S. Navy air station is established at Pensacola.

First flight is made of the four-engined Sikorsky *Ilya Mourometz*, the first of a series of reconnaissance-bombers built under the same name.

**January 1** Anthony Jannus of the Benoist Company flies a passenger from St. Petersburg to Tampa, Florida, in a Benoist flying-boat, completing the first scheduled service by an airline using aeroplanes.

**February 12** The first Russian *Ilya Mourometz* giant biplane carries 16 passengers and a dog to a height of 6,560ft (2,000m), setting a world load-to-altitude record.

**February 23** The prototype of the Bristol Scout single-seat biplane flies. Well ahead of its time in respect of design, the 'Baby Biplane' (as it is sometimes called) is capable of 95mph (153km/h). The improved Scout D production aircraft of 1916 carries a synchronized Vickers machine-gun.

**April** The Fokker M.5K appears. It becomes the forerunner of the famous Fokker Eindecker fighter.

**April 25** Lt. P.N.L. Bellinger makes the first American operational sortie by aeroplane when he searches for sea mines during the Vera Cruz incident. (A total of five Curtiss AB flying-boats are involved in this operation, flying from the battleship U.S.S. *Mississippi* and cruiser U.S.S. *Birmingham* and operating on 43 consecutive days.)

**May 6** Lt. P.N.L. Bellinger's Curtiss AB flying-boat is hit by rifle fire while on a reconnaissance flight during the Vera Cruz incident, making it the first U.S. military aircraft to be struck by enemy gunfire.

**May 9** W. Newell becomes the first person to descend by parachute from an aeroplane in the U.K.

**May 28** The full-size and restored Langley *Aerodrome* is flown briefly at Hammondsport by Glenn Curtiss, having been modified into a seaplane in order to help the Curtiss Company fight an injunction placed by the Wright Aeronautical Company over patents. A longer flight is achieved on October 25.

**July** R. Böhm (Germany), flying an Albatros B.I, remains airborne for 24 hrs 12 mins, establishing the last international flight endurance record before the First World War. H. Oelerich (Germany), flying a DFW B.I, reaches an altitude of 26,740ft (8,150m), establishing the last international altitude record before the First World War.

**July 1** The Naval Wing of the Royal Flying Corps separates and eventually forms the basis of the Royal Naval Air Service (R.N.A.S.).

**July 7** In the U.S.A. Dr. Robert H. Goddard receives a patent for his two-stage rocket that burns solid fuel.

**July 18** The Aviation Section of the U.S. Army Signal Corps is formed.

**July 27** Short brothers' test pilot Gordon Bell becomes the first pilot to drop a standard naval torpedo from an aeroplane, releasing a 14in (35.5cm) torpedo from a Short tractor seaplane.

**July 28** Sqdn. Cmdr. A. Longmore becomes the first Royal Navy pilot to drop a standard naval torpedo from an aeroplane when he releases a 14in (35.5cm) torpedo from a Short tractor seaplane.

**July 30** Norwegian Tryggve Gran makes the first flight across the North Sea by aeroplane (Blériot monoplane).

**August 1** France requisitions 50 Morane-Saulnier two-seat Parasols destined for export to Turkey. These equip French escadrilles MS 23 and MS 26.

**August 2** German military forces invade Luxembourg and the First World War begins in earnest.

**August 3** German forces invade Belgium after permission for free passage of its troops through Belgian territory had been denied.

**August 4** Great Britain declares war on Germany after refusing German requests to approve its forces entering Belgium. At midnight war is declared after Germany fails to guarantee Belgian neutrality.

**August 8** The observer of a French aircraft flown on a reconnaissance flight by Sadi Lecointe is wounded by a German rifleman, the first French casualty of the air war.

**August 11** R.F.C. personnel leave Southampton for Amiens, to prepare for the arrival of R.F.C. aircraft a few days later.

**August 12** Oberleutnant Reinhold Jahnow, German Air Service, is the first German airman to lose his life on active service. He is killed at Malmédy, Belgium.

2nd Lt. R. Skene and R. Barlow of No. 3 Squadron become the first members of the R.F.C. to be killed while on active service. They crash their Blériot monoplane while flying to Dover for the crossing to France by the first British warplanes.

Sgt. Bridou becomes the first French aviator to be killed in action when he has an accident while returning from a reconnaissance mission.

**August 13** Nos. 2, 3, 4 and 5 squadrons, R.F.C., begin crossing the English Channel to France. The first aircraft to land is a Royal Aircraft Factory B.E.2a, piloted by Lt. H.D. Harvey-Kelly.

**August 14** Lt. Cesari and Corporal Prudhommeau, French Air Force, attack the Zeppelin sheds at Metz-Frescaty.

**August 19** Lt. G. Mapplebeck, flying a Royal Aircraft Factory B.E.2a, and Capt. P. Joubert de la Ferté, flying a Blériot monoplane, carry out the first R.F.C. reconnaissance flight over German positions.

**August 22** R.F.C. aeroplanes on reconnaissance duty locate von Kluck's forces as they advance through Belgium.

Lt. V. Waterfall, R.F.C., is the first British airman to be shot down, when his Avro 504 is hit by rifle fire over Belgium.

**August 23** Zeppelins LZ 22 (ZVII) and LZ 23 (ZVIII) are shot down.

**August 24** French airship *Dupuy-de-Lôme* is shot down mistakenly by French ground troops.

**August 25** Lt. H.D. Harvey-Kelly and two other R.F.C. pilots flying unarmed aircraft force a German two-seat reconnaissance aircraft to land.

**August 26** Staff Capt. P.N. Nesterov, Imperial Russian Army, brings down an Austrian aircraft flown by Leutnant Baron von

Rosenthal by ramming it with his unarmed Morane Type M monoplane. The Austrian aeroplane had been attacking Nesterov's airfield at Sholkiv. Both Nesterov and von Rosenthal are killed.

**August 27** Wing Cmdr. C.R. Samson heads the first R.N.A.S. squadron to fly to France. The Eastchurch Squadron comprises a mixture of ten aeroplanes, including Sopwith Tabloids, Royal Aircraft Factory B.E.2s, Blériot monoplanes, a Short seaplane, Bristol and Farman biplanes, and the Astra-Torres No. 3 airship.

**August 30** Paris is bombed for the first time by a German Rumpler Taube monoplane flown by Lt. Ferdinand von Hiddeson. The five bombs, dropped near the Gare de l'Est railway terminal, Quai de Valmy, kill a woman and injure two others.

**September 22** Four aircraft of the Eastchurch Squadron, R.N.A.S., attack German airship sheds at Düsseldorf and Cologne. Only the three 20-lb (9-kg) Hales bombs dropped by Flt. Lt. Collet hit a shed (at Düsseldorf) but do not explode.

**September 27** The first French bomber *groupe* is formed, equipped with Voisin 'Chicken Coop' biplanes.

**October** The French Aéronautique Militaire has expanded to 34 escadrilles, by far the largest air arm in the world.

**October 5** Sgt. Joseph Frantz and Caporal Quénault, French Air Force, shoot down a

German Aviatik two-seater over Reims, with the machine-gun fitted to their Voisin biplane.

**October 8** Sqdn. Cdr. D.A. Spenser-Grey and Flt. Lt. R.L.G. Marix, Eastchurch Squadron, R.N.A.S., take off to make a second attack on the airship sheds at Düsseldorf and Cologne. Spenser-Grey attacks Cologne railway station instead, but Marix hits and destroys a shed at Düsseldorf and Zeppelin LZ 25 (Z IX) inside. Marix is shot down on the return flight to Antwerp but returns safely to his squadron by road.

**November 21** Three Avro 504s of the R.N.A.S. attack the Zeppelin sheds at Friedrichshafen. Each aircraft carries four 20lb (9kg) Hales bombs. One Zeppelin (LZ 32/L7) is badly damaged in its shed and the associated gasworks is blown up. This is the first-ever strategic bombing raid by a formation of aircraft.

**December 6** The German Navy seaplane unit, formed two days earlier, begins operations from its new base at Zeebrugge.

**December 10** Formation date of the Russian Army 'Flotilla of Flying Ships' (EVK), equipped with the first Ilya Mourometz long-range multi-engined reconnaissance-bombers. From then on all IM series aircraft are sent to this unit which, in time, comprise some 40-50 aircraft.

**December 16** Two U.S. Army lieutenants demonstrate two-way radio between the ground and an aeroplane. The aeroplane used is a Burgess-Wright.

**December 21** A German aeroplane, probably a Taube monoplane, makes the first air attack on Britain, dropping two bombs into the sea off Admiralty Pier, Dover.

**December 24** A bomb dropped from a German aeroplane explodes near Dover Castle.

**December 25** Seven R.N.A.S. seaplanes are launched from seaplane carriers H.M.S. *Empress*, *Engadine* and *Riviera* from a position north of Heligoland to attack the Zeppelin sheds at Cuxhaven.

## 1915

**January** Sikorsky S-16 two-seat armed biplanes appear, the first Russian aircraft designed specifically for aerial combat. Early examples are sent in March to the EVK unit operating Ilya Mourometz reconnaissance-bombers, for experimental trials. The synchronized machine-gun proves troublesome.

**January 6** A German Navy Friedrichshafen FF29a coastal patrol seaplane is launched from a submarine in trials to extend the aircraft's range.

**January 19** Two German Navy Zeppelins, LZ 24/L 3 and LZ 27/L 4 (LZ 31/L 6 returns early because of engine trouble), make the first airship raid on Great Britain, having taken off from Fuhlsbüttel and Nordholz. L 3 drops bombs on Great Yarmouth, while L 4 drops incendiary and high-explosive bombs on Sheringham, Thornham, Brancaster, Hunstanton, Heacham, Snettisham and King's

Lynn. Several British civilians are killed or injured in the raids.

**January 23** Reconnaissance aircraft spot Turkish forces massing for an attack on the Suez Canal area.

**February** The Russian Ilya Mourometz IM-V series four-engined reconnaissance-bombers are armed with three machine-guns, mainly for use against ground targets.

Armed Vickers F.B.5 'Gun Bus' pusher biplane fighters enter service on the Western Front.

**February 15** Sikorsky Ilya Mourometz reconnaissance-bombers attack targets in the Vistula-Dobrzhani area, Poland.

**February 17** Zeppelin LZ 24 (L 3) is stranded and destroyed on the coast of Jutland during a gale.

H.M.S. *Ark Royal* arrives off the Dardanelles and launches a seaplane to make a reconnaissance of Turkish ground forces. *Ark Royal* was designed as a merchant ship but converted in late 1914 to carry seaplanes, the first ship to be converted for this role,

**March 3** The U.S. National Advisory Committee for Aeronautics (NACA) is founded.

**March 5** Zeppelin LZ 33 (L 8) crashes near Ostend after being hit by gunfire over Nieuport during a mission to attack England.

**March 7** German Zeppelins raid Paris and its suburbs.

**March 10** British aircraft bomb railway targets in Menin and Courtrai to prevent reinforcements from reaching German front-line positions.

**March 31** Probably the first helicopter test from water takes place on Lake Cercey, France. The work of Frenchmen Papin and Rouilly, this pressure-jet machine has a single hollow rotor blade that is driven by air produced from a 80hp (59.7kW) Le Rhône engine-driven fan. In the trials, it oscillates and sinks.

**April 1** Lt. Roland Garros shoots down a German Albatros two-seater with the Hotchkiss machine-gun fitted to his Morane-Saulnier Type L monoplane. Steel wedge deflectors attached to the propeller protect the blades from damage as bullets pass through the turning propeller arc.

**April 11** The first flight of the Zeppelin V.G.O.I. prototype giant bomber is made at the hired Gotha works. This becomes the Zeppelin Staaken R.I., the first of 32 R-series bombers built by Zeppelin Staaken during the First World War.

**April 16** Lt. P.N.L. Bellinger in a U.S. Navy AB-2 flying-boat is catapult-launched from a barge. This follows earlier ground and wall experiments.

**April 19** Lt. Garros is forced down behind enemy lines and the details of the machine-gun arrangement on his Morane-Saulnier are studied by the Germans.

**April 26** Second Lt. W.B. Rhodes-Moorhouse, R.F.C., is killed after making a low-level bombing attack on the railway station at Courtrai in a Royal Aircraft Factory B.E.2c. He is posthumously awarded the Victoria Cross.

**April 30** German Navy Zeppelin L 9, commanded by Kapitänltn Mathys, attacks three British submarines within three hours, damaging the conning tower of one (D4).

**May 11** The German High Command orders continuous airship raids on England to bomb the country into submission.

**May 26** Seventeen French Voisin biplanes of Groupe de Bombardement I attack a strategic military target at Ludwigshafen, near Mannheim.

A Halberstadt C-type flown by Oberleutnant Kästner, and with Leutnant Georg Langhoff as observer/gunner, makes the first intended German air attack on another armed aircraft, the latter a French Voisin making an armed reconnaissance flight over the airfield at Douai. The Voisin is shot down but the crew survive.

**May 27** An Austrian Löhner L.l flying-boat is captured off the Italian coast. The Italian company Società Anonima Nieuport-Macchi produces a similar aircraft, which starts the company in the flying-boat business.

**May 31** Zeppelin LZ 38 makes the first bombing raid on London, killing seven civilians and injuring 14.

**June** René Paul Fonck, later to become the highest-scoring Allied pilot of the First World War, joins Escadrille C47 to fly Caudron G.IV bombing and reconnaissance aircraft.

**June 1** The prototype Airco (de Havilland) D.H.2 makes its maiden flight. In production form, the pusher-engined D.H.2 becomes the R.F.C.'s first true single-seat fighter and helps end the 'Fokker Scourge'.

**June 6/7** Flt. Sub-Lt. R.A.J. Warneford of No. 1 Squadron, R.N.A.S., wins the Victoria Cross when he destroys Zeppelin LZ 37. Warneford flies his Morane-Saulnier Parasol monoplane above LZ 37 and drops six 20lb (9kg) Hales bombs on the airship, the last exploding and causing it to fall at Ghent.

**June 17** Flt. Sub-Lt. Warneford VC is killed near Paris when the tail of the Farman biplane he is flying collapses in mid-air. His passenger, American journalist H. Needham, is also killed.

**July** German Fokker E.I 'Eindecker' monoplane fighters arrive on the Western Front for operational trials. These are the first purpose-prepared fighters with reliable synchronized machine-guns, able to fire through the propeller arc. They are flown by a small number of pilots from Douai airfield.

**July 1** Leutnant Kurt Wintgens destroys a French Morane-Saulnier monoplane while flying a Fokker M.5K reconnaissance monoplane fitted with a machine-gun with synchronization gear.

**July 19** Georges Marie Ludovic Jules Guynemer, destined to become the second highest-scoring French pilot of the First World War, gains his first aerial victory while flying a two-seat Morane-Saulnier Parasol monoplane.

**July 25** Major L.G. Hawker, R.F.C., gains victories over three armed German two-seat Albatros biplanes, while flying a Bristol Scout C armed only with a hastily fitted cavalry carbine mounted at an angle to fire outside the propeller arc.

**July 30** Leutnant Max Immelmann flies a Fokker M.8 in preparation for his first flight in an armed E.I Eindecker fighter the next day.

**August** A French strategic bomber escadrille at Malzeville is disbanded following the loss of nine aircraft from a similar escadrille to Fokker Eindeckers on August 2.

**August 1** Leutnant Max Immelmann, soon known as 'The Eagle of Lille', gains his first aerial victory by shooting down an enemy aircraft while flying a Fokker E.I monoplane.

**August 6** German Navy Zeppelin LZ 28 (L 5) has to make a forced landing in Russia after being hit by groundfire.

**August 10** German Navy Zeppelin LZ 43 (L 12) is damaged while on a raid over England. It is towed back to Ostend but is accidentally destroyed.

**August 12** Flt. Cmdr. C.H. Edmonds, R.N.A.S., flying a Short 184 seaplane from the seaplane carrier H.M.S. *Ben-My-Chree*, makes the first air attack with a torpedo (14 inch Whitehead torpedo, launched at just 15ft/4.5m above sea level) and sinks a 5,000-ton Turkish supply ship in the Sea of Marmara during the Dardanelles campaign.

**August 17** Flt. Cmdr. Edmonds sinks a second Turkish ship off the Dardanelles with a torpedo. Flt. Lt. G.B. Dacre, from H.M.S. *Ben-My-Chree*, also sinks a Turkish boat while flying a Short 184 type (No. 185), using a torpedo released from his aircraft while taxiing on the water.

**August 19** Col. Hugh Trenchard takes command of the R.F.C. in France.

**August 20** Italian Caproni Ca.2 triple-engined biplanes begin the first sustained bombing offensive against Austria-Hungary.

**August 23** Capt. A.J. Liddell, R.F.C., is awarded the Victoria Cross for valour while flying a Royal Aircraft Factory R.E.5.

**August 24** Maj. L.G. Hawker, R.F.C., receives the Victoria Cross for valour while flying a Bristol Scout. (q.v. July 25, 1915)

**September** The improved Fokker E.II monoplane fighter enters service, followed by the E.III.

**Autumn–Winter** The 'Fokker Scourge' begins and lasts throughout the winter, as Fokker monoplane fighters with synchronized machine-guns shoot down very large numbers of Allied aircraft.

**October** The Bulgarian Army Aviation Corps, disbanded after the Balkan War of 1912–13, is revived.

**October 1** Passenger airship LZ 11 *Viktoria Luise* is wrecked while docking.

**November 3** Flt. Sub-Lt. H.F. Towler, R.N.A.S., takes off in a Bristol Scout C from the seaplane carrier H.M.S. *Vindex* during launching experiments, subsequently ditching in the sea. This is the first occasion an aeroplane with a wheeled landing gear has taken off from a ship specifically designed as an aircraft (seaplane) carrier.

**November 5** A Curtiss AB-2 flying-boat becomes the first aircraft to be catapult-launched from an anchored American battleship, U.S.S. *North Carolina*, at Pensacola Bay, Florida.

**November 6** A Curtiss AB-2 flying-boat, piloted by Lt. Cmdr. Henry Mustin, is catapult-launched from U.S.S. *North Carolina* while underway. This is the first time an aeroplane has been so launched from a moving ship.

**November 18** German Navy Schütte-Lanz airship SL 6 (D 1) explodes while airborne and all the crew are killed.

**December 12** The Junkers J1 Blechesel (Tin Donkey) all-metal reconnaissance and close-support monoplane flies in Germany.

**December 17** The prototype Handley Page O/100 twin-engined heavy bomber flies for the first time.

**December 23** Lt. G.S.M. Insall, R.F.C., is awarded the Victoria Cross for valour, while flying a Vickers F.B.5.

**Winter 1915–16** Formation of the first Russian Fighter Aviation Detachments.

## 1916

Kampfgeschwader Nr. 1, the first German bomber wing, formed in November 1914 under the cover name Brieftauben Abteilung Ostende (Ostend Carrier Pigeon Detachment), receives Gotha IV bombers.

**January** Blueprints of the Russian Scarff-Dibovski machine-gun synchronization mechanism are sent on request to the British naval aviation authorities. Suitably adapted, this type of synchro-mechanism is later favoured for use on the Sopwith 1½ Strutter and several other fighters.

**January 1** Lt. R.B. Davis, R.N.A.S., is awarded the Victoria Cross for valour while flying a Nieuport fighter.

**January 12** German fighter aces Max Immelmann and Oswald Boelcke receive the Pour le Mérite.

**January 14** The R.F.C. is ordered to escort each reconnaissance aeroplane with a minimum of three fighters because of the Fokker Eindecker menace.

**February** No. 24 Squadron, R.F.C., stationed on the Western Front, is equipped with Airco (de Havilland) D.H.2 pusher-engined fighters.

**February 2** German Navy Zeppelin LZ 54 (L 19) is shot down by British aircraft over the North Sea, following a raid on England.

**February 6** Max Immelmann goes into action for the first time flying a specially-prepared three-gun Fokker E.IV.

**February 21** Zeppelin LZ 47 is attacked during a raid and bursts into flames.

The Battle of Verdun starts. This battle sees the first major use of large formations of fighter planes.

**April 1** German Navy Zeppelin LZ 48 (L 15) is struck by ground fire over England and alights off the coast at Knock Deep, but sinks. All but one of the crew of 18 survive.

**April 20** The Escadrille Américaine is established as an American volunteer unit flying with the French Aéronautique Militaire on the Western Front during the First World War. It later becomes the famed Lafayette Escadrille.

**May** The first American volunteer pilot serving with the French Aéronautique Militaire to receive the Médaille Militaire is Sgt. Maj. E. Cowdin, one of the seven original pilots. The 'American Squadron' had been formed on April 20, equipped with Nieuport 11 'Bébés'.

The prototype Armstrong Whitworth F.K.8 reconnaissance and light bombing biplane appears. No. 35 Squadron, R.F.C., becomes the first to operate the 'Big Ack' on the Western Front, from early 1917.

**May 4** The German Navy Zeppelin LZ 32 (L 7) is shot down by the cruisers H.M.S. *Phaeton* and *Galatea* and is finished off by the British submarine E 31.

**May 17** Experiments with parasite fighters begin with the air-launching of a Bristol Scout from a Porte Baby three-engined flying-boat.

**May 18** Lt. Kiffin Rockwell, a pilot with the Escadrille Américaine, gains his first air victory while on a bomber escort mission near Mulhouse. Rockwell is killed in action on September 23.

**May 22** Capt. Albert Ball gains his first two aerial victories.

**May 28** The prototype Sopwith Triplane 'Tripehound' single-seat fighter flies for the first time. Production Triplanes enter service with the R.N.A.S.

**June 18** Oberleutnant Max Immelmann is killed while flying his Fokker E.III in action against an F.E.2b of No. 25 Squadron crewed by 2nd Lt. McCubbin and Corp. J.H. Waller, R.F.C.

H. Clyde Balsley becomes the first American volunteer pilot serving with the Lafayette Escadrille to be shot down in action, near Verdun. He survives the incident.

**June 23** Victor Emmanuel Chapman, flying with the famous volunteer fighter group Lafayette Escadrille, is the first American pilot to be killed in action when he is shot down near Verdun.

**June 29** The first Boeing-built aeroplane flies as the B & W. Conceived by William Boeing and Commander G. Conrad Westervelt, U.S. Navy, it is a 125hp (93kW) Hall-Scott A-5-engined training and sporting biplane.

**July** No. 3 Wing, R.N.A.S., becomes the first British strategic bombing unit, flying Sopwith 1½ Strutters.

**July 1** The Battle of the Somme begins and both sides fight to gain air superiority. As the battle drags on for weeks and then months, the Allies begin to take control and are able to make successful sorties over enemy positions.

**July 14** The Bristol M.1A monoplane scout flies as a prototype. In its later M.1C form it is ordered in limited numbers and serves in Macedonia and the Middle East but not on the Western Front despite an excellent speed of 130mph (209km/h).

**August** The prototype Airco (de Havilland) D.H.4 day bomber flies for the first time.

**August 2/3** German Army airship Schütte-Lanz SL 11 is shot down over London with no survivors. (q.v. September 5, 1916)

**August 5** Maj. L.W.B. Rees, R.F.C., is awarded the Victoria Cross for valour while flying an Airco D.H.2 fighter.

**August 6** Frenchman Capitaine René Paul Fonck forces down a German Rumpler biplane, his first confirmed victory.

**August 29** The U.S. Naval Flying Corps is formed.

**September** The French Spad VII single-seat fighter enters service and contributes greatly to Allied aerial superiority. It eventually equips squadrons of 11 nations.

The Bristol F.2A Fighter flies. In production form the Fighter goes to the Western Front in April 1917, becoming one of the 'greats' of the war.

**September 5** Lt. William Leefe Robinson, R.F.C., is awarded the Victoria Cross for destroying German airship Schütte-Lanz SL 11 over Cuffley on the night of August 2/3, while flying a B.E.2c. (The destruction of SL 11 had far-reaching effects. It demoralised airship crews and, although not preventing large formations of German airships from attacking England, did stop the expected large-scale raid on London by demonstrating the effectiveness of the defences.)

**September 12** The Hewitt-Sperry radio-guided flying bomb is flight-tested in America. It is powered by a 40hp (29.75kW) engine and carries 308lb (140kg) of explosives.

**September 15** French submarine *Foucault* is sunk by an Austrian Löhner flying-boat.

**September 17** German Albatros D series fighters are flown on their first mission under the command of Oswald Boelcke.

Rittmeister Manfred Frhr. von Richthofen gains his first combat victory, bringing down an F.E.2b of No. 11 Squadron, R.F.C. Richthofen's aircraft is an Albatros D.II.

**September 23/24** Eleven Zeppelin airships raid England, three heading for London. LZ 76 (L 33), on its first mission, is badly damaged by anti-aircraft fire and is forced to land at Little Wigborough. LZ 74 (L 32) is attacked by 2nd Lt. F. Sowrey and catches fire, falling at Great Burstead. There are no survivors.

**September 24** The British Sopwith Pup single-seat biplane fighter claims its first victim, a German LVG two-seat biplane.

**September 26** Hauptmann R. Berthold is awarded the Pour le Mérite.

**October 2** German Navy Zeppelin LZ 72 (L 31) is shot down by British aircraft at Potters Bar, north of London.

**October 5** The first British airline, Aircraft Transport and Travel Limited, is registered in London.

**October 12** Raymond Collishaw gains his first aerial victory. He eventually becomes the highest-scoring R.N.A.S. pilot, with 60 victories.

**October 28** German fighter ace Hauptmann Oswald Boelcke is killed when the wing of his Albatros scout is struck by the undercarriage of another Albatros flown by Leutnant Boehme.

**November** A German Rumpler crewed by Leutnants Falk and Schultheis, operating in support of Turkish forces from Beersheba, drops some light bombs on the Cairo railway station.

Handley Page O/100 heavy biplane bombers enter service with the R.F.C.

**November 21** The prototype Bréguet 14 flies as a two-seat day bomber and reconnaissance biplane. It becomes one of the outstanding aircraft of the First World War.

**November 23** Manfred von Richthofen shoots down Maj. Lanoe G. Hawker, VC, who is flying a D.H.2.

**November 27** German Navy Zeppelin LZ 78 (L 34) is shot down off Hartlepool, England.

**November 28** German Navy Zeppelin LZ 61 (L 21) is shot down by British fighters off Lowestoft.

Deck Offizier R. Brandt, flying an LVG.C.II, drops six bombs near Victoria Station, London.

**December 28** German Navy Zeppelins LZ 53 (L 17) and LZ 69 (L 24) are destroyed after L 24 breaks its back across the entrance to its shed at Tondem and catches fire, igniting L 17 in turn. The same day Schütte-Lanz SL 12 (E 5) is wrecked in its shed.

## 1917

**January 16** Manfred von Richthofen receives the Pour le Mérite. (His brother Lothar receives the decoration the same year.)

**February** The first flight is made of the Junkers J4 armoured close-support biplane, featuring corrugated duralumin skinning. As the J1, it enters service in the late summer of 1917 and 227 are built.

**February 11/12** In the first (unintentional) successful night fighting between aircraft, Leutnants Peter and Frohwein in a DFW C.V shoot down two enemy bombers as they are coming in to land at Malzeville. (The C.V remains in use into 1918 and is extremely successful in reconnaissance and army co-operation roles.)

**February 12** Sgt. T. Mottershead receives the Victoria Cross for valour while flying in a F.E.2d.

**March** First flight of the Caudron R.11 twin-engined three-seat escort fighter. Developed from the Caudron R.4, the R.11 is the first of the French multi-seat fighters and proves quite successful in service.

Royal Aircraft Factory S.E.5 single-seat biplane fighters enter service with the R.F.C. Authority is given to convert the battle-cruiser being built as H.M.S. *Furious* into an aircraft carrier.

An 'AT' remotely controlled pilotless bomber is unsuccessfully tested at the R.F.C.'s flying school, Upavon. The aircraft is a monoplane designed by Geoffrey de Havilland.

**March 6** Airco (de Havilland) D.H.4s arrive in France, first going to No. 55 Squadron, R.F.C.

**March 8** Count Ferdinand von Zeppelin dies, the pioneer designer of large rigid airships.

**March 17** German Navy Zeppelin LZ 86 (L 39) is shot down by anti-aircraft guns over Compiègne, France.

**March 21** No. 100 Squadron, R.F.C., goes to France. It is the first British squadron to be formed for night bombing operations and is equipped with F.E.2b and B.E.2e biplanes.

**March 25** Canadian William Avery Bishop gains his first aerial victory over an Albatros. He ends the war with 72 victories.

**April** Leutnant W. Voss receives the Pour le Mérite.

The first two weeks of 'Bloody April' see the loss of nearly 140 R.F.C. aircraft brought together for an offensive. The main culprit is the German Albatros D.III fighter, which makes short work of several British types (especially the B.E.2c).

**April 5/6** No. 100 Squadron, R.F.C., makes its first raid, hitting Douai airfield. First planned night interception. Leutnant Frankl of Jasta 4, flying an Albatros D.III, shoots down a British B.E.2c of No. 100 Squadron over Quiéry la Motte.

**April 12** The French Aéronautique Militaire receives its first Bréguet 14s for use on the Western Front.

**April 20** The first non-rigid airship to be built for the U.S. Navy flies as the Al (DN-1) at Pensacola, Florida.

**April 26** Boeing Airplane Company is founded out of the Pacific Aero Products Company.

**April 29** U.S. Navy airship Al (DN-I) is abandoned after just three flights.

**May** French escadrilles begin to receive Spad XIII single-seat fighters. The Spad XIII is one of the fastest fighters of the First World War.

The first of two German experimental Link-Hofmann R I giant bombers breaks up in mid-air. It had been built to flight-test the results of wind-tunnel research at the Göttingen laboratory that suggested lift-to-drag ratio advantages for aircraft having the entire interplane gap between the wings filled by the fuselage.

**May 6** Capt. Albert Ball gains his 47th aerial victory, over an Albatros fighter of Jasta 20.

**May 7** Capt. Albert Ball, Britain's first really great fighter ace, dies when he dives his S.E.5 into cloud while chasing a German aircraft. The cause of his death is never established.

Edward 'Mick' Mannock, R.F.C., gains his first aerial victory when he destroys a balloon.

**May 14** German Navy Zeppelin LZ 64 (L 22) is shot down by a British flying-boat and all the crew of 21 are killed.

**May 15** Leutnant H. Gontermann receives the Pour le Mérite.

**May 20** The first German submarine to be sunk by aeroplane (U-36) is destroyed in the North Sea by a large America flying-boat commanded by Flt. Sub-Lt. C.R. Morrish, R.N.A.S.

**May 22** Italian mail services by aeroplane begin with an official military service between Turin and Rome.

**May 25** The first mass bombing raid on England by German aeroplanes takes place during daylight hours. The 21 Gotha bombers, attacking Folkestone, Shorncliffe and elsewhere, kill 95 people and injure 260 more.

**May 31** First defensive success against enemy night bombers over Austro-Hungarian territory: Austrian Linienschiffleutnant G. Banfield flying a Pfalz A.II single-seater forces down an Italian seaplane. For this deed, Banfield is awarded the Maria-Theresa Order which carries with it an hereditary peerage.

**June** The first of the German Staaken R.VI four-engined bombers is delivered to an operational unit.

**June 5** Twenty-two Gotha bombers attack Sheerness, England.

The U.S. Army's First Aeronautic Detachment arrives in France.

**June 8** Lt. F.H. McNamara and Capt. Albert Ball are awarded Victoria Crosses for valour.

**June 13** Fourteen Gotha bombers carry out the first large-scale bombing raid on London, killing 162 people and injuring 432 others in an area around Liverpool Street Station. The casualties of this raid constitute nearly 20 per cent of all British civilians killed or injured in bombing raids by aeroplanes during the 1914-18 war.

Hauptmann Ernst von Brandenburg wins the Pour le Mérite for leading the mass Gotha bombing raids on England.

**June 14** Leutnant K. Allmenröder is awarded the Pour le Mérite.

German Navy Zeppelin LZ 92 (L 43) is shot down over the North Sea by British aeroplanes.

**June 17** German Navy Zeppelin LZ 95 (L 48) is shot down over Suffolk, England, by British aeroplanes.

**June 28** Commercial airmail services in Italy begin with a flight from Naples to Palermo by Società Industrie Meridionali.

**June 30** Lt. Col. William 'Billy' Mitchell takes over as Aviation Officer, American Expeditionary Forces.

**July** The prototype Airco (de Havilland) D.H.9 bomber flies for the first time.

Sopwith Camel single-seat biplane fighters go into action with the R.F.C. for the first time.

**July 7** A mass formation of Gotha and Friedrichshafen bombers of KG 3 based at Ghent attacks London during daylight hours, killing 57 people and injuring many others.

**July 26** Formation date of German Jagdgeschwader Nr. 1 (Jastas Nos. 4, 6, 10 and 11). In action, it soon becomes known to the Allies as the 'Flying Circus' under the command of von Richthofen.

**July 27** A British Airco (de Havilland) D.H.4 two-seat bomber reaches the U.S.A. for evaluation with a Liberty engine. It arrives at the Dayton-Wright Airplane Company plant at Dayton, Ohio, on August 15. The first American-built example is completed in February 1918.

**July 31** The Battle of Ypres begins, with 850 Allied aircraft facing about 600 German aircraft.

**August 2** Sqdn. Cdr. E.H. Dunning lands his Sopwith Pup on the deck of H.M.S. *Furious*, which is steaming at 26 knots, thus making the first aeroplane landing on a moving ship.

**August 7** Sqdn. Cdr. Dunning tries to repeat the deck landing experiment on board H.M.S. *Furious* but stalls and his aircraft is blown over the side. Although he is killed, Dunning has proved that it is possible to land successfully and the Royal Navy goes on to perfect the concept.

**August 8/9** First enemy night bomber is shot down by fighters over Germany, near Frankfurt/Main.

**August 11** Canadian fighter pilot William Avery Bishop, serving with the R.F.C., is awarded the Victoria Cross for valour while flying over an enemy airfield on June 2.

**August 12** Gotha bombers make their last large-scale bombing raid on England during daylight hours, killing or injuring 78 people.

**August 13** The American 1st Aero Squadron leaves for France.

**August 17** The first French mail carried by air is flown between Paris, Le Mans and St-Nazaire. This starts a regular service.

**August 21** German Navy Zeppelin LZ 66 (L 23) is shot down near Jutland by Flt. Sub-Lt. B.A. Smart, who had flown his Sopwith Pup from a platform on board the cruiser H.M.S. *Yarmouth*.

Two new Fokker F.I (Dr. I) triplane fighters arrive at Courtrai, home of von Richthofen's fighter wing. The F.I was designed by Reinhold Platz.

**August 30** Leutnant Werner Voss flies a Fokker F.I (Dr. I) into combat for the first time, shooting down an R.F.C. aircraft.

**September** The prototype Handley Page O/400 heavy bomber flies for the first time.

**September 2/3** Dover receives the first large-scale night bombing raid by Gotha aeroplanes on Great Britain.

**September 3** The American 1st Aero Squadron arrives in France.

Brigadier-Gen. William L. Kenly becomes the first Chief of Air Service, American Expeditionary Force.

**September 5** An Airco (de Havilland) D.H.4 of the R.N.A.S. makes an unsuccessful attempt to bring down German Zeppelin LZ 93 (L 44) and has to alight in the North Sea. However, the airship is shot down by anti-aircraft fire over France on October 20.

**September 11** Fighter ace, Capitaine Georges Marie Ludovic Jules Guynemer, dies during a patrol over Poelcapelle, Belgium.

**September 17** First raid on England by German Staaken R.VI bombers. These 'R' or 'Giant' bombers can carry 2,205lb (1,000kg) bombs (the largest bombs used operationally in the First World War).

**September 23** Leutnant Werner Voss is killed in action while flying a Fokker Dr. I. Flying alone, he meets S.E.5s of No. 56 Squadron, R.F.C., and manages to cause considerable damage to them, finally being shot down by Capt. J.B. McCudden.

**September 29** Two Sopwith Camels of the R.N.A.S. carry out a unique night bombing raid on the balloon shed near Quiéry-la-Motte.

**October 2** Three Sopwith Pups carry out a low-level night bombing raid on the airfields at Cruyshautem and Waereghem.

**October 8** German Navy Zeppelin LZ 102 (L 57) explodes while entering its shed at Jüterbog, near Berlin.

**October 11** The 41st Wing of the R.F.C. is formed to carry out strategic bombing of targets of military importance inside Germany.

**October 20** In a disastrous day, the German Navy loses Zeppelin LZ 85 (L 45) that is forced to land in France behind enemy lines and has to be destroyed by the crew, LZ 93 (L 44) that is shot down by anti-aircraft fire over St-Clément in France, LZ 96 (L 49) that is forced to land in France and is captured, LZ 89 (L 50) that goes missing over the Mediterranean after losing a gondola, and LZ 101 (L 55) that is wrecked during a forced landing in Germany and has to be dismantled.

**October 21** A Curtiss HS-1 flying-boat test-flies the prototype Liberty engine. On August 12, the Secretary of War had announced that the engine had passed its final, presumably static, tests.

**October 29** A British-built Airco (de Havilland) D.H.4 is re-engined with an American Liberty engine and test-flown for the first time in this configuration.

**November 10** The bureau of Commissars of Aviation and Aeronautics (BKAV) is set up in Russia just three days after the Bolshevik seizure of power.

**November 18** U.S. Navy Tellier flying-boats begin air operations from Le Croisac, France. In total, 34 such aircraft are used by the Navy.

**November 20** The Battle of Cambrai begins and 289 British aircraft are brought together to support the army and to observe enemy forces and disrupt their communications. (The success of low-level air attacks on ground forces by the R.F.C., and later by the Germans, had far-reaching effects on the whole concept of aerial warfare.)

**November 21** The U.S. Navy's N-9 radio-guided flying bomb is demonstrated. (q.v. September 12, 1916)

**November 27** Brigadier-Gen. B.D. Foulois becomes Chief of Air Service, American Expeditionary Force, taking over from Brigadier-Gen. William L. Kenly.

**November 29** The Air Force (Constitution) Bill receives Royal assent in Britain.

**November 30** The prototype British Vickers Vimy heavy bomber flies for the first time.

**December** Sopwith Camels of No. 44 Squadron, R.F.C., force down a Gotha bomber, which lands near Folkestone.

**December 3** It is announced that the 'American Squadron' or Lafayette Escadrille (now Spa 124 with Spads) will be taken under AEF control from February 1918.

**December 17** German Navy Oberleutnant Christiansen, flying a Brandenburg W 12 floatplane fighter, shoots down the British non-rigid airship C 27.

**December 18** Riesenflugzeugabteilung S01 drops more than 59,525lb (27,000kg) of bombs on the U.K. without loss through enemy action between now and May 20, 1918.

**December 22** Russia begins peace negotiations with Germany following the Revolution. Particularly worrying for the Allies is the extra German manpower thus released for the Western Front.

## 1918

German fighter pilot Hermann Goering receives the Pour le Mérite.

**January** The German D-Type (fighter) competition at Berlin-Adlershof is won by the Fokker V.11 designed by Reinhold Platz. After some minor modifications it is put into production as the Fokker D.VII.

The first Gotha bomber to be shot down at night over England is destroyed by Sopwith Camels of No. 44 Squadron, R.F.C., at Wickford, Essex.

**January 2** Major-Gen. Sir Hugh Trenchard becomes the Chief of the British Air Staff.

**January 5** Five German Navy airships are destroyed in an explosion at the Ahlhorn sheds (LZ 87/L 47, LZ 94/L 46, LZ 97/L 51, LZ 105/L 58 and SL 20).

**January 18** Major-Gen. Sir Hugh Trenchard hands the command of the Royal Flying Corps in France to Major-Gen. Sir John Salmond.

**January 23** The first AEF balloon ascent is made at the Balloon School at Cuperly, France.

**February** British Handley Page O/400 heavy bombers first carry the 1,650-lb (748-kg) 'Minor' bomb.

The first combat aircraft to be mass-produced in America (Airco D.H.4s) come off the production lines.

The first operational squadrons of the American Expeditionary Force are formed in France. (Between now and the Armistice, American squadrons destroy 781 enemy aircraft.)

Lt. Stephen W. Thompson becomes the first American pilot to gain an aerial victory while serving with an American squadron (the 103rd Pursuit Squadron, formed from the Lafayette Escadrille on February 18 but still flying with French forces).

**February 16/17** Zeppelin Staaken R.VI No. 39 bomber becomes the first of the German 'giants' to drop a 2,205lb (1,000kg) bomb on England.

**February 18** The first American fighter squadron proper arrives in France as the 95th Aero (Pursuit) Squadron.

**March** The Aviation of the 1st Polish Corps is formed from the earlier 1st Polish Aviation Unit.

A helicopter designed by Dr. Ing. Theodor von Kármán (see 1944) and Wilhelm Zurovec is completed. It uses an electro-motor to power four rotors, as pioneered by Oberstlt. Stefan von Petroczy of the Austrian Army Balloon Corps, to produce a tethered observation helicopter with defensive armament (Petroczy's second helicopter, with three Le Rhône piston engines instead of electric motors, had remained aloft for an hour at low altitude). Built in Budapest, the electric-powered PKZ 1 performs four tethered lift-offs, all but one carrying three persons.

**March 3** The French-built Astra-Torres AT 1 non-rigid dirigible, the first French Navy airship, is operated by the AEF for the first time.

**March 4** The prototype three-seat de Havilland D.H.10 heavy bomber flies for the first time.

The American 94th Aero (Pursuit) Squadron arrives in France.

Edward Vernon Rickenbacker, eventually the highest-scoring U.S. pilot of the First World War, is transferred to the 94th Aero (Pursuit) Squadron (the famous 'Hat-in-the-Ring' squadron).

**March 5** The first U.S. balloon unit to serve operationally in France with AEF ground forces is the 2nd Balloon Company.

**March 10** The German Junkers D.I. (Junkers J9) all-metal single-seat cantilever monoplane fighter is flown as a prototype. Forty-one production aircraft are eventually built.

**March 11** The world's first scheduled international airmail service begins, operated between Vienna and Kiev with Hansa-Brandenburg C.I biplanes.

**March 14** Aircraft of the 95th Aero (Pursuit) Squadron begin patrol flights on the Western Front.

**March 19** The first American observation patrol over enemy lines takes place, by aircraft of the 94th Aero (Pursuit) Squadron.

**March 21** The German Spring offensives begin under the Michael plan, dubbed Kaiserschlacht or Emperor's battle. German strength includes 47 infantry attack divisions, thousands of field guns and hundreds of aeroplanes.

**March 26** French General Foch becomes the Commander-in-Chief of the Allied Armies fighting on the Western Front.

**March 27** The first production aircraft built by the U.S. Naval Aircraft Factory, Philadelphia Navy Yard, makes its first flight as the Curtiss H-16 flying-boat.

**April** R.A.F. Handley Page O/400 heavy bombers make the first of more than 200 cross-Channel flights between Lympne, England, and France, carrying passengers and goods. This service lasts until the following November, by which time many hundreds of people have been carried.

Fokker D.VII biplane fighters become operational on the Western Front with Jagdgeschwader I. The D.VII proves itself to be the best German fighter of the First World War.

**April 1** The R.F.C. and R.N.A.S. are amalgamated to form the Royal Air Force.

Bristol F.2B Fighters of No. 22 Squadron carry out the first official missions of the R.A.F. (see previous entry).

**April 2** Maj. J.T.B. McCudden, R.A.F., is awarded the Victoria Cross for valour.

The PKZ 2 helicopter, designed by Wilhelm Zurovec alone, is flown for the first time. With two contra-rotating rotors driven by three Gnome rotary engines, it thereafter makes tethered flights of up to approximately 164ft (50m), the longest lasting about one hour.

**April 7** Zeppelin LZ 104 (L 59), known as the 'African ship', burns while airborne over the Strait of Otranto off the Italian east coast.

**April 11** I Corps Observation Squadron becomes the first American observation unit to fly over enemy lines. (q.v. March 19, 1918)

**April 12** The final German Zeppelin raid on England causing casualties among the civilian population is carried out.

**April 13** Teniente Luis C. Candelaria, Argentine Army, makes the first crossing of the Andes by air, flying a Morane-Saulnier Parasol monoplane. His route takes him from Zapala, Argentina, to Cunco, Chile.

**April 14** The 94th Aero (Pursuit) Squadron becomes the first American fighter unit to see combat. 1st Lt. Douglas Campbell and 2nd Lt. Alan Winslow shoot down two German aeroplanes and the pilots are captured. The American pilots fly French-built Nieuport 28s.

Major-Gen. Sir Hugh Trenchard resigns as Chief of the Air Staff in Britain. His place is taken by Major-Gen. Sir Frederick Sykes.

**April 15** American fighters make their first combat patrol over enemy lines.

**April 21** 'Ace of aces' Manfred von Richthofen is killed while flying a Fokker Dr. I triplane during an engagement with No. 209 Squadron, R.A.F., over Sailly-le-Sec. Capt. A. Roy Brown is credited with the victory.

**April 22–23** The mole near Zeebrugge, Belgium, is attacked by Wing Cmdr. Fellows flying an Airco (de Havilland) D.H.4.

**April 29** Capt. Edward Vernon Rickenbacker shoots down the first of his 26 victims, an Albatros scout.

**May** The German AEG G.V heavy bomber appears as a longer-range development of the mass-produced but limited-performance G.IV of 1916-18 service. (Several G.Vs enter commercial service in 1919 with the first German post-war airline, DLR, each accommodating six passengers.)

**May 1** Lts. A.A. McLeod and A. Jerrard, R.A.F., are awarded Victoria Crosses for valour.

**May 10** German Navy Zeppelin LZ 107 (L 62) explodes while airborne over Heligoland.

**May 11** The American Expeditionary Force receives its first U.S.-built D.H.4.

**May 15** The U.S. Army Signal Corps establishes the first American airmail service between New York and Washington, using Curtiss JNs and Standard J biplanes.

**May 18** The first American bomber squadron, AEF, is formed in France as the 96th Aero Squadron.

**May 19** Hauptmann H. Kohl receives the Pour le Mérite, after flying 800 missions.

**May 19/20** Night raids on England by Gotha bombers end as losses become too high.

**May 20** Overman Act creates the Bureau of Aircraft Production and the Division of Military Aeronautics. The U.S. Army Air Service is formed from these on May 24.

**May 24** The All-Russian Air Board is replaced by the new Chief Directorate of the Workers and Peasants Military Air Fleet GU-RKKVF: Glavoce Upravlenie-Raboche-Krestyanskogo Krasnogo Vozdushnogo Flota).

**May 29** Brigadier-Gen. Mason Patrick is made Chief of the U.S. Air Service in France.

**June** Oberleutnant Ernst Udet receives the Pour Le Mérite.

**June 2** Oberleutnant Erich Löwenhardt receives the Pour le Mérite.

**June 5** The Independent Force, R.A.F., is established to operate heavy and light bombers in a strategic offensive role against industrial and military targets inside Germany. Major-Gen. Sir Hugh Trenchard is made Commander of the Force.

**June 6** The first Fairey IIIA two-seat naval light bomber makes its maiden flight. This is the first of the famous Fairey III series.

**June 12** The first bombing raid by U.S. aircraft on the Western Front is carried out by the 96th Aero Squadron on the railway at Dommany-Baroncourt.

**June 19** Maggiore Francesco Baracca, Italy's most successful fighter pilot with 34 victories, is killed during a ground-attack mission at Montello.

**June 24** Capt. Brian Peck, R.A.F., starts the first official airmail service in Canada.

**June 25** King George V grants the prefix 'Royal' to the U.K.'s Aeronautical Society.

**July 9** Maj. James Thomas Byford McCudden, VC, R.A.F., is killed at Auxi-le-Château when the engine of his S.E.5a fails and he crash-lands.

**July 10** Leutnant F. Rumney is awarded the Pour le Mérite.

**July 15** Gen. Ludendorff launches the final major attack of the German Spring offensive on Reims. By the 18th it is clear that the Spring offensive has failed.

**July 19** German Navy Zeppelins LZ 99 (L 54) and LZ 108 (L 60) are destroyed in their sheds at Tonden by aircraft from H.M.S. *Furious*.

**July 26** Maj. Edward 'Mick' Mannock, Britain's top ace with 73 victories, is killed when the petrol tank of his S.E.5a fighter is hit by German ground fire over the Western Front. (q.v. July 18, 1919)

**July 28** The first flight from England to Egypt is started by Maj. A.S. MacLaren and Brigadier-Gen. A.E. Borton in a Handley Page O/400 bomber. On August 8 they arrive in Egypt.

**August** German Fokker D.VII biplane fighters gain 565 'kills' over the Western Front in this month alone.

**August 1** Flt. Sub-Lt. Stuart Culley, Royal Navy, achieves the first take-off by aeroplane from a moving barge. The barge is towed behind H.M.S. *Redoubt*. (q.v. August 11, 1918)

**August 2** U.S.-built D.H.4s undertake their first patrol over enemy territory in France, an observation flight with the 135th Corps Observation Squadron.

**August 5/6** German Navy Zeppelin LZ 112 (L 70) is shot down off the Norfolk coast of England by Maj. Egbert Cadbury flying an Airco (de Havilland) D.H.4.

**August 9** No. 97 Squadron, R.A.F., joins the Independent Force to operate Handley Page O/400 heavy bombers.

**August 10** Oberleutnant E. Loewenhardt is killed in a mid-air collision with another German pilot, his score standing at 53 victories. (By the end of the war he was ranked third most successful German pilot.)

**August 11** German Navy Zeppelin LZ 100 (L 53) is shot down by Flt. Sub-Lt. Stuart Culley who had taken off in his Sopwith Camel from a towed barge in the North Sea.

**August 12** The U.S. Post Office takes over airmail services from the Army. The New York to Washington service is flown with Standard R.4s.

**August 17** The Martin MB-1 (or more correctly the GMB) flies. It becomes a standard bomber and observation aircraft with the U.S.A.A.S.

**August 21** The Nieuport-Delage NiD 29 single-seat fighter prototype flies for the first time. It becomes one of the most widely operated aircraft of the 1920s, flown in Belgium, France, Italy and Japan.

**August 31** Airco (de Havilland) D.H.9As of No. 110 Squadron arrive in France.

**September** The Sopwith Snipe enters R.A.F. service as a successor to the Camel. Although fewer than 100 see operational service before the Armistice, they are the best Allied fighters in use. (q.v. October 27, 1918)

**September 12–15** The largest number of aeroplanes brought together for a single operation is assembled for the assault on the *St.-Mihiel Salient* during the Battle of Bapaume. Under the command of Brigadier-Gen. William 'Billy' Mitchell, 1,483 aeroplanes of all types support American and French forces.

**September 14/15** Forty R.A.F. Handley Page O/400 heavy bombers launch an attack on German targets. In the same month, O/400s begin dropping the new 1,650lb (748kg) bomb.

**September 25** American air ace Capt. Edward V. Rickenbacker is awarded the U.S. Congressional Medal of Honor.

**September 26** Frenchman Capitaine René Paul Fonck shoots down four German Fokker D.VIIs, an Albatros D.V and a two-seater.

**September 28** Leutnant F. Büchner is awarded the Pour le Mérite.

2nd Lt. Frank Luke Jr. is killed after destroying three balloons while officially grounded for misconduct. Having been wounded, he landed his aircraft behind enemy lines and had a shoot-out with German troops. (His score of 21 victories made him the second-ranking American ace of the war.)

**September 29** Frank Luke is posthumously awarded the U.S. Congressional Medal of Honor.

**October** Sopwith Cuckoo torpedo-bombers go to sea on board the carrier H.M.S. *Argus*.

**October 4** The first Navy-Curtiss NC flying-boat makes its maiden flight as an anti-submarine aircraft. (q.v. May 8, 1919)

**October 5** Roland Garros is killed while flying a Spad fighter at Vouziers.

**October 6** 2nd Lt. Erwin R. Bleckley and 1st Lt. Harold E. Goettler are posthumously awarded U.S. Congressional Medals of Honor after an heroic supply-dropping mission at Binarville costs them their lives.

**October 12** Pilots of the 185th Aero (Pursuit) Squadron undertake the first U.S. night fighter operations in France.

**October 15** The 1st Aviation Unit of the Polish Forces is formed.

**October 24** The Fokker E.V arrives back at the Western Front as the strengthened D.VIII. It is an immediate success, its good rate of climb and manoeuvrability complementing a maximum speed of 127mph (204km/h).

**October 26** Major-Gen. Sir Hugh Trenchard becomes Commander-in-Chief of the Inter-Allied Independent Air Force.

**October 27** Maj. William G. Barker wins the Victoria Cross when he flies his Sopwith Snipe through five formations of German fighters during a single patrol, shooting down four aircraft. He is wounded three times but manages to land behind British lines.

**November** The international airmail service from Vienna to Kiev is discontinued. (q.v. March 11, 1918)

**November 1** More than 100 Fokker D.VIII monoplane fighters are operational with German aviation service and naval units.

**November 6** British airship R 31 makes its last flight before being grounded as a result of its rotting wooden framework. (Total flying time of the R 31 was about nine hours.)

**November 8** Capt. F.M.F. West is awarded the Victoria Cross for valour while flying an Armstrong Whitworth F.K.8 light bomber on August 10, 1918. (He was the second F.K.8 pilot to win the VC, the other being McLeod.)

**November 10** Dr. Robert H. Goddard demonstrates rockets at the Aberdeen Proving Ground, Maryland, U.S.A.

**November 11** The Armistice ends the First World War at the 11th hour of the 11th day of the 11th month. The R.A.F. finishes the war with the largest air force, comprising well over 22,000 aeroplanes, while the best-equipped air force is generally believed to be the French.

**November 25** The Italian airline Posta Aerea Transadriatica begins regular mail flights from Venice. The service is short-lived.

**November 29–December 12** Capt. Ross M. Smith, Brigadier-Gen. A.E. Borton, Major-Gen. W. Salmond and two other crew members start the first flight from Egypt to India on November 29, flying a Handley Page O/400 from Heliopolis bound for Karachi. They reach Karachi on December 12.

**November 30** Capt. A.W. Beauchamp-Proctor and Maj. Barker, R.A.F., are awarded Victoria Crosses.

**December 4–22** Four Curtiss JN-4 'Jennies' complete the first U.S. Army coast-to-coast crossing of the U.S.A., from San Diego to Jacksonville.

**December 16** No. 18 Squadron R.A.F. begins airmail flights to the British Army of Occupation in Germany. The flights end in August of the following year.

## 1918–1919
**December 13, 1918–January 16, 1919** In December 1918, Sqdn. Ldr. A. MacLaren, Lt. R. Halley and others begin the first flight from England to India in a Handley Page V/l500 heavy bomber *Carthusian*. They arrive in Delhi on January 16, 1919.

## 1919
Mme. la Baronne de Laroche is killed in a flying accident. (q.v. March 8, 1910)

The Argentine Marquis de Pateras Pescara begins constructing helicopters with cyclic-pitch control. (q.v. May 1921 and April 18, 1924)

**January 8** The German Air Ministry restores civil flying. This beats the British Air Navigation Regulations by several months in restoring civil flights.

**January 10** Regular passenger and mail services are started between London and Paris by No. 2 (Communications) Squadron, R.A.F. The R.A.F. service lasts until September, mainly for the benefit of the Peace Conference at Versailles. The aircraft used are Airco (de Havilland) D.H.4As, modified D.H.4s with enclosed accommodation aft of the pilot for two passengers.

**February** An express parcel air service between Folkestone and Ghent is started by Aircraft Transport and Travel Ltd., to carry food and clothing to Belgium. The flying is carried out by R.A.F. pilots using Airco (de Havilland) D.H.9s.

**February 5** Deutsche Luft-Reederei (DLR) begins the first sustained daily passenger airline service, flying modified ex-military AEG and DFW biplanes between Berlin and Weimar, Germany.

**February 8** The first airline passengers (military) to be carried from Paris to London are flown by a Farman F60 Goliath from Toussus-le-Noble to Kenley.

**February 12** The Department of Civil Aviation is formed in Britain.

**February 21** The prototype Thomas Morse MB-3 biplane makes its first flight. The MB-3 is the first U.S.-designed fighter to enter large-scale production.

**March** Italian Caproni aeroplanes are used to inaugurate a regular international air service between Padova (Padua) and Vienna.

**March 1** The German airline DLR extends its air network to Hamburg.

An Army airmail service is begun between Folkestone and Cologne.

**March 3** William Boeing and Edward Hubbard use the Boeing Model CL-4S to carry out the first U.S. international airmail survey flight between Seattle, Washington and Victoria, British Columbia, Canada. Regular airmail flights start that October.

**March 10** Brigadier-Gen. William 'Billy' Mitchell becomes the U.S. Director of Military Aeronautics.

**March 22** The first regular international passenger service is opened between Paris and Brussels by Lignes Aériennes Farman, using Farman F60 Goliath biplanes.

**April 6** Customs examination of airline passengers begins at Brussels.

**April 13** The prototype Vickers Vimy Commercial 10-passenger airliner makes its maiden flight.

**April 18** CMA (Compagnie des Messageries Aériennes) inaugurates a mail and cargo service between Paris and Lille. The service is daily using ex-military Bréguet 14s. Brussels and London are added to the growing network in August.

**April 19** Leslie Leroy Irvin makes the first recorded free-fall jump from an aeroplane before deploying his parachute.

**May** The prototype de Havilland D.H.16 4-passenger airliner enters service with Aircraft Transport and Travel Ltd. It flies to Amsterdam in July for demonstration at the Dutch First Air Traffic Exhibition. The D.H.16 is the first purely commercial de Havilland airliner.

**May 1** Civil aviation is once again allowed in Britain following publication of the Air Navigation Regulations.

**May 5** The Swiss airmail service begins, carrying civil mail in addition to military.

**May 8** Three U.S. Navy NC flying-boats set out from Rockaway, New York, in an attempt to make the first air crossing of the Atlantic under the leadership of Cmdr. John H. Towers. NC-1 and NC-3 fail in their attempt and alight near the Azores. (q.v. May 31, 1919)

**May 15** The U.S. Post Office inaugurates the first section of a transcontinental airmail service between Chicago and Cleveland. (q.v. February 22, 1921.)

**May 18** Harry Hawker and Lt. Cmdr. K.F. Mackenzie-Grieve attempt a non-stop transatlantic flight between Newfoundland and the U.K. They alight on the following day and are picked up by a Danish vessel. They are awarded £5,000 by the *Daily Mail* newspaper for the attempt.

**May 24** The Avro Civil Aviation Service begins the first domestic airline service in Britain. It offers daily flights linking Manchester, Southport and Blackpool. The service lasts four months.

**May 31** Navy-Curtiss flying-boat NC-4, commanded by Lt. Cmdr. A.C. Read, completes the first transatlantic crossing by air, landing at Plymouth, England. The journey, made in hops, covers stops in Chatham (Massachusetts), Halifax (Nova Scotia), Trepassy Bay (Newfoundland), Horta and Ponta Delgada (the Azores), Lisbon (Portugal) and Ferrol del Caudillo (Spain). Total flying time is 57 hrs 16 mins. (q.v. May 8, 1919)

**June** The German airline Lloyd Luftverkehr Sablatnig is founded as a domestic operator.

**June 7** The British airline Daimler Air Hire is established. It later becomes Daimler Airway.

**June 14** Handley Page Transport is established. Its first airline operation is between Cricklewood and Bournemouth, England.

**June 14/15** Capt. John Alcock and Lt. Arthur Whitten Brown make the first non-stop crossing of the Atlantic in a Vickers Vimy bomber, flying from St. John's, Newfoundland, to Clifden, County Galway, Ireland. Total flying time is 16 hrs 27 mins.

**June 23** German Navy Zeppelins LZ 46 (L 14), LZ 79 (L 41), LZ 91 (L 42), LZ 103 (L 56), LZ 110 (L 63) and LZ 111 (L 65) are wrecked by their crews at Nordholz to prevent them from being handed over to the Allies, due to be ordered under the Versailles Peace Treaty.

**June 25** The world's first purpose-built all-metal commercial aircraft flies as the German Junkers F 13; 322 are eventually built.

**June 28** The Versailles Peace Treaty is signed forbidding the Germans from having an air force or producing military aircraft. (Among many other terms included was the handing over of all Fokker D.VII fighters to the Allies. German aircraft manufacturers got round the manufacturing clause of the treaty by setting up factories abroad.)

**July** The Compagnie des Transports Aéronautiques du Sud-Ouest is formed as a charter operator flying to points around the Bay of Biscay.

**July 2–6** British airship R 34 makes the first airship crossing of the Atlantic, flying from East Fortune, Scotland, to New York.

**July 9–13** R 34 leaves Mineola, New York, for Norfolk, England, and arrives five days later having made the first two-way crossing of the Atlantic.

**July 14** An Italian Fiat B.R. light bomber makes the first non-stop flight between Rome and Paris. (q.v. December 23, 1924)

**July 15** Aircraft Transport and Travel Limited undertakes an experimental airline flight to Le Bourget. (q.v. August 25, 1919)

**July 18** Britain's top ranking ace of the First World War, Maj. Edward 'Mick' Mannock, is posthumously awarded the Victoria Cross. (q.v. July 26, 1918)

**August 7/8** Capt. Ernest Hoy, flying a Curtiss JN-4 Jenny, makes the first aeroplane flight across the Canadian Rocky Mountains, from Vancouver to Calgary.

**August 24** Delag airship *Bodensee* makes the first of its regular flights from Friedrichshafen to Berlin.

**August 25** A de Havilland D.H.16 belonging to Aircraft Transport and Travel Ltd. begins the world's first scheduled daily international airline service proper, flying from Hounslow, England, to Le Bourget, France.

**August 26** Handley Page Transport carries the first two women passengers to fly on an airline service between England and France.

**September** London to Paris services by No. 2 (Communications) Squadron, R.A.F. are discontinued after a total of 749 flights.

**September 2** Handley Page Transport begins a regular London-Paris airline service.

**September 19** Compagnie des Messageries Aériennes (CMA) begins its Paris to London passenger service with Bréguet 14s.

**September 28** The Supermarine Aviation Company inaugurates a flying-boat service to Le Havre.

**September 30** The British Aerial Transport Company (BAT) inaugurates a short-lived domestic airline service between London and Birmingham, flying Koolhoven F.K.26 4-passenger biplanes (first flown April 1919). A London-Amsterdam service is also flown for a short time.

**October 7** KLM (Koninklijke Luchtvaart Maatschappij voor Nederland an Kolonien/Royal Dutch Airlines) is formed.

**October 11** Handley Page Transport offers the first meals on board airliners, at a cost of 3 shillings per basket, on its London-Brussels service.

**October 13** The League of Nations sets up the Paris Convention to regulate international flying.

**November 1** The U.S. airline West Indies Airways begins services between Key West, Florida, and Havana, Cuba. It later merges with Aeromarine Airways to form Aeromarine West Indies Airways.

**November 11** An airline service between Berlin and Königsberg (later Kaliningrad) is started by Albatros Werke.

**November 12** Australian brothers Capt. Ross Smith and Lt. Keith Smith set off from Hounslow, England in a Vickers Vimy bomber in an attempt to be the first men to fly from England to Australia. (q.v. December 10, 1919)

**November 14** The American Railway Express Company hires a Handley Page V/1500 to carry 1,000lb (454kg) of parcels and other goods from Mitchell Field, New York, to Chicago. Mechanical problems force an early termination of the flight.

**November 16** Capt. H.N. Wrigley and Lt. A.W. Murphy become the first men to fly across Australia when they fly a B.E.2e from Melbourne to join Ross and Keith Smith. They land at Darwin on December 12 after a flying time of 46 hours.

**December 1** Delag's airship service between Friedrichshafen and Berlin is suspended on the orders of Allied Control Commission after more than 100 flights, carrying 2,400 passengers, have been made.

**December 2** The prototype Handley Page W.8 biplane airliner makes its maiden flight. It is among the first purpose-built British airliners to appear after the First World War and proves highly successful.

**December 5** Aérovias Nacionales de Colombia SA (Avianca) is formed. (A Colombian airline, it has the longest continuous record of scheduled services.)

**December 10** Ross and Keith Smith land their Vickers Vimy in Darwin, having made the first flight from England to Australia, a distance of 11,290 miles (18,170km).

**December 18** Sir John Alcock is killed in a flying accident at Rouen, France, while flying the Vickers Viking amphibian to the Paris Air Show.

**December 27** Boeing's first commercial aircraft and first flying-boat of its own design makes its maiden flight as the B-1.

## 1920

The Dayton-Wright RB Racer appears as the first aeroplane with a practical form of retractable landing gear. Built for the 1920 Gordon Bennett Aviation Cup Race, it has a maximum speed of 200mph (320km/h).

The first glider competition is held at Rhön, Germany, organized by the Aero Technical Association of Dresden.

**January 20** The Fédération Aéronautique Internationale announces that it is prepared to accept new official world records. However, speed records will require four runs (in both directions) over a 1km course, an average then being taken. The effect of wind speed is thus cancelled.

**January 24–March 31** Cmndt. Vuillemin, Aéronautique Militaire, crosses the Sahara by aeroplane.

**February** S. Instone and Company begins commercial airline services to Paris. The air organization becomes the Instone Air Line the following year. (q.v. May 15, 1920)

**February 4** Lt.-Col. Pierre van Ryneveld and Sqdn. Ldr. Christopher Q. Brand take off from

Brooklands in a Vickers Vimy bomber in an attempt to make the first flight from England to South Africa. (q.v. March 6, 1920 and March 17, 1920)

**February 7** Frenchman Sadi Lecointe sets the first post-war world speed record, achieving 171.01mph (275.92km/h) in a Nieuport-Delage 29.

**March 5** The first freight/passenger de Havilland D.H.18 biplane airliner is acquired by Aircraft Transport and Travel Ltd. Instone Air Line and Daimler Hire Ltd. share the other five. (q.v. April 7, 1922)

**March 6** Van Ryneveld and Brand (q.v. February 4, 1920) crash their second Vimy bomber at Bulawayo, Southern Rhodesia, and have to wait until a D.H.9 is provided for the rest of the journey (see below).

**March 17** Van Ryneveld and Brand set off in a D.H.9 to complete their England to South Africa flight, arriving at Wynberg Aerodrome, Cape Town, on March 20.

**March 29** Croydon Airport is first used as London's air terminal.

Grands Express Aériens (CGEA) introduces the Farman F60 Goliath on its Le Bourget-Croydon service. The Goliath dominates European aviation for a decade,

**April 23** Compagnie Franco-Roumaine de Navigation Aérienne (CFRNA) is established in France. The Potez IX 4-passenger biplane becomes its main aircraft.

**May 15** The Instone Air Line is formed in Britain to operate the London-Paris route established by the shipping firm S. Instone and Company.

**May 17** KLM begins an Amsterdam-London airline service in conjunction with Aircraft Transport and Travel Ltd. AT&T inaugurates the London to Amsterdam route using a de Havilland D.H.16.

**May 25** The Belgian airline SNETA (Syndicat National pour l'Étude des Transports Aériens) begins airline services to England. It becomes best known for its operations to the Belgian Congo.

**June 4** Army Re-Organization Act creates the U.S. Army Air Service.

**October 14** The Hubbard Air Service begins regular airmail services between Seattle and Victoria, using a Boeing B-1 flying boat.

**November 1** Aeromarine West Indies Airways is given the first contract for foreign mail by the U.S. Post Office.

**November 16** Qantas (Queensland and Northern Territory Aerial Services Limited) is registered. (q.v. November 2, 1922)

**November 24** The prototype Dornier Delphin 5/6-passenger commercial flying-boat makes its first flight. Later versions of the Delphin carry up to 13 passengers.

**November 25** The first Pulitzer Trophy Race is won by Capt. Corliss C. Moseley,

U.S.A.A.S., flying a Verville-Packard 600. Flown over a triangular course from Mitchell Field, Long Island, New York, competing aircraft had to have a landing speed of less than 75mph (121km/h).

**December 12** The prototype Blériot-Spad 33 4/5-passenger airliner flies for the first time. One of the most successful early French commercial aircraft, it is first operated on the regular Paris-London services of CMA in 1921. The type is developed throughout the 1920s, ending with the Type 126.

**December 14** The first fatal accident on a British scheduled commercial service takes place when a Handley Page O/400 crashes in fog at Cricklewood soon after taking off. Two crew members and two of the six passengers are killed.

**December 15** Aircraft Transport and Travel Ltd. (AT&T) makes its last commercial airline flight.

## 1921

Junkers Flugzeugwerke AG forms its own airline branch as the Junkers Luftverkehr. Similarly, Edmund Rumpler Flugzeug-Werke GmbH forms Rumpler Luftverkehr. Eventually, Junkers takes control of the Rumpler airline.

The German airline Aero-Union is formed to administer the operations of Deutsche Luft-Reederei (DLR) and Danziger Luft Reederei.

**January** R 34 is seriously damaged when it strikes a hill in fog. It is returned to Howden,

where ground crew cause further damage. Finally it is caught by gusting winds and rises and then plunges to the ground, causing its total destruction.

The first internal Soviet airline service is flown by demilitarized Ilya Mourometz bombers between Sarapul and Yekaterinburg. The second internal airline service between Moscow and Kharkov is inaugurated later the same year, also flown by demilitarized Ilya Mourometz bombers.

**February 18** C.C. Eversole, U.S. airmail pilot, makes a free-fall parachute jump from a disabled D.H.4.

**February 21–24** Lt. A. William Coney completes the first solo flight from San Diego, California, to Jacksonville, Florida. He completes the flight in a flying time of 22 hrs 30 mins.

**February 22** American transcontinental ailmail services begin between San Francisco and Mineola, New York. The route, flown in 14 sections in American-built de Havilland D.H.4Ms, takes a day and a half. The first flight is made by pilot Jack Knight. (q.v. July 1, 1924)

**March 19** British Government subsidy allows the British airlines Handley Page Transport and Instone Air Line to continue their London to Paris commercial services in the face of French competition.

**March 31** Croydon Airport is officially inaugurated.

**May** The U.S. Army's first production armoured aeroplane flies for the first time as the Boeing GA-1 triplane. Carrying eight 0.30in machine-guns and a 37mm Baldwin cannon, plus ten 25lb (11.3kg) fragmentation bombs, in addition to very heavy armour plating, it manages only 105mph (169km/h).

Marquis de Pateras Pescara's second helicopter lifts off, powered by a 170hp (127kW) Le Rhôn engine.

**June 8** Pressurized cabin experiments begin at Wright Field, U.S.A., using a D.H.4 biplane.

D.H.9As of Nos. 30 and 47 Squadrons, R.A.F., begin a regular Cairo-Baghdad desert airmail service.

**July 21** US Army MB-2 biplane bombers, under the command of Brigadier-Gen. William 'Billy' Mitchell, sink the anchored and unmanned ex-German battleship *Ostfriesland* in a demonstration of air power against naval vessels. Other ex-German and surplus American warships are also destroyed.

**July 30** François Durafour, flying a Caudron, lands on and takes off from Mont Blanc.

**August 1** The first Vickers Vernon troop-carrying biplane is delivered to the R.A.F. The Vernon is the first purpose-designed troop carrier.

**August 24** The British dirigible R 38 breaks up while airborne during flight trials, the wreckage ending in the river Humber. Forty-four of the 49 people on board lose their lives,

including 16 Americans, the dirigible having been sold to America.

**September 13** German Wolf Hirth makes a glider flight of 21 minutes, improving on the previous best set in 1911.

**September 17** The first Air League Challenge Cup race is held, initially for R.A.F. teams.

**September 23** The anchored battleship U.S.S. *Alabama* is sunk during aeroplane bombing trials in the U.S.A., just one of three unwanted U.S. Navy vessels sunk during further U.S.A.A.S. demonstrations by Brigadier-Gen. William Mitchell. Previously, *Alabama* had been hit by a 100lb phosphorus bomb that lifted the crow's nest.

**October 5** Major-Gen. Mason Patrick becomes the Chief of Air Services, U.S.A.A.S.

**October 15** The Spanish airline Compañiá Española de Trafico Aéreo begins services. It is the founding company of the present-day Iberia, formed on July 7, 1940.

**November** The French airline Aéronavale begins services to North Africa.

**November 12** Aviation fuel in a container is carried from one aeroplane to another in flight by Wesley May, who climbs from wing to wing.

**December 1** The U.S. Navy's dirigible Goodyear-Goodrich C 7 flies for the first time. One of 16 C-class dirigibles ordered, mostly for anti-submarine patrol, it uses helium gas.

Some C-class dirigibles are taken over by the U.S. Army.

## 1922

**February 9** Formation is announced of the Royal Air Force Reserve.

**March 13** Portuguese pilots Capt. Gago Coutinho and Capt. Sacadura Cabral set off from Lisbon on the first flight over the South Atlantic, flying a Fairey IIIC. On June 16 they arrive in Brazil flying their third aeroplane, Fairey IIID floatplane *Santa Cruz*, the earlier two planes having been wrecked en route.

**March 20** U.S.S. *Langley*, the U.S. Navy's first aircraft carrier, is commissioned.

**March 26** The first 8-passenger de Havilland D.H.34 makes its maiden flight. Eleven are eventually built, serving initially with Daimler Hire and Instone Air Line Ltd. These afford new standards of luxury for air passengers. (q.v. April 2, 1922)

**April** Shortly after signature of the Rapallo Treaty between Germany and the Soviet Union, preparations are made to establish a clandestine flying training centre at Lipetsk. Between 1924 and August 1933, when the centre is closed down, over 450 German military flying personnel are trained there.

**April 2** The British airline Daimler Hire starts London to Paris services using large-capacity de Havilland D.H.34s.

**April 7** The first mid-air collision between passenger-carrying airliners on scheduled

services takes place over Thieuloy-St.-Antoine, France, when a Daimler Hire de Havilland D.H.18 and a Grands Express Aériens Farman Goliath collide. The seven passengers and crew are killed.

**May** The prototype Bréguet 19 bomber and reconnaissance biplane flies. In production form it becomes one of the most widely operated military aircraft of the 'interwar' period.

**May 1** The Soviet airline Deutsche-Russische Luftverkehrs AG (Deruluft) begins domestic operations. Passenger services proper begin several months later.

**May 15** Instone Air Line starts commercial services from London to Brussels using D.H.34s.

**June 1** The Swiss airline Ad Astra begins an international service connecting Zurich and Geneva with Nuremberg, Germany.

**June 16** Henry A. Berliner demonstrates a helicopter of his own design at College Park, Maryland.

**August 12** The fifth Schneider Trophy contest is held at Naples. The Italians need to win this to hold the trophy for good, having won the two previous contests. It is won by Briton Henry Biard in the Supermarine Sea Lion II at an average speed of 145.7mph (234.48km/h).

**August 18** German glider pilot Martens in *Vampyr* makes the first glider flight of more than one hour's duration.

**September 4** Lt. James H. Doolittle flies coast-to-coast across America in a day, piloting his D.H.4 from Pablo Beach, Florida, to Rockwell Field, California. Flying time is 21 hrs 19 mins.

**September 8/9** Capt. F.L. Barnard wins the first King's Cup Air Race, piloting a de Havilland D.H.4A over the course from Croydon, England, to Glasgow, Scotland and back in a flying time of 6 hrs 32 mins.

**September 20** Sadi Lecointe sets up the first world speed record of over 200mph at Villesauvage, France, flying a Nieuport-Delage 29 and achieving 205.23mph (330.75km/h).

**September 27** Naval Aircraft Radio Laboratory technicians at Anacostia demonstrate radar signatures for the first time.

**October 1** The R.A.F. begins its air control operations in Iraq with the object of keeping the peace and enforcing law and order.

**October 9** Daimler begins its London to Amsterdam service.

**October 13** The Curtiss R-6 racing biplane flies for the first time. The R-6 comes first and second in the 1922 U.S. Pulitzer Trophy race and in the hands of William 'Billy' Mitchell achieves a world speed record of 222.970mph (358.836km/h) on October 18.

**October 17** Lt. V.C. Griffin, flying a Vought VE-7SF fighter, makes the first take-off from

an American aircraft carrier. (q.v. March 20, 1922)

**October 20** Lt. H.R. Harris, U.S. Army Air Service, makes the first parachute escape from a crippled aeroplane in America, jumping from a Loening monoplane.

**October 23** A reversible-pitch propeller is shown by the American Propeller Company.

**October 26** Lt. Cmdr. G. De Chevalier, U.S. Navy, flying an Aeromarine 39-B, makes the first landing on U.S.S. *Langley*.

**November 2** Qantas starts scheduled passenger and mail operations between Charleville and Cloncurry, Queensland.

**November 6** The prototype Dornier DoJ Wal flying-boat makes its maiden flight.

**November 11** The first flight is achieved by Etienne Oehmichen in his No. 2 multi-rotor helicopter in France. On April 14, 1924 he sets a distance in a straight line helicopter record of 1,181ft (360m), bettered on April 17 by a flight of 1,722ft (525m). Oehmichen also gains a time over a 1km closed-circuit helicopter record of 7 mins 40 secs. (q.v. May 4, 1924)

**November 19** The Hungarian airline Magyar Legiforgalmi (Malert) is established. Budapest and Vienna are linked by a regular service from mid-1923. The airline can be viewed as the founder of the current Malev, formed in 1946.

**November 24** The prototype Vickers Virginia heavy bomber for the R.A.F. makes its first flight.

**November 28** The prototype Fairey Flycatcher biplane fighter makes its maiden flight. The production Flycatcher becomes the first FAA fighter to be specially strengthened for catapulting so that it can be launched from warships without carrier-type decks.

**December 27** The *Hosho*, the first Japanese purpose-built aircraft carrier, is commissioned. (It survives the Second World War and is decommissioned after the war.) q.v. February 1923

**December 31** A Dornier Komet of Deutsche Luft-Reederei becomes the first German aeroplane to fly to England since the Armistice, landing at Lympne.

**1923**

American designer Turnbull demonstrates the first variable-pitch aeroplane propeller.

**January** The French airline Air Union is formed following the merger of CMA and Grands Express Aériens (CGEA).

**January 9** The C 4 Autogiro, designed by Don Juan de la Cierva, makes its first flight, marking the beginning of widespread interest in gyroplanes.

**February** The first take-off and landing of a Japanese fighter on a Japanese aircraft carrier (*Hosho*) are performed by Briton Capt. Jordan flying a Mitsubishi IMF1.

**March** Dobrolet, the original Soviet state airline, is founded. Operations begin with assistance from the Air Force. (q.v. 1929)

**March 23** The Italian Regia Aeronautica is formed.

**April 29** The prototype Boeing PW-9 biplane fighter takes off for the first time. On September 19, 1924, production examples are ordered for the U.S.A.A.S.

**May 2–3** Lt. O.G. Kelly and Lt. J.A. Macready, U.S. Army Air Service, make the first non-stop crossing of America by aeroplane, flying a Fokker T-2 from Roosevelt Field, Long Island, to Rockwell Field, California, in a flying time of 26 hrs 50 mins.

**May 14** The first prototype Curtiss PW-8 biplane fighter is received by the U.S.A.A.S.

**May 23** Sabena is formed in Belgium to develop routes within Europe and succeed the pioneer airline SNETA in the Belgian Congo.

**June** The first Supermarine Sea Eagle commercial amphibious flying-boat is flown. Three join the British Marine Air Navigation Co. Ltd. On August 14 one Sea Eagle (G-EBFK) makes the first flight by a commercial aircraft to Germany. Among the passengers is Sir Sefton Brancker.

**June 23** Flt. Lt. W.H. Longton, R.A.F., wins the first Grosvenor Challenge Cup for British aircraft of under 150hp (112kW), in a Sopwith Gnu.

**June 27** Capt. L.H. Smith and Lt. J.P. Richter, U.S. Army Air Service, successfully demonstrate in-flight refuelling in a de Havilland D.H.4B.

**July** The original JAL (Japanese Air Lines) is established as a domestic operator.

**July 19** Ceskoslovenske Statni Aerolinie (CSA) is formed.

**July 30** The de Havilland D.H.50 four-seat transport biplane makes its first flight. In early August it wins the reliability trial at the International Aeronautical Exhibition at Gothenberg, flown by Alan Cobham.

**August 14** British Marine Air Navigation Company inaugurates a flying-boat airline service to the Channel Islands and France.

**August 21** Ground-mounted electric beacons are first used in the U.S.A. to illuminate flight direction.

**August 23** First flight of the Polikarpov I-1(I1-400) cantilever low-wing monoplane fighter, powered by an American Liberty engine. Despite some stability problems the I-1 becomes the first Soviet fighter put into full production.

**August 27/28** Smith and Richter remain airborne in their D.H.4B for 37 hrs 16 mins, being refuelled 15 times by a D.H.4B tanker.

**September 4** The first flight of the rigid airship ZR-l *Shenandoah*, the U.S. Navy's first helium-filled airship, takes place over Lakehurst, New Jersey.

**September 9** The first flight is made of a Curtiss R2C-l. U.S. Navy pilots achieve first and second places in the 1923 Pulitzer Trophy race in R2C-1s, and on November 4 one sets a new world speed record of 267.16mph (429.96km/h).

**September 28** America gains first and second places in the Schneider Trophy contest with Curtiss CR-3 biplanes. The winner's average speed is 177.38mph (285.6km/h). America also wins the next contest, held in 1925.

**October** The Gloster Grebe biplane fighter enters service with the R.A.F. It is the first new fighter accepted by the force since the end of the First World War.

**October 2** The prototype de Havilland D.H.53 Humming Bird flies for the first time. The company's first light plane, it was designed and built as a small single-seater powered by a 750cc Douglas converted motorcycle engine and produced to compete in the *Daily Mail* Lympne Motor Glider Competitions (q.v. October 8, 1923). Other Humming Birds follow, powered by various engines, two being used by the R.A.F. for parasite experiments with the R 33 airship. (q.v. October 15, 1925).

**October 8** The Lympne (Kent, England) Motor Glider Competitions begin. The main prizes are awarded to the pilots of the English Electric Wren and the ANEC monoplane, both of which manage to fly 87.5 miles (140.8km) on one gallon of fuel.

**October 28** CSA begins scheduled services from Prague to Uzhgorod.

**November 1** The Finnish airline Aero O/Y is established. It begins operations on March 24 the following year. It later joins with Aktiebolaget Aerotransport on a service between Helsinki and Stockholm. It later becomes Finnair.

**December 12** The Italian airline Aero Expresso Italiana is established, although not beginning its services until 1926. It is the first Italian airline founded that eventually operates regular scheduled and sustained services.

## 1924

The Soviet Red Air Fleet is renamed Voenno-Vozdushniye Sily (VVS).

The Soviet naval aviation Voenno-Vozdushniye Sily-Voenno Morskovo Flota (VVS-VMF) is formed.

Huff Daland Dusters is formed as the world's first crop-dusting company. In 1929 Delta Air Service is formed when passenger services are inaugurated.

**March 31** Imperial Airways, the first British national airline company, is formed from Handley Page Transport, Daimler Airway, Instone Air Line and the British Marine Air Navigation Company.

**April** The Fleet Air Arm of the R.A.F. is formed in the U.K.

**April 6** Four Douglas DWCs (Douglas World Cruisers) under the command of Maj. F. Martin, U.S. Army Air Service, leave Seattle, Washington, in an attempt to circumnavigate the world. (q.v. April 30, 1924 and September 28, 1924)

**April 18** The Argentine Marquis de Pateras Pescara's third helicopter (with co-axial contra-rotating rotors) sets a world record flying a distance of 2,415ft (736m) at Issy-les-Moulineaux. Powered by a 180hp (134kW) Hispano-Suiza engine, No. 3 can lift a pilot but is directionally unstable

**April 28** Imperial Airways inaugurates its London-Paris service.

**April 30** Douglas World Cruiser *Seattle* (see above) crashes into a mountain in Alaska and the crew, including Maj. Martin, return to their base. DWC *Boston* later alights in the Atlantic close to the Faroe Islands, leaving two DWCs to continue the flight.

**May 4** The French Oehmichen No. 2 makes the first helicopter flight of over one kilometre. (q.v. November 11, 1922)

**May 19** Wing Cmdr. Gable and Flight Off. Mcintyre, R.A.A.F., return to base after flying around Australia in a Fairey IIID. The flying time is 90 hrs.

**May 26** First flight of the ANT-2 high-wing monoplane designed by Andrei N. Tupolev as the first Soviet all-metal aircraft. Its construction is based on German Junkers designs, but with some original modifications.

**July 1** Regular daily U.S. transcontinental airmail flights from San Francisco to New York begin, with sections flown at night. (q.v. February 22, 1921)

**August** The first flight is made of the prototype Savoia-Marchetti S.55 twin-hull flying-boat. Originally for military use as a torpedo-bomber, a commercial version is later produced as the S.55C. Aero Expresso Italiana (founded in December 1923) uses the S.55C to inaugurate its Brindisi-Constantinople route on August 1, 1926. A Brindisi-Rhodes route is added in 1930. (q.v. January 6, 1931)

**September 1** The British Air Ministry announces that it intends to help form light aeroplane flying clubs in the U.K.

**September 28** The Douglas World Cruisers *Chicago* and *New Orleans* arrive back in Seattle, U.S.A., having flown around the world in an actual flying time of 371 hrs 11 mins. Countries visited include Japan, China (Hong Kong), Indo-China, Siam, Malaya, Burma, India, Persia, Mesopotamia, Turkey, Romania, Hungary, Austria, France, England, Iceland and Greenland.

**October 11** Maj. Zanni, Argentine Servicio Aeronáutico de Ejército, ends his round-the-world attempt in Tokyo, having started from Amsterdam on July 26. His aircraft is a Fokker C.IV.

**October 12** ZR 3 (LZ 126) *Los Angeles*, the dirigible built under reparations in Germany for the U.S. Navy, leaves Friedrichshafen for Lakehurst, U.S.A. It arrives there 81 flying hours later.

**November 4** During the annual aerial review at Centocelle aerodrome, Rome, Italy, the new Fiat C.R.1 single-seat biplane fighter is demonstrated. The C.R.1 becomes the first new Italian-designed fighter to be adopted by the Regia Aeronautica,

**November 20–March 18, 1925** Alan Cobham, A. Elliott and Sir Sefton Brancker complete a return flight between London and Rangoon. The aeroplane used is the second de Havilland D.H. 50 built.

**December 13** 1st Lt. Clyde Finter, flying a Sperry Messenger, attempts to hook on to the U.S. Army TC-3 non-rigid dirigible. This fails and he makes an emergency landing.

**December 15** A Sperry Messenger biplane successfully hooks on to the U.S. Army airship TC-3.

**December 23** An Italian Fiat B.R.1 light bomber establishes a world record by carrying a 3,306lb (1,500kg) payload to an altitude of 18,220ft (5,553m).

## 1925
**February** The prototype Gloster Gamecock biplane fighter is flown for the first time. Production Gamecocks become the R.A.F.'s last biplane fighters of wooden construction.

**February 3–4** Capt. Ludovic Arrachart and Capt. Henri Lemaître set a distance in a straight line aeroplane record in a Bréguet 19, flying 1,967 miles (3,166km).

**February 22** The first flight takes place of the prototype de Havilland D.H.60 Moth, a small two-seat biplane that eventually revolutionizes private and club flying.

**April 13** Henry Ford starts the first regular U.S. aeroplane freight service, with flights between Detroit, Michigan and Chicago.

**May 1** The Japanese Army Air Corps is formed.

**May 10** The first flight takes place of the prototype Armstrong Whitworth Atlas. The Atlas becomes the R.A.F.'s first purpose-designed army co-operation aircraft.

**May 29** The prototype de Havilland D.H.60 Moth is flown by Alan Cobham from London to Zurich and back in a single day.

**July 6** The first Douglas mailplane flies as the DAM-1.

**July 7** The original Boeing Model 40 mailplane flies, having been designed to a U.S. Post Office Department specification, as had the Douglas Mailplane or DAM-1 (see above).

**September 3** U.S. Navy airship *Shenandoah* breaks into two in a squall over Caldwell, Ohio, and 14 men are killed.

**September 4** The prototype Fokker F.VIIa-3m three-engined monoplane airliner flies for the first time. It becomes one of the most widely known airliners in the world.

**October 15** A de Havilland Humming Bird (q.v. October 2, 1923) is released from the R 33 airship while at an altitude of 3,800ft (1,160m). Other successful releases follow.

**October 27–November 19** Three R.A.F. D.H.9s complete a return flight between Cairo, Egypt and Kano, Nigeria.

**November 16** Alan Cobham, A. Elliott and B. Emmott start their London to Cape Town and return flight in a de Havilland D.H.50. Cape Town is reached on February 17, 1926, and Croydon, England, on March 13, 1926.

**November 24** The prototype Tupolev TB-1 (ANT-4) twin-engined monoplane bomber flies, having been designed by V.M. Petlyakov. Production aircraft enter service as the first Soviet heavy bombers in 1929.

## 1926
The Junkers G 31 12/15-passenger low-wing monoplane airliner appears. Deutsche Luft-Hansa receives its first aircraft in 1928, being introduced on the Berlin to Amsterdam and London services in March.

**January 6** Deutsche Luft-Hansa is formed by the merger of Deutsche Aero Lloyd and Junkers Luftverkehr.

**January 22–February 10** The first east-west aeroplane crossing of the South Atlantic is made by Commandante Franco in a Dornier Wal flying-boat. The flight is in stages.

**March 1–June 2** The R.A.F.'s first official long-distance formation flight is carried out. Four Fairey IIIDs are led by Wing Cmdr. C.W.H. Pulford from Cairo to Cape Town, back to Cairo and then to Lee-on-Solent, England, a distance of 14,000 miles (22,530km).

**March 8** Dr. Robert H. Goddard statically tests a rocket at the Clark University. This has an oxygen pressure-feed system for the propellants.

**March 16** Dr. Robert H. Goddard launches the first successful liquid-fuelled rocket from a farm at Auburn, Massachusetts. It flies for just over 2 seconds, travelling 184ft (56m) at a speed of about 60mph (97km/h).

**April 6** Deutsche Luft-Hansa begins commercial operations, flying between Berlin, Halle, Erfurt, Stuttgart and Zurich. The aircraft used is a Dornier Komet III.

Varney Speed Lines begins the first U.S. commercial airmail between Pasco and Elko. The aircraft used are Swallow biplanes. In 1937 Varney becomes Continental Air Lines.

**April 17** Airmail flights by Western Air Express begin, operating between Los Angeles and Salt Lake City. Eventually becomes Western Airlines.

**May 9** Lt. Cmdr. Richard E. Byrd, U.S. Navy, and Floyd Bennett make the first aeroplane flight over the North Pole in Fokker EVIIA-3m *Josephine Ford*.

**May 11–14** Norwegian Roald Amundsen leads an expedition which makes the first airship flight over the North Pole, the airship *Norge* flying from Spitzbergen to Teller, Alaska. Other crew members include the American Lincoln Ellsworth and the Italian Umberto Nobile.

**May 23** Western Air Express begins the first sustained scheduled passenger services in the U.S.A., flying between Salt Lake City and Los Angeles. It had inaugurated its mail services on April 17.

**June 11** The prototype Ford 4-AT Tri-motor flies for the first time. It is an 11-passenger airliner.

**June 16** Imperial Airways starts using Argosy biplanes on its London to Paris service and for the first time the route becomes fully self-supporting.

**June 30–October 1** Alan Cobham completes the first England to Australia and return flight in a de Havilland D.H.50, finally landing on the Thames near the British Houses of Parliament.

**July 1** A Blackburn Dart makes the first night landing on an aircraft carrier, H.M.S. *Furious*.

**July 2** The U.S. Army Air Service becomes the U.S. Army Air Corps.

**July 24–September 26** Two Junkers G 24 airliners leave Berlin to fly to Peking and back, arriving back in Berlin on September 26. The G 24 is basically a re-engined G 23, becoming the major production version.

**July 28** A U.S. Navy submarine deploys and recovers a seaplane during experiments.

**September 16** The new French heavy bomber, the Lioré et Olivier 20, sets a world distance record while carrying a 4,409lb (2,000kg) payload.

**September 30** The prototype de Havilland D.H.66 Hercules 14-passenger biplane airliner flies for the first time. Production aircraft are used initially on Imperial Airways' Cairo-Karachi route.

**October 21** Two Gloster Grebe fighters are released while airborne from the airship R 33.

**November 3** The prototype Boeing F2B-l single-seat biplane fighter for the U.S. Navy flies for the first time.

**November 15–January 8, 1927** T. Neville Stack and B.S. Leete fly modified single-seat de Havilland D.H.60 Moth lightplanes from Croydon, England, to Karachi, India, a distance of about 5,500 miles (8,850km).

**December 20–January, 1927** An Imperial Airways Hercules airliner makes a proving flight for the proposed England-India air service.

## 1927

**January 7** Imperial Airways begins a Basra-Cairo air service. Cairo is then linked to Port Said, where ships continue to Marseille. In 1929 the route is extended to allow a full London to Karachi service.

**January 15** The U.S. Post Office's San Francisco-Chicago mail route is won by Boeing and forms Boeing Air Transport to do the flying.

**March 14** Pan American Airways is formed as a subsidiary of AVCO.

**March 21** Deutsche Luft-Hansa extends its European routes from Berlin, to take in Prague and Vienna.

**March 27** Charles Lindbergh's entry for the Raymond Orteig prize is accepted. (q.v. May 20-21, 1927)

**March 30–May 22** Four R.A.F. Fairey IIIDs make a return flight between Cairo and Cape Town.

**April 13** A Deutsche Luft-Hansa Rohrbach Roland I crosses the Alps.

**April 28** The Ryan NYP, an improved version of the M-l for Charles Lindbergh, is flown for the first time.

**May 1** Imperial Airways starts the first luxury air service, introducing the 'Silver Wing' service providing lunch on its London to Paris Argosy route.

**May 7** The airline Viação Aérea Rio-Gradense SA (VARIG) is formed in Brazil.

**May 8** Charles Eugène Jules Marie Nungesser takes off for an attempted east-west crossing of the Atlantic in a Levasseur PL8. He dies in the attempt. Nungesser is remembered as the third highest-scoring French fighter pilot of the First World War.

**May 17** The prototype Bristol Bulldog single-seat biplane fighter flies for the first time.

**May 20** Flt. Lt. C.R. Carr and Flt. Lt. L.E.M. Gillman take off in an attempt to fly a modified Hawker Horsley non-stop to India. They are forced to land in the Persian Gulf after completing 3,420 miles (5,505km). This flight nevertheless represents a new world long-distance record, which lasts for less than a day.

**May 20–21** Capt. Charles Lindbergh, flying the Ryan NYP monoplane *Spirit of St. Louis*, makes the first non-stop solo crossing of the Atlantic from Long Island, New York, to Paris, France. Flying time is 33 hrs 39 mins and the distance covered is 3,590 miles (5,778km).

**May 27** *Béarn*, the first French aircraft carrier, is completed after nearly seven years of construction.

**June 4–6** Clarence D. Chamberlin and Charles A. Levine fly the Wright-Bellanca W.B.2 *Columbia* from New York to Eisleben, Germany. This sets a new world record for distance in a straight line of 3,911 miles (6,294km).

**June 5** The Society for Space Flight (VfR) is founded in Germany. Its originators and first members include Prof. Hermann Oberth, Max Valier, Rudolf Nebel, Winkler, Willy Ley and the young Wernher von Braun.

**June 28/29** Lt. Albert Hegenberger and Lt. L. Maitland fly an Atlantic Fokker monoplane (Army C-2) non-stop from Oakland, California, to Honolulu, Hawaii.

**July 17** Five USMC DH-4s dive-bomb hostile forces that surround the Marine Corps garrison at Ocotal, Nicaragua.

**July 29** The first flight takes place of the Cierva C.6D, the first two-seat autogyro.

**July 30** Spaniard Don Juan de Ia Cierva becomes the first passenger to fly in a rotating-wing aircraft when he is carried aloft in his Cierva C.6D.

**August** The first Keystone bombers are delivered to the U.S.A.A.C. as single-engined LB-1. These begin the replacement of Martin bombers with Keystone types.

**September 1–28** Lt. R.R. Bentley, U.S.A.A.F., flies a de Havilland D.H.60X Moth lightplane named *Dorys* from London to Cape Town.

**September 7** Cessna Aircraft Company is incorporated, having been founded by Clyde V. Cessna.

**October 14–15** Capt. Dieudonné Costes and Lt. Cmdr. Joséph le Brix make the first non-stop aeroplane crossing of the South Atlantic in a Bréguet 19 named *Nungesser-Coli*, flying from St.-Louis, Senegal, to Port Natal, Brazil.

**October 19** Pan American Airways begins its first international route between Key West, Florida, and Havana, Cuba, with a Fairchild seaplane. Regular operations begin shortly after using a 10-passenger Fokker F.VIIa-3m (eventually five are operated).

**November 16 and December 14** The U.S. Navy's second and third aircraft carriers are commissioned as U.S.S. *Saratoga* and U.S.S. *Lexington* respectively. *Lexington* is sunk in 1942 by Japanese forces. *Saratoga* is destroyed in a 1946 atomic bomb test.

## 1928

Max Valier publicly demonstrates rocket propulsion in Germany, thereafter receiving financial support for his experiments from Fritz von Opel.

**January 27** The dirigible *Los Angeles* moors at sea to the aircraft carrier U.S.S. *Saratoga*. It had already proved that large rigid airships could be moored at sea by having first attached to the steamship *Potoka*.

**February 7** Sqdn. Ldr. H.J.L. 'Bert' Hinkler leaves Croydon in an Avro Avian III in an attempt to make the first solo flight from England to Australia. (q.v. February 22, 1928)

**February 12** Lady Heath leaves Cape Town in an Avro Avian III in an attempt to make the first solo flight by a woman from South Africa to England. (q.v. May 17, 1928)

**February 22** Bert Hinkler arrives in Darwin, Australia. having flown more than 11,000 miles (17,700km). His route has taken him to Italy, Malta, Libya, India, Burma and Singapore.

**March 1** Aéropostale inaugurates a mail service from France to Buenos Aires, Argentina.

**March 9–April 30** Lady Bailey, flying a de Havilland Moth, completes a flight from London to Cape Town. She makes the return flight between September 21, 1928 and January 16, 1929.

**March 30** Maj. Marto di Bernardi, Italian Air Force, sets the first world speed record of over 500km/h and first over 300mph in a Macchi M.52bis floatplane, achieving 318.57mph (512.69km/h).

**April** CMA (Compañiá Mexicana de Aviación) inaugurates scheduled airline services in Mexico.

**April 12/13** Junkers W33 *Bremen*, flown by Hermann Kohl, the Irish Capt. J. Fitzmaurice and Baron von Hünefeld, makes the first east-west crossing of the North Atlantic between Baldonnel, Ireland, and Greenly Island, Labrador.

**April 15–21** A Lockheed Vega flown by Capt. G.H. Wilkins and Lt. Carl B. Eielson makes the first west-east crossing of the Arctic.

**May** Luft-Hansa introduces the Junkers G 31 into service. Food and drinks are served during flights.

**May 15** The Australian Inland Mission and Qantas help inaugurate the Australian Flying Doctor service, founded by Rev. J. Flynn. The first aircraft is a modified de Havilland D.H.50 named *Victory*.

**May 17** Lady Heath arrives in Croydon, England, after her epic solo flight from South Africa. (q.v. February 12, 1928)

**May 23** The Italian airship *Italia* sets off for a flight over the North Pole under the command of Gen. Umberto Nobile, but crashes on the return flight. Amundsen (q.v. May 11, 1926) is killed while trying to rescue Nobile (who survives).

**May 29** Pan American Airways is awarded the first of six (of a total of seven) foreign airmail contracts from the U.S. Government, the first operating over the established Key West-Havana route on September 15, 1928.

**May 31–June 9** Capt. Charles Kingsford Smith and C.T.P. Ulm fly Fokker F.VIIB-3m *Southern Cross* from Oakland Field, San Francisco, to Honolulu, Suva (Fiji) and Brisbane (Australia) to complete a trans-Pacific flight. Actual flying time is 83 hrs 38 mins.

**June 11** The sailplane *Ente* (Duck), powered by two Sander solid-fuel rocket motors, becomes the first rocket-powered aeroplane to fly, at Wasserkuppe Mountain, Germany. It flies about 0.75 mile (1.2km) in the hands of pilot Friedrich Stamer.

**June 25** The prototype of the Boeing F4B and P-12 naval and army fighter biplanes makes its maiden flight.

**July 3–5** The first over 7,000km distance in a straight line record is set by an Italian Savoia-Marchetti S.64 three-seat monoplane, flown by Capt. Arturo Ferrarin and Major Carlo Del Prete.

**August** The British *Daily Mail* newspaper buys a modified de Havilland D.H.61 for use as a flying newspaper office. It is fitted with a desk for a typist, a dark-room for a photographer and a motorcycle for a reporter.

**September 18** German airship LZ 127 *Graf Zeppelin* is launched.

Don Juan de La Cierva flies his C8L Mark II Autogiro from Croydon to Le Bourget, making the first Channel flight by a rotary wing aircraft,

**October 11** German passenger airship LZ 127 *Graf Zeppelin* crosses the North Atlantic from Friedrichshafen to Lakehurst, New Jersey, U.S.A. The journey takes about 71 hrs.

**October 29–November 1** The LZ 127 *Graf Zeppelin* flies 3,967.137 miles (6,384.50km). This remained thereafter the longest distance ever covered by a dirigible in a straight line.

**December 19** Harold Pitcairn flies the first American autogyro in Philadelphia. (The Pitcairn experiments are subsequently overshadowed by the Kellett autogyros which became the U.S. Army's first rotary-wing aircraft.)

**December 20** Australian Hubert Wilkins and Carl Ben Eielson fly over the Antarctic in a Lockheed Vega. Earlier, between April 15 and 20, 1928, they had made the first trans-Arctic flight from Point Barrow to Spitsbergen.

**December 23–February 25, 1929** Eight R.A.F. Vickers Victoria transport aircraft and a Handley Page Hinaidi evacuate 586 people and 24,1931b (10,975kg) of baggage from Kabul, Afghanistan, during tribal disturbances.

## 1929

**January** The Italian General Umberto Nobile accepts an offer to design airships in the Soviet Union.

A modified Soviet TB-1 heavy bomber named *Strana Sovietov* (Soviet Land) flies from Moscow to New York, covering a total distance of 13,200 miles (21,243km).

American Edward Albert Link sells the initial model of the world's first electrical-mechanical flight simulator, later known as the Link Trainer.

Dobrolet merges with the Ukrainian airline Ukvozdukhput to become Dobroflot. Reorganized as Aeroflot in 1932.

Professor Hermann J. Oberth completes a liquid-propellant rocket while living temporarily in Berlin. During the Second World War he works on the A-4 (V2) at the secret Peenemünde establishment, and from the 1950s helps with the U.S. rocket programme.

The prototype Gloster Gauntlet flies. In production form, it becomes the R.A.F.'s last open-cockpit fighter.

**January 1** Polskie Linie Lotnicze – LOT is formed by the Polish Government.

**February** United Aircraft and Transport Corporation is formed from a merger of all Boeing's aviation operations with those of Pratt & Whitney, the Standard Steel Propeller Company and others.

**March 5** Línea Aeropostal Santiago-Arica is formed. Later becomes Línea Aerea Nacional de Chile.

**March 30** Imperial Airways inaugurates a

commercial passenger service from Croydon, England, to Karachi, India, via Switzerland, Italy and Egypt. Sections of the journey, which takes seven days, are flown in Armstrong Whitworth Argosy, Short Calcutta and de Havilland Hercules aircraft.

**April 24–26** Sqdn. Ldr. A.G. Jones-Williams and Flt. Lt. N.H. Jenkins complete the first non-stop flight from England to India in a Fairey Long-Range Monoplane. The distance covered is 4,130 miles (6,647km).

**July 3** Lt. A.W. Gordon, U.S. Navy, successfully hooks on to the airship *Los Angeles* in a modified Vought VO-l observation biplane during 'parasite' experiments.

**July 7** Transcontinental Air Transport inaugurates a two-day transcontinental service. This is not a through journey, as part of the distance is covered by train.

**July 10** Eastern Air Transport Inc. is formed from Pitcairn Aviation Inc.

**July 17** Dr. Robert H. Goddard successfully fires a rocket carrying a camera.

**July 22** A Heinkel He 12 postal seaplane is used in attempts to speed up transatlantic mail services, flying from the German ship Bremen while 250 miles (400km) from New York,

**July 25** The Dornier Do X, the largest flying-boat built before the Second World War, makes its maiden flight.

**August 1** The LZ 127 *Graf Zeppelin* leaves Friedrichshafen for Lakehurst, New Jersey, U.S.A. (This was considered in Germany to be the start of the round-the-world flight, making Germany the starting and finishing point. However, by arriving back at Friedrichshafen on September 4, this was slower than the Lakehurst to Lakehurst section of the overall journey.) (q.v. August 8-29, 1929)

**August 8–29** The LZ 127 *Graf Zeppelin* becomes the first airship to circumnavigate the world, flying from, and returning to, Lakehurst, New Jersey via Germany, Japan and Los Angeles. The journey of over 21,873 miles (35,200km) takes 21 days 5 hrs and 31 mins. (q.v. October 11, 1928)

**September 24** Lt. James H. Doolittle undertakes successfully the first blind-flight take off, level flight and landing at Mitchell Field, Long Island, NY.

**September 27–29** A Bréguet 19 'Super Bidon' named *Point d'Intérrogation* is flown by Capt. Dieudonné Costes and Maurice Bellonte from Le Bourget to Manchuria. The flight sets up a new world distance record of 4,912 miles (7,905km). (q.v. September 1–2, 1930)

**September 30** Fritz von Opel pilots the Opel-Hatry Rak-1 rocket-powered glider near Frankfurt, Germany. It flies for more than 1.1 mile (1.8km) and reaches a speed of 100mph (160km/h).

**October 18** Launch of the French submarine cruiser *Sourcouf* which carries a seaplane with folded wings in a watertight container on deck. The only operational European submarine designed to carry an aircraft, *Sourcouf* is accidentally rammed in February 1942 in the Gulf of Mexico.

**October 21** The Dornier Do X takes off with ten crew, 150 passengers and nine stowaways. (q.v. July 25, 1929)

**November 6** The first of two remarkable Junkers G 38 monoplane airliners, at that time the world's largest landplane, flies for the first time. Each has passenger accommodation for 34 in main fuselage cabins, in the fuselage nose and in wing-root cabins.

**November 28–29** Cmdr. Byrd, Bernt Balchen, Ashley McKinley and Harold June crew the Ford 4-AT Tri-motor *Floyd Bennett* during the first flight over the South Pole. (q.v. May 9, 1926)

## 1930

The service test Douglas YIB-7 flies, becoming the U.S.A.A.C.'s first monoplane bomber.

**January 25** American Airways is established, becoming American Airlines on May 13, 1934.

**April 10–19** C. Barnard, R. Little and the Duchess of Bedford fly from London to Cape Town in a Fokker. They start the return flight two days later.

**May 4** The German rocket-powered Espenlaub/Sohldenhoff E.l5 tailless glider makes its first flight near Bremerhaven.

**May 5–24** Amy Johnson becomes the first woman to fly solo from England to Australia when she pilots her de Havilland D.H.60G Gipsy Moth *Jason* from Croydon to Darwin. The *Daily Mail* newspaper awards her a prize of £10,000 for the flight.

**May 6** Boeing's famous Model 200 Monomail flies for the first time. This introduces cantilever low wings, a retractable landing gear and other modern features and is used as a mail/cargo aeroplane with a payload of 2,300lb (1,043kg).

**May 15** Registered nurse Ellen Church becomes the world's first airline stewardess, making her first flight with Boeing Air Transport between San Francisco, California and Cheyenne, Wyoming, in a Boeing Model 80.

**May 17** German rocket pioneer Max Valier is killed while testing a liquid-fuelled rocket unit.

**May 18** LZ 127 *Graf Zeppelin* makes its first crossing of the South Atlantic.

**June 4** Lt. Apollo Soucek sets a new world seaplane altitude record in a Wright F3W-1 Apache single-seat experimental fighter, attaining 43,166ft (13,157m) at Anacostia.

**June 12** The prototype Handley Page H.P.38 Heyford bomber flies for the first time. It enters R.A.F. service in 1933 in production form, becoming the R.A.F.'s last biplane heavy bomber.

**July 16** Transcontinental and Western Air (TWA) is formed from Transcontinental Air Transport and Western Air Express.

**July 29** The British dirigible R 100 sets out on its first passenger-carrying flight between Cardington, England, and Montreal, Canada. The flight takes 78 hrs 51 mins.

**August** Wolfgang von Gronau, flying a Dornier Wal, makes the first east-west crossing of the Atlantic by flying-boat.

**August 6** The bodies of Salomon August André, Nils Strindberg and Knut Fraenkel are found on White Island. (q.v. July 11, 1897)

**August 13–16** R 100 makes the return flight from Canada in a little over 56 hrs. This is also its last commercial flight. (q.v. July 29, 1930)

**September 1–2** The first east-west crossing of the North Atlantic is achieved by Capt. Dieudonné Costes (see October 14-15, 1927) and Bellonte in a Bréguet 19 named *Point d'Intérrogation*. They fly from Paris to New York in 37 hrs 18 mins.

**September 27** The world's first rocket-launching drome is founded at Berlin-Reinickendorf.

**October** The Polish PZL P-7 single-seat fighter appears. When P-7a fighters equip all of Poland's fighter squadrons (by Autumn, 1933), the Polish Air Force becomes the first in the world with only all-metal monoplane (gull wing) fighters in front-line service.

**October 4** British airship R 101 sets off from Cardington, England, to fly to Egypt and India, having received a temporary Certificate of Airworthiness.

**October 5** The R 101 makes two unexpected dives over Beauvais, near Paris, the second causing it to strike the ground. Only six of the 54 persons on board survive the impact and subsequent fire. The dead include Lord Thompson, Secretary of State for Air, and Major-General Sir Sefton Brancker, Director of Civil Aviation.

**October 13** The prototype Junkers Ju 52 single-engined transport aircraft makes its first flight.

**October 19–November 25** R.A.F. Fairey IIIDs make a return flight between Khartoum and West Africa.

**October 25** Transcontinental and Western Air inaugurates the first passenger service across the U.S. continent, from New York to Los Angeles.

**November 2** A Dornier Do X begins a flight in stages from Friedrichshafen to New York. Damage caused to the wing in Lisbon and to the hull in the Canary Islands, and engine changes, means that the journey is not completed until August 27, 1931. The pilot is Capt. Christiansen, a former seaplane fighter ace.

**November 14** The prototype Handley Page H.P.42 flies as a luxury long-range biplane airliner for Imperial Airways.

**November 25** The prototype Fairey Hendon makes its maiden flight. It is the first British heavy bomber with cantilever monoplane wings and in production form becomes the R.A.F.'s first monoplane heavy bomber (except for experimental aircraft like the Beardmore Inflexible).

**December 2** The Airship Guarantee Company that built the R100 airship ceases trading.

**December 22** The first Soviet Tupolev four-engined heavy bomber, the TB-3, makes its first flight as the ANT-6 prototype. At that time it is the largest landplane in the world.

## 1931

First trials of the Soviet 67-mm recoilless guns mounted on the experimental TsKB-7 fighter and a modified I-4.

The Rocket Propulsion Study Group (GIRD) is founded in Moscow. One of its leading scientists is Fridrikh Tsander, a rocket expert of Latvian origin.

German Wolf Hirth makes the first thermal flight over a city, piloting a sailplane over New York.

**January 6** Twelve Savoia-Marchetti S.55A flying-boats of the 93rd Seaplane Bombers Group of Orbetello, under the command of Gen. Italo Balbo and flying in four squadrons (including two reserve aircraft), complete the first formation flight across the South Atlantic, flying from Bolama in Portuguese Guinea to Natal, Brazil, taking over 18 hours. The epic flight had actually begun on December 17,

1930, when 16 aircraft had made staged flights to Bolama for the Atlantic crossing that began on the 5th (four S-55As had accidents or alighted during the Atlantic cruise). Ten were sold to Brazil thereafter.

**February 26–March 1** A Blériot 110 two-seat monoplane sets a new distance in a closed circuit record at 5,481.928 miles (8,822.325km), flown by Lucien Bossoutrot and Maurice Rossi.

**February 28** Imperial Airways inaugurates the first commercial service from England to Central Africa, carrying passengers from Croydon to Khartoum (the Sudan) via Greece, Crete and Egypt, and airmail on to Lake Victoria.

**March 26** Swissair is formed from Ad Astra Aero AG and Basler Luftverkehr.

**April** The prototype Ju 52/3m (three-engined) transport aircraft makes its first flight.

**April 1–9** C.W. Scott makes a solo flight in a de Havilland Moth lightplane from Lympne, England, to Darwin, Australia.

**April 2** Grumman receives a U.S. Navy contract which leads to the development of the FF-1 fighter, the first U.S. Navy fighter with an enclosed cockpit and retractable landing gear.

**April 15** The world's first airmail by rocket is flown near Osnabrück in Germany.

**May 27** A full-scale wind tunnel is first used at the NACA's Langley Field Laboratory.

**June 23–July 1** Wiley Post and Harold Gatty fly Lockheed Vega *Winnie Mae* around the world in a record time of 8 days 15 hrs 51 mins. (q.v. July 15-22, 1933)

**July 1** United Air Lines is formed as a holding company for Boeing Air Transport, National Air Transport, Pacific Air Transport and Varney Air Lines.

**July 22–September 1** Sir Alan Cobham and a crew of five make a return flight between Rochester, England, and the Belgian Congo in a Short Valetta. The round trip covers 12,300 miles (19,800km).

**July 23** A non-stop flight from New York to Istanbul, Turkey, is made by Russell N. Boardman and John Polando in a Bellanca. Five days later they set a world distance record in a Wright J6, covering 5,011 miles (8,065km).

**July 28–August 6** Amy Johnson flies from England to Tokyo in under nine days in a de Havilland D.H.80A Puss Moth.

**August 18** Professor Auguste Piccard and Kipfer perform the first stratosphere flight in a balloon, reaching an altitude of 51,775ft (15,781m).

**September 13** Britain wins the Schneider Trophy outright, having won three competitions in a row, the last with the Supermarine S.6B flown by Flt. Lt. J.N. Boothman.

**September 25** U.S.S. *Akron* is flown for the first time. (q.v. October 27, 1931 and April 4, 1933)

**September 29** Flt. Lt. G.E. Stainforth sets a new world speed record and the first over 400mph by flying the Supermarine S.6B at 406.94mph (654.9km/h) at Ryde, Isle of Wight.

**October 3–5** Americans Clyde Pangborn and Hugh Herndon make the first non-stop flight from Japan to America in a Bellanca aeroplane.

**October 27** A Curtiss F9C Sparrowhawk parasite fighter hooks on to the airship *Los Angeles*.

U.S.S. *Akron*, the first of two purpose-built aircraft carrier airships for the U.S. Navy, is commissioned. *Akron* carries Sparrowhawk parasite fighters.

**October 27–28** Sqdn. Ldr. O.R. Gayford and Flt. Lt. D.L.G. Bett fly a Fairey Long-Range Monoplane from Cranwell, England, to Abu Sueir, Egypt, a distance of 2,857 miles (4,600km).

**October–December 7** Bert Hinkler makes the first solo flight from New York to London in a light aircraft, flying a de Havilland Puss Moth.

**November 3** U.S.S. *Akron* lifts off with 207 persons on board, a new record.

**December 3** First flight of the Soviet Zveno-1 ('Link-1') carrier/fighter combination proposed by V.S. Vakhmistrov. This first combination consists of a TB-1 heavy bomber with two I-4 fighters attached on its wing surfaces. Both fighters successfully leave their 'carrier' in flight and return to base. Later, more advanced experiments lead to the final Zveno-2 combination that is used operationally during the early stages of the German assault on the Soviet Union. (q.v. August 1, 1941)

## 1932

Walter H. Beech and his wife Olive Ann form the Beech Aircraft Company. The Company's first product is the Model 17 'Staggerwing', which flies on November 4, 1932.

**January 20** Imperial Airways extends its weekly mail service from England to Central Africa to take in Cape Town. The first stage is flown by Handley Page HP 42W *Helena*, covering Croydon, England, to Paris, France. The first return flight, which has many mishaps, begins on January 27.

**February 14** Flying a Lockheed Vega with diesel power plant at Floyd Bennett Field, New York, R. Nichols sets a new world altitude record for diesel-powered aircraft of 19,928ft (6,074m).

**March 23–26** Frenchmen Lucien Bossoutrot and Maurice Rossi set a world distance record in a closed circuit, flying the Blériot 110 F-ALCC *Joséph le Brix* for 6,587.442 miles (10,601.48km) at Oran, Algeria.

**March 24–28** J.A. Mollison makes a solo flight in the D.H. Puss Moth G-ABKG from Lympne, Kent to Cape Town, South Africa in 4 days 17 hrs 30 mins.

**April 19–28** C.W.A. Scott flies solo in the D.H.60M Gipsy Moth VH-UQA (originally G-ACOA) from Lympne, Kent to Darwin, Australia, for his second record attempt, in 8 days 20 hrs 47 mins.

**May 9** A first blind solo flight entirely on instruments, with no check pilot on board the aircraft, is made at Dayton, Ohio, by Capt. A.E Hegenberger, flying a Consolidated NY-2 trainer, a feat which wins him the Collier Trophy.

**May 20–21** Flying a Lockheed Vega monoplane, American Amelia Earhart becomes the first woman to make a solo flight across the North Atlantic, from Harbor Grace, Newfoundland, to Londonderry (Derry), Northern Ireland.

**May 24** The giant Dornier Do X flying-boat returns to Friedrichshafen, Germany, after a journey to New York and back that had taken about 19 months. It had left New York on May 19.

**June 18** The prototype of the Dewoitine D. 500 makes its first flight and is to eventually become the first cantilever low-wing monoplane fighter to serve with the French Armée de l'Air.

**July 21** A Dornier Wal, with von Gronau and crew, begins a round-the-world flight, the first to be made in a flying-boat and completed in 111 days.

**August 13** First flight of the startling Granville Brothers Gee Bee R-1 Super Sportster at Springfield, Massachusetts.

**August 14–23** In America, Frances Mersalis and Louise Thaden establish a women's flight-refuelled endurance record of 8 days 4 hrs 5 mins.

**August 18** Auguste Piccard and Max Cosyns ascend from Dübendolf, Switzerland, to set a new balloon height record at 53,l53ft (16,201m).

**August 18–19** Taking off in the D.H.80A Puss Moth *The Heart's Content* (G-ABXY), from the beach of Portmarnock Strand, north of Dublin, J.A. Mollison records the first east-west solo flight across the North Atlantic to land at Pennfield Ridge, New Brunswick 31 hrs 20 mins later.

**August 25** Amelia Earhart, flying a Lockheed Vega, becomes the first woman to achieve a non-stop transcontinental flight across the United States, from Los Angeles, California, to Newark, New Jersey.

**September 3** In winning the national Air Race at Cleveland, Ohio, in a Granville Gee Bee monoplane, Maj. J.H. Doolittle sets a new world speed record of 296.287mph (476.828km/h).

**September 7** Taking part in an International Balloon Race held at Basle, Switzerland, U.S. Navy Lts. T. Settle and W. Bushnell not only win the event, but in landing at Vilna, Poland, establish a new balloon world distance record of 963.12 miles (1,550km).

**September 25** Capt. Lewis A. Yancey sets a new world altitude record for autogyros at

Boston, Massachusetts, of 21,500ft (6,553m). The aircraft is a Pitcairn PCA-9.

**October 15** Tata Sons Ltd. begin a Karachi-Madras mail service to connect with the Imperial Airways London-Karachi route. The first mail is carried by J.R.D. Tata from Karachi to Bombay, and by Nevill Vintcent from Bombay to Madras in a D.H. Puss Moth (VT-AND), marking the beginning of Indian air transport.

**November 14–18** Amy Johnson (Mrs J.A. Mollison) flies solo in the DH.80A Puss Moth *Desert Cloud* (G-ACAB) from Lympne, Kent to Cape Town, South Africa in a new record time of 4 days 6 hrs 54 mins.

**December 11–18** On her return flight from Cape Town, Amy Johnson lands in *Desert Cloud* at Croydon, Surrey on December 18, having established a new South Africa to England record time of 7 days 7 hrs 5 mins.

## 1933

**January 2** Orville Wright is awarded the first Honorary Fellowship of the U.S. Institute of Aeronautical Sciences,

**February 6** The Fairey Long-Range Monoplane Mk.II (K1991), crewed by Sqdn. Ldr. O.R. Gayford and Flt. Lt. G.E. Nicholetts takes off from R.A.F. Cranwell. Landing at Walvis Bay, South Africa, on February 8, they have established a new non-stop world long distance record of 5,309.24 miles (8,544.37km).

**February 6–9** J.A. Mollison takes off from Lympne, Kent, again in the Puss Moth *The*

*Heart's Content* with Port Natal, Brazil as his target for a new U.K.-South America record. When he lands at Natal on February 9 he has become the first pilot to achieve an England-South America solo flight, the first to fly the South Atlantic solo east-west, and the first to have made solo flights across both the North and South Atlantic.

**February 8** The first flight is recorded of the Boeing Model 247, representing an important step towards the modern airliner. It is of all-metal construction, has a cantilever low-set monoplane wing, retractable landing gear, twin-engine power plant with controllable pitch propellers, and carries up to 10 passengers and 400lb (181kg) of mail.

**March 30** Boeing's new airliner, the Model 247, enters service with United Air Lines.

**April 3** Two biplanes built by the Westland Aircraft Company of Yeovil, Somerset, become the first to fly over the 29,028ft (8,848m) peak of Mount Everest. These are the P.V.3 (G-ACAZ) with Sqdn. Ldr. the Marquis of Douglas and Clydesdale and L.V.S. Blacker, and the P.V.6 (G-ACBR) with Flt. Lt. D.F. McIntyre and S.R. Bonnet.

**April 4** The U.S. Navy dirigible U.S.S. *Akron* crashes into the sea off the New Jersey coast during a violent storm, killing 73 personnel. Among them is Rear Adm. William A. Moffett, Chief of the U.S. Navy's Bureau of Aeronautics.

**April 21** Less than three weeks after the loss of the U.S.S. *Akron* a new dirigible for the

navy, the U.S.S. *Macon*, makes its first flight. It, too, was destined to end its useful life in the sea.

**June 6** A Dornier Do 8-t Wal crosses the South Atlantic with one stop only at a refuelling ship.

**June 23** The new dirigible U.S.S. *Macon* is commissioned by the U.S. Navy. One of its tasks is to take over a role carried out formerly by the U.S.S. *Akron*, as 'mothership' for the Sparrowhawk parasite fighters.

**July 1** Unable to acquire Boeing Model 247s until the requirements of competing United Air Lines have been met, Transcontinental & Western Air requests the Douglas Aircraft Company to develop a worthy competitor. The resulting Douglas DC-1 records its first flight on this date, from Clover Field, Santa Monica.

**July 1–15** Under the command of the Italian Gen. Italo Balbo, 24 Savoia-Marchetti S-55X flying-boats fly from Italy to Chicago, Illinois, to take part in the Century of Progress Exposition. In the process, they record the first formation flight across the North Atlantic.

**July 15–22** Flying the Lockheed Vega *Winnie Mae*, American Wiley Post records the first round-the-world solo flight. His 15,596 mile (25,099km) route is from and to Floyd Bennett Field, New York, via Berlin, Moscow, Irkutsk, and Alaska.

**July 22–24** Flying the D.H.84 Dragon Seafarer (G-ACCV), Amy and Jim Mollison make an east-west crossing of the North

Atlantic from Pendine Sands, Wales. Their objective was to reach New York, but low on fuel and attempting to land at Bridgeport, Connecticut, the Seafarer overturned and was wrecked. Fortunately, neither of Britain's record-breaking pilots is seriously injured.

**August 17** The Soviet Union flight-tests its first rocket, the GIRD-X, with semi-liquid fuel.

**August 30** Air France (Compagnie Nationale Air France) is established, following acquisitions that had combined Air Orient, Air-Union, Compagnie Aéropostale, and some smaller airlines,

**October 4–11** Sir Charles Kingsford Smith, flying the Percival Gull Four *Miss Southern Cross* (G-ACJV), takes off from Lympne, Kent on a solo flight to Australia. Landing at Wyndham, Western Australia on October 11, he has established a new record time of 7 days 44 mins over the England-Australia route.

**October 12** Crewed by C.T.P. Ulm, P.G. Taylor, G.U. Allen and J. Edwards, the Avro Ten *Faith in Australia* (VH-UXX) takes off from Fairey's West Aerodrome, Hayes, Middlesex, en route to Australia. Landing at Derby, Western Australia on October 19, the flight from England is made in a record 115 hour's flying time.

**October 31** Australia's Queensland and Northern Territory Air Service (Qantas) announces that it has completed its first 2 million miles (3.2 million kilometres) of route flying.

*1933: A Curtiss F9C-2 Sparrowhawk hooking on to U.S. S.* Macon

**November 4** The Brazilian airline VASP (Viação Aérea São Paulo SA) is established.

**December 31** The prototype of the Polikarpov 1-16 (TsKB-12) is flown for the first time. When the type entered service with Soviet squadrons in the autumn of 1934, it had the distinction of being the first monoplane fighter in the world to have a fully enclosed cockpit and fully retractable landing gear.

## 1934

**January 18** Qantas Empire Airways is registered, and thereafter known as Qantas. The new company combines the interests of Qantas and Imperial Airways, with each company holding 50 per cent of the capital, and is formed to operate the Singapore to Brisbane section of the England to Australia air route.

**February 1** South African Airways is founded, beginning operations with aircraft and staff that it took over from South Africa's Union Airways (Pty) Ltd., which had been established during 1929.

**February 3** Start of the first scheduled transocean airmail service between Europe and South America by the German airline Deutsche Luft-Hansa, flown from Stuttgart to Buenos Aires via Seville, Bathurst and Natal.

**February 19** Following a number of complaints from small airline companies in the U.S. who believed that major airlines were being given preferential treatment in the allocation of U.S. airmail contracts, President Roosevelt cancels all existing contracts with

effect from midnight February 19. Simultaneously, the U.S. Army Air Corps is given the task of flying the U.S. domestic airmail.

**February 25** American airwoman Laura Ingalls begins a solo flight around South America, a distance of some 17,000 miles (27,359km). This is completed successfully on April 25.

**April 16** The Brazilian airline VASP begins its first scheduled services.

**April 17** Originating from Pitcairn Aviation Inc. and renamed Eastern Air Transport during 1929, this large U.S. airline adopts its current title of Eastern Air Lines.

The first flight is made by the Fairey TSR.2, the Swordfish prototype.

**May 8–23** New Zealand airwoman Jean Batten takes off from Lympne, Kent, in a third attempt to establish a new England-Australia solo flight record. Flying a de Havilland D.H.60M Moth (G-AARB), she lands at Darwin, in Australia's Northern Territory, on May 23. Her time for the flight, 14 days 22 hrs 30 mins, beats the record set by Amy Johnson in 1930 by more than four days.

**May 13** U.S. airmail pilot Jack Fyre sets a new U.S. coast-to-coast record carrying mail from Los Angeles, California, to Newark, New Jersey, in a flight time of 11 hrs 31 mins.

Formation date of American Airlines Inc. as a direct successor of American Airways Inc. which had been incorporated during 1930.

**May 16** Initial revenue use by Imperial Airways of the then giant four-engined Short Type L.17 biplane landplane. The first of two, named *Scylla* (G-ACJJ), is used to carry passengers and airmail on the airline's London-Paris route.

**May 19** The world's largest aircraft flies as the Soviet Tupolev ANT-20MG *Maxim Gorki*. Powered by eight 900hp M-34FRN engines mounted on or above the 206ft 8in (63m) span wings, it was equipped for government propaganda work that included filming, printing and illuminating slogans using external lighting. It is lost on May 18, 1935 when it is struck by an escorting Polikarpov I-5 biplane fighter, killing all in the two aircraft.

**May 28** Capt. Maurice Rossi and Lt. Paul Codes of the French air force land at Brooklyn, New York, after a 38 hr 27 min flight from Paris, France. This had been an attempt to beat the world distance record they set in 1933, but the long transatlantic flight against long head winds forced them to abandon their attempt.

**May 29** Britain's first regular domestic airmail service is inaugurated by Highland Airways with a de Havilland Dragon (G-ACCE), between Inverness and Kirkwall.

**June 1** The U.S. Army Air Corps ceases to be responsible for the carriage of U.S. domestic airmail. During its short period of responsibility, flown during a period of extremely bad weather, the service had carried some 347 tons of mail and flown about 1.6 million miles (2.6 million km).

**July 28** A balloon flown as a combined U.S. Air Corps/National Geographic Society effort, carrying Maj. W.E. Kepner and Capts. A.W. Stevens and O.A. Anderson, attains an altitude of 60,613ft (18,475m).

**August 8–9** L.G. Reid and J.R. Ayling, flying the de Havilland Dragon *Trail of the Caribou* (G-ACJM), record the first non-stop flight from Canada to England. Taking off from Wasaga Beach, Ontario, they land at Heston Airport, Middlesex 30 hrs 50 mins later.

**September 1** Formation date of the Mexican airline AeroMexico which begins initial operations later that month.

**September 28** Luft-Hansa carries its 1,000,000th passenger.

**October 7** First flight of the Tupolev-Arkhangelsky SB-1 (ANT-40.1) tactical bomber. It is of very advanced conception at the time it is ordered into production six months before completion of the prototypes. In developed form as the SB-2, it is first operational in Spain (where named 'Katyusha') and forms the mainstay of the Soviet tactical bomber force in 1941. From 1938 it is also licence-built in Czechoslovakia as the B.71.

**October 9** For his achievement in completing the world's first solo round-the-world flight, Wiley Post is awarded the Gold Medal of the Fédération Aéronautique Internationale.

**October 20** The MacRobertson England-Australia air race starts, flown from

Mildenhall, Suffolk, to Flemington Racecourse, Melbourne. Prize money of £15,000 is given by Sir Macpherson Robertson as part of the centenary celebrations of the foundation of the State of Victoria. Winner is the D.H. 88 Comet *Grosvenor House* (G-ACSS), flown by Charles W.A. Scott and Tom Campbell Black, in a time of 70 hrs 54 mins 18 secs.

**October 22–November 4** Flying a Lockheed Altair, Sir Charles Kingsford Smith and Capt. P.G. Taylor accomplish the first flight from Australia to the United States. Take-off is from Brisbane, Queensland with the route via Fiji and Hawaii to Oakland, California.

**October 23** Flying the Macchi MC. 72 seaplane, the design of which had been initiated by Italy for participation in the Schneider Trophy Contest of 1931, Francesco Agello establishes a new world speed record and a record in its own FAI sub-class C-2. This speed of 440.683mph (709.209km/h) has since been bettered many times as a world speed record, but in 1982 the piston-engined seaplane record was still unbeaten.

**November 8** Capt. E.V. Rickenbacker, with Capt. Charles W. France and Silas Morehouse as crew, establish a new U.S. coast-to-coast record for a commercial transport aircraft. They record a time of 12 hrs 3 mins 50 secs for the flight from Los Angeles, California to Newark, New Jersey.

**December 8** Inauguration date of a regular weekly airmail service between England and Australia. The London to Karachi sector is the responsibility of Imperial Airways which also shares with Indian Trans-Continental Airways the route between Karachi and Singapore. Qantas flies the sector from Singapore to Brisbane.

**December 20** The U.K. Government gives first details of its proposed (for 1937) Empire Air Mail Programme. This plans that all letters from the U.K. for delivery over Empire air routes would be carried without any special surcharge.

**December 31** Airwoman Helen Richey becomes the first woman in the U.S. to pilot an airmail transport aircraft on regular schedule. Her first scheduled flight, flown on this date, is with a Ford Tri-motor from Washington, D.C. to Detroit, Michigan.

## 1935

**January 11–12** Taking off from Wheeler Field, a U.S.A.A.C. base on the Hawaiian island of Oahu, Amelia Earhart flies solo in a Lockheed Vega to Oakland, California in 18 hrs 15 mins. In completing this journey, Amelia Earhart becomes the first person to accomplish a flight over the route.

**January 15** Maj. J.H. Doolittle, flying a commercial transport carrying two passengers establishes a new U.S. coast-to-coast transport aircraft record from Los Angeles, California to Newark, New Jersey of 11 hrs 59 mins.

**February 12** The U.S. Navy dirigible U.S.S. *Macon* crashes into the sea off the California coast, fortunately with the loss of only two of her crew.

**February 22** Flying a transport aircraft over the same coast-to-coast route as Maj. J.H. Doolittle (q.v. January 15), American airline pilot Leland S. Andrews sets a new record time of 11 hrs 34 mins.

**February 24** First flight of the Heinkel He 111a prototype, ostensibly a twin-engined transport, but intended as a bomber for the still-secret Luftwaffe.

**March 1** General Headquarters Air Force, a new formation within the U.S. Army Air Corps, is established with Brigadier Gen. Frank M. Andrews commanding. This is seen by the proponents of air power as a first move towards an autonomous U.S. air force.

**March 9** It is announced in Germany that the Luftwaffe, a new national air force, has been established.

**March 16** Blaming the failure of other nations to disarm, Germany repudiates the disarmament clauses of the Versailles Treaty and announces a massive rearmament programme.

**March 28** In the U.S.A., Dr. Robert Goddard achieves the first successful launch of his gyroscopically controlled rocket. It is stated to have gained a height of 4,800ft (I,463m) and speed of 550mph (885km/h).

**April 1** Swissair inaugurates its first regular service to the U.K, between Zürich and Croydon, Surrey via Basle, operated with Douglas DC-2 transports.

**April 12** First flight of the Bristol Type 142, a 6-passenger twin-engined monoplane which has been designed as an executive aircraft for *Daily Mail* owner Lord Rothermere. Its outstanding performance results in him presenting it to the nation (named *Britain First*), leading to development of the Bristol Blenheim bomber/fighter,

**April 13** Imperial Airways, in conjunction with Qantas (q.v. April 17), opens the London-Brisbane route to passengers. The first through passengers (two) are carried on the service that leaves London on April 20.

**April 16/17** A Pan American Clipper flying-boat makes the airline's first proving flight from Alameda, California to Honolulu, Hawaii. This is the first stage in creating a transpacific route from the U.S.A. to the Philippines.

**April 17** The Australia-England air service for the carriage of passengers is inaugurated with the departure of the first aircraft from Brisbane, Queensland.

**May 18** What is then the world's worst air disaster involving a heavier-than-air aircraft occurs when the Soviet ANT-20 *Maxim Gorky* is destroyed after collision with another aircraft, near Tushino, killing 56 persons.

**May 28** First flight of the Messerschmitt Bf 109V1 prototype, powered by a Rolls-Royce Kestrel engine and piloted by Hans D. Knoetzsch at Augsburg-Haunstetten. It is the first of more than 33,000 Bf 109s built during the subsequent years, one of the most famous and longest-serving piston-engined fighters of all.

**June 26** The first flight is recorded of the Bréguet-Dorand Gyroplane Laboratoire helicopter in France. This has counter-rotating co-axial two-blade metal rotors to offset the effects of torque, and such features as cyclic pitch control for lateral and longitudinal movement, and collective pitch for vertical movement.

**July 23** A first report on radio direction finding, later to become named as radar, is made to Britain's Air Defence Research Committee.

**July 28** The Boeing Airplane Company's private-venture Model 299 prototype makes a successful first flight with Boeing's test pilot Leslie R. Tower at the controls. It becomes the famous B-17 Flying Fortress bomber.

**August 8** First flight of the Morane-Saulnier MS.405 prototype. Ordered into production as the MS.406 in 1937, it is numerically the most important French fighter in autumn 1939.

**September 17** First flight of the Junkers Ju 87 prototype powered by a Rolls-Royce Kestrel engine. Soon to be known and dreaded as the Stuka, it is the only dive bomber to make a real impact on history.

**September 30** Allied British Airways is registered in the U.K. as a new company formed by a merger of Hillman's Airways, Spartan Air Lines and United Airways. In retrospect, the name British Airways seems more commercial, and is adopted instead on October 29, 1935.

**October 3** With no prior warning and without an official declaration of war, Italy invades Abyssinia (now Ethiopia), making early use of aircraft and artillery for close support.

**November 4–11** The Parnall Heck (G-ACTC), which had been built by Westland aircraft, is used by Flt. Off. David Llewellyn and Jill Wyndham to establish a new Cape Town-England record. The route from Cape Town to Lympne, Kent, is flown in 6 days 12 hrs 17 mins.

**November 8** The Hawker Hurricane prototype, Sydney Camm's single-seat monoplane fighter designed to the British Air Ministry Specification F.36/34, flies for the first time piloted by the company's test pilot P.W.S. Bulman. This eight-gun fighter (in its Mk I configuration) is remembered especially in British aviation history for its vital role in the Battle of Britain.

**November 11** With assistance from the National Geographic Society, Capts. A.W. Stevens and O.A. Anderson establish a new balloon world altitude record of 72,395ft (22,066m) following launch from Rapid City, South Dakota.

**November 11–13** Jean Batten, flying the Percival Gull Six *Jean* (G-APDR) takes off from Lympne, Kent in an attempt to establish a record time for the England-South America route. Landing at Natal, Brazil after an over-ocean flight in a heavy storm, she sets a time for the route of 2 days 13 hrs 15 mins, almost a day less than the previous record gained by Jim Mollison. (q.v. February 6, 1933)

**November 22** Pan American inaugurates its first scheduled transpacific airmail service, flown by the Martin M.130 flying-boat *China Clipper* with Capt. Edwin C. Musick and crew. Its route is from San Francisco's Alameda Airport to Manila, Philippines via Honolulu and the islands of Wake and Guam.

**December 17** A popular date for first flights in the U.S.A., recalling that made by the Wright brothers at Kitty Hawk in 1903, is the date chosen in 1935 for the first flight of the Douglas Sleeper Transport (DST). Better known later under the designations C-47, DC-3, or the name Dakota, many remained in service in the 1990s.

**December 27** The year closes with a peaceful use of military air power; the U.S.A.A.C. drops bombs at Hilo, Hawaii to divert the lava flow of Mauna Loa away from the local waterworks.

## 1936

Early in the year, the Special Purpose Air Arm (AON), an independent strategic force, is formed in the Soviet Union. Subsequently reorganized as Supreme Command's Long Range Bomber Arm (DBA-GK), in 1940, it is renamed Long-Range Air Arm (ADD) in March, 1942.

**February** The Soviet I-16UTI two-seat fighter trainer passes its State Acceptance tests. Also known as the UTI-4, it is the first such two-seat modification of an operational single-seat fighter to assist conversion training.

**March** First flight test of a liquid-fuel rocket motor developed by Wernher von Braun fitted into an He 112. The aircraft explodes but the pilot, Erich Warsitz, is thrown clear.

**March 4** First flight of the German Zeppelin Company's LZ 129 *Hindenburg*, the world's largest rigid airship with a length of 803.8ft (245m) and maximum diameter of 134.5ft (41m). This airship, and its sister ship the LZ 130 *Graf Zeppelin II*, are the world's last two rigid airships to be built.

**March 5** First flight of the Supermarine Type 300 Spitfire prototype (K5054), incorporating eight-gun armament and with power provided by a Rolls-Royce Merlin piston-engine. Designed by R.J. Mitchell, it benefited from his experience in the design and development of the Supermarine seaplanes that won the Schneider Trophy outright for Britain in 1931.

**March 10** First flight of the Fairey Battle light bomber prototype (K4303). Obsolescent in 1939, it was nevertheless built and used in substantial numbers. The first two VCs awarded to the R.A.F. during the Second World War were gained by Battle aircrews.

**March 14** Imperial Airways inaugurates a weekly London-Hong Kong air service which, reportedly, is used initially for the carriage of mail.

**March 17** First flight of the Armstrong Whitworth A.W.38 prototype (K4586), later named Whitley which, together with the Hampden and Wellington, forms the mainstay of R.A.F. Bomber Command in the early years of the Second World War.

**April** First flight of the Fieseler Fi 156 Storch (Stork) prototype (D-1KVN) light army co-operation monoplane. Fitted with extensive high-lift devices and stalky landing gear, it is the first true STOL aircraft to be built. It subsequently serves in many roles throughout the Second World War and afterwards.

The German Research Institute for Rocket Flight is established.

**May 4–7** Flying a Percival Gull Six (G-ADZO), Amy Mollison takes off from Gravesend, Kent, in an attempt to establish a new England-South Africa record. Following the shorter West Coast route, she lands at Wingfield Aerodrome, Cape Town, on May 7, setting a new time of 3 days 6 hrs 26 mins and beating the existing record by just over 11 hrs.

**May 5** Following what had been virtually a campaign of terror in which the Italian Air Force had used modern weapons, including poison gas, against a primitive people armed with almost medieval weapons, Italian forces capture Addis Ababa, marking the collapse of Ethiopian resistance.

**May 6–14** First crossings of the North Atlantic by Germany's new Zeppelin, the LZ 129 *Hindenburg*. The outward journey, from Friedrichshafen to Lakehurst, New Jersey, is completed in 61 hrs 50 mins, the return flight in 49 hrs 3 mins.

**May 10–15** Endeavouring to set a new time for the return flight from South Africa to England, Amy Mollison takes off from Wingfield. Flying over the orthodox route, she

lands at Croydon, Surrey, after taking 4 days 16 hrs 17 mins to gain both the outward and return records.

**May 12** First flight of the Messerschmitt Bf 110V-1 twin-engined strategic fighter prototype from Augsburg-Haunstetten airfield. Regarded as a *zerstörer* (destroyer) of enemy fighters, it is soon discovered during the Battle of Britain that Goering's much vaunted Zerstörergeschwader could not operate in daylight unless themselves escorted by highly manoeuvrable fighters. Nevertheless, the Bf 110 proved an effective nightfighter.

**May 19** First flight of the Consolidated XPBY-1 amphibian, a development of the XP3Y-1, the first of the many Catalinas. A very successful design, it is later also manufactured under licence in the Soviet Union as the GIST.

**May 22** Aer Lingus Teoranta is established in Dublin, Eire, as a private company, originally under the name Irish Sea Airways.

**May 27** Using a de Havilland D.H.84 Dragon, Aer Lingus begins its first daily service between Dublin and Bristol, Somerset. The route is operated in conjunction with the U.K.-registered Blackpool and West Coast Air Services.

**June 15** A first flight is made by the Vickers Type 271 bomber prototype (K4049). To become better known as the Wellington, its design incorporates the geodetic construction developed by designer B. N. Wallis, enabling it to retain structural integrity despite heavy

punishment from enemy weapons.

**June 25** The Bristol Blenheim I light bomber prototype (K7033), developed from the Type 142 *Britain First* (q.v. April 12, 1935), makes its first flight.

**June 26** Piloted by Ewald Rohlfs, the Focke Wulf Fw 61 twin rotor helicopter prototype makes its first flight of about half-a-minute's duration. Development over the ensuing 12 months is to establish this aircraft as the world's first completely successful helicopter.

**July 3** First flight at Rochester, Kent, of the first of the Short S.23 'C-class' flying-boats for Imperial Airways, piloted by John Parker and flown almost unintentionally for 14 minutes. This is G-ADHL, which was named subsequently as *Canopus*.

**July 18** Simultaneous revolt by 12 military garrisons in Spain, and of five in Spanish Morocco mark the beginning of the Spanish Civil War.

**July 20** Twenty Ju 52/3m g3e bomber-transports arrive in Seville and begin transporting nationalist troops from Morocco. It is the first large-scale airlift operation in the world; a total of 7,350 troops with artillery and other equipment are carried to Spain in about six weeks, followed by two more airlift operations the following month.

**August 7** The first six Heinkel He 51 fighters with their pilots and ground crew arrive in Cadiz, Spain, as the initial consignment of German military assistance promised to General Franco.

**September 4–5** South Africa's Mrs Beryl Markham, flying the Percival Vega Gull *The Messenger* (VP-KCC), takes off from Abingdon, Berkshire to achieve the first east-west solo transatlantic crossing by a woman pilot. She force-lands due to fuel shortage at Baleine Cove, Cape Breton Island, after a flight of 21 hrs 35 mins.

**September 29–October 1** The Schlesinger Air Race (U.K.-South Africa), held in conjunction with the Empire Exhibition in Johannesburg, is won by Charles W.A. Scott and Giles Guthrie. Their Percival Vega Gull (G-AEKE) is the only aircraft to complete the course, in a time of 2 days 4 hrs 56 mins.

**October 5–16** Flying her Percival Gull Six *Jean* (G-ADPR), Jean Batten leaves Lympne, Kent in an attempt to establish a new England-Australia solo record. She arrives at Darwin, Northern Territory on October 11 in a time of 5 days 21 hrs 3 mins, beating the previous record by more than a day. From Darwin she flies to Sydney, NSW, then across the Tasman Sea to Auckland, New Zealand on October 16. Hers was then the fastest solo crossing of the Tasman Sea, and she had set a new solo U.K.-New Zealand record of 11 days 1 hr 25 mins.

**October 13** The first Soviet I-15 fighters arrive at Cartagena, Spain. Subsequent Soviet help to the Republicans totals over 1,400 military aircraft, paid for by Spanish gold reserves.

**October 15** First flight of the Nakajima Ki-27 prototype, the first low-wing monoplane fighter with an enclosed cockpit to enter service with the Japanese Army Air Force.

**October 29–30** Taking off from Harbor Grace, Newfoundland, and flying the rebuilt Bellanca 28-70 monoplane *The Dorothy* (NRl9OM), J.A. Mollison sets a new transatlantic west-east solo record by landing at Croydon, Surrey 13 hrs 17 mins later.

**October 30** The Imperial Airways' C-class flying-boat *Canopus* (G-ADHL), records the first scheduled flight of the type on the airline's trans-Mediterranean Alexandria-Brindisi route.

**November** The German Legion Condor is formed in Spain in response to the increasing number of Soviet aircraft on the Republican side. It begins operating on November 15.

**November 4** First operational use of Soviet fighters on the Republican side in Spain as I-15 biplanes are flown by Soviet pilots.

**November 6** Intensive air bombardment of Spain's capital city, Madrid, fails to dislodge Republican troops holding the city against siege forces.

**December 21** First flight of the Junkers Ju 88V-1 prototype (D-AQEN) at Dessau. Designed as a high-speed bomber, it is to see extensive service with the Luftwaffe throughout the Second World War, being used in a wide variety of roles.

**December 27** First flight of the ANT-42 (functional designation TB-7) prototype. After prolonged trials, it is redesigned in 1938 and becomes operational in 1940 as the Pe-8, the only modern four-engined Soviet heavy bomber to see service during the Second World War.

## 1937

**January 12** Imperial Airways' 'C-class' flying-boat *Centaurus* (G-ADUT) makes the airline's first all-air trans-Mediterranean service, Alexandria to Southampton, on the final leg of the India-U.K. route.

**January 16** First flight of the Lioré et Olivier LeO 45 prototype, destined to be the only really modern medium bomber in the French Armée de l'Air service at the time of the German attack in 1940.

**February 9** First flight of the Blackburn Type B-24 prototype (K5178) is made at Brough, Yorkshire. To become known as the Skua, it is the first monoplane to enter service with the Fleet Air Arm, and its first dive bomber of British construction.

**February 18** A non-stop flight of 2,222 miles (3,576km) from Southampton, Hampshire to Alexandria, Egypt is made by the 'C-class' flying-boat *Caledonia* (G-ADHM) of Imperial Airways.

**March 5** Airmail-carrying Allegheny Airlines is formed, becoming known as All American Airways when it becomes a passenger carrier in March 1949. The name is changed to Allegheny Airlines in 1953, but adopts the name USAir during October 1979.

A flying-boat base at Hythe, Hampshire, on Southampton Water, is opened by Imperial Airways as the terminal for its Empire services.

**April 6–9** The second prototype of the Mitsubishi Type 97 (Ki-l5) is acquired by the proprietors of Japan's *Asahi Shimbun* newspaper to be used in a Japan-England record attempt. Named *Kamikaze* (Divine Wind) and registered J-BAAI, it is flown by Masaaki Iinuma with his navigator/mechanic Kenji Tsukagoshi from Tashikawa, arriving at Croydon, Surrey on April 9. They secured the record in an FAI-accredited flying time of 51 hrs 17 mins 23 secs for the 9,542 mile (15,356km) route.

**April 10** Trans-Canada Air Lines (TCA) is formed, its first scheduled services being inaugurated on September 1, 1937. The current name of Air Canada was adopted in 1964.

**April 12** Frank Whittle (later Sir Frank) bench tests successfully for the first time the world's first gas-turbine engine designed specifically for aircraft propulsion.

**April 19** The first letter to encircle the world by commercial airmail services is despatched from New York. Routed via San Francisco, Hong Kong, Penang, Amsterdam and Brazil, it is returned to New York on May 25, 1937.

**April 26** Guernica, the seat of Spain's Basque government, is bombed by Luftwaffe aircraft with heavy loss of life.

**April 28** A Pan American Clipper arrives at Hong Kong, marking the end of the first complete crossing of the Pacific Ocean by a commercial aircraft.

**April 30** The battleship *España*, being operated as the major component of the Spanish Nationalist fleet, is sunk in an air attack by Republican aircraft.

**May 2** The Handley Page HP 45 (alternatively HP 42W) Heracles (G-AAXC) records the 40,000th crossing of the English Channel by Imperial Airways aircraft.

**May 6** The pride of German air transport, the Zeppelin LZ 129 *Hindenburg* is destroyed by fire in an accident at Lakehurst, New Jersey. Remarkably, 61 of the 97 on board survive. This disaster brings an end to the development of commercial passenger-carrying airships.

**May 7** First flight is made by the Lockheed XC-35 high-altitude research aircraft, introducing the world's first completely successful pressurized cabin.

**May 28** Spanish Republican SB bombers with Soviet crews bomb the German armoured ship *Deutschland* while at anchor off Ibiza.

**May 31** In retaliation for the attack on the armoured ship *Deutschland*, aircraft of the German Condor Legion in Spain make a heavy raid on the coastal town of Almeria, which also comes under shellfire from the German warships, *Admiral Scheer* and *Leipzig*.

**June 2** The 'C-class' flying-boat *Canopus* (G-ADHL) of Imperial Airways inaugurates the airline's first through flying-boat service from Southampton to Durban, South Africa.

**June 18–20** The Soviet ANT-25 RD monoplane crewed by V.P. ChkaIov, G.F.

Baidukov and A.V. Belyakov, makes a non-stop flight from Moscow via the North Pole to the U.S.A., a distance of 5,673 miles (9,130km).

**June 29** Imperial Airways' 'C-class' flying-boat *Centurion* (G-ADVE) departs from Southampton to inaugurate the U.K.'s Empire Air Mail Programme.

**July** Projekt X, the development of a rocket-powered research aircraft designed by Dr. Alexander Lippisch at DFS, is initiated by the German Air Ministry. It becomes the DFS 194. (q.v. August, 1940)

**July 1** The name Continental Airlines is given to the former Varney Air Transport, itself derived from Varney Speed Lines of 1926.

**July 7** Following a night clash with Chinese troops at Lukouchiao, near Peiping (Peking), Japan initiates a full-scale invasion of China. This date is regarded by some military historians as the beginning of the Second World War.

**July 12–14** Flying an ANT-25 (RD-2), Col. M.M. Gromov, Cmdt. A.B. Yumashev, and Ing. S.A. Danilin establish for the Soviet Union a new world distance record. The flight from Moscow via the North Pole to San Jacinto, Colombia covers a distance of 6,306 miles (10,148km).

**July 27** The first flight is made by the Focke-Wulf Fw 200V-1 Condor prototype. Designed as a 26-seat passenger aircraft for service with Deutsche Luft-Hansa, it is to be adopted by

the Luftwaffe for long-range anti-shipping patrols over the North Atlantic during the early years of the Second World War.

**August 9** A London-Berlin night airmail service is inaugurated as a co-operative effort by British Airways and Deutsche Luft-Hansa.

**August 11** First flight of the Boulton Paul Defiant prototype (K8310), the first two-seat fighter to be used in R.A.F. squadron service with a power-operated four-gun turret.

**August 15** Deutsche Luft-Hansa initiates North Atlantic trials between the Azores and New York. This involves the use of seaplane depot ships which can retrieve and catapult-launch specially-designed Blohm und Voss Ha 139-engined seaplanes. Trials are inaugurated with Ha 139V-2 *Nordmeer* (D-AMIE), which lands at Long Island, New York.

**August 23** The first completely automatic landing by a heavier-than-air craft is made at Wright Field, Ohio being accomplished without assistance from a pilot on the aircraft or by radio control from the ground.

**August 24** A Luft-Hansa Junkers 52/3, crewed by Flugkapitän Untucht, Freiherr von Gablenz and mechanic Kirchoff, leaves Kabul on a trial flight to China; they arrive back on September 27.

**October 16** First flight of the Short S.25 prototype (K4774), which in production form is to become well known as the Sunderland flying boat.

**October 18** Jean Batten, flying the Percival Gull Six *Jean* (G-ADPR), establishes a new solo record flight time from Darwin, Australia to Lympne, Kent of 5 days 18 hrs 15 mins.

**October 25** Hanna Reitsch flying his Focke-Wulf Fw 61 establishes a world distance record for helicopters of 67.71 miles (108.974km).

**November 14–20** Flying the de Havilland DH.88 Comet G-ACSS, then renamed *The Burberry*, Flt. Off. A.E. Clouston and Mrs Betty Kirby-Green establish a record U.K./South Africa out and return flight. Total time, Croydon, Surrey to Cape Town and back to Croydon is 5 days 17 hrs 28 mins, beating the existing record by nearly 4 days.

**December 3–27** Capt. J.W. Burgess is in command of Imperial Airways' first flying-boat survey from the U.K. to Australia and New Zealand, flown in the Short 'C-class' *Centaurus* (G-ADUT).

## 1938

Bristol Aeroplane Company starts series production of the 665hp (490kW) Perseus radial engine developed by Roy Fedden as the world's first sleeve-valve aero engine.

**January** First flight of the Aichi D3A carrier-borne dive bomber. Known under the Allied SW Pacific reporting name of 'Val' it is the first Japanese all-metal, low-wing monoplane dive bomber and plays an important role in the Japanese surprise attack on Pearl Harbor in December, 1941.

**February 6** First separation in flight of the Mercury upper component from the Maia lower component of the Short-Mayo composite aircraft. This represents one approach to the problem of long-range flight.

**February 10** Flown by Sqdr. Ldr. J.W. Gillan, commanding officer of the R.A.F.'s No. 111 squadron, the new Hawker Hurricane makes headline news. This results from a night flight made between Edinburgh, Scotland and Northolt, Middlesex at an average speed of 408mph (657km/h), achieved with assistance from a strong following wind.

**February 20** Under the direction of Sir Alan Cobham, Imperial Airways carries out a first flight refuelling test of a 'C-class' flying-boat. The tanker aircraft is the Armstrong Whitworth A.W.23 bomber/transport prototype, loaned by the Air Ministry to Flight Refuelling Ltd. and registered G-AFRX.

**February 23** The DH.88 Comet G-ACSS, now renamed *Australian Anniversary*, takes off from Gravesend, Kent on a new record attempt. Flown by Arthur Clouston and Victor Ricketts, it completes a 26,500-mile (42,648-km) U.K.-New Zealand and return flight in 10 days 21 hrs, establishing not only a new record for the route but many new point-to-point records.

**March 27–29** Catapult-launched from Start Point, Devon, Luft-Hansa's Dornier Do 18F D-ANHR is flown by Capt. H.W. von Eagle to Caravelas, Brazil. This non-stop flight of 5,215 miles (8,392km), completed in 43 hrs 5 mins, establishes a new world distance record for seaplanes.

**April 16–22** The last of the pre-war Australia-U.K. solo lightplane flight records is established by H.F. Broadbent. Taking off from Sydney, NSW in the Percival Vega Gull (G-AFEH), he lands at Lympne, Kent having covered 9,612 miles (15,469km) in 5 days 4 hrs 21 mins.

**April 20** Air Cmdr. A.H. Harris leads the first British purchasing mission to the U.S.A. seeking suitable aircraft of American manufacture for use by the R.A.F.

**April 21** The U.K. Government announces an expansion of the 'shadow factory' scheme, under which new factories would be built at government expense. When completed these would be managed by approved aircraft manufacturers.

**June** The Heinkel HeS 3B turbojet, designed by Pabst von Ohain, is test-flown attached beneath an He 118 – the first 'flying test bed' for a jet engine.

**June 9** It is announced in the U.K. Parliament that as a result of evaluation by the purchasing commission sent to the U.S., the government has decided to buy 200 aircraft each from Lockheed and North American. These duly enter service as the Hudson and Harvard respectively.

**July 10** Howard Hughes and crew, flying a Lockheed 14, take off on a round-the-world flight. The route – New York, Paris, Moscow,

Omsk, Yatutsk, Fairbanks and Minneapolis to New York – is completed in 3 days 19 hrs 8 mins.

**July 11–August 10** Severe fighting breaks out between Japanese and Soviet forces disputing territory at the frontiers of Korea, Manchuria, and Siberia. Later known as the 'Lake Khasan incident', it is the first occasion the Soviet Air Force uses large numbers of fighters and bombers against the Japanese.

**July 21–22** Mercury (G-ADHJ), the upper component of the Short-Mayo composite, records the first commercial crossing of the North Atlantic by a heavier-than-air craft. Flown by Capt. D.C.T. Bennett with radio operator A.J. Coster, it was launched from Maia near Foynes before flying non-stop to Montreal, Canada in 20 hrs 20 mins.

**July 28** The U. K. Empire Air Mail Programme is extended to Australia, New Zealand and a number of Pacific destinations. The inaugural flight is by Imperial Airways' 'C-class' flying-boat *Calypso* (G-AEUA).

**August** Soviet Air Group in Spain begins its withdrawal, leaving its aircraft to the Spanish Republican crews.

**August 2** Qantas' 'C-class' flying-boat *Carpentaria* (VH-ABA) leaves Sydney, NSW with the first airmail carried from Australia under the Empire Air Mail Programme. However, the first official service is made on August 4 by Imperial Airways' *Camilla* (G-AEUB).

**August 10/11** The Fw 200 Condor prototype, designated Fw 200S-1 and named Brandenburg (D-ACON), is piloted by Dipl. Ing. Alfred Henke on a non-stop flight from Berlin to New York, returning two days later. Less than three months later, on November 28, the same Fw 200 attempts to fly from Berlin to Tokyo and back but is forced to ditch off Manila on the return flight due to a fuel shortage.

**August 22** The United States Civil Aeronautics Act becomes effective, co-ordinating all non-military aviation in the U.S.A. under the Civil Aeronautics Authority (CAA).

**September 10** All foreign aircraft making flights over Germany are prohibited to stray from specified air corridors established for civil aircraft.

**September 14** First flight in Germany of the sister-ship of the ill-fated *Hindenburg*, the Zeppelin LZ 130 Graf Zeppelin II.

**September 23** Because of the German-Czech political crisis, Imperial Airways' Handley Page H.P.45 Heracles (G-AAXC) is used to evacuate British residents from Prague to London.

**September 29** Agreement is finally reached at a Munich conference dominated by Axis representatives. With Britain and France too weak, particularly in terms of air power, Germany is pacified by the 'gift' of the Czech Sudetenland with its approximately 3 million Germans. Neville Chamberlain flies back to Britain claiming 'peace in our time'.

**October 2** First flight of the Dewoitine D.520 prototype, the most advanced French fighter to participate in the Second World War.

**October 6** Imperial Airways' Short-Mayo *Mercury*, flown by Capt. D.C.T. Bennett with First Off. I. Harvey, is used to establish a new seaplane world distance record. Released from Maia just north of Dundee, Scotland, *Mercury* lands at Port Nolloth, Orange River, South Africa on October 8, having flown 5,997.43 miles (9,651.9km) non-stop in 41 hrs 56 mins.

**October 11** First flight of the Westland Whirlwind prototype (L6844), the only twin-engined single-seat fighter to serve operationally with the R.A.F. during the Second World War.

**October 14** First flight of the Curtiss XP-40 Warhawk prototype. Almost 14,000 of these single-seat aircraft are built and used in a variety of roles, many serving with the R.A.F. under the names of Tomahawk and Kitty Hawk.

**October 22** Flying the Caproni 161*bis* at Montecello, Italy, Lt. Col. M. Pezzi establishes a new world altitude record of 56,046ft (17,083m). This has since proved to be the greatest altitude attained by a piston-engined aircraft.

**November 1** R.A.F. Balloon Command is formed, deploying some 1,500 barrage balloons by the outbreak of the Second World War.

**November 5–7** Two Vickers Wellesleys of the R.A.F.'s Long-Range Flight establish a new world distance record. Flown from Ismailia, Egypt to Darwin, Australia, L2638 captained by Sqdn. Ldr. R.G. Kellett and L2680 by Flt. Lt. A.N. Combe land at Darwin on November 7, completing the 7,158.5-mile (11,520-km) flight in 48 hrs.

**November 10** The U.K. Secretary of State for Air, giving details of R.A.F. expansion in the House of Commons, states that fighter strength is to be increased by 30 per cent.

**December 6** A Franco-German pact is signed, this serving to guarantee existing frontiers between the two countries.

**December 8** *Graf Zeppelin*, the first German aircraft carrier, is launched. It never becomes operational.

## 1939

**January** First flight of the Nakajima Ki-43 Hayabusa prototype (c/n 4301) allocated the Allied SW Pacific reporting name of 'Oscar'.

**January 17** The U.K. Air Ministry announces the formation of an Auxiliary Air Force Reserve.

**January 27** First flight of the Lockheed XP-38 prototype is made. Built in large numbers, the unusual twin-boom configuration of the P-38 Lightning is to make it one of the best-known of the U.S.A.A.F.'s fighter aircraft of the Second World War.

**February 5** Flying a specially-modified Percival Mew Gull (G-AEXF), Alex Henshaw establishes a new record time for a U.K-South Africa return flight. His total time of 4 days 10 hrs 20 mins, from Gravesend, Kent, to Wingfield Aerodrome, Cape Town, and return, included 21 hrs 19 mins on the ground at Cape Town.

**February 24** The first Boeing Model 314 flying-boat for service with Pan American is officially handed over at Baltimore.

**March 28** Madrid and Valencia surrender to the Nationalists, thus marking the end of the Spanish Civil War.

**March 30** Flying the Heinkel He 100V-8 (D-IDGH) at Oranienburg, Germany, Flugkapitän Hans Dieterle establishes a new world speed record of 463.82mph (746.45km/h).

**April 1** The first flight is made at Kagamigahara, Japan, of the prototype Mitsubishi A6M1 monoplane fighter for the Imperial Japanese Navy. Easily the best-known of the nation's Second World War aircraft, it is later designated Navy Type 0 Carrier Fighter, becoming nicknamed the Zero. It was subsequently allocated the Allied codename 'Zeke'.

**April 26** The Heinkel He 100's recently-gained world speed record is broken by another German aircraft. Flown by Flugkapitän Fritz Wendel at Augsburg, Germany, the Messerschmitt Me 209VI attains a FAI-accredited speed of 469.22mph (755.138km/h). (q.v. August 16, 1969)

**May 7** The first flight of the Petlyakov VI-100 prototype, later designated Pe-2 in production form. From mid-1942 onwards, progressively improved variants of the Pe-2 form the backbone of Soviet tactical bombing operations over the Eastern Front. Total Pe-2 production amounts to 11,427 aircraft.

**May 14** First flight of the Short Stirling four-engined bomber prototype (L7600), which ends in disaster when the aircraft crashes on landing.

**May 20** The first regular scheduled transatlantic airmail service is inaugurated. Pan American Boeing 314 flying-boat *Yankee Clipper* flies from New York via the Azores, Lisbon and Marseille to Southampton, which it reaches on May 23.

First of the large-scale aerial battles between Soviet and Japanese aircraft in Outer Mongolia near Khalkin Gol.

**June 1** First flight of the Focke-Wulf Fw 190V-1 (D-OPZE) prototype is made at Bremen, Germany. Designed by Dipl. Ing. Kurt Tank, it has since come to be regarded as the outstanding radial-engined fighter of the Second World War.

A plan is inaugurated in the U.S.A. that uses civilian flying schools to provide primary flight training for U.S.A.A.C. cadets.

**June 20** First flight of the He 116 research aircraft powered by one Walter HWK R.I-203 rocket motor at Peenemünde, piloted by Erich Warsitz. It is the first flight of a manned rocket-powered aircraft specifically designed for that purpose.

**July 1** The Women's Auxiliary Air Force is founded, intended to allow women to serve in the R.A.F. during wartime.

**July 25** First flight of the Avro Type 679 twin-engined heavy bomber, later named Manchester. Although not very successful due to its underdeveloped Rolls-Royce Vulture engines, the airframe design proves sound when re-engined with four Merlins as the Lancaster. (q.v. January 9, 1941)

**August 5** Imperial Airways inaugurates an experimental weekly transatlantic airmail service over the route Southampton, Foynes, Botwood, Montreal and New York. Operated by Short S.30 'C-class' flying-boats, flight refuelled after take-off by Handley Page Harrow II tankers, the initial service is flown by Capt. J.C. Kelly Rogers and crew in *Caribou* (G-AFCV), fuelled after take-off by Harrow tanker G-AFRL.

**August 22** Adolf Hitler gives final orders for the invasion of Poland. In Moscow, von Ribbentrop and Molotov sign a 10-year non-aggression pact, the secret clauses of which detail the partition of Poland.

**August 27** The world's first flight by a turbojet-powered aircraft is made at Heinkel's Marienehe airfield. The Heinkel He 178, piloted by Flugkapitän Erich Warsitz, is powered by a Heinkel HeS 3b engine designed by Dr. Pabst von Ohain.

**September 1** Preceded by a heavy pre-dawn air bombardment, Germany invades Poland.

Announcing the invasion of Poland in the Reichstag, Hitler says: 'I will not war against women and children. I have ordered my air force to restrict itself to attacks on military objectives.'

**September 2** Ten squadrons of Fairey Battle bombers of the Advanced Air Striking Force are deployed to bases in France.

**September 3** A Blenheim IV aircraft (N6215) of the R.A.F. is the first to cross the German frontier following the declaration of war, and photographs German naval units leaving Wilhelmshaven.

**September 3/4** R.A.F. Whitley IIIs of Nos. 51 and 98 Squadrons drop propaganda leaflets on Bremen, Hamburg and the Ruhr.

**September 4–9** Thirteen R.A.F. squadrons, comprising Blenheim, Hurricane and Lysander aircraft, fly to bases in France as components of the British Expeditionary Force.

**September 5** The United States proclaims its neutrality in relation to the conflict in Europe.

**September 14** The Vought-Sikorsky VS-300, with a single main rotor, makes a first tethered helicopter flight in the U.S.A.

**September 17** In accordance with agreed clauses of the recently-signed German-Soviet Treaty, Soviet forces invade Poland at its eastern border.

**October 5** The war in Poland ends with the surrender of 17,000 Polish troops at Kock; Germany and the Soviet Union divide the defeated nation between them.

**October 8** A Lockheed Hudson of the R.A.F.'s No. 224 Squadron shoots down a German Dornier Do 18 flying-boat. This is the first victory recorded by an American-built aircraft in the Second World War.

**October 10** Institution of the Empire Air Training Scheme which, with the participation of Australia, Canada and New Zealand, is to cover the training of air crew in their countries.

**October 16** In an attack by Luftwaffe aircraft on warships in the Firth of Forth anchorage, the first enemy aircraft to be destroyed over Britain in the Second World War, a Ju 88A, is credited to Spitfires of No. 603 (City of Edinburgh) Squadron of the Auxiliary Air Force.

**October 23** The prototype of the Japanese Mitsubishi G4N1 bomber is flown for the first time. It is subsequently to be given the Allied codename 'Betty'.

**October 25** The first flight is made at R.A.F. Bicester, Oxfordshire, of the Handley Page H.P.57 four-engined bomber prototype (L7244). Later named the Halifax, and together with the Avro Lancaster, it is to form the mainstay of the R.A.F.'s heavy bomber force.

**November 18** German aircraft drop the first anti-shipping magnetic mines in British coastal waters.

**November 19** The Heinkel He 177V-1 heavy bomber prototype makes its first flight from Rostock-Marienehe airfield.

**November 20** Forty-one magnetic mines are dropped by the Luftwaffe on the east coast of England. One is recovered intact by the British forces, enabling counter-measures to be devised.

**November 21** First flight of the Piaggio P.108B heavy bomber prototype, the only four-engined Italian bomber to see operational service in the Second World War.

**November 24** British Overseas Airways Corporation is established under the BOAC Act, merging British Airways and Imperial Airways.

**November 25** First flight is made by Bell's XP-39B prototype, an improved version of the earlier XP-39, which is to be built in large numbers as the P-39 Airacobra. It has a unique power plant installation so far as U.S.A.A.F. fighters are concerned, the engine being mounted within the aft fuselage.

**November 30** The Soviet Air Force makes attacks on Helsinki and Viipuri without declaration of war, followed by invasion of Finnish territory, marking the beginning of the Russo-Finnish War.

**December 18** The loss of 12 of 24 R.A.F. Wellingtons making a reconnaissance flight of Wilhelmshaven and the Schillig Roads, brings an end to R.A.F. daylight bomber formations.

**December 26** The first Royal Australian Air Force squadron for active service against Germany arrives in the U.K.

**December 29** The Consolidated XB-24 prototype (39-680) makes its first flight at Lindberg Field, San Diego, California. It is to he more extensively produced than any other American aircraft of the Second World War, with more than 18,000 B-24 Liberators of all versions built for the U.S.A.A.F. and its allies.

**December 30** First flight of the Soviet TsKB-55 (BSh-2) armoured ground attack aircraft prototype. In its developed form as the Il-2, and later Il-2m 3, it gains renown as the Shturmovik. (q.v. October 12, 1940)

## 1940

**January 1** The first flight is recorded of the Yakovlev 1-26 (Yak-1) prototype, a design which leads to a valuable and closely related family of Yakovlev fighters to be used by the Soviet air force throughout the Second World War.

**February 14** A Lockheed Hudson of R.A.F. Coastal Command locates the German prison ship *Altmark* in Norwegian territorial waters.

**February 22** Sqdn. Ldr. Douglas Farquhar of No. 602 (City of Glasgow) Squadron, Auxiliary Air Force, takes the first British gun-camera film of the war while attacking and destroying a Heinkel He 111 over Coldingham, Berwickshire.

**February 22/23** Luftwaffe He 111s accidentally bomb German naval vessels during Operation Wikinger. The destroyers *Lebrecht Maas* and *Max Schultz* run into a British minefield and are lost.

**February 24** First flight of the Hawker Typhoon prototype (P5212) powered by a Napier-Sabre II engine.

**February 25** The first unit of the Royal Canadian Air Force arrives in the U.K.

**February 26** The United States War Department forms the U.S. Air Defense Command to integrate defences against possible attack from the air.

**March 12** Overwhelmed by the sheer weight of the Soviet attack, Finland capitulates to its invaders.

**March 25** U.S.A.A.C. contractors are authorized to sell to anti-Axis governments modern types of Army combat aircraft. This is seen as a means of expanding production facilities to the future benefit of the U.S.A.A.C. should the U.S.A. become involved in war.

**March 30** First flight of the Lavochkin 1-22 or LaGG-l fighter, from which is developed an improved LaGG-3, to be used extensively by the Soviet Air Force during the early stages of the German invasion.

**April 5** The first flight is made of the Mikoyan and Gurevich MiG-1 prototype, built in comparatively small production numbers before development of the improved MiG-3. (q.v. August, 1940)

**April 13** The first anti-shipping mines of the war to be air-dropped by the R.A.F. are released by Handley Page Hampden bombers into Danish coastal waters.

**April 20** The training begins of air crews under the Empire Air Training Scheme, to be retitled later as the British Commonwealth Air Training Plan.

**April 23** The British aircraft carriers H.M.S. *Ark Royal* and H.M.S. *Glorious* are despatched to give support off Andalsnes and Namsos to British, French and Norwegian forces resisting the German invaders in Norway.

**April 24** Gloster Gladiators of No. 963 Squadron are flown off H.M.S. *Glorious* some 180 miles (290km) from shore, landing on the frozen Lake Lesjaskog near Andalsnes.

**May 4** A Messerschmitt Bf 109E-3 of the Luftwaffe's II/JG 54, one of the first two just captured in France, is test flown at the Aircraft and Armament Experimental Establishment at Boscombe Down, England, allowing the first full evaluation of this front-line fighter by the Allies.

**May 7** Aer Lingus operates its first service with a Douglas DC-3 (EI-ACA), on its Dublin-Liverpool route.

**May 10** The German invasion of the Low Countries begins, preceded by extensive and effective deployment of paratroops and airborne troops. Belgium's 'impregnable' Fort Eban Emael is easily subjugated by the unexpected use of glider-borne assault troops. According to Luftwaffe records, its aircraft losses on the first day of the Belgium/Netherlands/France invasion are 304 destroyed and 51 damaged.

**May 13** In the United States, the Sikorsky VS-300 single-rotor helicopter, which uses a small rotor at the tail to overcome the torque effect of the main rotor, makes its first free flight.

**May 14** Germany threatens the destruction of all Dutch cities by aerial bombardment in surrender discussions at the Hague. The remainder of the world is shocked by the bombing of the business centre of Rotterdam by the Luftwaffe as these surrender negotiations are in progress. All bomber formations had been recalled when negotiations began but one group failed to receive radio instructions to abort the mission.

**May 18** The British battleship H.M.S. *Resolution* is hit but not sunk by a 1,000-kg bomb from a Junkers Ju 88 near Narvik.

**May 29** First flight of the Vought XF4U-l prototype in the U.S. As the F4U Corsair, more than 12,000 are built to serve with the United States Navy and Marine Corps, and with America's Allies. Most air historians regard it as the best of the carrier-based fighters developed during the Second World War.

**June 4** The British evacuation from the Dunkirk beaches is completed. More than 338,000 men are carried to Britain to fight again, this total including some 112,000 Belgians and French.

**June 5** German forces regroup and begin the Battle of France. This proves to be an impressive demonstration of air power used in close-support of armour and infantry.

**June 8** The British 27,560-ton aircraft carrier H.M.S. *Glorious*, returning from operations off Norway with the remnants of Nos. 46 and 263 Squadrons aboard, is sunk by the German battleships *Gneisenau* and *Scharnhorst*.

**June 11** The Italian air force, the Regia Aeronautica, makes its first attack on Malta.

**June 11/12** The R.A.F. reacts to the Italian declaration of war by sending a force of 36 Whitley bombers to attack the Fiat works at Turin.

**June 14** Jersey Airways begins to evacuate its staff and equipment to the U.K. mainland by air with assistance from the R.A.F.'s No. 24 (Communications) Squadron.

**June 17–18** The last serviceable aircraft of the British Expeditionary Force are flown from Nantes, France to R.A.F. Tangmere, Sussex.

**June 21** Hitler meets French officials in a railway carriage in Compiègne Forest, where the Armistice of 1918 had been signed, to accept their capitulation. Hostilities between France and Germany officially end four days later.

**July 1/2** The R.A.F. drops its first 2,000-lb bomb in an attack on the battleship *Scharnhorst* at Kiel.

**July 3** Aircraft of the Fleet Air Arm take part in an attack on the French fleet at Oran. This is made in an attempt to ensure that the vessels do not fall into German hands.

**July 7** The Spanish airline Iberia is reformed as the national airline, financed originally by the Spanish Government and Deutsche Luft-Hansa.

**July 10** Date regarded generally as the opening phase of the Luftwaffe/R.A.F. confrontation known as the Battle of Britain.

**July 14** Air reconnaissance provides evidence of a build-up of barges and materials at cross-Channel ports, clearly intended for a German invasion of Britain.

**July 16** Bombardier training begins in U.S.A.A.C. schools, initially at Lowry Field, Colorado.

**August** First flight of the DFS 194 research aircraft under full rocket power at Peenemünde, piloted by Heini Dittmar.

First flight of the Focke-Achgelis Fa 223 Drache transport helicopter. After prolonged trials, small numbers are built and become operational late in 1943. (q.v. also September, 1945)

The Soviet I-200 (MiG-l) fighter, designed by Artyom I. Mikoyan and Mikhail I. Gurevich, successfully passes its State Acceptance tests. Ordered into production, it becomes the first of the famous MiG series of fighters.

**August 16** Flt. Lt. J.B. Nicholson, R.A.F., wins the only Victoria Cross awarded to a pilot of Fighter Command by remaining in his blazing Hurricane in order to destroy a German aircraft over Southampton before baling out.

**August 17** P.O. William M.L. Fiske, first regular American pilot to serve with the R.A.F., dies from wounds received on the previous day.

**August 19** First flight of the North American B-25 medium bomber prototype, subsequently built in large numbers for service with the U.S. and its allies.

**August 24/25** First German bombs fall on central London.

**August 25/26** To maintain the status quo, 43 aircraft of Bomber Command comprising Hampdens, Wellingtons and Whitleys, make the R.A.F.'s first attack of the war on Berlin.

**August 28** First flight of the experimental Italian Caproni-Campini N-1 monoplane, powered by a turbine that is driven by a piston engine.

**September 2** The U.S.A. transfers 50 U.S. First World War destroyers to the U.K. in exchange for air and naval bases at eight strategic points.

**September 6** An invasion alert is given to forces in Britain when air reconnaissance shows that barge and material concentrations in Channel ports has reached a high level.

**September 7** The Luftwaffe begins to make heavy bombing attacks on London.

**September 17** With the failure of the Luftwaffe to eliminate the R.A.F., Hitler orders Operation Sea Lion (the invasion of Britain) to be postponed.

**September 27** Germany, Italy and Japan conclude a pact, each pledging total aid to the others.

**October** The Luftwaffe Gruppe Rowehl special high-altitude reconnaissance unit is instructed to start photographic mapping of western Russia and the frontier districts.

**October 8** It is announced in the U.K. that the R.A.F. is to form a so-called Eagle Squadron, a Fighter Command unit to consist of volunteer pilots from the U.S.A.

**October 12** First flight is recorded of the Ilyushin Il-2 third prototype, this being of similar configuration to the production version. The Il-2 is the first and most famous of the Soviet Shturmoviki (ground attack) aircraft used throughout the Second World War, and built to the tune of more than 36,000.

**October 18** It is announced in the House of Commons that because of Luftwaffe attacks, almost half a million children have been evacuated from London and that thousands are still leaving daily.

**October 26** The first flight is made of the North American NA-73 fighter prototype which had been designed to meet a British requirement for use in Europe. Better known as the P51 Mustang, more than 15,000 are built and the extensively-produced P-51D/K versions (almost 8,000) are regarded as classic examples of Second World War fighter aircraft.

**November 10** The first organized transatlantic ferry flights of U.S.-built aircraft begin.

**November 11** Italy's Regia Aeronautica makes its one and only major air attack on the U.K.

In what is now an historic action, Fairey Swordfish torpedo-bombers of the Fleet Air Arm decimate the Italian Fleet in a night attack on Taranto harbour.

**November 14/15** Guided by X-Gerät radio beams, nearly 300 Luftwaffe bombers cause major damage to the city of Coventry, Warwickshire.

**November 15** Resulting from the U.S.A.'s gain of bases by its destroyer deal with the U.K., U.S. Navy aircraft begin operations from Bermuda.

**November 25** The first de Havilland DH.98 Mosquito prototype (W4050) makes its first flight at Hatfield, England. Designed as a bomber aircraft that would be fast enough to dispense with defensive armament, it has a level speed of almost 400mph (644km/h). It is to see wide-scale service in a variety of roles.

First flight of the Martin B-26 Marauder prototype (40-1361), a medium-range bomber to be used widely by the U.S.A.A.F.

**November 29** A Lockheed Hudson, on delivery flight from the U.S.A., completes the first transatlantic ferry flight to terminate with a landing at Prestwick

**December** First flight of the Yokosuka D4Y1 Suisei naval dive bomber, subsequently allocated the Allied SW Pacific reporting name 'Judy'.

**December 18** In Germany, the first successful flight is made by a Henschel Hs 293A radio-controlled bomb.

First recorded flight of the Curtiss XSB2C-1 Helldiver prototype, a carrier-based scout-bomber which is to see service on U.S. Navy carriers in the Pacific theatre.

## 1941

**January** First flight of the Kawanishi H8K1 long-range flying-boat. Considered by many air historians to be one of the outstanding water-based aircraft of the Second World War, it is later allocated the Allied SW Pacific reporting name 'Emily'.

**January 9** First flight of the Avro Lancaster prototype (BT308), then known as the

Manchester III. It was, in fact, a converted Manchester airframe but powered by four Rolls-Royce Merlins. The production Lancaster becomes the best-known and most successful of the R.A.F.'s wartime heavy bombers.

**January 16** Grand Harbour at Malta is bombed by Axis aircraft, H.M.S. *Illustrious* being damaged.

**January 29** Luftwaffe aircraft air-drop mines into the Suez Canal.

**February 25** First flight of the Me 321 Gigant large-capacity glider, designed for the airborne invasion of Britain which was later indefinitely postponed.

**February 10** British paratroops, dropped by Whitley Vs of the R.A.F.'s Nos. 51 and 78 Squadrons, carry out the first British airborne operation of the Second World War, an unsuccessful attack on a viaduct at Tragino, Campagna, Italy.

**February 10/11** The R.A.F.'s No. 7 Squadron, its first unit to fly four-engined bombers since the First World War, uses Stirlings operationally for the first time in an attack on Rotterdam.

**February 24/25** First operational use of the Avro Manchester is made by the R.A.F. in an attack on targets at Brest, France.

**March 10/11** First operational use by the R.A.F. of the Handley Page Halifax bomber, deployed against targets at Le Havre, France.

**March 11** The Lend-Lease Act is authorized by President Roosevelt, allowing the supply of goods and services to nations that are considered vital to the defence of the U.S.A.

**March 28** It is announced in the U.K. that the R.A.F.'s Eagle Squadron, composed of volunteer pilots from the U.S.A., is fully operational.

**March 30/31** In the first of many attacks, 109 R.A.F. bombers are deployed against the German battleships *Gneisenau* and *Scharnhorst* at Brest, France.

**April 1** In an attack on Emden, a Wellington of the R.A.F.'s No. 149 Squadron drops the first 4,000-lb 'block-buster' bomb to be used operationally.

**April 2** First flight of the Heinkel He 280V-l prototype. the first aircraft to be designed as a jet fighter and also the first with twin-engined turbojet power plant.

**April 9** An agreement is concluded between the United States and the Danish Government in exile, allowing the U.S. to build and operate airfields in Greenland.

**April 15** Demonstrating his VS-300 at Stratford, Connecticut, Igor Sikorsky makes an officially recorded flight of 1 hr 5 mins 14.5 secs duration.

**April 18** First flight of the Messerschmitt Me 262V-l (PC-UA), powered by a single piston-engine because its intended turbojet engines have not materialized.

**May** First Soviet RUS-1 and RUS-2 air defence radar sets are put into service.

First flight of the Nakajima JlNI Gekko twin-engined fighter. Modified to a night fighting role as the JINI-S in 1943, it becomes the first Japanese aircraft to carry primitive AI radar and oblique-firing armament.

**May 4** First operation on the North Atlantic Return Ferry Service is flown by Capt. D.C.T. Bennett, in a Consolidated Liberator I (AM258) from Montreal to Squires Gate, Blackpool.

**May 6** First flight of the Republic XP-47B prototype (40-3051) designed by a team under the leadership of Alexander Kartveli. It is to be developed as the excellent Thunderbolt, built to more than 15,000 examples. It becomes one of the three outstanding U.S.A.A.F. fighters of the Second World War.

The Luftwaffe attacks several U.K. midland towns, claiming that the Rolls-Royce factory has been destroyed. Fortunately for the U.K., the attack has been diverted into open country by use of a 'beam bending' technique.

**May 10/11** Rudolf Hess, Deputy Führer of Germany, flies to Britain in a Messerschmitt Bf 110 and lands by parachute in Scotland.

**May 13–14** First mass flight of bomber aircraft over the Pacific, when the U.S.A.A.C. deploys 21 B-17s from Hamilton Field, California, to Hicknam Field, Hawaii.

**May 15** The first flight is made at R.A.F. Cranwell of the Gloster E.28/39 experimental jet-powered aircraft (W4041), piloted by P.E.G. Sayer. It is the first flight of a British turbojet-powered aircraft.

**May 20** Operation Mercury, the largest airborne assault mounted by the Luftwaffe during the Second World War, lands 22,750 men on the island of Crete. A successful operation, it results in seizure of the island, but losses of about 5,600 men and some 150 transport aircraft bring an end to Luftwaffe paratroop operations.

**May 26** A Catalina of the R.A.F.'s No. 209 Squadron spots the 50,150-ton German battleship *Bismarck* in the Atlantic. Its steering gear is subsequently damaged in an attack by Swordfish from H.M.S. *Ark Royal*, enabling her to be sunk by British warships.

First flight of the Japanese Kayaba Ka-1 artillery observation autogyro. Converted to an anti-submarine role carrying light bombs, the Ka-1 later becomes the first armed rotary wing aircraft used in action.

**June 20** The United States Army Air Force is formed, with Major Gen. H.H. Arnold as its chief.

**June 22** Operation Barbarossa, the German invasion of the Soviet Union, begins with a massive surprise air strike. By nightfall, Soviet losses amount to 1,811 aircraft (1,489 destroyed on the ground for the loss of only 35 Luftwaffe aircraft), but this success is never repeated.

At 043 hrs, Lt. Kokorev of the 124th Fighter Rgt. Red Air Force, deliberately rams a Luftwaffe Bf 110 – the first instance of a taran (battering ram) attack during this war.

**July 8** The R.A.F. makes a daylight attack on Wilhelmshaven using Fortress Is received from the U.S.; this represents the first operational use of the Boeing B-17 Flying Fortress.

**July 18** The formation of R.A.F. Ferry Command is announced.

**July 21/22** Luftwaffe bombers make their first night attack on Moscow.

**August 1** First operational use of Soviet 'parasite' I-16SPB high-speed dive bombers (variant of the standard fighter) carried under the wings of TB-3 heavy bombers. These make a successful attack on Constanta, Rumania. (q.v. December 3, 1931)

The U.S. bans the export of aviation fuel, except to the U.K. and unoccupied nations resisting the Nazis. This comes as a severe blow to the Japanese, involved in a continuing war with China, and hastens a decision to unite with its Axis partners in war against the Allies.

First flight of the German XTBF-1 Avenger prototype destined to become the U.S. Navy's standard torpedo-bomber of the Second World War.

**August 3** To provide interim air cover for North Atlantic convoys, the U.K. develops a 'Catafighter' scheme. The first success is

gained on this date when a Sea Hurricane, catapulted from H.M.S. *Maplin*, destroys a German Focke-Wulf Fw 200 Condor on maritime patrol.

**August 7/8** A small number of Soviet DB-3F bombers of the Soviet Naval Aviation take off from the Estonian islands of Dagö and Saaremaa and raid the Berlin area, which is brightly lit. From then on, Berlin is under strict blackout regulations.

**August 13** First flight of the Me 163A prototype under full rocket power at Peenemünde.

**August 18** President Roosevelt announces that Pan American Airways is to ferry U.S.-built warplanes to British forces in the Middle East.

**August 27** Following determined attacks by a Lockheed Hudson of the R.A.F.'s No. 269 Squadron patrol in the North Atlantic, the German submarine U-570 surrenders to the Hudson. This is the first U-boat to be captured by the R.A.F.

**September 7** Hawker Hurricane I fighters of Nos. 81 and 134 Squadrons fly off H.M.S. *Argus* to land on a Soviet airfield near Murmansk, to help bolster the local defences. The aircraft were later handed to the Soviet air force.

**September 14** Messerschmitt Me 321 giant assault transport gliders of Staffel [G-S] 1 are first used operationally during the airborne attack on the Saaremaa island in the Baltic, as part of an attempt to capture the fort at Kübassaare.

**September 16** Following an attack of the previous week, the Luftwaffe drops leaflets on Leningrad, threatening its immediate destruction if the city does not surrender,

**September 23** Oberleutnant Hans-Urich Rudel, flying a Ju 87, succeeds in hitting the 26,170-ton Soviet battleship *Marat* at Kronshtadt with a 2,205-lb (1,000kg) bomb. The ship is badly damaged and sinks in shallow water. This is almost certainly the greatest single success achieved by a dive bomber pilot in the Second World War.

**September 24** BOAC carries out its first operation on the North Atlantic Return Ferry service, using Liberator Is provided by R.A.F. Ferry Command.

**September 30** To date, the Luftwaffe claims to have destroyed more than 4,500 Soviet aircraft since the beginning of the invasion.

**October** First flight of the Heinkel He IIIZ, a five-engined heavy glider tug specifically designed to tow the Me 321. It unites two He IIIH fuselages by a constant-chord wing section mounting the fifth engine.

**October 2** The third Me 163A rocket-powered prototype, piloted by Heini Dittmar, achieves a speed of 623.85mph (l,004km/h), an unofficial world speed record that remains secret until the end of hostilities.

**October 12** BOAC begins a U.K. to Cairo service, the first flight operated by C-class flying-boat *Clare* (G-AFCZ) routed via Lisbon, Gibraltar and Malta.

**October 30** A Consolidated B-24 Liberator with Maj. Alva L. Harvey in command completes a round-the-world flight carrying personnel of the Harriman Mission.

**October 31** It is announced that R.A.F. aircraft operating from Malta have destroyed some 76,500 tons of enemy shipping in the Mediterranean.

**November 12** The British aircraft carrier H.M.S. *Ark Royal* is sunk by the German submarine U-81 off Gibraltar.

**November 30** First Whitleys to be equipped with ASV Mk 11 long-range radar are those operated by the R.A.F.'s No. 502 Squadron. On this date, a Whitley VII (Z9190) of the squadron scores Coastal Command's first ASV destruction of an enemy submarine, the U-206, in the Bay of Biscay.

**December** First flight of the Kawasaki Ki-61 'Hien' fighter prototype. Allocated the Allied SW Pacific reporting name of 'Tony', it is the only Japanese fighter powered by a liquid-cooled engine to see operational service during the Second World War.

First flight of the Soviet Lavochkin La-5 fighter prototype, radial-engined development of the LaGG-3. La-5 fighters first became operational near Stalingrad in September, 1942. (q.v. March 30, 1940)

**December 1** The U.S. Civil Air Patrol is established, formed to utilize American civil pilots and their aircraft for wartime duties.

**December 7** Using carrier-based aircraft, and without any declaration of war, the Japanese attack Pearl Harbor, Hawaii, causing extensive damage to the U.S. Pacific Fleet and shore installations,

**December 8** Following intensive air attacks on R.A.F. bases in Malaya and Singapore, the Japanese invade northern Malaya.

Lockheed Hudsons are used by the Royal Australian Air Force in its first attacks of the Second World War, made against Japanese forces invading Pacific islands.

**December 10** U.S.A.A.F. B-17 Flying Fortress bombers make the first American air offensive of the year attacking Japanese shipping.

Aircraft from the U.S.S. *Enterprise* record the first U.S. victory of the war against a Japanese combat ship, sinking a submarine north of the Hawaiian Islands.

The British battleships H.M.S. *Prince of Wales* and H.M.S. *Impulse* are sunk by Japanese Mitsubishi G3M 'Nell' bombers.

**December 18** Lt. 'Buzz' Wagner of the U.S.A.A.F. becomes the first American 'ace' of the Second World War, destroying his fifth Japanese aircraft over the Philippines.

**December 21/22** An ASV-equipped Fairey Swordfish of the FAA's No. 812 Squadron sinks the first German U-boat (U-451) to be destroyed by an aircraft at night.

**1942**
**January–May** German troops cut off by Soviet forces at Kholm are supplied by air by using DFS 230 and Go 242 cargo gliders, the first large-scale use of air supply to own forces behind enemy lines.

**January 1** Following the signature of the United Nations Declaration on this date, the name United Nations is adopted by the coalition of powers fighting the Axis. The name is perpetuated in the United Nations Organization.

**January 14** The first flight is made at Stratford, Connecticut of the Sikorsky XR-4 helicopter prototype (41-18874). (q.v. October 30, 1943)

**January 28** Two of the earliest North American Mustang Is used by the R.A.F. (AG360 and AG365) are sent to the Air Development Fighting Unit at Duxford. The first operational squadron to receive them is No. 26, in February 1942, with the first operational sortie flown over France on May 5, 1942.

**February 1** First carrier offensive made by the U.S.S. *Enterprise* and U.S.S. *Yorktown*, their aircraft attacking enemy installations on several of the Marshall and Gilbert Islands.

**February 8–9** Following heavy air bombardment, Japanese forces land on Singapore, capturing Tengah airfield.

**February 10** The last R.A.F. fighters are withdrawn from Singapore to bases in Sumatra.

**February 12** The German warships *Gneisenau*, *Scharnhorst* and *Prinz Eugen*, protected by a strong defensive air cover of fighters, escape through the English Channel.

**February 19** A first practical demonstration of Australia's vulnerability is made clear when Japanese bombers attack shipping in harbour at Port Darwin, Australia.

**February 22** The first U.S.A.A.F. Headquarters in Europe is established in the U.K. under the command of Brigadier-Gen. I.C. Eaker.

Air Marshal Arthur Harris is appointed Commander-in-Chief, R.A.F. Bomber Command.

**February 27** The U.K. Army Air Corps is formed, comprising the Glider Pilot Regiment, the Airborne Infantry Units and the Parachute Regiment.

**February 27–28** A first British combined operation against Europe, and involving air, land and sea forces, is made against Bruneval in northern France, After overcoming German resistance, components are removed from a Würzburg ground radar station which is then destroyed before the forces withdraw.

**March** First flight of the Focke-Achgelis Fa 330 Bachstelze submarine-borne rotor kite. It becomes operational in summer 1942, but is never very popular with the submarine crews due to the delays in submerging when attacked.

First flight of the Messerschmitt Me 323 Gigant six-engined large-capacity transport, a powered version of the Me 321 glider.

**March 3** The R.A.F.'s No. 44 Squadron makes the first operational sortie with its new Avro Lancaster bombers, a mine-laying operation in the Heligoland Bight.

**March 20** First flight of the Mitsubishi J2MI Raiden naval fighter prototype at Kasumiga-ura. It was subsequently allocated the Allied SW Pacific reporting name of 'Jack'.

**March 25** Unsuccessful flight test of the first Me 262 Vl prototype powered by two early BMW 003 turbojets and a central Jumo 210G piston engine.

**April 2** The U.S. Tenth Army Air Force makes its first combat operation, heavy bombers attacking shipping off the Andaman Islands.

**April 2–9** Japanese carrier-based aircraft operating off the coasts of Ceylon and India cause considerable damage to installations at Colombo and Trincomalee. Royal Navy operations to intercept the enemy fleet are disastrous, the aircraft carrier H.M.S. *Hermes*, the cruisers H.M.S. *Cornwall* and *Devonshire* and the destroyer *Vampire* all being sunk by carrier-based aircraft.

**April 6** Carrier-based aircraft from the Japanese formation mentioned above are the first to make air attacks against India.

**April 12** Three U.S.A.A.F. B-17s and ten B-25s based in Australia make the first attack against Japanese shipping and installations in the Philippines.

**April 13** In a one-way attack on Tokyo, 16 B-25s led by Lt. Col. J.H. Doolittle are flown off the carrier U.S.S. *Hornet* some 400 miles (640km) at sea. Having completed the attack, most of the aircraft force-land in China.

**April 19** First night of the Macchi C.205 fighter prototype, arguably the best Italian fighter of the Second World War.

**April 20** Malta's air defence is reinforced by 47 Spitfires flown off the U.S.S. *Wasp* about 660 miles (1,062km) west of the island.

**April 22** The Assam, Burma, China Ferry Command is established to air-ferry supplies to China over the Himalayas ('Hump route').

**April 26** Winston Churchill instructs the U.K. Petroleum Warfare Department to investigate ways of dispersing fog from emergency airfields.

**May 7–8** The Battle of the Coral Sea is fought by carrier-based aircraft of opposing Japanese and U.S. fleets. It was the first vital naval battle to be fought without a surface ship of either side sighting the enemy fleet. The U.S. Navy loses U.S.S. *Lexington* and 69 aircraft. The Japanese lose *Shoho* and 85 aircraft and *Shokaku* is damaged, which prevents its use during the Battle of Midway.

**May 10** The U.S. carrier U.S.S. *Ranger*, off the African Gold Coast, flies off 60 U.S.A.A.F. Curtiss P-40s to Accra. They were then flown in stages to join with the U.S. Tenth Army Air Force in India.

**May 26** The first flight is made by the Northrop XP-61 prototype. The U.S.A.A.F.'s first purpose-designed radar-equipped night fighter, the P-61 Black Widow enters operational use in the Pacific theatre in 1944.

**May 30/31** R.A.F. Bomber Command mounts its first 'thousand bomber' raid against a German target. Deployed against Cologne, 1,046 aircraft are involved, 599 of them being Vickers Wellingtons.

**May 31** The R.A.F. uses de Havilland Mosquitos operationally for the first time in a daylight follow-up attack on Cologne by aircraft of No. 105 Squadron.

**June 3/4** A Vickers Wellington of the R.A.F.'s No. 172 Squadron is the first to make a night attack on an enemy submarine by using a Leigh light to illuminate its target.

**June 3–4** The Battle of Midway is fought, one of the decisive battles of history in which the Japanese aircraft carriers *Akagi*, *Hiryu*, *Kaga* and *Soryu* are destroyed by carrier-based aircraft of the U.S. Navy (the cruiser *Mikuma* is also lost). The Japanese Navy, deprived of its in-being carrier force, had lost the initiative and from that moment forward is compelled to fight the defensive. The U.S. Navy loses the original U.S.S. *Yorktown* and the destroyer U.S.S. *Hammann*.

**June 12** Twelve U.S.A.A.F. B-24 Liberators make an unsuccessful strike against the Ploesti oil refineries. It is the U.S.A.A.F.'s first attack against a strategic target in the Balkans.

**June 13** The German A4 (V2) rocket is launched for the first time at Peenemünde, but quickly goes out of control and crashes.

**June 18** Major Gen. Carl Spaatz is appointed to command the U.S. Eighth Army Air Force in the U.K.

**June 26** First flight of the Grumman XF6F-3 Hellcat prototype (02982), a significant Allied shipboard fighter of the Second World War.

**July 1** A Boeing B-17 Flying Fortress, the first aircraft to begin equipping the U.S. Eighth Army Air Force in the U.K., lands at Prestwick.

**July 4** Six crews of the U.S. 15th Bombardment Squadron make the first U.S.A.A.F. bomber mission over Europe in the Second World War. Flying R.A.F. Douglas Bostons, they make attacks on four enemy-held airfields in Holland.

**July 18** A first jet-powered flight is made by the Messerschmitt Me 262V-3 prototype (PC-UC), fitted with two Junkers 109-004A turbojets, each developing 1,852lb (840kg). The pilot is Fritz Wendel.

**August 15** The R.A.F.'s Pathfinder Force is formed under the command of Air Commodore D.C.T. Bennett.

**August 16/17** The first exploratory use of the Pathfinder Force is made in an attack on Emden, Germany.

**August 17** The U.S.A.A.F. makes its first Second World War heavy bomber attack against targets in Western Europe. B-17s of the 97th Bombardment Group attack the Rouen-Scotteville marshalling yards in occupied France.

**August 20** The U.S. Twelfth Army Air Force is activated at Bolling Field, Washington D.C., in preparation for the invasion of North Africa.

**August 24** The first Junkers Ju 86P-2 very high altitude pressurized reconnaissance aircraft is intercepted and destroyed. This is achieved by an R.A.F. Spitfire VC from Alexandria, making its interception at about 42,000ft (12,800m) although the pilot had no pressurized protection against operation at that height.

**September** A Yokosuka E14YI ('Glen') light submarine-home reconnaissance floatplane, launched from the Japanese submarine I-25, makes two overflights of the wooded Oregon coast and drops four incendiary bombs. It is the first and only time Japanese fixed-wing aircraft raid the U.S.A. during the Second World War.

**September 1** R.A.F. and U.S. Navy Catalinas disperse a 'wolf pack' of German submarines attacking a west-bound North Atlantic convoy. One of the submarines is sunk.

**September 2** A first flight is made by the

Hawker Tempest prototype (HM595), a Mk V built as a conversion of a Hawker Typhoon.

**September 12** The first use of para-fragmentation bombs in the Second World War is made by the U.S.A.A.F.'s 89th Attack Squadron during sweeps over Buna airstrip, New Guinea.

**September 16** Shortly after the third anniversary of the formation of the U.K.'s Air Transport Auxiliary, it is announced that its pilots had ferried some 100,000 aircraft of 117 different types.

**September 21** First flight of the Boeing B-29 Superfortress prototype (41-2) is made at Seattle, Washington.

**September 23** Brigadier Gen. J.H. Doolittle is appointed commander of the U.S.A.A.F.'s new Twelfth Air Force.

**September 25** A low-level attack on the Gestapo headquarters in Oslo, Norway, is made by Mosquito bombers of the R.A.F.'s No. 105 Squadron.

**September 29** The Eagle Squadrons serving with the R.A.F. are formally taken over by the U.S.A.A.F.'s VIIIth Fighter Command and integrated with its 4th Fighter Group.

**October 1** The first flight of a Bell XP-59A Airacomet prototype, the first turbojet-powered aircraft to fly in the United States.

**October 3** The first fully successful launch of a German A4 (V2) ballistic rocket is made at Peenemünde.

**October 21** Using B-24 Liberators, the U.S.A.A.F.'s India Air Task Force makes its first attack north of the Yellow River, China.

The U.S.A.A.F.'s VIIIth Bomber Command flies its first operation, attacking German submarine bases in occupied France.

**October 21–22** BOAC makes an experimental flight from Prestwick to Ramenskoye, near Moscow. The non-stop flight of 13 hrs 9 mins is made in a converted Liberator 1.

**October 25** In a first attack on Japanese-occupied Hong Kong, U.S. bomber aircraft cause damage to Kowloon docks.

**November 2** The Patuxent River Naval Air Station is established by the U.S. Navy as a test unit for aircraft, equipment and materials.

**November 8–11** U.S.A.A.F. aircraft operating from offshore U.S. Navy aircraft carriers contribute air cover for the Allied invasion of North Africa under Operation Torch.

**November 9–10** To counter the Allied invasion, large numbers of Luftwaffe fighters and bomber aircraft are flown into Tunis and troop reinforcements are brought in by air and sea.

**November 12** The U.S. Ninth Army Air Force is established in the Middle East.

**November 15** First flight of the Heinkel He 219 twin-engined night fighter prototype. Operational from June 1943, it is the

Luftwaffe's first operational aircraft with retractable tricycle landing gear and the first in the world with crew ejection seats.

**November 25** Start of Luftwaffe supply flights into Stalingrad. The last remaining landing field at Tatsinskaya is lost to Soviet tanks on December 24.

**November 28** The U.S.A.A.F.'s 7th Bomb Group makes a first attack on Bangkok, capital of Japanese-held Thailand, involving a 2,760-mile (4,440-km) round trip from Gaya, India.

**December 4** Making the U.S.A.A.F.'s first attack on Italy, B-24 Liberators of the Ninth Air Force bomb Naples.

**December 20/21** Japanese bombers make the first night attack on Calcutta, India.

Mosquito bombers of the R.A.F.'s No. 109 Squadron, equipped with Oboe radar, are used in a night Pathfinder operation for the first time.

**December 22** Consolidated B-24 Liberators of the U.S.A.A.F.'s 307th Bombardment Group make the first major air attack on a Japanese air base in the Central Pacific,

**December 23** The U.K. Government sets up a committee under the chairmanship of Lord Brabazon of Tara to make recommendations on suitable civil transport aircraft for early post-war development.

**December 27** First flight of the Kawanishi NIKI-J Shiden naval fighter prototype, allocated the Allied SW Pacific reporting name of 'George'.

## 1943

**January 5** The U.S.A.A.F.'s Northwest African Air Forces are activated with Major Gen. Carl Spaatz in command.

**January 9** The first flight is recorded of the first Lockheed Model L-49 Constellation at Burbank, California. Commandeered on the production line for service with the U.S.A.A.F. under the designation C-69, it is still bearing its civil registration NX67900.

**January 14–23** In a conference at Casablanca, Morocco, Churchill, Roosevelt and their chiefs-of-staff reach some important decisions: to step up round-the-clock bombing of targets in Germany, to begin an invasion of Europe's 'soft underbelly' with Sicily as the initial objective, and to defer the cross-Channel invasion until 1944.

**January 27** Attacking Emden and Wilhelmshaven, B-17s of the 1st Bombardment Wing, Eighth Air Force, make the U.S.A.A.F.'s first heavy-bomber attack on Germany.

**January 30** Mosquito bombers of the R.A.F.'s No. 105 Squadron make the first daylight raid on Berlin.

**February 11** Air Marshal Sir Arthur Tedder, R.A.F., is appointed to be Air C-in-C Mediterranean Air Command.

**February 13** The first operational use is made of Vought F4U Corsair aircraft of Marine Fighter Squadron 124 escorting Navy PB4Y Liberators in an attack on Bougainville.

**March 5** A first flight is made by the Gloster Meteor prototype (DG206). The Meteor becomes the first turbojet aircraft to enter service with the R.A.F. and the only Allied turbojet to see operational service during the Second World War.

**March 10** The U.S. Fourteenth Army Air Force is activated, commanded by Major Gen. Claire Chennault.

**March 24** Battle of the Bismarck Sea, during which a major Japanese attempt to reinforce Lae is foiled by aircraft of the Southwest Pacific Air Forces. Some 40,000 tons of Japanese shipping is sunk and almost 60 enemy aircraft destroyed.

**April 5** Operation Flax is initiated to make concentrated air attacks on German and Italian transport aircraft shuttling arms and reinforcements from Italy to Tunisia.

**April 18** Massacre of German transport aircraft off Cape Bon, Tunisia. Claims of 52 aircraft destroyed are made by British and U.S. fighters.

Admiral Isoroku Yamamoto, Japan's protagonist of naval air power, is killed when the Mitsubishi G4M 'Betty' carrying him and his staff is ambushed and destroyed over Bougainville. This attack is made by Lockheed P-38G Lightnings of the

U.S.A.A.F.'s 339th Fighter Squadron, flying 550 miles (885km) from their base to make the interception.

**May 17/18** Historic attack by the R.A.F.'s No. 617 Squadron, led by Wing Cmdr. Guy Gibson, against the Ruhr dams. So-called 'bouncing bomb' mines are used, conceived by Barnes Wallis.

**May 23** In a new demonstration of the versatility of the Fairey Swordfish, one operating from the escort carrier H.M.S. *Archer* sinks the German submarine U-572 by rocket attack.

**June** The Messerschmitt Me 262A jet-powered fighter is ordered into series production.

**June 1** In advance of receiving its Boeing B-29 Superfortresses, the U.S.A.A.F.'s 58th Very Heavy Bombardment Wing is activated at Marietta, Georgia. It is created to make strategic attacks on Japanese targets.

**June 11** The surrender of the Italian garrison on the island of Pantellaria, midway between Tunisia and Sicily, followed intensive bombing by Allied aircraft. It is the first occasion that a large defended area is conquered by air power alone.

**June 15** The Arado Ar 234V-I Blitz (Lightning), the prototype of the world's first turbojet-powered recce-bomber, makes its first flight.

**June 28** First mention is made that air reconnaissance of Peenemünde had revealed large rockets which might be intended for long-range attack.

**July 9** Following a month-long bombardment of Axis air bases on Sicily, Sardinia and Italy, the British Eighth Army and U.S. Seventh Army invade Sicily. The amphibious landings are preceded with an assault by paratroops and a large number of troop and cargo-carrying gliders.

**July 18** The U.S. Navy airship K-74 is shot down by a German submarine off the Florida coast. It was the only U.S. airship to be destroyed by enemy action during the Second World War.

**July 22** The Canadian Government's transatlantic service for mail, military personnel and VIPs is inaugurated, being operated by Trans-Canada Air Lines.

**July 24/25** The anti-radar device known as 'Window' is used by the R.A.F. for the first time during an attack on Hamburg.

**July 30** First flight of the Arado Ar 234A jet reconnaissance bomber prototype.

**August 1** U.S.A.A.F. Mediterranean-based B-24 Liberators make a low-level attack on the Ploesti oil refineries in Romania. This is the U.S.A.A.F.'s first low-level attack by heavy bombers against a strongly defended target, and its longest-range bombing mission to date.

**August 2/3** R.A.F. Bomber Command makes its fourth major attack on Hamburg within ten days. More than 3,000 bombers are employed in these attacks, but thanks to the use of 'Window' the 87 aircraft which were lost represented 2.6 per cent of the total, rather than the more usual average of about 6 per cent for such operations.

**August 17** In daylight attacks against Regensburg and Schweinfurt, the U.S. Eighth Army Air Force loses 59 heavy bombers.

**August 17/18** R.A.F. bombers make a heavy attack on the German research establishment at Peenemünde, intended to destroy or delay the design and production of advanced weapons.

First operational use by the Luftwaffe of the Henschel HS 293A-1 rocket-powered remotely-controlled glide bomb, when Dornier Do217E-5s of Il/KG 100 carry out an anti-shipping strike against British ships in the Bay of Biscay.

**August 27** The British corvette H.M.S. *Egret*, on patrol in the Bay of Biscay, is sunk by an air-launched Henschel Hs 993 radio-controlled bomb.

**August 31** First operational use of the Grumman F6F Hellcat by U.S. Navy squadron VF-5 flown off the carrier U.S.S. *Yorktown* in an attack by Navy Task Force 15 against Japanese positions on Marcus Island.

**September** First flight of the DFS 228 rocket-powered high-altitude reconnaissance aircraft

prototype in glider form, released from a Do 217K carrier.

**September 3** Peace negotiations between the Allies and Italy are concluded in secret. The armistice became effective on September 8.

**September 9** The Italian 46,200-ton battleship *Roma* is sunk by two Ruhrstahl/Kramer Fritz X-1 radio-controlled bombs air-launched by Luftwaffe Dornier Do 217s.

**September 12** Benito Mussolini, being held prisoner at an hotel in the Gran Sasso mountains, is rescued by German glider troops and airlifted to safety in a Fieseler Fi 156 Storch.

**September 13** In attempts to enable the Allies to break out from the beachhead at Salerno, a reinforcing 1,200 paratroopers of the U.S. 82nd Airborne Division are airdropped.

**September 15/16** An R.A.F. Lancaster makes the first operational use of a 12,000-lb bomb, this being dropped on the Dortmund-Ems canal in Germany.

**September 20** The prototype of the de Havilland Vampire turbojet-powered single-seat fighter (LZ548) makes its first flight at Hatfield, Hertfordshire.

**October 14** In a second major attack on ball bearing factories at Schweinfurt, the U.S.A.A.F. loses 60 out of 288 bombers despatched on the mission. Following this attack, the German ball bearing industry is dispersed.

**October 16** The U.S. Ninth Army Air Force is reorganized in the U.K. to serve as a tactical arm of the U.S.A.A.F.

**October 26** First flight of the Dornier Do 335 single-seat multi-role fighter prototype (CP+UA), powered by both tractor and pusher engines.

**October 30** In order to evaluate the capability of the helicopter, the U.S. Navy acquires a single Sikorsky YR-4B from the U.S.A.A.F. (46445), redesignating it HMS-1.

**October 31** The U.S. Navy scores its first aerial victory by the use of airborne interception radar when an AI-equipped Vought F4U-2 Corsair destroys a Japanese aircraft in New Guinea.

**November 2** First operation of the newly-formed U.S. Fifteenth Army Air Force is an attack by 112 heavy bombers on aircraft factories at Wiener Neustadt, Austria.

**November 5** Carrier-based aircraft from U.S.S. *Princeton* and U.S.S. *Saratoga* seriously damage Japanese cruisers and destroyers steaming from Truk through Rabaul.

**November 11** Further severe damage is caused to Japanese naval vessels off Rabaul by aircraft from the U.S. Navy carriers *Bunker Hill*, *Essex* and *Independence*.

Aircraft of the U.S. Fifth and Thirteenth Army Air Forces co-operating with U.S. Navy carrier-based aircraft launch a major attack on Rabaul.

**November 25** A force of Lockheed P-38s, North American B-25s and P-51s of the U.S. Fourteenth Army Air Force make a first attack on Formosa from bases in China.

**November 27** The U.S.A.A.F.'s 20th Bomber Command is activated at Smoky Hill Army Air Field, Salina, Kansas.

**November 30** The U.S. Navy's giant Martin Mars flying-boat makes a first operational non-stop flight of 4,375 miles (7,040km) from its Patuxent River base to Natal, Brazil.

**December 13** Marking the beginning of long-range operations with fighter escort, the U.S.A.A.F.'s 8th and 9th Air Forces eventually fly 1,462 daylight sorties.

**December 17** Orville Wright, on the 40th anniversary of making his first powered flight, presents the Collier Trophy for outstanding achievement in aviation to his former pupil Gen. H.H. ('Hap') Arnold.

**December 20** Allied aircraft begin intensive bombing attacks on V-1 launching sites that are being prepared in Northern France. It causes the Germans to change over to quick-assembly prefabricated sites.

## 1944

Dr. Ing. Theodor von Kármán takes the post of chairman to the Scientific Advisory Board, U.S.A.A.F. (He initiated the first U.S. Army rocket motor project while holding positions at the California Institute of Technology during 1926–49.)

**January 1** The United States Strategic Air Forces in Europe (U.S.S.A.F.E.) is activated.

**January 4** The first high-altitude mine-dropping operation is made by an R.A.F. Halifax bomber off Brest, France.

**January 9** First flight of the Lockheed XP-80 Shooting Star prototype (44-83020) is made at Muroc Dry Lake, California. It becomes, in December 1945, the first single-seat turbojet-powered fighter/fighter-bomber to enter service with the U.S.A.A.F. in P-80A form.

**January 18** U.S. Navy Catalinas equipped with magnetic anomaly detection (MAD) equipment begin to patrol the Straits of Gibraltar. This is intended to prevent German submarines from getting into the Mediterranean.

**January 22** Large-scale Allied landings, protected by massive air support, put some 50,000 Anglo-American troops ashore at Anzio, Italy without opposition.

**February 15** Several hundred Allied medium/heavy bombers attack the monastery of Monte Cassino, Italy, ahead of the advancing American 5th Army.

**February 17** A massive air attack is made against German formations endeavouring to push the Allied forces off the Anzio beachhead.

Twelve radar-equipped Grumman TBF-1C Avengers of the U.S. Navy, operating from the U.S.S. *Enterprise*, attack Truk by night. This

was the first night bombing attack to be made from a U.S. aircraft carrier.

**February 18** Mosquito bombers make a daring low-level daylight attack on the German prison at Amiens, France, attempting to liberate patriots awaiting execution for aiding the Allies.

**February 29** Aircraft of the U.S. Fifth Army Air Force support the first landing made on the Admiralty Islands, thus completing the isolation of Rabaul.

**March 4** First U.S.A.A.F. bombing raid on Berlin, undertaken by Boeing B-17G Flying Fortresses of the 8th Air Force.

**March 5** Brigadier Gen. Orde Wingate's special force lands at 'Broadway', North Burma, in a night glider operation.

**March 6** In its first major attack on Berlin, the U.S.A.A.F. deploys a force of 660 heavy bombers. A total of 69 bombers and 11 escort fighters are lost.

**March 25** In landing aboard H.M.S. *Indefatigable*, the pre-prototype of the de Havilland Sea Mosquito (LR359) becomes the first British twin-engined aircraft to land on the deck of an aircraft carrier.

First operational use by the U.S. 15th Air Force of the VB-I Azon bomb, a general-purpose bomb with a pair of radio-controlled rudders in the tail.

**April** The Rolls-Royce Derwent I begins flight tests in a Gloster Meteor flying test bed.

**April 4** The U.S. Twentieth Army Air Force is activated in Washington, D.C.

**May 1** Allied aircraft begin a major offensive against the rail transport system of Western Europe.

**May 10** Completion of the Chengtu Project, the construction of bomber and fighter airfields in China. This has been accomplished by some 400,000 Chinese coolies using primitive equipment.

**June 1** The U.S. Navy records a first Atlantic crossing by non-rigid airships, from South Weymouth, Massachusetts to Port Lautey, Morocco, via Argentina and the Azores.

**June 3** A Luftwaffe Junkers Ju 290A transport lands in Greenland to evacuate 26 men of the Bassgeiger weather station, who had been there for ten months.

**June 6** Preceded by airdrops, the D-Day landings on the Normandy coast begin. The biggest amphibious assault in history, it is supported by massive Allied air force operations involving almost 5,000 sorties. By nightfall some five divisions are established ashore.

**June 7** The first Allied airstrip to be completed in Normandy following the D-Day landings becomes operational at Asnelles, northeast of Bayeux.

**June 11** U.S. Navy Task Force 58, comprising seven heavy and eight light aircraft carriers, is assembled and begins to deploy its aircraft in the opening of the campaign to occupy the Mariana Islands.

**June 13** The first German V1 flying bombs are launched from sites in France against British targets.

**June 15** With massive air support from the Task Force carriers, U.S. forces begin making landings on Saipan, Mariana Islands.

Boeing B-29 Superfortresses of the U.S.S.A.F.'s 20th Bomber Command make a first attack on Japan, deployed from their new bases in Chengtu, China.

**June 15–16** With growing experience, German launching crews begin to step up the number of V1 flying bombs being despatched against targets in England.

**June 24/25** First use by the Luftwaffe of its Mistel composite. The initial variant comprises an upper piloted Messerschmitt Bf 109F-4, mounted above a Ju 88A-4 carrying a warhead containing 3,803lb (1,725kg) of high explosive. In this initial night operation, five composites are deployed against Allied shipping in the Seine Bay. (q.v. March 9, 1945)

**June 25** Some 2,400 Allied bomber aircraft make a three-hour saturation raid on German positions forward of the American lines at St.-Lô, France.

**July 5** A first powered flight is recorded by the Northrop MX-324, the first American rocket-powered military aircraft.

**July 12** The first two operational Gloster Meteors are delivered to the R.A.F.'s No. 616 Squadron, then based at Culmhead, Somerset.

**July 17** The first operational use of napalm incendiary material is made by U.S.S.A.F. P-38 Lightnings during attacks on a fuel depot at Coutances, France.

**July 20** First operational use of the Arado Ar 234A turbojet-powered reconnaissance aircraft, flying from Juvincourt, near Reims.

**July 27** Gloster Meteors are used operationally for the first time in attacks on V1s. These are unsuccessful because of gun-firing problems.

**July 28** First flight of the de Havilland Hornet prototype (RR915). These single-seat long-range fighter/fighter-bombers, which enter service with the R.A.F. after the war, prove to be the fastest twin piston-engined combat aircraft in the world.

**July 29** A battle-damaged B-29 of the U.S.A.S.F.'s 20th Bomber Command lands near Vladivostok and is immediately seized by the Soviet authorities. This B-29 is followed by another three on August 20, November 11 and November 21, 1944. These B-29s are carefully dismantled, examined and serve as pattern aircraft for the Tupolev Tu-4, the first modern Soviet heavy long-range bomber. (q.v. August 3, 1947)

**August 2** The First Allied Airborne Army is formed under the command of Lt. Gen. Lewis H. Brereton, U.S.A.A.F.

**August 4** Destroying a V1, by flying alongside it and using the wing of his Gloster Meteor to tip the missile and force it to the ground, Flt. Off. Dean of No. 616 Squadron scores the Meteor's first combat success.

In a first mission code-named Aphrodite, radio-controlled B-17s, each packed with 20,000lb (9,072kg) of TNT, are launched against German V2 sites being constructed at Pas de Calais, France.

**August 7** The U.S. Navy Carrier Division 11 is commissioned. Comprising the aircraft carriers U.S.S. *Ranger* and U.S.S. *Saratoga*, it is the first division intended specifically for night operations.

**August 8/9** The Mediterranean Air Forces drop arms and supplies to the Polish Home Army in Warsaw that has been uprising against German forces since August 1. This is the first of several such operations.

**August 14/15** Mediterranean Allied Air Forces fly more than 4,000 sorties and transport more than 9,000 airborne troops to begin the invasion of southern France, between Cannes and Hyères. The paratroops are dropped at night and in thick fog.

**August 16** Messerschmitt Me 163B-1 Komet rocket-powered interceptor fighters are used operationally for the first time, attacking a formation of U.S.A.A.F. B-17 Flying Fortresses.

**August 28** The U.S.A.A.F.'s 78th Fighter Group claims the destruction of a Messerschmitt Me 262, the first jet-powered aircraft to be shot down in air combat.

**September** First operational use of the Arado Ar 234B Blitz in a reconnaissance role.

**September 1** The Germans begin to launch their V1 flying bombs against targets in Europe.

**September 4** German V1 attacks on Britain from cross-Channel launching sites come to an end.

**September 5–6** Start of the German Operation Zeppelin, an unsuccessful attempt to assassinate Stalin. The task group is flown from near Riga, Latvia, to a point near Moscow by an Ar 232B transport of KG 200.

**September 8** Two German V2 ballistic rockets land in Paris. Later that day, the first of these weapons launched against England detonates in Chiswick, West London, killing two people and injuring several others.

Basic specifications for a Volksäger (People's Fighter) are drawn up by the German Air Ministry and issued to seven leading aircraft manufacturers

**October** First unpowered test flight of the Yokosuka MXY-7 Ohka manned rocket-powered suicide weapon, Allied SW Pacific reporting name 'Baka'.

**October 23** Beginning of the Battle of Leyte Gulf, during which the Japanese introduce the use of Kamikaze attacks by suicide planes, these sinking the U.S.S. *St. Lo* and several other vessels. When the battle had ended (October 25) the Japanese had lost three battleships, 10 cruisers and 11 destroyers, marking the end of the Japanese fleet as an effective fighting force.

**October 27** Mission flown by the U.S.A.A.F.'s 9th Fighter Squadron from Tacloban airstrip marks the first U.S. air operation from the Philippines since 1942.

**November 1** A U.S.A.A.F. F-13 (a reconnaissance variant of the B-29 Superfortress) is the first U.S. aircraft to fly over Tokyo since the Doolittle raid of 1942. (q.v. April 18, 1942)

**November 3** Start of the Japanese 'Fu-Go Weapon' (balloon bomb) offensive against the U.S.A. (q.v. May 22, 1945)

**November 12** The 52,600-ton German battleship *Tirpitz*, anchored in Tromsø Fjord, Norway, is sunk by bombs dropped from Avro Lancasters of the R.A.F.'s Nos. 9 and 617 Squadrons.

**November 15** A first flight is made by the Boeing XC-97 Stratofreighter prototype (43-27470).

**November 24** First major bombing attack on Tokyo from the Mariana Islands by 88 B-29s of the U.S.A.A.F.'s 21st Bomber Command.

**December** The TR-1 (VDR-3), the first Soviet turbojet engine, reportedly completes its official bench running tests.

**December 6** A first flight is made by the Heinkel He 162V-1 Salamander turbojet-powered fighter prototype (200 001) at Vienna-Schwechat.

**December 7** The U.S.S. *Chourre* is commissioned as the U.S. Navy's first aviation repair ship.

**December 17** The U.S.A.A.F.'s 509th Composite Group, assembled to carry out U.S. atomic bomb operations, is established in Utah.

Maj. Richard Ira Bong, the U.S.A.A.F.'s most successful fighter pilot of the Second World War, scores his 40th and final victory.

**December 18** First vertical launch of the German unmanned Bachem Ba 349 Natter, intended for operational use as a manned, vertically launched rocket-powered interceptor.

## 1945

**January 1** In Operation Bodenplatte the Luftwaffe, in its last major attack, attempts to destroy the maximum number of Allied aircraft on the ground. About 800 Luftwaffe aircraft are involved in this surprise air strike. A total of 465 Allied aircraft are destroyed or damaged and more than 220 Luftwaffe aircraft are lost during this operation.

**February 13–15** R.A.F. and U.S.A.A.F. night and day attacks on Dresden, Germany, create a devastating fire storm which virtually destroys the city. The estimates as to the number of dead vary between 35,000 and 220,000.

**February 17** The softening-up of Iwo Jima, which is the most strongly defended of all Japanese positions, begins with a combined attack from carrier-based aircraft naval heavy guns and U.S. Seventh Air Force B-24 Liberators.

**February 19** With massive air and sea support, the U.S. Marines begin landing on Iwo Jima.

**February 21** First flight is made by the Hawker Sea Fury prototype (SR661), which proves to be the last piston-engined fighter to serve in FAA first-line squadrons.

The U.S. Navy aircraft carrier *Saratoga* is hit and badly damaged by Kamikaze attack.

**February 22** Some 9,000 Allied aircraft make a concentrated attack on the German transport system.

**February 23** The Luftwaffe sinks its last ship of the war, the *Henry Bacon* belonging to convoy RA.64.

**February 25** First flight is made by the Bell XP-83 prototype, a pressurized turbojet-powered escort fighter developed from the P-59 Airacomet.

**February 28** First manned flight test of the vertical take-off Bachem Ba 349 Natter (Viper) rocket-powered target defence interceptor kills the pilot, Oberleutnant Lothar Siebert. Three subsequent manned launches in March are successful, and the Natter is approved for operational use.

**March 9** Allied aircraft provide support in operations against German armour attempting to eliminate the Remagen bridgehead, established two days previously.

In one of the first attacks by the Luftwaffe's Mistel 2 composites of II/KG 200, which operates Junkers Ju 88Gs and Focke-Wulf Fw 190s as the lower and upper components respectively, four composites strike the Görlitz bridges spanning the Neisse.

**March 9/10** In a change of tactics, more than 300 Marianas-based B-29 Superfortresses armed with incendiary bombs make a low-altitude night attack on Tokyo.

**March 11** Allied air forces make an all-out bombing attack on Essen to cut German rail communications prior to the Rhine crossings.

**March 14** First operational use of the 22,000-lb (9,979kg) 'Grand Slam' bomb, dropped by a Lancaster of No. 617 Squadron on the Bielefeld Viaduct, Germany.

**March 16** The U.S. Navy claims that in attacks on Japanese bases during the previous month they have destroyed 648 enemy aircraft.

Organized Japanese resistance on Iwo Jima ends. U.S. Marine casualties total 6,891 dead and 18,070 injured, but this small island is to prove a valuable emergency landing field for bomber aircraft attacking the Japanese homeland. By the war's end, 2,251 B-29 Superfortresses have found refuge there.

**March 17** Following the success of the first incendiary attack on Tokyo, 307 B-29s drop 2,300 tons of incendiary weapons on Kobe, Japan.

**March 18** First flight of the Douglas XBT2D-1 Skyraider prototype, a single-seat carrier-based dive-bomber/torpedo-bomber, which is the first aircraft of this category to be used by the U.S. Navy. It enters service too late to see operational use during the Second World War.

More than 1,250 bombers plus an escort of some 670 fighters make the U.S.A.A.F.'s biggest daylight attack on Berlin.

**March 20/21** Luftwaffe aircraft attack Britain. This was the last German attack on the U.K. by piloted aircraft.

**March 21** The first but unsuccessful sortie is made by the Japanese Yokosuka Ohka purpose-built suicide aircraft.

**March 21–24** The Allied air forces in Europe mount a large-scale attack against the Luftwaffe and its bases. This great strategic effort virtually destroys the Luftwaffe as an effective force.

**March 27** The last V2 rocket falls on Britain, at Orpington, Kent.

**March 31** The British Commonwealth Air Training Plan is officially terminated. It has produced 137,739 trainees, including 54,098 pilots.

**April 1** Scoring their first major success, Japanese Ohka suicide aircraft severely damage the battleships U.S.S. *West Virginia* and three other vessels. One of them is the British aircraft carrier *Indefatigable*.

**April 7** While making a final effort to try and hamper U.S. landings on Okinawa, the 71,000-ton Japanese battleship *Yamoto*, a cruiser, and four of eight destroyers are sunk by endless attack from U.S. Navy carrier-based aircraft.

The U.S.A.A.F. is able to begin fighter-escorted B-29 missions against targets on the Japanese homeland.

**April 10** The last Luftwaffe wartime sortie over Britain is made by an Arado Ar 234B turbojet-powered reconnaissance aircraft operating from Norway.

In an attack on targets near Berlin, the U.S.A.A.F. loses 19 of its bomber aircraft and eight escort fighters to attacks by Messerschmitt Me 262 turbojet-powered fighters.

**April 12** The American destroyer U.S.S. *Mannert L. Abele* is sunk by a Japanese Ohka suicide aircraft off Okinawa.

**April 19** First flight is made of the de Havilland Sea Hornet prototype (PX212). When the type enters service post-war, it is the first twin-engined single-seat fighter to be operated from aircraft carriers of the Royal Navy.

The International Air Transport Association (IATA) is formed at Havana, Cuba, succeeding the International Air Traffic Association.

**April 23** The U.S. Navy's PB4Y Liberators of Patrol Bombing Squadron 109 launch two Bat missiles against Japanese shipping in Balikpapan harbour, Borneo. This is the first known combat use of automatic homing missiles during the Second World War.

**April 26** Flying a Fieseler Fi 156 Storch, Hanna Reitsch carries Gen. Rittel von Greim from Berlin-Gatow into Berlin. There he is promoted by Hitler to command the Luftwaffe, replacing Hermann Goering.

**April 28** Benito Mussolini is captured at Dongo, near Lake Como, and shot by Italian Communist partisans.

**April 29** War in Italy comes to an end, with German envoys signing terms of unconditional surrender.

R.A.F. Bomber Command begins airdrops of food and clothing to the Dutch people. Some 6,600 tons are supplied in just over a week.

**May 7** R.A.F. Coastal Command sinks its 196th and last German submarine of the Second World War, the U-320, by No. 210 Squadron, west of Bergen.

Documents for the unconditional surrender of all German forces are signed at General Eisenhower's headquarters.

The unconditional surrender of the German forces is ratified in Berlin, and the war in Western Europe ends officially at midnight.

**May 22** It is announced in the U.S. that the Japanese have been attempting to attack the continental United States by means of balloons carrying incendiary material. Released in Japan, they were carried by jet streams across the Pacific.

**May 29** The advance party of the U.S.A.A.F.'s 509th Composite Group (the atom bomb team) arrives in the Mariana Islands.

**May 31** BOAC and Qantas begin a joint weekly Hurn, Hampshire to Sydney, NSW service with Lancastrian aircraft.

**June 11** B-29s of the U.S.A.A.F.'s 393rd Very Heavy Bomber Squadron, the only combat aircraft of the 509th Composite Group, land at Tinian, Marianas.

**June 17** The U.S.A.A.F.'s 21st Bomber Command begins a series of incendiary attacks on all major Japanese towns.

**June 25** National Skyway Freight Corporation is established in the U.S.A. First all-cargo airline in the U.S., in early 1946 it adopts the title of Flying Tiger Line Incorporated.

**July 2** The Japanese begin a major evacuation of the people of Tokyo, due to continuous and devastating air attacks.

**July 5** The United States CAB authorizes American Overseas Airlines, Pan American and TWA to operate over the North Atlantic.

**July 10** The final U.S. Navy aircraft carrier actions of the Second World War begin, the ship-based aircraft attacking targets on the Japanese homeland.

**July 14** Attacking Japanese-held oilfields at Boela, Ceram Island, U.S.A.A.F. Douglas A-20s from Hollandia make the first use of rocket bombs in the southwest Pacific

**July 15** The R.A.F.'s 2nd Tactical Air Force is reformed as the British Air Force of Occupation, Germany.

**July 16** Major Gen. Curtis LeMay takes command of the U.S.A.A.F.'s 20th Air Force.

**July 20** The 393rd Squadron of the 509th Composite Group begins making practice bombing attacks against Japanese cities, using conventional HE bombs.

**July 21** Japanese forces in Burma are decimated by air attack from Mustangs and Spitfires as they attempt to cross the Sittang river.

**July 25** Gen. Carl Spaatz is instructed that the 509th Composite Group should make its first atom bomb attack on Japan as soon as possible after August 3, 1945.

**July 30** The Mediterranean Allied Air Forces are disbanded.

**August 1** 851 aircraft are deployed against targets in Japan in the largest operation mounted by B-29 Superfortresses.

**August 2** The operational orders for the atom bomb attack are signed. Hiroshima is named as the primary target, with Kokura or Nagasaki as alternatives.

**August 6** The B-29 Superfortress *Enola Gay*, captained by Col. Paul W. Tibbets Jr., drops the world's first operational atomic bomb over the city of Hiroshima.

**August 7** Japan's first turbojet-powered aircraft makes its first flight as the Nakajima J8N1 Kikka Special Attack Fighter prototype.

**August 9** Lieutenant Robert H. Gray of the Royal Canadian Navy Volunteer Reserve, the pilot of a Corsair fighter-bomber, is killed attacking a Japanese destroyer. Attached to the Fleet Air Arm, he is posthumously awarded the last Victoria Cross to be won during the Second World War.

The second atomic bomb is dropped over Nagasaki from the B-29 *Bock's Car* captained by Maj. Charles W. Sweeney.

**August 14** Flying its last wartime mission, the U.S.A.A.F.'s 20th Air Force despatches 754 B-29s and 169 fighters to attack targets in Japan
.

**August 15** Seven Japanese suicide aircraft make the last Kamikaze attack of the war.

Andrei G. Kochetkov, Head of NII-VVS Fighter Test section, becomes the first Soviet

pilot to fly a jet-powered aircraft – a captured Me 262A fighter at Shcholkovo near Moscow.

**August 19** Two Mitsubishi G4M Betty transports carry the Japanese surrender delegation to Ie Shima.

**August 21** All existing contracts under the U.S. Lend-Lease Act are cancelled.

**August 27** B-29 Superfortresses airdrop supplies to Allied prisoners of war in the Weihsien camp near Peiping, China.

**September** A captured Fa 223 Drache becomes the first helicopter to cross the English Channel, flown by its ex-Luftwaffe aircrew to Brockenhurst, Hampshire.

**September 2** Surrounded by the U.S. Pacific Fleet, the Japanese surrender documents are signed aboard the battleship U.S.S. *Missouri* anchored in Tokyo Bay.

**September 10** The U.S.S. *Midway*, the first of the U.S. Navy's 45,000-ton class carriers, is commissioned at Westport News, Virginia.

**September 15** Spitfires lead a formation of some 300 R.A.F. fighters in the first Battle of Britain anniversary fly-past over London.

**September 29** Swissair resumes operations to the U.K., making a first post-war flight on its Zurich-London route.

**October 4–8** Qantas operates its first post-war flight to Singapore, flown by the C-class flying-boat *Coriolanus* (VH-ABG).

**October 22** Sabena resumes operations on its Brussels-London route.

Air France's Paris-London route is reopened.

**October 23** American Overseas Airlines inaugurates post-war transatlantic routes using Douglas DC-4 airliners.

**November 6** Flying a mixed power plant Ryan FR-1 Fireball, which has a conventional piston-engine plus a turbojet engine in the aft fuselage, Ensign J.C. West uses the latter engine only to make the first turbojet-powered landing on an aircraft carrier, the U.S.S. *Wake Island*.

**November 7** Flying a Gloster Meteor F.4, Gp. Capt. H.J. Wilson establishes a first post-war aircraft world speed record of 606.25mph (975.67km/h).

**November 10** BOAC and South African Airways inaugurate a joint 'Springbok' service between Hurn, Hampshire, and Johannesburg.

**November 30** The U.K. Air Transport Auxiliary is disbanded. During the course of the war, its pilots had ferried 307,378 aircraft.

**December 3** The third prototype of the de Havilland Vampire 1 (LZ551), which had been modified for deck landing trials aboard the H.M.S. *Ocean*, becomes the first pure-jet aircraft in the world to operate from an aircraft carrier.

**December 4** A Lockheed Constellation of TWA sets a record transatlantic flight time for a commercial aircraft making the first scheduled service from Washington to Paris.

**December 8** A first flight is made by the prototype Bell Model 47 helicopter.

## 1946

**January 1** Heathrow, which is to become the site of the future London Airport, is handed over from the Air Ministry to the Ministry of Civil Aviation.

The British European Airways Division of BOAC (BEA) is established to take over the U.K.-Europe services which had been operated by No. 110 Wing, 46 Group, R.A.F. Transport Command.

The flying restrictions that had been imposed in the U.K. at the beginning of the Second World War are rescinded.

**January 10** A U.S. Army Sikorsky R-5 sets an unofficial helicopter height record of 21,000ft (6,400m) at Stratford, Connecticut.

**January 19** A first unpowered flight is made by the Bell X-1 research aircraft, following launch from a Boeing B-29 Superfortress 'motherplane'.

**January 26** The U.S.A.A.F. establishes its first experimental guided missile group at Eglin AFB, Florida.

**January 31** BOAC resumes its flying-boat services from the U.K. to Singapore.

**February 4** Pan American flies its first scheduled Constellation flight from La Guardia, New York to Hurn, Hampshire in a flight time of 14 hrs 9 mins.

**February 10** A Consolidated Liberator (AM920) completes BOAC's 2,000 transatlantic crossings of the Return Ferry Service.

**February 28** The Republic XP-84 Thunderjet prototype makes its first flight from Muroc Dry Lake.

**March 4** BEA begins operations with its aircraft in civil markings and its crews in BOAC uniform.

**March 8** The Bell Model 47 is granted the first commercial helicopter certificate to be awarded by the U.S. CAA.

**March 10** After RMA *Berwick* arrives at Baltimore, Maryland, BOAC ends transatlantic operations with Boeing Model 314s.

**March 21** The U.S.A.A.F. establishes its Air Defense Command, Strategic Air Command, and Tactical Air Command.

**April 24** First flights of the Yakovlev Yak-15 (one Jumo 004B) and Mikoyan MiG-9 (two BMW 003A) jet fighter prototypes, the first pure jet Soviet aircraft to fly.

**May 31** London's Heathrow Airport (formerly Heathrow Airfield) is officially opened. Its

facilities include one runway and several tents for passenger handling.

**June 1** A Pan American Constellation lands at London Heathrow on the airline's first scheduled New York-London service.

**June 14** BOAC's last scheduled service from Hurn Airport, Hampshire.

**June 22** Two U.S.A.A.F. Lockheed P40 Shooting Star fighters carry the first U.S. airmail to travel by turbojet-powered aircraft, from Shenectady to Washington D.C. and Chicago, Illinois.

**June 25** First flight of the first Northrop XB-35 at Muroc, the world's first full-size flying-wing bomber intended for service (though cancelled after a further 13 development aircraft had been built). (q.v. October 21, 1947)

**July 1** BOAC inaugurates a twice-weekly London-New York service operated with the Lockheed Constellation.

In an exercise codenamed Operation Crossroads, a U.S.A.A.F. B-29 drops an atomic bomb over 73 naval vessels anchored at Bikini Atoll in the Pacific Ocean.

**July 21** The McDonnell XFH-1 Phantom becomes the first pure turbojet aircraft to operate from a U.S. aircraft carrier, the U.S.S. *Franklin D. Roosevelt*.

**July 24** Bernard Lynch makes the first

recorded manned ejection from an aircraft on the ground, a Gloster Meteor, by means of a Martin-Baker ejection seat. It is reported that ejections were made from German jet aircraft during the Second World War.

**July 25** Just over ten years after his death, Brigadier Gen. William 'Billy' Mitchell is posthumously awarded the U.S. Congressional Medal of Honor.

**July 31** SAS (Scandinavian Airlines System) is formed in a unique post-war collaboration of the national airlines of Denmark, Norway and Sweden.

**August 1** British European Airways Corporation is established, primarily to operate routes in the British Isles and to Europe.

**August 8** The first prototype of the giant Corsair XB-36 bomber (42-13570) makes its first flight.

**August 17** Sgt. L. Lambert, U.S.A.A.F., becomes the first person in the U.S. to make a manned test of an ejection seat from a Northrop P-61 Black Widow flying at 300mph (483km/h) at 7,800ft (2,375m).

**September 11–12** First post-war meeting of the Fédération Aéronautique Internationale (FAI).

**September 16** Alitalia (Aerolinee Italiane Internationale) becomes incorporated in Italy. BEA was initially a 40 per cent shareholder.

**September 19** TAP (Transportes Aéreos Portugueses SARL), which had been formed as a division of the government's Civil Aeronautics Secretariat during 1944, becomes established as an airline and inaugurates its first Lisbon-Madrid service on this date.

**September 24** Cathay Pacific Airways is incorporated in Hong Kong, originally as a small charter airline.

**September 27** The de Havilland DH.108 sweptwing research aircraft breaks up in the air over the Thames estuary killing the pilot, Geoffrey de Havilland Jr.

**September 29–October 1** A U.S. Navy Lockheed P2V Neptune crewed by Cmdr. T. Davis and E.P. Rankin sets a new non-stop world distance record of 11,235.6 miles (18,081.99km) flying from Perth, Australia to Columbus, Ohio.

**October 1** Beginning of the first U.S. experiments of airmail delivery in the Chicago suburbs are made by the U.S. Post Office in conjunction with the U.S.A.A.F., using Sikorsky helicopters.

**October 6** The first non-stop Hawaii-Egypt flight over the North Pole is made in a U.S.A.A.F. Boeing B-29, covering a distance of 10,873 miles (17,498km).

**November 1** The U.S. Navy non-rigid airship XM-l completes a flight of 170 hrs 3 mins which is a world record for flight unsustained by any form of refuelling.

**December 9** The first powered flight is made by a Bell X-1 rocket-powered research aircraft.

## 1947

**March 14** Saudia (Saudi Arabian Airlines Corporation), which had been formed by the Saudi Arabian government during 1946, begins scheduled operations.

**April 1** JAT (Jugoslovenski Aerotransport) is established by the Yugoslavian government as the national airline.

**April 4** The International Civil Aviation Organization (ICAO) is established, with headquarters in Montreal, Canada.

**April 15** BOAC begins a weekly Constellation service between London and Montreal, this being BOAC's first commercial operation to Canada.

**May 28** British South American Airways begins a series of non-stop flight refuelling trials over a route from London to Bermuda. These are flown by the Avro Lancaster G-AHJV, which is flight-refuelled by an Avro Lancaster tanker over the Azores.

First full flight is made by the Douglas D-558-l Skystreak research aircraft from Muroc Dry Lake, California. The Skystreak later establishes two world speed records, the first on August 20, 1947, flown by Cmdr. T.F. Caldwell, U.S. Navy, at a speed of 640.60mph (1,030.95km/h). The second record is made five days later, by Major M. E. Carl of the U.S.M.C., at a speed of 650.78mph (1,047.33km/h).

**June 17** Pan American inaugurates a nearly-round-the-world service, flown the long way round from New York to San Francisco.

**June 19** A new world speed record of 623.61mph (1,003.60km/h) is set by Col. Albert Boyd flying a Lockheed P-80R Shooting Star at Muroc Dry Lake, California.

**July 2** The first Mikoyan I-310 (Type 'S') jet fighter prototype makes its first flight. This forerunner of the MiG-15 is believed lost in a flying accident, but a second prototype is more successful. (q.v. December 30, 1947)

**July 16** The Saunders-Roe SR.A/1, the world's first turbojet-powered flying-boat, makes its first flight. An experimental fighter, it is the first flying-boat to be flown at a speed in excess of 500mph (805km/h).

**July 24** The first flight of the Ilyushin Il-22, the first Soviet jet-powered bomber. The design is unsuccessful and flight tests are terminated soon afterwards.

**July 26** President Truman signs the United States Armed Forces Unification Act.

**July 27** The Tupolev Tu-12, the first Soviet turbojet-powered bomber to gain production status, makes its first flight.

**August 3** First public appearance during the Soviet Aviation Day parade of the Tupolev Tu-4 heavy bomber, a direct Soviet copy of the Boeing B-29 Superfortress. (q.v. July 29, 1944)

**August 10** BEA inaugurates a scheduled all-cargo service. This is operated by Douglas DC-3s over a route from London to Prague via Brussels.

**August 14** Following the partition of India, the Royal Pakistan Air Force is established on this date. It becomes the Pakistan Air Force on March 23, 1956.

**September 18** Foundation date of the United States Air Force, which becomes an independent service within the new united U.S. armed services.

**September 22** A U.S.A.F. Douglas C-54 Skymaster makes a fully-automatic flight from Stephenville, Newfoundland to the U.K.

**October 1** Los Angeles Airways inaugurates its first scheduled helicopter airmail services operated by Sikorsky S-51s.

The first flight is made by the North American P-86 Sabre prototype (NA-140), which becomes the U.S.A.F.'s first sweptwing fighter (redesignated F-86 Sabre).

**October 14** Piloted by Capt. Charles Yeager, the Bell X-I *Glamorous Glennis* rocket-powered research aircraft becomes the first in the world to exceed the speed of sound in level flight, attaining Mach 1.06 or 700mph (1,126km/h) at 42,000ft (12,800m).

**October 21** The first Northrop YB-49 flying-wing heavy bomber, powered by eight 4,000-lb (l,814kg) Allison J35-A-5 turbojets, makes its first flight.

**November 1** BEA operates its last scheduled services from Croydon Airport, Surrey.

**November 2** The eight-engined Hughes H-4 Hercules, the largest flying-boat ever built, makes its one and only flight over Los Angeles harbour, covering a distance of about 1 mile (1.6 kilometres).

**December 1** Qantas operates its first through service from Sydney, NSW to London's Heathrow Airport, flown by the Lockheed Constellation *Charles Kingsford Smith* (VH-EAD).

**December 17** On the 44th anniversary of the Wright brothers' first flight, the prototype of the Boeing XB-47 swept-wing jet bomber (46-065) makes its first flight from Boeing Field, Seattle, to Moses Lake AFB.

**December 30** First flight of the second Mikoyan Type 'S' fighter prototype powered by an imported Rolls-Royce Nene 2 turbojet. After successfully passing its State Acceptance tests the fighter is assigned the designation MiG-15, its entry into service giving the Soviet Air Force an early performance lead in turbojet-powered fighters.

## 1948

**January 30** The death is announced of Orville Wright, at Dayton, Ohio at the age of 76.

**February 4** The U.S.A.F. Military Air Transport Service (MATS) is established.

**February 18** The Spanish airline Aviaco (Aviación y Comercio SA) is established to operate all-cargo services, but turns to scheduled passenger operations during 1950.

**March 23** A new world altitude record of 59,445ft (18,119m) is set by John Cunningham flying a de Havilland Vampire I from Hatfield, Hertfordshire.

**April 3** Alitalia operates its first post-war service to the U.K. with the inauguration of its Rome-London route.

**April 5** Growing transatlantic passenger traffic is highlighted by a BOAC announcement that its Lockheed Constellations have made 1,000 North Atlantic crossings.

**April 14** The official opening of the Southampton, Hampshire flying-boat terminal by the U.K. Minister of Aviation shows that, so far as the U.K. is concerned, the age of the flying-boat has not passed.

**April 25** The YP-86A prototype of the North American F-86 Sabre is flown at a speed in excess of Mach 1, making it the first turbojet-powered aircraft to attain such a speed.

**May 20** The Israeli air force is in action against Arab forces for the first time.

**May 23** The U.S.A.F. announces the activation of a new wind tunnel at Aberdeen, Maryland, with a test section having a continuous capability of 3,000mph (4,828km/h).

**May 27** It is announced in the U.K. that the

government had awarded a £100,000 tax-free payment to Air Cdre. Frank Whittle for his pioneering work on aircraft turbojet engines.

**June 1** BEA begins the first helicopter public airmail service in the U.K., operated by Westland/Sikorsky S-51s from Peterborough, Cambridgeshire, to points in East Anglia.

**June 18/19** All road traffic between Berlin and West Germany is stopped at midnight by the Soviet military authorities.

**June 24** Due to so-called 'technical reasons', all rail services between Berlin and West Germany are terminated by the Soviet military authorities.

**June 26** A first airlift of supplies into Berlin is organized by the U.S.A.F. using C-47s based near Frankfurt, marking the beginning of the Berlin Airlift.

**June 28** The first British and international Class G helicopter record is established by Sqdn. Ldr. Basil H. Arkell, flying the Fairey Gyrodyne G-AIKF at an average speed of 124.31mph (200.06km/h).

British air operations in connection with the Berlin Airlift begin.

**July 16** First flight of the Vickers Viscount prototype (G-AHRF) is made at Wisley, Surrey. On its entry into service it becomes the world's first turboprop-powered civil transport.

**July 20** A first west-east crossing of the North

Atlantic by turbojet-powered aircraft is recorded by 16 Lockheed F-80 (formerly P-80) Shooting Star fighters. They complete a flight from Selfridge Field, Michigan, to Scotland.

**July 23** The U.S.A.F.'s Military Air Transport Service is ordered to establish an Airlift task force for, if necessary, the long-term sustenance of Berlin.

**August 4** British independent civil operators become involved in the Berlin Airlift.

**August 16** First flight of the Northrop XF-89 Scorpion prototype at Edwards AFB, California. When the type enters service during 1950 it becomes the U.S.A.F.'s first all-weather turbojet-powered interceptor.

**August 21** Douglas C-54 Skymasters of the U.S.A.F.'s MATS begin operations on the Berlin Airlift.

**August 23** A first free flight is made by the McDonnell XF-85 Goblin prototype. It is intended to be used as a parasite escort fighter, carried by the giant Convair B-36; but subsequent analysis shows the concept to be of little worth.

**September 1** First flight of the Swedish Saab J-29, which becomes the first European sweptwing jet fighter to enter operational service, in May 1951. The late 'F' production version eventually introduces an afterburning engine and air-to-air missiles.

**September 6** The de Havilland DH.108 research aircraft becomes the first British

aircraft to exceed the speed of sound, recording more than Mach 1 in a dive.

**September 14** Royal Australian Air Force crews join operations on the Berlin Airlift.

**September 15** Flying an F-86A Sabre at Muroc Dry Lake, California, Maj. R.L. Johnson, U.S.A.F., establishes a new world speed record of 670.84mph (1,079.61km/h).

**October 15** The R.A.F. and U.S.A.F. combine their efforts as an Airlift task force.

**October 16** South African Air Force crews join operations on the Berlin Airlift.

**November 3** Royal New Zealand Air Force crews join in the continuing Berlin Airlift.

**November 15** El Al Israel Airlines is formed, beginning operations from Tel Aviv to Paris and Rome in mid-1949.

**November 22** Growing concern about the sale of Rolls-Royce turbojet engines to the Soviet Union leads to questions being raised in the U.K Parliament, a deal which had been approved by Stafford Cripps.

**November 30** First commercial use of FIDO (fog dispersal system) at Blackbushe, Surrey, to allow an urgent take-off by a Vickers Viking in thick fog.

**December 5** A U.S.A.F. Consolidated B-36 completes a 9,400mile (15,128km) unrefuelled non-stop flight from Fort Worth, Texas to Hawaii and return.

**December 29** The U.S. Defense Secretary announces that work has been initiated on 'an earth satellite vehicle program'.

## 1949

**January 3** The U.S.A. introduces a bill to speed guided missile research.

**February 4** The U.S. CAA authorizes the use of GCA (ground-controlled approach) radar as a primary landing aid in bad weather.

**February 14** BEA begins the first U.K. helicopter night airmail experiments, flown with Westland/Sikorsky S-51s.

**February 24** In the U.S.A., Project Bumper sees the first completely successful two-stage rocket launch into space, reaching a height of 244 miles (393km).

**February 26–March 2** The first non-stop round-the-world flight is made by the U.S.A.F.'s Boeing B-50 Superfortress *Lucky Lady II*, piloted by Capt. James Gallagher. The aircraft is flight-refuelled four times during its 94-hr 1 min, 23,452-mile (37,742-km) flight.

**March 30** A bill is authorized in the U.S.A. for the establishment of a permanent radar defence network.

**April 2** Trans-Australia Airlines takes over responsibility from Qantas for several services, including the Flying Doctor services operated from Charleville and Cloncurry.

**April 4** The North Atlantic Treaty Organization becomes established following signature of the treaty by 12 nations at Washington. It becomes effective on August 24, 1949.

**April 16** Peak day of the Berlin Airlift; within 24 hours, 1,398 sorties are made, carrying a total of 12,940 tons.

**April 21** An R.A.F. Sunderland lands on the Yangtse River, taking a doctor and medical supplies to the British frigate H.M.S. *Amethyst* following an attack on it by Chinese Communists,

**April 26** Completion of a flight-refuelled world endurance record in the U.S., made by Bill Barris and Dick Reidel flying the Aeronca Chief lightplane *Sunkist Lady*. During flight, fuel and food is hauled up four times daily from a jeep speeding below. The Chief was kept airborne for 1,008 hrs 1 min (one minute over six weeks).

**May 12** The Soviet Union ends its blockade of Berlin, but the Allied airlift continues until September 30, 1949 (q.v.), in order to build up stocks in the city.

**May 13** The English Electric Canberra prototype (VN-799) makes its first flight at Warton, Lancashire. It becomes the first jet bomber to be produced in the U.K. and the first to serve with the R.A.F.

**May 14** Aérolineas Argentinas is established to operate domestic and international routes.

**May 18** The first New York helicopter station is established at Pier 41, East River.

**May 19** The U.S. Navy flying-boat *Marshall Mars*, flying from Alameda, Idaho to San Diego, California, carries a new record total of 301 passengers plus a crew of seven.

**May 21** A Sikorsky S-52 helicopter establishes a new helicopter altitude record of 21,220ft (6,468m) over Stratford, Connecticut.

**June 3** Pan American introduces Boeing Model 377 Stratocruisers on its North Atlantic services. Others later go to Northwest Airlines, United Air Lines, American Overseas Airlines, BOAC and SAS.

**June 26** After one year of the Berlin Airlift, about 1.8 million tons of supplies have been airlifted into the city. Outsize items have included a steam roller and 3.5-ton (3.56-tonne) girders.

**July 27** The de Havilland DH.106 Comet I prototype (G-ALVG) makes its first flight at Hatfield, Hertfordshire.

**August 1** The SBAC (Society of British Aircraft Constructors) Challenge Cup race, open to jet-powered aircraft from any nation, is won by Sqdn. Ldr. T.S. Wade flying the Hawker private-venture P.1040 prototype (VP401). Won at an average speed of 510mph (821km/h), one lap was flown at 562.5mph (903km/h).

**August 9** In the U.S.A., the first use of an ejection seat emergency escape from an aircraft is recorded. It is made by Lt. J.L. Fruin, U.S. Navy, from a McDonnell F2H-l Banshee flying in exces of 575mph (925km/h) near Walterboro, South Carolina.

**September 4** The Avro 707 (VX784) makes its first flight from Boscombe Down, Wiltshire. This first British delta-wing research aircraft had been built to test the wing configuration of the future Vulcan bomber.

The Bristol Brabazon I prototype (G-AGPW), the largest landplane ever constructed in Great Britain, makes its first flight.

**September 23** The Soviet Union detonates its first atomic bomb and thus ends the U.S. nuclear monopoly.

**September 30** Allied aircraft end the Berlin Airlift. During the 15 months that it had been operated, almost 2.25 million tons of supplies and equipment had been flown into Berlin.

**October 17** BEA begins the first night helicopter airmail service in the U.K. Flown by Westland/Sikorsky S-51s between Peterborough, Cambridgeshire and Norwich, Norfolk, the service continues until mid-April 1950. (q.v. February 14, 1949)

**November 7** First flight of the Sikorsky S-55 helicopter prototype at Stratford, Connecticut. It is the first helicopter to have the centre fuselage free from a power plant installation, it being mounted instead in the fuselage.

**November 18** AC-74 Globemaster I of the U.S.A.F.'s MATS lands at Marham, Norfolk, after a non-stop flight from the U.S. It carries a total of 103 passengers and crew which is then the largest number of people carried across the North Atlantic in a single flight.

**1950**
**January 23** The U.S.A.F. Research and Development Command is established.

**February 1** The U.S.A.F.'s Continental Air Command is directed to establish a civil Air Raid Warning system.

**April 12** L. Welch makes the first cross-Channel sailplane flight from London to Brussels.

**April 24** A DH.106 Comet 1 establishes a new London-Cairo point-to-point record en route to Khartoum and Nairobi for tropical trials.

**May 9–19** In connection with the British Industries Fair, Westland Helicopters (in conjunction with Rotor Stations Ltd.) operates the U.K.'s first scheduled helicopter passenger services. These are flown between London and Birmingham using a Westland/Sikorsky S-51.

**May 17** The U.S. airline Transcontinental & Western Air (TWA), which had been established during 1930, changes its name to Trans World Airlines (TWA) to reflect the world-wide operations of the company.

**June 1** BEA inaugurates the world's first scheduled and sustained helicopter service. This is flown between Liverpool and Cardiff, operated by Westland/Sikorsky S-51s and continues until March 31, 1951.

**June 25** The Korean War begins, with North Korean forces making a dawn crossing of the 38th Parallel borderline into South Korea.

**June 27–28** The United Nations Security Council calls upon its member nations to assist South Korea in any way possible.

**July 3** The first U.S. jet fighter to be involved in air combat is a Grumman F9F-2 Panther of the U.S. Navy. This is flown off the aircraft carrier U.S.S. *Valley Forge* to enter action against North Korean forces.

**July 24** The first rocket is launched at the Cape Canaveral test range, this being a V2 first stage with a WAC Corporal as its second, known as Bumper-WAC. (q.v. February 24, 1949)

**July 28** The world's first certificate of airworthiness for a turbine-powered civil airliner is awarded to the Vickers V630 Viscount.

**July 29** The Vickers V630 Viscount G-AHRF is used by BEA to navigate the world's first scheduled service to be flown by a turboprop-powered airliner. The type is introduced for a short period on the airline's London to Paris service.

**August 15** Using the V630 Viscount which has been operating the London-Paris route, BEA provides a London-Edinburgh service for just over a week. This is the first U.K. domestic service to be flown by a gas-turbine-powered airliner.

**September 22** Colonel David C. Schilling, U.S.A.F., lands at Limestone, Maine, after a non-stop flight from the U.K. in a Republic EF-84E Thunderjet fighter. Two of these aircraft had been converted by Flight Refuelling Ltd., for refuelling by its probe and drogue system which is being adopted by Tactical Air Command. It is by using this system for three inflight refuellings that the Thunderjet records the first non-stop crossing of the North Atlantic by a turbojet-powered fighter aircraft.

**September 29** At Holloman AFB, New Mexico, Capt. Richard V. Wheeler makes a parachute jump from a height of 42,449ft (12,938m).

**November 7** Replacing Solent flying-boats with Handley Page Hermes aircraft on its U.K.-Johannesburg service, BOAC brings to an end the flying-boat services that had been operated by the airline and its predecessors for some 26 years.

**November 8** The first victory to be scored in the first allied combat is by Lt. Russell J. Brown Jr., U.S.A.F. 51st Fighter-Interceptor Wing, flying a Lockheed F-80C. His victim is a Mikoyan MiG-15 jet fighter of the Chinese People's Republic Air Force.

**November 9** In the first encounter between U.S. Navy jet fighters and MiG-15s, Lt. Cmdr. W.T. Amen flying a Grumman F9F-2 Panther becomes the first U.S. pilot to destroy another jet fighter in combat.

**December 17** North American F-86A Sabres go into action in Korea with the 4th Fighter-

Interceptor Wing. In their first day of combat operations, four MiG-15s are claimed as destroyed.

**1951**
**January 1** Reinforced by some 400,000 Chinese troops, the North Koreans begin a new major advance into South Korea.

**February 5** The U.S.A. and Canada jointly announce the intention to set up a DEW (distant early-warning) system for North America.

**February 21** In flying from Aldergrove, Northern Ireland to Gander, Newfoundland, an English Electric Canberra B. Mk 2 becomes the first jet aircraft to fly the North Atlantic non-stop and unrefuelled. The distance of 2,072 miles (3,335km) is flown in 4 hrs 37 mins.

**April 18** An Aerobee research rocket carrying a monkey in a special capsule for a space biology experiment is launched from Holloman AFB, New Mexico.

**May 18** First flight of the Vickers Valiant prototype (WB210). The type is to become the first of the R.A.F.'s V-bombers to enter service.

**May 20** Capt. James Jabara, an F-86 Sabre pilot of the U.S.A.F's 4th Fighter-Interceptor Wing in Korea, becomes the first jet pilot to score five confirmed victories over jet aircraft, destroying his 5th and 6th MiG-15s on this date.

**May 29** The first solo transpolar flight is made by American C. Blair, flying a North American P-51 Mustang from Bardufoss, Norway to Fairbanks, Alaska.

**July 20** The first flight of the first of three Hawker Hunter prototypes (WB188) is made from Boscombe Down, Wiltshire.

**August 15** Two of BEA's DC-3s are given Rolls-Royce Dart turboprop power plant for engine development flying. They are used by BEA on cargo services between Northolt, Middlesex and Hanover, Germany, and the service which starts on this date is the first cargo service to be flown by turboprop-powered aircraft.

**August 22** The Supermarine Attacker enters service with the FAA's No. 800 Squadron at Ford, Sussex. It is the first jet fighter to be standardized in the FAA's first-line squadrons.

**September 20** The U.S.A.F. makes a first successful recovery of animals which have been launched into space by a research rocket. The payload of a monkey and 11 mice is recovered with no apparent ill-effects.

**October 3** Squadron HS-I, the U.S. Navy's first ASW helicopter squadron, is commissioned at Key West, Florida.

**November 26** First flight of the first of three Gloster Javelin prototypes (WD804). When the type enters service with the R.A.F in early 1956, it is the R.A.F.'s and the world's first twin-jet delta-winged fighter. It is also the first R.A.F. fighter designed specifically for all-weather operations.

**December 17** The U.S.A.F. claims that during the previous 12 months its No. 4 Fighter-Interceptor Wing in Korea, operating with F-86 Sabres, had destroyed 130 MiG-15s.

## 1952

**January 3** First flight of the Bristol Type 173 prototype (G-ALBN) at Filton, near Bristol. This is the first twin-rotor, twin-engined helicopter to be designed and flown in Britain.

**January 5** Pan American inaugurates its first transatlantic all-cargo service, this being operated by Douglas DC-6s.

**January 22** The de Havilland Comet I gains the first certificate of airworthiness to be awarded to a turbojet-powered airliner.

**April 15** First flight of the Boeing YB-52 prototype (49-231), which does not enter service with the U.S.A.F. until late 1957. A strategic heavy bomber, it is designed to carry nuclear weapons to any target in the world.

**May 2** The de Havilland DH.106 Comet I (G-ALYP) flies BOAC's inaugural jet service between London and Johannesburg. This is the world's first regular-scheduled airline service to be operated by a turbojet-powered aircraft.

**June 17** The U.S. Navy takes delivery at Lakehurst, New Jersey, of the world's largest non-rigid airship. Designated ZPN-1, it has an overall length of 324ft (98.76m) and a maximum diameter of 35ft (10.67m).

**July 3** BOAC begins Comet 1 proving flights on its London-Tokyo route.

**July 13–31** Two Sikorsky S-55 helicopters, flown in stages, achieve the first west-east crossing of the North Atlantic by helicopters.

**July 19** The U.S.A.F. announces that for periods of over three days it has successfully flown free balloons at controlled constant altitudes in the stratosphere.

**July 29** The first non-stop transpacific flight by a jet aircraft is completed by a North American RB-45, a reconnaissance version of the B-45 Tornado light tactical bomber. This is flown from Elmendorf AFB, Alaska, to Yokota AB, Japan.

**August 11** BOAC inaugurates a weekly London-Colombo service with Comet 1s.

**August 20** The first giant Saunders-Roe S.R. 45 Princess flying-boat (G-ALUN) is launched at Cowes, Isle of Wight. It flies two days later. It is intended to accommodate 105-220 persons. The giant aircraft has a 219ft 6in (66.9m) wing span and is powered by ten 3,780 shp Bristol Proteus 2 turboprop engines.

**August 30** The Avro Vulcan B.1 prototype (VX770) makes its first flight. This large delta-wing long-range bomber is the second of the RAF's V-bombers.

**September 30** A Bell GAM1-63 Rascal air-to-surface missile is launched for the first time.

**October 3** The first British atomic bomb is detonated over the Monte Bello Islands, off north-western Australia.

**October 14** BOAC introduces Comet 1s on its London-Singapore route reducing the scheduled time by more than 50 per cent.

**October 26** A first shadow on the de Havilland Comet's horizon occurs when BOAC's G-ALYZ is severely damaged in a take-off accident at Rome. A similar accident to a Canadian Pacific Comet during March 1953 gives proof that if the nose is held a little too high on take-off the aircraft cannot attain flying speed. Remedial action includes the installation of drooped-wing leading-edges.

**October 28** First flight of the Douglas XA3D-1 Skywarrior carrier-based attack bomber prototype. When the A3Ds begin to enter service in March 1956, they are the heaviest aeroplanes used as standard equipment aboard aircraft carriers.

**November 2** A U.S. Navy Douglas F3D Skyknight destroys a MiG-15, the first time a jet fighter successfully intercepts another jet at night.

**November 3** The first flight is made by the Saab-32 Lansen two-seat all-weather attack fighter, powered by a Rolls-Royce Avon turbojet. Production aircraft have a Svenska-Flygmotor licence-built version of the Avon with reheat.

**November 12** First flight of the Russian Tupolev Tu-95 Bear long range strategic bomber powered by huge turboprop engines with contra-rotating propellers.

**November 19** SAS (Scandinavian Airlines

System) makes the first unscheduled commercial airline flights over the polar regions between Europe and North America. These are flown by Douglas DC-6Bs, but it is not until 1954 that the airline operates scheduled commercial flights over this route.

**December 16** The U.S.A.F. Tactical Air Force Command activates its first helicopter squadron.

**December 24** The Handley Page Victor prototype (WB771) makes its first flights. This is the third and last of the long-range medium bombers for the R.A.F's V-bomber programme.

## 1953

**January 3** BEA takes delivery of the first of its Vickers V.701 Viscount turboprop airliners (G-ALWE).

**January 6** Luftag is formed as a German airline following the closure of Luft-Hansa after the end of the war. In the following year (1954) it becomes Deutsche Lufthansa.

**January 12** The U.S. Navy begins operational flight tests with its first angled-deck carrier. the U.S.S. *Antietam.*

**April 9** The first flight is made by the Convair F2Y-l Sea Dart experimental twin-jet delta-wing seaplane fighter. This uses retractable hydro-skis to take off from and land on water.

**April 18** BEA begins the world's first sustained passenger service to be operated by turboprop-powered airliners. This is the

airline's London-Nicosia route, the first scheduled flight being made by Viscount V.701 *Sir Ernest Shackleton* (G-AMNY).

**May 2** On the first anniversary of the inauguration of Comet operations, a BOAC Comet 1 (G-ALYV) suffers structural failure and crashes near Calcutta with the loss of 43 lives.

**May 4** A new world altitude record is established by W.F. Gibb, flying an English Electric Canberra to a height of 63,668ft (19,406m).

**May 18** The first flight of the Douglas DC-7 piston-engined transport is made. In its DC-7C long-range version, the type is remembered as a piston-engined airliner at the peak of its development.

**May 19** The American airwoman Jacqueline Cochran pilots a Canadian-built version of the North American F-86 Sabre at a speed of Mach 1.01, becoming the first woman in the world to fly faster than the speed of sound.

**May 25** The first North American YF-100A Super Sabre prototype makes its first flight. It has a significant place in world aviation history as the first combat aircraft capable of sustained supersonic performance in level flight.

**June 18** The world's first air disaster involving the death of more than 100 persons occurs. This is suffered by a U.S.A.F. C-124 Globemaster II which crashes after engine failure on take-off from Tachikawa AFB, Tokyo, killing 129 people.

**July 7** The first international helicopter flight into central London is made by a Sikorsky S-55 operated by Sabena. This is flown from the Allée Verte Heliport at Brussels, landing at the South Bank Heliport, Waterloo.

**July 13** BEA introduces a helicopter all-cargo service between London Airport and Birmingham, flown by Bristol Type 171s.

**July 16** Lt. Col. W.F. Barnes, U.S.A.F., flying a North American F86D Sabre, sets the world's first 'more-than 700mph' speed record, the FA1-ratified record being at 715.60mph (1151.64km/h).

**July 17** Lt. Guy Bordelon, flying a piston-engined Vought F4U Corsair, becomes the first U.S. Navy pilot involved in the Korean War to score five confirmed victories.

**July 27** After a little over three years of fighting, the Korean War terminates with the signature of Armistice terms.

**August 25** Following successful tests carried out during May 1953, the U.S.A.F. announces that the Convair B-36 bomber, in a GRB-36F configuration, is able to launch and retrieve Republic GRF-84F Thunderflash reconnaissance aircraft from an under-fuselage trapeze. About 12 of these bombers are converted to the GRB-36F configuration, enabling them also to launch and control missiles in support of development programmes.

**August 27** The first flight of the first production de Havilland Comet 2 (G-AMXA) is made at Hatfield, Hertfordshire.

**September 1** The Belgian airline Sabena inaugurates the first scheduled international helicopter services, flown from Brussels to link with Maastricht and Rotterdam in the Netherlands, and Lille in France.

**September 7** Flying a Hawker Hunter 3, Sqdn. Ldr. Neville Duke, R.A.F., establishes a new world speed record off Littlehampton, West Sussex of 727.48mph (1,170.76km/h).

**September 11** The U.S.A.F. announces that the Sidewinder air-to-air missile has made its first completely successful interception, destroying the Grumman F6F Hellcat drone that was its target.

**October 1** Japan Air Lines becomes reorganized and adopts this, its current title.

**October 3** Lt. Cmdr. J.B. Verdin, U.S.N., flying a Douglas F4D-1 Skyray at Salton Sea, California, sets a new world speed record of 752.78mph (1,211.48km/h).

**October 24** The first flight is made by the Convair YF-102A Delta Dagger prototype from Edwards AFB, California. When it enters service in April 1956, initially with the 327th Fighter Interceptor Squadron, it is the U.S.A.F.'s first delta-wing aircraft.

**November 29** The Douglas DC-7 enters scheduled airline service in the U.S.A. with American Airlines.

**December 12** Capt. Charles Yeager flies the air-launched Bell X-1A rocket-powered high-speed research aircraft at a speed of Mach

2.435, or approximately 1,650mph (2,655km/h), at an altitude of 70,000ft (21,340m).

**December 29** ICAO announces that for the first time the world's airlines have carried more than 50 million passengers during the preceding 12 months.

## 1954

**January 10** The BOAC Comet 1 G-ALYP, en route from the Far East to London, breaks up in the air. The wreckage falls into the Mediterranean about 10 miles (16 km) south of Elba, but none of the 35 persons on board survives. Immediately the news of the Comet accident is received, BOAC grounds its Comet fleet for the completion of airworthiness checks.

**February 28** The first flight is recorded by the first prototype Lockheed XF-104 Starfighter air superiority fighter. When it enters service in early 1958 its Mach 2 performance and wing span of just under 22ft (6.71m) causes the Press to refer to it as the 'missile with a man in it'.

**March 17** BOAC announces that 20 new Comet 4s have been ordered from de Havilland; these will allow the carriage of full payload over the North Atlantic route.

**March 20** The de Havilland Sea Venom enters service with No. 890 Squadron which re-formed at Yeovilton, Somerset on this date.

**March 23** After inspection reveals no apparent fault in BOAC's Comet fleet, they are returned to service.

**April 1** An R.A.F. photo-reconnaissance Spitfire makes the last operational sortie of the type while on duty in Malaya.

**April 8** BOAC's Comet 1 G-ALYY breaks up and falls into the sea south of Naples with the loss of its passengers and crew. The type is immediately withdrawn from service and subsequent investigation reveals metal fatigue problems adjacent to windows in the pressurized structure, causing an explosive decompression.

**May I** The U.S.A.F. forms an Early Warning and Control Division, using specially-equipped RC-121C and RC-121D (later EC-121C/D) aircraft for radar surveillance.

**May 25** A U.S. Navy ZPG-2 airship flown by Cmdr. M.H. Eppes and crew lands at Key West, Florida, after being airborne for just over 200 hours.

**July 1** Following Japanese-U.S. agreement on the formation of defence forces for Japan, the three air arms become officially established with U.S. aid. They comprise and are still known as the Japan Air Self-Defence Force (Koku Jiei-tai), Japan Maritime Self-Defence Force (Kaijoh Jiei-tai) and the Japan Ground Self-Defence Force (Rikujye Jiei-tai).

**July 15** The Boeing Model 367-80 turbojet-powered prototype of a flight refuelling tanker transport for the U.S.A.F. makes its first flight. It is to be built extensively for the U.S.A.F. as the C-I35/KC-135, and to be developed as the Boeing Model 707 civil transport.

**August 2** The first free flight is made by the Rolls-Royce test rig that is built to evaluate the potential of jet lift for vertical take-off and the means of controlling such a vehicle in flight. It is dubbed the 'Flying Bedstead' by the Press.

**August 3** The second prototype of the Convair XF2Y-1 Sea Dart exceeds a speed of Mach 1 in a shallow dive, thus becoming the first water-based aircraft in the world to exceed the speed of sound.

**August 4** The first flight is made by the first English Electric P.I.A. prototype (WG760), later to become known as the Lightning. When production aircraft enter service in December 1959, the Lightning is the R.A.F.'s first true supersonic fighter able to exceed the speed of sound in level flight.

**August 26** A height of about 90,000ft (27,430m), then the greatest height attained by a piloted aircraft, is set by the Bell X-lA research aircraft over the Mojave Desert.

**September 1** The U.S.A.F. Continental Air Defense Command is established, with its headquarters at Colorado Springs.

**September 29** The first flight of a McDonnell F-101A Voodoo is made at Edwards AFB, California. This supersonic single-seat fighter has been developed for the U.S.A.F. from the company's XF-88 Voodoo.

**October 17** The Sikorsky XH-39 helicopter sets a new world altitude record for rotary-wing aircraft of 24,500ft (7,468m).

**October 23** The Western nations agree to terminate occupation of West Germany and to fully incorporate the German Federal Republic into NATO.

**November 1** The U.S.A.F. retires all its Boeing B-29 Superfortresses that are serving in a bomber capacity.

**November 2** The Convair XFY-1's first transitions from vertical to horizontal flight and vice versa are accomplished. (q.v. August 3, 1954)

**November 11** Fairey Aviation announces that its Delta 2 research aircraft has exceeded a speed of Mach 1 in a climb.

**November 25** In Hungary, Malev (Magyar Légiközlekedesi Vállalat) becomes established as the state airline. This follows acquisition by the Hungarian government of the Soviet Union's holding in the original Maszovlet airline, which had been formed with Soviet assistance in March 1946.

## 1955

The Regulus I nuclear or conventionally armed surface-to-surface attack missile is first tested. It becomes operational on some U.S. Navy aircraft carriers, cruisers and submarines from 1955, being finally phased out (from submarines) in 1965.

**February 26** Ejecting from a North American F-100 Super Sabre after the controls had jammed, the company's test pilot George F. Smith becomes the first man in the world to live after ejection from an aircraft travelling at supersonic speed, in this case Mach 1.05.

**March 25** The first flight is made by the first of two Ling-Temco-Vought (LTV) XF8U-1 Crusader prototypes. The last fighter designed by the Chance Vought company before becoming a component of the LTV organization, this carrier-based fighter has an unusual variable-incidence wing.

**April 1** Lufthansa, the re-established German airline, flies its test domestic service from Hamburg.

**April 15** A Convair CV-340 makes the first post-war landing in the U.K. by a German-operated civil airliner. This is Lufthansa's D-ACAD on a Hamburg-London proving flight.

**April 17** London (Heathrow) Airport Central becomes operational, the first departure made by a BEA Viscount.

**May 16** Germany's newly-formed Lufthansa begins European international (as opposed to domestic) airline operations.

**May 27** The first of two Sud-Est Aviation SE.210 Caravelle prototypes makes its first flight. The Caravelle is the first multi-engined monoplane airliner to preserve a clean wing uncluttered by engine installations, its two Rolls-Royce Avon turbojets mounted in pods, one on each side of the rear fuselage.

**June 3–4** Canadian Pacific Air Lines inaugurates a polar route, linking Sydney, Australia with Amsterdam, Netherlands via Vancouver. The first service is flown by Douglas DC-6B *Empress of Amsterdam* (CF-CUR).

**June 15** The first Tupolev Tu-104 prototype (SSSR-L5400), a turbojet-powered civil transport, makes its maiden flight. The first jet airliner to be flown by Aeroflot, its entry into service from September 1956 completely revolutionizes many of the airline's routes.

**June 29** The Boeing B-52 Stratofortress enters service with the U.S.A.F., initially with the 93rd Bomber Wing at Castle AFB, California.

**July 13** The U.S.A.F. gives authorization to the Boeing Airplane Company to proceed with the development and production, in the government-owned plant at Renton, Washington, of a civil transport version of the KC-135 tanker/transport. This new airliner is to become known as the Boeing Model 707.

**July 26** Egypt's President Nasser announces that the international company controlling the Suez Canal is to be terminated and the operation of the Canal nationalized. This follows U.S. withdrawal from a plan to help finance construction of the Aswan Dam, Nasser intending that revenue from the Canal should finance building of the dam.

**August 1** The U.S. begins its first zero-gravity research experiments, using Lockheed T-33 trainers to study the effects of weightlessness.

**August 20** Flying a North American F-100C Super Sabre from Edwards AFB, California, Col. H.A. Hanes sets a new world speed record of 822.09mph (1,323.03km/h).

**August 29** A new world altitude record of 65,889ft (20,083m) is established in the U.K.

by W.F. Gibb flying an English Electric Canberra.

**September 3** The first parachute escape from an aircraft travelling at speed on the ground is made by Sqdn. Ldr. J.S. Fifield, R.A.F. This is made to test a Martin-Baker ejection seat installed in a modified Gloster Meteor which is travelling at about 120mph (194km/h) at the moment of ejection.

**October 16** During the course of experimental flights, Boeing's Model 367-80 flies non-stop from Seattle, Washington, to Washington D.C. in 3 hrs 58 mins and back to Seattle in 4 hrs 8 mins. These times represent average speeds of 589mph (947km/h) and 564mph (907km/h) respectively.

**October 19** The United States' Federal Communications Commission authorizes the American Telephone and Telegraph Company to work on a computer-controlled defence radar and communications system known as Semi-Automatic Ground Environment (SAGE).

**October 22** The Republic YF-105A Thunderchief prototype makes its first flight. This supersonic single-seat fighter-bomber is to prove of great value to the U.S.A.F. during subsequent operations in Vietnam.

**October 25** The first flight is recorded in Sweden by the Saab-35 Draken prototype, a double-delta-winged supersonic single-seat fighter.

**November 1** A United Air Lines DC-6MB

explodes in mid-air and crashes near Longmont, Colorado, killing all 44 occupants. It is subsequently established as one of the most bizarre accidents in aviation history, caused by a bomb introduced onto the aircraft by John G. Graham, intended to destroy the aircraft and his mother who is a passenger. Her death is planned to allow him to claim heavy compensation from large-scale pre-flight insurance.

First guided missile cruiser, the U.S.S. *Boston*, is commissioned by the U.S. Navy.

Having been responsible for placing a requirement with Lockheed in 1939 for a transcontinental airliner that instigated the design of the original Constellation that had to wait until December 1945 to make a civil transatlantic proving flight, TWA (formerly Transcontinental & Western Air) subsequently puts the improved L-1049G Super Constellation into service on the Atlantic route on this date. Not the first Super G on the Atlantic route, it was nevertheless probably the most famous service. (q.v. December 4, 1945)

**December 19** An agreement is concluded between Aeroflot and BEA covering the mutual operation of air services between the Soviet Union and the U.K.

# 1956

**January 10** The first U.S.-built rocket engine with a thrust in excess of 400,000lb (181,437kg) is run successfully for the first time at Santa Susana, California.

**January 11** The U.K. Air Ministry announces the formation of a task force to conduct British atomic tests off the Monte Bello Islands in the Indian Ocean.

**January 17** The U.S. Department of Defense for the first time publicly reveals the existence of the SAGE defence system. (q.v. October 19, 1955)

**February 17** The first flight is made by the first production Lockheed F-104A Starfighter, a single-seat air superiority fighter for service with the U.S.A.F.

**February 24** The Gloster Javelin all-weather fighter enters service with the R.A.F.'s No. 46 Squadron at Odiham, Hampshire.

**March 10** Pushing the world speed record upwards by almost 310mph (500km/h) in a single jump, Lt. Peter Twiss establishes the world's first over 1,000mph speed record. This is accomplished flying the Fairey Delta 2 research aircraft off the English coast at Chichester, West Sussex, and gaining a record ratified at 1,131.76mph (1,821.39km/h).

**March 14** The first successful launch is made from Cape Canaveral of a Chrysler Redstone or Jupiter-A tactical bombardment missile. This has been developed in the U.S.A. by a team headed by Dr. Wernher von Braun, the designer of Germany's V2 (A4) rocket of the Second World War.

**May 21** A U.S. hydrogen bomb, the first to be released from an aircraft, is detonated over Bikini Atoll in the Pacific.

**June 20** The U.S. Navy commissions its first helicopter assault carrier, the U.S.S. *Thetis Bay*.

**July 7** The de Havilland Comet 2 enters service with R.A.F. Transport Command at Lyneham, Wiltshire, becoming the world's first turbojet-powered aircraft to see service in a military transport role.

**July 24** The first flight is made by the French Dassault Étendard IV prototype which has been built by the company as a private venture. Failing to enter production as a land-based strike fighter for which it had been intended, it is developed into a successful carrier-based fighter-bomber/reconnaissance aircraft.

**July 26** Egypt seizes control of the Suez Canal from the privately owned Suez Canal Corporation.

**August 23–24** A specially-prepared Hiller H-21 ('Flying Banana') twin-rotor helicopter of the U.S. Army becomes the first rotary-wing aircraft to complete a non-stop transcontinental flight from San Diego, California to Washington, D.C.

**August 31** The first production example of the Boeing KC-135A tanker/transport for the U.S.A.F. makes its first flight.

**September 2** A Vickers Valiant records the first non-stop transatlantic flight to be made by one of the R.A.F.'s V-bombers, from Lowring, Maine, to Marham, Norfolk.

**September 7** The Bell X-2 research aircraft is flown by Capt. Iven C. Kincheloe to an altitude of 126,200ft (38,466m).

**September 15** The Tupolev Tu-104 turbojet-powered airliner enters service with Aeroflot, initially on its Moscow-Irkutsk route.

**September 20** The American Jupiter C rocket is first launched, attaining a record height of 682miles (1,097km).

**September 24** Formation date of the post-war German air force, the Luftwaffe der Deutschen Bundesrepublik.

**September 27** The Bell X-2 is destroyed in a fatal accident following a flight in which its pilot, Capt. Milburn Apt, U.S.A.F., had achieved a speed of Mach 3.2, the highest then recorded by a manned aircraft.

**October 10** NACA discloses that a speed of Mach 10.4 has been attained by a four-stage research rocket.

**October 11** The first atomic bomb to be dropped by a British aircraft is released by a Vickers Valiant of No. 49 (Bomber) Squadron over Malalinga, South Australia.

**October 24** In secret meetings, an Anglo-French-Israeli agreement is reached to co-ordinate military operations against Egypt. This requires Israel to pose a threat to the security of the Suez Canal, thus precipitating Anglo-French intervention.

**October 29** Israeli forces begin their planned attack to threaten the Suez Canal, making an airdrop of paratroops at Mitla Pass in the Sinai Peninsula.

**October 30** An Anglo-French ultimatum calls upon Egyptian and Israeli troops to cease fighting and allow British and French troops to occupy key points to secure the safety of the Suez Canal.

**October 31** Following rejection of the ultimatum by Egypt and Israel, British and French air forces begin attacks on Egyptian air bases.

**November 5** British and French paratroops are airdropped at Port Fuad and Port Said, Egypt.

**November 6** An Anglo-French amphibious landing at Port Said, carried out with air cover, is followed by a midnight cease-fire.

**November 8** Ascending from Rapid City, South Dakota, Lt. Cmdr. M.L. Lewis, U.S. Navy, and Malcom D. Ross establish a world altitude record for manned balloons of 76,000ft (23,165m).

**November 11** The first flight is made at Fort Worth, Texas, of the Convair XB-58 Hustler prototype, a four-turbojet delta-wing medium bomber. When the B-58 enters service in early 1960 it is the U.S.A.F.'s first supersonic bomber.

**November 12** A Sikorsky S-56 helicopter in service with the U.S. Marine Corps records a speed of 162.7mph (261.8km/h).

**November 17** The first flight is made by the

Dassault Mirage III prototype, a delta-wing high-altitude interceptor/fighter.

**December 13** In the U.S.A.F.'s altitude research chamber at its Air Research and Development Command, Dayton, Ohio, Maj. Arnold I. Beck attains the equivalent of a flight altitude of 198,770ft (60,585m).

**December 26** Convair's F-106A Delta Dart prototype makes its first flight. This supersonic delta-wing all-weather interceptor is to become an important weapon of the U.S.A.F.

## 1957

**January 18** Three of the U.S.A.F.'s Boeing B-52 Stratofortresses, commanded by Major Gen. Archie J. Old Jr., make the world's first round-the-world non-stop flight by turbojet-powered aircraft. This is completed in 45 hrs 19 mins at an average speed of 534mph (859km/h).

**March 15** A U.S. Navy ZPG-2 airship, with Cmdr. J.R. Hunt and crew, establishes a new unrefuelled endurance record of 264 hrs 12 mins.

**April 2** The Short SC.1 VTOL research aircraft with five Rolls-Royce RB.108 turbojets, four being used for jet-lift, makes its first flight in a conventional take-off mode.

**April 4** The first flight is made by the first of three English Electric P.1B prototypes (XA847), upon which is based the production version of the Lightning.

**May 15** A Vickers Valiant of the R.A.F.'s No. 49 (Bomber) Squadron drops the U.K.'s first thermonuclear (hydrogen) bomb over the Pacific, close to Christmas Island.

**May 30** The U.S.A.F. discloses development of the Hughes Falcon air-to-air guided missile armed with a nuclear warhead.

**July 31** The North American DEW line early warning system, extending across the arctic areas of Canada, is reported to be fully operational.

**August 1** A joint U.S.-Canada North American Air Defense Command (NORAD) is informally activated.

**August 19–20** Ascending from Crosby, Minnesota, Maj. David G. Simons, U.S.A.F., sets a balloon world altitude record of 101,516ft (30,942m).

**August 21** The Soviet R7 rocket is successfully launched. (q.v. October 4, 1957)

**September 11** Pan American inaugurates a London-San Francisco service with Douglas DC-7Cs. This is flown via Frobisher Bay, Baffin Island, and is to become known as the polar route.

**September 20** The U.S.A.F. Chief of Staff announces the development of a radar system with the capability to detect ICBMs at a range of 3,000 miles (4,830km).

**September 30** Trans World Airlines inaugurates a Los Angeles-London service

with Lockheed L-l649A Starliners, flying over the so-called polar route.

**October 4** The Soviet Union puts into Earth orbit the world's first artificial satellite. Named Sputnik 1 ('Fellow Traveller'), it is launched by a newly-developed R7 ICBM from the U.S.S.R.'s Tyuratam Baikonur cosmodrome.

**October 16** The U.S.A.F. achieves its first successful experiment to boost a man-made object to a velocity at which it can escape from the Earth's gravitational pull. This is accomplished by a special Aerobee rocket which, at a height of 54 miles (87km), detonates a shaped charge to boost small metallic pellets to a speed of some 33,000mph (53,100km/h).

**October 22** Under Operation Far Side, a four-stage research rocket is launched from a U.S. balloon flying at some l00,000ft (30,480m) above Eniwetok Atoll. This succeeds in travelling some 2,700 miles (4,345km) into space.

**November 3** The Soviet Union launches *Sputnik 2*, carrying the dog Laika which is destined to die when its oxygen is exhausted.

**November 7** Showing American TV audiences a Jupiter nose-cone which has been recovered after launch from Cape Canaveral, President Eisenhower states that the U.S. has solved the missile re-entry problem.

**December 6** The first flight is made by the Lockheed L-188 Electra short-to-medium-

range turboprop airliner prototype (N1881). This is achieved more than a month ahead of schedule.

The U.S.A. attempts to launch a satellite into space, but the Vanguard booster rocket explodes.

**December 12** Maj. Adrian Drew, U.S.A.F., using a McDonnell F-101A Voodoo, sets a new world speed record of 1,207.34mph (1,943.03km/h).

**December 17** The U.S. Atlas booster rocket is successfully launched.

**December 19** BOAC introduces Bristol Britannia Srs 312s on its London-New York route, marking the first transatlantic passenger services to be operated by a turboprop airliner.

**December 20** The first production example of the Boeing Model 707-120, the basic domestic version, makes its first flight.

## 1958

**January 14–20** Qantas inaugurates the airline's first scheduled round-the-world route. The first services are flown by the Super Constellations *Southern Aurora* (VH-EAO) eastbound, and *Southern Zephyr* (VH-EAP) westbound.

**January 31** *Explorer 1*, the first U.S. satellite to enter Earth orbit, is launched by a Jupiter C rocket from Cape Canaveral. Travelling in an elliptical orbit, data that it transmits lead to discovery of the Van Allen radiation belts that girdle the Earth.

**February 18** The U.S.A.F. discloses that an airflow speed of approximately 32,400mph (52,140km/h) has been briefly attained in the test section of a wind tunnel at Arnold Research and Development Center, Tullahoma, Tennessee.

**March 17** *Vanguard 1*, the second U.S. satellite to enter Earth orbit, is launched from Cape Canaveral.

**April 9** The two-man crew of a Canberra bomber which explodes over Monyash, Derbyshire, makes the highest reported emergency escape from an aircraft, 56,000ft (17,070m).

**April 18** In the United States, Lt. Cmdr. G.C. Watkins, U.S. Navy, establishes a new world altitude record of 76,932ft (23,449m) while flying a Grumman F11F-1 Tiger. This is the last of Grumman's famous 'cat' family to serve with the U.S. Navy.

**April 27** The first production de Havilland DH.l06 Comet 4, for service with BOAC (G-APDA), makes its first flight at Hatfield, Hertfordshire.

**May 2** Lt. Commander G.C. Watkins' two-week-old world altitude record is broken by R. Carpentier in France. Flying the Sud-Ouest SO.9050 Trident (F-ZWUM), he attains an altitude of 79,452ft (24,217m).

**May 7** Maj. H.C. Johnson, flying a Lockheed F-104A Starfighter in the U.S.A., plays his part in keeping the FAI busy by setting a third new world altitude record in less than three weeks, attaining a height of 91,243ft (27,811m).

**May 12** The North American Air Defense Command (NORAD), which was informally activated on August 1, 1957, is formally established with headquarters at Colorado Springs.

**May 15** The Soviet Union launches *Sputnik 3*, carrying an automatic scientific lab.

**May 16** The first 'over-2,000km/h' world speed record is set over southern California by Capt. W.W. Irvin, U.S.A.F. Flying a Lockheed F-104A Starfighter, he attains a speed of 1,403mph (2,259.18km/h).

**May 27** The first flight is made by the McDonnell F4H-1 Phantom II carrier-based fighter and tactical strike fighter.

**May 30** The first Douglas DC-8 Srs 10, a domestic version of the company's turbojet sweptwing civil transport, makes its first flight.

**June 9** London's new Gatwick Airport is officially opened by H.M. Queen Elizabeth II.

**August 6** The Short SC.1 VTOL research aircraft makes a first tethered vertical flight.

**August 7** A de Havilland DH.106 Comet 4 on a proving flight from New York to Hatfield, Hertfordshire, completes its flight in 6 hrs 27 mins.

**September 9** The Lockheed X-7, a pilotless test vehicle for ramjet engines and missile components, achieves a speed of Mach 4 following launch from a Boeing B-50. Recovery is effected after each flight by an automatically-opening parachute.

**September 14** The de Havilland Comet 4 G-APDA makes a proving flight from Hong Kong to Hatfield, Hertfordshire within the day, in a flight time of 16 hrs 16 mins.

**September 30** U.K. commercial flying-boat operations come to an end when Aquila Airways withdraws its Southampton-Madeira service.

The U.S. National Advisory Committee for Aeronautics (NACA) issues its final report and then ceases to exist.

**October 1** The U.S. National Aeronautics and Space Administration (NASA) is established to absorb the functions of NACA, and to control all U.S. non-military space projects.

President Eisenhower appoints an administrator for the newly-formed Federal Aviation Agency (FAA), which absorbs the former Civil Aeronautics Administration (CAA).

**October 4** BOAC inaugurates simultaneous London-New York and New York-London services with the de Havilland Comet 4. These are the first transatlantic passenger services flown by turbojet-powered airliners.

**October 11** The U.S.A.F. makes a second attempt to put a research probe in orbit around the Moon. This is *Pioneer 1B* which, because its third stage cuts out fractionally too soon, travels about 70,700 miles (113,780km) before falling back towards Earth.

**October 26** Pan American inaugurates its first transatlantic services operated by the Boeing 707-121 turbojet-powered airliner.

**December 18** The United States places in Earth orbit a small communications relay satellite. Carrying a pre-recorded tape, on the following day it transmits President Eisenhower's Christmas message to the nation. This is the first U.S. active communication from space.

## 1959

**January 2** The Soviet Union launches a scientific probe named *Luna 1*, which is intended to impact on the Moon's surface. It misses its target by some 3,700 miles (5,955km), passing the Moon to enter a solar orbit.

**February 11** A U.S. weather balloon climbs to a record height of 146,000ft (44,500m).

**February 17** The U.S. Navy launches the weather reporting *Vanguard II* satellite into Earth orbit.

**February 28** Vandenberg Air Force Base in California is used for the first time to launch a satellite, *Discoverer 1*.

**March 3** The U.S. *Pioneer 4* space probe is launched in an attempt to obtain crude pictures of the Moon's surface while making a fly-past at a distance of about 20,000 miles (32,200km). It passes the Moon at almost double this range and travels on into solar orbit.

**March 13** Aviation Cadet E. R. Cook becomes the U.S. Navy's first student pilot to fly solo in a turbojet-powered trainer without prior experience in a propeller-driven aircraft.

**April 6** It is announced in the U.S. that seven pilots have been selected from the nation's armed services for training as space vehicle pilots.

**April 23** The U.S. Hound Dog thermonuclear stand-off missile makes a successful first flight following launch from a Boeing B-52D bomber.

**May 15** The last operational flight is made by an R.A.F. Sunderland, also marking the last use of water-based aircraft by the Royal Air Force.

**May 28** Two monkeys, named Able and Baker, are recovered unharmed after a 300-mile (483km) flight in a compartment in the nose-cone of a Jupiter rocket.

**June 3** The American satellite *Discoverer 3* is launched carrying four mice for a biological experiment.

**June 8** The first unpowered free flight of the North American X-15A high-performance research aircraft is made following launch from beneath the wing of its Boeing B-52 'mother plane'.

**June 17** The first flight is made by the Dassault Mirage IV-A strategic bomber prototype.

**July 13–23** A London-Paris air race, held throughout this period to mark the 50th anniversary of Louis Blériot's first crossing of the English Channel (q.v. July 25, 1909), is won by Sqdn. Ldr. Charles Maughan, R.A.F. Using a combination of two motor-cycles, a Bristol Sycamore helicopter and a Hawker Hunter T.Mk 7, his city-centre to city-centre time is a remarkable 40 mins 44 secs.

**July 14** Maj. V. Ilyushin of the Soviet Union sets a new world altitude record of 94,659ft (28,852m) flying the Sukhoi T-431.

**July 27** Air France introduces the Sud-Aviation Caravelle on its services to the U.K., the initial operation flown by Caravelle *Lorraine* (F-BHRB).

**July 29** Qantas operates its first jet service from Sydney to San Francisco with the Boeing 707-138 *City of Canberra* (VH-EBC). This is also the airline's first scheduled transpacific flight by a turbojet-powered airliner.

**July 30** The first flight is made by the Northrop N-156C prototype, which exceeds a speed of Mach 1 during this initial flight test. It is to become known internationally as the F-5 Freedom Fighter.

**August 7** NASA's *Explorer 6* is launched into Earth orbit from Cape Canaveral, and is to send the first TV pictures from space.

**August 17** A NASA research rocket ignites a sodium flare at an altitude of some 150 miles (240km) in a project to provide information on high-altitude wind direction and velocity and the rate of matter diffusion in the upper atmosphere.

**August 24** The data capsule of an Atlas-C rocket is successfully recovered after a 5,000-mile (8,050-km) flight down-range. It provides the first cine films of Earth taken from an altitude of 700 miles (1,125km).

**September 4** An unmanned U.S. scientific balloon records an altitude of some 150,000ft (45,720m).

**September 9** *BigJoe*, which was NASA's test version of the Mercury astronaut capsule, is successfully recovered in the Caribbean Sea after a 1,500-mile (2,415-km) flight following launch by an Atlas rocket.

**September 12** The Soviet Union's *Luna 2* space probe is launched. On the 14th it becomes the first man-made object to impact on the Moon, between the craters Archimedes, Aristillus and Autolycus.

**September 17** The second example of the North American X-15A research aircraft makes a successful first powered flight following launch from its B-52 mother plane.

**September 18** The Douglas DC-8 Srs 10 turbojet-powered airliner makes its first entry into U.S. domestic service, flown by Delta Air Lines and United Air Lines.

**October 4** The Soviet *Luna 3* space probe is launched towards the Moon. It is to record the first circumlunar flight, and is the first to photograph the Moon's hidden surface. The photographic images are transmitted over a TV link to Earth.

**October 10** The Pan American Boeing 707-321 *Clipper Windward* inaugurates the first round-the-world passenger service by turbojet-powered airliners.

**October 30** The first of an initial batch of 50 production English Electric Lightning F.Mk 1 interceptors for the R.A.F. flies. First joining the R.A.F. with No. 74 Squadron in July 1960, the Lightning gives the R.A.F. its first warplane with Mach 2 performance.

**October 31** Flying a Mikoyan Type Ye-66 at Sidorovo, Tyumenskaya, Col. G. Mosolov establishes a new world speed record of 1,665.89mph (2,681.00km/h).

**November 16** Capt. Joseph W. Kittinger Jr. makes a balloon ascent from White Sands, New Mexico. Having gained an altitude of 76,400ft (23,285m) in an open gondola, he parachutes to the ground, recording a free-fall of 64,000ft (19,505m).

**December 4** NASA tests the Mercury capsule escape system, launching a capsule with a rhesus monkey aboard which is recovered alive and quite unharmed.

**December 6** A U.S. Navy McDonnell F-4 Phantom II piloted by Cmdr. L. Flint establishes a new world altitude record of 98,556ft (30,040m).

**December 9** At Bloomfield, Connecticut, a Kaman H-43B rescue helicopter, crewed by U.S.A.F. officers Maj. William J. Davis and Capt. Walter J. Hodgson, sets a helicopter altitude record of 29,846ft (9,097m).

**December 14** The eight-day-old world altitude record of Cmdr. L. Flint, U.S.N., is broken by a Lockheed F-104C Starfighter piloted by Capt. J.B. Jordan to a height of 103,389ft (31,513m).

**December 15** A new world speed record of 1,525.93mph (2,455.74km/h) is set by Maj. J.W. Rogers, U.S.A.F., flying a Convair F-106A Delta Dart at Edwards AFB, California.

## 1960

**January 21** In a further low-altitude test of the Mercury escape system, NASA launches a monkey named Miss Sam. She is recovered unharmed after the escape system is activated almost immediately following launch.

**February 9** The U.S.A.F. activates a National Space Surveillance Control Center at Bedford, Massachusetts.

**February 13** France explodes an atomic weapon in the Sahara Desert, thus becoming the world's fourth nuclear power.

**April 6** The second Short SC.1 research aircraft makes the first full transitions from vertical to horizontal flight and vice-versa by a British VTOL aircraft.

**April 29** First test firing by NASA of all eight Rocketdyne H-l engines of the Chrysler Saturn 1 first stage produces a combined 1,300,0001b (589,670kg) stagic thrust.

**May 6** At a first public demonstration for the Press, a U.S.A.F. Minuteman is successfully launched from an underground launch pad (not a silo) at Edwards AFB, California.

**May 7** A Lockheed U-2 high-altitude reconnaissance aircraft, overflying the Soviet Union and piloted by Gary Powers, is shot down from an altitude of some 65,000ft (19,810m) by a Soviet SAM near Sverdlovsk.

**May 24** The U.S. launches *Midas II* into orbit, the first early-warning satellite.

**June 22** The U.S.A. becomes the first to launch a rocket carrying multiple independently-instrumented satellites.

**July 20** The Short SC.1 becomes the first jet-lift aircraft to fly the English Channel.

**August 12** Following successful test launches in which balloons are inflated to a large diameter in space, NASA places into orbit the *Echo I* passive communications satellite. This is of plastic material with an aluminium film, and serves as a test vehicle for the relay of several types of communication signals.

Maj. Robert White, U.S.A.F., pilots the North American X-15A research aircraft to a height of 136,500ft (41,600m).

**August 16** Following the success of his earlier parachute jump (q.v. November 16, 1959), Capt. Joseph W. Kittinger Jr., U.S.A.F., jumps from a balloon at 102,200ft (31,150m), making a free fall of 84,700ft (25,815m).

**August 19** The Soviet Union's *Sputnik 5* satellite is launched into Earth orbit carrying two dogs named Belka and Strelka. They are successfully recovered after completing 18 orbits.

**October 1** A U.S. BMEWS (Ballistic Missile Early Warning System) radar site becomes operational at Thule, Greenland.

**October 16** Marking the end of what had once seemed to be a great success story for the British aviation industry, BOAC operates its last scheduled Comet 4 New York-London service.

**October 21** The first tethered flight is made by the Hawker Siddeley P.1127 Kestrel experimental V/STOL tactical fighter.

**October 24** In the worst space-related accident ever, 91 people lose their lives in the Baikonur Space Centre in the U.S.S.R. (since Kazakhstan), when an R-16 booster blows up.

**November 12** Launching *Discoverer 17* from Vandenburg AFB, a restartable rocket engine is used for the first time.

## 1961

**January 31** Extending from the last unmanned Mercury experiment on December 19, 1960, NASA launches a Mercury capsule containing a chimpanzee named Ham. Although subjected to 17g during the launch phase, Ham is successfully recovered after a 420-mile (676km) down-range sub-orbital flight, with no apparent ill effects.

**March 13** The Hawker Siddeley P.1127 Kestrel experimental V/STOL tactical fighter makes its first conventional flight.

**March 28** Air Afrique (Société Aérienne Africaine Multinationale) is formed as a joint venture involving Air France and several now independent African states.

**March 30** NASA pilot Joe Walker attains a height of 169,600ft (51,695m) in the North American X-15A research aircraft.

**April 12** The Soviet Union staggers the world by announcing that it has launched the spacecraft *Vostok 1* into Earth orbit carrying Yuri Gagarin, the first man in space. He lands successfully after one orbit of the Earth in a total flight time of 1 hr 48 mins.

**April 21** Maj. Robert White, U.S.A.F., pilots the North American X-15A during the first test flight at full throttle. A speed of 3,074mph (4,947km/h) is attained at 79,000ft (24,080m), before coasting upward to an altitude of 105,100ft (32,034m).

**April 28** Col. G. Mosolov, flying a Mikoyan Ye-66A, regains the world height record for the Soviet Union at an altitude of 113,898ft (34,714m).

**May 5** Alan B. Shepard becomes the first American in space, with a flight time of 15 mins 28 secs. Carried in the Mercury ballistic capsule *Freedom 7*, following launch by a

Redstone rocket, this is a sub-orbital trajectory during which a height of 116.5 miles (187km) and range of 297 miles (478km) is attained.

**June 28** Announcement is made of the termination of U.S. Navy airship operations, prompted by the collapse of one of four Goodyear ZPG-3W Airborne Early Warning airships. First flown in 1958, the ZPG-3W was the largest non-rigid airship to date.

**June 29** The U.S. Navy's *Transit IV* satellite is launched, the first known to carry a nuclear power source in the form of a radioisotope-powered battery.

**July 1** NORAD begins the operation of SPADATS, designed to electronically catalogue all man-made space objects.

**July 10** A Tactical Air Command pilot flies a Republic F-105D Thunderchief for more than 1,500 miles (2,410km) without any external vision. This is a test to ensure that the instrumentation and radar system of the F-105 is adequate for a squadron pilot to make a long-range IFR mission at altitudes between 500 and 1,000ft (152 and 305m).

**July 21** The U.S. puts its second man in sub-orbital flight down the Atlantic Missile Range; Virgil Grissom in the Mercury capsule *Liberty Bell 7*.

**August 6** The Soviet Union launches its second man into Earth orbit in *Vostok 2*. Cosmonaut Herman Titov completes 17 Earth orbits before landing after 1 day 1 hr 19 mins.

**September 13** The world-wide tracking network which has been set up for the U.S. Mercury programme is used for the first time to observe the orbit of an unmanned Mercury capsule. Data from this network convinces NASA that the Atlas is capable of putting a manned Mercury capsule into Earth orbit.

**October 4** Launch of the world's first active communications satellite *Courier 1B* (U.S.A).

**November 9** In the last high-speed flight made by the X-15A during 1961, Maj. Robert White, U.S.A.F., attains a speed of 4,093mph (6,587km/h) at 101,600ft (30,970m).

**November 22** At Edwards AFB, California, Lt. Col. R.B. Robinson establishes a new world speed record in a McDonnell F4H-1F Phantom II at a speed of 1,606.51mph (2,585.43km/h).

**November 29** In its last unmanned Mercury capsule test, NASA launches the chimpanzee Enos into Earth orbit.

**December 11** The first direct military support for South Vietnam is provided by the arrival at Saigon of a U.S. Navy aircraft carrier transporting two U.S. Army helicopter companies.

**December 15** NORAD's SAGE system becomes fully operational with the completion of a 21st and final control centre at Sioux City, Iowa.

## 1962

**January 10–11** Maj. Clyde P. Evely and crew establish a new world distance record in a

Boeing B-52H Stratofortress, flying from Okinawa, Ryukyu Islands to Madrid, Spain, a distance of 12,532.3 miles (20,168.78km).

**February 20** Launched by an Atlas booster, the Mercury capsule *Friendship 7* carries America's Lt. Col. John H. Glenn (U.S.M.C.) into Earth orbit (the first U.S. astronaut to go into orbit). He completes three orbits to record a flight time of 4 hrs 55 mins 23 secs before splash-down.

**February 28** In the first manned test of the steel cocoon-type escape capsule carried by the General Dynamics/Convair B-58A Hustler, W.O. Edward J. Murray is ejected from the aircraft which is travelling at 565mph (909km/h) at 20,000ft (6,100m). After a 26-second free-fall, a parachute is automatically deployed, bringing him safely to the ground eight minutes after ejection.

**April 30** Flown by NASA pilot Joe Walker, the North American X-15A attains a new record height of 246,700ft (75,195m).

**May 24** NASA's Mercury capsule *Aurora 7* is launched into Earth orbit carrying Lt. Cmdr. M. Scott Carpenter, U.S. Navy, on a similar three-orbit mission to that of *Friendship 7*. Experiencing re-entry problems, he guides the spacecraft manually through re-entry but splashes down some 260 miles (420km) from the target area after a 4 hr 56 minute mission. He remains in his life raft until rescued.

**June 27** The North American X15A flown by NASA pilot Joe Walker attains its highest recorded speed of 4,159mph (6,693km/h).

Flying the Mikoyan Type Ye-166 at Sidorovo Tyumenskaya, Col. G. Mosolov establishes a new world speed record of 1,665.89mph (2,681km/h).

**July 10** The *Telstar 1* communications satellite is placed in Earth orbit by a Delta booster from Cape Canaveral. It makes possible the first transatlantic exchanges of TV programmes, proving to 'the man in the street' that he might gain some benefit from the space race.

**August 8** In tests carried out to determine the effects of kinetic heating, the second North American X-15A attains a surface temperature of 900°F (482°C) at an altitude of 90,000ft (27,430m) and speed of 2,900mph (4,665km/h).

**August 11** and **12** Respective launch dates of the Soviet Union's *Vostok 3* (Andrian Nikolayev) and *4* (Pavel Popovich) into Earth orbit. The two spacecraft make a rendezvous in orbit, approaching to within 3 miles (5km) of each other. TV cameras in the spacecraft provide the first TV transmission from a manned vehicle in space.

**September 29** The Canadian built and designed *Alouette 1* satellite, the first to be built outside of the U.S. or U.S.S.R., is successfully launched by a Thor-Agena B booster.

**October 3** Cmdr. Walter M. Schirra, U.S.N., completes a 9 hr 13 minute space mission in the Mercury-Atlas 8 *Sigma 7*.

**October 22** President Kennedy announces that U.S. reconnaissance aircraft have established that offensive missile sites are being erected in Cuba.

**October 24–29** Lengthy exchanges between Kennedy and Khrushchev end the 'Cuban missile crisis'. The U.S. pledges that it will not invade Cuba and, in return, the U.S.S.R. agrees to halt construction of missile bases and remove its missiles.

**December 13–14** Under the designation Project Stargazer, a balloon manned by Capt. Joseph W. Kittinger, U.S.A.F., carries civilian astronomer William C. White and a specially-mounted telescope to a height of 82,000ft (25,000m). This enables White to make a number of observations under ideal conditions.

**December 14** NASA's *Mariner II* scans the surface of Venus for 35 mins as it flies past at a distance of 21,642 miles (34,830km). A surface temperature of 834°F (428°C) is recorded. *Mariner II* is the first man-made satellite to reach another planet.

## 1963

**January 7** The U.S.S. *Buck*, having completed qualification trials, is the first U.S. warship to become operational with Gyrodyne GH-50C ASW drone helicopters.

**January 17** NASA pilot Joe Walker flies the North American X-15A to a height of 271,000ft (82,600m). He qualifies for 'astronaut's wings', having exceeded a height of 50 miles (80km).

**February 9** The Boeing 727 prototype is flown for the first time, a short/medium-range jet transport. Incorporating three rear-mounted engines and a T-tail, it is in other respects similar to the Model 707/720 that had preceded it.

**April 30–May 12** American airwoman Betty Miller makes the first transpacific solo flight by a woman. This is accomplished in a four-stop flight from Oakland, California to Brisbane, Australia.

**May 1** Flying a Lockheed TF-104G Starfighter near Edwards AFB, California, Jacqueline Cochran successfully sets a 100-km closed-circuit world speed record for women of 1,203.686mph (1,937.14km/h).

**May 15–16** In the longest U.S. space mission to date, Maj. L. Gordon Cooper, U.S.A.F., orbits the Earth 22 times in Mercury Atlas 9 *Faith 7*. Cooper carries out experiments related to the navigation and guidance of spacecraft, is monitored by a TV camera, and makes a manually-controlled re-entry, to record a total mission time of 34 hrs 19 mins 49 secs.

**June 7** Following a merger of Air Liban and Middle East Airlines, the title Middle East Airlines Air Liban is adopted.

**June 14–19** The Soviet Union's *Vostok 5* spacecraft carrying Valery Bykovsky, records the longest space mission to date of 119 hours 16 minutes.

**June 16** With the launch of a second spacecraft within two days, the Soviet Union's

*Vostok 6* carries the first woman into space, cosmonaut Valentina Tereshkova.

**July 19** NASA pilot Joe Walker flies the North American X15A to an unofficial height record of 347,800ft (106,010m).

**July 25** A nuclear test ban treaty is finalized after almost three years of discussion; subsequently signed by most nations of the world, it brings an end to tests in the atmosphere.

**July 26** The U.S. *Syncom 2* is the world's first geosynchronous satellite, remaining static over the Atlantic.

**August 28** The first test in the U.S. Apollo programme is made when a Little Joe II booster, which has been designed for unmanned sub-orbital testing of this vehicle, makes a first test with a dummy Apollo spacecraft.

**October 1** Under the command of Rear Adm. James R. Reedy, a ski-equipped Lockheed C-130 Hercules makes a first transpolar non-stop flight from Capetown, South Africa to McMurdo Sound, Antarctica.

**October 17** The United Nations General Assembly confirms earlier unilateral declarations made by the U.S. and U.S.S.R. that no weapons will be mounted in or used from space.

The *Vela Hotel* satellite makes the first detection of a nuclear explosion from space.

**November 20** The U.S.A.F. formally accepts its first two McDonnell F-4C Phantom II fighters at MacDill AFB, Florida.

**November 29** By an executive order, President Johnson renames Cape Canaveral Cape Kennedy, and its space facilities as the John F. Kennedy Space Center.

**December 15** Alia (Alia Royal Jordanian Airline) begins operations. Formed in October 1963, it is the successor to Air Jordan.

**December 17** The first flight is made by the Lockheed C-141A four-turbofan long-range military transport ordered for service with the U.S.A.F.'s MATS.

## 1964

**January 29** *Saturn I* SA-5 is successfully launched, recording the first flight with a live second stage.

**February 29** For the first time, President Johnson publicly reveals the existence of the Lockheed A-11 high-altitude reconnaissance aircraft.

**April 8** The first unmanned *Gemini* spacecraft is placed in Earth orbit by a Titan II booster.

**April 17** At the end of a 29-day flight in her Cessna 180 *Spirit of Columbus*, U.S. airwoman Jerrie Mock lands at Columbus, Ohio, so becoming the first woman pilot to fly solo round the world.

**May 11** Piloting a Lockheed TF-104G Starfighter, Jacqueline Cochran sets a new world speed record for women over a 15/25km course of 1,429.246mph (2,300.14km/h).

**May 12** American Joan Merriam, flying a Piper Apache, becomes the second woman to make a solo round-the-world flight, taking 56 days to cover the route which had been planned by Amelia Earhart.

**June 28** The North American X-15A No. 2 research aircraft, which following an accident has been rebuilt with new large external fuel tanks, makes its first flight under the new designation X-15A-2.

**July 27** The Daniel Guggenheim Medal for 1964 is posthumously awarded to Dr. Robert H. Goddard in recognition of his important contributions to rocket theory and design.

**July 28** NASA's unmanned *Ranger 7* is launched from Cape Kennedy, subsequently taking 4,316 TV pictures of the lunar surface in the last 13 minutes of flight before it impacts on the Moon.

**July 31** In the U.S.A., A.H. Parker sets the first over 646-mile (1,000km) sailplane distance record using a Sisu-1A.

**August 5** In retaliation for the unprovoked attack by the North Vietnamese patrol boats on U.S. destroyers, President Johnson orders carrier-based aircraft from U.S.S. *Constellation* and *Ticonderoga* to attack North Vietnamese naval bases. A U.S. Navy pilot killed in the action was this service's first loss of the Vietnam War.

**September 21** The North American XB-70A Valkyrie prototype makes its first flight. This Mach 3 strategic bomber programme is subsequently abandoned.

**September 27** The BAC TSR.2 two-seat all-weather supersonic attack reconnaissance aircraft prototype (XR219) makes its first flight. It proves to be the only one of the type to fly as the programme is subsequently cancelled.

**October 12** The Soviet Union launches the *Voskhod 1* spacecraft into Earth orbit. It is the first to carry a multiple crew consisting of Vladimir Komarov, Konstantin Feoktistov and Boris Yegorov, who are able to carry out their mission without wearing spacesuits.

**October 14** The first flight is made by the Sikorsky CH-53A Sea Stallion prototype, a heavy assault helicopter accommodating up to 38 combat troops which has been developed for the U.S. Marine Corps.

**October 16** The People's Republic of China detonates its first atomic bomb, becoming the world's fifth nuclear power.

**October 30** NASA pilot Joe Walker makes the first flight with the Bell Lunar Landing Research Vehicle (LLRV). This has a variable-stability system that allows pilots to gain the reactions and sensations of operating in a lunar environment.

**November 28** The U.S. space probe *Mariner 4* is launched. This passes within 5,400 miles (8,690km) of Mars on July 14, 1965,

transmitting 21 pictures of the Martian surface.

**December 14** In Operation Barrel Roll, U.S.A.F. fighter-bombers attack the Ho Chi Minh Trail communist supply route in Laos.

**December 21** The first General Dynamics F-111A variable-geometry (swing-wing) multi-purpose fighter makes its first flight. This is carried out with the wings locked at 26° sweepback but full wing sweep, from 16° to 72.5°, is first accomplished on January 6, 1965.

**December 22** President Johnson approves development by Lockheed of the CX-HLS military transport for the U.S. Air Force. This becomes the C-5A Galaxy.

**December 22** The first flight is made by the Lockheed SR-71A strategic reconnaissance aircraft.

## 1965

**January 27** The potential of geostationary satellites for emergency communications is demonstrated. For the first time, a comsat is used as a link between a Pan American Boeing 707 in flight and a remote ground control station.

**February 23** The first flight is recorded by the Douglas DC-9 short/medium-range airliner, powered by two rear-mounted turbofan engines.

**March 6** A Sikorsky SH-3A Sea King makes the first non-stop helicopter flight across the

North American continent. Taking off from the carrier U.S.S. *Hornet* at San Diego, California, it lands on the carrier U.S.S. *Franklin D. Roosevelt* at Jacksonville, Florida having completed a distance of 2,116 miles (3,405km). This establishes a new international straight-line distance record for helicopters.

**March 18** The Soviet Union launches *Voskhod 2* with cosmonauts Pavel Belyayev and Alexei Leonov. During their mission, Leonov makes the first 'spacewalk', tethered to the spacecraft while floating in space for about ten minutes.

**March 23** Launched by a Titan II booster, NASA's *Gemini 3* spacecraft is placed in Earth orbit. It carries the first U.S. two-man crew, astronauts Maj. Virgil Grissom and Lt. Cmdr. John Young, on a 4 hr 53 min mission. They make the first-ever piloted orbital manoeuvre.

**April 1** Tasman Empire Airways, which had become wholly nationally owned in 1961, adopts the name Air New Zealand.

**April 6** The Hughes *Early Bird 1* comsat is launched into geostationary Earth orbit. When it becomes operational, on June 28, 1965, it is the world's first commercial satellite for public telephone services.

**May 1** Flying a Lockheed YF-12A from Edwards AFB, California, Col. R.L. Stephens establishes a new world speed record of 2,070.11mph (3,331.507km/h).

*1965: U.S.A.F. F-4Cs taking fuel from a KC-135 over Vietnam*

**May 7** The Canadair CL-84 Dynavert, a twin-engined tilt-wing VSTOL close-support/transport prototype, achieves its first vertical take-offs and landings.

**June** U.S.A.F. McDonnell Douglas F-4C Phantom II tactical fighters are first deployed to Vietnam,

**June 3** The NASA spacecraft *Gemini 4* is launched into Earth orbit carrying astronauts James McDivitt and Edward White. During this mission, Maj. White makes a 21-minute spacewalk (the first by a U.S. astronaut), known in U.S aerospace terminology as an extra-vehicular activity (EVA).

**August 21** NASA's *Gemini 5* spacecraft, with astronauts Gordon Cooper and Charles Conrad on board, carries out the first exploration 'long' space mission, lasting 7 days 22 hrs 56 mins. *Gemini 5* is the first manned spacecraft to use fuel cells to provide electrical power (instead of batteries).

**September 7** The first flight is made by the prototype Bell Model 209 HueyCobra armed helicopter, which has been developed as a private venture for the U.S. Army from the UH-1B Iroquois.

**September 13** The Fédération Aéronautique Internationale homologates its first hot-air balloon record, an altitude of 9,780ft (2,978m) attained by B. Bogan in the U.S.

**September 27** The first of three evaluation LTV A-7A Corsair II single-seat carrier-based attack aircraft makes its first flight. The type is

to prove a valuable addition to U.S. Navy carrier-based aircraft operating off Vietnam.

**November 15** A first circumnavigation of the world, overflying both poles, is made by a Boeing 707 of the Flying Tiger Line.

**November 16** The Soviet interplanetary space probe *Venera 3* is launched, later becoming the first man-made object to impact on the surface of Venus.

**November 26** Using a Diamant launch vehicle, the French *Asterix 1* (*Matra A1*) test satellite is placed in Earth orbit. France thus becomes the first nation, other than the U.S. or U.S.S.R., to develop and orbit a satellite by its own efforts.

**December 4** NASA's *Gemini 7* spacecraft is launched into Earth orbit carrying astronauts Frank Borman and James Lovell. In addition to carrying out a longer-stay mission (13 days 18 hrs 35 mins), *Gemini 7* serves as a rendezvous target for *Gemini 6*.

**December 15** The *Gemini 6* spacecraft is launched with astronauts Walter Schirra and Thomas Stafford on board. Manoeuvring to within 6ft (l.8m) of *Gemini 7* in orbit, this is the first manoeuvred rendezvous in space.

## 1966

**January 31** The Soviet Union launches the unmanned spacecraft *Luna 9*, which becomes the first man-made vehicle to soft-land on the lunar surface and transmit panoramic still pictures of the terrain.

**March 16** NASA's *Gemini 8* spacecraft, carrying astronauts Neil Armstrong and Maj. David Scott, is launched into orbit to carry out docking manoeuvres with an Agena docking target. Although they achieve the first manual docking of two spacecraft in orbit, this has to be aborted almost immediately because of uncontrollable spinning.

**May 18** British airwoman Sheila Scott takes off from London (Heathrow) Airport in a Piper Comanche 260B in an attempt to make a solo round-the-world flight. (q.v. June 20, 1966)

**May 30** NASA launches the *Surveyor 1* lunar probe, which makes the first fully-controlled soft landing on the Moon on June 2. It transmits 11,150 high-resolution pictures of the lunar surface.

**June 3** NASA launches *Gemini 9* with Thomas Stafford and Eugene Cernan on board. Cernan performs a 2 hour spacewalk during the 3-day 21 minute mission.

**June 20** Sheila Scott lands at London (Heathrow) Airport at the conclusion of her solo round-the-world flight. She is not only the first British airwoman to complete such a flight, but she has established a new record for women of 33 days 3 minutes.

**July 18–21** During the *Gemini 10* mission (Michael Collins and John Young), a scientific experiment package is retrieved from an orbiting Agena craft. This gives evidence of a capability to rendezvous with and repair/service satellites in Earth orbit.

**August 2** First flight of the Soviet Sukhoi Su-17 as a variable-geometry derivative of the Su-7.

**August 10** NASA launches the Lunar *Orbiter 1* unmanned spacecraft which duly goes into orbit around the Moon and obtains high resolution pictures of potential Apollo landing sites.

**August 31** The first of six Hawker Siddeley Harrier development aircraft (XV276) makes its first hovering flight at Dunsfold, Surrey.

**September 12** NASA launches *Gemini 11* with Charles Conrad Jr. and Richard Cordon Jr. on board, to carry out docking tests. The mission lasts 2 days 23 hrs 17 mins.

**September 24** In the Soviet Union Marina Solovyeva, flying a Ye-76 (MiG-21), sets a new women's world speed record of 1,270mph (2,044km/h).

**November 4** The Hawker Siddeley Trident G-ARPB, fitted with Smiths' Autoland system, makes three test landings at London Heathrow. These are made in conditions of 150ft (46m) visibility when all other operations have been cancelled.

**November 11** NASA launches *Gemini 12* with James Lovell and Edwin Aldrin on board. Three spacewalks and a docking manoeuvre are performed during the 3 day 22 hr 34 min mission.

**December 23** The first flight of Dassault's Mirage Fl single-seat fighter prototype is successfully made.

## 1967

**January 2** It is announced in the U.S. that Boeing has been awarded a contract for the design of an SST, and that General Electric is to develop the power plant for it.

**January 25** Soviet *Cosmos 139* anti-satellite satellite conducts the first fractional orbit bombardment.

**January 27** In a tragic accident on the ground, U.S. astronauts Roger Chaffee, Virgil Grissom and Edward White are burnt to death in a flash fire during tests of the *Apollo 1* command module. They had been scheduled to make the first Apollo orbital flight on February 21, 1967. These are the first losses of the U.S. space programme.

**March 9** The Royal Aeronautical Society announces that the Kremer prize, which had been offered for a first significant manpowered flight, has been increased to £10,000 and that any nation is eligible to compete.

**April 6** Trans World Airlines becomes the first of the U.S. airlines to complete the transition to an all-jet fleet.

**April 9** The first flight is made by the Boeing Model 737-100 turbojet short-range transport. This basic version provides accommodation for 80-101 passengers.

**April 23** Launch date of *Soyuz 1* in which Soviet cosmonaut Col. Vladimir Komarov is killed when the spacecraft crashes during the final stages of landing. He is the first man known to have died in the course of a space flight.

**May 5** *UK-3* (*Ariel 3*), the first all-British satellite, is launched into Earth orbit from the Western Test Range, California.

**June 5** The Boeing Company delivers its 1,000th jet airliner, a Model 707-120B for American Airlines.

Outbreak of the '6-day war' between Israel and the Arab states. Pre-emptive air strikes by the Israeli Air Force make the Egyptian, Jordan and Syrian air forces virtually ineffective.

**June 10** Following the enforcement of a cease-fire the '6-day war' ends. It is theoretically an Israeli victory, due largely to their skilful deployment of air power.

**June 17** The Chinese People's Republic detonates its first thermonuclear weapon.

**July 2** First flight of the T6-l delta-winged prototype for the Soviet Sukhoi Su-24 Fencer variable-geometry strike bomber. (q.v. January 17, 1970)

**July 7** A Pan American Boeing 707-321B (N4l9PA) records the first fully-automatic approach and landing by a four-engined turbojet aircraft with passengers on board.

**July 21** In Operation Pershing, CS riot-control gas is dropped from helicopters onto suspected VC emplacements at Binh Dinh in Vietnam.

**August 7** Aérolineas Argentinas and Iberia jointly inaugurate the world's longest non-stop air route, between Buenos Aires and Madrid.

**August 17** The U.S. lunar probe *Surveyor 3* is launched to the Moon, achieving a soft-landing in the Ocean of Storms. A mechanical scoop, activated from Earth, allows soil samples to be taken for photographic transmission to Earth and, in addition, more than 6,000 pictures are taken of the landing site.

**September 8** U.S. *Surveyor 5* makes the first chemical analysis of the Moon's surface.

**October 3** Flown by Maj. William Knight, U.S.A.F., the North American X-15A-2 attains its highest speed of Mach 6.72 (4,534mph or 7,297km/h).

**October 20** The first emergency escape using the crew module of a U.S.A.F. F-111 is made over Texas, the two crew members remaining within the module until reaching the ground unhurt.

**November 3** The U.S. Defense Secretary states that the U.S.S.R. has developed a fractional-orbit bombardment system (FOBS) that will allow orbiting satellites to release nuclear weapons against Earth targets.

**November 29** Australia's *Wresat 1* research satellite, the nation's first, is launched into Polar orbit from Woomera using a modified Redstone missile as booster.

**December 11** The Aérospatiale-built Concorde 001 prototype is rolled out at Toulouse, France.

**December 16** The Dornier Do 31E experimental V/STOL transport makes its first transition from vertical to horizontal flight. The first transition from horizontal to vertical is made on December 21.

**December 28** The first production Hawker Siddeley Harrier GR.l (XV738) makes a 20-minute flight at Dunsfold, Surrey.

## 1968

**January 21** A U.S.A.F. Boeing B-52 of Strategic Air Command, carrying four nuclear weapons, crashes on sea ice on its approach to Thule AFB, Greenland.

**January 29** It is announced that the highly successful North American X-15 research programme is to terminate at the end of 1968.

**March 17** U.S.A.F. General Dynamics F-111As are used operationally for the first time in Vietnam. Two are lost by the end of the month.

**March 18** The U.K. Minister of State, Mintech, announces that talks have been held with Canadian, Dutch, German and Italian ministries to consider British participation in the design and development of a European multi-role combat aircraft (MRCA).

**March 28** Col. Yuri Gagarin, Soviet cosmonaut and first man in space, is killed when the MiG-15UTI that he is flying crashes near Kirzhatsk, north of Moscow.

**April 13** Martin-Baker announces that a successful ejection on that date marks the 2,000th life to be saved by the company's escape system.

**April 15** The Soviet Union's unmanned spacecrafts *Cosmos 212* and *213* dock and undock automatically in Earth orbit.

**April 26** The *Daily Mail*, a long-term sponsor of aviation, announces an Atlantic Air Race for 1969 to commemorate the 50th anniversary of the first non-stop transatlantic flight. Prize money is to total £45,000.

**May 1** The U.K. Hot Air Group's inaugural meeting, at the Balloon and Airship Flying Centre, Blackbushe, Hampshire, is opened by an ascent of the hot-air-balloon *Bristol Belle* (G-AVTL).

**May 16** Carbon-fibre-reinforced plastics turbine compressor blades are exhibited for the first time at a meeting of the Royal Society.

BOAC's Super VC 10 G-ASGK, carrying 146 passengers, makes the airline's first fully automatic approach and landing at the completion of a scheduled flight from Chicago and Montreal.

**June 26** Demonstrating the development that is being made in nuclear propulsion, a Phoebus 2A nuclear reactor on test at the Nuclear Rocket Development Station, Jackass Flats, Nevada, generates a thrust of 200,000lb (90,718kg) for a 12-minute test run.

**June 30** The Lockheed C-5A Galaxy makes its successful first flight at Dobbins AFB, Georgia, the largest landplane then flown.

**August 24** France detonates a 2-megaton thermonuclear weapon suspended from a balloon over Mururoa Atoll.

**September 8** The Anglo-French Jaguar E-01 prototype makes a successful first flight from the Centre d'Essais en Vol at Istres, France.

**September 30** The Boeing Model 747 prototype, the world's first wide-body jetliner, is rolled out at Everett, Washington.

The New York City Police, which was the first police force in the world to make regular use of helicopters, celebrates the 20th anniversary of their introduction into daily use.

**October 11–22** The first Apollo test mission is made, lasting for 10 days 20 hrs 9 mins. This is *Apollo 7*, launched by a Saturn 1B and carrying astronauts Walter Schirra, Don Eisele and Walter Cunningham.

**October 20** Soviet satellites *Cosmos 248* and *249* undertake the first co-orbital anti-satellite trials.

**October 26** The Soviet Union launches *Soyuz 3* with Georgi Beregovoi on board. The mission, which lasts 3 days 22 hrs 51 mins, includes a rendezvous with unmanned *Soyuz 2*.

**November 12** NASA announces that its *Apollo 8* mission, scheduled for December 21, 1968, will put the Apollo spacecraft in orbit around the Moon.

**December 21–27** The *Apollo 8* spacecraft is launched by a Saturn V booster carrying astronauts Frank Borman, James Lovell and William Anders. During its 6 day 3 hr 1 min mission, this spacecraft completes the first manned flight around the Moon (on December 24).

**December 31** The prototype of the Soviet Union's Tupolev Tu-144 SST makes its successful first flight, the world's first supersonic transport aircraft to fly.

## 1969

**January 14** and 15 Respective launch dates of the Soviet Union's *Soyuz 4* and 5 spacecraft. They accomplish the first docking of two manned spacecraft in Earth orbit and the first crew exchange carried out by EVA methods.

**February 9** The Boeing Company achieves the successful first flight of the Model 747 wide-body transport. Dubbed 'jumbo-jet' by the world's Press, it is the first aircraft of this class to be flown.

**February 12** Three days after the first flight of the world's largest fixed-wing civil transport, there is an announcement in the Soviet Union to the effect that Russia has developed the world's largest helicopter, the giant Mil Mi-12. This is confirmed early the following month when it is established that on February 12 the helicopter set a number of load-to-height records.

**March 2** The first Sud-Aviation/BAC Concorde 001 SST prototype makes its completely successful first flight at Toulouse, France, piloted by Sud's chief test pilot André Turcat.

**March 3–13** The U.S. astronauts Col. James McDivitt, Col. David Scott and Russel Schweickart are launched into Earth orbit aboard *Apollo 9*. During this mission the first in-space tests of the Lunar Module are carried out, and it is the first occasion that a crew-transfer is made between two space vehicles through an internal connection.

**March 19** A weekly return service between Montreal, Canada and Resolution Bay, Cornwallis Island, is inaugurated by Nordair. This is the world's first scheduled jet service inside the Arctic circle.

**March 28** BAC announces the formation by BAC, Fiat, Fokker and Messerschmitt-Bölkow of a new aerospace company. This is the international Panavia GmbH, created to develop the multi-role combat aircraft (MRCA).

**April 9** The first U.K.-built SST prototype, Concorde 002, makes its successful first flight piloted by Brian Trubshaw.

**April 28** A V/STOL Hawker Siddeley Harrier GR.1 of the R.A.F. records a first transatlantic crossing by the aircraft type, flying from Northolt, Middlesex to Floyd Bennett Field, New York.

**May 11** The *Daily Mail* Transatlantic Air Race ends at midnight. Beginning a week earlier to allow time for a maximum number of individual efforts, it is won by Lt. Cmdr. Brian Davis, Royal Navy, with a time of 5 hrs 11 mins 22 secs to get from the top of the Post

Office Tower, London, to the top of the Empire State Building, New York.

**May 18–26** The *Apollo 10* spacecraft, carrying astronauts Thomas Stafford, Eugene Cernan and John Young, carries out a Moon-landing rehearsal. While the *Apollo 10* travels in lunar orbit, Stafford and Cernan detach the Lunar Module and make two descents to within 8.7 miles (14km) of the Moon's surface.

**June 15** An Ilyushin Il-62 long-range airliner is used by Aeroflot to inaugurate a joint service with Pan American, linking Moscow and New York.

**July 16–24** NASA's *Apollo 11* is launched to the Moon, carrying astronauts Neil A. Armstrong, Edwin E.A. Aldrin and Michael Collins. On July 21, Neil Armstrong becomes the first man on the Moon after he and Aldrin have descended to the Moon's surface in the Lunar Module *Eagle*. The mission is completed by a successful splashdown on July 24, the total time being 8 days 3 hrs 19 mins.

**July 30** NASA's *Mariner 6* interplanetary probe transmits 24 pictures of Mars, taken some 2,130 miles (3,428km) from its surface and relayed over a distance of 0.77 million miles (1.24 million kilometres).

**August 16** Flying a modified Grumman F8F-2 Bearcat over a 3-km course at restricted altitude, U.S. test pilot Darryl Greenamyer sets a new world speed record for piston-engined aircraft of 477.98mph (769.23km/h). This beats by just over 8mph (13km/h) the

record set by a Messerschmitt Me 209VI in 1939.

**August 30** First flight of the Soviet Tupolev Tu-22M Backfire intermediate-range supersonic variable-geometry bomber, piloted by Vasili Borisov. Deliveries to the 185th Heavy Bomber Regiment of Guards at Poltava, Ukraine, begins in 1975.

**October 11, 12** and **13** The respective launch dates of the Soviet Union's *Soyuz 6, 7* and *8* spacecraft, which are the first to make a group flight without docking.

**October 20** Finnair becomes the world's first airline to operate aircraft with an inertial guidance system on scheduled passenger services. This dispenses with the requirement for a navigator as a member of the aircrew.

**October 29** The U.S. Secretary of Defense states that as an economy measure, the U.S.A.F.'s B-58A Hustler, the world's first supersonic strategic bomber, is to be phased out of service.

**November 7–10** Flying the unorthodox BD-2, James Bede sets an unrefuelled closed-circuit world distance record for piston-engined aircraft of 8,973.4 miles (14,441.26km). (q.v. December 5, 1981)

**November 8** West Germany's *Azur* research satellite is launched into orbit by a NASA Scout from the Western Test Range. It is the first West German space satellite.

**November 14–24** The second Moon landing

is made by the *Apollo 12* mission, its all-U.S. Navy crew comprising Charles Conrad, Richard F. Gordon and Alan L. Bean. Major experiments are conducted on the Moon for the first time.

**November 17** The first U.S./Soviet SALT (Strategic Arms Limitation Talks) begin in Helsinki, Finland.

**December 1** The U.S. Federal Air Regulation Pt 36 is introduced, the first legislation to limit aircraft noise at airports.

**December 17** The first Lockheed C-5A Galaxy for service with the U.S.A.F. is officially handed over at Marietta, Georgia.

**December 18** Aircraft competing in the England-Australia Commemorative Air Race begin taking off from London's Gatwick Airport. Marking the 50th anniversary of the first England-Australia flight, and the bi-centenary of the discovery of Australia, it is won by Capt. W.J. Bright and Capt. F.L. Buxton in the Britten-Norman BN-2A Islander G-AXUD.

## 1970

**January 12** The first Boeing Model 747 wide-body transport lands at London Heathrow, a Pan American aircraft on a proving flight from New York.

**January 17** First flight of the Soviet T6-2I variable-geometry prototype to the Sukhoi Su-24 Fencer strike bomber. (q.v. July 2, 1967)

**February 1** Capt. Raymond Munro makes the

first hot-air balloon crossing of the Irish Sea, from Brittis Bay, Co. Wicklow to Ennerdale, Cumberland.

**February 11** Japan becomes the fourth nation in the world to launch a domestic satellite using a nationally-built launch rocket, the *Ohsumi*, boosted by a Lambda 4S carrier rocket from the Kagoshima Space Centre.

**March 26** The British 'Gee Chain', which provided valuable navigational services during the Second World War, is finally closed down.

**April 1** Air Jamaica begins scheduled operations. This airline was formed during 1968 to succeed an earlier company of the same name.

**April 11–17** NASA's *Apollo 13* mission focuses the world's attention when an oxygen tank explodes during the outward flight. The resulting emergency is resolved by brilliant evaluation and improvisation, returning astronauts James Lovell, John Swigert and Fred Haise safely to Earth.

**April 24** The Chinese People's Republic launches its first satellite into Earth orbit using an indigenous booster rocket. A basic research satellite, it is identified as *Chicom 1* by NORAD.

**May 25** The U.S. Government announces that Multiple Individual Re-entry Vehicles (MIRVs), or multiple warheads, have been developed and are available for deployment on the nation's ICBMs.

**June 1** The first production Lockheed C-5A Galaxy to enter operational service with the U.S.A.F. is delivered to Military Airlift Command (MAC) at Scott AFB, Charleston, Virginia.

The Soviet Union's *Soyuz 9* spacecraft is launched into Earth orbit carrying cosmonauts Andrian Nikolayev and Vitali Sevastyanov. They land successfully after completing what is then the longest space mission, totalling 17 days 16 hrs 59 mins.

**July 2** The first flight is made by the Saab Sk 37 Viggen two-seat trainer prototype from the company's airfield at Linköping.

**August 17** The Soviet Union launches the inter-planetary probe *Venera 7*. The instrument capsule from this probe makes the first confirmed landing on Venus in January 1971, transmitting a weak data signal for 23 minutes.

**August 22** Two Sikorsky HH-53C helicopters complete a non-stop transpacific flight of some 9,000 miles (14,484km), refuelled en route by Hercules tankers.

**August 29** The first flight of the McDonnell Douglas DC-10 widebody jet (N10DC) is made at Long Beach, California.

**September 12** The Soviet Union's *Luna 16* moon probe is launched. This remarkable vehicle makes an unmanned automatic soft-landing on the lunar surface and scoops up a sample of surface soil which it stores within

the vehicle before taking off and returning to Earth on September 24.

Three commercial transports which had been hijacked by Arab guerrillas are destroyed by dynamite on the desert airstrip known as Dawsons's Field near Amman, Jordan. They comprise a Boeing 707 of Trans World Airlines, a McDonnell Douglas DC-8 of Swissair, and a BAC VC 10 of BOAC.

**October 24** The last flight of the North American X-15 research programme is made by NASA pilot William H. Dana.

**November 4** The Concorde 001 prototype attains its design cruising speed of Mach 2 for the first time. The U.K.-built 002 achieves this milestone nine days later.

**November 6** The U.S.A.F. launches a military reconnaissance satellite into a geostationary orbit above the Indian Ocean. It is reported to have sensors able to detect infra-red emissions from rocket plumes.

**November 10** The Soviet Union launches the *Luna 17* moon probe. This soft-lands on the lunar surface to deploy a Lunokhod rover vehicle on November 17 which travels more than 6 miles (9.5km) during the ensuing nine months, conducting experiments and transmitting the results to Earth.

**November 16** The first Lockheed L-1011 TriStar wide-body jet airliner (N1011) makes its first flight.

**December 18** Aérospatiale, Deutsche-Airbus

and Fokker-VFW establish Airbus Industrie to be responsible for the A300B programme.

**December 21** The first flight is recorded by the prototype of the Grumman F-14 Tomcat carrier-based variable-geometry multi-role fighter for the U.S. Navy.

## 1971

**January 22** The crew of a US Navy Lockheed P-3C Orion, led by Cmdr. Donald H. Lilienthal, establish a new world long-distance record for aircraft with turboprop engines at just over 7,010 miles (11,281km). On January 27 the same aircraft sets up a speed in a straight line record at 500.89mph (806.10km/h) also in Class C, Group II.

**January 31–February 9** NASA's *Apollo 14* is launched to make the third U.S. Moon landing, a mission which is successfully completed by astronauts Alan Shepard, Stuart Rossa and Edgar Mitchell. It is the first landing on the Moon's highlands.

**March 24** By a single vote, the U.S. Senate decides not to provide funding for development of an American SST, bringing cancellation of the Boeing 2707-300 project.

**April 12** The U.S.A.F. announces the use of a so-called 'daisy cutter' bomb in Vietnam. This is a conventional high-explosive bomb designed to clear jungle areas.

**April 14** Trans-Mediterranean Airways, which was formed during 1953 to provide non-scheduled freight services from Beirut, inaugurates the first round-the-world cargo service.

**April 15** The U.S. Marine Corps' first Harrier squadron, VMA-513, becomes operational at Beaufort Air Station, South Carolina.

**April 19** The Soviet Union launches the *Salyut 1* into Earth orbit, the first space station.

**April 22–24** The Soviet Union's *Soyuz 10* spacecraft is launched into orbit, docking with *Salyut 1*, but no crew board the space station.

**May 3** H.M.S. *Ark Royal* embarks the R.A.F.'s No. 1 Squadron with its Harriers for sea trials off the Scottish coast.

**May 13** Concorde 001 makes its first fully automatic approach and landing at Toulouse, France.

**May 20** The U.S. Supersonic Transport Program is officially terminated by Congress.

**May 28** The Soviet Union launches the interplanetary space probe *Mars 3*, which subsequently puts the first data capsule on the Martian surface.

**May 30** Launch date of NASA's *Mariner 9* interplanetary probe, which becomes the first artificial satellite of Mars. It transmits more than 7,000 pictures, many of which provide remarkable detail of the Martian surface.

**June 6** The Soviet Union puts the *Soyuz 11* spacecraft in orbit with cosmonauts Georgi Dobrovolski, Vladislav Volkov and Viktor Parsayev. They dock with *Salyut 1* and make a stay of more than three weeks; but all three during the landing phase of their mission.

**June 11–August 4** The first flight by a lightplane from equator to equator via the North Pole is made by U.K. airwoman Sheila Scott flying a Piper Aztec D.

**July 26–August 7** The U.S. achieves its fourth Moon landing with the *Apollo 15* mission. It is distinguished by the first use of the Lunar Roving Vehicle.

**August 5** The U.K. Civil Aviation Act 1971 bill is approved, establishing the Civil Aviation Authority (CAA) and British Airways Board.

**October 4** The Soviet Union announces that its Lunokhod 1 lunar roving vehicle has ended its useful life.

**October 10** Derived from Misrair, then assuming the name United Arab Airlines under President Nasser, Egypt's national airline becomes Egyptair on the above date.

**October 11** The Soviet Union's orbiting space laboratory *Salyut 1* is destroyed as it re-enters the Earth's atmosphere after its mission had been terminated.

**November 2** The first U.S. Defense Satellite Communications System Phase II satellites, or DSCS IIs, enter geosynchronous orbits.

**November 23** Carried by an Aero Spacelines Super Guppy operated by Aeromaritime, the first set of Airbus A300B wings is delivered from Hawker Siddeley's Chester Factory to Toulouse, France.

**December 6** The Spanish Government states that the nation's aircraft industry is to participate in the Airbus A300 programme.

**December 13** A new Soviet deep space tracking and research ship, the *Kosmonaut Yuri Gagarin*, sails from Odessa on its maiden voyage.

## 1972

**January 4** Bangladesh Biman is formed as the national airline of the state of Bangladesh, formerly known as East Pakistan.

**March 8** The Goodyear non-rigid airship *Europa*, which has been assembled in the U.K., makes its first flight from Cardington, Bedfordshire.

**March 27** The Soviet Union's interplanetary probe *Venera 8* is launched towards Venus. An instrument capsule is landed successfully on the surface of the planet on July 22, 1972, transmitting data for a period of 50 minutes.

**April 1** The British Airways Board combines the activities of BEA and BOAC under the title of British Airways.

The U.K. Civil Aviation Authority (CAA), the nation's first independent body for regulating civil aviation and providing air traffic control and navigation service, begins its functions.

**April 16–27** NASA's *Apollo 16* mission, and the fifth Moon landing, is successfully carried out. Crewed by Lt. Col. Charles Duke, Lt. Cmdr. Thomas Mattingly and Capt. John

Young, the Moon is used for astronomical purposes for the first time.

**April 25** A Schleicher ASW 12 flown by Hans Gross (Germany) establishes a new world distance record for single-seat sailplanes of 907.7 miles (1,460.8km).

**April 29** A specially-equipped McDonnell Douglas F-4 Phantom II becomes the first aircraft to be flown in the U.S. with a fly-by-wire control system.

**May 10** India and the U.S.S.R. sign a development agreement under which the Soviet Union will launch India's first nationally-designed and built satellite.

The prototype of the Fairchild A-10A, one of the two contenders for the U.S.A.F.'s AX close-support requirement, makes its first flight.

**May 26** At a summit meeting in Moscow, President Nixon and Leonid Brezhnev sign the first SALT agreement.

Cessna Aircraft Corporation announces completion of the company's 100,000th aircraft, the first company in the world to achieve such a production figure.

**June 21** Jean Boulet flies an Aérospatiale Lama helicopter to a world record height of 40,820ft (12,442m).

**July 23** The first U.S. Earth Resources Technology Satellite, or ERTS A, is launched. It is later renamed *Landsat 1*.

**July 26** NASA announces that Rockwell International Corporation has been selected to build the Space Shuttle Orbiter, awarding the company an initial $450 million to cover the first two years of development.

**July 27** The first flight is made by the first pre-production McDonnell Douglas F-15A Eagle fighter (71-0280) from Edwards AFB, California.

**August 28** H.R.H. Prince William of Gloucester and his passenger are killed in a flying accident at the beginning of a Goodyear Trophy Race in the U.K.

**September 22** Receipt by the Boeing Company of an order for 14 Model 727s from Delta Air Lines brings total sales for this aircraft to 1,000. It is the first jetliner to attain such a sales figure.

**September 29** The People's Republic of China and Japan sign a peace treaty, officially ending a state of war that had started 35 years earlier.

**October 1** Malaysian Airline System (Sistem Penerbangan Malaysia Berhad), which had been established as the government-owned national airline during April 1971, begins scheduled operations.

**October 20** The first flight is made at Toulouse-Blagnac of the first Airbus A300B1 (F-WUAB), piloted by Max Fischl.

**December 7–19** NASA's successful *Apollo 17* mission is the last of the Moon landings. It, like those that preceded it, makes use of a Lunar Roving Vehicle, and a 75-hour stay on the lunar surface is the longest of the Apollo missions.

**December 23** The Hertfordshire Pedal Aeronauts (HPA) Toucan man-powered aircraft makes a first flight of 2,100ft (640m) at Radlett. It is the first to have a two-man crew/power unit.

## 1973

**January 7** The world's first hot-air airship (G-BAMK), developed in the U.K. by Cameron Balloons of Bristol, makes its successful first flight.

**January 15** President Nixon orders a halt to air strikes and all other offensive military action against North Vietnam.

**January 24** An agreement to end the war in Vietnam is initialled in Paris. It calls for a cease-fire at 23.59 hrs GMT on January 27.

**February 23** The Aérospatiale/BAC Concorde 002 flies non-stop from Toulouse to Iceland and return. This represents a greater distance than the guaranteed entry-into-service range.

**April 13** A deep-space tracking antenna with a diameter of 210ft (64m) is commissioned at Tidbinbilla, Australia.

**May 14** The last Saturn V booster is used to launch NASA's *Skylab 1* Orbital Workshop into Earth orbit. Air pressure causes damage to a micrometeoroid shield immediately after lift-off.

**May 20** Because of a 50 mile (80m) fishing limit dispute with the U.K., the government of Iceland bans R.A.F. use of the NATO base at Keflavik.

**May 22** Aero Perú (Empresa de Transporte Aéreo del Perú) is formed as the Government-owned national airline.

**May 25** NASA's *Skylab 2* is launched into orbit to rendezvous with *Skylab 1*. Astronauts Charles Conrad, Joseph Kerwin and Paul Weitz are able to effect repairs to *Skylab 1* during several EVAs. Total mission time is 28 days 49 mins.

**May 30** The first production SEPECAT Jaguar GR.Mk 1 for R.A.F. Strike Command is delivered to R.A.F. Lossiemouth, Morayshire.

**June 3** The 30th Paris Air Show closes on a tragic note with the loss during a flying display of the second pre-production Tupolev Tu-144 SST, killing all six crew members

**June 26** A Pan American Boeing 747 carrying 220 passengers makes a completely uneventful fully-automatic landing at London Heathrow. This is made because storm damage to the flight deck windscreen had completely cut off all forward view.

**July 25** A. Fedotov flying the Mikoyan Ye-266 in the Soviet Union, establishes a new world altitude record of 118,898ft (36,240m).

**August 14** The U.S.A.F. ends its bombing attacks on Cambodia terminating more than

nine years of U.S. air combat in South-East Asia.

**September 24** A Memorandum of Understanding is concluded between NASA and ESRO (European Space Research Organization). As a result, ESRO is given responsibility for design and construction of the Spacelab to be used in conjunction with NASA's Space Shuttle.

**September 27–29** The Soviet Union's *Soyuz 12* mission carries cosmonauts Vasily Lazarev and Oleg Makarov into Earth orbit This is the first Soyuz mission since the tragic loss of the *Soyuz 11* crew (q.v. June 6, 1971), and is the first flight of an improved Soyuz vehicle intended to serve as an Earth space ferry to the Salyut space workshops

**October 6** A massive air strike by the Egyptian Air Force against Israeli artillery and command positions marks the beginning of the October or Yom Kippur war.

**October 6–8** Israeli air counter-attack against Egypt's air and ground forces is frustrated by large-scale use of Soviet-made and effective SAMs.

**October 21** At Linz, Austria, the Militky MB-E1 (Militky Brditschka Electric 1) becomes the first electrically-powered manned aircraft to fly. A specially modified Brditschka HB-3 sailplane, it has a Bosch electric motor driven by rechargeable batteries.

**October 22** The first cease-fire is negotiated in the Yom Kippur war but fighting flares up again on the following day.

**October 24** The second cease-fire of the Yom Kippur war is negotiated but only slowly comes into effect.

**October 25** Tom Sage of the U.K. Cameron Balloon company establishes a hot-air balloon duration record of 5 hrs 45 mins.

**November 16–February 8** NASA's *Skylab 4* is launched to rendezvous with *Skylab 1*, carrying astronauts Gerald Carr, Edward Gibson and William Pogue. This is the final Skylab mission and when the astronauts land they have completed a record 84 days 1 hr 15 mins in space.

**December 3** The unmanned U.S. *Pioneer 10* is the first spacecraft to near Jupiter.

## 1974

**January 1** Sikorsky S-61N helicopters operated by Bristow Helicopters mount a rescue operation, evacuating the 50-man crew of North Sea drilling platform *Transocean 3* shortly before it overturns.

**January 4** Teledyne Ryan rolls out two YQM-98A RPV long-endurance reconnaissance prototypes. Built for the U.S.A.F.'s Compass Cope programme, they are designed to take off from and land on normal runways.

**February 2** The first flight is made by the first General Dynamics YF-16 lightweight fighter prototype (72-01567) at Edwards AFB, California. The same aircraft had made a brief unofficial first flight on January 20, when it lifted off during high-speed taxi tests.

**February 18** U.S. Army reservist Col. Thomas Gatch lifts off from Pennsylvania in an attempt to make a North Atlantic balloon crossing. (q.v. February 21, 1974)

**February 21** The distinctive balloon of Col. Gatch, comprising ten small balloons supporting a sealed and pressurized gondola, is reported by a merchant ship some 1,000 miles (1,600km) west of the Canary Islands, but is never seen again.

**March 3** To date the world's worst air disaster involving a single aircraft occurs soon after a THY Turkish Airlines McDonnell Douglas DC-l0 takes off from Orly Airport. All 346 people on board are killed, and subsequent investigation shows that the failure of a cargo door had caused decompression, resulting in loss of control.

**March 8** Charles de Gaulle Airport at Roissy-en-France, 15.5 miles (25km) from the centre of Paris and Europe's newest international airport, is officially opened by the French Prime Minister.

**April 10** A Martin Marietta Titan III-D launches an additional *Big Bird* reconnaissance satellite into Earth orbit from Vandenberg AFB, California.

**April 13** At Kennedy Space Center a Thor-Delta launcher is used to put the first of two *Westar* domestic comsats into geostationary orbit.

**April 23** Bell Helicopters announce the delivery of the company's 20,000th helicopter. Of this total, some 80 per cent have been delivered since the beginning of 1964.

**May 23** Europe's first wide-body jetliner, an Airbus A300B2 of Air France, makes its inaugural revenue flight on the airline's Paris-London route.

**June 9** The first of Northrop's two YF-17 lightweight fighter prototypes (72-01569) makes its first flight. They are built for the U.S.A.F. LWF programme and are to be flown in competition against the General Dynamics YF-16s. (q.v. February 2, 1974)

**August 14** The Panavia 200 MRCA prototype (D-9591) makes its first flight at Manching, West Germany, piloted by BAC's Paul Millet.

**August 19** The Cameron balloon *Gerard A. Heineken* is flown for the first time at Bristol, Somerset. Then the world's largest hot-air balloon with a volume of 500,000cu ft (14,158m³), its two-tier basket could accommodate a total of 12 passengers.

**August 26** The death is announced of Charles Lindbergh, one of the best known pilots in aviation history. His solo west-east crossing of the North Atlantic, 47 years earlier, had captured the imagination and interest of the world.

**August 30** Launch of the first Dutch satellite *ANS*.

**August 31** The Apollo command module for the 1975 U.S/U.S.S.R. space flight is delivered to Kennedy Space Center by a Lockheed C-5A Galaxy.

**October 17** The first flight is made at Stratford, Connecticut of the first of three Sikorsky YUH-60A prototypes (21650). This is a utility transport helicopter that has been designed to meet the U.S. Army's UTTAS (Utility Tactical Transport Aircraft System) requirement, to be flown in evaluation against Boeing Vertol YUH-61A contenders.

**November 15** Launch of the first Spanish satellite *INTASAT*.

**December 2–8** The Soviet Union places *Soyuz 16* into Earth orbit for a final rehearsal of the ASTP (Apollo-Soyuz Test Project) planned for 1975.

**December 18** *Symphonie A*, Europe's first communications satellite, is launched into geostationary orbit by a Delta vehicle from Cape Kennedy.

**December 23** The first flight is made by the first Rockwell International B-l prototype (71-40158) at Palmdale, California.

## 1975

**January 14** It is announced in Washington that the U.S.A.F. has selected the General Dynamics YF-16 as the winner of its LWF (lightweight fighter) programme.

**February 1** During a 16-day period that ended on this date, all eight world time-to-height records are captured by the McDonnell Douglas F-15 Eagle, named 'Streak Eagle'. The final record set a time of 3 mins 27.8 secs from standstill on a runway to a height of 98,425ft (30,000m).

**February 22** First flight of the Soviet Su-25 Frogfoot subsonic close-air support aircraft, piloted by Vladimir Ilyushin. (q.v. February 4, 1981)

**May 30** The European Space Agency (ESA) is founded.

**June 3** The first flight is made by the first prototype Mitsubishi FS-T2-KAI, a single-seat supersonic close-support fighter developed from the T-2 jet trainer. Required to replace the JASDF's F-86F Sabres, it becomes designated F-1 when it enters service.

**June 8** The Soviet Union's *Venera 9* interplanetary 250 probe is launched towards Venus. This is very successful and later becomes the first artificial satellite of Venus. The data capsule which it ejects makes a successful landing on the planet's surface, its 53 minutes of transmission including TV pictures.

**June 22** A new world speed record for women is established in the Soviet Union by Svetlana Savitskaya, flying a Mikoyan Ye-133 at a speed of 1,667.42mph (2,683.44km/h).

**July 15–24** Combined U.S/U.S.S.R. space mission, during which the Soviet Union's *Soyuz 19* spacecraft and the U.S. Apollo ASTP (Apollo-Soyuz Test Project) dock together in Earth orbit for crew exchanges and combined experiments.

**August 20** NASA's interplanetary probe *Viking 1* is launched. It subsequently places a landing module on Mars which transmits the first pictures of the planet's surface.

**September 1** The fourth production Aérospatiale BAC Concorde becomes the first aircraft to make two return transatlantic flights (London-Gander-London) or four transatlantic crossings in a single day.

**September 16** The first flight of the Soviet Mikoyan MiG-31 Foxhound long-range interceptor.

**September 30** A test flight is made by the first of two Hughes Model 77 (YAH-64) prototypes (22248). The YAH-64 is designed to meet the U.S. Army's Armed Attack Helicopter (AAH) requirement, and for fly-off evaluation against the Bell YAH-63.

**November 17** The Soviet Union launches the unmanned *Soyuz 20* to conduct experiments in the resupply of Salyut space stations.

**December 6** Carrying airmail between Moscow and Alma Ata, the Soviet Union's Tupolev Tu-144 SST makes the first airmail flight by a supersonic airliner.

**1976**
**January 21** The world's first passenger services by a supersonic airliner are made, with Concorde SSTs of British Airways and Air France taking off simultaneously for Bahrain and Rio de Janeiro.

**May 24** Air France and British Airways begin transatlantic Concorde passenger services from Paris and London, respectively, to Washington's Dulles International Airport.

**June 22** The Soviet Union launches into Earth orbit the unmanned *Salyut 5* space station.

**July 1** Clive Canning arrives in the U.K. after a solo flight from Australia in a homebuilt Thorp T-18 Tiger. This is the first Australia-England flight made in an aircraft of amateur construction

**July 3** It is reported that in an Israeli commando assault on Entebbe airport on this date, the Israelis destroyed four MiG-17s and seven MiG-21s.

**July 6** The Soviet Union launches *Soyuz 21* to dock with *Salyut 5* in orbit. Cosmonauts Boris Volynov and Vitali Zholobov carry out a 49 day 5 hr 24 min space mission.

**July 28** Flying a Lockheed SR-71A strategic reconnaissance aircraft, Capt. E.W Joersz and Maj. G.T. Morgan Jr., U.S.A.F., establish a new world speed record of 2,193.17mph (3,529.56km/h).

**December 22** The prototype of the Soviet Union's Ilyushin Il-86 wide-body-jetliner (CCCP-86000) makes its first flight from the old Moscow Central Airport of Khodinka, piloted by Hero of the Soviet Union A. Kuznetsov.

**December 23** The Sikorsky S-70 (UH-60A) is declared winner of the U.S. Army's UTTAS competition for a primary combat assault helicopter.

**1977**
**January 21** Bell makes the first tie-down test of the Model 301 (XV-15) tilt-rotor research aircraft.

**February 17** Beech Aircraft Corporation completes production flight testing of its 10,000th Model 35 Bonanza.

**February 18** The first flight of the Boeing 747 Space Shuttle carrier, with the Space Shuttle *Enterprise* mounted above the fuselage, is successfully made at NASA's Dryden Flight Research Center. In this test, and the five that are planned to follow, the *Enterprise* is unmanned.

**March 24** The first operational Boeing E-3A AWACS aircraft is delivered to the U.S.A.F.'s 552nd Airborne Warning and Control Wing at Tinker AFB, Oklahoma.

**March 27** The world's greatest air tragedy to date (583 fatalities) occurs when Pan Am and KLM Boeing 747s collide on the runway at Santa Cruz Airport, Tenerife.

**May 3** The first of two Bell XV-l5 tilt-rotor research aircraft (702) makes its first hovering flight.

**May 19** The Soviet Union's *Cosmos 909* satellite is launched to serve as the target for a space interceptor satellite.

**May 20** First flight of the Soviet Sukhoi Su-27 Flanker long-range fighter, piloted by Vladimir Ilyushin. (q.v. January 7, 1987)

**June 13** President Carter gives his approval to the U.S. CAB's recommendation that Laker Airways should be allowed to operate a Skytrain service between London and New York for a one-year trial period.

**June 17** The Soviet Union's *Cosmos 918* satellite is launched and intercepts the *Cosmos 909* target. (q.v. May 19)

**June 30** President Carter announces cancellation of the Rockwell International B-1 supersonic strategic bomber programme: the U.S. is thus expected to rely on cruise missiles for strategic attack.

**August 12** The U.S. Space Shuttle *Enterprise* makes its first free gliding flight following launch from the Boeing 747 Shuttle Carrier aircraft at a height of 22,800ft (6,950m).

**August 20** NASA launches the unmanned spacecraft *Voyager 2*, which flies past Jupiter in July 1979 then continues via Saturn. Having passed Saturn, it is scheduled to reach Uranus in 1986.

**August 23** *Gossamer Condor*, designed under the leadership of Dr. Paul MacCready in the U.S., and piloted by racing cyclist Bryan Allen, wins the £50,000 Kremer prize for the first 1-mile (1.6km) figure-of-eight flight by a man-powered aircraft.

**August 31** In the Soviet Union, Alexander Fedotov, flying the Mikoyan Ye-266M, establishes a new world altitude record for air-breathing aircraft of 123,524ft (37,650m).

**September 26** Six years after making initial proposals, Laker Airways inaugurates its London-New York Skytrain service. Almost immediately, six scheduled airlines introduce low-cost transatlantic fares.

**October 6** First flight of the Soviet 9-01 prototype to the Mikoyan MiG-29 Fulcrum fighter, piloted by Alexander Fedotov.

**November 22** After seemingly endless delays, Air France and British Airways inaugurate Concorde services to New York.

**November 23** Launch of the first European weather satellite *Meteosat*.

**December 1** First flight of the first of two Lockheed XST Have Blue stealth aircraft technology demonstrators at Groom Lake, Nevada. These assisted in the development of the F-117A stealth fighter. They are lost in 1978 and 1979.

**December 4** British Airways, in conjunction with Singapore Airlines, begins Concorde services from Bahrain to Singapore.

**December 14** First flight of the Soviet Mil Mi-26 Halo very heavy helicopter, the world's largest production helicopter, featuring an 8-blade main rotor.

## 1978

Introduction of the McDonnell Douglas Advanced Concept Ejection Seat II, also known as ACES II. (Subsequently used in the F-15, F-16, B-lB, B-2, A-10 and F-117A, it had saved over 200 lives by 1995, including nine ejections during the Gulf War.)

**January 1** The assets and business of British Aircraft Corporation, Hawker Siddeley Aviation, Hawker Siddeley Dynamics and Scottish Aviation are transferred to British Aerospace. The latter corporation had been established by U.K. Government Act on April 29, 1977 and became technically the owner of the companies named above, although they had continued to trade under their original titles until this date.

**January 10** The Soviet Union's *Soyuz 27* is launched to dock with *Salyut 6*/*Soyuz 26* in Earth orbit, its cosmonauts carrying mail and supplies to record the first mail delivery in space.

**January 20** The Soviet Union's unmanned space ferry *Progress 1* is launched, carrying supplies to and docking automatically with *Salyut 6*.

**February 22** The first Global Positioning System satellite is launched into Earth orbit.

**March 2** Vladimir Remek is carried as a crew member aboard *Soyuz 28*, thus becoming the first Czechoslovakian to take part in a space mission.

**March 10** The first flight is made at Istres of the first Dassault Mirage 2000 prototype, a single-seat interceptor and air superiority fighter that was selected in 1975 as the primary combat aircraft for service with the French Air Force from the mid-1980s.

**April 19** ICAO delegates meeting in Montreal vote in favour of the U.S.-developed Time Reference Scanning Beam microwave landing system, selecting it for introduction as the standard international landing system by 1995.

**May 9** David Cook, flying a Revell VJ-23-powered hang-glider, records the first crossing of the English Channel by such an aircraft.

**May 21** Some four years later than planned, largely because of action by protesters, Tokyo's new Narita International Airport becomes operational.

**June 6** It is reported that Aeroflot's Tu-144 services between Moscow and Alma Ata have been suspended because of excessive fuel consumption.

**June 27** The Soviet Union launches *Soyuz 30* to dock with *Salyut 6*. In an operation similar to that of the *Soyuz 28* mission, Miroslaw Giermaszewski becomes the first Pole to take part in a space mission.

**August 12–17** A balloon duration record of 137 hrs 5 mins 50 secs, a record distance of 3,107.62 miles (5,001.22km), and the first transatlantic crossing by a gas balloon, is recorded by *Double Eagle II* crewed by Ben L. Abruzzo, Maxie L. Anderson and Larry M. Newman.

**August 20** The first flight is made by the British Aerospace Sea Harrier FRS.Mk 1 (XZ45O) from the company's airfield at Dunsfold, Surrey.

**August 26** The Soviet Union launches *Soyuz 31*, crewed by Valery Bykovsky and the East German Sigmund Jahn. They return to earth in *Soyuz 29*, having previously docked with the *Salyut 6* space station.

**October 2** Aeroflot begins route-proving trials with the Ilyushin Il-86 on its Moscow-Mineralnye Vody route.

**November 9** The McDonnell Douglas YAV-8B Advanced Harrier prototype (158394) makes its first flight, a development of the British Aerospace Harrier to give increased weapons payload/combat radius.

**November 18** The first flight is made by the McDonnell Douglas F/A-18 Hornet prototype (160775), a single-seat carrier-based fighter developed jointly by McDonnell Douglas and Northrop from the latter company's YF-17 prototype (that had taken part in the U.S.A.F.'s LWF programme).

**December 19** Britons David Williams and Fred To fly *Solar One* the world's first solar powered aircraft.

**December 19** First flight of the Soviet Beriev A-50 Mainstay airborne early warning and control aircraft based on an Ilyushin Il-76MD airframe. Pilot is Vladimir Demyanovsky.

## 1979

**January 1** Boeing E-3A Sentry AWACS aircraft of the U.S.A.F.'s 552nd Airborne Warning and Control Wing begin to assume a role in U.S. air defence.

**January 6** The first General Dynamics F-16A single-seat lightweight air combat fighter is officially handed over to the U.S.A.F.'s 388th Tactical Fighter Wing at Hill AFB, Utah.

**February 3** An unusual first flight is recorded at Cardington, Bedfordshire, by the Aerospace Developments AD 500 non-rigid airship (C-BECE). This has an overall length of 164ft (50m).

**February 27** Production of the McDonnell Douglas A-4 Skyhawk ends after 26 years with the delivery of the 2,960th and last (an A4-M) to the U.S.M.C.'s Marine Attack Squadron VMA-331.

**April 15** The first flight is made by the Dassault Mirage 50 prototype, a multi-mission fighter retaining the basic airframe of the Mirage III/5 series but incorporating the higher rated SNECMA Atar 9K-50 turbojet.

**April 20** The 16th and last production Concorde makes its first flight.

**June 5** The Chrysalis man-powered biplane built at the Massachusetts Institute of Technology makes its first flight. When dismantled in September 1979, 345 flights have been made by 44 different pilots.

**June 12** The *Gossamer Albatross*, designed and built under the leadership of Dr. Paul MacCready, wins the £100,000 Kremer prize for a first crossing of the English Channel by a man-powered aircraft.

**July 11** The U.S. *Skylab* space station re-enters Earth's atmosphere and breaks up,

pieces falling on Australia and in the Indian Ocean.

**September 19** The Royal Navy's first Sea Harrier squadron, No. 700A, is commissioned at R.N.A.S. Yeovilton, Somerset. No. 700A later becomes the shore-based No. 899 H.Q. Squadron. Front line Sea Harrier units become Nos. 800, 801 and 802 Squadrons.

**October 15** The 4450th Tactical Group, U.S.A.F., is formed to receive F-117A stealth fighters. (q.v. August 23, 1982)

**1980**

**March 28** Gates Learjet announces that it has delivered its 1,000th Learjet.

**April 18** The name Air Zimbabwe is adopted from the former temporary Air Zimbabwe Rhodesia. It had been formed originally as Air Rhodesia in September 1967.

**April 24** An attempt to rescue American hostages held in Iran is initiated as Operation Evening Light. Sikorsky RH-53 Sea Stallion helicopters from U.S.S. *Nimitz* are among aircraft used, but the rescue fails as accidents at a desert landing area bring an end to the mission.

**June 5** The Soviet Union's first manned *Soyuz T* capsule, incorporating an automatic docking system, is launched into Earth orbit.

**July 18** The Indian Space Research Organization (ISRO) successfully launches into Earth orbit the *Rohini RS-1* test satellite, designed primarily to evaluate the efficiency of the SLV-3 launch vehicle.

**August 7** The MacCready *Gossamer Penguin* makes its first straight (no turns) solar-powered flight of about 2 miles (3km), piloted by Janice Brown.

**September 19** Fighting breaks out between the nations of Iran and Iraq, with extensive use of air power being made.

**September 22** The Royal Navy's last conventional aircraft carrier, H.M.S. *Ark Royal*, sails from Plymouth en route to the scrapyard.

**October 2** A Westland Sea King helicopter is used in the rescue of 22 crew and passengers from the Swedish freighter *Finneagle* on fire at sea. The operation is carried out in 80mph (129km/h) winds with very high sea conditions, and with a crew of four and a doctor, a total of 27 persons is carried by the Sea King on its return flight to Kirkwall, Orkney Islands.

**October 11** Soviet cosmonauts Valeri Ryumin and Leonid Popov land successfully in *Soyuz 37* after spending 185 days in space on board the *Salyut 6* orbiting laboratory. During that period they have received visits and supplies from three manned spacecraft, and supplies and equipment from three unmanned Progress cargo spacecraft.

**October 11–15** The Goodyear airship *Europa* is used for pollution monitoring in the Golf of Genoa as part of a Mediterranean Pollution Monitoring Research Programme.

**November 6** First battery-powered flight test

is made at Shafter, California, of the *Solar Challenger* designed under the leadership of Dr. Paul MacCready.

**November 9** The last revenue flight of a de Havilland Comet 4C (G-BDIW) is made from London Gatwick, a special flight for air enthusiasts and recalling the first flight more than 30 years earlier.

**November 11** NASA's *Voyager 1* spacecraft flies past Saturn's largest moon, Titan, at a distance of about 2,796 miles (4,500km). It subsequently passes below Saturn's rings before travelling on out of the solar system.

**November 18–21** British airwoman Judith Chisholm, flying a Cessna Turbo Centurion, establishes a new woman's solo flight record between England and Australia of 3 days and 13 hrs.

**November 20** The MacCready *Solar Challenger* makes its first short-duration test flight solely on solar power.

**December 3** Judith Chisholm (q.v. November 18) lands at London Heathrow after completing her solo round-the-world flight in 15 days 22 mins 30 secs and thus virtually halving the previous time set by Sheila Scott.

**December 5** Piloted by Janice Brown, Dr. Paul MacCready's *Solar Challenger* records a flight under solar power only of 1 hr 32 mins.

**December 6** The MacCready *Solar Challenger* is flown for a distance of 18 miles (29km) between Tucson and Phoenix, Arizona, the flight being terminated by a heavy rainstorm.

**1981**

**January 1** In accordance with U.K. Government plans to return British Aerospace to private ownership, British Aerospace Ltd. is vested with all assets, liabilities and obligations of the nationalized corporation. It is then re-registered as British Aerospace Public Limited Company.

**January 15** Operating in a 80mph (129km/h) blizzard, Bell 212s of Bristow Helicopters, a Sikorsky S-61N of British Airways Helicopters and Westland Sea Kings of the Royal Norwegian Air Force combine efforts to rescue nine men from a sinking vessel some 115 miles (185km) north-east of the Shetlands.

**January 18** A Bell Model 222 light commercial helicopter delivered to Omniflight Helicopters is the company's 25,000th production helicopter.

**January 26** Pan American flies its last service with the Boeing Model 707-320C: Model 707s had been operated by the airline for just over 22 years.

The Soviet Union's *Progress 12* unmanned cargo spacecraft docks with and automatically refuels *Salyut 6* in Earth orbit. Two days later, *Progress 12* is used to raise the space station's orbit.

**January 30** British Airways makes a record 96 automatic landings at London Heathrow on a day when fog has virtually closed the airport to other airlines, with an RVR of 410-492ft (125-150m) throughout the day.

**February 4** The first Sukhoi Su-25 unit becomes operational as the 200th Independent Attack Air Flight of the Soviet air force, formed with 12 aircraft at the Sital-chai base in Azerbaijan. (q.v. February 22, 1975)

**February 12** U.S. balloonists Max Anderson and Don Ida lift off from Luxor, Egypt in the helium-filled balloon *Jules Verne*. Their round-the-world flight attempt is aborted two days later after travelling some 2,900 miles (4,667km) to a point east of New Delhi.

**April 12** U.K. hot-air balloon manufacturer Thunder-Colt Balloons records the first flight of its new AS 80 hot-air airship.

NASA's Space Shuttle *Columbia* is successfully launched from Cape Kennedy on mission STS-1, under the power of its own rocket engines and two jettisonable boosters. It is crewed by John Young and Robert Crippen and makes 37 orbits. The flight lasts for 2 days 6 hr 21 mins. (q.v. April 14, 1981)

**April 14** After 37 orbits of the Earth, *Columbia* makes a controlled re-entry into the atmosphere before completing a near-perfect unpowered landing on the dry bed of Rogers Lake at Edwards AFB, California.

**June 5** Flying a specially-prepared Rutan Long-EZ lightplane, Richard G. Rutan sets a world straight-line distance record in the FAI-class C-1-b. The distance of 4,563.7 miles (7,344.56km) is subsequently ratified by the FAI.

**June 7** Eight Israeli Air Force F-16s, escorted by F-15s, attack the Osirak nuclear reactor near Baghdad, Iraq. As a result, the U.S. imposes a temporary embargo on the supply of further F-16s to Israel.

**June 19** Launch of the French *Meteosat 2* weather satellite by Ariana LO 3 rocket booster from Kouron, French Guyana.

**July 7** The MacCready *Solar Challenger* makes the first crossing of the English Channel by a solar-powered aircraft. The 5 hr 23 min (180 mile/290 km) flight from Cergy Pontaire, near Paris to Cranston Airfield, Kent is piloted by Steve Ptacek.

**August 3** The Boeing Company attains a new production milestone with the delivery of its 4,000th jetliner, a 727-200 for Ansett Airlines of Australia.

**August 25** The NASA *Voyager 2* spacecraft makes its closest approach to the planet Saturn, returning spectacular pictures of its moons and rings. Next rendezvous for *Voyager 2* is with Uranus in January 1986.

**September 7** Edwin A. Link, inventor of the Link trainer, dies at the age of 77. His ground-based flight trainer was the first stepping-stone towards the sophisticated flight simulators now used for a major portion of all flight training.

**September 20** The People's Republic of China launches three satellites into Earth orbit with a single booster rocket. It is the nation's first multiple launch.

**September 22** An Ilyushin Il-86, captained by G. Volokhov, establishes for the Soviet Union a new world-class record for speed in a 2,000-km closed circuit, carrying payloads of 35,500 to 65,000kg, of 606.02mph (975.3km/h). Two days later the same aircraft/crew combination sets a new record over a 1,000-km closed circuit of 597.8mph (962km/h) carrying payloads from 30,000 to 80,000kg.

**September 26** The first flight of the Boeing Model 767 is successfully completed at Paine Field, Everett. This 2 hr 4 min flight is made three days ahead of a target that was set in 1978.

**September 30** The last de Havilland Comet airliner flight in the U.K. is made by the Srs 4C G-BOIX, flown by Dan-Air to East Fortune for the Royal Scottish Museum.

**October 2** President Reagan announces that 100 Rockwell B-1B SAL (Strategic Air-launched cruise missile Launchers) are to be procured for the U.S.A.F.

**October 6** The first flight is recorded of an Airbus A300 with a two-man Forward Facing Crew Cockpit (FFCC). The FFCC flight deck has advanced avionics and improved system automation, making it possible for a flight crew of two to operate this wide-body airliner.

**October 9** Ascending from a site near Los Angeles, California, Fred Gorrell and John Shoecroft in the helium-filled balloon *Superchicken III* record the first non-stop trans-America flight in a balloon, landing in Georgia 55 hrs 25 mins after lift-off.

*1982: A  F-117A stealth fighter*

**November 4** NASA's second flight by the Space Shuttle *Columbia* is aborted 31 seconds before lift-off due to a computer mismatch.

**November 12** The NASA Space Shuttle *Columbia*, on mission STS-2, makes a successful lift-off from Kennedy Space Center with Joe Engle and Richard Truly as crew. Thirty-six orbits are performed, the mission lasting for 2 days 6 hrs 13 mins. A fuel cell fault halved the expected 5-day mission.

**November 13** Ben Abruzzo, Larry Newman, Ron Clarke and Rocky Aoki complete the first manned crossing of the Pacific by balloon. Carried in the helium-filled balloon *Double Eagle V*, their journey from Nagashima, Japan, ends in a crash-landing in severe weather some 170 miles (274km) north of San Francisco.

**November 14** With its mission cut short because of a fuel cell failure, the Space Shuttle *Columbia* makes a successful landing at Rogers Lake, Edwards AFB, California.

**November 24** Two Sikorsky S-61Ns of Bristow Helicopters, operating in winds of about 87mph (140km/h), rescue 48 oilmen from the production rig *Transworld 58* after it had been blown from its moorings.

**November 25-26** Crewed by French balloonists Hélène Dorigny and Michael Arnould, the Cameron A-530 hot-air balloon *Semiramis* is flown from Ballina, Ireland, to St.-Christophe-en-Boucherie, France. This is later ratified by the FAI as a new hot-air balloon distance record of 717.5 miles (1,154.74km).

**December 4** NASA accepts the first flight-standard ERNO Spacelab module at ERNO's Bremen factory.

**December 5** Jerry Mullen takes off in an aircraft named *Phoenix*, used formerly by Jim Bede as the BD-2 *Love One*, to attempt a closed-circuit distance record for piston-engined aircraft in Class C-1-d. He lands on December 8 after 73 hrs 2 mins in the air, having flown a distance of 10,007.1 miles (16,104.9km), which considerably exceeds the previous world record.

**December 19** First flight of the Soviet Tupolev Tu-160 Blackjack supersonic heavy bomber, initially intended to carry cruise missiles, (q.v. April 25, 1987)

## 1982

**January 6** A Gulfstream III executive transport, operated by the U.S. National Distillers and Chemical Corporation, begins a round-the-world flight. Landing on January 10, the flight (from and to Teterboro, New Jersey) is completed in 47 hrs 39 mins, breaking three existing records and setting 10 new records in the appropriate FAI class.

**January 27** Cessna Aircraft Company announce delivery of its 1,000th business jet, a Citation II.

**February 19** The Boeing Model 757 makes its first flight at Renton, Washington. The successful 2 hr 30 min flight terminates at Paine Field, Everett, where it is to be based until cleared by the FAA for operation from the company's airfield at Seattle.

**April 2** Argentine Forces invade the Falkland Islands and, on the following day, the island of South Georgia.

**April 3** The United Nations Security Council passes Resolution 502, calling for the withdrawal of Argentine forces from the Falklands.

The first Airbus A310 (F-WZLH) makes a successful first flight of 3 hrs 15 mins at Toulouse, France.

The main elements of the British task force for operations against the Argentine forces on the Falklands sail from Portsmouth. These include the carriers H.M.S. *Hermes* and *Invincible*.

**April 6** A new Sea Harrier squadron, No. 809, is formed at R.N.A.S. Yeovilton. Nos. 800, 801, 809 and 899 Sea Harrier squadrons carry out 2,376 sorties and complete 2,675 hrs 25 mins of operational flying during the Falklands conflict that follows.

**April 7** The British Government declares a 200-mile (322km) exclusion zone around the Falkland Islands.

**April 21** Two Westland Wessex helicopters of the British task force crash on South Georgia in bad weather. A third recovers the men of the SAS.

**April 25** Aircraft attached to the British task force despatched to the Falkland Islands are in action for the first time. Lynx helicopters flying from the frigates H.M.S. *Alacrity* and

*Antelope* attack the Argentine submarine *Santa Fe* off Grytviken harbour, South Georgia. Later that day, Sea Kings escorted by Lynx helicopters land Royal Marines on South Georgia. The Marines subsequently recapture the island.

**April 28** The British Government gives Argentina 48 hours warning that an air blockade is to be imposed over a 200-mile (322km) radius from the Falklands.

**May 1** The first British air attack against Argentine positions on the Falkland Islands is made by a single Vulcan B2 operating from Ascension Island. It requires flight refuelling on both the outward and return flights. The Vulcan bombs Port Stanley airfield, and an attack on the same airfield is made immediately afterwards by nine Sea Harriers from H.M.S. *Hermes*. Three Sea Harriers also attack the airstrip at Goose Green. The Vulcan operation against Port Stanley from Ascension Island ranks then as the longest-ever operational sortie.

In the first Sea Harrier combat victory, an Argentine Mirage IIIEA is destroyed by a Sidewinder missile. Argentine losses on the same day include a second Mirage III and a Canberra bomber.

**May 2** A Royal Navy ASW Sea King helicopter under fire from the Argentine patrol vessel *Alferez Sobral* reports its position to the task force. Soon afterwards the *Sobral* is severely damaged in an attack by two Lynx helicopters deploying Sea Skua missiles and an accompanying patrol vessel, the *Comodoro Somellera*, is sunk.

The Argentine Navy cruiser *General Belgrano* is sunk by the British nuclear-powered submarine *Conqueror*.

**May 4** A Sea Harrier is lost during an attack on Port Stanley.

H.M.S. *Sheffield*, a Type 42 destroyer, has to be abandoned and later sinks after being hit by an Exocet missile launched from an Argentine Navy Dassault-Bréguet Super Étendard recently supplied from France.

**May 5** Two British Airways L-1011 TriStars make safe touch-downs at London's Heathrow Airport in totally blind conditions. The landings are made with an absence of runway visual range and reference height measurements.

**May 7** The British Government declares a 'safe zone' extending 12 miles (19.3km) from the Argentine coast.

Two Sea Harriers from H.M.S. *Invincible* are lost; it is believed they collided in poor visibility.

**May 8** About 20 Harriers and Sea Harriers fly non-stop from R.N.A.S. Yeovilton, Somerset, to Ascension Island, air-refuelled several times during the 9-hour flight.

**May 9** The Argentine vessel *Nawal*, shadowing the British task force, is attacked by two Sea Harriers. Its crew subsequently surrenders to a boarding party from H.M.S. *Hermes*.

**May 13** The *Soyuz T-5* is launched successfully from Baikonur, carrying cosmonauts Anatoli Berezovoy and Valentin Lebedev. A successful link-up is made on May 14 with the Soviet Union's new orbiting laboratory, *Salyut 7*.

**May 14** The British task force raids Pebble Island; three Argentine Skyhawk attack-bombers are lost in action.

India's combined communications and weather satellite, *Insat 1A*, becomes operational.

**May 17** In what is believed to be the first launch of a satellite from an orbiting space station, the crew of *Salyut 7* place the amateur radio satellite *Iskra 2* in Earth orbit via an airlock in the space laboratory (q.v. May 13, 1982)

**May 21** Royal Marine Commandos and a Parachute Regiment battalion make a successful landing at Port San Carlos on the East Falklands. Royal Navy Sea Kings play a major role in this action; for example, a detachment of Sea King Mk. 4 Commando helicopters of No. 846 Squadron airlift more than 407 tons of stores and 520 troops on this day alone. The Type 21 frigate H.M.S. *Ardent* is lost after air attack. Nine Argentine aircraft are lost in action.

**May 24** Following several hits by rockets and bombs launched from Argentine aircraft on the previous day, the frigate H.M.S. *Antelope* explodes and sinks. Seven Argentine aircraft are lost in action.

**May 25** The Type 42 destroyer H.M.S. *Coventry* of the British task force is hit by bombs from Argentine Skyhawks and sinks following serious fire damage. In another attack, the container ship *Atlantic Conveyor* is hit by an Exocet missile launched from an Argentine Navy Super Étendard and is abandoned after serious fire damage. Twenty-four task force personnel lose their lives.

**May 28** Goose Green and Darwin are retaken by British forces. Seventeen British soldiers are killed in the action.

**June 3** An R.A.F. Vulcan is intercepted in Brazilian airspace and escorted to Rio de Janeiro by Brazilian F-5Es.

**June 8** Argentine aircraft attack task-force ships at Bluff Cove. Fifty task-force personnel lose their lives. Eleven Argentine aircraft are lost in action.

**June 12** H.M.S. *Glamorgan* is struck by a land-based Exocet fired from Port Stanley. Thirteen sailors are lost but the destroyer remains operational.

**June 14** Argentine forces on the Falklands surrender. Argentine losses amount to more than 700 killed, five ships and well over 100

aircraft. British air losses total four Sea Harriers lost in accidents, two lost to ground fire, three Harrier GR Mk 3s lost to ground fire and helicopters. No Harrier/Sea Harrier has been lost in air-to-air combat.

**July 27** Space Shuttle *Columbia* is launched on mission STS-4, its last proving flight. Crewed by Mattingly and Hartsfield, the mission lasts for 7 days 1 hr 10 mins and sees the first Shuttle landing on a concrete runway.

**August 5** Australian Dick Smith begins the first solo helicopter flight around the world. (q.v. July 22, 1983)

**August 23** The first of 59 Lockheed F-117A stealth fighters are delivered to the U.S.A.F. (last on July 12, 1990). Initial operational capability by the 4450th Test Squadron is in October of the following year.

**September 30** The first round-the-world flight by helicopter is completed by H. Ross Perot Jr. and Jay W. Coburn in a Bell Model 206L LongRanger II named *The Spirit of Texas*. Begun on September 1, the crew made 29 landings in 23 different countries during the staged flight, with fuel also being taken on from S.S. *President McKinley* in the North Pacific. The calculated distance flown is 26,000 miles (41,850km). Modifications to the helicopter include the addition of a 151 U.S. gallon auxiliary fuel tank in the cabin, increasing the helicopter's range to 750 miles (1,207km). This also establishes an FAA world speed record for helicopters flying around the world of 35.4mph (56.97km/h).

**November 4** Pan American Boeing 747SPs inaugurate services between Los Angeles (U.S.A.) and Sydney (Australia), a distance of 7,487 miles (12,049km). It is said by the airline to be the world's longest non-stop commercial route.

**November 8** An R.A.F. Tornado GR.Mk 1 makes a non-stop two-way flight between England and Cyprus. Flight-refuelled by Victors and a Buccaneer, it is one of No. 9 Squadron's aircraft, the R.A.F.'s first operational Tornado squadron (since June 1, 1982).

**November 11** Space Shuttle mission STS-5 using *Columbia* begins. Lasting 5 days 2 hrs 14 mins, it is the first operational flight, deploying *Anik-3*. Crew comprises Allen, Brand, Lenoir and Overmyer.

**December 16** The Boeing AGM-86B air-launched cruise missile (ALCM) attains initial operational capability on Boeing B-52 Stratofortress bombers.

**December 20** Launch of the first Defense Meteorological Satellite Program satellite.

**December 21** With the disbanding of No. 44 Squadron, the R.A.F. finally gives up its last Avro Vulcan bombers. This leaves the R.A.F. with no operational bombers as such.

**December 26** The prototype Antonov An-124 Condor flies for the first time. It is then the world's largest aircraft.

## 1983

**February 17** When an Italian Air Force pilot ejects from his Aeritalia F-104S Starfighter, he becomes the 5,000th person to be saved using Martin-Baker ejection seats.

**April 5** Space Shuttle mission STS-6 using *Challenger* begins after a long delay caused by leaks. It sees the first EVA from an Orbiter. Crew comprises Bobko, Musgrave, Peterson and Weitz.

**April 26** A sum of £100,000 is given to the Royal Aeronautical Society by Henry Kremer to further promote the development of man-powered aircraft. Intended to encourage greater speeds, an initial award of £20,000 is offered by the Society for a man-powered flight of one mile in under three minutes.

**May 14** The Hughes Flying Boat Exhibition, housing the H-4 Hercules *Spruce Goose*, is opened to the public at Long Beach, California.

**May 22** A French Aviasud Sirocco makes the first flight across the Mediterranean by a microlight aircraft.

**June 18** Space Shuttle mission STS-7 using *Challenger* begins. It lasts 6 days 2 hrs 24 mins. *Anik-C2* and *Palapa-B1* are deployed (Canadian and Indonesian satellites). Also sees the first satellite retrieval and the first American woman in space (Dr. Sally Ride, at 32 the youngest U.S. astronaut). Other crew members are Crippen, Fabian, Hauck and Thagard.

**July 22** Australian Dick Smith completes the first solo flight around the world in a helicopter. The 35,258-mile (56,742-km) journey was made in stages, with the Bell JetRanger III *Australian Explorer* accumulating an actual flying time of some 320 hrs.

**August 19** Lockheed rolls out its 250th and last TriStar airliner at Palmdale, California.

**August 30** Space Shuttle mission STS-8 begins, lasting 6 days 7 mins. Crewed by Bluford, Brandenstein, Gardner, Thornton and Truly, it is the first night launch and landing.

**September** Soviet *Soyuz T-10* launch ends with an explosion on the Tyuratam launch pad. The two crew fly to safety using the launch escape system.

**September 6** It is acknowledged that a Soviet Air Force Sukhoi Su-15 interceptor is responsible for shooting down a Korean Air Lines Boeing Model 747, with the loss of 269 lives. The airliner had flown off-course, taking it over Sakhalin Island.

**September 30** Roll-out of the first production McDonnell Douglas (Hughes) AH-64A Apache attack helicopter. IOC is achieved by the 6th Cavalry Regiment's 3rd Squadron in July 1986.

**October 26** With a special Boeing 707 flight between New York and Paris, Pan American commemorates the 25th anniversary of 707 transatlantic services.

**November 28** Space Shuttle mission STS-9/41-A begins Spacelab 1 mission.

**December 16** The Chiefs of Staff of the British, French, West German, Italian and Spanish air forces sign a preliminary design agreement for a Future European Fighter Aircraft. France withdraws in July 1985. (q.v. June 1986)

## 1984

**January 12** The U.S. Marine Corps receives its first McDonnell Douglas/BAe AV-8B Harrier II.

**February 3** Space Shuttle mission 41-B begins using *Challenger*, lasting 7 days 23 hrs 17 mins. *Palapa B2* and *Westar 6* satellites are lost. Bruce McCandless makes the first untethered EVA using the Martin Marietta Manned Manoeuvring Unit.

**March 6** The British Airship Industrie's Skyship 600 makes its first flight at Cardington, Bedfordshire.

**March 27** British Airways starts a thrice-weekly return service between London, Heathrow and Miami, using Concorde.

**March 31** No. 50 Squadron, R.A.F., is disbanded at Waddington, Lincolnshire. This sees the Avro Vulcan finally out of service in all roles.

**April 4** Space Shuttle mission 41-C begins using *Challenger*, lasting 6 days 23 hrs 40 mins. During the mission, the *Solar Maximum* satellite is retrieved, repaired and redeployed.

**May 15** The first flight of the Aeritalia/Aermacchi/EMBRAER/AMX close-support aircraft.

**June 22** Voyager Aircraft Inc.'s *Voyager* flies for the first time, with Dick Rutan at the controls (30 mins). Designed by Rutan, it is expected to attempt a non-stop and unrefuelled flight around the world. The next test flight takes place on the 24th, lasting three hours. (q.v. December 14-23, 1986)

**July 2** Escadron de Chasse (EC) 1/2 Cigognes at Dijon is the first squadron to become operational with the Dassault-Bréguet Mirage 2000.

**July 25** Soviet cosmonaut Svetlana Savitskaya makes the first EVA 'spacewalk' by a woman, leaving the *Salyut 7/Soyuz T-10B/Soyuz T-12* complex for 3 hrs 35 mins 4 secs. She is also the first woman to fly twice in space.

**August 30** Space Shuttle mission 41-D using *Discovery*, the 12th mission, begins. It lasts 6 days 56 mins and carries the first commercial payload specialist.

**September 1984–March 1987** Frenchman Patrice Franceschi makes the first staged around-the-world flight in a microlight. Piloting an Aviasud Sirocco, some 27,960 miles (45,000km) are covered in a flying time of about 700 hrs.

**September 14–18** Famous high-altitude parachute jumper, ex-U.S.A.F. Colonel Joe Kittinger, makes the first solo non-stop balloon flight across the North Atlantic. His 101,000cu ft (2,160m$^3$) balloon *Rosie O'Grady* took off from Carbon, Maine, and lands at Savona, Italy.

**October 2** *Soyuz T-10B* lands after setting a new space duration record of 237 days.

**October 5** Space Shuttle mission 41-G begins using *Challenger*, following two cancelled missions. Lasting 8 days 5 hrs 23 mins it has the first 7-person crew. Sally Ride becomes the first U.S. woman to fly into space twice. Kathryn Sullivan makes the first 'spacewalk' by a U.S. female astronaut. Also on board is Canadian Marc Garneau.

**October 18** The first production Rockwell International B-1B strategic bomber makes its first flight. 100 are on order.

**November 3** As part of an international relief effort to help starving Ethiopia, the first of two R.A.F. Hercules transports arrive at Addis Ababa Airport. Seven-days-a-week flying begins on November 5, ending at the close of the year.

**November 9** No. 849 Squadron, R.N.A.S. Culdrose, Cornwall, England, becomes the world's first helicopter airborne early-warning squadron.

**November 20–22** Briton Julian Nott establishes a new world altitude record for manned pressurized balloons, taking ULD1 to a height of 17,767ft (5,415.4m). It also sets new duration and distance records for pressurized balloons, at 33 hrs 8 mins 42 secs and 1,485.98 miles (2,391.46km) respectively.

**1985**

A U.S. Boeing B-29 Superfortress of the 46th Reconnaissance Squadron based in Alaska is rediscovered virtually intact in Greenland, where it had been abandoned after running short of fuel during the return leg of a possibly-secret mission on February 21, 1947. Landed at night in snow on a frozen lake, the crew had been rescued by a C-54 transport a few days later.

**January 27** Space Shuttle mission 51-C begins, using *Discovery*. Lasting 3 days 1 hr 33 mins, it is the first U.S. Department of Defense military mission, with the DoD Flight engineer Payton on board. A signal-intelligence satellite is launched.

**April 12** Space Shuttle mission 51-D begins, using *Discovery*. Lasting 6 days 23 hrs 56 mins, Senator Jake Garn is the Shuttle's first passenger/observer.

**April 30** The first Harrier GR.Mk 5 development aircraft is flown by British Aerospace.

**May 4** The second production Rockwell International B-1B bomber makes its first flight. It is delivered to the 96th Bomb Wing at Dyess Air Force Base, Texas on July 7. Initial Operational Capability is achieved in September 1986.

**May 14** A prototype AIM-120A AMRAAM air-to-air missile is successfully test-fired at a QF-100 Super Sabre drone flying over White Sands, New Mexico.

**May 29** The Antonov An-124, then the world's largest aircraft, flies into Le Bourget to make its first public appearance at the Paris Air Show.

**June 23** An Air India Boeing Model 747 is blown up by a bomb some 120 miles (193km) off Ireland. 321 people are killed.

**August 2** West Germany, Italy and the U.K. sign an agreement for the development and production of the European Fighter Aircraft.

**August 12** A Japan Air Lines Boeing 747SR crashes in mountains north of Tokyo. 520 persons are killed, the highest number of fatalities ever in a single aircraft to this date.

**September 13** A U.S.A.F. McDonnell Douglas F-15 Eagle launches an anti-satellite missile from an altitude of about 40,000ft (12,190m). It destroys the inert *Solwind* research satellite in Earth orbit.

**September 30** The new aircraft carrier, *Giuseppe Garibaldi*, is handed over to the Italian Navy. Although initially flying helicopters, its design allows for V/STOL jets of BAe Sea Harrier type.

**October 3** Space Shuttle mission 51-J begins, using *Atlantis* for the first time. Lasts 4 days 1 hr 45 mins.

**October 28** The Hazeltine Microwave Landing System installed at Westland Helicopter's Yeovil airfield is declared operational. It is the first in Europe.

**October 30** Space Shuttle mission 61-A begins, paid for by West Germany and using *Columbia*. First eight-person crew, including Germans.

**November 26** Space Shuttle mission 61-B begins, using *Atlantis*. Lasting over 6 days 22 hrs, the Mexican Neri is among the seven crew.

**December 5** The Soviet Union launches its first nuclear-powered aircraft carrier at the Nikolayev South yard, which is commissioned on January 21, 1991 and becomes *Admiral Kuznetzov* (formerly *Tbilisi*).

## 1986

**January 28** Space Shuttle mission 51-L, using *Challenger*. The crew of seven are killed in an explosion 73 seconds after lift-off. Planned future Shuttle missions are cancelled while investigations take place.

**March 13** The British Aerospace *Giotto* satellite, launched on July 2, 1986, intercepts Halley's Comet. It passes within 375 miles (605km) of the comet's nucleus.

**March 26** The British Aerospace Terprom aircraft navigation system completes its technology demonstration trials. It has an accuracy of 150–300ft (45.7–91.4m) regardless of flight duration.

**April 23** Scheduled passenger services over London landmarks are begun using an Airship Industries Skyship 500 airship.

**May 10** A U.S.A.F. Boeing B-52H, flying from Carswell Air Force Base, Texas, for the first time carries a full load of 20 AGM-86B air-launched cruise missiles.

**June** Eurofighter Jagdflugzeug GmbH is formed in Munich to oversee the European Fighter Aircraft programme. (q.v. December 16, 1983)

**July 1** Six Soviet Mikoyan MiG-29 Fulcrum fighters begin a courtesy visit to Rissala Air Base in Finland. It gives the West the first opportunity to see this new combat aircraft close up.

**July 4** The Dassault-Bréguet Rafale A experimental advanced combat aircraft makes its first flight, during which it achieves Mach 1.3+.

**July 10** Dick Rutan and Jeana Yeager begin a five-day and 11,336.9-mile (18,245-km) non-stop test flight in *Voyager*.

**July 28** Seven American aircraft companies submit design proposals for the future AFT (Advanced Tactical Fighter). On October 31, the U.S.A.F. announces the Lockheed-Burbank YF-22A and Northrop YF-23A are to be developed.

**August 11** The Westland Lynx demonstrator G-LYNX sets a new world speed record for helicopters by flying at 249.09mph (400.87km/h) over a 15/25km course. It uses the new BERP III main rotor blades for the record flight.

**August 12** The first Japanese H-I rocket is launched, carrying an experimental geodetic satellite into orbit.

**August 17** Boeing rolls out of its Seattle factory its 5,000th commercial jet airliner, a Model 737-300 for KLM.

**August 28** Richard Meredith-Hardy begins a flight using a Mainair Gemini Flash 2 microlight that takes him in stages from London's Dockland to Cape Town, South Africa, in the British Trans-Africa Microlight Expedition. The journey of 10,700 miles (17,220km) takes 330 flying hours.

**September 2** Henk and Evelyn Brink of the Netherlands make a record-breaking flight across the Atlantic in a Cameron R-225 combined hot air/helium balloon, taking 50 hrs to fly from St. John's, Newfoundland, to a point near Amsterdam.

**November 6** The worst civilian helicopter accident to date happens off Sumburgh, Shetland Islands, when 45 of the 47 persons on board a commercial Boeing 234 Chinook helicopter belonging to British International Helicopters are killed. (On May 10, 1977, 54 had been killed in an Israeli military Sikorsky Sea Stallion.)

**December 8** First flight of the Russian Beriev A-40 ASW and SAR jet amphibian.

**December 14–23** The *Voyager* composites trimaran aeroplane makes a successful non-stop and unrefuelled around-the-world flight, beginning and ending at Edwards Air Force

Base. Crewed by Dick Rutan and Jeana Yeager, the actual time is 9 days 3 mins 44 secs. It establishes a world absolute distance record in a straight line and closed circuit for aeroplanes of 24,986.664 miles (40,212.139km).

## 1987

**January 7** A Norwegian F-16 makes the first contact with a Soviet Sukhoi Su-27 fighter over the Barents Sea.

**January 21** The Massachusetts Institute of Technology (MIT) *Michelob Light Eagle* human-powered aircraft is used to set world distance in a straight line, distance in a closed circuit and duration records for women at 4,255 miles (6.83km), 9.59 miles (15.44km) and 37 mins 38 secs respectively, piloted by American Lois McCallin.

**January 22** The MIT *Michelob Light Eagle* sets a world distance record in a closed circuit for a human-powered aircraft of 36.452 miles (58.664km), piloted by Glenn Tremml.

**February 5** The Soviet Union launches spacecraft *TM2* with full television coverage. Col. Yuri Romanenko and Flight Engineer Alexander Laveikin (the 200th person in space) dock with the *Mir* space station on the 7th.

**April 25** First two operational Soviet Tupolev Tu-160 Blackjack supersonic heavy cruise-missile bombers are delivered to the 184th Heavy Bomber Regiment of Guards at Priluki, Ukraine.

**May 15** The Soviet Energia heavy rocket booster is first launched, capable of carrying a 100-ton payload.

**July 2** The first transatlantic crossing by hot-air balloon begins from Sugar Loaf, Maine, U.S.A. Crewed by Richard Branson and Per Lindstrand, the *Virgin Atlantic Flyer* (at this time the world's largest hot-air balloon at 2,130.000cu ft/60,314.8m³) lands near Limavady, Northern Ireland the following day. Having entered a jetstream during its crossing, it achieved a computed maximum speed of 153mph (246km/h).

**August 17** First flight of the first real prototype Russian Sukhoi Su-33 carrier-borne fighter and anti-shipping aircraft.

**October 9** The first pre-production EH Industries EH 101 helicopter makes its maiden flight at Yeovil, England.

**October 14** A de Havilland Canada DHC-7 Dash 7 of Brymon Airways makes the first passenger-carrying flight from Britain's new London City Airport. The destination is Paris, France.

**October 26** The first revenue flight is made from London City Airport.

**November 29** A Korean Air Lines Boeing Model 707 is destroyed in the air by a bomb reportedly planted by a North Korean woman. All 115 persons are killed.

**December 8** The United States of America and the Soviet Union sign an Intermediate-range Nuclear Forces (INF) treaty. It is later ratified by Congress.

**December 10** Two prisoners are helped to escape from the U.K.'s Gartree maximum security prison by a hijacked Bell Model 206L LongRanger helicopter.

**December 21** Soviet cosmonauts Musa Manarov and Vladimir Titov are launched to the *Mir* space station. (q.v. November 11, 1988)

**December 29** Soviet cosmonaut Yuri Romanenko returns to Earth in *Soyuz TM3* after a 326-day stay in space.

## 1988

**February 25** India launches the *Prithvi*, a tactical surface-to-surface missile of its own development.

**April 15** The first aeroplane fuelled by liquid hydrogen makes its maiden flight as the Soviet Tupolev Tu-155. It is basically a converted Tu-154 airliner.

**June 1** Per Lindstrand pilots a 600,000cu ft (17,000m³) hot-air balloon to an altitude of 65,0000 (19,810m) over Texas, U.S.A., setting a new record.

**June 7** The Soviet *Phobos* satellite is launched from Baikonur on a mission to Mars. A second satellite follows shortly after. They are to orbit Mars and land monitoring experiments onto the moon Phobos. The satellites carry equipment from 12 other nations and America's NASA Deep Space network helps with communications and other aspects of the mission.

**June 28** First flight of the prototype Russian Sukhoi Su-35 advanced air-superiority fighter and attack aircraft.

**July 1** The Chinese state airline, CAAC, becomes Air China.

**July** A cease-fire is proposed between Iraq and Iran.

**August 1** In accordance with the INF Treaty, the first four Soviet SS-20 missiles with their warheads removed are blown up at the Sary Ozek base.

**August 2** U.S. Defense Secretary Frank Carlucci inspects an example of the new Soviet Tupolev Blackjack bomber at Kubinka air base, near Moscow.

**August 17** A Pakistan Air Force Lockheed C-130 Hercules crashes soon after take-off from Bakawalpur. Among the 30 killed is President Zia.

**August 18** Indian industrialist Vijay Singhania flies from Biggin Hill, England, in the CFM Shadow microlight *L'Esprit D'lndian Post* in an attempt to fly to Bombay in 23 days.

**August 28** Three Italian Air Force pilots are killed, together with 39 spectators when three Aermacchi MB-339PANs of the Italian Pattuglia Acrobatica Nazionale Frecce Tricolori aerobatic team collide during a display at the U.S.A.F.'s Ramstein Air Base in West Germany.

**September 19** Israel launches its first satellite, the *Offeq 1*, from a Shavit booster.

**September 28** The Soviet Ilyushin Il-96-300 wide-body airliner makes its maiden flight.

**September 29** The U.S. Space Shuttle Orbiter programme resumes with the launch of STS-26, using *Discovery*. A Tracking and Data Relay Satellite System satellite is launched (TDRSS-C). The mission ends on October 3.

**November** Antonov displays its massive An-225 Mriya transport aircraft. Powered by six Lotarev D-18T turbofan engines, it weighs some 590 tons (600 tonnes) and is therefore nearly half as heavy again as the world's previously largest aircraft, the Antonov An-124. (q.v. December 21, 1988)

**November 11** Soviet cosmonauts Musa Manarov and Vladimir Titov set a new space endurance record of 326 days. (q.v. December 21, 1987)

**November 15** The Soviet Space Shuttle *Buran* is launched for the first time from the Baikonur Cosmodrome on a 3 hr 25 min unmanned flight. This was the third launch attempt and it uses an Energia booster rocket.

**November 22** The Northrop B-2A advanced technology bomber is rolled out. B-2As will eventually complement B-1Bs as the U.S.A.F.'s main strategic bomber in the next decade.

**December 9** Saab JAS 39 Gripen, a Swedish multi-role combat aircraft makes its first flight from Linköping. (q.v. June 1996)

**December 21** First flight of the world's largest aircraft, the Ukrainian Antonov An-225 Mriya six-engined very heavy freighter. Only a single example is completed. Its first commercial flight takes place in May 1990, having earlier been used for the first time to transport the Russian *Buran* space shuttle on its back.

## 1989

The first hot-air airship with cargo-carrying capability flies as the Thunder & Colt AS 261. With a length of 156ft 10in (47.8m) and volume of 261,000cu ft (7,391m³), it is also (in 1989) the world's largest hot-air airship. Capable of carrying five crew and a 0.75-ton (0.76-tonne) suspended payload, it is used to air-lift an inflatable platform to the tree tops in the Brazilian rain forest to help with botanical investigations.

**January 2** The first flight is recorded of the Soviet Tupolev Tu-204, from a Moscow airport.

**January 8** The Soviet Union announces its intention to begin destroying its huge stockpile of chemical weapons. Western estimates for the size of the stockpile vary from 50 to 500,000 tons/tonnes. The U.S.A. is thought to have 30–42,000 tons/tonnes.

**January 22** The Massachusetts Institute of Technology manpowered aircraft, *Michelob Light Eagle*, flies 36,452 miles (58.664km) under the pedal-power of Glenn Tremml.

**March 15** Canadian Hilda Wallace becomes the oldest recorded person to gain a pilot's licence, at 80.3 years old.

**April 11** Australian Eric Winton flies a Tyagarah Aerodrome to a new world altitude record of 29,999ft (9,144m).

**May 8** First flight of the AIDC Ching-Kuo indigenous fighter and attack aircraft in Taiwan. Production deliveries began in January 1994, with initial operational capability achieved by No. 8 Squadron a year later.

**June 8** Russian pilot Anatoli Kvochur ejects from his stricken Mikoyan MiG-29 at an altitude of just 400ft (122m) at the Paris Air Show after an engine cut-out. Having ensured that the nose-diving aircraft would miss the crowd, he ejects horizontally, just two seconds before impact.

**July 17** First flight of the Northrop Grumman B-2A Spirit strategic stealth bomber, which had been under secret development since 1978. (q.v. December 11, 1993)

**August 15** A McDonnell Douglas/BAe GR.Mk 5 Harrier II records the fastest climb to date, taking just 2 mins 6.63 sees to reach 39,370ft (12,000m) from a standing start.

**August 21** A new world speed record for landplanes with piston engines is established by American Lyle Shelton, flying a modified Grumman F8F Bearcat with a 3,800hp (2,834kW) Wright R-3350 radial engine. He achieves over 528mph (850km/h) over a 3-km course at Las Vegas.

**November 1** A Sukhoi Su-27K (T10K-2, also known as Su-33) lands on the aircraft carrier T*bilisi* (since renamed *Admiral Kuznetsov*), the first conventional fixed-wing aircraft to land on a Russian aircraft carrier. The same day an Su-25UTG shipborne trainer and Mikoyan MiG-29K fighter land on the carrier.

**December** A Bell Model 47B, accommodating Doug Daigle, Dave Meyer, Brian Watts and Ron Anderson, makes the longest helicopter hovering flight yet recorded, at 50 hrs 50 secs.

**December 10** The California Polytechnic University's composites-built (balsa wood, carbon and plastics) *Da Vinci III* makes the first recognized and official flight by a human-powered helicopter, lasting 7.1 seconds and attaining a height of 8in (0.2m). Earlier flights, in November, had seen the helicopter lift off the ground, but very briefly.

**December 20/21** First operational use of the U.S.A.F.'s Lockheed F-117A stealth fighter, when two aircraft release 2,000-lb laser-guided bombs on the Rio Hato barracks in Panama, under Operation Just Cause.

**December 30** First flight of the Russian Sukhoi Su-30 Flanker two-seat long-range interceptor development of the Su-27.

## 1989–90

The Russian Tupolev Tu-160 Blackjack supersonic heavy strategic bomber sets 44 speed, payload and height records, including a Class C-l-r record of 1,075mph (1,731km/h) over a 1,000-km closed circuit with a 66,140lb (30,000kg) payload.

## 1990

January 30 Northwest Airlines' flight attendant, Connie Walker, retires at the age of 70, after 42 years in the air.

**February 25** No-smoking flights are compulsory for all U.S. airlines flying over North America.

**March 10** The 6,000th Boeing jet airliner is delivered, a 767-200 to Britannia Airways.

**March 29** First flight of the Russian Ilyushin Il-114 short-haul airliner.

**April 13** First flight of the Russian Sukhoi Su-34 two-seat (side-by-side) tactical and theatre bomber, intended to replace the Su-24 and other combat types.

**April 28** David Cook sets the current British altitude record for microlights, flying to 27,064ft (8,249m) over Aldeburgh, Suffolk.

**May 1** First flight of the actual prototype McDonnell Douglas MD 520N NOTAR (no tail rotor) helicopter.

**May 6** First cross-country flight by a Bell Boeing V-22 Osprey tilt-rotor transport, flying from Dallas to Wilmington, a distance of 1,393 miles (2,241km). First sea trials by two Ospreys take place on board U.S.S. *Wasp* during December 4–7.

**June 10** A British Airways BAC One-Eleven, in the early part of its flight to Malaga, makes an emergency landing at Southampton after a cockpit windscreen blows out at 23,000ft

(7,000m), sucking Captain Tim Lancaster half out. Fortunately, having been grabbed by the co-pilot and steward, he was then held by his legs for the 18 minutes it took to land the aircraft.

**July 3** The longest straight-line distance flown to date in a hang-glider is set at 303.36 miles (488.2km), between New Mexico and Kansas by American Larry Tudor in a Wills Wing.

**August 2** Iraqi forces advance into Kuwait, so beginning the Gulf War.

**August 7** 2,300 paratroops of the U.S. Army's 82nd Airborne Division are airlifted to Saudi Arabia at the start of Operation Desert Shield, the largest-ever military airlift. To protect Saudi Arabia, coalition forces are massed over the coming 22 days, with a C-141B StarLifter, C-5 Galaxy or other aircraft landing at Dhahran every seven minutes (average) in the early days of the operation.

The longest operational deployment of fighters to date is recorded during Operation Desert Shield, when 48 U.S.A.F. McDonnell Douglas F-15C/D Eagles of the 27th and 71st TFSs, 1st Tactical Fighter Wing, are flown non-stop from Langley AFB, Virginia to Dhahran, Saudi Arabia, each fighter carrying air-to-air armament and requiring several aerial refuellings.

**August 8** The U.S. Navy aircraft carrier U.S.S. *Dwight D. Eisenhower* and battle group station in the Red Sea, while U.S.A.F. Boeing B-52s begin deployment to Diego Garcia in the Indian Ocean. The carrier U.S.S. *John F. Kennedy* sets out for the Gulf on the 15th.

**August 9** The United Nations' Security Council pass Resolution 662, requiring Iraqi forces to withdraw from Kuwait.

**August 10** The first squadron of R.A.F. aircraft, Panavia Tornado F.Mk 3 interceptors, arrive in Dhahran. R.A.F. SEPECAT Jaguar GR.Mk 1A attack aircraft arrive in Thumrait, Oman, the following day.

**August 13** The French Navy aircraft carrier *Clemenceau* sets sail for Djibouti, carrying 42 anti-armour helicopters for the French rapid action force in the Gulf.

**August 19** Twenty-one U.S.A.F. F-117A stealth fighters of the 37th TFW leave their base at Tonopah to take part in Operation Desert Shield during the Gulf War. After touch-down at Langley, they fly non-stop to the King Khalid Air Base in Saudi Arabia (arriving on the 21st), having been refuelled in mid-air by KC-10A tankers. Others from the 417th TFW arrive between December 4 (1990) and January 26 (1991). (q.v. 1991)

**August 25** United Nations' Security Council Resolution 665 is granted, authorizing the use of some force if needed to ensure that the blockade on trade from Iraq and Kuwait is not broken. U.S.S. *Saratoga* takes over from U.S.S. *Dwight D. Eisenhower* in the Gulf. Other aircraft carrier movements followed during the conflict.

**August 29** A U.S.A.F. Lockheed C-5A Galaxy heavy transport crashes on take-off in Germany, with the loss of the crew and cargo bound for Saudi Arabia. This is the first non-combat air loss of the Gulf conflict.

**September** A Ukrainian-built Antonov An-124 is used to emergency airlift 451 refugees from Amman to Dacca.

**September 27** On a flight from San Francisco to Hong Kong, United Airlines becomes the first to use satellite data communications on a commercial service.

**September 29** First flight of the first of two prototype Lockheed F-22 Advanced Tactical Fighters for the U.S.A.F., from Palmdale to Edwards Air Force Base. The first supersonic flight by an F-22 followed on October 25.

**October** The Cameron combination helium gas and hot-air balloon *Roziere* R-60 makes the first balloon flight from Great Britain to the U.S.S.R.

**October 7** As coalition forces gather under Operation Desert Shield, 12 Canadian CF-18 Hornets of No. 419 Squadron arrive in Qatar.

**October 18** An R.A.F. Tornado GR.Mk 1 of No. 16 Squadron becomes the first (non-U.S.) coalition air loss of Operation Desert Shield when an arrester barrier catches the landing gear and causes the aircraft to strike the runway. The two crew safely eject and the aircraft is returned to the U.K. for repair.

**November 29** United Nations' Security Council Resolution 678 is granted, authorizing the use of force against Iraq unless it withdraws from Kuwait by January 15,1991.

**December 2** U.S. Astronaut Vance DeVoe Brand lifts off on board Space Shuttle *Columbia*, mission STS 35. At 59, he is the oldest astronaut/cosmonaut to date (still the oldest in 1996).

**December 17** U.S. Army General H. Norman Schwarzkopf orders deployment of the two Northrop Grumman E-8A Joint STARS development aircraft to the Gulf for surveillance during the conflict with Iraq. They return to the U.S.A. in March 1991 after flying 535 operational hours in 49 missions with 4411 Squadron.

**December 31** The 6,000th life is saved by Martin-Baker ejection seats, when the four crew of a U.S. Navy Grumman EA-6B Prowler of VAQ-141 Squadron from U.S.S. *Theodore Roosevelt* eject safely.

## 1991

**January 13** The first Boeing 727-100 (N700IU, *Spirit of Seattle*) is withdrawn from service, after 64,492 flight hours with United Air Lines.

**January 15–17** The fastest speed recorded to date for a manned hot-air balloon is 239mph (385km/h), set by the *Virgin Otsuka Pacific Flyer* crewed by Richard Branson and Per Lindstrand during this first-ever transpacific flight by a hot-air balloon, between Miyakonojo (Japan) and the North West Territories, Canada. The distance covered is 6,761 miles (10,878km), a record (then) for balloons (q.v. January 7, 1997)

**January 16** Eight U.S. Army McDonnell Douglas AH-64 Apache attack helicopters of the 101st Airborne Division plus a CH-53 Pathfinder, head out to attack two Iraqi air defence radar sites west of Baghdad. These are the first aircraft to take off for an actual attack mission during Operation Desert Storm. The Apaches begin their attack at 2.38 am on the 17th, firing Hellfire missiles, rockets and guns, destroying their targets.

**January 17** The start of Operation Desert Storm (Gulf War), the United Nations Coalition forces' military action to expel Iraqi forces from Kuwait. (q.v. January 16, 1991)

The first fixed-wing aircraft to take off under Operation Desert Storm are U.S.A.F. Lockheed F-117A stealth fighters and U.S.A.F., U.S. Navy and R.A.F. tankers in the early minutes of the 17th, the latter to flight refuel attacking tactical aircraft. The F-117As make the first fixed-wing aircraft attack of Operation Desert Storm, striking at air defence installations near Baghdad and a communications centre in Baghdad, the latter at about 03.00 am.

Tomahawk missiles, fired from U.S.S. *Missouri*, *Wisconsin* and *San Jacinto* in the Persian Gulf, hit targets in Baghdad in the very early hours of the 17th.

The first Iraqi Air Force loss of the Gulf War was a Dassault Mirage Fl interceptor that hit the ground during a low-level manoeuvre while attacking a U.S.A.F. Grumman EF-111A Raven electronic warfare aircraft.

The first Coalition victory in air-to-air combat of Operation Desert Storm was at about 03.20 am, when Captain Steve Tate flying a McDonnell Douglas F-15C Eagle with the 71st Tactical Fighter Squadron fired a Sparrow missile at an Iraqi Dassault Mirage F1, which was hit.

The U.S. Navy records its first air victories of Operation Desert Storm when two bomb-carrying McDonnell Douglas F/A-18C Hornets of VEA-81 claim two Iraqi Mikoyan MiG-21s in air-to-air combat.

Lt. Cmdr. Michael Scott Speicher, flying a McDonnell Douglas F/A-18C Hornet from U.S.S. *Saratoga*, is killed when his aircraft is hit by an SA-6 anti-aircraft missile. This is the first American combat air loss of the Gulf War.

The first (non-U.S.) Coalition air loss of Operation Desert Storm was an R.A.F. Panavia Tornado GR.Mk 1 of No. XV Squadron, while mounting an attack on the Shaibah air base. Loss was not caused by combat damage and the crew ejected, to become POWs of Iraq.

**January 18** Coalition forces begin the hunt for Iraqi Scud missile launchers, after five (of seven launched) Scuds with conventional warheads hit Israel (other Scud attacks followed). Among many other actions, French Jaguars attack a munitions store at Ras Al Qulayah.

**January 19** First operational missions by R.A.F. Tornado GR. Mk 1A reconnaissance aircraft, one of which pinpointed a Scud site for attack.

**January 20** Heavy action by Iraqi and Coalition forces includes the launch of two Iraqi Scuds and three Frog surface-to-surface missiles against Saudi Arabia (Scuds intercepted by U.S. Patriot missiles).

**January 22** Three Iraqi transport aircraft fly to Iran and out of the conflict. Others follow from the 23rd, with combat types also leaving from the 26th to avoid destruction in the air or on the ground in their (still vulnerable) hardened shelters.

**January 24** Capt. Ayehid Salab al-Shamrani of No.13 Squadron, Royal Saudi Air Force, records the first non-U.S. victory in air-to-air combat, claiming two Iraqi Mirage F1s, his F-15C Eagle having been guided to the targets by E-3 AWACS.

**January 27** Actions include three U.S.A.F. General Dynamics F-111Fs of the 48th TFW attacking two oil pumping stations in Kuwait (in Iraqi hands) with GBU-15 precision bombs that had been releasing a giant oil slick into the Persian Gulf to hinder Coalition naval activities.

**January 30** Iraqi ground forces with armoured support launch five separate incursions into Saudi Arabia. After one is detected by an unmanned aerial vehicle, four are stopped by AV-8B, HueyCobra and other counter attacks. One incursion reaches Khafji, where it is attacked by HueyCobras and A-10As.

Naval air actions include Royal Navy Lynx helicopters and U.S. Navy Hornets and Intruders attacking many Iraqi fast patrol boats (a number armed with Exocet anti-ship missiles), causing several to be sunk.

The Coalition claims air supremacy over Iraq.

**February 6** Captain Robert Swain of the U.S.A.F.'s 706th Tactical Fighter Squadron, shoots down an Iraqi BO 105 helicopter while flying a Fairchild A-10A Thunderbolt II attack aircraft. On February 15, Captain Todd Sheehy of the 511th TFS shoots down an Iraqi Mil Mi-8 helicopter. Thus, to these A-10As go the unusual distinction of gaining the only gun air-to-air 'victories' of the Gulf War.

**February 13** Among other actions, 46 U.S.A.F. General Dynamics F-111Fs of the 48th TFW, each carrying four laser-guided bombs, strike 132 Iraqi armoured vehicles.

**February 19** U.S. Navy squadron VS-32, operating Lockheed S-3B Vikings, sinks a patrol boat during Operation Desert Storm.

**February 23** Reconnaissance shows that Iraqi forces have set alight more than 300 oil wells in Kuwait. Many more will be fired in the coming days.

**February 24** Massive Coalition ground forces begin the ground war offensive against Iraqi forces in Kuwait and southern Iraq, supported by heavy air activity.

The largest-ever helicopter-borne attack takes place when more than 2,000 troops of the U.S. Army's 101st Airborne Division are air-lifted

*1992: Airbus A330*

by Chinook and Black Hawk helicopters to strategic points during Gulf War, supported by AH-1 HueyCobra, AH-64 Apache and AH-58 Warrior escort gunship helicopters. The total force comprises about 550 helicopters.

**February 26** Iraq orders its forces out of Kuwait.

**February 28** The end of the Gulf War, with the Coalition air forces having flown over 110,000 sorties, recording the first occasion when air power alone had rendered one of the world's largest land armies ineffective, though ground and naval forces had played important roles in the final victory. Since January 17, Iraq has lost 40 aircraft in air combat, with a huge number of others having been either destroyed on the ground or flown to Iran. Coalition combat losses are 35 U.S. aircraft, six R.A.F. Tornados, a Kuwaiti Skyhawk (January 17th) and an Italian Tornado (January 17th), though none were lost in air-to-air combat (many brought down or very badly damaged by ground fire/missiles). Thousands of Iraqi tanks have been destroyed, along with thousands of personnel carriers, artillery pieces and other equipment, radar sites, communications centres and much more.

**March 1** Major Marie T. Rossi dies when the Chinook helicopter she is piloting strikes a microwave tower while flying a low-level mission. Having flown troops into action during Operation Desert Storm, she is reportedly the highest-ranking American to be killed during the Gulf War and its aftermath.

**April 27** First flight of the Eurocopter Tiger (Tigre) anti-armour and combat support helicopter.

**May 24** An El Al Boeing 747 airliner with its galleys and all except four toilets removed, carries the largest number of passengers ever recorded on a flight by a commercial airliner, at 1,087. This occurs during Operation Solomon, when Falasha people are evacuated to Israel from Ethiopia. The airliner has a staggering 760 seats installed, with six persons occupying every four seats by folding away the armrests. During the flight, three babies are born.

**June 1** A Python is found in a baggage locker on board a Delta airliner en route from Orlando.

**July 17** A Lockheed S-3B Viking records the longest flight ever made after taking off from an aircraft carrier, at 5,873 miles (9,445km), lasting 15.5 hours.

**July 22** American Kari Castle establishes the current world hang gliding distance record for women at 201.66 miles (335.8km), at Owens Valley, California.

**September 15** First flight of the McDonnell Douglas C-17A Globemaster III heavy-lift transport for the U.S.A.F. First delivery to an operational unit, the 437th Air Wing, takes place on June 14, 1993, having earlier gone to the 6517th Test Squadron (September 15, 1991).

**October 21** Chris Dewhirst and Leo Dickinson in *Star Flyer 1*, together with Andy Elson and Eric Jones in *Star Flyer 2*, make the first balloon flights over the summit of Mount Everest.

**October 25** First flight of the Airbus A340 long-range airliner.

**December 4** Following financial difficulties, the original Pan Am airline makes its last commercial flight, flown by a Boeing 727 between Bridgetown, Barbados and Miami. In charge is Captain Mark Pyle.

## 1992

**February** Production of the Russian Tupolev Tu-95 Bear bomber finally comes to an end.

**April 15** First flight of the prototype McDonnell Douglas AH-64D Longbow Apache attack helicopter for the U.S. Army and export.

**April 17** Gérard Herbaud and Jean-Noël Herbaud establish a new world distance record for two-seat gliders, flying over 859 miles (1,383km) from Vinon, France to Fez, Morocco in a Schleicher ASH 25 glider.

**May 13** Astronauts Rick Hieb, Pierre Thuot and Tom Akers undertake the longest-ever spacewalk (EVA), at 8 hrs 29 mins, during Space Shuttle Endeavour Mission STS 49. It is the first triple spacewalk and recovers the *Intelsat 6*.

**June 1** The U.S.A.F. establishes Air Combat Command from the former Tactical Air Command and Strategic Air Command. Headquartered at Langley AFB, it is expected to provide combat air forces that include fighters, bombers, reconnaissance and related aircraft types as well as providing nuclear-capable forces for U.S. Strategic Command.

The U.S.A.F. establishes Air Mobility Command from the former Military Airlift Command, to operate transport and aerial refuelling aircraft. It is the Air Force arm of the U.S. Transportation Command.

**July 1** The U.S.A.F. establishes Air Force Materiel Command.

**August 26** Dr. Glenn Singleman and Nicholas Feteris make the highest-ever recorded parachute jump from land, leaping from the Great Trango Tower ledge in the Karakoram mountains, Pakistan.

**September 10** The first production JAS 39 Gripen fighter flies.

**September 12** 15 persons parachute from a hot-air balloon flying over Somerset and Devon, U.K. This is the largest number ever to parachute from a balloon.

**September 22** First flight of the all-weather, day-and-night-attack, and air-to-air STOVL-capable McDonnell Douglas/BAe Harrier II Plus, with Hughes APG-65 multi-mode radar.

**September 16–22** Americans Richard Abruzzo and Troy Bradley set a new world duration record for balloons, by flying for 144 hrs 16 mins in the Cameron R-77 *Team USA*, from Bangor, Maine, U.S.A. to Ben Slimane, Morocco.

**October 1–2** American Maynard Hill sets the current world record for the longest endurance flight by a model aircraft, at 33 hrs 39 mins 15 secs.

**October 7** Sea deployment starts on board the aircraft carrier U.S.S. *John F. Kennedy* of Northrop Grumman F-14A Tomcats converted for bombing, known unofficially as Bombats. (The last newly built F-14 of any version was delivered to the U.S. Navy on July 20, as a F-14D.)

**October 22** Russian Kh-55 Kent advanced cruise missiles are launched for the first time from a Tupolev Tu-160.

**October 23** The current FAI official world record for the largest-ever free-fall formation is set at 200 persons at an altitude of 16,500ft (5,000m) over South Carolina U.S.A. (q.v. August 19, 1994)

**November 2** First flight of the Airbus A330 medium-range wide-body airliner.

**December 1** Briton Judy Leden establishes the current world height-gain hang gliding record for women at 13,025ft (3,970m), at Kuruman, South Africa.

**December 14** 61 refugees are killed in a Russian helicopter shot down over Georgia. This is the world's worst helicopter loss.

**December 29** Certification is gained for the Russian Ilyushin Il-96 wide-body airliner, having first flown on September 28, 1988.

## 1993
**January 6** Briton Robby Whittal sets a paragliding height-gain record (after towed launch) at Brandvlei, South Africa, of 14,850ft (4,526m).

**January 13** Major Susan Helms, U.S.A.F., is launched on Space Shuttle *Endeavor*. She is the first American military woman to enter space.

**January 22** Briton Robby Whittal sets a distance paragliding record from Kuruman, South Africa, of 157 miles (253km). (q.v. December 25, 1995 for towed)

**March 11** First flight of the Airbus A321 airliner.

**March 19** First known loss of a Sukhoi Su-27 in combat, hit by a surface-to-air missile over Sukhumi.

**July 13** The new Russian Beriev Be-12P fire-fighting conversion of the military ASW and SAR amphibian drops 248 tons (252 tonnes) of water in just two runs to tackle a fire at the village of Listvianka.

**September** An Antonov An-124-100 carries the heaviest single load ever air-lifted (to date), comprising a 122 ton (124-tonne) power plant generator core plus its load-spreading skid, totalling 133 tons (135.2 tonnes), transported from Düsseldorf in Germany to New Delhi in India.

**December 2–13** U.S. Space Shuttle *Endeavor* undertakes a successful mission to repair the Hubble Space Telescope.

**December 11** The first production Northrop Grumman B-2A Spirit (AV-8 *Missouri*) stealth bomber is delivered to the 509th Bomb Wing at Whiteman Air Force Base.

## 1994
**January 25** The unmanned *Clementine* spacecraft is launched on the first American lunar mission since the Apollo flights.

**February 7** The first U.S. *Milstar* satellite is launched into orbit.

**March 27** First flight of the first Eurofighter development aircraft (DAI) at Manching, Germany. (q.v. December 23, 1997)

**April 10** Under Operation Blue Sword, NATO air forces, for the first time in the history of the organization, undertake their first air strikes against ground targets when two U.S.A.F. F-16Cs drop bombs on a Bosnian Serb artillery command centre, following the shelling (by a tank) of the Moslem sector of Gorazde.

**June 12** First flight of the Boeing 777 long-range wide-body airliner.

**June 2–July 22** American Ron Bower sets the current world record for the fastest around-the-world flight by helicopter. Using a Bell 206B-3 JetRanger, he left Fort Worth on the 28th and took 24 days 4 hrs 36 mins 24 secs, flying eastward, with 81 stopovers en route.

**June 29** An American Space Shuttle first flies to a Russian *Mir* space station.

**August** Two U.S.A.F. Boeing B-52 bombers from Barksdale Air Force Base undertake the first around-the-world bombing mission, releasing 27,000lb (12,250kg) of bombs in the Kuwait desert during a 47-hour practice mission.

**August 19** 216 persons perform the largest-ever free-fall formation (though not officially recognized as a record), at an altitude of 21,000ft (6,400m) over Slovakia. (q.v. October 23, 1992)

**September 18** A world altitude record for microlights is set by Frenchman Serge Zin, who reaches 31,890ft (9,720m) over St.-Auban, France.

**October 6–11** A Beriev Be-12NKh civil transport conversion of the Be-12 (q.v. July 13, 1993) delivers 29.5 tons (30 tonnes) of supplies to earthquake victims in Yuzhno-Kurilsk.

**October 12** At Davis, California, 46 persons perform a parachute canopy stack lasting over 37 seconds, the greatest number so far recorded.

**October 19** First flight of a Boeing 767 AWACS aircraft, prior to having its specialized equipment fitted. (It first flies after 'fitting out' on August 9, 1996 and delivery will take place in March 1998.)

**November 5** The *Ulysses* spacecraft passes over the Sun's southern pole.

**December 16** First flight of the Ukrainian Antonov An-70 medium freighter.

**December 28** First flight of the Russian Sukhoi Su-32FN long-range maritime strike aircraft.

## 1995

Alaska Airlines becomes the first U.S. airline to book travel and sell tickets via the Internet. Previously, in 1989, it had been the first airline in the world to manually land a passenger jet in FAA Category III weather conditions, using a revolutionary 'fog busting' head-up flight guidance system; in 1990 an Alaska Boeing 727 with the guidance system became the first passenger jet to take off in under 600ft (183m) of runway visibility.

**February 6** The U.S. Space Shuttle *Discovery*, on Mission STS 63, joins the Russian *Mir* space station in space, the first U.S.-Russian rendezvous for two decades. *Discovery* is piloted by U.S.A.F. Lt. Col. Eileen Collins, the first woman to pilot an American spacecraft. (q.v. June 29, 1995)

**February 17–21** Steve Fossett establishes a new world distance record for balloons by flying a Cameron R-150 from Seoul, South Korea to Mendham, Saskatchewan, Canada, a distance of over 5,435 miles (8,748km). This is also the first solo balloon flight across the Pacific. (q.v. 1997)

**March 14** Astronaut Norman Thagard is the first American to be launched with Russian cosmonauts on board *Soyuz TM21*. On the 16th he enters the Russian space station *Mir*,

the first American to do so. The 14th also marks the occasion when the largest number of astronauts and cosmonauts are in space at the same time, comprising the seven crew of U.S. Space Shuttle *Endeavor* (Mission STS 67), two cosmonauts and an American on board Russian *Soyuz TM21*, and three cosmonauts on the *Mir* space station.

**March 22** Russian cosmonaut Dr. Valeriy Poliyakov returns to Earth on board *Soyuz TM20* after the longest-ever spaceflight lasting 437 days 17 hrs 58 mins 16 secs. Launched on *Soyuz TM18* on January 8, 1994, most of the time had been spent on the *Mir* space station.

**April 4** The British Government announces that the R.A.F. will end its nuclear capability in 1998 when WE177 free-fall nuclear bombs are finally withdrawn.

**June 2** A U.S.A.F. F-16 on patrol in the 'no-fly zone' over Bosnia is brought down by a Bosnian Serb anti-aircraft missile. After six days of avoiding capture, the pilot, Capt. Scott O'Grady of the 555th Fighter Squadron, is rescued by U.S.M.C. CH-53 helicopters from the assault ship U.S.S. *Kearsage*, supported by attack helicopters and warplanes.

**June 26** Americans Robert Rosenthal and Maynard Hill establish the current world distance record for model aircraft flying in a closed circuit, at 776 miles (1,250km).

**June 29** U.S. Space Shuttle *Atlantis*, on Mission STS 71, docks with the Russian *Mir* space station, the first-ever docking of a U.S. spacecraft with a Russian space station.

**July** The largest radio-controlled model aircraft in the world flies as a scale-model of the Ukrainian Antonov An-225 Mriya. Constructor is Briton Simon Cocker.

**August 4** The Grob G 850 Strato 2C sets a new world altitude record for manned piston-engined aircraft, at 60,867ft (18,552m).

**August 5** A Delta II booster launches South Korea's *Koreasat-1* communications satellite into space.

**August 10** First flight of the Indonesian IPTN N-250 regional airliner.

**August 11** First flight of tbe Brazilian EMBRAER EMB-145 regional jet airliner.

**August 15–16** An Air France Concorde supersonic airliner, flown by Michel Dupont and Claude Hetru and carrying 96 other persons, sets a speed record for flying around the world at over 811mph (1,305km/h). The elapsed time is a record 31 hrs 27 mins 49 secs.

**August 16** American Col. Clarence Cornish flies a Cessna 172, making him the world's oldest pilot, at 96. He first flew in 1918.

**August 25** First flight of the Airbus A319 short/medium-range airliner.

**August 30** Under Operation Deliberate Force, NATO aircraft under the sanction of the United Nations begin the first large-scale attacks on Bosnian Serb air defence, radar,

communications, ammunition and other targets, following a Serbian mortar attack on Sarajevo on the 28th (37 civilians killed) and some three years of hostilities in the region. (Earlier NATO raids, such as those in November 1994 and May 1995, had been on a much smaller scale.) A French Dassault Mirage 2000N is shot down by an SA-7 ground-launched missile.

**September 1** The German Luftwaffe undertakes its first combat mission since the end of the Second World War when a Panavia Tornado ECR reconnaissance aircraft of JBG 32 flies a reconnaissance sortie over former Yugoslavia from a base in Italy, in support of United Nations' Operation Deliberate Force.

**October 7** First flight of the Japanese Mitsubishi F-2 (then known as FS-X) close support and anti-shipping fighter.

**October 20** The astronauts on U.S. Space Shuttle *Columbia*, on Mission STS 73, undertake microgravity experiments, useful for possible future chemical and pharmaceutical manufacturing.

**November 8–9** American Cheryl Stearns sets the current world record for the greatest number of parachute jumps in 24 hours, at 352, from Raeford, North Carolina.

**November 12–20** U.S. Space Shuttle *Atlantis*, on Mission STS-74, makes the second Shuttle docking with the Russian *Mir* space station. The Shuttle carries food and water to *Mir*.

**November 17** Roll-out of the prototype Indian Light Combat Aircraft at Bangalore.

**December** In the Russian Navy's first major deployment into the Adriatic and the first operational deployment of its new aircraft carrier, *Admiral Kuznetsov*, it and escorting ships assist in supporting the Bosnia peace agreement.

**December 2** A U.S. Atlas IIAS rocket launches the European Space Agency's Solar and Heliospheric Observatory into orbit.

**December 7** The *Galileo* satellite, launched by U.S. Space Shuttle *Atlantis* in 1989, launches a parachute probe into Jupiter's atmosphere.

**December 18** First flight of the NHIndustries NH90 tactical transport helicopter.

**December 25** British woman K. Thurston sets a new (and current) paragliding distance record after a towed launch from Kuruman in South Africa, of 177 miles (285km).

**December 28** China uses its Long March booster rocket to launch the American *EchoStar-1* direct-broadcast satellite.

### 1996

**January 4** First flight of the Boeing Sikorsky RAH-66 Comanche battlefield helicopter, intended for U.S. Army service from 2006.

**January 11–20** U.S. Space Shuttle Mission STS 72, using *Endeavor*, retrieves the Japanese Space Flyer Unit satellite among other objectives.

**February** American Nicholas Piantanida sets an unofficial world altitude record at 123,800ft (37,735m) for piloted balloons. Having taken off from Sioux Falls, South Dakota, he was killed during the landing in Iowa.

**February 17** American Hildegarde Ferrera becomes the oldest person ever to make a tandem parachute jump, at the age of 99 (over Mokuleia, Hawaii).

**February 26** U.S. Space Shuttle *Columbia* fully deploys the Italian Tethered Satellite during Mission STS 75. With the tether extending more than 12 miles (19km) from the Shuttle, the combined shuttle/satellite becomes the largest-ever object in space.

**March 15** Fokker of the Netherlands is declared bankrupt, having been an aircraft manufacturer since 1919. Various revival attempts follow.

**March 21** First flight of the Russian Tupolev Tu-214 airliner.

**March 22** U.S. Space Shuttle *Atlantis* lifts off on Mission STS 76 carrying American Shannon Lucid, at 53 the oldest woman astronaut to date. Spending 181 days on board the Russian *Mir* space station before returning to Earth on Shuttle Mission STS-79 in November 1996, she establishes a new endurance record for an American living in space and broke the world's record for a woman in space. She received the U.S. Congressional Space Medal of Honor in December. Mission STS-76 itself lasts until March 30, and includes the first Shuttle-*Mir* EVA.

**March 31** Delta Air Lines establishes a world record when the 2-millionth passenger boarded a Delta flight at Hartsfield Atlanta International Airport, the first occasion this number of passengers had ever been recorded at a single airport during one month.

**April 5** First flight of the C-130J Hercules, the latest version of this long-serving transport. (q.v. August 26, 1998)

**May** The first edition of *Brassey's World Aircraft & Systems Directory* is published, conceived and edited by Michael J. H. Taylor. Formerly the Assistant Editor on *Jane's All the World's Aircraft*, Michael Taylor conceived Brassey's WA&SD to be the world's most comprehensive aviation work.

American Don Kellner records his 22,000th parachute jump, the greatest-ever number for one person.

**May 30** French Armée de l'Air Dassault Mirage IV-P nuclear-armed strategic bombers fly their last mission, so ending 33 years of service (originally as IV-As). The Bretagne operating unit is disbanded at Cazaux on July 4. The five strategic reconnaissance conversions will continue operations until 2005.

**June** The Saab JAS 39A Gripen combat aircraft is officially accepted into the Swedish Air Force with a ceremony at F7 Wing.

**June 24** The 5,000th aircraft of the Beech King Air range is delivered to a customer.

**July 27** After a long and distinguished career, General Dynamics F-111 fighter-bombers are finally retired from the U.S.A.F. (with the exception of Grumman EF-111 A Raven electronic warfare conversions).

**August 6** First flight of the Japanese Kawasaki OH-X armed scout and observation helicopter, also capable of attack. Production began in mid-1998 as the OH-1 Kogata Kansoku.

**September 3** In Operation Desert Strike, the U.S. Navy launches 14 Tomahawk cruise missiles from two ships and the U.S.A.F. launches 13 AGM-86C cruise missiles from two Boeing B-52Hs against air defence and command/control centre targets in southern Iraq following Iraq's assault on the town of Arbil in northern Iraq on August 30. The B-52s had flown from Guam, making a 34-hour and 27,000-mile (43,450-km) round flight. A further 17 Tomahawks are launched from three destroyers and a submarine on the 4th.

**October 17** The last airworthy Vickers Vanguard makes its final flight, landing at the Brooklands Museum.

**November 12** A Saudia Boeing 747 and a Kazakhstan Airlines Ilyushin Il-76TD collide near New Delhi, India. The 312 crew and passengers of the 747 and 39 of the Il-76TD are killed or die from their injuries.

**November 29** First flight of the upgraded Russian Tupolev Tu-144LL supersonic airliner at Zhukovsky. With new engines, it will be used for research into the next

*1996: Northrop Grumman B-2A*

generation of supersonic airliners on behalf of NASA and various U.S. and U.K. companies.

**December 15** It is announced that Boeing is to take over McDonnell Douglas in a $13.3 billion agreement, creating the world's largest aerospace company.

**December 19** U.S. Navy Grumman A-6E Intruders complete their last-ever operational deployment, so ending the 34-year career of this strike bomber. The final 14A-6Es of VA-75 had been on board U.S.S. *Enterprise* and are being replaced by Hornets.

## 1997

**January** Boeing, the world's largest producer of commercial aircraft, announces that orders for the 737, the world's best-selling airliner in history, have exceeded 3,600.

**January 4** A Hong Kong newspaper reports that China is likely to have its first aircraft carrier completed by the year 2000, a full five years earlier than expected.

**January 6** Airbus Industrie announces plans to virtually double production of its airliners over the coming two years.

**January 7** The 194.88-ft (59.4-m) total height, 1.1 million cu ft (31,148m³) combined helium gas and hot air balloon *Virgin Global Challenger* lifts off from Marrakech in Morocco at 11.19 am to attempt the first non-stop circumnavigation of the world by balloon. On board are Richard Branson, Per Lindstrand and Alex Ritchie. The balloon rises

far more quickly than anticipated, reaching its 30,000-ft (9,150m) maximum altitude in just an hour, thereafter making a series of very rapid descents, causing near disaster. The attempt ends at 07.20 am on January 8 at Bechar in Algeria.

**January 12** *Breitling Orbiter* lifts off from Château d'Oex in Switzerland in an attempt to make the first non-stop circumnavigation of the world by balloon. Crewed by Swiss Bertrand Piccard and Belgian Wim Verstraeten, the flight finishes in a controlled landing in the Mediterranean just six hours later, after kerosene fumes had leaked into the crew capsule.

**January 14–20** American J. Stephen Fossett (aged 52) lakes off from St. Louis, Missouri, U.S.A., in his 170-ft (52-m) high helium gas/hot-air balloon Cameron R-210 *Solar Spirit*, in an attempt to make the first non-stop circumnavigation of the world by balloon. Flying alone, he is forced to use more fuel than anticipated and lands 6 days 2 hrs and 54 mins later at Nonkhar, Sultan Par, India, having failed to fly around the world but having broken his own world endurance record for ballooning by 1 hr 38 mins. The distance flown of 10,360 miles (16,673km) is also a record.

**January 31** This date sees the decommissioning of Indian Navy aircraft carrier I.N.S. *Vikrant*.

**February 1** The new aircraft carrier *Charles de Gaulle* is handed over to the French Navy.

Still undergoing fitting out, it will enter operational service in 1999.

**March 14** Last official flight of the final airworthy de Havilland Comet (XS235 *Canopus*) takes place at Boscombe Down, This Comet 4C was first flown in 1963 and has been used for research duties.

**April 1** Initial operational capability is achieved by the Northrop Grumman B-2A Spirit bomber, with 393rd Bomb Squadron of the 509th Bomb Wing.

**May 17** An ex-Air France Boeing 747-128 dating from 1971 is deliberately destroyed by four remotely detonated explosions at Bruntingthorpe Airfield in Leicestershire as part of the Civil Aircraft Explosion Hardening Project to improve airliner safety against terrorist threats.

**June 25** First flight of the Russian Kamov Ka-52 Alligator Hokum-B two-seat combat helicopter, flown by Alexander Smirnov and Dmitri Titov.

**July 8–9** AV-15 *Alaska* makes the longest Northrop Grumman B-2A stealth bomber flight to date, of 25 hrs 30 mins.

**August 4** Boeing and McDonnell Douglas begin operating as a merged company, under the Boeing name.

**August 8** First flight of the Zeppelin NT series LZ N 07 rigid helium airship demonstrator.

**August 14** The U.S.A.F. retires its last Lockheed T-33, an NT-33A in-flight simulator aircraft. It had undertaken its final mission on April 22.

**September 7** First flight of a Lockheed Martin F-22 Raptor EMD prototype, piloted by Paul Metz.

**September 25** First flight of the Russian Sukhoi S-37 fifth-generation tactical fighter, piloted by Igor Votintsev. S-37 features forward-swept wings.

**December 23** Eurofighter DA2 makes the first Mach 2 flight of the Eurofighter test programme. The first in-flight refuelling is demonstrated in January 1998.

## 1998

**January 28–February 7** A new world duration record for free-flying balloons is established by Bertrand Piccard of Switzerland and Andy Elson of the U.K. in the Cameron gas/hot-air balloon *Breitling Orbiter 2*, flying from Château d'Oex, Switzerland to Sitkwin Minhla, Myanmar. The record set is 233 hrs 55 mins.

**February 28** First flight of the Teledyne Ryan RQ-4A Global Hawk unmanned air vehicle reconnaissance aircraft.

**March 28** The Chinese Nanchang Aircraft Manufacturing Company changes its name to Hongdu Aviation Industry Group.

**April 1** The Royal Air Force becomes a fully non-nuclear force as the WE177 tactical nuclear weapon is withdrawn earlier than expected from first-line service by the Labour Government's Defence Secretary.

**April 27** The U.S.A.F. announces that the Lockheed SR-71 Blackbird supersonic strategic reconnaissance aircraft is to remain retired from operational use.

**May 19** Dassault Aviation of France presents the design concept for a 2-crew and 8-passenger supersonic Falcon business jet, to be capable of cruising at Mach 1.8 and have a range of 4,000 nautical miles.

**May 31** Boeing announces that since the beginning of the year it has received orders worth US$15.459 billion, having a backlog of 1,793 aircraft to deliver.

**June 24** The U.S.S. *Harry S. Truman* (CVN-75) nuclear-powered aircraft carrier completes its acceptance sea trials. It is to be commissioned by the U.S. Navy the following month.

**July 4** The prototype EMBRAER RJ135 (ERJ135) 37-passenger regional jet flies. Production deliveries are then expected to begin in October 1999.

**July 15** First flight of the initial production Beech T-6A Texan II trainer, 711 having been ordered for the U.S.A.F. and U.S. Navy under the JPATS programme.

**July 26** First flight of the uniquely configured tandem-wing Scaled Composites Proteus proof-of-concept sensor platform aircraft,

with future roles to include communications relay, remote sensing and monitoring.

**July 30** The 98,000lb (435.93kN) thrust Pratt & Whitney PW4098 turbofan, the world's most powerful commercial aircraft engine intended for the Boeing 777, receives its Type and Production certificates from the FAA.

**August 26** First delivery of a Lockheed Martin C-130J Hercules takes place to the R.A.F. as a C-130J-30.

**September 2** Boeing first flies its new Model 717 at Long Beach Airport, having been designed as the McDonnell Douglas MD-95.

**September 14** Israel records the first successful launch of its Arrow 2 anti-ballistic missile missile.

**September 18** Contracts are signed by Eurofighter GmbH, Eurojet GmbH and NETMA for production of the first 148 Eurofighters.

**September 24** First flight of the Russian Beriev Be-200 twin-turbofan amphibian from Irkutsk.

**September 25** The first production WAH-64 Apache helicopter for the British Army flies. It is one of eight being built by Boeing prior to British assembly.

The U.S. Navy assumes responsibility for the command, control and communications of U.S. strategic nuclear forces under the Looking Glass role, using E-6B Tacamo

aircraft. This role had, up to today, been the responsibility of the U.S.A.F. using now retired C3 variants of the EC-135s.

**September 28** The last newly-built Panavia Tornado is delivered. Going to the Royal Saudi Air Force, it marks the end of production after 974 aircraft.

**September 30** H.M.S. *Ocean*, the British Royal Navy's new helicopter carrier, is commissioned. It will carry 12 EH 101s and six Lynx, or can instead deploy (but not operationally support) up to 20 Sea Harriers.

**October 7** King Harald of Norway opens a new airport at Gardermoen, Oslo. The same day the final flight from the old Fornebu airport is recorded.

**October 24** NASA's Deep Space 1 (DS1) technology demonstrator spacecraft is launched from Cape Kennedy in Florida, U.S.A., by a Delta II booster. DS1 has a xenon ion propulsion system.

**October 29** Launch of U.S. Space Shuttle mission STS 95 using *Discovery*, the crew including 77-year-old John Glenn. (q.v. February 20, 1962)

**November** Airbus Industrie announces that it has delivered 1,840 airliners of 3,142 ordered, leaving a backlog of 1,302 to deliver.

**November 15** Air attacks on Iraq by U.S. and U.K. aircraft are aborted just 14 minutes before the first attacking aircraft, six U.S.A.F. Boeing B-52H Stratofortresses, were to launch cruise missiles. Other airborne aircraft,

including U.S. Navy F-14 Tomcats and F/A-18 Hornets and U.S.A.F. A-10 Thunderbolts and F-16s, are also airborne at the time. Recall is due to a diplomatic solution found at the last possible moment, when Iraq agrees to fully co-operate with United Nations weapon inspectors following diplomatic efforts by Kofi Annan, U.N. Secretary-General. However, in December, further difficulties lead to scaled-down air attacks by U.S. and U.K. forces.

**November 20** Assembly of the International Space Station begins, with the launch of Russia's *Zarya* control module from Baikonur. The first module to be attached to *Zarya* is the U.S. Node 1/Unity, carried into spare in December on board U.S. space shuttle *Endeavor* on mission STS 88. (q.v. December 10, 1998)

**December 10** Astronauts from *Endeavor* connect the first two modules of the International Space Station (q.v. November 20, 1998), allowing the doors to be opened for the first time and preparing the way for the first occupants in 1999.

**December 18** Richard Branson, Steve Fossett and Per Lindstrand lift off from Marrakech at the start of Branson's fourth attempt to circumnavigate the world in a balloon, the *ICO Global Challenger*. The attempt ends short of its goal on the 25th.

**December 22** First flight of the Raytheon Premier I business aircraft from Beech Field which lasted 62 minutes.

**December 23** First flight of the Sikorsky S-92A Helibus civil and military medium helicopter.

## 1999

During 1999, U.S.A.F. Northrop Grumman B-2A Spirit stealth bombers undertake their first ever operation missions, flying 30-hour sorties from Whitman Air Force Base, Missouri, to Europe and return to launch JD AM missiles against targets in Serbia/Yugoslavia.

**March** Publication of the 1999/2000 edition of *Brassey's World Aircraft & Systems Directory*, considered by many to be the world's most comprehensive aviation reference book.

**March 1–21** *Breitling Orbiter 3*, crewed by Bertrand Piccard of Switzerland and Brian Jones of Great Britain, becomes the first balloon to complete a round-the-world flight. Take-off was from Château d'Oex in Switzerland on March 1, and the balloon finally landed on March 21 in Egypt, at a point some 45 miles (70km) from Mut.

**March 25** NATO forces and ship-launched cruise missiles strike at military targets in Serbia, in an attempt to halt the conflict in Kosovo and force a political solution to a long-standing crisis.

**May** Anticipated U.S. space shuttle mission STS 96 using *Discovery*, intended for logistics supply to the International Space Station.

**July** Anticipated launch by Russia of the International Space Station's service module.

**December 3** First export order for the Saab JAS Gripen (28 to South Africa in 2007–2012).

## 2000

**January 4** First flight of the Indian Aeronautical Development Agency Light Combat Aircraft (LCA) This is India's first modern fighter designed specifically for the Indian Air Force and claimed to be the smallest multi-role combat aircraft in the world.

**January 24** Sukhoi Su-47 Berkut (formerly S-37) forward-swept-wing fifth-generation heavy tactical fighter makes its first supersonic flight, reportedly attaining Mach 1.3. It had first flown on September 25 1997.

**February 29** Long awaited first flight of the Russian RAC 'MiG' 1-44 proof-of-concept new-generation tactical fighter at Zhukovsky, lasting 18 minutes.

**April** 4,000 Lockheed Martin F-16 delivered, as an F-16C to Egypt.

**July 10** The European Aeronautic Defence and Space Company EADS N.V. began operations, merging the aerospace and defence business of Aérospatiale Matra of France. DaimlerChrysler Aerospace AG (DASA) of Germany, and CASA of Spain.

**September 18** The Boeing X 32A Concept Demonstrator for the Joint Strike Fighter makes its first flight, intended to compete for orders to replace several different types of warplanes with the U.S.A.F., U.S. Navy, U.S. Marine Corps and overseas forces from 2008.

**October** Launch of the first crew to man the International Space Station.

**October 24** The Lockheed Martin X-35A Concept Demonstrator for the Joint Strike Fighter makes its first flight, intended to compete against the Boeing X-32.

**December 19** Official approval is given to launch the Airbus A380, the world's first very high capacity, double deck, airliner. First delivery is expected in 2006. Accommodation in the A380-200 version will be for 656 passengers plus 46 LD3 cargo pallets.

## 2001

**March** The Russian Space Agency Mir 1 space station is de-orbited after a long and successful career. It had suffered damage in 1997 in a docking collision.

**May 7** The only operational example of the Antonov An-255 Mriya, the world's largest aircraft, begins flying again after 7 years in storage and a multi-million dollar overhaul. It enters commercial service later this year.

**June 19** Tests are initiated in the U.K. on the first of 7 British Airways Concordes fitted with Kevlar/rubber fuel tank liners and armoured electric cabling in the area of the undercarriage, in the hope of getting the supersonic airliner back into commercial service after the accident to an Air France Concorde in 2000 grounded the fleet of both nations.